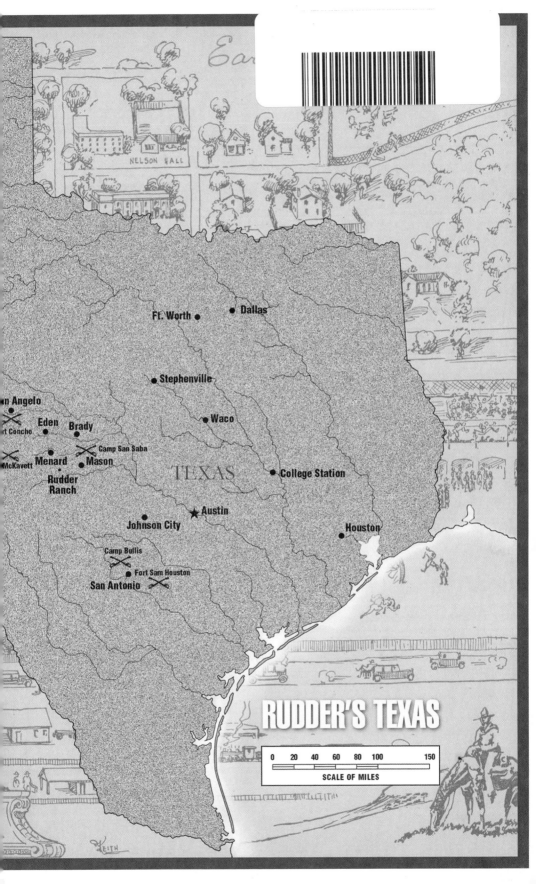

NELSON HALL

Ft. Worth •   • Dallas

• Stephenville

n Angelo
Eden   Brady
t Concho
Camp San Saba
McKavett   Menard   Mason
Rudder
Ranch

• Waco

TEXAS

• College Station

★ Austin
Johnson City

Houston

Camp Bullis
• Fort Sam Houston
San Antonio

RUDDER'S TEXAS

0   20   40   60   80   100   150

SCALE OF MILES

RUDDER

NUMBER 115

*Centennial Series
of the Association of Former Students,
Texas A&M University*

*With the support and cooperation of the
Dolph Briscoe Center for American History,
University of Texas at Austin*

RUDDER
FROM LEADER TO LEGEND

THOMAS M. HATFIELD

TEXAS A&M UNIVERSITY PRESS
College Station

This paper meets the requirements of
ANSI/NISO Z39.48-1992
(Permanence of Paper).
Binding materials have been
chosen for durability.

Library of Congress Cataloging-in-Publication Data
Hatfield, Thomas M.
Rudder : from leader to legend / Thomas M. Hatfield.—1st ed.
p. cm.—(Centennial series of the Association of Former Students,
Texas A&M University ; no. 115)
Includes bibliographical references and index.
ISBN-13: 978-1-60344-262-6 (cloth : alk. paper)
ISBN-10: 1-60344-262-6 (cloth : alk. paper)
ISBN-13: 978-1-60344-263-3 (deluxe cloth : alk. paper)
ISBN-10: 1-60344-263-4 (deluxe cloth : alk. paper)
[etc.]
1. Rudder, James Earl, 1910–1970. 2. United States. Army. Ranger Battalion,
2nd—Biography. 3. United States. Army—Officers—Biography. 4. World War,
1939–1945—Campaigns—Europe. 5. Mayors—Texas—Brady—Biography. 6. Texas.
General Land Office—Officials and employees—Biography. 7. Texas A & M University—
Presidents—Biography. 8. College presidents—Texas—Biography. 9. Texas—Politics
and government—1951– I. Title. II. Series: Centennial series of the Association of
Former Students, Texas A&M University ; no. 115.
E745.H375 2011
940.54'1273092—dc22
[B] 2010034085

"Dirty Old Egg Suckin' Dog"
Words and Music by Jack Clement
Copyright © 1965 Jack Music, Inc.
Rights Administered by Universal-Songs, Polygram Int'l., Inc.
Reprinted by permission of Hal Leonard Corp.

Front endpaper map: "Rudder's Texas," a map of the state imposed on a drawing of
the Texas A&M campus in 1932, with Rudder's signature in upper right corner.
Back endpaper map: "Rudder's Europe," a map of Western Europe showing
locations that were significant in Rudder's wartime service.

FOR THREE GRAND LADIES
OF TEXAS A&M UNIVERSITY—

Margaret Williamson Rudder
(1916–2004)

Sadie Hatfield
(1895–1990)

Nelda Rowell Green,
executive secretary to President Rudder from 1965 to 1970

and

THREE STRONG HATFIELD WOMEN—

Carol, Alice, and Sara

CONTENTS

ILLUSTRATIONS

MAPS

PREFACE

The theme of this book is the triumph of humane and purposeful leadership in war and peace. The theme's medium is character—what it is, how it was formed, and how it was manifest in the life of James Earl Rudder.

Why Rudder? Because he rose from obscurity and deprivation in the American heartland to be widely admired by heads of state, soldiers, mechanics, and scholars; because he combined hardheaded leadership with altruistic motives for service to others; because his life illustrates the supreme importance of community and family in character formation; and because his accomplishments are proof that in a free society where education is accessible to all, greatness can come from anywhere.

As a young adult, I was fortunate to observe Earl Rudder at close hand several times. The first time occurred when he was commissioner of the General Land Office of Texas (1955–58), where I had a part-time job while an undergraduate at the University of Texas. Three years later I returned to the university for graduate study and was a lieutenant in the G-2 section (intelligence) of the 90th Infantry Division, USAR, which he commanded. When we went for summer training at Fort Hood, Texas, or Fort Polk, Louisiana, I was usually assigned to his headquarters. My services were so critical that once in Louisiana swamps I was charged with the construction of his latrine, with the assistance of two professional architects and a squad of other equally redundant army reservists. My military specialty was interpreting aerial photographs. From this, colonels on his staff presumed that I took them as well as explained them, and they would send me aloft in a small fixed-wing plane to shoot pictures of the division deployed in the field. After the film was developed and I had oriented the colonels to the photos, they would show them to Rudder, if he had not already come to look over my shoulder as I talked about them. I never showed the colonels where the guys had buried the beer, iced down in a tarpaulin removed from a truck, with brush pulled over it until after dark.

Rudder became a serious subject when I began teaching the history of World War II at the University of Texas at Austin in the 1980s, with emphasis on the Battle of Normandy, where he played a significant role. This

led to taking groups—students, veterans and other adults—across battlefields of Western Europe, lecturing, and living for extended periods in Normandy, where Rudder's name and likeness are carved on monuments. With
no idea of writing his biography, I interviewed men in England and France
who had known him during the war. The Pointe du Hoc battlefield, where
he emerged as a legendary figure, was as familiar as my neighborhood park,
and I strolled along the shoreline and bluffs above Omaha Beach with maps,
planning documents of the invasion, and memoirs of men who were there.
Similarly, I studied the Ardennes in Belgium and Luxembourg. In this book
the reader has for the first time a detailed account of Rudder's extraordinary
exploits in five major battles of the European War: Normandy, Brittany, the
Huertgen Forest, the Ardennes, and the Colmar Pocket. I composed the text
for the non-specialist and put technical information in endnotes.

Delving into Rudder's life coincided with my serious interests in
twentieth-century Texas history, U.S. political history, military history, and
higher education. I had a special interest in Rudder's close friend, Lyndon B.
Johnson, whose tenure as U.S. senator, vice president, and president, 1948–
69, was almost the same as Rudder's public service career, 1946–70. The fact
that Rudder and I had similar origins in the Texas Hill Country made him a
more compelling subject, although I am exactly a quarter-century younger.
Fortuitously, too, as a youngster I was a regular visitor to Texas A&M and
formed many of my basic ideas about education from observing its land-
grant functions in action, which were his passions as well.

Tracking Rudder from Texas to Britain, across France, Belgium, Luxembourg, and into Germany was high adventure. I went to every place that
was significant in his life, from his birthplace in Eden, Texas, to an enemy
fortress at the tip of Brittany, where he persuaded its commander to surrender fourteen hundred combatants in September 1944, to the wine cellar of
a small hotel in the Huertgen Forest south of Aachen that was his forward
command post during the following November, to the city square in Colmar
where he was decorated with the French Croix de Guerre and the Legion of
Honor in February 1945. Back home, I pored through the archives of the
Land Office, Texas A&M University, the National Archives, and his personal
correspondence to assemble the pieces of his life.

This biography includes the worst and the best that I learned about Earl
Rudder. His positive accomplishments can easily withstand the inevitable
mistakes and omissions of an active life. He was frequently, in Theodore Roosevelt's memorable phrase, the "man in the arena." Members of the Rudder
family were unfailingly helpful, but no one suggested restraints of any kind.
Although I owe them, and especially Margaret Rudder, a profound debt, this
book is not in any sense compensation for their favors and friendship.

ACKNOWLEDGMENTS

So many people and institutions helped me produce this book that I can most efficiently express my appreciation by describing their assistance in categories, beginning with those whose assistance was comprehensive and affected the development of the entire manuscript, followed by those whose help was significant in the three sections of the book: The Early Years, The War Years, and Public Servant.

Comprehensive. My wife, Carol Sutherland Hatfield, was steadfast and indispensable. Seeing Carol, an accomplished editor and journalist, work and apply her extraordinary organizational skills made me realize how lucky I have been to have her beside me for most of my life. Two other women read the entire manuscript: Nelda Rowell Green and Carolyn Culbert Osborn. Nelda was Earl Rudder's executive secretary for the last five years of his Texas A&M presidency. She directed me to sources, provided original documents, and responded positively to the many requests that I made. Carolyn Osborn—novelist, short story writer, and friend from undergraduate days—is a stylist whose suggestions elevated the manuscript. My copy editor, Noel Parsons, improved the work in similar ways.

Margaret Williamson Rudder gave me exclusive, unlimited access to her personal papers, as well as her husband's. She died while the book was in progress, and her children—Bud, Anne, Linda, and Bob—continued to give their wholehearted support. Texas Governor Rick Perry encouraged and supported the project from beginning to end.

At all times I was aware of the influence of my aunt, Sadie Hatfield (1895–1990), a career professional in the Cooperative Extension Service of Texas A&M University. She was an inexplicable blessing, always expanding my perceptions, whether of the natural world or the cultured world. Her inspiring legacy is both tangible and intangible. Dave H. Williams, Ralph Ellis, and John Mobley gave crucial material and moral support to the entire project.

Dr. David Chapman, director of Texas A&M University's Cushing Memorial Library and Archives, guided me to documents in the Rudder collection. In the office of the Texas A&M System Board of Regents, Vickie Spillers and Laura Powers were unfailingly helpful. Regent Phil Adams allowed me free use of an apartment on the campus, and Regent Richard Box made numerous contacts for me.

Earl Rudder would see no contradiction in the fact that the University of Texas at Austin, my alma mater and academic home, cooperated with Texas A&M, his university, to publish his biography. His original base of statewide political support was with alumni of the University of Texas whose leaders later helped him as A&M's president. Rudder was not parochial and worked for the improvement of education at all levels, once commenting, "A rising tide lifts all boats." Except for about three hours each year, his support of the University of Texas is undeniable. He attended Longhorn football banquets and joined in singing the Texas fight song and "The Eyes of Texas." His wife was a UT graduate, and four of his children attended the university.

The magnificent libraries and information technology services of the University of Texas were essential to the production of this book. Colleagues at the university who helped me include Sharry Kahanek, Judy Evans, Ramona Kelly, Echo Uribe, David Grosvenor, David Zepeda, Dr. Holly Taylor, and Dr. Don Carleton, executive director of the Dolph Briscoe Center for American History. Professors Jean-Pierre Cauvin and Robert D. King translated French and German documents. At Texas A&M University Press, Charles Backus, Mary Lenn Dixon, and Thom Lemmons gave reliable advice and encouragement, which earned them my respect and admiration.

The Early Years. Carolyn Moody, the director of the Don Freeman Memorial Museum in Eden, Texas—Rudder's birthplace—oriented me to the area and sent me numerous documents that she surely spent hours searching to find. Margaret Rose Loveless afforded me family documents with photographs and accounts of the funeral of her uncle, John R. Lapp Jr., which forms the opening scene of the book. Two interviews with Evelyn Whitfield Hendricks, as she approached her one hundredth birthday, were extraordinary for their clarity and detail about the Rudder family, in whose home she worked in the late 1920s. The Concho County clerk, Barbara Hoffman, and Gail Scott helped me reconstruct the difficulties of Rudder's father in reconciling business transactions. Tarleton State University librarian Glenda Stone was resourceful in finding documents and photos from Rudder's two periods there, first as a student, 1927–30, and as a teacher-coach, 1938–41. Don D. Carter, Texas A&M's registrar and admissions officer, retrieved records from Rudder's student days, 1930–32, including his earliest existing letter.

The publisher of the *Brady Standard,* Larry Smith, sorted through morgue files and told me of the friendship that developed between his father (then sports editor of the newspaper) and Rudder after Rudder became the Brady high school football coach in 1933.

The War Years. Several of Rudder's associates during the war gave extraordinary assistance, beginning with James W. "Ike" Eikner. As the communications officer and later Headquarters Company commander in the 2nd Ranger Battalion, 1943–45, Eikner was necessarily in close proximity to Rudder from July 1943, when Rudder took command (Eikner was already there), until Rudder was promoted to a regimental command in December of 1944. Ike published a chronology of headquarters company shortly after the war and accumulated extensive files on the battalion. Equally important, he has not embellished his memory with fantasies, as is often the case.

Maj. Gen. John C. Raaen Jr., USMA 1943 and a Ranger who fought under Rudder's command in the Normandy invasion, gave valuable insights to operations throughout the war, enriching every account about Rudder's combat experience. Leonard G. Lomell and Frank E. South were enlisted men in the 2nd Ranger Battalion before Rudder took command, observed him at close range, and were associated with him after the war.

In Washington, D.C., Gene Buck found valuable material in the National Archives about various units connected to Rudder during the war. John Slonaker in Carlisle, Pennsylvania, sent important materials from the army's Military History Institute. Mark J. Reardon of the U.S. Army's Center of Military History convinced me that he is possibly the finest researcher of the American army in Europe during World War II.

Although Rudder was in Greenock, Scotland, only a few hours on December 1, 1943, I got vivid accounts of the day from George Munro, who watched his battalion march up Campbell Street; Margaret Chatters, then a WREN, who served the Rangers lunch in the Glebe sugar warehouse; and Vincent Gillen, curator of the McLean Museum and Art Gallery. In Bude, County Cornwall, Bryan Dudley Stamp gathered twenty residents, who were children during the war, for a party hosted by Councillor Ann Davies, mayor of Bude-Stratton. The gathering led to numerous interviews, notable among them those with Judyth Gwynne and Brian Woolcott, whose family home was near Rudder's billet. Laura Jacobs, archivist and librarian at the University of Wisconsin–Superior, sent background material on Jim Dan Hill, who served with Rudder in Cornwall.

In Weymouth, Norman Carter and John Braddock, whose second careers are pro bono World War II projects, drove me along the coast to Swanage and inland to places that were significant to Rudder's Rangers. Mrs. Poppy Collins Butcher displayed her collection of American uniforms and decorations as well as a 1942 Willys Jeep. Dawn Yardy, once a Red Cross girl, told of watching the GIs march along the esplanade on June 1, 1944, to embark for Normandy.

Traveling down the country roads of Devon, Dorset, and Cornwall was easy, because I was driven by Dorothy Jeffries, a friend from student days in England, in her car. In addition, she copied documents from the Somerset County Library, and she paid a bill for copy and postal charges for me in pounds sterling in Blandford Forum that only surfaced after I had left. Professors Roger Louis and William S. Livingston made suggestions about the Britain chapter. Charles Messenger was a reliable source for information about Commandos and Rangers.

Donald G. Cook, retired United States Air Force four-star general, provided letters from his father, Harvey Cook, Rudder's operations and intelligence officer, which, with other documents, enabled me to reconstruct the events of June 4–5, 1944, that led to Rudder's assuming personal command of the Pointe du Hoc assault. Dr. Simon Trew, senior lecturer in the Department of War Studies at the Royal Military Academy Sandhurst, provided important sources in British archives and suggestions about my Pointe du Hoc narrative. Joe Balkoski, the historian of U.S. Army engagements in Normandy and Brittany, also reviewed the Pointe du Hoc chapter. Ranger historian Robert W. Black generously shared materials. Jan Houterman of the Netherlands is an outstanding researcher on Royal Navy and British army officers during the war, which is reflected in my narrative about Rudder in Britain and the crisis that occurred while approaching Pointe du Hoc.

In Normandy, André Heintz—retired professor at the University of Caen and a member of the French resistance during the German occupation—has taught me much about the war over the last twenty-five years. In the same period, the Pierre Colmant and Denise Preél families have become like family to me while accepting me in their homes in Caen, Saint-Aubin-sur-Mer, and Bény Bocage. In similar ways, Denis and Marie-Christine de Kergorlay of Château de Canisy have been inspirational, providing a home-away-from-home that brings to mind Thomas Jefferson's well-worn phrase that "Every man has two countries, his own and France." Louis Ledevin, longtime mayor of Cricqueville-en-Bessin, helped me gain access to church and private properties near Pointe du Hoc, which is within the jurisdiction of his mayorship.

In Brittany, I was a guest in the home of Yannick and Flo Creac'h and their three children: Sterem (5), Maëla (4), and Yoran (2). Most of their multilevel home in Morlaix is a children's palace, but one level is a museum with collections of U.S. Army uniforms and artifacts of the war that Yannick has unearthed. Accompanied by his friends Eric Pillon and Ronan Urvoaz, Yannick drove me around Le Conquet Peninsula, where Rudder and the 2nd Ranger Battalion were heavily engaged in September 1944. Ronan is a scholar on the fighting around Brest and provided me with related books and maps.

In the German village of Germeter, with the information I provided, Bernd Henkelmann realized that Rudder's command post could only have been in what is now the wine cellar of a local inn, Zum Alten Forsthaus, owned by Barbara and Rainer Gübbels. Walking into the cellar was a mystical experience, one of the most exciting moments in the preparation of this book. For several days I had been so profoundly absorbed in reliving Rudder's ordeal in the Huertgen Forest and the Ardennes that I had the powerful feeling that I had been in the cellar before. It was as though I had overlapped with a past life that was mine rather than his.

Luxembourg's leading historian of the war, Roland Gaul, took me over the terrain along the Sûre River that was familiar to Rudder during the Battle of the Bulge. Gaul is the founder-director of the National Museum of Military History in Diekirch. In the French province of Alsace, Mme. Lise Pommois, the leading historian of the liberation, provided me with interpretations and materials, especially regarding the liberation of Colmar, in which Rudder played a conspicuous part. In Schleiden, Germany, Karl Lüttgens is the leading local historian of the war. He oriented me to the area, located Rudder's February 1945 command post, and obtained German military archive materials.

While I was writing about the war, I thought often of two great friends and tutors on World War II: Charles B. MacDonald (1922–90) and Martin Blumenson (1918–2005). Both lectured at the University of Texas, and each was a preeminent historian of the European war as well as a veteran. From the early 1980s until they became frail, we traversed European battlefields from Sicily to the Rhineland and west to the Atlantic, and I saw them often in Washington, where we seldom talked about anything except the war, its leaders, and their decisions.

Public Servant. In 1948, Rep. Lyndon B. Johnson solicited Rudder's help in his successful run for the U.S Senate. The two men got along well and remained close, personally and politically. As a result, there is considerable material about their mutual interests in the Lyndon B. Johnson Presidential Library, where Deputy Director Tina Houston gave me broad direction and Claudia Anderson found Rudder-related materials from the pre-presidential period. Oliver Sadberry and Leroy Sterling, among the first African American students at Texas A&M, vividly described their experiences.

For Rudder's twelve years at the helm of Texas A&M University, I relied mainly on A&M's holdings, notably of the Sterling Evans Library, the records of the Association of Former Students, and, as mentioned earlier, the Cushing Memorial Library and Archives and the Board of Regents.

Thomas M. Hatfield
Austin, Texas
August 1, 2010

Texas A&M University Press and author Thomas M. Hatfield gratefully acknowledge the support, in many forms, of many individuals in the writing of this book. Without the crucial material and moral support of Dave H. Williams, Ralph Ellis, and John Mobley, in particular, as well as the interest and generosity of all those listed below, the publication of this comprehensive account of the life of James Earl Rudder would not have been possible:

Robert H. Allen, A&M '50

Joyce S. Aronson

Ben Barnes

Roy Butler

The Effie and Wofford Cain
    Foundation

Donald M. Carlton

Frank Denius

Wayne C. Edwards, A&M '72

J. Ralph Ellis Jr., A&M '52

Diane Finch Grant

Eleanor M. Hill

Benjamin L. Hinds, A&M '55

Betty M. MacGuire

Nethery S. Marrow

Barry McBurnett

Donald P. McClure

William B. Miller

John Mobley, A&M '51

Robert C. Pate

N. David Porter

James A. and Betsey Reichert

The James and Mayne Rowland
    Foundation

John P. and Ellie Schneider

Jason B. Sowell

Celika Storm

Sam L. Susser

DeWitt and Muffy Waltmon

The James M. West Endowment

Clayton W. Williams Jr., A&M '54

The Dave H. and Reba W. Williams
    Foundation

RUDDER

PROLOGUE

London, 1943. Plans go forth for the Anglo-American attack across the English Channel on Nazi-occupied Europe in the spring of 1944. The cross-channel attack will be the main effort in Western Europe against Germany to end the war. A landing on the coast of Normandy in northwestern France will require breaching Hitler's vaunted Atlantic Wall, a series of fortifications along the coast with powerful guns reaching out to sea. The most formidable are on a promontory called Pointe du Hoc, which juts with hundred-foot cliffs into the sea between two sandy beaches, code-named Omaha and Utah, where fifty thousand American troops will land on D-Day, the first day of the invasion. The guns of Pointe du Hoc endanger the success of the invasion.

The only certain way to destroy the guns is a ground attack, and the most feasible approach is from the sea to scale the cliffs, which the enemy believes are unassailable. The task will require a specialized Ranger force, well trained, disciplined, and led by a dauntless commander. A senior American naval officer speaks for many when he says, "It can't be done. Three old women with brooms could keep the Rangers from climbing those cliffs."

Gen. Omar N. Bradley, the American ground commander, assigns the mission to a thirty-three-year-old U.S. Army reserve lieutenant colonel from Texas, James Earl Rudder. Bradley says it was the most difficult decision he made during the entire war. Rudder tells him, "My men can do it," referring to the 2nd Ranger Battalion, a group of some five hundred men he has recruited and trained. On June 6, 1944, half of the Rangers will scale the cliffs of Pointe du Hoc and destroy the guns, while the other half will assault Omaha and knock out more guns that imperil the landings there. As the decades pass, multitudes of visitors to Pointe du Hoc stare in disbelief at the cliffs the Rangers climbed under fire. Even Rudder says, "How did we do this? It was crazy then, and it's crazy now."

In planning and leading the assault on Pointe du Hoc, Rudder demonstrated exceptional qualities of leadership. His task required physical and moral courage, conceptual ability, and personal skills. The success of the Pointe du Hoc mission makes him an icon in the U.S. Army and marks him for future leadership. Before the war ended, he was awarded every decoration for valor and gallantry except the Medal of Honor. Preeminent professional soldiers acclaimed him "the bravest of the brave" and the model of the American citizen-soldier.

After the war Rudder achieved a distinguished career in public service that ended with his death while president of Texas A&M University at fifty-nine. Following his death, Gen. Matthew B. Ridgway, perhaps America's outstanding battlefield general of the twentieth century, wrote that Rudder "deserved all the honors that come his way." They were not long in coming and continued for forty years.

The first was on Memorial Day after his death when the Earl Rudder Memorial Park was dedicated in his birthplace, Eden, Texas. In Normandy, the parish church in the village of Cricqueville-en-Bessin, near Pointe du Hoc, began conducting a memorial service in his memory on a Sunday near the date of his death. A white marble plaque was affixed to the interior wall of the ancient church calling worshippers not to "forget the American soldiers who risked and sacrificed their lives for you on the 6th of June, 1944." In time, a sculptured likeness of Rudder's countenance, in bas-relief on a disc of sea green marble, was placed above the plaque.

In Weymouth, England, his image is embedded in a dockside monument where he and his Rangers embarked for France. In Florida, the U.S. Army operates the Rudder Ranger Training Center, and in Kaiserslautern, Germany, the Rudder Army Reserve Center. In Washington, D.C., the Association of the U.S. Army annually awards the James Earl Rudder Medal to a person who has made an outstanding contribution to the integration of the active and reserve forces.

San Antonio, Texas, has its Earl Rudder Middle School and the Rudder Army Reserve Center, and Austin has the James Earl Rudder State Office Building. The Earl Rudder Freeway connects the cities of College Station and Bryan, where James Earl Rudder High School was dedicated in 2008.

His statue, larger than life, stands on the campus of Texas A&M University not far from Rudder Tower, which memorializes his accomplishments in war and peace. "His vision of what Texas A&M could be," said Aggie graduate Tom DeFrank, "is the underpinning of today's world-class university," which is but one of many reasons to honor his memory.[1]

PART ONE

THE EARLY YEARS

"Earl, don't tell your father that I gave you five dollars for college."
—*His mother, 1927*

CHAPTER 1

EDEN, TEXAS
1910–1927

The remote West Texas town of Eden had never been so still or seen such crowds. Hundreds of people were standing quietly along the streets, waiting for a black-trimmed farm wagon drawn by six white horses. From farms and ranches across Concho County the mass of humanity had thronged down dirt roads on horseback, in buggies and hacks. Some walked and others rode in America's first dream car, the Ford Model T, easily doubling the usual population of half a thousand. Now they stood in the lengthening shadows of late afternoon for the funeral cortege of Pvt. John R. Lapp Jr.

The ill-fated John Lapp was the only man from Eden to lose his life in the First World War. His flag-draped coffin arrived back home on Wednesday, July 27, 1921, on the 5:20 once-a-day train from Brady.[1] When the locomotive ground to a stop, the local American Legion post took charge with an elaborate plan to honor John Lapp for the last time. An honor guard of a dozen veterans attired in uniforms brought home from the Great War stood at attention with rifles at their sides while others removed the coffin from the baggage car and lashed it to the wagon for the half-mile drive to the center of town. From the railway station the ceremonial guards led the way as the solemn procession followed the road that came north from Menard past the home of Frederick Ede, the founder of Eden but thirty-nine years before. So quiet were the crowds that only the steady clomping of hooves and the squeak of the horses' rigging disturbed the evening air.[2]

Finally, the procession entered the town square, the same area that a half-century later would be designated the Earl Rudder Memorial Park. All business houses were closed except the hardware store, where the body was taken to lie in repose for four days and nights. In simple dignity, John Lapp's friends kept a vigil beside his bier while his fellow citizens came to pay homage to his sacrifice and console his family. On Sunday afternoon the body was moved to the Methodist church for a memorial service conducted by the Lutheran pastor, whose congregation had no sanctuary of its own.[3]

Then the cortege formed again for the final journey to the cemetery a mile and a quarter north of town on the Paint Rock road. Some two thousand people lined the way, the Lutheran pastor estimated, the largest gathering in the history of Eden. The Sons of Herman, whose purpose ironically was to preserve German culture, organized car pools from San Angelo, forty-five miles west; others came from Brady, thirty-five miles east, and Ballinger, an equal distance to the north. So impressive were the crowds and the ceremonies that more than eighty years later the scenes remained fixed in the minds of then small children as the most memorable event ever to occur in Eden. Pulling the farm wagon were four dapple gray percherons—stout and muscular with crested necks—and two white horses, ridden and guided by former doughboys dazzlingly impressive in their campaign hats with gold braid, army brown pullover shirts, and khaki pants. Three of John Lapp's four brothers walked behind the wagon. Six-year-old Blu Bell Maddox took advantage of her mother's absence attending the funeral service by climbing to the forbidden highest gable of their two-story home to watch the pageantry. Almost certainly Earl Rudder, two months into his twelfth year, stood along the road with his chum, M. J. Green, watching the cortege with its unforgettable images of flags, soldiers, and sailors. It would have been his first view of soldiers marching with a color guard bearing his country's flag.[4]

John Lapp was buried with full military honors in the traditions of the U.S. Army. While his coffin was suspended over the grave, seven men clad in their wartime uniforms stepped forward in a straight line and fired three volleys from their .30-caliber Springfield rifles. The sudden blasts shattered the stillness and then trailed away, resounding across the rolling countryside. Two of the honor guards removed the flag from the coffin and folded it crisply thirteen times to the shape of the three-cornered hat worn by colonial soldiers in the American Revolution. Holding the folded banner with both hands, the white-gloved captain of the guard presented it to John Lapp's mother as she murmured, "I do not have my son, but I have this flag," as though mere possession of the nation's emblem was due compensation for her loss.[5]

All across America, the First World War aroused strong sentiments of devotion to the nation, a shared sense of nationalism so pervasive that it mostly healed the North-South resentments that had persisted since the Civil War two generations earlier. Patriotism was, or became, a secular religion for most Americans. New patriotic customs took hold. The date the war ended in 1918—November 11—became a national holiday called Armistice Day, not celebrated with fireworks like the Fourth of July but quietly remembered like Thanksgiving.

In Eden, the graves of veterans were decorated with flowers, business houses closed, and the high school band marched to the town square to play music for the assembled townspeople, songs such as "America the Beautiful" and "My Country 'Tis of Thee," the de facto national anthem until the adoption of "The Star-Spangled Banner" in 1931. The music stopped just before eleven o'clock, the exact time—the eleventh hour of the eleventh day of the eleventh month—when the cease-fire was declared in 1918. Then a lone trumpeter sounded "Taps." Its haunting notes seemed to hang in the air as a pastor gave the benediction and called for remembrance of those who had served their country. Conducted again and again, these community rituals would have lasting effects on the minds of the young, not least on the boy, James Earl Rudder, whose ideas about service and country were then taking form.

THE GREAT AMERICAN DESERT

The community of Eden and Concho County that Earl Rudder knew as a boy are keys to understanding his basic values and motivations. That understanding begins with the fact that the economic existence of every family depended on two factors beyond their control. One was the market price of cotton, wool, and beef, and the other was rainfall: when it fell and how much fell. The region was on the edge of the Great American Desert, where prolonged dry periods—droughts—came unannounced and stayed for extended visits.[6] Rainfall, usually the lack of it, was always a topic of conversation. The uncertainty about rain made gamblers of farm and ranch families. Each year they bet 365 days of their collective manual labors on the dampness of the soil at the right times. If rainfall was insufficient, they were in trouble unless they had substantial savings from bountiful years, which was unlikely except for a few.

Nature was capricious with weather patterns, luring and deceiving newcomers in good years only to disappoint and often defeat them later. Six-year-old Mallie Jones was misled about the bountifulness of the country when she came with her family about when the Rudders arrived. For the remainder of her long life she talked about the "beautiful fields of bluebonnets, waving in the wind and rolling like ocean waves."[7] The vivid scene stuck in her memory because it was so unusual, an aberration from the norm that she seldom saw again.

The reality was closer to the recollection of rancher Tom McCall. Looking back on a lifetime of hard work on the range, he told of times when "the creeks went completely dry, not a drop for the poor, thirsty animals to drink" nor a "blade of grass for miles around." He went to his grave troubled by the recurring memory of thirsty cows wandering into a streambed—once flowing with water but now merely a mud hole—and dying miserably, bawling in their tracks, so weakened from the lack of food and water that they could not free themselves from the mud. McCall called his constant worry about rain "drought anxiety," a condition that also affected Earl Rudder, who worried about the next drought—when it would come and its effect on wildlife and livestock, trees, streams, and people.[8]

When a multiyear drought afflicted much of Texas in the 1950s, Rudder became a conspicuous advocate of government financial support to relieve hardships on farm and ranch families. Testifying before a government committee, he stated his philosophy of serving others with earnest clarity: "I came from a family that had a hard time making a living. I find it hard to turn down people who say they need help. I have been helped down the road a lot when I needed it, and I just want to reciprocate."[9] He did not merely sympathize with people in need; he empathized. He had been in their place and could see the world as they saw it.

Like many newcomers to Eden about 1900, the Rudder family came because the town was a market and trading center for farmers and ranchers. Immigrants attracted with illusions of a biblical paradise were certain to be disappointed, because "Eden" was an adaptation of the family name of Frederick Ede, who set aside forty acres of his land in 1882 for the new town. Most families survived by applying the muscle power of men, women, children, horses, and mules. Eking out a livelihood in a hardscrabble, semiarid land was demanding and endless. Practical solutions were required without dawdling.

Although most people in Concho County were cash poor, no one went hungry. Living close to the land, they were well nourished, and Earl Rudder better than most. The staple was beef—inexpensive and available—and the Rudder family's table fare was abundant. Visiting in the home of his cousin, Eunice Stephens, he disparaged the selection of prepared foods. Eunice disagreed. "There was plenty," she insisted, "maybe only about three items, but lots of that. The Rudders always set a big table with two or three meats and many vegetables."[10]

Unless a family owned considerable acreage, which the Rudders did not, its means of support was marginal even in the best of times. The Rudder family lived on the economic edge, without land, a business enterprise, or professional skills. Earl's father, Dee Forrest Rudder, could read, write, and figure but was otherwise uneducated. Known as a "commission man," he relied on his wits and congeniality to sell anything of value from which he could reap a percentage of the sale. His advertisement in the local newspaper, the *Eden Echo,* was brief and direct: "If you're in the market to buy or sell real estate, live stock, oil royalties, oil leases, see D. F. Rudder."[11] His family did without many things that others had, which informed Earl's attitudes about thriftiness, self-denial, and charity. "Waste not, want not" and "Live simply" were more than slogans; they were necessities. Like many in his and earlier generations, he grew up happy without the material goods and conveniences that later generations took for granted.

WESTWARD MOVEMENT

The Rudder family came to live in Concho County in 1906, led by their patriarch, Earl's grandfather, Alexander Perry Rudder.[12] Born in Virginia in 1835, Alexander Rudder immigrated to Texas and married Alabama-born Francis Jane Tyler in 1857 in Trinity County, a pine forest of immense trees north of Houston and only a hundred miles from the Louisiana line.[13] Four years later the Civil War broke out, and he enlisted in the 22nd Texas Infantry Regiment. He saw action in half a dozen battles in Louisiana and Mississippi before he was captured and made a prisoner of war by the Federals. He was mustered out of the Confederate army as the first sergeant of his company, a significant advance in rank in an army where most men were privates.[14]

Returning to Texas, he found Trinity County was a lawless and troubled area. During the war the deep, dense woods had become a hideout for Confederate deserters and criminals. Public order had broken down, and lawlessness continued after the war. The white population, especially Confederate veterans, resented the presence of an occupation force: three companies of Union soldiers from Illinois. White Southerners were leaving Trinity County, and the Rudders pulled out with them, moving 250 miles southwest to Goliad County on the coastal prairie of Texas, where their son, Dee Forrest, who would become Earl's father, was born on December 21, 1872. By 1880, Alex and Francis Jane had moved again, 150 miles northwest to Mason County. On Christmas Eve 1891, Dee married Annie Clark Powell in adjacent McCulloch County.[15]

The Rudders were lured a few miles west to Concho County by several wet years about the turn of the century. In such bountiful periods, people might convince themselves that the climate had changed permanently and become wetter. Owners of big cattle ranches were selling off partials known as stock farms—small ranches that combined pastureland for livestock with cultivated fields for farming. Dee Forrest Rudder intended to be a stock farmer, but he arrived too late to acquire good land at bargain prices and could not afford the higher prices for better land. His land was the kind that West Texans said was "useful to hold the earth together." Driven by a protracted dry

Eden, Texas, 1910, the year of Rudder's birth. His father's office was in the building to the right with "Rudder-Wallace Real Estate" on the facade. (Courtesy of Carolyn Moody, director, Don Freeman Memorial Museum, Eden, Texas)

spell, in 1910 Dee Rudder gave up farming and moved his family into Eden, where Earl was born on May 6 in a small frame house on the Brady road.

In her first fifteen years of marriage, Annie Powell Rudder gave birth to ten children, six of whom died in infancy or early childhood. The four survivors, all boys, were, in order of birth, Francis Simmie, A. P., J. D., and John. After the family moved to Eden, three more boys were born, of whom two would survive: James Earl, called Earl from birth, born five years after John, and Marshall, the youngest, three years after Earl.[16] In all, Earl's mother gave birth to thirteen children.

There is a mystery about what happened to A. P., the second son. His mother stated in a 1939 affidavit that his place of residence was unknown, consistent with the usual family explanation that he disappeared. In Eden it was rumored that he had been sentenced to prison in Oklahoma, but the Texas and Oklahoma prison systems claim no record of an inmate with his name.[17]

NEW JERUSALEM

As did many pioneers on the American frontier, the early white settlers of Eden saw themselves as fulfilling the biblical prophesy of building a New Jerusalem. In their city upon a hill, people would have a fuller relationship with

*The Rudder family,
late 1910.* Left to right:
*John; the father, Dee
Forrest Rudder; Francis
Simmie "Sim"* (standing);
*J.D.; and the mother,
Annie Powell Rudder,
holding Earl, born May 6,
1910. Not pictured: A.P.
and Marshall, born three
years later. (Courtesy of
John Rudder Jr.)*

their God by helping each other, practicing virtue and brotherly love.[18] Their theology harmonized with the reality that nearly everyone was dependent on others in times of need. Helping a family afflicted by sickness or crop failure was not only virtuous but was enlightened self-interest in the long term. The social safety net was reciprocated altruism—doing good for others because it was both right and carried with it the implicit understanding that it would be repaid in kind, if needed. When a mother was stricken ill, others went to her home and cared for her and her children. People called each other "sister" and "brother" even if their relationship was only proximity and a shared past, however recent. In these circumstances self-reliance was necessary and charity was wise, and the adult Earl Rudder practiced both.

Eden was Christian and ecumenical before the latter term was widely used. When the town was but a cluster of small frame houses, a common Sunday school was held in the first schoolhouse, built in 1885. There, too, itinerant preachers delivered fiery sermons to people of all denominations. Their exhortations brought a reprieve from the loneliness and tedium of rural Texas life. The tedium was particularly difficult for homebound women with an unrelenting daily routine of caring for children, cooking, washing, cleaning, and gardening. The Methodist church was organized in 1904, and the whole community pitched in to erect the Baptist church in 1905. Until the Lutherans had their own building, they met in the Methodist church, conducting their worship services on Sunday afternoons, alternately in English and German. Although the town was overwhelmingly Protestant, Roman Catholics made an early entrance into Eden, with immigrants arriving directly from Ireland. Like them and nearly everyone else in Eden, the Rudders' ancestors had come to America from the British Isles. The first Rudder in the New World entered Virginia in 1716.[19] The family name, Rudder, was Old English, derived from the Anglo-Saxon (fifth to twelfth centuries) word *rothor,* meaning a steering oar.[20]

Earl's mother expected her sons and husband to be with her in the Methodist church on Sunday mornings. To people outside the family, Earl's father seemed indifferent to church attendance. Men and boys wore coats and ties to church, their shirts stiffly starched and ironed. Earl sang in the church choir. He could not avoid learning Wesleyan hymns from eighteenth-century England, and his favorite became "A Charge to Keep," composed by Charles Wesley in 1762. Eunice Stephens attributed much of his success to his mother: "She prayed for her sons and counseled with them. Those boys would sit and listen to her read the scriptures." Besides the Bible, she had a small shelf of books that were traded among women in the town. The King James version of the Bible (and a Sears Roebuck mail order catalog) lay on a table beside her reading lamp.[21]

"THE NEXT GREATEST THING"

By 1920 electrical power was connected to most populated areas of the United States—but not Eden, Texas. The magic of electricity came to Eden homes five years later, when Earl was fifteen.[22] The nitty-gritty of living every hour of every day without electricity is difficult to comprehend for anyone who has never lived without it. In Earl Rudder's Eden, it meant no electric lights, stoves, or irons for clothing; no electric water well pumps or indoor plumbing; rub boards instead of washing machines; and no refrigerators. It meant that ordinary housework was sheer drudgery.

Without electricity, Earl's mother did her homemaking tasks—washing, cooking, ironing, canning (preserving food)—by hand as had his grandmother, his great-grandmother, and a long line of maternal ancestors. She cooked on a stove heated by burning wood that he or one of his brothers had cut into useable lengths, split with an axe, and carried indoors. Even boiling water was hard work that began when the water was carried indoors in buckets drawn from a well that had been dug by hand. Clothes were washed once a week, normally on Monday, followed by ironing on Tuesday, because of the time and labor required. Saturday was bathing day, and several people bathed in the same water (but not at the same time). Children washed their feet every night because they went barefoot during the day. For drinking water, a bucket with a dipper sat on the Rudders' back porch, and everyone drank from the same dipper.[23] So profound were the wonders of electricity that a story was told about an elderly woman who, soon after her home was electrified, arose in church to proclaim for all to hear, "The greatest thing in the world is to have the love of the Lord in your heart, and the next greatest thing is have electricity in your house."[24]

Many men who served under Rudder during the war would have been surprised to know that he learned to read by the light of a kerosene lantern with the illumination of a twenty-five-watt bulb and that he grew up in a home with an outdoor privy and no refrigeration. Without refrigeration, the only way to have vegetables was to buy them from neighbors or to raise them, which required tilling the soil, planting the seeds, hoeing the weeds, irrigating the plants, and harvesting the yield, all by hand. The Rudders had ten acres of land adjoining their home, enough for a garden, for chickens to range free, and for a cow milked by hand morning and night. Without refrigeration, milk that was fresh in the morning would clabber by evening on a warm summer day. After the whey was drained off, the clabber was stirred to make buttermilk. Mrs. Rudder wanted butter churned every day, and extra made on Saturday for Sunday's meals, when unnecessary work was not done. With the help of her boys, she may have sold butter and eggs to Eden grocers and other families, as was a common practice.

A ridge southeast of Eden is called Smoothing Iron Mountain for its contours, which resemble the cast-iron implement once used to smooth out the wrinkles in clothing. The smoothing iron was heated on a stove or hot coals. So hot was the iron that it could be gripped only by using a glove, a potholder, or rags for protection. Mrs. Rudder occasionally hired teenaged Evelyn Whitfield to help with household chores. Two years younger than Earl, Evelyn remembered the summer heat of the kitchen while ironing: "We had to keep the fire going to iron the shirts of all those boys. The shirts had lots of heavy starch. That's why the iron had to be so hot and heavy." As a practical joke, Evelyn starched Earl's undershorts and hung them on the outdoor clothesline to dry with other clothing. But he noticed they were stiff, swinging like wooden planks in the West Texas wind, removed them from the line, rinsed out the starch, and hung them back to dry.

Day or night, when Earl was leaving his home his grandmother might say, from a habit formed in her early life, "Look out for Indians."[25] She still

called a full moon a Comanche Moon for the time when those master horse-
men swept across the plains during bright lunar phases to burn houses, steal
horses, kidnap children, and take scalps. One night Evelyn Whitfield was
leaving the Rudder home to walk to her own home through Eden's unlighted
streets, when Earl called out, "No, you can't go there alone after dark. I'll go
with you." He insisted because he knew a young man along the way had been
pestering her. This was a sign of his lifelong tendency to intrude in the concerns of people he cared about when he believed they were making a mistake
or needed protection. His intervention was not always welcome, but he had
internalized the lesson of the Good Samaritan and believed it was his duty to
help people, even when they did not want help. All the same, Evelyn Whitfield was grateful when he escorted her through Eden's dark byways.[26]

"The darkness was familiar and I loved to take a quilt outside, lie on the
ground, and look at the stars," said Blu Bell Maddox.[27] However, walking
outdoors on summer nights involved more than overcoming fears of hob-
goblins and ghosts in the darkness. There was a real danger from the potentially aggressive western diamondback rattlesnake, whose bite could be
fatal or crippling. Almost of necessity, people had to walk outdoors in the
darkness knowing that a rattlesnake could be in their path. It was a way of
life instilled from childhood that required grit and a willingness to risk the
odds, if only for privy trips and chasing fireflies. With the pluck and self-
assurance thus acquired, Rudder later trained and fought his battalion and
regiment at night.

INCUBATOR OF PATRIOTISM

When Earl Rudder was a child, men still lived in Concho County who had
fought in the Civil War (1861–65), fended off Indian raids (the last in the
early 1870s), and ridden horses to drive immense herds of cattle to railroad
terminals in Kansas and beyond (1865–75). They were the heroes and story-
tellers of the era. Many had heard the Comanche war whoop and had given
the Rebel yell. Their stories depicted boldness in the face of danger, comradeship, injury, and sometimes death. Listening to them, a boy might make up
his mind that a real man should be as they had been: skillful with weapons,
physically strong, calm under life-threatening pressure, and loyal to friends.

The largest gathering of these legendary figures of the Texas frontier occurred each year during Eden's Fourth of July celebration in a grove of oak
trees just west of town called the Pfluger Motte for its owner, Lee Pfluger. The
gatherings were grassroots Americana, three-day patriotic rallies with flying

banners, barbecue, baseball, a rodeo, horse races, speeches by politicians, and dances in the evenings set to fiddle music. Farm and ranch families came from miles around and stayed for the whole shindig. For many it was the only time they got away from home in the entire year. A rancher would donate a beef or two for the barbecue, and the women prepared the sides, as the other dishes were called. Under the big trees there were domino games and the steady clink of steel on steel as people pitched horseshoes.

At age eighty-nine, Blu Bell Maddox mused, "We lived from one year to the next for the Fourth of July." She loved seeing the people gather. "Usually a

Rudder, age five, Eden, Texas, 1915. (Courtesy of Margaret Rudder)

traveling carnival would come with cheap sideshows, and I wanted to see the fat lady. There was a platform for speakers, and there were lots of politicians in an election year."[28]

Imagine a chubby eight-year-old Earl Rudder with curly brown hair, dressed in blue overalls, seated on the ground in the shade of the Pfluger Motte on July 4, 1918. He hears the old trail drivers, Indian fighters, and Texas Rangers tell their harrowing tales. Rudder has come along just in time to see and talk with the men who had fought to preserve and extend civilization on the American frontier. It was a fleeting moment in the history of the American West. In their company a boy could be transposed in time and place, his mind enthralled with images of a scrape with the Apaches at Packsaddle Mountain in nearby Llano County in 1873 and in the charge against the Yankees at Shiloh eleven years earlier. Their linguistic influence can be seen in his unaffected use of the word *damnyankee* in reference to the wife of an officer on his staff from New York in 1944. He uttered and wrote it as he had learned it: uncapitalized, neither vulgar nor profane, simply the accepted term for a northerner in the Eden of his childhood.[29]

All about the Pfluger Motte young Earl witnessed the vivid scenes of intense nationalistic fervor that swept the United States during the war to end wars: speeches, flags waving, and young men in uniforms on leave from training at Camp Bowie near Fort Worth, where they were preparing for the battlefields in France.[30] Adding depth and substance to these lasting impressions, forty miles west and southwest of Eden lay the crumbling ruins of two abandoned U.S. Army posts, Fort Concho and Fort McKavett. From 1852 to the early 1880s, soldiers from the forts kept watch over settlers on the frontier.[31] Above the scattered stones, chimney towers stood like lonely sentinels, affirming the truth that the power of the federal government had been required for homesteaders to settle the land. Public safety, law and order, civilization itself depended on an effective government willing to enforce its policies with military power.

As Fourth of July celebrations imprinted patriotic images on the minds of children, the schools of Eden molded ideals and habits. Each morning one lucky child was selected to pull the colors up the pole while all recited the "Pledge of Allegiance," a prayer for the nation. At school assemblies teachers and children sang the cherished songs of the nation as well as "Dixie," a popular song in the Southern states during the Civil War. Earl's civics class, taught by the superintendent, E. Walter LeFevre, included lessons on family responsibilities and moral excellence as well as the rights and duties of citizenship. LeFevre virtually forced his students to learn by requiring them to write the entire lessons in longhand in their Red Chief notebooks.[32]

In history, character was taught by inference as qualities exemplified by the nation's founders—Washington, Jefferson, Patrick Henry, and others—who were held in awe without compromise or psychological analysis. Most children took to heart the romanticized qualities and values attributed to the founding fathers and never forgot the lines, "I cannot tell a lie," "All men are created equal," and "Give me liberty or give me death." Robert E. Lee's famous maxim, "Duty is the sublimest word in the English language," was heard by every school child in the South, and Rudder came to admire Lee as America's greatest captain. In 1959, not long after he became president of Texas A&M, Rudder told a group of students, "Robert E. Lee stands out above all as the epitome of military leaders. There is no finer example of leadership to emulate." He spoke from a prepared text, but he made notes in the margin. After writing, "Duty is the," he stopped and drew a line through those three words. (After all, *sublimest* is not a proper word; General Lee should have said "most sublime.") Rudder then wrote these notes to describe Robert E. Lee:

"Reverent, modest, compassionate"
"Highest type of character, brilliant"
"His life before, during, and after military worth studying."[33]

Eden was a virtual incubator of patriotism, a place where the people's pride as Americans gave cohesion to community life. Everything that Rudder saw and heard in those formative years contributed to his adult character. Years of maturing and testing on fields afar would season his judgments and define his character, but the imprint of his Eden boyhood can be seen in every major endeavor of his life. The core was the tight hold of his family, especially of his mother; then, the school, where lifelong friendships were forged; followed by the larger community, which imposed standards with an invisible web of constraints that connected to his school and family. In all the goals that he would pursue, Earl Rudder was branded as a product of Eden, Texas, as it was in the first quarter of the twentieth century.

HIGH SCHOOL AND FOOTBALL

Although Eden was isolated, local citizens made resources available that were the basis of a sound education for young people. The town had a free lending library and an "exceptional high school," in the judgment of Ira Eaker, an Eden boy a dozen years older than Rudder, who became one of the founders of the U.S. Air Force, rising to four-star rank. Eaker credited the local school superintendent, David Crockett Broyles, with setting the tone of the community. He was, Eaker believed, "a man of great character who made us think about problems beyond our small environment" and encouraged us "to adopt professions that would be useful to the state and the country." Broyles established a newspaper, the *Eden Echo,* and as the county superintendent remained influential during Rudder's era when the high school was selected as one of the hundred best in Texas. In Eaker and Rudder, Eden, Texas—where the railroad dead-ended and people lived without electricity, running water, or paved roads—produced two prominent military leaders, innovative thinkers, purposeful with their lives and faithful to duty.[34]

High school football gave Earl Rudder a handhold on the challenges of adulthood, and he made the most of it. His first games at the age of fifteen infected him with a passion that set him apart from his peers. As a youngster he lived to play the game, and he made coaching football his initial profession an adult. As a vehicle for personal development, football capitalized on his innate capabilities and enhanced the man he was becoming. Eden enthusiasts applauded his achievements and built his confidence. Upon completing high school, football unexpectedly became his exit ticket from Eden, sending him to college and launching him on his early career.

As the fifth of six brothers, Earl took to a sport that epitomized male companionship and burly competition at close quarters. The game evoked mental qualities and demanded physical skills that were important preparation for leadership in both war and peace. "War," he said in his understated way while home on leave at the end of World War II with scars of a bullet wound in his leg and shell fragments across his chest and arm, "is all teamwork. Fighting a battle is a lot like playing football, only in war the teams are bigger and the stakes are deadly."[35]

If Earl had entered high school two years earlier, he would have played no football games in Eden. The school sponsored its first team in 1925, the same year that Eden High School published its first yearbook, the *Bulldog,* named for the school mascot, always Earl's favorite canine breed. Stories about Earl Rudder abound in the tributes written by his teachers and fellow students in his yearbooks for 1925–26 and 1926–27. The commentaries were sentimental, but they were also the equivalent of a public discussion about him, because all the writers knew that others would read what they had written.

Nicknamed "Curly," he was popular and admired as an athlete who had little interest in academics or in extracurricular activities other than sports. Excelling in football drew attention to his likeable personality and his muscular physique, but he was never elected class officer or selected most popular boy, as were his closest friends, M. J. Green, Carl Pfluger, and John Miller, who virtually rotated those honors among them.[36]

The foursome—M. J., John, Carl, and Earl—were well known and fun loving. John was artistic and jovial; M. J., thoughtful and contemplative; Carl, reflective and generous; and Earl, competitive and striking. John Miller captured Earl's adolescent appearance when he called him "The Bulldog of Eden High, the guy with the massive physique. The big, true, loyal, and foolish—still capable—friend when necessity commands." As for his "massive physique," at age sixteen Earl was almost six feet in height, when the average American adult white male stood a shade over five feet, eight inches.[37]

Forty years after Rudder's high school days, when he was president of Texas A&M University, his daughter Anne asked why he had left Eden. He replied that he did not want the other boys to get ahead of him—the "other boys" being M. J., Carl, and John. An important consideration in his competition with friends involved a comparison of their fathers' attainments. In that regard, the other boys were so far ahead of him that his best option was to seek his fortune elsewhere. Although in adulthood Rudder was characterized

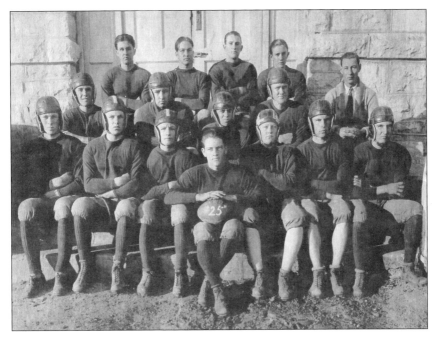

Eden High School 1925 football team, the first in the school's history. Rudder is in the
front row, second from the left. (Bulldog, Eden High School, 1926)

by supreme self-confidence, recollections of his status in Eden relative to his
best friends motivated him in ways that no written record reveals.

As teenagers in Eden, Earl and his friends were far from perfect—and
closely watched. Their problem in getting away with mischief was that virtually every person they encountered had an ongoing relationship with their
parents; their mothers might hear what they had done before they returned
home. Corporal punishment was in vogue, and Earl got it like most other
boys. With a "gleam of fond memory in his eye," M. J. Green told how he and
Earl were "cutting up in class," and the teacher sent them to the school superintendent, who decided they should receive a few licks with the paddle. M. J.
went first, and when Earl saw the effect on his friend, he refused to follow. He
persuaded his father to go with him to see Tom Drinkard, president of the
school board. Drinkard brooked no sympathy for Earl and told his father,
"Mr. Rudder, if you want that boy to grow up to amount to anything, you'll
let him take those licks." Earl considered the whipping an important lesson
in his life; it was also a precedent for his disciplinary methods as a father.[38]

With football emerging as a national pastime in the mid-1920s, Eden
High School had no money for suits, as uniforms were called then. But so
great was football fervor that for the first games in 1925 a "few loyal boosters

*Rudder's stellar performance on the 1926 Eden High School football team earned him a scholarship to play for John Tarleton Agricultural College. (*Bulldog, Eden High School, *1927)*

[Eden businessmen] bought the suits on credit and paid for them with receipts from the games." Not many suits were required, because only fifteen boys came out for the team, and only three of them had ever seen a football game. The team's practice and playing field was actually grazing land for livestock, merely an unimproved clearing surrounded by undersized mesquite trees a mile away from the school on the other side of town. Littered with small stones, it had only sprigs of grass. Spectators stood along the sidelines or sat in their horse-drawn buggies or cars. Fans who came on horseback had to learn not to tie their horses to the goalposts.[39]

The team ran between the school and the practice field, but that was not enough for Earl. After each practice he insisted on running extra laps around the field. M. J. Green would "always remember [Earl for] causing me to take the extra trip around the football track."[40] Earl had already learned the value of physical conditioning, which became one of his cardinal principles as a football coach in the 1930s and as a wartime commander.

Rudder was a stalwart in the center of the line, a pillar on offense and defense, the acknowledged leader of the team before team captains were customary. Eleven players from each team were required on the field at all times. For a small school like Eden, a full complement on the field was only possible if most boys played the entire game, injured or not. They played before the advent of pain-killing medications and without medical personnel on the sidelines. In the absence of antibiotic medications, trivial cuts and abrasions that became infected could be life-threatening. Newspaper accounts of the period have frequent references to serious injuries—broken legs, arms, collarbones, and ribs as well as paralyzing spinal injuries—and death. Brain concussions, with symptoms of dizziness, headaches, or blurred vision, were usually ignored as long as the boy was still on his feet; their cumulative, adverse effects on cognition and mental health were not even suspected.

Essential safety standards for the players were not recognized. Rules were inadequate and violated wholesale. Protective equipment was almost nonexistent by later standards. Helmets, made of thin leather layers, could be folded and carried in a boy's pocket and were frequently knocked off. Padding was not required.[41] Coaches and officials were not professionally prepared. There was no consensus about how to best protect the players. Some parents could calculate the odds of injury to their sons, but the enthusiasm of coaches and community boosters, coupled with the desire of the boys to engage in this daring and exciting game, was difficult to resist. Football was the ultimate challenge in teamwork, requiring mutual support and cooperative effort of all players. Boys quickly learned the ethic of the game: team and teammates come first, not personal well-being. Those who persisted in playing the game eventually realized the essential quality for success was fearlessness.

A rare photograph of a play in action shows Rudder as a presence on the field. He stands above the churning bodies of his teammates and the opposing team, his helmet knocked from his head, his face calm and his gaze fixed on the ball carrier across the field. Despite the emotion and turmoil around him, his mind is focused on the decisive action occurring elsewhere, an early insight into his steadfast leadership and calm presence that men noticed again and again. His subordinate, Elmer H. "Dutch" Vermeer, would write about Rudder under great stress and danger in Normandy in 1944: "Seeing [him] in command all the time saved our day. He was the strength of the whole operation in spite of his wounds. Under his leadership, miracles seemed possible."[42]

Rudder's high school principal, Kathryn Torrance, told him she might "forget some people, but I can never forget you. Neither will I forget the Santa Anna game when you cried so hard." It was only Earl's second game in organized play, but it revealed his passion and his commitment to play and win. The opposing team flagrantly violated the rules by playing an adult man whose wife and child watched from the sidelines. The older man repeatedly plunged into the center of the line where Rudder anchored the defense. An Eden student described "watching Santa Anna's two hundred pound, twenty-five year old back, slash thru [sic] the defense for gain after gain in spite of all efforts to stop him. The Bulldogs lost their confidence and went down by 13–0."[43] Observing Earl's determination and despair, Kathryn Torrance put her finger on a distinctive quality that would characterize Rudder for life: when he undertook a task, he pursued it with his whole heart.

Eden High School 1926 basketball team, district champions. Rudder is standing third from the right. (Bulldog, Eden High School, 1926)

In the spring of 1927, the class prophet forecast a bright future for Earl if he put forth the effort: "At last we have found perpetual motion in Earl's smile. All who remember how he won football fame in '26 know that he can succeed at anything he tries."[44] The younger boys looked up to him, and they wrote affectionately, "Don't forget me," "I hope we are always friends," and "I will always remember you for your sportsmanship."[45] M. J. Green wrote, "I will always remember playing at your right side."[46] In the community ambience of Eden—with its sense of unity, where people chipped in to help each other and talked face-to-face without the interference of cell phones, computers, or television—he developed an empathetic understanding and caring for people.

A NEGATIVE ROLE MODEL

"Earl's father never found his niche," Margaret Rudder would say when asked about the elder Rudder. Of Earl and Margaret's children, only their oldest daughter, Anne, recalls her father ever speaking of his father and then only to say, "You would have liked him." That's the entire recollection of Earl's family about his father, Dee Forrest Rudder (1872–1935), who died before they were born.[47]

After trying farming and ranching, Dee Rudder decided to make his living buying and selling anything of value, mainly selling real estate. Although he sold many properties in Concho and neighboring counties, he was negligent in filing and recording deeds for his clients, sometimes leaving a buyer without clear title to property duly purchased. Court records show that he had misunderstandings with men who did business with him regarding deeds, promissory notes, and contracts of sale. As a result, he was occasionally summoned to court for a judge to reconcile a transaction. The judges usually ruled in his favor, but he was not a stranger in the Concho County courthouse for the resolution of his business activities.

In contrast to his father, Earl was focused, well organized, and meticulous in his record keeping. He personally set up his filing system and, when he held public office, he hired an assistant at his expense to work after normal business hours to help with filing and responding to correspondence.

Evelyn Whitfield knew the Rudder family quite well from her employment to help Mrs. Rudder in their home. To boost the family income, Mrs. Rudder took in boarders and hired Evelyn for all manner of household chores. When Evelyn stayed overnight in the Rudder home, she slept on a single bed in the same room with Mr. and Mrs. Rudder. At times Mrs. Rudder had seven boarders, her husband, her sons Earl and Marshall, Evelyn, and herself—eleven persons—in the small house. Thinking of them three-quarters of a century later, she reminisced, "I loved them, and I think they loved me too." She remembered the house so well that she could draw a sketch of it showing the location of the furniture in each room. In one room, five highway workers slept in two double beds and one single bed; two teachers slept in another room in one bed; Earl and Marshall slept together in a screened-in section of the back porch that had been converted into the kitchen. With money from the boarders, the Rudders purchased a windmill that pumped water from the backyard well up to an elevated storage tank that provided running water with modest pressure in the house. Indoors, they constructed a small indoor bathroom that was usually reserved for the women, while the men used the outdoor privy.

Dee Rudder had likeable qualities that he capitalized on as a commission man. At the same time, Evelyn Whitfield observed, "I never knew Mr. Rudder to do much of anything."[48] Unfortunately, he came of age in Texas in the aftermath of the Civil War, a period of economic impoverishment and limited possibilities for an education. Poverty was almost certain for a man like Dee Rudder, the son of a Confederate veteran who had gone to war with

scant material possessions and returned with nothing to a lawless land that
afforded few opportunities. Dee married at the age of nineteen, was soon the
father of several children, and never accumulated the capital necessary to
acquire productive land for farming or ranching.

After he died in September 1935, his widow discovered she could not probate their community property. Her husband had not obtained clear title to
the property where they had made their home since they bought it in 1921
with a vendor's lien attached. Seeking a court judgment to clarify her title to
the homestead, Mrs. Rudder instigated a friendly suit against her husband's
creditors, all of whom disclaimed ownership in the property. The court ruled
in her favor and conveyed clear title to the property in 1939, eighteen years
after Rudder bought it on a note to be paid within one year. If he had paid
off the note, he did not obtain a release of the lien. In Dee Rudder's death,
as in his life, a judgment of the court was required to clarify his personal
business.

When Mrs. Rudder probated their joint estate, it showed no material assets except their home and 10.4 acres of adjoining land, which she sold for
two thousand dollars. She then moved permanently to Brady to live in a du-
plex built for her by her sons Earl and John. With her departure, not one
member of her large family remained in Eden. Longtime residents lament
that after graduating from high school, Earl rarely came back for a civic or
community event. He returned to Eden many times for private visits with
friends, but only twice for public occasions. Both were for reunions of Eden
High School's first football team, in 1948 and 1959.[49] As a renowned native-
born son schooled in Eden, his presence would have been appreciated at any
public event, but he did not come—not to victory celebrations after the war,
not when he was mayor of Brady (1946–52), not while he was Texas state land
commissioner (1955–58), and only one time while president of Texas A&M
University (1958–70).

Why did Rudder ignore the place of his birth and boyhood home? Self-
consciousness about the relative standing of his father may have been a factor.
In the years immediately after high school, he could have been embarrassed
by the comparison of his father to the fathers of his friends. Staying away
from Eden's celebratory occasions was a tendency that, once begun, he never
stopped. In comparison to Ira Eaker, Rudder slighted Eden. Except for the
war years, Rudder lived his entire life in Texas, and a trip to Eden would have
been easy for him in comparison to the distances that Eaker traveled. Almost
until his death in 1986 at the age of ninety, Eaker journeyed to Eden from
Washington, D.C., and California to reunions and served as grand marshal

for parades. He was lionized at Eden's victory parade after the war and was "grateful and excited with the invitations" from Eden.[50]

As Earl learned from his father how *not* to conduct personal business affairs, the larger lesson was to avoid failure, which became a wellspring of his determination to succeed at whatever he did. In adulthood he coupled this determination with the habit of purposeful improvement, which was obvious to those closely associated with him. Even so, the foundation of Earl Rudder's accomplishments was the influence of his mother, who taught values based on the commandments and exemplified loving selflessness. Evelyn Whitfield made the point when, reflecting on Earl's life, she concluded, "He pulled himself up by his bootstraps and the love of his mother."[51]

CHAPTER 2

TARLETON COLLEGE

1927–1930

On a summer day in 1927, a stranger driving across the vast, open spaces of West Texas stopped in Eden for his noon meal. Although anonymous in Eden, the traveler was well known a hundred or so miles northeast toward Fort Worth, especially in the vicinity of Stephenville, where he was the football coach at John Tarleton Agricultural College.[1] His name was William Jones "W. J." Wisdom, and he was canvassing West Texas for players to fill out his team. Before the advent of widely circulated newspapers and radio networks, outstanding high school athletes gained acclaim mostly by word of mouth and were recruited to colleges by coaches who searched them out and enticed them to enroll.

Long years later Wisdom thought back on that fortuitous day. "I asked the cafe man if there were any football players in town. He immediately replied there was one! He said it in a way that interested me so I asked if I could see him."[2] Wisdom learned the boy's name was Earl Rudder; he had just graduated from high school and, at that moment, was clerking in the Eden Drug Store across the square. Finding Rudder, Wisdom quickly sized him up and proposed that he enroll at Tarleton College in September and play football. To Rudder's protest that he had no money, Wisdom vaguely promised a scholarship. "Come on and we'll work out something," which meant he did not actually have football scholarships, as they were later formalized. Wisdom's "scholarship" was his assistance in getting odd jobs around the campus—mowing the grass, tending flower gardens, cleaning classrooms, waiting tables—as well as lodging in the least expensive dormitory. From yet undetermined sources, maybe from his own pocket, he would help pay tuition.[3]

Rudder could not agree then to Wisdom's proposal. The ramifications were too complicated for a seventeen-year-old to resolve before talking them through with his family and friends. Merely the idea of going to college was a radical departure from the aimless future then before him. Of the nineteen graduates in his class, only one of the eight boys, Raymond Pfluger, was definitely college bound. An indifferent student, Earl, like his friends John Miller and M. J. Green, expected to remain in Eden and find a way to get by. They had hashed over hitchhiking to California, but that ended when Earl took the job in the drugstore. Without goals or purposeful intentions, chance and circumstance would determine their fortunes. Now Wisdom had presented Rudder with another possibility, and the question was not whether he could go to college but whether he had the courage to go. He needed time and told Wisdom he would let him know. Wisdom tantalized him with his favorite recruiting tag line: "At Tarleton, we set the best training table in the state."[4]

Rudder, age seventeen, in his graduation year. (Bulldog, Eden High School, 1927)

Although Wisdom went away from Eden without a firm commitment, he had gained Rudder's confidence. His firm but soft manner of speaking inspired trust, and the muscular development of his five-foot, ten-inch frame impressed a fellow athlete. Wisdom was a gifted self-taught coach who achieved remarkable win-loss records coaching two team sports that he had never played: football and basketball. He was first employed at Tarleton in 1920 as the business manager of the college store and began coaching four years later when budget reductions threatened his job. He took on the assignment at the suggestion of Tarleton's executive dean (president in all but title), J. Thomas Davis, who had hired him. In the nine years that he coached football, his teams won almost three-fourths of their games.[5]

When the Great Depression of 1929 further reduced the college budget, Wisdom also became Tarleton's basketball coach. Starting from scratch, he studied and read books about the game, recruited "athletes" rather than specialized players, and "gave them the freedom to use their natural tendencies rather than mine." He encouraged them to "cut up on the court" and emphasized the elimination of errors. His record was astonishing. In a five-year winning streak Wisdom's basketball teams won 111 of 112 games, including 86 in a row, a performance so remarkable that he was featured in Ripley's "Believe It or Not!"[6] Wisdom could have been a big fish in a big pond, but he preferred to remain a big fish in a small pond—John Tarleton Agricultural

W. J. Wisdom (1887–1981), Rudder's coach and role model at the John Tarleton Agricultural College. (Courtesy of Tarleton State University)

College in Stephenville, Texas. Truly the atypical athletic coach, his secret diversion was listening to symphonic music, a lingering passion from his student years at North Texas State Teachers College, when he was the first chair violinist in the orchestra.[7]

Wisdom's proposal created a dilemma for Rudder. To decline or ignore the offer was as much a decision as to accept. His father was no help, quibbling, "You're already making more money than I was when I married your mother." His mother may have swayed him to accept with biblical allusions in the vein of "Keep moving toward the Light." Not one of his four older brothers had gone to college, although John would earn a license to practice pharmacy. From the standpoint of a robust young athlete, Wisdom's offer coupled an adventure into unfamiliar territory with playing the game that he loved. Other events in that phenomenal year of 1927 almost certainly stirred his aspirations. In May the boyish Charles A. Lindbergh flew nonstop from New York to Paris, capturing the imagination of the world and opening a new era for human potential. While Rudder was deciding about Tarleton, Lindbergh was piloting the *Spirit of St. Louis* on a victory tour of the United States. He flew near Eden and Stephenville and stayed overnight in Abilene.[8] More in line with Rudder's athletic interests, by midsummer Babe Ruth was on a torrid pace to hit a record sixty home runs in a single season. Why should a vigorous, high-spirited boy remain in a situation with limited prospects when fascinating possibilities beckoned elsewhere?

Whatever Rudder's rationale, he decided to take up Wisdom's offer. The absolute minimum expenses for the fall semester of 1927 at Tarleton College were $247.50, including tuition and fees ($20.25), food and lodging ($152.25), and $75.00 for military uniforms, because the Reserve Officer Training Corps (ROTC) was required for men.[9] When Rudder counted all of his money, he had about $100.00, less than half the minimum required for only one-half of the school year. Wisdom would have to provide the difference or Rudder could not remain at Tarleton.

So Rudder went to college to play football for W. J. Wisdom. In the progression of his career, seven distinguished men would see in him the qualities of a champion and promote his interests, usually while advancing their own. (The others were his father-in-law, Willie W. Williamson; three generals, Lloyd R. Fredendall, Omar N. Bradley, and Troy H. Middleton; Texas governor Allan Shivers; and President Lyndon B. Johnson.) Wisdom was the first. Rudder's chance encounter with Wisdom was the essential turning point that enabled him to position himself for those that followed. Not long before Rudder died, he affirmed Wisdom's incomparable lift at this crucial juncture in his life: "In 1927 . . . I had few resources and a small amount of ability to achieve success in an educational institution. The one person who helped me personally and who inspired me to achievement was W. J. Wisdom."[10]

Earl had to be in Stephenville on Wednesday, September 14, to register for classes. He could have taken the train, but the fare was $6.15. Hitchhiking was less expensive, available at almost any time, and maybe faster. He could pack his entire belongings in one cardboard suitcase, kiss his mother good-bye, walk fifteen minutes from their home on Duke Street to U.S. Highway 385 (the east-west road through Eden), and hold up his right thumb.

Few cars were on the road, but he probably did not wait long. Motorists would readily pick up a clean-cut teenage boy. His route to Stephenville was through Brady, Brownwood, Blanket, Comanche, and Dublin, 125 miles of unimproved roads, merely graded, with the topsoil pushed to the sides, except for two stretches of about five miles each. Through the hamlet of Blanket the road was simply dirt, either muddy or dusty, with deep, challenging ruts for drivers to straddle. The last four miles into Stephenville were the best of all; gravel was spread over the sod.[11] He may have ridden part of the way in the back of one of the popular 1925 Ford Model T pickup trucks, perhaps sitting on a bale of hay with the driver's children. In Stephenville he was farther from home than he had ever been, but not too far to walk back, if necessary.

Coach Wisdom had arranged for him to live in a World War I barracks that had been converted into a men's dormitory. Everyone called it "Fort John," and its residents ridiculed themselves as "Fort John Slime." Fort John was not even mentioned in the college catalog. Rudder declared that civil engineering was his major. Why not? Much road building was underway in West Texas, and jobs were plentiful for men trained in road construction.

Most of Tarleton's 1,011 students that fall of 1927 came from within fifty miles of Stephenville. Eden was twice that distance away, and Rudder may not have known another student, but he would not remain an outsider for long. Granted that college freshmen are aggressive social animals, the evidence is clear that he made strong first impressions on them that did not

diminish with time and familiarity. Nine months later they wrote effusively
in his yearbook about their first meetings: "I have enjoyed you since I saw you
the first time. . . . I shall never forget you," and "I won't forget the first time
I met you." Even two years later, a co-ed acknowledged fantasizing about
him: "I think of you real often. Do you remember the first nite [*sic*] I was ever
around you? You were at the skating rink." Their positive reactions foretold
similar responses to him by many people for the remainder of his life.[12]

Over the previous weeks and months Earl Rudder had morphed from an
awkward high school lad to an extroverted young man with an easygoing,
self-confident manner. He was casual, relaxed, neither pretentious nor self-
conscious. The other students found him fun-loving, engaging, and sympathetic to their concerns. One noted that his "million-dollar smile" shone
through in all circumstances, even when he "came up with a mouth full of
sand" from the football field.[13] This bursting forth, the newfound exuberance of Rudder's personality, reflected the influence of W. J. Wisdom. Confidence begets confidence, and Wisdom made Rudder's self-confidence soar.
Another factor was the effect of breaking away, disconnecting from Eden and
the restraints of life at home, releasing childhood inhibitions amid the excitement of meeting new and interesting companions. In his Eden birthplace
his face was familiar, and he was seen as "just an ordinary boy," as rancher
Will Loveless would say.[14] The social whirl of Tarleton College stimulated his
gregarious instinct and challenged his natural desire to be recognized.

TARLETON CULTURE

To his good fortune Earl had entered a collegiate environment that had been
intentionally crafted for young men and women like him—kids from small
towns, farms, and ranches away from home for the first time. "They had
grown up having to work hard," said one of them seventy years later. "They
had strong family roots, and good discipline." Although Tarleton had been
founded as an agricultural college, it had evolved into a liberal arts junior
college that included agriculture in its diverse course offerings. It had a good
academic reputation, and women made up almost half of the student body
and the faculty. The curriculum accommodated feminine interests in the
fine arts with a music conservatory, theater, graphics arts, and courses in
home economics, including one, nicknamed the "college of etiquette," for
young men, on table manners and conversation.[15] Women further influenced
the tone of the college through their social clubs and their literary and artistic societies.

Rules and customs imposed a high level of decorum, and all students were expected to attend chapel every day.[16] Using tobacco and frequenting "public dance hall[s]" were forbidden. All students—men and women—wore uniforms. Men were required to wear their military uniforms within five miles of the campus; they held cadet ranks, exchanged salutes, drilled, stood for reviews and inspections, fired weapons, and were taught military science by a regular army officer.

The women wore a blue chambray dress that was not available for purchase. Rich or poor, they were required to make four sets "with white Cambric collar and black Windsor tie" from a specific pattern that was available from mail-order houses. Low-heeled shoes, either black or brown, completed their regular attire. In physical training, which was required, they wore white middy blouses, white high-top tennis shoes, and black cotton bloomers.[17] All students ate in the college dining hall, and female students were required to live in the women's dormitory. In many ways Tarleton College was a contradiction, with characteristics of both an East Coast finishing school for girls and a military academy for boys.

"John's Rules" was the students' term for the school's numerous regulations, which were enforced with a system of "military discipline and demerit[s]" that were recorded on their official transcripts.[18] Rudder got his share. Sixty-five was the dismissal threshold in a student's first semester, and he got thirty-five for unspecified offenses, such as wearing a nonregulation uniform, failing to douse lights by 10:30 PM, or merely loitering on the grounds, perhaps on the lawn of the women's dormitory. A catchall rule covered "offenses against good order, propriety, and delinquencies not specifically enumerated." The rules were published in the fifty-six-page *Purple Book,* which urged students to "make the most of yourselves, physically, mentally and morally, then you will be best serving your home, your God, and your country."[19] Students did not protest the restrictions and moralizing; they and their parents accepted them when they enrolled.

Surprisingly, the emphasis on conformity in the appearance of women did not extend to hairstyles. Someone with authority—no doubt, Dean J. Thomas Davis—realized that the aim of a college education was not to produce carbon copies, and the girls made the most of it. Photographs captured their glamour and playful allure, enticing smiles, bobbed hair curled coquettishly in the mode of Irene Castle and Clara Bow, sideward poses while glancing over their shoulders, and flirtatious cutting of the eyes under shapely brows. The girls were animated by the lyrics and melodies of the flapper era: "Five Foot Two, Eyes of Blue" (1925), "Yes Sir, That's My Baby" (1926), and "Ain't

*J. Thomas Davis (1880–1950). As executive
dean of the John Tarleton Agricultural
College, he was a wise and trusted
counselor of Rudder the student (1927–30)
and the teacher-coach (1938–41). (Courtesy
of Tarleton State University)*

She Sweet" (1927). The term *sex appeal* was coined in the 1920s, and the young women at Tarleton had it. Some called a wisp of hair over the brow an "S-C," for sex curl. Samuel Hopkins Adams's description of the young people of the 1920s—"all desperadoes, all of them with any life in their veins, maybe the girls more than the boys"—aptly described the girls at Tarleton.[20] They were unlike the generation that came before or after them. Since their parents had sent them to a college that stressed culture and social life, even providing handsome young men in uniforms strutting about the premises, they would leverage the situation, have fun, and maybe snare a spouse. Tarleton was a marriage market par excellence on the Texas prairie, and Earl Rudder would have to fend off the prospects.

Tarleton was a sophisticated anomaly for its time and place, balancing traditional restraints with progressive approaches to education. The person responsible for this academic and political juggling act was Dean Davis, another personality who would influence Rudder for life. Educated in the classics, with two degrees from the University of Texas, Davis was a compelling classroom teacher, the austere head of the faculty, and the unquestioned academic leader of the institution. He had come to Tarleton in 1919 to create a collegiate culture that enhanced student appreciation for the finer things of life and of the world beyond West Texas. Although his rules were excessive by later standards, they were consistent with regional mores and gave him cover to offer music and art programs—considered frills by some public opinion makers—and to invite to the campus mildly controversial speakers who could come by train from Dallas in three hours.

Dean Davis's seeming omnipresence was not difficult, because his home was in the center of the campus. He attended chapel and sporting events. When the cadets stood for inspection, he towered above all, front and center in the reviewing stand. As he walked the campus at night, students snickered,

Rudder at John Tarleton Agricultural College in the fall of 1927. He enrolled in September 1927 and withdrew in November after playing in the last football game of the year without earning an academic credit. He worked on a road crew until the next fall when he returned to Tarleton as an increasingly serious student. (Grassburr, John Tarleton Agricultural College, 1928)

"If a sparrow falls to ground, Dean Davis will know about it."[21] Humane, dignified, and definite, he fostered an attitude within the faculty of helping students succeed rather than proving they could not. To avoid stigmatizing them as failures, the faculty did not award the grade of F for failure to attain a specified numerical average in a course. Instead, they gave Es and Ks. An E was for an average below 60 percent, and a K was for not completing the course requirements. The academic transcript of Earl Rudder is sprinkled with Es and Ks.

COACH'S ETHIC

When Rudder tried out successfully for the football team—the Plowboys—it was the beginning of his close association with Coach Wisdom. The affinity that developed between them was based on similarities that became more pronounced as the younger man absorbed the values and methods of his mentor. They played by the rules, played hard, and treated referees and opponents with respect. Rudder's teammates at Eden High School had praised his good sportsmanship. With similar zeal, Wisdom preached, practiced, and posted in his players' locker room the challenging principle for athletes proposed by the legendary sportswriter Grantland Rice. The poetic words stuck with them. Even when frail with age, they spoke with affection for Coach Wisdom, and some quoted the lines exactly:

> *For when the One Great Scorer comes to mark against your name,*
> *He writes—not that you won or lost—but how you played the Game.*[22]

From Wisdom, Rudder would learn much more than coaching techniques and game strategies. He would gradually absorb the subtleties of managing and motivating young men to perform demanding tasks while working together at the upper limits of physical exertion. Wisdom's players claimed his effect on them was mystical. He inspired them to be better than they were. Marshall Hughes, a basketball player, said, "I've never seen another man like him. He asked us to play as well as we could and we did. If he said we could beat another team, we simply went out and won."[23] Wisdom's greatest satisfaction came from fellowship with his players. He was their friend. He listened to them, counseled with them, and tried to persuade them to his philosophy of games and competition. As a mentor, he helped them develop as men rather than just athletes. His winning teams were as much, or more, byproducts of his relationships with the players as physical conditioning, clever and deceptive plays, or game plans. One of Rudder's teammates captured the visible essence of Wisdom's approach by describing him as a "coach with a smile that makes a slave of every man who works under him."[24]

At the same time, Wisdom was a fierce competitor who much preferred winning to explaining a loss. Although he kept the results in mind, he focused on processes. If the proper procedures were followed—from recruitment to practice to execution on the playing field—he believed his teams would win most of their games. Rudder adopted Wisdom's approach. If asked to explain, he might well have replied, "If you do everything right, you will come out ahead." In Wisdom, Rudder saw the kind of man he would aspire to be.[25]

Tarleton College's football team had an illustrious season in Rudder's first year, that autumn of 1927. In five conference games they scored 135 points while their opponents scored but 13, and they won the state junior college championship. Rudder gradually took over the starting center's position and usually played the entire game, since the rules did not permit free substitution. There were no special teams for kickoffs or field goals, and the same eleven men played on offense and defense.

All the while, his financial situation deteriorated. Halfway through the semester, he was virtually broke and informed Wisdom that he would have to withdraw from Tarleton. Wisdom asked him to postpone his decision until he could discuss Rudder's predicament with the Stephenville Lions Club. Presto! The Lions Club immediately announced a new scholarship, known casually as the "milk cow scholarship," that Wisdom promptly awarded to Earl Rudder. The Lions Club donated a two-year-old jersey heifer to Tarleton College, and Dean Davis permitted it to graze on college grounds. Rudder milked the cow each morning and evening and took the milk pail to the dining hall, where the value of the milk was deducted from his meal charges. A complication arose when the heifer did not yield a full pail, and the kitchen manager declined to give Rudder full credit. Rudder solved the problem with a nearby water hydrant and never again delivered less than a full pail, however diluted.

Over the years, rumors about the scholarship became legend. Wisdom did not tell the whole story until Rudder became president of Texas A&M in 1959. He had bought the cow in the name of the Lions Club for twenty dollars. In a congratulatory letter to Rudder, he wrote: "The twenty dollars I put up with the Lions Club to purchase a jersey cow was one of the best investments I ever made. I've had wonderful dividends." Rudder insightfully replied that Wisdom's satisfaction "was part of the remuneration that you did not get while active in coaching and teaching."[26]

With the various forms of financial aid that Wisdom arranged, Rudder managed to remain in school through the last football game of the season, and not one day longer. On Thanksgiving Day, Tarleton played for the state junior college championship against their traditional rival, North Texas Agricultural College in Arlington, also a branch of Texas A&M. The *Eden Echo* noted that "Mr. and Mrs. Dee Rudder and sons, J. P. and Marshall, motored to Stephenville," and Earl's brother John came from Fort Worth to see the game, which Tarleton won, 18–7.[27] Rudder then withdrew from Tarleton with no grades on his transcript and returned to Eden, in all probability with his parents immediately after the game. Evelyn Whitfield was helping Mrs. Rudder with boarders and recalled when "Earl ran out of money and had to come home." He got a job working on the Eden to Brady road construction crew and did not reenroll in Tarleton until the fall of the next year.

HEADWAY

In Rudder's second year at Tarleton (1928–29) he began telling classmates that he wanted to be a football coach. This decision reflected the deepening influence of W. J. Wisdom. In addition to playing ball for Wisdom, he made his best grades in Wisdom's course on the theory and practice of coaching. His other top grades were in military science. Thus, while a student at Tarleton he discovered the two professional passions of his adult life—coaching and soldiering—that he would follow until he was drafted to run for public office in 1946. Having reached these important conclusions about his future while a student at Tarleton College assured that the campus would always be one of his favorite places, a haven to which he returned as often as possible.[28]

The 1928 Tarleton football team was again the state junior college champion, and Rudder was elected team captain.[29] The big change from the

At Tarleton College Rudder was selected to the all-male Lucky 13 Club. The thirteen members were dandies, who decked out in tuxedoes for their parties held on the thirteenth of each month to make fun of bad luck symbols such as black cats and walking under ladders. (Grassburr, John Tarleton Agricultural College, 1930)

previous year was his broader participation in social life with money saved from nine months of working on the road crew. He joined the West Texas Club and was selected to the exclusive all-male Lucky 13 Club. The club had a party on the thirteenth of each month to make fun of bad luck symbols such as black cats and walking under ladders. Members were dandies, decked out elegantly in tuxedoes at their parties. Yet Rudder's main interests remained football, military science, and girls without entanglement.

In his third and last year at Tarleton (1929–30), Rudder marginally improved his grades to a B or C, clearly doing best in courses with practical applications. He took not one course in history, political science, literature, or a foreign language. Two courses in English composition were required; he made a D in the first course, which was sufficient to take the second course, but when he did, he got behind and dropped it. When he tried the same course again, he made yet another D. Since no course completed with the grade of D was acceptable for transfer to Texas A&M, he had to take both courses again when he got there. Still, his teacher at Tarleton, Irene Ellis, did not give up on him. Recognizing his potential, she nailed him with this assessment: "You have an extremely likeable personality that will always win for you many friends. Sometimes you don't do your best, but you will, won't you? And if you do the best you can, you are sure to have much success and happiness."[30]

However mediocre Rudder was in the classroom, he was a hit socially and made headlines in every football game. "Captain Rudder led his hard fighting Plowboys in a brilliant fight" and "Earl Rudder was without a doubt the outstanding player on the field for both teams" appeared in game accounts. Sportswriters speculated (correctly) that he was striving for a scholarship to play at Texas A&M the following year.[31] After he "led the Plowboys to victory over Gainesville Junior College, the whole town [of Stephenville, population four thousand] was roused with a downtown pep meeting and glorious shirt-tail parade."[32] Rudder was the man of the hour as they tramped around the red granite and white stone gothic courthouse in the town square. It was a scene for the canvas of Thomas Hart Benton, an idealized tableau of a spontaneous celebration by young and old in a small college town in the American heartland.

The celebrants that November evening seemed blissfully ignorant of transcending events that would soon subsume their lives: the crash on Wall Street only two weeks before—"Black Thursday," October 24, 1929—and the rise of fascism in Europe. One would precipitate the Great Depression, and the other would eventually bring war. Those harsh realities were in the future for students at Tarleton College, where many concurred with Katherine Smith, who wrote, "Whenever I think of Tarleton, I'll always think of Rudder."[33]

Although he was an object of football-hero worship, Rudder did not hang out exclusively with the jocks. Ann Maness thanked him for encouraging her to return to college: "Each time I think of what this year has meant to me I think that [but] for you I might not have put forth the effort to come back." The obstacles she faced are unknown, but many families were in economic distress. Another acknowledged that she did not expect to see him again: "I can honestly say I have never gone with any boy that treated me any nicer than you have." And yet another, at the end of a two-year infatuation, thanked him for not taking advantage of her, declaring, "I am proud that we did not break any of John's old rules such as 'out after hours,' 'car riding,' and 'dates other than [on the campus].'" Yet another complained that he declined her invitation to a picnic: "You went out and played football instead of going with me." He was not wholly indifferent. F. Scott Fitzgerald's view of flappers as "lovely, expensive, and about nineteen" is a clue about why Rudder did not have a serious girlfriend in college. Otherwise, he was more interested in football.[34]

To his teammates he was "a damned good sport and a real man." With self-effacing vulnerability, they praised him. "So many good things have been written to and about you that I feel unable to add anything." "It has been an honor for me to be mistaken for you." Dan Slater wrote, without further explanation, "I know damn well that you will make good, for you have more business ability than the rest of the Gym bunch put together. You could make money in the middle of the Sahara Desert."[35]

One student that Rudder did not meet was Lawrence Williamson, the son of a prominent rancher in Menard. When Williamson took his yearbook home, his twelve-year-old sister, Margaret—"Chick" to her family and friends—pored over it. She could never remember when she saw Earl the first time, but five years later in the summer of 1933 they began seeing each other, and four years later they were married. Late in life she would say, "I'd had my eye on Earl from the time I saw his photograph in my brother's yearbook from Tarleton."[36]

TARLETON LEGACY

The admiring comments of Rudder's fellow students obscured a quality that would distinguish him for the remainder of his life; he was not a self-promoter. In the yearbook it was customary to print each graduating senior's major and a list of activities and honors beneath his or her photographs. His could have been lengthy, but he listed none for his entire three years at Tarleton. All that appeared by his photograph was "Earl Rudder, Civil Engineering."

Further, as at Eden High School, he was not elected to office in any organization. He was one of sixteen first lieutenants in ROTC, all outranked by eleven other student officers.[37] Maybe he shunned leadership responsibilities because he had too much to do. As a mature adult, he was assertive and he looked after his interests, but, with one exception, others would choose him and put him into positions of influence and authority. The one exception was his pursuit of an opportunity to return to Tarleton as its football coach to work under W. J. Wisdom and Dean J. Thomas Davis.

Before Rudder took leave from Tarleton for the last time as a student, he asked Wisdom and Davis to write a farewell note in his yearbook. Each man addressed the virtues of gratitude, fealty, and perseverance. Wisdom, closer to Rudder than Davis, was personal: "With sincere appreciation for your loyalty and friendship, and for what you have done for Tarleton." In ten words, Davis made clear his undiluted dedication to Tarleton College: "Something to do, something to love, something to live for."

Davis found Wisdom, who found Rudder, whose conduct was thenceforth informed by the character traits he found in them. In the course of his life, Rudder would encounter many admirable men, but none would rival Wisdom and Davis, whose continuing influence was his legacy from Tarleton College.

CHAPTER 3

TEXAS A&M COLLEGE
1930–1932

Inspired by completing his basic course work at Tarleton College, Earl Rudder entered Texas A&M in the fall of 1930 with unprecedented motivation and self-direction. His new objectives would require an intense, consistent effort that solidified three distinct habits of his adulthood: setting personal goals, concentrating his mind, and improving himself, intentionally and selectively. He did not aspire to be a renaissance man, but this combination, plus his engaging personality, would progressively set him apart from most men. From this transitional period he became rightly known as a "fighter who never quit anything until it was finished," distinguished for his determination and persistence toward whatever goal he had set or had become his responsibility.[1]

An academic counselor evaluated his record and concluded that he would require three years to complete his bachelor's degree,[2] but he finished in twenty-one months by taking half a dozen courses each semester, which required up to thirty-five hours a week in classes and laboratories, and by attending summer school. He also participated in weekly drill practices, marching and calling cadence; held numerous part-time jobs; won the intramural wrestling championship in his weight classification; and starred on the football team. The wonder is when he had time to study, except on weekends. Given his financial straits and initial academic deficiencies, it was a blessing that there were no female distractions and few temptations to leave the campus on weekends. Few students left the campus on weekends in the early 1930s because classes were held on Saturday, and they had little cash during the Great Depression. Another motive for studying hard was to avoid expulsion for poor grades, mocked as a "one-way Corps trip" by the cadets.

In the summer between the two nine-month academic years when Rudder was a student at A&M, he did not go home to Eden but went for six weeks of military training, then returned to the campus.[3] By remaining there through the summer, he did more than earn credits toward his degree; he kept other students from taking his jobs, and he was available when other jobs came open, as they usually did near the beginning of the new school

Three Rudder brothers with their parents, ca. 1930. Left to right: *Earl, Marshall, and John behind their mother and father. (Courtesy of Margaret Rudder)*

year. By minimizing the time required to complete degree requirements, he saved money as well as time. In an era before grade inflation, his grades improved steadily, and, with one exception, a history course that he had to repeat, every course he attempted counted toward his degree. His many obligations forced him to plan each day carefully, with the result that his most important lesson at Texas A&M may have been learning to budget his time.

Thenceforth, he was always a busy man whose attitude about time was a distinctive quality. "If we only had more time we could get so much more done," he often said. He did not believe in extended vacations for himself, his family, or students. After he had a family, his idea of a summer vacation was a weekend on the coast with plenty of good food; otherwise, the two weeks of military training in the summer were his vacation, with the added benefit that he got paid for it. A winter vacation was a week during the Christmas holidays on the family ranch, where he also attended to the business side of the enterprise.

For similar reasons he never learned to fish or play golf, because he would not take the time away from other obligations. He was an expert with a revolver and a rifle; they were innate to his boyhood in rural Texas, military training, and ranching. Wild turkeys and white-tailed deer inhabited the same rangeland as his cattle, and with a rifle at hand he converted them to

meat on the table. The firearms were also employed on rattlesnakes and pred-
ators. He was not proficient with a shotgun for shooting birds on the wing
such as dove, quail, and pheasants.[4] Hunting game birds was a recreational
sport that would take him away from his vocations. Photographs of him in
the well-known Texas hunting camps with other prominent state officials
show him wearing a white dress shirt (with tie removed) and the trousers of a
business suit, suggesting that he came only to visit or had arrived late. Yet he
knew more about wildlife and livestock than most men because he had spent
much of his youth in the outdoors and was active in ranching. From the time
he enrolled at Texas A&M, his adult life centered on responsibilities rather
than recreations. His inability to distinguish between work and play defined
him as "a truly happy man," in the words of Mark Twain.

Rudder demonstrated his newfound single-mindedness even before
classes began. His first roommate, Al Davies, arrived at A&M as a freshman
("fish" in Aggie jargon) in mid-September 1930, a few days after Rudder did.
Al was given his room number in a dormitory called Goodwin Hall and told
that his "old lady" (roommate) was Earl Rudder, a third-year transfer student ("frog"). Upon finding the room, Al saw that no one was there, but that
mops, brooms, buckets, and dustpans were stacked on the floor. Puzzled, he
returned to the housing office for correct information about his room assignment. There was no mistake. Aggie cadets were responsible for cleaning
their rooms, and Rudder had a part-time job outfitting those in Goodwin
Hall, which entitled him to a reduction in charges for his room. Rudder and
Davies formed a lifelong friendship. Davies would earn two degrees from
A&M, have an outstanding career with Sears, Roebuck and Co., and serve on
the Texas A&M System Board of Regents in the 1980s.[5]

Rudder got the mop and broom concession by getting to the campus before other students and, probably, by having recommendations from Tarleton College's Dean J. Thomas Davis and Coach W. J. Wisdom. In addition,
Rudder had a well-placed and unexpected advocate in A&M's administration in the person of Tarleton's former registrar, E. J. Howell, who had relo-
cated to A&M over the summer. Before Rudder arrived at A&M, Howell sent
him a welcoming letter: "We are looking forward to your contact with A&M
and personally, I am counting on you making good, especially in the way of
athletics. Come to see me when you arrive."[6]

Although Howell approved Rudder's admission to A&M, he denied the
transfer of several courses because of subpar grades. Rudder appealed. In his
earliest surviving letter, he wrote. "Dear Mr. Howell, I never did pass Junior
English at Tarleton and I want to know if [I can] take an examination on it.
I had an average of about 68%."[7] Howell denied the appeal, leaving Rudder

with no choice but to spend an entire year retaking the courses that he had attempted three times at Tarleton. He passed with higher grades than at Tarleton, not because English composition was easier at A&M, but because he was a better student.

At the time, people usually got jobs by personal contact instead of formal application through a personnel office. Howell spread the word that Rudder was an exceptional young man who needed part-time work to remain in school. Since A&M had fewer than twenty-five hundred students in 1930, and the administrative staff was proportionately even smaller than it would become later, Howell easily made Rudder's name known to his colleagues.[8] Rudder reciprocated Howell's help in extraordinary ways thirty years later. In September 1945 Howell succeeded J. Thomas Davis as Tarleton's executive dean and was still in that position when Rudder became president of the Texas A&M University System in 1965. In the intervening years, Rudder was instrumental in elevating Tarleton to four-year status as Tarleton State College in 1959, thereby upgrading Howell's title from dean to president. Rudder's rise to prominence reversed their roles; he became Howell's benefactor, and he eventually treated Howell to a well-deserved retirement party.

But in 1930 Rudder was near the bottom of the pecking order, pleading for any kind of job that would enable him to stay in school. Some of his revenue-producing activities were waiting tables in the legendary Sbisa Hall, the "largest dining hall under one roof in the world," according to Aggie lore; working in the Aggieland Inn, a hotel on the campus; selling bookcases to freshmen and sophomores; and selling peanuts and candy from a table in his dormitory's "bull pen," the Aggies' name for the entrance hallway where the cadets gathered.[9]

Rudder officiated at intramural games, and he sold soft drinks during varsity football games at Kyle Field, a lucrative concession during his first year that he shared with seven other athletes on scholarship. Under Southwest Conference rules in 1930, transfer students had to play on the freshman squad during their first year. Hawking the beverages through the grandstands was the fun part, but in addition they ordered the soft drinks (hundreds of cases), received and iced them down, and cleaned up the premises afterwards.[10]

Rudder also loaned money to cadets who were broke before the end of the month. With his savings he set up a small-loan business and qualified applicants by lending only to those in advanced ROTC, who received a monthly stipend from the federal government. He collected the loans (with interest) by sitting at his peanuts-and-candy table in the bull pen where cadets gathered informally and his debtors could not escape him.[11]

In addition, as an advanced student in ROTC, Rudder received thirty cents a day in federal money for food—"subsistence" or "rations"—and a total of forty dollars for uniforms, an inadequate allowance spread over two years. In 1930 the A&M registrar estimated total necessary expenses for the nine-month academic year at less than nine hundred dollars, including seventy-five dollars for uniforms.[12]

To prepare for a career, Rudder changed his major from civil engineering to industrial education, probably on the advice of E. J. Howell, whose name appears on the document, and from whom he also learned that coaches were expected to teach other subjects and that industrial education was one of them. And by changing his major to education, his new degree plan allowed him to take courses about coaching and physical education. Thus, when Rudder completed his degree he was in the first generation of high school football coaches in Texas with both practical experience and theoretical preparation in concepts, principles, and emerging professional ethics, which were important in his first job.[13]

CORPS LIFE

The Texas A&M that Rudder entered in the fall of 1930 enrolled only white male students, almost all between the ages of eighteen and twenty-two. In going to College Station, some left their home counties for the first time. Like Rudder, most came from small towns, farms, and ranches, so much alike that they could easily identify with each other. For many, the A&M campus was the most impressive collection of buildings they had ever seen and the most densely populated place they had ever been. Merely being there with masses of other young men was a mind-expanding experience.

All students lived in a dormitory, ate in Sbisa Hall, and wore a prescribed uniform unless they were disabled, foreign, or pursuing a graduate degree.[14] The entire student body was organized as a military unit under the commandant of the Corps of Cadets, Col. C. J. Nelson, a regular army officer. Students could not leave the campus without first obtaining a "furlough" from Nelson, and they were not "permitted to keep motor vehicles or to make frequent use of motor vehicles kept by others."

Cadets marched with their unit three times each day from their dormitory along the Military Walk to Sbisa Hall, the mess hall, or "Soupy." Sbisa Hall was at the north end of Military Walk, sixteen hundred feet in a straight line from the south end at Guion Hall, an auditorium torn down in 1970 to provide space for the construction of the Rudder Tower and Conference Center.[15] Military Walk was the axis of the campus—exactly 640 steps at the regulation drill stride of 30 inches—and passed in front of all the dormitories. At a normal cadence of 120 steps a minute, it could be traversed in just over five minutes. Marching to Sbisa did more than instill discipline; it fostered pride in being an Aggie. Visitors gathered at Sbisa to view the whole Corps of Cadets marching along Military Walk to the commands of student officers. It was a stirring scene that evoked nostalgia in old soldiers and inspired young boys to be Aggies.

Tom Morris of Waxahachie waited tables with Rudder in Sbisa Hall. Their meals were their compensation. "Earl was a 'mealhound,'" laughed Morris. "He got a full plate and more every time." Morris and Rudder quickly learned new terms for the food that were shockingly different from those back home: Sugar was "sawdust"; catsup was "blood"; spaghetti, "worms"; eggs, "cackle"; coffee, "dope"; dessert, "cush"; cornflakes, "scabs"; bread, "gun wadding"; and peas, "shot."[16]

Hazing was deeply entrenched at Texas A&M despite specific prohibitions in state law and college regulations. The harassment of first-year students during meals was routine. At other times, the proverbial board of education was laid on their buttocks, and the bruises photographed and printed in the yearbook.[17] If Rudder was hazed, it was slight, because he entered as a third-year student and was either working or engaged in athletics, which made him inaccessible to upperclassmen. He was not harassed at meals because he was serving the tables. Circulating around the tables, however, he saw freshmen compelled to eat square meals (only ninety-degree arm movements permitted) while sitting on the edge of their chairs and deprived of cush (dessert).

When he became president of A&M, one of his first official acts was to forbid mealtime hazing, and he made other decisions discouraging all forms of hazing. If hazing was important to forming the Aggie spirit, he was deprived of the experience, yet by playing on the varsity football team and diligently performing his duties in the Corps of Cadets, Rudder participated in the two activities that for many Aggies were the spiritual essence of Texas A&M.

At the same time, Rudder was thoroughly inculcated with the egalitarian traditions that made Texas A&M a congenial college for poor boys. Ideally, cadets earned status by their achievements at A&M rather than by their family's wealth, political influence, or social prestige. The important differences between them were performance in three areas: academics, the Corps, and athletics. They lived together, marched together, ate together, attended class together, wore khaki uniforms, and, not surprisingly, stuck together. In those fundamental ways A&M was in Rudder's time, as it had been during the formative presidency of Lawrence Sullivan Ross in the 1890s, a college where the "sons of the rich and poor, high and low [were] treated as equals." In 1930 it was still true, as the first student yearbook proclaimed in 1895, that "here we all dress alike, eat alike and sleep alike."[18] And when Rudder became president of A&M, he emphasized to the state legislature the importance of A&M as a high-quality institution for "poor boys" with meager resources.

In addition to the egalitarian spirit and traditions that infused Texas A&M, the difficulties of most students during the Depression era uniquely bonded them to one another and to the institution. Henry C. Dethloff, A&M's centennial historian, discerned that the "spirit of Aggieland was at no time before or since so keen as it was during the 1930s and the early 1940s. The camaraderie and student unity at A&M . . . truly reached the pitch of the one great fraternity during the Depression decade."[19] At an impressionable period in their lives, more than two thousand young men lived in relative isolation, bound by the contagious magnetism of an institutional culture that combined the unifying influences of an army regiment, an academic college, and athletic teams. To diminish one Aggie was to diminish all.

Studies in military science prepared cadets for reserve commissions in several branches of the army, and Rudder selected the infantry over the artillery, the cavalry, the engineers, and the Signal Corps. Decades later, when he was a general, he used his influence on army policy to ensure that all soldiers went through basic infantry training, regardless of their branch of service. The choice of the infantry was right for him. He was skillful with his hands rather than technically inclined. Topography, recognizing and describing the surface features of land, was a required course for infantry cadets in which Rudder excelled, a natural consequence of walking over the countryside from early childhood and helping ranchers build barbed-wire fences across the irregular terrain of Concho County.

Rudder attracted attention for his military decorum. Mike Dillingham observed Rudder for the first time supervising intramural games. "I could tell immediately," Dillingham recalled, "that he had something in him." His perfectly pressed uniform and his military bearing were exceptional. At the age of ninety, Dillingham retained a sharp mental image of Rudder wearing an officer's service cap with a perfectly round brim, which was unusual. Many cadets removed the cap's internal expandable band, allowing the brim to sag along the edges, giving them a nonchalant, laid-back appearance. They called such a cap a "crusher." Dillingham also noticed that Rudder's cap was not tilted to the side but set straight toward the front of his head so that the brown leather visor actually shaded his eyes. The brass badge on the front (an eagle inscribed with "AMC") glistened. Crushed and tilted caps

*Rudder as a regimental staff officer in the Texas A&M Corps of Cadets. (*Longhorn, Agricultural and Mechanical College of Texas, *1932)*

were never Rudder's style. "He was dressed immaculately. He looked the part of an officer all the time," Dillingham remembered.[20]

Summer camp was an important part of the training required of ROTC cadets between their third and fourth years in college. The War Department decreed six weeks of training in tactics and weaponry on an army post under the direction of regular army officers with the intention of teaching all cadets the same fundamental principles, giving them a common view for the conduct of military operations. From early June to mid-July 1931, Rudder and other A&M infantry cadets trained at Camp Bullis, a military reservation in the hardscrabble Hill Country about twenty-five miles northwest of downtown San Antonio. Diamondback rattlesnakes were prevalent in the area, and the cadets made a game of finding and killing them. Shirtless, tanned, laughing, and filled with the excitement of young men merrily playing at war, the Aggies draped the carcasses of the malevolently handsome reptiles over their shoulders.

Individual marksmanship was fundamental to the way the army believed the next war would be fought, and the cadets spent much time firing rifles, pistols, and machine guns left over from World War I. They dug and built World War I trench–style field fortifications with firing steps even though this type of training was contrary to an army doctrine adopted in 1923 after extensive analysis of the American experience in the recent war. In theory, the army endorsed infantry and tanks operating together. In fact, the cadets did not train with tanks because the army's tank component was disbanded that very year, 1931, for lack of money. Gen. Douglas MacArthur, the army's chief of staff, concentrated his meager appropriation on personnel rather than equipment, in the belief that equipment would become obsolete but leadership would not.[21] MacArthur was correct in his decision, but the country would pay a price for this omission. In Normandy, American commanders—Rudder among them—would be compelled to take time out from fighting to have specialized training in tank and infantry coordination. Overall, Rudder's summer camp experience in 1931, except for the disciplinary value of drilling, digging, and marksmanship training, was the old story of the army's preparing to fight the last war.

FOOTBALL

Although Rudder had played three years of collegiate football at Tarleton, as a transfer student he was required to play on the freshmen team in his first year at Texas A&M. Even so, he was a star and photogenic. His performance propelled him to recognition on a campus where, as a classmate said, athletics were "all-important [because] in our situation, we are practically isolated from the outside world, non co-educational and enjoying limited social activities. Athletics fills this huge gap in student life."[22]

While Rudder enjoyed stardom on the 1930 freshman team, the varsity had a miserable season. Sportswriters speculated that the next year would be better because "Rudder and others would move up to the varsity and leave nothing to be desired." During most of the season the freshmen team was used as cannon fodder for the varsity's practice. It was boring, but it gave Rudder more contact with another remarkable coach, Madison "Matty" Bell. Bell was appreciated for the respect he gave each player and for never using a word of profanity. His coaching technique was repetitive exercises to perfect specific plays for a wide-open style of play.[23] He was admired, which enhanced his profession, but his influence on Rudder did not compare to W. J. Wisdom's.

Rudder's career on the varsity in the fall of 1931 began auspiciously when he set up a touchdown in the first game against Sam Houston State Teachers College, won by A&M 32–0. "Earl Rudder intercepted a pass and ran 20 yards before being downed at the Sam Houston twenty-three yard line."[24] Nonetheless, he competed for the starting center's position with Willis Nolan and Pete Robertson. Nolan had lettered the previous year, and Robertson's heftiness, at 205 pounds, gave him the upper hand because coaches concluded that bigger men were better blockers on offense and harder for the opposing team to move aside on defense. At 179 pounds, Rudder was disadvantaged, but he was tough, as evidenced by his winning the intramural wrestling championship in the 175-pound class.

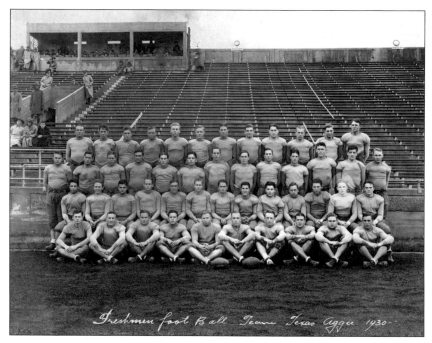

Texas A&M's freshman football team of 1930 in Kyle Field. Rudder is seated, second row, second from the right. As a transfer student he was required by the Southwest Conference rules to play on the freshman team in his first year. (Courtesy of Margaret Rudder)

On Friday evenings before a game the next day, the Aggie band marched in formation along Military Walk to the YMCA Building, playing "Goodbye to Texas University" and the Aggie battle song, "Wildcat." The "Y" had four Doric columns set on a porch nineteen steps above ground level. The entire team stood on the steps, and each member of the team was introduced. As they gazed over the assembled cadets for the first time, the scene was etched in the minds of new men like Rudder. Matty Bell captured the moment when he told the cheering crowd and his players, "To me the spirit of Aggieland is loyalty and a never-give-up attitude."[25]

When A&M played Tulane University in New Orleans, Rudder traveled outside of Texas for the first time. A photograph snapped as the team left the train in New Orleans caught him beaming. The team stayed in the famous Roosevelt Hotel. A slew of cadets got there somehow and slept twelve to a room. If Rudder dropped in on the Saint Charles Bar, he encountered scenes unlike any in Eden, Stephenville, or College Station. The walls, painted with figures of nude women, reeked with cigar smoke and the aroma of bourbon despite prohibitions against alcohol mandated by the eighteenth amendment.

Tulane, with its elephantine—for that era—forward wall averaging 201 pounds a man, eighteen pounds more than the Aggies, prevailed, 7–0, before seven thousand fans. "A light drizzle turned to a heavy shower and the weight of the ball became a factor" in the game. The ground was "too soggy and the ball was too wet and heavy for either team to flash its skill."[26]

Back on campus and preparing for future games, Coach Bell had an idea to gain more practice time, which was limited by late classes or labs and the gradual decline of daylight hours. He placed five searchlights on the practice field, and "when night [began] to fall and the lights [were] turned on, the players abandoned the usual tan colored football [for] a white one."[27]

Against formidable Texas Christian University, a winner over A&M the previous six years, Rudder played the entire game. Most of A&M's twenty-four hundred students went to Fort Worth for the game on special trains. The Southern Pacific Railroad assigned its crack train, the *Sunbeam,* known for its gleaming orange and black colors, to carry the team and hyped its speed and reliability by advertising the departure time from College Station at 2:12 PM on Friday before the Saturday afternoon game. Mike Dillingham was among only 350 students who remained in College Station. They crowded into a frame movie house west of the "Y" to watch Western Union's play-by-play ticker-tape account of the game projected on the screen, only a few minutes behind the actual game play. At that time, before radio broadcasts of games were commonplace, watching the projected paper strip, on which telegraphed accounts of the game were printed, was a way to follow the action of out-of-town games. Yet for all the Aggie spirit, the Horned Frogs scored in the fourth quarter and came out ahead, 6–0.[28]

When A&M played Southern Methodist University, Rudder collided across the line with another future university president, Willis McDonald Tate, who was named that year to the all–Southwest Conference team. Willis Tate served as SMU's president from 1954 until 1971. He and Rudder became well acquainted when their presidencies overlapped in the 1960s.[29] En route to the conference crown in 1931, SMU defeated the Aggies 8–0.

In mid-November, Matty Bell began preparing for the last game of the season, the Thanksgiving Day clash with the University of Texas, on A&M's historic Kyle Field, "more than steel and concrete" to the Aggies. The game was the thirty-eighth annual match between the Aggies and the vaunted Longhorns, prompting an A&M undergraduate to describe Texas as an "ancient foe." Rudder reminisced about this game against the "Tea-sips" more than any other. In the 1960s he told Wayne C. Hall, A&M's academic vice president, "how he enjoyed butting heads, and relished sacking [Wilson] 'Bull' Elkins," UT's star quarterback.[30] Elkins became president of the

University of Maryland. Twenty-five years later Elkins, Rudder, and Willis
Tate were named to the "Silver Anniversary All-American" football team by
Sports Illustrated.

Preparations for the Texas game proceeded at a feverish pitch around the
A&M campus and in Bryan, four miles north with 6,500 inhabitants. "Cadets
Make Bad Medicine at Big Fire," and "Thousands Coming by Auto, Train,
Plane for Big Contest," the newspaper headlines read. Bryan was in "festi-
val spirit" as hundreds of guests began arriving to stay in private homes. In
the absence of an established airport, landing fields were cleared for private
airplanes, and seventeen special trains were scheduled to bring more than
20,000 spectators. An overflow crowd was expected for Kyle Field's seating
capacity of 33,760.[31]

Gov. Ross Sterling tossed out the ball to start the game, but dreary weather,
"cold chilling winds from the north," and threatening rain kept many people
away, and a crowd of only about 22,000 saw the Aggies prevail over Texas,
7–6.[32] From down on the field that day, Rudder witnessed a method of conveying information by air that he would employ on D-Day in Normandy
when radios failed—homing pigeons. Before photographs were transmitted via telephone lines (or radio), pigeons carried undeveloped game photographs from A&M to Houston newspapers. The Kyle Field public-address
speaker announced the release of the pigeons, which soared up and circled to
get their bearings before heading for their Houston roosts, where they usually arrived by the copy deadline of 7:00 PM for Sunday morning editions.[33]

CAREER DEFERRED

Under the rules for transfer students, Rudder could have remained at A&M
and played football another year, but he declined in favor of beginning his
coaching career. He was commissioned a second lieutenant in the Army Reserve on Monday, May 28, 1932, five days before Texas A&M's commencement ceremony, where he received his bachelor of science degree. The early
commissioning date gave Aggie officers seniority over officers commissioned
in the spring at other military schools. Seniority, even by one day, could give
an officer an advantage over others of the same rank in the choice of assignments or duties.

From Rudder's commissioning until he retired thirty-five years later as
a major general, he was active in the army reserves. Even before the war,
he took army correspondence courses, met voluntarily (unpaid) with other
officers to discuss issues and problems, and without fail participated in summer training programs. Remembering his commissioning on the twentieth

anniversary of D-Day, Rudder commented to a *Newsweek* reporter, "Thank God I lived in a country which gave me ROTC so that I was ready [when war came]."[34]

The single individual photograph of Rudder in the 1932 A&M yearbook illustrates his frugality. Students were required to pay a fee for individual photos of themselves with organizations they joined but not the one with their class.[35] As Rudder had refused to pay the extra fees at Tarleton College, so did he at A&M. No fee was charged for incidental and group photos, such as for football, the Corps, and snapshots, and he is shown in several. The citation beside his class photograph in the 1932 yearbook is as follows:

J. Earl Rudder, Spike, 21, I. E., Eden, Captain, Inf. Reg. Staff, Co. H Inf., T Club, Sbisa Volunteers, Industrial Arts Club, Fish Numeral, Intramural Wrestling Champ, 175-lb. weight.[36]

His nickname, "Spike," did not stick.

With similar frugality, he purchased the least expensive Aggie ring available, a ten-carat version for $10.50 from Caldwell's Jewelry Store in Bryan rather than the $13.50 eleven-carat version from Sanky Park Jewelry near the campus. "J. E. Rudder" was engraved on the inner surface. If he took the bus to Bryan to make the purchase, the roundtrip fare was sixteen cents. For another $7.00 he had a diamond mounted on the ring. In the recollections of his family, he never once removed the ring from his finger. When asked to give his ring for the collection of the Association of Former Students, he declined, saying "There are two things you cannot have: my ring and my wife—in that order!"[37]

After five years of striving, Rudder left A&M with a degree but without a job. Few new college graduates got jobs in 1932. In a country with a population of about 120 million, 12 million people were unemployed. It was the nadir of the Depression. The national income of $83,326,000,000 in 1929 had fallen 52 percent to $39,963,000,000 in 1932. One month after he graduated, the Dow Jones industrial average hit 41, its lowest point in the twentieth century. Henry Dethloff determined that A&M's class of 1932 was the hardest hit of the Depression era. "Only one engineer in the graduating class [had] a job at commencement."[38]

Finding himself in the same predicament, Rudder explained much later, "I went all over the state, but finally had to go home to Eden to eat. They were building a highway from Eden to Menard then, and that gave me a chance for a job digging ditches at 25 cents an hour."[39] His parents still lived in the home on Duke Street where they had been since he was nine. He would work on the road crew for fifteen months. It was not entirely wasted time. He rekindled his friendships with Chunky Pfluger and M. J. Green. The work disabused him of any notion that his college degree had created a gulf between himself and men who work with their hands. He saw again the importance of a living wage to families and gained new appreciation for ordinary workers, a perspective on their working conditions, and a realization of their importance to society.

His associates would always be impressed at his rapport with people in all walks of life. "I always admired the way you could mix with your subordinates and still retain their respect as their commander," was a line in a letter he got nine years after the war from a man who had been a noncommissioned officer in his regimental headquarters for the last six months of the war. Rudder was more likely than most executives to recognize that seemingly ordinary tasks often require exceptional skills—and that almost any request or order required subordinates to work with their hands.

CHAPTER 4

COACHING YEARS
1933–1941

Rudder's year-long search for a job ended in April 1933 when he was offered a position at Brady, Texas, High School to start in September. He accepted without knowing the salary and was on the job when it was approved at one hundred dollars a month for the nine-month school year. He was expected to coach football and basketball while teaching history, mathematics, and chemistry. Without teaching experience, he would learn about teaching while teaching. Years later he acknowledged that "planning those courses was quite an education for me."[1] His daily routine was to teach for the first five periods before going to the gymnasium to prepare for team practices after school. He did not complain about the workload or the salary. At last he was doing what he wanted to do and, by chance, was exactly where he wanted to be.

Rudder's arrival in Brady (population about four thousand) was splashed across the front page of the *Brady Standard,* along with his photograph and the caption: "The Brady School Board was fortunate in securing the services of Earl Rudder, former Texas A&M star." L. B. "Smitty" Smith, the sports editor, praised Rudder's experience and preparation at Texas A&M and Tarleton College, leaving no doubt that Rudder was well qualified to coach football.[2] Nothing was mentioned about his qualifications to teach history or chemistry, and they could hardly have been worse. One year of chemistry was required for his degree; he twice attempted the first half at Tarleton College, managing to pass it the second time with a C, and he completed the second half at Texas A&M, also with a C.

His interest in history rivaled Henry Ford's, whose quip, "History is bunk," was more widely quoted at the time than anything said by a historian. In five years of college Rudder enrolled for exactly one history course—not once but twice, because he failed the first time; he got by with a C on second effort. Furthermore, the course, History 305 at Texas A&M, was history in name only; the actual subject matter was state and federal government.[3] So it was that history—one of the most subtle and elusive of all subjects—was assigned to a poorly prepared coach who was sent to the classroom without

Rudder during the first year of his appointment as a teacher and coach at Brady High School. (Bulldog, *Brady High School, 1934)*

broad knowledge of the subject matter or insight about the issues other than the commonplace interpretations found in textbooks. In this mismatch Rudder continued a combination that became a deplorable practice.

In spite of his initial deficiencies, Earl was a popular teacher and respected by his students, some of whom became outstanding teachers, university professors, and medical doctors. He succeeded by his native intelligence, his diligence, and his likeable personality. He overcame his shortcomings by studying at night and concentrating on the welfare of his students. When he married in 1937 after four years of teaching, he knew the subject matter, but he still "burned the midnight oil," his bride lamented, "preparing for his classes."[4]

Rudder did not compromise academic standards for his players, even the stars. "You got what you made," recalled Bill Roberts, who played under him for three years. "He did not overlook anything. Whatever he did, he was fair about it, and it didn't matter if you were captain of the football team, you had to do your work. It didn't make any difference if he liked you or not, he'd help you but he expected you to do your part. We tried not to get behind because we knew he wouldn't pass us, and we wouldn't be able to play."[5]

CHICK WILLIAMSON

As 1933 was the turning point of Rudder's professional life, so it was for his personal life. That summer he began seeing the young woman he would marry four years later. Her name was Margaret Williamson, called "Chick" until mid-life. She had just completed her freshman year at the University of Texas and was home for the summer with her family on their ranch near Menard.

Chick—the valedictorian of her class of thirty-six students in Menard's high school in 1932—smiled easily and often. Her voice was low, vibrant, and not soon forgotten. Her father said she had been vaccinated with a phonograph needle, meaning she seldom stopped talking. Third in a family of three boys and two girls, she played a vigorous game of tennis and rode horseback as naturally as she walked. Her father kept a string of thirty or forty horses for men to ride while tending livestock. At the age of twelve, she rode horseback fourteen miles round-trip each day to the nearest school in London, Texas.[6]

She entered the University of Texas at sixteen, oblivious, she observed late in life, "to how young I was." Nonetheless the other young women in her residence hall elected her their president, and at the end of her freshman year, the dorm's paid staff asked her to stay on as a counselor, which she did each year until she graduated in 1936. She went into the Alpha Delta Pi social sorority and was elected to the student government assembly, where she counted among her acquaintances two future governors of Texas: Allan Shivers and John B. Connally. While waiting in line for her first classes, she met J. J. "Jake" Pickle, destined to serve thirty-two years in Congress (1963–95), and their friendship endured to the end of their lives. This triumvirate of her friends—Shivers, Connally, and Pickle—would push Earl's rise in Texas politics after the war. As Jake Pickle remarked, "My connection to Earl was through Chick." He was the nexus of Rudder's original band of supporters and friend of an ambitious New Dealer named Lyndon B. Johnson.[7]

In the summer of 1933, Chick and Earl began meeting at an upscale dance hall in Menard. "We started dancing together, that's all," she told her husband's biographer. The dance hall was the Crystal Ballroom on the top level of the four-story Bevans Hotel in the center of Menard (population two thousand), twenty-six miles from the Williamson ranch. Earl drove down the road he was helping build for the Texas Highway Department from Eden, twenty-one miles north. His car did not compare to her green 1930 Ford Model A Roadster Coupe with a rumble seat, a spare tire on the back, and a forty-horsepower engine.

Clouds of dust followed as she drove toward Menard. It streamed in around windows and through the factory-made holes in the floor for the brake pedal and the clutch and covered the interior. She covered her hair with a bonnet, pulled gloves over her hands, and at times held a handkerchief to her face. Because the mixture of dirt and sweat formed a brown ring inside the collar of her blouse, she put tissue paper between her neck and collar until she reached Menard, where she applied her makeup.

By reading the odometer, Chick's father kept track of the miles she put on the car. He paid the bills; gasoline was $0.15 a gallon, and a set of four new Goodyear tires sold for $6.35. Only her younger brother Alton, called Rusty, knew that she drove miles and miles in reverse to roll back the odometer. To the end of her driving days her friends admired her ability to maneuver a car backward into a tight parking place, but they never knew that she learned by deceiving her father.

Chick and Earl did not have to be introduced. He knew about her vaguely in the way that people in sparsely populated areas know of others, especially members of prominent families. Most everyone in the region knew about her father, Willie Walter Williamson (1871–1952), a prosperous rancher with large landholdings and livestock. Called Uncle Bill, he made his fortune from scratch by industrious application of his native abilities with minimal benefits of a formal education. Williamson capitalized on the generosity of the State of Texas with its public lands, acquiring vast acreages, much of it from other men who were unable to convert the state's beneficence into profit as he did. So often asked for advice about how to make money, he had a standard reply: "Buy land and strike oil," his own hard physical labors remaining unstated.

Willie Williamson became an important person in Earl Rudder's life because his accumulated wealth and generosity enabled Rudder to devote himself to public service when he returned from the war. At the age of sixteen, Williamson left his home in East Texas, penniless, without even a horse. He walked and hitched rides for three hundred miles to reach a half-brother in West Texas who had promised to help him. He applied for a 640-acre section of unimproved public land, where he cleared brush by hand with a double-bladed axe and dug a well. Success at ranching in the arid region was not easy, and many of his neighbors failed. When they did, he acquired their property for pennies on the dollar and gradually increased his holdings, eventually stocked with thousands of sheep and goats for their wool and mohair. Until they became too numerous, he sheared them by hand with the help of his wife, Lucy Striegler (1880–1949). With such efforts the Williamsons accumulated the wealth that ultimately made their son-in-law, Earl Rudder, almost financially independent.

On Saturday nights at the Crystal Ballroom the music began at half past nine and ended at two in the morning. Jazz aficionados in San Antonio or Austin who thought Menard—almost 150 miles west—was at the edge of the earth would have been shocked to know there were few better venues for their music. The railroad brought dance bands from afar and drew people from across the region to listen, dine, dance, and stay in Mr. Bevans's hotel. As the romance of Chick and Earl bloomed, they were serenaded by the trombonist, Jack Teagarden, playing his big hits—"Chances Are," "Tiger Rag," and "Have You Ever Been Lonely?"

From the sweltering dance floor couples took breathers in the coolness of American Legion Park across a side street from the hotel. With natural beauty and relaxing allure, the park's two acres were a refuge from summer's heat. It was their lovers' lane, the perfect rendezvous for a courting couple who abided by conventional middle-class restraints of the 1930s. In Chick's memory the summer was over almost as quickly as it began. The interlude came down to the usual questions: Was their mutual attraction real love? Would the time and distance between them spoil what might have been? When September came, she returned to Austin for her second year of university studies, and he went to Brady for his first professional assignment. They saw each other briefly during the holidays until summer came again and they renewed the cycle as they would for three years.

BRADY COACH

Shortly after arriving in Brady, Rudder moved in with Vivian and L. B. "Smitty" Smith, sports editor of the *Brady Standard* and later its editor and publisher. The Smiths had been married fourteen months and had a new two-bedroom home. Earl came to stay a month and remained four years. Each month he paid Vivian forty-five dollars, enough to buy food for the three of them. Earl was, she said at age ninety-two, "a good man, such a handsome man, and very popular. I got mad at him only one time. He told Smitty that I was a good cook but we needed more variety in our food." When Vivian asked why he had not married, Earl replied that he hadn't found the right girl. "Well, what are you looking for?" she asked. He replied, "She has to be able to play the piano, be a good athlete, and be a good cook."[8] Chick Williamson could play the piano and had a slashing tennis serve—and Earl sent her to cooking school after they were married.

By making his home with the sports editor of the local newspaper, Rudder gave his viewpoint to the town's only news medium, and Smitty Smith had ready access to his most important beat, the Brady High School sports program. They became such good friends that Smitty's son, Larry, could say, "My dad truly loved Earl." On a typical evening after supper, Earl and Smitty sat in the backyard of 801 West 12th Street and talked about sports. Vivian joined them after washing the dishes and cleaning up the kitchen. Two weeks after Earl went on the job, Smitty informed his readers, "If Coach Rudder can mold a crack forward wall with the material at hand, he will be a proverbial miracle man."[9]

In Rudder's first season coaching football—the fall of 1933—he assisted Brady's head coach, E. J. Powell, who was practically driven from the game by the passions it produced. Hard-fought football games were barely concealed fistfights. Brady's games with the archrival San Saba Armadillos usually featured a fight between Powell and the San Saba coach, Andrew Locklear.[10] Rudder was not involved in such fights. He understood the dynamics of the game and how its intensity could be emotionally overwhelming. His personal qualities restrained would-be adversaries. He stood six feet tall, and although he had a kind face and genial manner, he was unlikely to walk away from a challenge or confrontation, while his presence and bearing caused anyone contemplating a physical encounter to think before acting.

Rudder issued a standing challenge to high school athletes that he would wrestle three of them at the same time. His challenge was accepted only once and by a trio who seventy years later said it as the biggest mistake of their high school careers. "He wasn't mean," they agreed, "just tough and he was strong as a bull." Another youngster said Earl "did not know how strong he was."[11]

Seventy years after playing football for Rudder, three men reminisced about him. Charlie Dye was such a spectacular running back in 1937 that in 1996 he was still recognized as the best in the history of Brady High School. Karl "Corky" Steffens was voted the best player of the district in 1934 and served on the city council while Earl was mayor after the war. Bill Roberts played under Rudder for three years. Steffens considered Rudder "most of all, a motivator. . . . He made us rough, tough, and ready. When we went on the field we thought we were better than the other guy. We did push-ups and sit-ups and we ran to get in condition. We ran and ran and ran and ran. He was a hard man in certain ways . . . , but he was a gentle man in other ways." So rigorous was Rudder's training drills that a player's mother called him the "meanest man in town."[12]

Charlie Dye compared Rudder's attitudes. "On the field he was strictly football. When we left the field, we could be personal. On the field, he showed you what to do and expected you to do it. Off the field, we could be friends. He would come to a practice with no shoulder pads and run plays at you, taking the role of an offensive runner against you and he wanted you to tackle him. If you didn't knock him down, he ran right over you." Dye witnessed a startling display of strength by Rudder. "One of our linebackers missed some tackles in a game. During the next practice, the boy was in position on the line and Earl was standing behind him. Earl was telling him what he wanted him to do and how he wanted him to do it. All of a sudden he picked that boy up and threw him across the line right into the tackle on the other side."[13]

Steffens cited an unusual coaching technique. "I fumbled three times in one game. Earl went to a leather shop and got them to make a little mitt-like carrying strap that wrapped around my hand, holding it to a football. He gave it to me and told me to carry it with me all the time until I quit fumbling. I even took it to bed with me." Rudder's sympathetic attitude was important to Charlie Dye. "If you went to him and asked him for advice or for help, you got it. I came from a broken home, and it was pretty rough at times. He always helped me."[14]

In the final game of Rudder's inaugural season as head coach, the opposing team came from his hometown of Eden. The game was a major event in both towns. Scheduled on a Friday afternoon in late November, local newspapers promoted it with front-page publicity, urging their readers to attend. Given Rudder's ties to both towns, the *Eden Echo* and *Brady Standard* played him up in human interest stories that promoted the contest. Brady's mayor "declared Friday afternoon a half holiday" and "issued a proclamation urging all Brady merchants to close between the hours of 3 and 5 o'clock, and to attend the game en masse."[15]

In Eden there were similar appeals, and a special train conveyed fans and students those thirty miles to Brady. When Smitty interviewed Brady players, he was told that they wanted to win "for their coach, Earl Rudder, whose hometown friends in Eden have sent word that they are 'coming here to bury the Bulldogs.'"[16] By coincidence, the English bulldog was the mascot of both teams, which may explain why it became Rudder's favorite breed.

Eden's mayor and town council were welcomed at the railway station by their Brady counterparts. Led by a band, they walked with citizens of both communities to the courthouse square, where each mayor made a speech, poking fun at the other. The greetings and hurrahs were good-natured and congenial between the neighboring towns that were rival trading centers. Three hours later the sweet-tempered mood had changed dramatically.

Smitty Smith wrote up the game as "hard-fought" and "played in perfect football weather." "The Brady boys had the stuff of champions. . . . They came back in the last two minutes to score the winning touchdown and win 14–12."[17] On the other side of the field, Eden fans and players were angry. Many thought the referees had cheated them of the victory in the final seconds by not ending the game when, as they saw it, the clock had run out while they were ahead twelve to seven. Leonard Jacoby played left guard on the Eden team. Seventy-one years later, in a voice tinged with rancor, he claimed that the officials favored Rudder and ran back the game clock, allowing the Brady team time to complete its final scoring drive and win the game. Jacoby added bitterly, "And Rudder knew it."[18] Eden's grievance aside, Rudder ended his first season as a head football coach on a high note. His popularity may have suffered in Eden, but in Brady he was the winner.

MARRIAGE

During Chick's graduation year from the University of Texas, 1936, Earl learned that the Brady school trustees planned to employ a female teacher of physical education, her major field of study. "Earl came down to Austin," she recalled, "and told me to apply for a teaching position in Brady." She was hired for nine months at $100.00 per month in the 1936–37 school year; Earl was appointed for ten months at $130.00 per month. Chick said, "I made the grand sum of nine hundred dollars. If it had not been for my parents paying my first month's room and board and buying my fall clothes, I would have been in the hole."[19]

Chick took a room with the Whiteman family, around the corner from Vivian and Smitty Smith, where Earl lived. Neither Chick nor Earl had a car, and as Vivian said, "They courted in my living room after Smitty and I went to bed." In Chick's view, "Earl worked long hours. I worked long hours. I was so young and full of life at the time. They made me sponsor of everything they could think of—volleyball, pep squad, senior play. Earl's workload was murder."[20]

The year in close proximity confirmed their love, and she set the wedding date for Saturday, June 12, 1937. Preferring a small wedding, she chose her parents' new home thirty miles from Brady on unpaved roads and another quarter-mile through the pasture to the creamy brick house with three gables under large pecan boughs. They honeymooned for two weeks in the mountains of New Mexico and Colorado.[21]

In the custom of their time and place, Earl assumed a controlling role in making their decisions, a practice that would always annoy her. She was intelligent, strong-willed, articulate, and as educated as he. He would hear her opinions whether he wanted them or not. Long after he was gone, she sighed, "Earl knew how to give orders, and I took 'em."

At the time of their marriage, Earl had eighty dollars in cash and Chick had forty, their savings from the previous year.[22] Her parents' generosity would soon change that, but it would never be openly revealed to others, not even to their children. Chick had never experienced the money crunch that Earl had known, but both had been reared with an ethic of deferred

The wedding photo-graph of Margaret "Chick" Williamson and Earl Rudder a few days before they married on June 12, 1937. (Courtesy of Margaret Rudder)

benefit, involving saving for the future. In their religious upbringings they were relatively freethinking Methodists, infused with enough Calvinism to restrain excessive materialistic indulgence. Comfort rather than conspicu-ous consumption was their lifestyle.

Within a year of his marriage Earl Rudder became a man of property and financially secure to a degree he would not have thought possible in his early life. The transition began in 1938 when Chick's father and mother began transferring their landholdings of some 12,800 acres and accumulated cash to three of their four surviving children and their spouses. For their oldest son, Lawrence, they made a different bequest. Willie and Lucy Williamson put Earl's name as well as Chick's on the deeds when they divided approxi-mately twenty sections of ranchland in Menard County between their two daughters, Jewel and Chick, and their son Rusty. In the division, fourteen-year-old Rusty got eight sections, while Jewel and Chick each got six sections, or about 3,840 acres. To compensate Jewel and Chick for the additional two sections that Rusty received, the parents gave cash to each daughter at a rate of $22.00 an acre, the going price of land in the area, or about $28,160—ap-proximately $400,000 in 2008 purchasing power. Chick's parents distributed the real estate and the cash over several years. Rusty eventually sold his eight sections to Earl and Chick, bringing their holdings to fourteen sections, or about 9,000 acres, which became known as the Rudder Ranch.[23]

With a ranch, Rudder possessed the most iconic symbol of Texas. It gave him a measure of social, financial, and political credibility as well as income in seasonable years. People saw him as both a man of the soil and of sub-stance. Aside from the material importance of the ranch, Rudder was deeply attached to the land, the trees, the streams, the valleys and hills, the wild-life—all of the natural world. The ranch became part of his being. Although

Rudder's father-in-law, rancher Willie W. Williamson (1871–1952), whose industriousness, wealth, and generosity—combined with that of his wife, Lucy Striegler—made possible Rudder's public service career after the war. (Courtesy of Alton Williamson)

he never ranched full-time, the ranch and the mythology of Texas shaped his persona. Many wartime comrades would remember him as a "rancher from Brady, Texas."[24]

Twelve days after Chick and Earl returned from their honeymoon, he left for two weeks of summer camp with the army's Organized Reserve Corps. His departure foretold a distinctive part of their marriage: he was frequently absent to fulfill his public responsibilities. As Martha Washington and Mamie Eisenhower grieved over the absence of their husbands in military service, so did Chick. Apart from the loneliness, his absences presented her with decisions for which she was ill prepared because he had not kept her informed. "Every summer we were together," she emphasized, "every summer, he had two weeks of summer camp."[25]

That fall of 1937, Earl's football team won eleven games and lost but one, the best record in the history of the school. Charlie Dye, the star running back, was voted the outstanding player in the district and made the all-state team. With eleven consecutive victories behind them, the Brady Bulldogs entered the regional playoff game against the San Saba Armadillos, still coached by Andrew Locklear. In ten games the Armadillos had run up 444 points to their opponents' mere 20; Brady had outscored its opponents, 343 to 91. Both teams were undefeated and untied. Before the game, Smitty Smith's front-page story began with, "This town will be as dead and desolate as a desert Friday afternoon, with most of the populace to follow its football team to San Saba to meet the Armadillos for the Region 7 championship." At noon a "football special train" left the Brady station, and school was dismissed at 11:45 AM to permit students to catch the train.[26]

But there would be no victory for Brady in San Saba in 1937. The Bulldogs went down 12–6 "in one of the most ferociously fought games of the year. They had little luck in a game that was played on the coldest day of the year [before] 2,500 fans from all sections of the country." Smitty concluded his coverage of the 1937 Brady Bulldogs' football fortunes with the observation that Rudder would field another good team the following year.[27] No one could have predicted that Earl Rudder had coached his last high school game.

TARLETON COLLEGE COACH

In March of 1938 the job of head football coach at Tarleton College opened up, and Rudder went after it like no other job in his entire life. He began by writing Tarleton's executive dean, J. Thomas Davis. Davis replied with a friendly letter that was not encouraging. "Dear Earl: You certainly have a right to apply for the position. . . . Mr. Wisdom and I had both concluded that next to Taylor [unidentified candidate] we preferred you, and the only reason we put Taylor first was because of his more maturity and experience. I suggest that if you file an application you file it with me, sending a copy to Mr. G. R. White and a copy to [Texas A&M] President Walton."[28]

"Mr. G. R. White," better known as G. Rollie (pron. Rah-lee) White, was a banker and civic leader in Brady as well as rancher and philanthropist. He was also a member of the Texas A&M board of directors, nine men who governed Tarleton College and approved its budget and personnel appointments. White was a close friend of Chick's parents and well acquainted with Rudder. He was well-positioned to help Rudder, which he did in spite of the fact that Rudder refused to do business with White's Commercial National Bank in Brady.[29] Two years earlier Rudder had been denied a loan at the bank while White was out of town. He then took his application to the rival Brady National Bank, where it was promptly approved. From then on Rudder banked with Brady National and shunned White's appeals for his account, even as White was helping him get the Tarleton job. Rudder wanted to be Tarleton's head football coach more than anything, but he would not compromise his loyalty to the Brady National Bank to curry favor with White. He was faithful to Brady National Bank for the remainder of his life.

As Davis suggested, Rudder wrote him a letter applying "for the position of Football Coach and assistant instructor of Physical Education in John Tarleton College." He claimed he was well qualified, having attended and played football at both Tarleton and Texas A&M. He emphasized his successful record in four years as Brady High's head coach: "My football teams have lost seven games out of forty-two played, winning the district and bi-district championship the past season. . . . Ever since leaving John Tarleton College, I have looked forward to the time that I might return there as coach."[30]

Rudder sent copies to President Thomas O. Walton and, of course, to G. Rollie White. Then he heard nothing for almost four months, except that several applicants were considered and rejected.[31] The selection process was stalemated in confusion about who should make the next move. Was the hiring decision up to the A&M board? Was it Walton's decision? Or was it Davis's?

In August, with the new academic year and football season fast approaching, Davis pleaded with Walton to present the issue to the A&M board. Suddenly, on August 9, Walton was bypassed and Rudder was appointed. G. Rollie White was the hidden hand behind the appointment. He had been prodding the chairman of the A&M board to take action. Finally, the chairman asked White to poll other board members about whether Davis should be authorized to make the appointment. White's poll confirmed that members wanted Davis to make the appointment. White then called Davis and told him, "Go ahead with the work"—meaning, make the appointment. Davis replied, "The man I want is Mr. Earl Rudder." Knowing White would deliver the message to Rudder, Davis added, "Send him on." Rudder may have been sitting in White's office during this conversation. He reported to Dean Davis in Stephenville that very night and was on the job the next day as Tarleton's head football coach. We know these details because Walton asked Davis to explain why he (Walton) had been left out of the process.[32]

The *Brady Standard* broke the news, and Smitty Smith got to the heart of Rudder's sentiments. "Going back to Tarleton as coach, Rudder realizes one of his ambitions. He has had his eyes on the job since he entered the coaching profession here five years ago." Rudder's farewell statement appeared on the front page. "I want to thank my many friends for the many kindnesses and courtesies that have been extended during my five years here. Brady, which gave me my first coaching opportunity, will always be home to me."[33]

The year 1938 was another important turning point for Rudder, professionally and financially. As Tarleton College's head football coach, he advanced in pay from $1,500 for ten months' work to $2,400 for nine months' work, plus extra pay for teaching in the summer.[34] He coached only football and taught physical education as a member of the college faculty with more autonomy and flexibility in his schedule than at Brady High School. Regular conversations with W. J. Wisdom, Tarleton's director of athletics and Rudder's supervisor, were a bonus.

In the financial realm, 1938 was the year that Chick's parents began distributing her inheritance. Their cash gift to Earl and Chick in 1938 was $14,400, followed by $9,600 in 1939, the purchasing power equivalent of about $358,000 in 2007, based on the consumer price index. The gifts provided the young Rudders with a healthy cash reserve, and they bought a small frame house at 360 North Ollie Street near the main entrance to the

Tarleton campus.[35] It was to this home that Chick and Earl brought their first child, James Earl Jr., born May 9, 1940.

In Rudder's first football season at Tarleton, his team won four, lost four, and tied one. During the games Rudder sat on the bench with the players, usually wearing a dark suit with a tie and an equally dark fedora. In cold weather he added a vest. The bitterest rival was, as when Rudder was a Tarleton student, Texas A&M's two-year branch, the North Texas Agricultural College, in Arlington. In Rudder's first year Tarleton lost by a score of 6–0.

In the run-up to the next year's game (1939) with NTAC, Tarleton ROTC cadets beat a drum without stopping day and night for a week, and student pranks overshadowed the game in preliminary press reports. Tarleton won the game 6–0; it was the last of the year and the most important from the fans' point of view. The record for the year was six wins and four losses. In the next year, 1940, Rudder's team beat NTAC 13–7 while compiling a season record of eight wins and two losses.[36]

At the age of thirty, Rudder was a success in his profession. With a secure faculty appointment at Tarleton, he and Chick purchased five vacant lots near the college, presumably on which to build a larger home for the family they anticipated.[37] He began taking courses toward a graduate degree at Texas Christian University, perhaps hoping to succeed Wisdom as athletic director.

Rudder was probably better informed about international developments than most citizens on account of his participation in the Organized Reserves. He could not have been indifferent to the rise of Hitler and increasing tensions between the United States and Japan in the late 1930s. Conscientious about his duties as a reserve officer, he enrolled in the army's extension courses, attended special schools, and, as previously stated, participated in two weeks of training each summer. He studied at nights and on weekends, often with other officers around the kitchen table in his home. Some were regular or active-duty officers from the ROTC faculty of the college, and others were reserve officers like himself. As Chick summarized his weekly schedule, from Monday through Friday, he taught classes during the day and conducted practice sessions for his team in the late afternoon. On Saturday he coached the team in games against other teams, and on Sunday after church he devoted himself to military matters.

Germany's invasion of Poland at the beginning of September 1939 was followed by declarations of war on Germany by Britain and France. Texans, like most Americans, opposed the totalitarian government of Germany and favored the democracies of Britain and France. After France surrendered to Nazi Germany in June 1940, American sentiment turned toward support for Britain but not for intervention in the war. Texas newspapers and most Texas citizens and congressmen supported the program of national defense mounted by the Roosevelt administration. On August 27, 1940, Congress approved the calling up of the Organized Reserves. Earl knew then that it was only a question of time before he was called to active duty. Across the nation, others like him were going on active duty as fast as the army could construct camps to house them. No member of the Texas delegation voted against the lend-lease bill for all-out aid to Britain in early 1941.[38]

"He was so anxious to go," Chick said much later, "that he sold our home before he got his orders and without telling me what he had done."[39]

PART TWO

THE WAR

*The essential thing is action. Action has three stages:
the decision born of thought, the order or preparation for execution,
and the execution itself. All three stages are governed by the will.
The will is rooted in character, and for the man of action
character is more important than intellect.
Intellect without will is worthless,
will without intellect is dangerous.*
—*Hans von Seeckt,* Thoughts of a Soldier, *1930*

CHAPTER 5

STATESIDE

JUNE 1941–NOVEMBER 1943

T he United States went to war reluctantly in 1941. Historically, the nation had generally abided by George Washington's advice to avoid "foreign entanglements" and conducted an isolationist foreign policy. However, in 1917 it had joined with Britain, France, and other allies to defeat Germany, only to become disillusioned with the results. In the aftermath, isolationist sentiments surged and continued into the 1930s despite aggressive acts by Germany and Japan that were contrary to American interests. President Roosevelt, elected in 1932, seemed inclined toward an active role on the world scene, but he was restrained by public and congressional opinions and by his own domestic priorities.

The fall of France to Nazi Germany in June 1940, leaving only Britain and its empire to face Hitler, was a turning point in public opinion that was soon reflected in Congress. In August, Congress approved calling the National Guard and the Organized Reserves to active duty. Three weeks later, Congress passed the first peacetime draft of untrained civilians in American history, and men began going on active duty as fast as the army could construct camps to house them.[1] Rudder knew it was only a question of time before he would be a full-time soldier. When his orders came, he had two weeks to transition from civilian to military status at Fort Sam Houston in San Antonio. Expecting to return within a year, he stored some of their household furnishings in the Tarleton College gymnasium and took Chick and one-year-old Bud to her parents' home on their ranch near Menard.

On June 18, 1941, he reported for active duty; he was now 1st Lt. James E. Rudder, serial number O-294916. Assigned to the 2nd Infantry Division, he was promoted to captain the next day and enrolled in a five-week course to learn, as he put it, "what Reserve officers need to know before they are put on the job with troops."[2]

The war would test his four-year marriage. There was always uncertainty and worry, but initially only inconvenience and discomfort. At the end of his first week away from Chick, he emphasized the positive: "I know we will come through stronger than we were." Since he went where the army sent him, she soon posed a question that applied to every day of the war: "Where will you go when you leave there? My best wish is for us to be together." As long as he was in the United States, she would follow, beginning in the summer heat of 1941 when she drove with their toddler son the 150 miles from Menard to Fort Sam Houston to see him and to search for lodging.[3]

In late July Earl was sent almost a thousand miles east to Fort Benning, Georgia, for three months of field training and instruction on "The Rifle and Heavy Weapons."[4] The rifle was the army's new M1 Garand; the rest of the course was about machine guns, pistols, the Browning automatic rifle (BAR), mortars, and how to teach soldiers to use them. Chick remained on her parents' ranch with more privacy than a vigorous twenty-five-year-old extrovert normally preferred.

Earl spoke first about the strain of their separation. On a Sunday afternoon in mid-August, he was lonely in a barracks room "too hot to study or sleep." He wrote, "What's wrong on that end of the line? . . . I haven't had a letter since Thursday—and that is too damn long. You don't know how lonesome it is. It wouldn't have taken much time to write me a note." Her reply was equally curt. "Your scorching letter just came and I think, if you had counted to ten, you wouldn't have written it. Remember, you don't have a monopoly on being lonesome." He apologized at the first opportunity: "Honey, I am sorry, but I had not had a letter in 4 days, and I was getting plenty lonesome. Get about $100 and pay the expenses to come down here."[5] He found an apartment, and her parents drove her to Georgia.

The Fort Benning course ended in late October, and they returned to San Antonio. Chick located two rooms, one of three improvised apartments in a one-family, frame house at 225 Muncey Street across the railroad tracks from Fort Sam Houston's south gate. They hung their clothes on nails driven in the wall. The bedroom was the daytime sitting room, and they shared the kitchen and bathroom with two other couples. It was an unaccustomed living arrangement for them but not unusual near military bases during the war.

That's where they were on the early afternoon of Sunday, December 7, 1941, when they heard the radio announcement that the Japanese had attacked Pearl Harbor. Four days later, Germany and Italy declared war on the United States, and the lineup of adversaries for a global war was almost complete. No one needed to tell them that Earl was now in the army "for the duration," a well-worn phrase for "until the war is over."

GULF COAST DUTY

With Germany in the war, industrial plants along the Texas coast were vulnerable to saboteurs coming ashore from the German submarines that were sinking oil tankers only a few miles out to sea.[6] Within walking distance of the beach, the Dow chemical plant at Freeport employed a new chemical process to extract magnesium from seawater, high-priority material for aircraft construction and explosives. Rudder and his company of 165 infantrymen were sent to protect the plant. Once again, Chick retired to the Williamson ranch while keeping the Muncey Street rooms under lease.

The couple resolved that he would try to call her once each week. A generation accustomed to cell phones and text messaging cannot imagine the frustration of making a long-distance telephone call during the war, when millions of homesick men and women yearned to hear the voices of loved ones. Long-distance calls were operator-assisted and required several operators to manually connect their switchboards before, in this case, Earl could speak to Chick on the boxy, hand-cranked telephone mounted on the wall at the ranch. Voice quality was poor, made worse because fourteen ranch families shared the same strand of wire strung on poles for thirty miles between the Brady switchboard and the Williamson home.

The last step in the connection occurred when the switchboard operator in Brady sent two electronic impulses—one long and one short—the Williamson's unique signal. When the other thirteen families on the Brady line heard that signal, they knew the Williamsons had an incoming call. Isolated, longing for news, and snoopy, they could eavesdrop, which diminished the voice quality. "If you move into Brady, I'll be able to hear you better," Earl advised. Despite their telephone conversations, he insisted, "Don't ever stop writing me, I need your letters and look forward to them each day."[7]

In early March, Earl was back at Fort Sam, and Chick returned to San Antonio, where their second child, Anne Margaret, called Sis, was born on May 28, 1942. Six weeks after her birth, Earl was transferred to the 83rd Infantry Division at Camp Atterbury, Indiana, and Chick went with him, along with both children. They drove the twelve hundred miles in their black 1941 Ford coupe and rented a house in Edinburgh, thirty miles south of Indianapolis.[8]

On the morning of August 18, hours before reveille at Camp Atterbury and half a world away, a Royal Air Force Mosquito bomber equipped for photoreconnaissance took off from an airfield known as RAF Benson near Oxford, England. Climbing to an altitude of thirty-one thousand feet, the high-performance twin-engine plane flew south, crossed over the English

Channel, and intersected the French coast near Cherbourg, where it turned east to photograph the coastline for 120 miles to Le Havre. When photo interpreters studied the images captured on film, they noted that the Germans were building concrete emplacements for long-range guns on a wedge-shaped promontory thirty-five miles southeast of Cherbourg at 49° 23′ 48″ north, 0° 59′ 21″ west. Their report described it as "a three-gun medium battery . . . right on the cliff edge. The whole area is enclosed by well concealed wire. There is a road to possibly a fourth emplacement under construction." The destruction of the guns in these fortifications would be Rudder's rendezvous with history, and his success the pivotal event of his adult life.[9]

Rudder's assignment to the 83rd Division's planning staff for operations and training was a springboard to advances in rank and responsibility. He was selected to attend the army's Command and General Staff School at Fort Leavenworth, Kansas, a choice assignment for promising officers. The subject matter was tactical doctrine and army procedures, both intended to enhance the ability of officers to serve in different capacities and advance in rank. His orders to Leavenworth included the proviso: "Quarters for dependents are not available." Chick chose not to make the long journey back to Texas but to remain in an unfamiliar town with winters more severe than any she had ever known. Her aggravations were similar to those of other young mothers during the war. Both children were hospitalized with high fevers that led to bronchial pneumonia. Automobile tires were strictly rationed, and she awoke on a bitterly cold morning to discover that all four had been stolen from their car. "It was a tough winter," she remembered, "and Earl was gone."[10]

"HERE I BE A RANGER"

Earl arrived in Fort Leavenworth by train on November 28, 1942, to learn that he had been promoted to major the previous day. He called Chick, and she wrote, "Oh, how I'd like to see you don those gold leaves for the first time."[11] She saw them when he returned for two days at Christmas, but not again until February, when his course ended.

Rudder's proficiency as a training officer in the 83rd Division led to his selection to command the 2nd Ranger Battalion. The army commander of the region encompassing Indiana, Lt. Gen. Ben Lear, believed every soldier should have disciplined and realistic training that emphasized teamwork, initiative, problem solving, strength, and endurance. He mandated that each division in his region should have Ranger-type training, and Rudder was given the job of organizing the program in the 83rd Division. Lear also established a Ranger training school at Camp Forrest, Tennessee, seventy miles north of Chattanooga, and activated the 2nd Ranger Battalion there on April 1, 1943, probably on orders from Washington. That same month Lear was succeeded by Lt. Gen. Lloyd R. Fredendall, recently returned from commanding a corps of about sixty thousand men in North Africa, where he had been impressed with Rangers commanded by William O. Darby. When Fredendall inspected the 83rd Infantry Division at Camp Atterbury, he came away convinced that Rudder's Ranger training program was the best he had seen. Meanwhile, at Camp Forrest, the newly formed 2nd Ranger Battalion was not living up to expectations and considered a "rag-tag, orphan mob in want of military bearing and dis-

Rudder while a student in the Command and General Staff School at Fort Leavenworth, Kansas, during late 1942 and early 1943. (Courtesy of Margaret Rudder)

cipline." Fredendall, searching for the right officer to take over the battalion, remembered the impressive young major he had met in Indiana.[12]

On June 18, Fredendall's aide, Col. R. T. Beurket, called Rudder's boss, Colonel Van Brunt. A clerk-typist listened to the conversation and typed his notes for the record:

> **Colonel Beurket:** *General Fredendall is very complimentary about your Ranger Training. He would like for you to appoint a Major to take over the 2nd Army's Ranger Bn. This would be an incentive for a topnotch youngster. He must be a volunteer.*
>
> **Colonel Van Brunt:** *We've got a topnotch man here for you.*
>
> **Colonel Beurket:** *Get his name, number, and assign him to 2nd Army Ranger Bn, Camp Forrest.*

Van Brunt presented the possibility to Rudder and returned the call to Beurket at 8:45 AM the next day:

> **Colonel Van Brunt:** *We've got a fine officer for the job. He is a Ranger and we consider him the best Major in the division. He is the only man for the job.*

Colonel Beurket: He must be a volunteer. We want to hear from you as soon as he makes the decision.[13]

Rudder seized the opportunity, although he later soft-pedaled his eagerness by saying, "When a general asks you to volunteer for a job, you just volunteer." His new orders granted him "eight days delay en route" to Camp Forrest and directed him to go by way of Fredendall's headquarters in Memphis.[14] Once again, he drove Chick and the children to her parents' home. They decided she should live in Brady for the rest of the war and chose a house at 1108 South Bridge Street near the homes of his mother and his brother, John.

Leaving Brady for Camp Forrest, Rudder caught a ride by car to Dallas, where he hopped on a military flight from Love Field to Memphis and Fredendall's headquarters. Finally, on the night of Sunday, July 4, he wrote from Camp Forrest with unconcealed delight about events of recent days. "Well, here I be a *Ranger* [his emphasis]. I arrived Wednesday. I flew all the way and really sailed along. In Memphis, I went to Second Army Hdqs and went over the set up here, and met the general [Fredendall]. . . . I got to fly up here with the general in his private plane that afternoon."[15]

Rudder's predecessor believed that men in Ranger training should live under difficult conditions. Although barracks were available, he housed them in rows and rows of pyramidal tents with dirt floors along dirt streets. Six men slept in each tent, with their clothing hung on the center pole or shoved under their cots. The showers were half a mile away. Most men cleaned up using tin washbasins. The latrine and mess hall were as inconvenient as the showers, and the "chow was miserable."[16]

In Rudder's first meeting with the battalion, he did not call the men to a military formation. Instead he gathered them around him, told them to sit down, and gave them a speech that they remembered for three simple points: "Men, I'm your new battalion commander. I've come here so you can teach me how to be a Ranger. Company commanders, take charge of your companies."[17]

Rudder then moved the battalion into barracks with indoor plumbing and began regular gripe sessions in which any man could complain about conditions or suggest improvements or just speak his mind. He sent the cooks to cooking school and sent them again when complaints about the food continued. The men quickly realized that the battalion had a commander who cared about their welfare and demanded two things: superb physical performance and soldierly conduct. They saw, too, that he was as unsparing of himself as he was of them. After a twelve-mile speed march, 1st Lt. Ralph E.

Goranson observed Rudder cutting off his bloody socks and bandaging his feet. Goranson also noticed Rudder was with them on the next march.[18]

Nonetheless, disciplinary and morale problems persisted. The end of Rudder's "concerned about your welfare" approach was precipitated by a poor showing of the battalion at a pass-in-review ceremony for senior officers from Fredendall's headquarters. Rudder was reprimanded for the Rangers' lack of military bearing and discipline. Furious, he called the battalion to formation. Shouting with anger, he ridiculed and taunted them. He challenged them, one man at a time, to "step forward and take him on in a fight." No one came forward. Rudder was as tough physically as he was mentally. He could personally enforce his orders, and he was dedicated to molding the battalion into a premier organization that could carry the fight to the enemy.[19]

Several of Darby's Rangers who had fought against the Germans came from North Africa to advise Rudder about training. Ten- or twelve-mile speed marches were the heart of it, but some were longer, even a seventy-mile march in three days with full packs. "If a man fell out, that was the end unless he had a very good excuse." Discipline was so strict that an all-night march was punishment for a company because "a couple of men took off for town." Three weeks after Rudder took command, the entire battalion completed a speed march of seven and one-half miles in an average of ninety minutes, whereas Rudder's headquarters company covered the distance in sixty-seven minutes. In another memorable talk with three points, Rudder told them, "First, I'm going to make men out of you. Then, I'm going to make soldiers out of you and, then, I'm going to make Rangers out of you."[20]

Because each Ranger was a volunteer, it followed that any man could quit the Rangers on his own accord, and many did. In July and August, the first two months that Rudder was in command, sixteen officers and 227 enlisted men transferred from the battalion. Meanwhile, Rudder traveled to interview prospective Rangers on other army posts. When he interviewed a man, he usually began with two questions. Although Eden, Texas, had not had a Boy Scout troop when he was a boy, he had seen Scouts in action in Stephenville, and he would ask whether the soldier had been in the Boy Scouts. Then, what sports had he played? On August 1, 1943, one month after taking command of the battalion, he cleaned house, announcing, "If you don't want to belong, transfer out." New recruits were arriving, and the hardy men who remained could see that he had the battalion on an upward trend. Rudder had winning ways, but he winnowed by the "ruthless elimination of the less rugged."[21]

In training, realism was more important than safety. The sawdust pit was the Rangers' version of boys playing king-of-the-mountain. Two platoons—about seventy men—crawled over the wall of an eighteen-foot-square enclosure formed by logs stacked four to five feet high. A thick layer of sawdust covered the earth floor of the pit. The goal for each platoon was to throw the men of the other platoon out of the pit. The rules were simple: anything goes, and the game was over when only one man was left standing in the pit. Casualties were numerous, and there were plenty of "black eyes, broken toes, sprained wrists," and displaced shoulders or other joints. Training with explosives was more dangerous. Some men learned to respect explosives only with tragic consequences. Joe Camelo held on to an improvised grenade too long and lost an arm. Joe Antonelli suffered an unspeakable loss when a charge detonated between his legs while he was setting up a booby trap.[22] Every minute of the training day was filled with activity. Night exercises—firing weapons, infiltrating under fire, mock assaults—were routine, normally ending about two in the morning, followed by reveille at a quarter to six.

In late August, Chick drove from Brady to Camp Forrest, more than a thousand miles, with three-year-old Bud and Sis, now fifteen months old. There were no interstate highways, and her route was on two-lane roads through hundreds of towns, crossing thousands of intersections. The reunion was necessarily brief, as the battalion was packing up to leave for an undisclosed destination. Earl anticipated the coming perils, and their departure was difficult for him. After she drove away, he wrote, "I acted like a child when I left you but it is tough to think of being away from you and the kids for such a long time."[23] The reality that he might never see them again was left unsaid.

FLORIDA

In early September 1943, Rudder took the 2nd Ranger Battalion by train to Fort Pierce, on Florida's Atlantic coast, for twelve days of training in amphibious operations, a subject so neglected in his previous training that he could not spell the word.[24] Under the command of the joint Army-Navy Amphibious Scout and Raider School, most of the training was in five-man rubber boats and flat-bottomed British vessels, which could carry about thirty-five men, called landing craft, attack, or LCA—three letters that would become familiar to men still with the battalion in England.

The final exercise was a mock raid at night on the city of Fort Pierce from the sea. The Rangers were taken several miles out into the Atlantic, where they transferred to rubber boats and paddled toward the blacked-out Florida coast. Civil Defense authorities were informed about the Rangers' assignment and planned to use it to test their preparations against German agents who might come ashore from U-boats. They assumed the Rangers would approach the city through a passage cut in the barrier island that gave the city direct access to the sea. Augmented by sailors, the local police waited near the passage for the Rangers to arrive but they never came. Instead, they beached their rubber boats on the barrier island and carried them a quarter of a mile across it. With their hands and faces streaked green and black, they rowed across the intervening lagoon to the mainland and infiltrated the darkened city unseen and unheard. The attack plan "went off like clock-work" as they quickly took up positions around key sites in the city and the airport. They could have done more, but Rudder denied their plea to take over the electric power plant.[25]

The commandant of the school, naval captain Clarence Gulbranson, was proud of the Rangers and declared them the best trainees ever. Rudder was so pleased that he rewarded them with passes the following night, and they took Fort Pierce again. It was a night of drinking, carousing, and fighting with sailors that left broken windows, chairs, tables, and bones. They even roughed up the navy's Shore Patrol.[26]

Captain Gulbranson was a hard-boiled 1912 Annapolis graduate and stickler for military bearing and appearance. As the proud founder and the only commandant the school would have during the war, he was not amused by the Rangers' celebration, and he called Rudder in and held him person-ally responsible for the conduct of his men. Rudder contended that Rangers were a special kind of soldier, full of energy and exuberant with the success of their amphibious exercise against the city. Since they would soon be asked to give their lives for their country, he asked the commandant to leave the disciplinary action to him. Gulbranson agreed, and Rudder court-martialed several men, filing twelve charges against one man. Many were reduced in rank, others transferred from the battalion, and the rest were confined to quarters for their remaining two days at Fort Pierce.[27]

NEW JERSEY

The next destination was Fort Dix, New Jersey, for advanced tactical train-ing, the last phase of their training before leaving the United States. The two days and three nights required for the trip was not a recess from physi-cal training. At stops along the way, Rudder's order rang out, "Everyone off the train!" and then he would send the Rangers on a two-mile run. At Fort Dix they concentrated on coordinated firing problems, artillery demonstra-tions, and simulated demolition of bridges, dams and power plants. They

Walter E. Block, M.D., spirited and
beloved medical officer of the 2nd Ranger
Battalion, from Sept. 24, 1943, until
killed in action, at Bergstein, Germany,
December 8, 1944. (Courtesy of Frank E.
South)

conducted day-and-night exercises across the northern New Jersey countryside, sleeping in concealed sites during the day and practicing patrols at night, frightening civilians with their soot-blackened faces. In preference to Spam, they reduced the population of squirrels, rabbits, and unchaperoned chickens. Rudder forbade the taking of chickens, but his order was not much of a deterrent. Ranger Al Baer noted that the "Colonel made them pay for every damn one of those chickens," but they had to be caught violating the order.[28]

Rudder's winnowing—training, recruiting, and expelling—continued. In Dr. Walter E. Block he finally found the medical officer he wanted. A family practitioner from Chicago, Block quickly gained the affection and admiration of the battalion. A graduate of Northwestern University, he was humane, tough, and combative. The story went around that in college he had slugged a professor who had made fun of his Polish family name, which was more complicated before being shortened to a single syllable.

At Camp Ritchie, Maryland, the battalion went through "final readiness" training and made a night attack on a steep hilltop held by G.I.s in German uniforms firing enemy weapons. In a presentation on hand-to-hand fighting, their instructor on knives was a lieutenant "with a glib tongue and a way of talking that made the Rangers believe he knew what he was talking about." He impressed them as a smart soldier, and Rudder persuaded him to join the battalion as its operations and intelligence officer. His name was Harvey Cook, and he became Rudder's resourceful comrade and friend.[29]

Training intensified as Rudder instigated frequent spot-checks and inspections. He confided to Chick, "We have been training seven days a week . . . lots of night problems . . . keeps me going day and night. . . . We are short on jeeps and I have taken up motorcycle riding. I would give anything to see you and the kids again before we shove off but I guess that is impossible.[30]

EMBARKATION

Then he changed his mind about her visit. "He called me on a Wednesday night," she remembered, "and wanted me to be at Fort Dix by Saturday noon, and I had to figure out how to get there. I took my first plane ride, but I got bounced off in Indianapolis. I finally got there by train and stayed ten days."[31]

When he could pull away from battalion duties, they saw the sights of New York and Philadelphia. He tried to prepare her for the future, forewarning that "there will come a time soon when it will be impossible for me to write for two or three weeks at a time." Their reunion ended in the familiar wartime scene of lovers embracing in a railroad station moments before she boarded the train for Texas. The date was November 2, 1943. However dampened his spirits were, he got a lift on the following day when he was promoted to lieutenant colonel.[32]

Packing for the coming ocean voyage, Earl got rid of nonessentials by giving them away or sending them to Chick. He would not need civilian

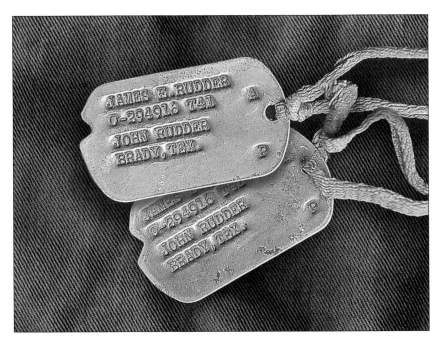

Rudder's wartime dog tags designating his brother, John Rudder, as the recipient of official notification in case of his death. He wanted John to convey the news to his wife rather than have her learn from a telegram. (Courtesy of Ron Walley Photography and James Earl Rudder Jr.)

clothes or dress uniforms where he was going. Everything he took had to
fit in one barracks bag, a footlocker, and his Valpak—the brand name of a
folding suitcase used by many officers. A subordinate said his looked like a
"stuffed pig without legs."

On November 11 the battalion moved north to Camp Shanks, New York,
on the west bank of the Hudson only forty-five minutes by train from Manhattan. They got more vaccinations, physical exams, and dental work and
prepared their wills. Rudder sent Chick his will with a note that it would
"make things much easier—just in case."[33] She would not know until after
the war about the unusual arrangement he made for her to learn of his death.
Every person in the American military wore two dog tags on a cord or chain
around the neck. Earl's dog tags were stamped with the his name, service
number, blood type, and religion and the name of the person to be notified
in case of death. Normally a married man named his wife as the person to be
notified, but Earl named his brother John, a pharmacist in Brady, to receive
the first news in case of Earl's death. Earl did not want the devastating news
to reach Chick by telegram or by an unknown army officer and chaplain in
uniform knocking on her door.

Early on the morning of Sunday, November 21, 1943, the battalion traveled by train into Manhattan and down a spur to 49th Street, two blocks
from the Hudson River.[34] They marched to pier 94, where they were startled
by the first sight of their transport, the Cunard's *Queen Elizabeth,* then the
largest ship in the world. Even in her camouflage grey and without gleaming trim on her hull and decks, she was stately. Rudder had a private cabin,
while most men of the battalion were housed in the great ballroom without
its prewar mirrors, crystal, marble, and mahogany paneling.

After boarding the *Queen Elizabeth,* he went ashore for a final emotional
telephone call to Chick. Then he wrote his last letter from the United States
for almost two years. "You will have to pardon my weakness," he wrote, al-
luding to their telephone conversation, "but somehow I couldn't help it."[35]

CHAPTER 6

BRITAIN

1943–1944

Early on the first day of December 1943, the *Queen Elizabeth* lay still in the River Clyde, a quarter-mile out from Greenock, Scotland, with more than 15,000 American troops eager to disembark. The last to leave were the 513 men of the 2nd Ranger Battalion. In the six-day crossing from New York to Greenock they had been the ship's military police and Rudder its provost marshal, charged with maintaining order. The Rangers detested MP chores as the "lowest form of duty." Some fancied the assignment was punishment for the trouble they had caused for real MPs in bars from Florida to New Jersey. Nonetheless, they supervised boat drills and blackouts and restrained would-be rowdies on the strength of their Ranger reputations and authority symbolized by a round, white badge worn over the right vest pocket with MP printed boldly in black.[1]

Their final assignment was to supervise the long lines of GIs exiting through the passageways. Then they trudged down ramps to paddle-wheeled ferryboats that usually carried people to villages along the Clyde. In mid-morning they were shuttled to the red brick Princes Pier, whose four ornate Italian-styled towers were landmarks that would help them find their way back for a six o'clock train departure.

As the Rangers formed up in their companies and platoons, two uniformed officers, one civilian and one military, came to meet Rudder. The civilian was a local police officer who would guide the battalion through the town. There was no formal welcoming ceremony, only policemen, spiffy in their dark blue uniforms and peaked caps, shaking hands with the American officers. American troops had been passing through Greenock for eighteen months and were now streaming through as fast as ocean liners could bring them across.[2]

The military officer was a U.S. Army Ranger, Maj. Max F. Schneider. He had come to escort the battalion on the five-hundred-mile journey to their new duty station in southwest England. Rudder studied Schneider with special interest. Schneider had been assigned to the battalion on November 11 while Rudder was still in the States. Given the limitations in trans-Atlantic

Max F. Schneider, one of the original Rangers selected by William O. Darby, is shown here in Scotland in 1942 in training conducted by British Commandos. He was in the spearhead of three assault landings in the Mediterranean and, as Rudder's subordinate, commanded the 5th Ranger Battalion in the Omaha Beach landing on D-Day. (Courtesy of James F. Schneider)

communications, Rudder knew little about Schneider, a veteran of fighting in the Mediterranean, where he was decorated with the Silver Star and a Purple Heart. War correspondents acclaimed him as the first American soldier ashore in the invasion of Italy, which, if true, meant he was the first to set foot on the European continent in the war. As a Ranger company commander, he had led three assault landings: the first in Algeria on November 8, 1942, followed by Sicily six months later and Italy, where he was injured by a concussion grenade, on September 28 near Salerno.[3]

Schneider was eligible to return home, but men with his experience were in high demand because most of them were either dead or in hospitals. He had no visible wounds, and his psychic injuries were normally obscured by a boyish smile that charmed his doctors, who understood little about "battle fatigue," as posttraumatic stress disorder was then called.[4] After his injury, he was placed on limited duty for recuperation and sent to London, where senior officers were planning for the arrival of two fresh Ranger units from the United States: Rudder's 2nd Battalion and the 5th Battalion following in January.[5] Both units desperately needed officers with combat experience. Regardless of Schneider's brilliant record, Rudder was now the senior Ranger officer in Britain, and he would decide whether Schneider remained with the battalion. The winnowing of the 2nd Ranger Battalion was continuous, and Schneider was no exception.

Clad in their "WOGs" (wool olive green uniforms), heavy overcoats, and steel helmets, with backpacks and barracks bags slung over their shoulders, the battalion marched in route step up the wet, gray granite cobblestones of Campbell Street.[6] Their destination was the Glebe sugar warehouse, now a transit camp for feeding incoming Americans.

Rudder probably adjourned for the afternoon to the pub of a hotel run by the British military. His Majesty's Services had taken over most hotels in Greenock and would welcome an American colonel, especially the commander of an elite battalion that was the counterpart to their own tough Commandos. Rudder relaxed that afternoon with his key staff officers—Pete Staples (executive officer), Fred Wilkins (adjutant for administration and personnel), and Harvey Cook (intelligence and operations)—as Schneider briefed them on their new duty station in the town of Bude, in Cornwall on the Atlantic coast, 250 miles west of London, beyond Stonehenge and Bath. He had just come from Bude. As Schneider talked, Rudder must have considered whether he should replace Staples with Schneider, who had been the executive officer of the 4th Ranger Battalion in Italy. He was a natural for the same job in the 2nd Battalion, if Rudder agreed that he was fit for duty and they could get along. Rudder soon decided in favor of Schneider, and Staples left the battalion.

In Bude, arrangements for the battalion were in the hands of a four-man advance party that Rudder had dispatched to London in September from Florida. The leader was 1st Lt. Gerald W. Heaney, the battalion's training officer. Without further communication with Rudder, Heaney had organized Bude to receive the battalion.[7] In Heaney, a lawyer from Minnesota, Rudder chose the right man for the job despite Heaney's one self-appraised disadvantage: an intense prejudice against the English acquired from his Irish grandparents. Heaney would be liberated from his bias in Bude, where he waited, hoping Rudder would be satisfied with what he had done.

The train pulled away from the Princes Pier on time. Through the night and into the next day it sped southward, stopping more often than the travelers preferred, but their irritation was soothed when local people came aboard

with tea and tarts. Rudder revealed nothing about the journey to Chick except that he had a comfortable trip. He ended his first letter from Britain
with a suggestion that would tantalize her often in the coming twenty-one
months: "The experience will make interesting conversation on an evening
in the future." Censorship was enforced, and he did not tell her about troop
movements.[8]

BUDE, CORNWALL

Nineteen hours out of Greenock, the train lurched to a halt in a small railway
station at end of the tracks where the roar of the sea never stopped. This was
Bude, a middle-class resort town on the west side of the craggy peninsula
that had been called Land's End for as long as the English language had been
spoken.

Descending from the train, the Rangers were greeted by a small U.S.
Army band playing the music that lifts American spirits: "You're a Grand
Old Flag," "Stars and Stripes Forever," and "The Caissons Go Rolling Along."
The revelation of how the band came to be in such a remote place led to more
surprises. Another U.S. Army unit, the 190th Field Artillery Regiment, was
already there and, with evacuees from London and other cities, had filled
the hotels, leaving none for the Rangers. Since there were no barracks, they
would lodge like boarders—"billet"—in the homes of local people.[9]

The hour was early afternoon, and they went first to the mess hall that
Heaney had improvised in a large garage half a mile from the railway station.
Still carrying their barracks bags and backpacks and unbathed since they
left New York on November 21, they tramped onto Beecoolen Road, which
merged with The Strand along the right bank of the narrow River Neet.
Further on they veered from the river, passed a small, triangular park, and
slogged "up the hill through the winding street to the center of the town."[10]

At first glance, Bude's main similarity to Eden, Texas, was its location at
the end of the railroad tracks. But other similarities soon became apparent
that made the town and the region congenial for Rudder and the Americans.
Most of the Americans came from farms or small towns with agricultural
economies; the same was true of Bude. Unlike many parts of England, local
farmers had small tracts rather than large estates. There was neither a landed
gentry nor an aristocratic class. Of course, some people thought they were
better than others, but that was true back home, too. Rudder had cautioned
Chick, "Don't let the snobs of Brady get you down."[11]

Bude's churches were also similar to those in many American towns: an
evangelical congregation whose members sometimes spoke in tongues, two

Methodist chapels, and a High Anglican church whose vicar complained to Rudder that Rangers came to church with poorly concealed knives and pistols. One of them was a South Carolinian, Capt. Cleveland A. Lytle, who knelt at the communion bar with a bulge in his right hip pocket that was too thick to pass for a plug of chewing tobacco. The Americans found that the people of Bude also believed in equal rights and privileges for everyone, and they got along without major problems. In the nature of things, "some families had an unintended child, but life went on as in the past." Referring to the prevalence of such births, a London stage comedian quipped to an audience of American servicemen, "In the next war, you will only have to send the uniforms."[12]

Bude was divided north and south by a wedge-shaped golf course that, in earlier times, had been common grazing land for folk who had none of their own. Heaney had located Rudder's headquarters on the north side of town in an area called Flexbury, which had numerous three- and four-level houses with several small apartments to accommodate vacationers. For Rudder's headquarters Heaney had selected the Links Hotel, a boxy, three-level house with more than a dozen rooms, enough for the colonel's immediate staff. Heaney's decision to concentrate the battalion in Flexbury was an unintended bonus for training. He anticipated using the golf course and the beach, but not the towering, seemingly endless succession of granite cliffs to the north. At the time, no one in the battalion knew that the Rangers would have to become experts in cliff climbing. Like a wall abutting the sea, the cliffs had been a historic barrier to invasion. Now they would be the training ground for an invasion.

Rudder was billeted with two other officers in the home of Mrs. Duke at 11 Downs View Road, in a row of connected houses overlooking the golf course. When he went to his headquarters, he turned left from her front door for a short walk to the Links Hotel; the beach was a little farther in the other direction. Mrs. Duke had a severe and gloomy reputation with the children of Bude. "She was a rather stately woman," remembered David Dobson, "who always dressed in black with her hair done in a bun." The children did not know that she worried about her son, who had been wounded in Italy. Mrs. Duke was unfailingly considerate to Rudder, who described her as "very kind to me, about fifty years old, and a small, soft spoken person." Only his second day in Bude, December 3, he informed Chick that he was "comfortably quartered and everything is fine with me." Two weeks later, he could say, "The landlady has made my quarters most comfortable," and on Christmas Day he would write, "I think of you so much, I am afraid I neglect my job. The main thought of everyone here is to get on with the war so we can get home again.

If it weren't for the fact that the British are so nice to us, I don't know what it would be like." And a month later, he reported, "I received the Bible you sent. I shall make good use of it."[13]

After their ocean voyage, the Rangers were physically stale. Their strength and endurance had to be rebuilt, and the method was the familiar routine of calisthenics and speed marches of up to twelve miles with full packs or thirty miles without them. At the end of the training day, classes were held on British customs and the British military forces. The Americans were embarrassed that the children of Bude could have taught their classes on aircraft recognition, whether by sight or sound, friend or foe. Rudder held a formal retreat ceremony four times a week and sent a battalion officer to inspect each man's billet on Saturday mornings.[14]

In an amazing coincidence, the commander of the 190th Field Artillery Regiment, Col. Jim Dan Hill, hailed from Schleicher County, Texas, in Rudder's home area. "I met a Col. Hill," Earl confided to Chick, "and he knows your father well." Hill had attended Texas A&M, had taken his first degree from Baylor University, and had earned a Ph.D. in history from the University of Minnesota. When called to active duty in 1940, he left the presidency of Superior State Teachers College in Wisconsin.[15]

Although their backgrounds were similar, they could have clashed without Rudder's forbearance. More than anyone else in Rudder's life—including generals, governors, even presidents—Hill was condescending. He lorded over Rudder his seniority in rank, seniority in age (thirteen years), and precedence in Bude (two months). He billeted with the vicar and wrote for public consumption that he was "the senior officer present," that the Rangers "came under his general command," and that he had been told by higher authority in the army "to keep them out of trouble."[16] Rudder tried to avoid people who annoyed him, but he could not entirely ignore Hill. Instead, he relegated him to the status of an acquaintance or perfunctory comrade-in-arms.

By the mid-1960s their relationship had flip-flopped, and Hill was solicitous of Rudder, then president of Texas A&M University and influential in state politics. The presidency of the University of Texas opened up, and Hill was interested. Rudder was genial when Hill visited him at A&M, but Hill was not an overnight guest in the president's home, as were many other dignitaries and friends. Neither did he become president of the University of Texas.

Rudder arrived in Bude without knowing the Rangers' mission for the coming invasion of Europe. He presumed, as everyone else did, that there would be an attack across the English Channel on German-occupied Europe. On the day he arrived in Britain, President Franklin Roosevelt and

Prime Minister Winston Churchill promised Soviet premier Josef Stalin that their nations would launch the attack, codenamed Overlord, during May of 1944. The "Big Three" were meeting in Teheran, and on the following day, December 2, Roosevelt chose an American officer, Gen. Dwight D. Eisenhower, to command Overlord.[17]

Even without knowing his D-Day mission, Rudder had plenty to do. He had a capable staff, but he was the key decision maker, chief planner, and instigator or overseer of every major activity. He had to specify objectives, monitor developments, and resolve problems while maintaining order and discipline and training endlessly. His attention to matters away from Bude was essential for the right things to happen in Bude. Under the army's concept of a Ranger battalion, every man was a fighting soldier. The battalion was minimally staffed, sparingly equipped, and intentionally dependent on larger units for supplies and equipment such as weapons, radios, and stoves. If the battalion was to have the things it needed, Rudder had to have the confidence of the people with whom he was working (higher headquarters staffs) and his superior officers.[18]

Rudder's essential tasks were to assure that the battalion had satisfactory food and housing; to establish effective relationships with local civilian authorities and nearby military units, British and American; to cultivate higher levels of command; to recruit new Rangers from other U.S. Army units and purge misfits from the battalion; and to conduct a general training program until he had a specific D-Day mission for which to prepare. Demanding as these tasks were, they were minor in comparison to his duties once he was assigned his D-Day mission. Then he would have to learn the guiding principles of the invasion, keep up with changes in the evolving plan, prepare the Rangers' attack plan, and write (or supervise) the precise five-part operations order for each component. These complex tasks would require his close collaboration with a multitude of people and his practically taking up residence in London to draw on the knowledge of British officers. When the Rangers' attack plan was completed, he would have to adapt it to the overall invasion plan in consultation with senior American commanders at their headquarters in southwest England, especially in the city of Bristol and the Dorset village of Blandford Forum.

From his first days in England, he traveled a lot, beginning with Bristol, a hundred miles north of Bude and the location of two major U.S. Army headquarters: V Corps, commanded by Maj. Gen. Leonard T. Gerow, and Lt. Gen. Omar N. Bradley's First Army. The 2nd Ranger Battalion was attached to First Army, whose headquarters he visited to get acquainted and explain the needs of the battalion. Jim Dan Hill observed, "There was always about him an air of patient deliberation. A natural drawl gave a slowness to his words, and his voice was as soft as a presiding elder saying Sunday grace over a chicken dinner." Upon seeing Rudder the first time, John C. Raaen Jr., a 1943 Military Academy graduate, sized him up as "the kind of man that when he walked into a room, you just naturally wanted to stand up and salute." Raaen, son of a career army officer, also noticed that Rudder "was at ease with high-ranking officers and that was a tremendous advantage."[19]

Rudder held battalion formations for the men to see him, to hear his expectations, and to voice their complaints. "He had a way of speaking," wrote Ranger historian Ronald Lane, "that promised of coming excitement, keeping the men keyed up, expecting formidable, but achievable missions ahead." His standards of decorum were high, and he talked to them about their off-duty conduct. Sixty years later the people of Bude produced photographs of Rangers in uniforms clean and properly pressed, with headgear straight on their heads, though not always wearing gloves, as Rudder preferred. "All that was required," Morris Prince told an interviewer, "was that when we went to town, we remembered we were gentlemen and that we were Rangers." Rudder insisted that officers should know the names of every man in their company.[20]

Ten-year-old Brian Woolcott was with a group of friends near the battalion's canteen on Crooklet's Beach when he overheard one Ranger complain to another about food in the mess hall. "I will not eat that shit anymore," he said. The other man quickly admonished his buddy by quoting Rudder: "Don't talk like that around here. You know what the colonel said about not using foul language where children can hear."[21]

When the Rangers were settling into Bude, some were consistently late to the 6:30 AM reveille formation. For the tardiness of a few, first sergeants were penalizing whole platoons by sending them on fast marches of an hour or more. Rudder laid down the rule that, if anyone was late, everyone would be penalized by changing reveille to 6:15 AM. The problem was that Rangers were spread over the town, and not everyone had a clock. As one man noted, "No two clocks in Bude read the same time." In one of Rudder's periodic gripe sessions, a young Ranger rose to say: "Sir, most everyone has been issued a watch and I don't have one. When can I expect to get a watch?" Rudder handed his own watch to the man and asked, "How about right now, son?" The gesture made a memorable impression, and Rudder arranged for every Ranger to have a new Hamilton wristwatch.[22]

Young men have difficulty remembering and complying with rules, and Rudder's Rangers were no exception. The army's *Manual for Courts Martial*

(1928) authorized trials before a military tribunal for certain offenses. As the battalion's commanding officer, Rudder decided whether charges should be preferred against an alleged offender and appointed the tribunal to try the accused. In one case he appointed Heaney, the Minnesota lawyer, to preside over a trial. The tribunal found the man innocent, and Heaney was summoned to Rudder's office for a brief lecture. "Heaney," he said, "I want you to know that when I prefer charges against a man, he is guilty."[23] There were few disciplinary problems in the battalion, because Rudder chose the men who got in and got rid of incompetents and malcontents. Rather than endure the distraction of a court-martial, he transferred the offender to the replacement depot.

Some of the battalion's disciplinary measures were in plain view of the townspeople. The street in front of Rudder's billet and two other streets around the golf course formed an equilateral triangle almost exactly one mile long. As punishment, a Ranger might be required to run around and around the golf course wearing his helmet and carrying a full backpack while holding his rifle over his head."[24]

The Woolcott family lived half a dozen houses from Rudder's billet with Mrs. Duke. Young Brian's third-story bedroom window overlooked the golf course. He was mesmerized by the Rangers' pranks and escapades. The scene, he said, was "continuous theatre, all the time." In the evening after taps, a group of Rangers would often form up on the golf course for a night exercise. A hundred men, more or less, would march out of Bude and make a mock attack toward town on another hundred or so who defended the golf course, mostly in the sand traps. For a people who love sports and were wearied by war, it was grand entertainment. "Someone might tie cans on the tails of several dogs that ran around making a lot of noise. [Everyone] would sit on the walls outside the houses shouting and cheering for the side they wanted to win, together with the children who should have been in bed."[25]

Rudder is the central figure in an anecdote passed down in the Woolcott family. Brian was stricken with double pneumonia. The boy's strength was ebbing away, and his father, a major in British army, came home on emergency leave. Major Woolcott objected to the endless noise produced by the many Rangers billeted in homes near the Woolcotts. It was a roar exceeding that of the sea. "We have to win the war," he told his family, "but we also have to get some rest. I'm going to see their commanding officer." When he explained the situation, Rudder's quick response was, "We've got the stuff!" Penicillin was not yet available, but Dr. Block gave Brian a new medication called sulfathiazole, and the boy soon recovered while Rudder took his father

Brian Woolcott was ten years old in December 1943 when Rudder brought the 2nd Ranger Battalion to Bude on the Atlantic coast in southwest England. From his home near Rudder's billet and the battalion headquarters he watched the Rangers in fun-making as well as training. His parents attributed his recovery from double pneumonia to Rudder's decision to provide a new medication, sulfathiazole, administered by Dr. Block. (Courtesy of Brian Woolcott)

to watch a live firing exercise. In Brian Woolcott's judgment, "Colonel Rudder saved my life," and Rudder's phrase "We've got the stuff!" became a favorite catch phrase in the Woolcott family.[26]

The battalion's training program included night attacks on make-believe enemy installations along the coast. While Rudder was away, one of his Rangers got the idea of attacking an installation that was neither make-believe nor the enemy but an RAF airfield, called Cleave Camp, perched high on the cliffs five miles up the coast from Bude. In the darkness, several Rangers slipped along the base of the cliffs, skirted concrete antitank obstacles at the mouths of ravines, and scaled the cliffs beneath the airfield near Duckpool Beach. Without disturbing an indifferent sentry, they got in the hangers and among the airplanes with chalk and paintbrushes and left rather disrespectful evidence as to what would have happened to the RAF station had they been Germans. All returned to their billets by dawn. The episode did not improve Rudder's diplomatic relations with the RAF commander. It cost him a dinner, a carton of cigarettes, and a solemn promise that no higher headquarters would ever hear of it.[27]

December of 1943 was the fifth consecutive Christmas season that Britain had been at war. Essential items—including food and clothing—were strictly rationed, and there were no sweets. Rudder told Chick about the battalion's plan for the children of Bude. "Xmas is just around the corner but there is very little sign of it here. We gave up our rations of candy and sweets for two weeks and are having a party for the kids in the community on the 23rd." It was really his plan. Long after the war, company commander Sidney Salomon recalled how Rudder "made it clear that this was to be the party of all parties for local children. The men were told to spend their Christmas leave in Bude and not in London. During the run-up to Christmas, Rudder paid as much attention to planning the party as he did to training for D-Day."[28]

The party also diverted the Rangers' longing for their homes with their families and friends. Ranger Ed Sorvisto confirmed the party's success as a distraction: "It did everyone's heart good to watch the children. When you see a husky American lad driving a three-quarter ton truck laden with children . . . holding a cute blond English girl of three, tears form in your eyes and a lump swells in your throat." Another Ranger wrote, "It was a big event when we handed out our rations to all the wee ones and some not so wee." After the party, the children of Bude had no doubts they were on the winning side of the war. On Christmas day Rudder wrote with obvious satisfaction: "The party our boys gave for the kids was a real success. There were 535 present. I have never seen a group of kids have as much fun. It is difficult to say [who] had the greatest fun, the kids or our boys."[29]

Two weeks after arriving in Bude, Rudder got orders from General Bradley for the battalion to begin training with British Commandos in preparation for raids on the coast of Nazi-occupied Europe. He was told to take his instructions from the Commandos' parent organization, Combined Operations headquarters. Rudder's orders were premised on the original reason for creation of the Rangers in early 1942: to gain combat experience by joining in the Commandos' raids along the coast of occupied Europe. Only Rudder's closest associates knew about the new orders or that he had gone to London with Schneider and Cook to confer with British officers at Combined Operations. The three Rangers quickly realized that Combined Operations had evolved from an organization concerned with pinprick hit-and-run raiding parties into an embryonic invasion headquarters. Under Admiral Lord Louis Mountbatten, Combined Operations developed amphibious assault tactics, landing craft, and equipment that Commandos tested with actual raids on German territory. From the raids they gained experience and gathered information about enemy defenses for the full-fledged invasion. After four difficult years, the Commandos were the acknowledged experts on amphibious landings in Europe, and Combined Operations was the best source of experts and specialized equipment for the coming cross-channel invasion.[30]

D-DAY MISSION

Rudder was summoned to General Bradley's headquarters in London on Tuesday, January 4, 1944.[31] Bradley had moved his main headquarters from Bristol to Bryanston Square, a row of fashionable West End apartments four blocks north of Marble Arch and a brisk five-minute walk from Paddington railway station. From Bude, the fastest way to the West End was to drive a staff car fifty miles to Exeter and catch the train to Paddington. The Great Western Railroad had one on its schedule that went straight through from Exeter in less than four hours.

Rudder took with him Max Schneider, who, like his commander, balanced audacity with prudence.[32] Schneider, aggressive but not foolhardy, had been well schooled by his former commander, William O. Darby. "Max," Darby once advised, "You have to learn to combine cautiousness with recklessness."[33] Both Rudder and Schneider were invigorated by the challenge of a tough contest. Schneider was a competitive diver who had dropped out of Iowa State College to become an airline pilot. Like Rudder, he came of age in a small town in the American heartland: Shenandoah, Iowa, near the Nebraska line on the edge of a vast, sparsely populated prairie.

For a visit to the city they wore the standard browns and tans for infantry officers of their grade: olive drab trousers, a green blouse, brown shoes and gloves; tan socks, shirt, tie, and field jacket. Their headgear was the army's soft brimless service cap, resembling a cloth envelope with one long side slit open to fit across the head. Rudder carried a stocky 218 pounds on his six-foot frame, and Schneider, at five foot, nine, was lithe, slender, and light on his feet. Their diamond-shaped Ranger patch, navy blue embroidered in bright yellow gold with the word RANGERS, sewn on the left jacket shoulder, drew the attention of onlookers. The exploits of Commandos and Rangers in North Africa and Italy had been widely publicized in Britain.

Leaving the cavernous Paddington Station, grimy with the accumulated soot of coal-fired steam engines, they passed scenes of damage from the Blitz. Their destination was numbers 29–32 Bryanston Square, a five-level building with a white stone façade at street level and red brick above. A heavy German bombing attack on May 10, 1941, had spoiled the elegant late Georgian symmetry of the square by destroying several buildings. The once handsome iron railings around its central park were gone, cut down and

The Ranger shoulder patch worn during World War II

smelted for munitions. From the arched entrance doorway an armed guard escorted them to the war room, formerly an ornate apartment on the second level, where they were exposed to the most closely guarded secrets of the European war. The floor-to-ceiling windows were covered with heavy blackout cloth, blocking any external view of the maps and aerial photographs on the walls, all of which were marked Top Secret. The fireplace was barely visible behind desks and filing cabinets.[34]

Bradley's operations officer, Col. Truman "Tubby" Thorson, was the briefing officer. Detailed maps and high-quality aerial photographs of the French coast, covered with clear acetate sheets for marking pencils, were spread across tables. Unit boundaries and objectives were scrawled on the sheets. Heavy black arcs were drawn out from the beaches, indicating the range of German coastal guns. Thorson called their attention to a triangular geologic feature, a sharp promontory of land that jutted into the sea, rising vertically a hundred feet above a narrow shoreline. Its name was Pointe du Hoc, misspelled then and later as "Hoe." The original word was *haca*, "promontory," and came, like the word *Normandy*, from the Norsemen who swept along the coast of Europe in the ninth and tenth centuries.

Above the beach, on the flat headlands of Pointe du Hoc, the Germans had installed six long-range 155 mm guns, several antiaircraft guns, a concrete observation bunker, and other fortifications. The guns had a range of about twenty-five thousand yards, or fourteen miles. Most German defenses were on the inland side of the *pointe*, as the enemy believed it was unassailable from the sea.[35] Air strikes alone could not guarantee that the guns were out of action. The only certain way to silence them would be to go in on the ground. The mission would require an elite band of warriors commanded by a bold and inspirational leader.

Rudder noted Schneider's reaction to Thorson's description of Pointe du Hoc. "When we got a look at it, Max just whistled once through his teeth. He had a way of doing that. He'd made three landings already, but I was just a country boy coaching football [two and a half years] before. It would almost knock you out of your boots."[36]

The main American landings would occur four miles east of Pointe du Hoc on a slightly curving four-mile stretch of sandy beach codenamed Omaha. Three weeks after the briefing, a second beach, Utah, on the eastern shore of the Cherbourg Peninsula, was added to the landing plan.[37] Utah was nine miles northwest of Pointe du Hoc and within easy range of the German guns on the *pointe*. In addition to knocking out the guns, the Rangers were assigned a second mission: to block the coastal road behind Pointe du Hoc; otherwise, the Germans could use it to rush forces to Omaha. Later, a third

The forbidding cliffs of Pointe du Hoc in 1943 before bombardment, a photograph that may have been shown to Rudder on January 4, 1944, when he was assigned the mission to knock out the six guns whose emplacements have been marked P1 through P6 by the photo interpreters. (U.S. National Archives)

objective was added to take out the enemy guns on a steep bluff at the west end of Omaha called Pointe et Raz de la Percée. These three objectives were the Rangers' D-Day mission.

Without exception, the American high command apparently believed the success of the landings on Omaha and Utah depended on the destruction or neutralization of the guns on Pointe du Hoc. The *pointe* ranked number one on the U.S. Army's list of the most dangerous German coastal gun batteries. War correspondents briefed in secret on the invasion came away with the impression that, as combat historian Forrest Pogue recalled, the "Pointe du Hoc operation was the crucial one on Omaha Beach," and "the Rangers were the most interesting troops in the invasion." At the same time, well-informed skeptics thought taking out the guns on Pointe du Hoc by a ground attack was impossible. "It can't be done," said one doubter. "Three old women with brooms could keep the Rangers from climbing that cliff."[38]

Since Omar Bradley was in charge of the entire American landing force on the two beaches, Earl Rudder was central to his thinking about D-Day. He would praise Rudder for the remainder of his long life (1893–1981).[39]

After Rudder learned the battalion's D-Day mission, the Rangers continued training with Commandos and the Royal Navy along England's south coast. They practiced night landings on unfamiliar beaches. They landed in rough waters along the edge of cliffs and made mock assaults where Commandos, firing from hidden positions, shot up the ground and surf around them, even shattering their boat paddles. After blowing up fake coastal guns, they withdrew as Commandos fired live ammunition over and around them.

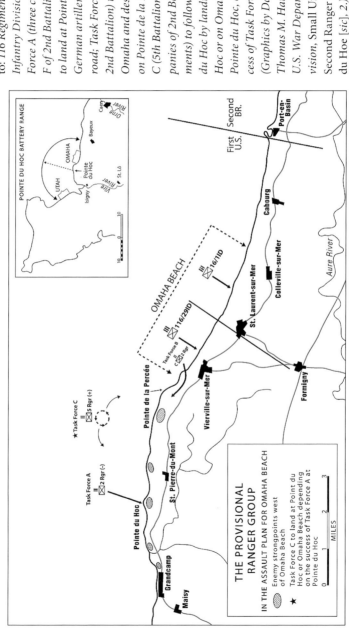

Map 6-1. Commander: Lt. Col. James E. Rudder. Components: 2nd and 5th Ranger Battalions. Attached to: 116 Regimental Combat Team, 29th Infantry Division. Deployed as: Task Force A (three companies—D, E, and F of 2nd Battalion plus attachments) to land at Pointe du Hoc to destroy German artillery and block the coastal road; Task Force B (C Company of 2nd Battalion) to land on west end of Omaha and destroy German weapons on Pointe de la Percée; and Task Force C (5th Battalion plus A and B companies of 2nd Battalion and attachments) to follow Task Force A to Pointe du Hoc by landing either at Pointe du Hoc or on Omaha, then overland to Pointe du Hoc, depending on the success of Task Force A at Pointe du Hoc. (Graphics by David Zepeda, copyright Thomas M. Hatfield. Map reference: U.S. War Department, Historical Division, Small Unit Actions: France: Second Ranger Battalion at Pointe du Hoe [sic], 2.)

British Commando Lt. Col. Thomas H. Trevor (center), an expert on cliff climbing, was an advisor to the 2nd Ranger Battalion in England. He influenced the development of Rudder's assault plan as well as the training program and accompanied the Rangers to Pointe du Hoc. The photo was enhanced from a panorama of Commandos taken in 1943. (Courtesy of the Commando Veterans Association, U.K.)

They trained only in British landing craft manned by seamen of the Royal Navy because those were the boats that would carry them to the far shore on D-Day. They learned the Brits' seafaring rules, their jargon, and their customs. The awkward part was catching on to their ironic sense of humor, the habit of stating literally the opposite of the intended meaning, and their exasperating tendency to phase an assertion as a question.

When not practicing amphibious assaults, Commandos taught cliff climbing, hand-to-hand fighting, and getting out of tight corners by disarming or killing the enemy with their famous Fairbairn-Sykes knife. The Commandos maintained that cliff climbing was an essential part of their training because much of the enemy-occupied coastline, especially in France, was rimmed with steep, perpendicular cliffs. For specialized training on sea cliffs, the battalion went to the Isle of Wight, where they were joined by an advisor from Combined Operations, Commando Lt. Col. Thomas H. Trevor. Trevor was known for his expertise in cliff climbing, which stemmed from boyhood fantasies as a medieval knight surmounting castle walls. He had distinguished himself during the Anglo-American invasion of North Africa in November 1942, where he was mentioned in dispatches and decorated with the Order of the British Empire. General Eisenhower told him in a personal letter that he "exemplified those rugged, self-reliant qualities which the entire world

associates with the very name 'Commando.'" Trevor was an important addition to Rudder's inner circle and would influence the D-Day assault plan.[40]

Although Rudder was informed of the Rangers' D-Day mission, he was
not told how to accomplish it. He had a directive for planning rather than a
plan. The same was true for other ground commanders from his level (the
battalion) all the way up to the supreme commander. Based on the overall concept of the invasion, planning proceeded simultaneously at all levels,
from army to corps to divisions to regiments down to battalions. The entire
invasion plan was assembled from these unit plans, which changed as the
overall concept evolved. Problems identified at a higher level had a cascading
effect that required adjustments in the plans of lower levels. When Rudder
began planning, final decisions had not been made about the date of the attack, whether it would occur in daylight or darkness, or the preferred level of
the tide for the first wave going ashore. Through the "early spring planning
proceeded on the assumption that overall German strength and dispositions
would remain substantially unchanged" until D-Day; this assumption was
necessary to have a firm basis for planning.[41]

As Rudder was considering how to approach his planning task, he had
to deal with a dilemma in his staff. The issue was Max Schneider's posttraumatic stress disorder. Three days after they had gone to London, Rudder
submitted a request in writing to General Bradley for Schneider's return to
the United States. Rudder emphasized the rigors of Schneider's combat in the
Mediterranean: "He fought the entire African Campaign" and participated
in the invasions and campaigns in Sicily and Italy before he was transferred
to the 2nd Ranger Battalion.[42] Whether this request was on Rudder's initiative, at Schneider's request, or by mutual agreement cannot be determined.

A week later, Dr. Block forwarded a supporting memorandum with a
medical diagnosis and prognosis. Block said Schneider was "suffering from
a Neurasthenic condition brought on by overwork and mental fatigue" and
strongly recommended his transfer to the United States. Further, Block predicted, "unless such a radical measure is resorted to," he "may suffer a mental 'crack up.'" The request was approved and then retracted after review by
General Eisenhower "in order to utilize [Schneider's] services in the initial
invasion of the continent."[43]

Thus did the army knowingly disregard Max Schneider's physical pains
and psychic difficulties. His physical impairment went back to 1933, when
surgeons had placed a silver plate in his skull to repair an injury suffered
in an air crash. The grenade explosion in Italy probably aggravated the old
head wound and may have caused other minute cranial injuries. The least
of his pain was from festering sores as the internal shell fragments of the

grenade worked their way out through the skin. Symptoms of his "battle fatigue" were recognized, but the disorder was poorly understood and usually
ignored unless the afflicted person was unable to function. However heart-
less Eisenhower's decision may seem, in the light of Schneider's heroic leadership on D-Day the supreme commander made a wise determination.

RECRUITING RANGERS

For almost two months after receiving his D-Day mission, Rudder applied
himself to recruiting and mostly left the preparation of the preliminary assault plan to Combined Operations headquarters, where it was the responsibility of Lt. Col. Dermot L. Richardson, a British army staff officer. Rudder
had always recruited to improve the 2nd Ranger Battalion, but he now had
another reason. Told to expect 70 percent casualties on D-Day, he was recruiting replacements to come to France after the invasion.[44]

As in the United States, he handpicked the Rangers, and no soldier became a Ranger unless he wanted to be. Many commanders were reluctant
to lose their best soldiers, but if Rudder wanted a man and the man wanted
to be a Ranger, no one except General Bradley could stop it. Rudder was
enough of a schoolteacher to know a really dumb soldier when he saw one
and enough of a football coach to recognize one who lacked physical ability.
When he decided that a man did not measure up to his standards, he crossed
him off his list. The men who remained gained confidence in the knowledge
that they met Rudder's expectations. In the words of Morris Prince, those
transferred out "didn't quite meet the rigid standards and moral requirements of the Rangers."[45]

Second Lt. Conrad Epperson was appointed to the headquarters staff in
February and usually saw Rudder every day. "If you didn't cut the mustard,
you were gone," he said. "It was the same with officers as with men and we
appreciated it. If you had a dough-dough in your group, you wanted to get
rid of him and only Colonel Rudder could do it." Epperson added, "He was a
quiet disciplinarian. Nothing bothered him. I never heard him lose his temper or even raise his voice."[46]

"Rudder shaped us up," said Sidney Salomon. "He had expertise in coaching and administration and the managerial experience to weld us together
as a battalion. We got rid of officers who did not measure up to Rudder's
standards."[47]

The style of Rudder's interviews with prospective Rangers can be seen in
the account of Bob Edlin, who reveals that Rudder appreciated an unconven-
tional approach to solving a problem and a nonconformist who challenged

those in authority for a good reason. Edlin entered the room, stood at attention, and saluted. Rudder told him to be seated and that he had two questions.

> **Rudder:** *"Why do you want to be in the Rangers?"*
>
> **Edlin:** *"The outfit I'm with now has a battalion commander who is going to get a lot of people hurt and I need to be in an outfit that believes in itself."*
>
> **Rudder:** *"I've looked at your records. You've had lots of training, however you have some bad reports. They say you're a rebel and a renegade. Were you ever in the Boy Scouts?"*
>
> **Edlin:** *"Yes, sir, I was for a short time."*
>
> **Rudder:** *"What was their motto?"*
>
> **Edlin:** *"Be prepared."*
>
> **Rudder:** *"All right. If you were leading a company of Rangers and you were on a hillside, completely surrounded by Germans and they were attacking you and you were plumb out of ammunition, what would you do?'*
>
> **Edlin:** *"Well, I'd surrender."*
>
> **Rudder:** *"Why would you surrender?"*
>
> **Edlin:** *"There might be a chance that some of us could get away and tie up some of the Germans guarding us."*

Rudder then stood up, shook Edlin's hand, and told him, "Go tell the first sergeant to put you on the Ranger roster."[48]

Sgt. William L. "L-Rod" Petty may have been the only man who persuaded Rudder to remove his name from the purge list. Petty's front teeth had been knocked out playing football in his native Georgia. When Rudder accepted him in the battalion, Petty promised to get false teeth, which he had not done. After Petty learned that Rudder intended to purge him, he appealed. When Rudder mentioned that he had not gotten his false teeth, Petty replied, "Colonel, I don't want to bite 'em. I want to fight 'em." After that cunning retort Rudder let him remain, and he was a splendid battlefield soldier. The other men said, "He loved his B-A-R" (Browning automatic rifle), and he was an expert with it. But Petty was often difficult. As a boy, his father had brutally beaten him on a "fairly regular but unpredictable basis." Not surprisingly, Petty was defiant and disobedient to those in authority. He would be reduced in grade, only to be promoted for his combat performance.[49]

Rudder's main recruiting territory was in southwest England because most American ground units were there. But a sizeable American contingent was also in Northern Ireland, where he prospected the 2nd Infantry Division for Rangers. Rudder knew many men in the division from having served with them when called to active duty in 1941. From near Belfast he wrote to Chick: "I have seen most of the Northern Ireland and Scotland. I did some flying a few days ago and the country looks exactly like an old patch quilt. The country is divided into little fields of about 10 acres with a hedge rock fence around each one. There isn't one inch of wasted space here. I [will] see Frank Corder this afternoon."[50]

Frank Corder, Texas A&M class of 1940, was a captain in the division and one of Rudder's closest friends. He was qualified to be a Ranger, but Rudder tried to persuade him to remain where he was. When Corder insisted, Rudder relented. Tom Morris, another Aggie friend in the 2nd Infantry, had been Rudder's classmate, football teammate, and fellow table waiter in Sbisa Hall. Now, fourteen years later and forty-five hundred miles from Sbisa, Rudder and Morris shared K-rations under a field tent in a marshy meadow in the rain of Northern Ireland. When Rudder offered to make Morris a Ranger, Morris declined, saying, "Earl, I have enough war where I am."[51] Elsewhere, Rudder attended the closing exercises of a Ranger training course near Portsmouth, where one of the graduates was nineteen-year-old Frank Denius of Athens, Texas. Denius was admitted to the Texas state bar after the war, and Rudder would seek his help in the 1960s to resolve legal issues related to Texas A&M.

While Rudder was actively recruiting, the 5th Ranger Battalion arrived in Liverpool to augment the 2nd Battalion in the D-Day assault. Its arrival was a further indication of the higher command's great concern about the guns on Pointe du Hoc. A few weeks later, company commanders from the 5th Battalion began contacting Rudder with complaints about their commanding officer. Without an official announcement, they somehow understood that Rudder was the number one Ranger in Britain. Before long, the battalion commander was relieved, and Max Schneider replaced him. To succeed Schneider as the 2nd Battalion's executive officer, Rudder appointed Cleveland A. Lytle, a regular army officer and a 1936 honors graduate of Clemson University. Before the invasion, the two battalions were joined temporarily as the Provisional Ranger Group—almost a thousand of the U.S. Army's elite soldiers—with Rudder in command.[52]

PRELIMINARY PLAN REJECTED

By the end of February, Colonel Richardson had a draft of the Rangers' attack plan for review by Rudder and Maj. Gen. Leonard T. Gerow, under whose

U.S. Army V Corps the Provisional Ranger Group would operate on D-Day. On March 3, Richardson met Rudder and Gerow in the latter's headquarters in Bristol's Clifton College, a public school whose students and faculty had moved, by coincidence, to Bude, which was less at risk to German bombs.[53]

Richardson recommended the Rangers land in two places, each about four miles east and west of Pointe du Hoc, and converge overland toward it in conjunction with an airdrop on the promontory of about thirty-five men. He hedged his bets on the attack from the west because the shoals might hinder an amphibious approach. His proposal, therefore, rested on the airdrop and an attack from the east originating from Omaha Beach, the site of the main landing. Gerow refused to approve the airdrop, perhaps because airborne forces were fully committed elsewhere. That left Richardson's plan with only the attack overland from Omaha, which was ruled out because it would arrive at Pointe du Hoc too late. The guns had to be out of operation when the Omaha and Utah landings began, not hours afterwards. Otherwise, they might fire on the beaches crowded with troops and vehicles. Richardson did not propose a frontal assault to scale the Pointe du Hoc cliffs.[54]

Rudder then took over planning the attack with Harvey Cook and Max Schneider as his principal aides. Although Rudder was as proud as any American, he knew he needed the help of British officers at Combined Operations. The Rangers' assault plan had to conform to the overall concept of the invasion and mesh with the details of the landing schedule. Coordination was essential, and he became the go-between for his battalion and Combined Operations with the American high command, mainly Maj. Gen. Clarence R. Huebner, commanding general of the U.S. 1st Infantry Division. Huebner was Gerow's subordinate to command all forces landing on Omaha Beach, including those going to Pointe du Hoc. As preparation of the Rangers' assault plan proceeded, Rudder shuttled between four headquarters: Huebner's in Langton House near Blandford Forum, 140 miles over back roads from his own headquarters in Bude; Gerow's in Bristol; and Combined Operations in central London.

Combined Operations' contribution was indispensable, beginning with Commando Trevor as an advisor on tactics and training. For equipment and technical advice, Rudder turned to Combined Operations' Department of Miscellaneous Weapons Development, directed by Royal Navy captain Francis W. H. Jeans, and three Royal Navy Volunteer Reserve officers: Lt. Cdr. R. C. Byng, Lt. Donald F. Currie, and Lt. Ronald F. Eades, Trevor's assistant.[55]

Devising the assault plan was at an impasse unless other approaches to Pointe du Hoc could be identified. The planners reexamined an approach from the west but dropped it when the Germans flooded an inland area with

Harvey Cook, Rudder's confidant and the 2nd Ranger Battalion's intelligence and operations officer, 1943–45. (Courtesy of Gen. Donald G. Cook, USAF, ret)

seawater that would force the Rangers to attack through prepared defensive positions that Trevor termed a "killing ground." By eliminating the east and west options and an airdrop, Rudder arrived at the decision to recommend an attack from the sea. Trevor had favored it all along, counseling that "bold conception and cautious execution leads to quick and favorable decisions" on the battlefield.[56]

Clearly defining a problem creates a mind-set for imaginative solutions. Rudder's decision for a frontal assault up the cliffs had that effect. The challenge was how to quickly raise about 250 men up one-hundred-foot vertical heights. Combined Operations evaluated several mechanical devices. Metal spikes and anchors were found ineffective on crumbling cliffs. Another idea was a "special roller" similar to a large wheel installed at the top of the cliff with a rope looped around it that men on the beach would pull to lift other men to the top.[57] Trevor was fascinated with a naval balloon that could "waft" (his word) a few men to the top who could then help others up; it was silent and fast but rejected as difficult to handle and too vulnerable to gunfire.

Two types of equipment for cliff climbing were ready and available from Combined Operations: one was a lightweight tubular steel ladder in four-foot sections that could be assembled one on top of the other by a person climbing up them, and the other was a rocket-propelled grapnel to shoot over a cliff rim with ropes attached so men could then pull themselves up if the grapnel's hooks caught on the cliff top. The rocket-propelled grapnels were too large for a man to carry but could be mounted on landing craft; Rudder accepted them and requested a smaller model that a man could carry, and they were fabricated especially for the Rangers.

In London, Rangers saw firemen using long, electric-powered extension ladders. Someone made a mental association between the extension ladders and a new amphibious truck he had seen in the Mediterranean. The vehicle was a DUKW, called a "duck," a pun-like term derived from terminology used for military vehicles: D for designed in 1942; U for utility; K for all-wheel drive; and W for two powered rear axles. Thus Rudder adopted three methods for scaling the cliffs: rocket-propelled grapnel hooks with ropes attached, hand-held ladders, and DUKWs with extension ladders.

Rudder's tactical challenge was how to organize and arrange the Provisional Ranger Group to attack the three objectives: the guns on Pointe du Hoc, the coastal road, and the guns on Pointe de la Percée. An important question was how to approach Pointe du Hoc from the sea. Aerial photographs showed German fortifications regularly spaced back from the tip of the *pointe*. He decided to land his Pointe du Hoc assault force in about equal numbers on each side of the tip. Another concern was the almost certain loss of surprise, since the German garrison would see them approaching in slow-moving landing craft. To offset this disadvantage, plans were made with naval and air commanders for heavy, intensive bombardments that would stop just moments before the landing craft hit the beach. Timing was crucial. Disaster loomed if the bombardments stopped too soon and permitted the Germans to leave their dugouts, or if it continued past the Rangers' arrival, which could subject them to the bombardments.

Planning was in high gear at the end of March when Rudder began meeting with Huebner in his headquarters at Langton House, an elegant Georgian mansion in the Palladian style constructed in 1830 on the edge of Blandford Forum. An aide to Huebner kept notes on his office conferences. On March 27 Rudder spent the afternoon with Huebner "in the Bigot Room . . . discussing the employment of the Ranger battalions in coming operations. [Bigot was the code word for anyone who was briefed on invasion plans.] Lt. Col. Richardson of Combined Operations came at 1400. [They] discussed various details concerning the target." Rudder remained after Richardson left. Four days later, Rudder was back again. "During the day," Huebner's assistant recorded, "the CG (commanding general) spent much time in the Bigot Room with Lt. Col. Rudder."[58]

Meanwhile, the 2nd Battalion trained in Bude. Although Rudder knew their D-Day assignment, he did not yet know how the attack would be made, so they trained in skills that infantrymen need when they meet the enemy: teamwork in small group assaults; violent attacks against fortified positions; map-and-compass courses; and marksmanship with weapons a man could carry in his hands: rifles, BARs, bazookas, flamethrowers, and pistols.[59]

Trevor coached them in cliff climbing, beginning with strolls along the top. The cliffs scared men as dauntless as Bob Edlin: "The first time I looked up at those 90-foot cliffs, it just scared the crap out of me. Sheer cliffs. Rope ladders and ropes were hanging on them and some guys were climbing up them. I thought, 'What kind of nut would climb up something like this?'" Morris Prince was surprised at the ease of assembling four-foot steel ladders up to a hundred feet high while climbing on them.[60]

Local people came to watch the Rangers, including thirteen-year-old Judyth Gwynne and her friends. "We watched them run through the surf. They climbed cliffs while we walked all in amongst them. It looked like fun and we wondered why grown men were doing such things." At the same time, she encountered her first overtures from men. "There were wolf whistles, a new phenomena to us, but we stuck our noses in the air and walked past them on our daily journey to and from school."[61]

Despite their instructions, some Rangers were occasionally irresponsible with live ammunition. British authorities had arranged for them to have a practice rifle range in an isolated ravine that notched the cliffs above the beach. High shots and ricochets went into the sea. While Rudder was away, Cleveland Lytle, his second in command, decided to conduct an exercise by attacking up the narrow valley that led to a village, several farmhouses, and a crossroads pub. The telephone in Rudder's headquarters in the Links Hotel began ringing about the time the first shot was fired.

The raiding party was recalled to Bude, and the incident was investigated. Cornwall was cattle country, dotted with tough, brawny bulls, slender-shouldered milk cows, and young spring calves. Given the strict meat rationing, no one should have been surprised by what happened. The only casualty was a well-fattened yearling steer with one clean shot through its upper neck. Death was instantaneous. Rudder and the farmer could agree on two points: the selection of the steer and the marksmanship of the sharp-shooter. The farmer was not assuaged. Rudder tried to make a deal with him. Since Uncle Sam would not pay damages on the steer, officers of the battalion would be punished by chipping in to pay for the animal at 10 percent above the pegged price of beef. The offer was refused. Others followed, and only the invasion ended Rudder's correspondence on the subject. "There was always excitement," three Rangers bragged in their 1946 chronology. "More than once, we ran afoul of the Home Guard and had the whole countryside in an uproar."[62]

On April 1 the battalion celebrated the first anniversary of its activation at Camp Forrest, Tennessee, with a party and stage performances that satirized and ridiculed, as a Ranger wrote, "everything and everyone from our battalion commander on down. Our colonel was the butt of many a witty remark, and gave out with mighty guffaws every time he was slandered; a swell sport and a great leader."[63] In the evening the battalion sponsored a dance that drew a large turnout from the people of Bude, who could not be told it was their last gathering with Rangers.

Two days later the entire battalion left Bude, never to return.[64] Their movement was secret, and they slipped away quietly in the early morning. No good-byes, no more chewing gum, and no more chocolates. The people awoke to find they were all gone. In the words of one child, Brian Woolcott, "The party was over."

From Bude the battalion moved about forty miles up the coast to the newly established assault training center on Morte Bay near the village of Braunton. Most men realized, as did Morris Prince, "the big dealers at

battalion headquarters knew the part that we would play in the coming assault on *Fortress Europa,* so we started to undergo problems that were similar
to those in the coming invasion plans."[65] The 5th Ranger Battalion joined
with the 2nd Battalion for the first time—a tip-off they would fight under
one command on D-Day.

CENTRAL LONDON

When Rudder went to Combined Operations headquarters in London, he
often stayed at the Savoy Hotel on The Strand. He became sufficiently well
known that his only two postwar returns to the famous Savoy Grill were
memorable for the waiters and his companions. In 1969, a medical doctor,
William Green, son of his lifelong friend in Eden, M. J. Green, dined with
him and heard waiters calling to others from twenty-five years earlier, "Colonel Rudder is back!" They remembered the convivial Colonel Rudder, so
fond of good food and company.

A new acquaintance from this period saw him as "not the swash-buckling
type in personal appearance or attitude." His demeanor left an impression
because it contrasted with that of many Rangers, who emulated the swag-
ger of British Commandos, including their conspicuous mustaches.[66] Rudder
had an aversion to facial hair that became well known while he was president
of Texas A&M.

From the Savoy Hotel it was a ten-minute stroll to Combined Operations headquarters on Richmond Terrace, a short connecting street between
Whitehall and the Victoria Embankment along the Thames. He walked
along The Strand to Charing Cross and Trafalgar Square, usually crowded
with American soldiers. Shop windows were boarded up, and shrapnel dings
on buildings were visible and widespread. The base of Nelson's Column was
covered with sandbags, but the four huge bronze lions were exposed, and GIs
might be seen reaching up to stroke their paws. The midsection of one lion
was holed by bomb damage, and its paw had been blown away. Brick bomb
shelters had been built over the water fountains, and the square was splotched
with patches over filled-in bomb craters. "An air of gray resolution seemed to
hang over the city," as Sayre Van Young saw it.[67] From Trafalgar Square, Rudder entered Whitehall, a broad thoroughfare that led to the Houses of Parliament. In two blocks he came to Richmond Terrace. Five minutes further, he
reached the Houses of Parliament. Westminster Abbey was nearby.

Two towering events in his life occurred in London during the Easter
week of 1944. On Good Friday, April 7, he attended a presentation of the
entire Overlord plan organized by British general Bernard L. Montgomery,

Eisenhower's subordinate to command all ground forces in the invasion. The briefing was conducted at Saint Paul's School for a select audience of senior land, naval, and air officers. Attendance by a mere lieutenant colonel was an exception, but Rudder's friends at Combined Operations arranged a pass for him, a small card that he kept spotless and unfolded among his memorabilia. All the top brass were in the room: Churchill; Eisenhower; Gen. Alan Brooke, the head of the British army; and Bradley. A relief map of Normandy as wide as a city street was spread across the floor. It began with naval and air commanders giving their overviews. After lunch, Monty summarized, trampling over the map, Bradley said, "with rare skill . . . like a giant through Lilliputian France."[68]

Then Churchill spoke, "looking old and lacking a great deal of his usual vitality," in Brooke's judgment. Churchill's opinion was otherwise, and he telegraphed Roosevelt, "I gave a good talk to all the Generals, British and American, expressing my strong confidence in the result of this extraordinary but magnificent operation." Eisenhower said the conference consumed an entire day, presenting the "completed picture of the detailed plan for the ground assault against the beaches."[69] No lieutenant colonel in the U.S. Army was better informed about plans for the invasion than Earl Rudder.

Two days later, he was still at the Savoy Hotel and attended Easter services in Westminster Abbey. That evening he wrote to Chick, exhilarated by events of recent days yet longing to be home: "If I could have had you here with me this would be the most perfect weekend of my career. Occasionally I have to stop and ask myself if this isn't just a dream. Here's hoping next Easter finds me back with you."[70]

FINAL PREPARATIONS

While working from the assault training center in Braunton, Rudder appointed his staff for the Provisional Ranger Group (PRG). He took them from both battalions, and they retained their battalion duties while taking on their PRG assignment as temporary. At Braunton he took for his personal quarters a hut large enough for himself and three key subordinates: Max Schneider, commander of the 5th Battalion, promoted to lieutenant colonel on May 30; Maj. Richard P. "Sully" Sullivan, 5th Battalion's executive officer, who had the same role in the PRG; and Capt. Richard P. Merrill, Rudder's adjutant in the 2nd Battalion, who also had the same job in the PRG. No doubt he wanted to talk about the still incomplete assault plan. Merrill recalled that Rudder fell asleep early, while Schneider stayed up later than the others, sitting on the edge of his bed, making notes, and

The 2nd Ranger Battalion on June 1, 1944, marching through Weymouth, England, to board troopships bound for the Normandy invasion. Rudder is in the right foreground. (U.S. National Archives)

writing letters. He told his wife that he "admired Rudder's courage and can-do attitude."[71]

Rudder continued traveling to London and to Langton House to confer with General Huebner. He was there when Huebner arrived from Mass on Sunday, April 23. An aide to Huebner wrote sparsely in his diary: "Lt Col Rudder, CO of the Ranger Group, was in. Many subjects and problems were discussed in the Bigot Room, including lack of complete equipment." Rudder did not yet have the DUKWs with extension ladders for which the Rangers had high hopes. Huebner called Gerow "for a solution to Rudder's problem," and they decided that he should go immediately to Gerow's headquarters sixty miles north in Bristol for a decision.[72] He would get the DUKWs, but not until the final days before embarking for Normandy.

On April 27 the battalion moved toward the Channel coast in a vast stream of traffic. Along the roads were endless stacks of bombs, hundreds of artillery pieces, jeeps, and tanks. The crescendo of preparations for the invasion was continuing at a feverish pitch. Invasion forces were concentrating in marshaling areas near the ports of embarkation, and the south coast of England was closed to visitors.[73]

On May 11 General Huebner issued the field order for the Omaha Beach landings with details about the PRG based on Rudder's plan. The PRG would be attached to the 116th Regimental Combat Team commanded by Col. Charles D. W. Canham and organized in three task forces. Ranger Task Force A, about half of the 2nd Battalion, would make the assault on Pointe du Hoc. Task Force B, one company of the 2nd Battalion, would knock out the guns on Pointe de la Percée. The rest of the entire PRG, Task Force C, would land at Pointe du Hoc or on Omaha, depending on the success of Task Force A at Pointe du Hoc. Huebner ended his order with "Good luck, God bless you, and shoot to kill."[74]

On May 19 the battalion moved to their final staging area behind barbed wire on a British airfield called RAF Warmwell about ten miles inland from Weymouth. During the last week in May the briefings were completed, and they were sealed in the marshaling areas. When Morris Prince looked over the bivouacked 2nd Battalion, he was proud: "We were strong in every sense of the word. We had trained and worked hard." Using models and aerial photographs, they studied and memorized their assignments. "Each and every terrain feature was sharply imbued in our minds. Every man could have maneuvered over this land blindfolded. Each man got to know not only his part, but that of his buddies. [We knew] our company's mission, our battalion's mission and [those] operating alongside."[75]

On May 28, the second birthday of his daughter, Anne, Rudder wrote to Chick that "this would probably be the last letter for a few days, but I'll be loving you and thinking of you all the while." On May 29 he went to see Huebner again; there were still unresolved details about the Rangers' assault plan, including exactly where Rudder would be when the landings began.[76]

On the day before loading on the troopship for Normandy, Rudder wrote a final letter to his mother: "I know your prayers will give me the necessary blessing so that I cannot fail to do the task ahead of me to the best of my ability. The price we are having to pay is tremendous but not out of proportion to the results we shall achieve. Don't worry for me because we are all well taken of and I am certain we will overcome all obstacles. Your son, Earl."[77]

On the morning of June 1, trucks conveyed the two Ranger battalions to the Weymouth esplanade, a half-mile crescent along Weymouth Bay that ended at the docks where landing craft waited to take them to troopships anchored in the bay. In columns of two, the battalion marched along the promenade with civilians cheering, waving, and singing the U.S. national anthem and "God Bless America."[78] They were not allowed to talk to the G.I.s, but

1st Lt. Robert T. Edlin loading up for Normandy in Weymouth, England, June 1, 1944. Later renowned for leading daring patrols into enemy territory, Edlin declined Rudder's recommendation for the Medal of Honor in Brittany when advised that his acceptance of the decoration would require him to leave the 2nd Ranger Battalion. (U.S. National Archives)

they recognized the Ranger shoulder patch and gaped, knowing these men were not ordinary soldiers.

Lines of DUKWs were along the beachfront, and farther out, at the edge of the surf, tank barriers stood as a precaution against an enemy attack. Coils of barbed wire lay along the esplanade to foul enemy raiders coming from the sea. Barrage balloons soared overhead. Hundreds of ships for the invasion fleet were anchored in the bay. The Rangers' landing craft bobbed in the quiet waters of the River Wey, tied up at piers separating the river from Weymouth Bay. Edlin, the first man to board a landing craft, grinned broadly for a photograph that made him forever a local celebrity. The LCAs ferried them to their troopships flying the white ensign of the Royal Navy.

The Rangers boarded their ships convinced that the enemy was doomed to defeat. Ranger Alfred Baer captured their spirit: "The German Army didn't have a chance against the Rangers." Earl's final letter to Chick was tinged with humility, confident without arrogance: "No one has ever had the privilege of leading a finer bunch of men and officers into battle than I will have."[79]

CHAPTER 7

POINTE DU HOC
JUNE 6–8, 1944

R udder's attack plan for D-Day was definite when the Rangers boarded their troopships in Weymouth Bay on June 1, 1944. He was in command of all Rangers in the invasion, some to land on Omaha Beach and others, four miles west at Pointe du Hoc, considered part of Omaha in the invasion plan. Each Ranger would cross to Normandy in two vessels, going most of the 130 miles in a modified civilian troopship before transferring to a landing craft for the run-in to the beach. The troopships were converted channel steamers, which in peacetime carried tourists from England to the Continent or to the Isle of Man and Ireland. The landing craft were LCAs, the acronym for landing craft, assault. The LCAs and troopships were Royal Navy vessels and operated by British crews. The former channel steamers were often called by their civilian names—*Prince Charles, Ben-my-Chree, Prince Baudouin, Prince Leopold, Emperor Javelin,* and *Amsterdam*—and each had been modified to accommodate Commandos in raids along the coast of occupied Europe.[1]

Rudder had organized the Provisional Ranger Group (PRG) in three task forces. Task Force A, slightly more than 250 men, was three companies (D, E, F, and part of Headquarters Company) of the 2nd Battalion, plus about forty others. Led by Maj. Cleveland A. Lytle, Task Force A would assault Pointe du Hoc from the sea and scale the cliffs to destroy or neutralize its guns, then penetrate inland to block the coastal road.

Task Force B, sixty-nine Rangers (C Company of the 2nd Battalion) under Capt. Ralph E. Goranson, would land on the extreme west end of Omaha Beach, go sharply to the right, and climb the ninety-foot bluffs of Pointe de la Percée to destroy two 75 mm guns, several machine guns, and mortars. The 75 mm guns were placed to fire laterally the length of the beach, potentially endangering every man on Omaha Beach. Rudder told Goranson, "You have the toughest goddamn job on the whole beach."[2]

Task Force C, about 665 men and the main body of the PRG, was all of Max Schneider's 5th Battalion plus two companies (A and B) and part of Headquarters Company of the 2nd Battalion, as well as Rudder with his PRG headquarters staff. Where Task Force C would land depended on the success of Lytle's Task Force A at Pointe du Hoc. If the essential men in Task Force A got up the cliffs by 7:00 AM (thirty minutes after the scheduled landing), Task Force C would follow them in. But if Task Force A failed, Task Force C would land on Omaha Beach and fight its way overland to Pointe du Hoc—four to five miles of countryside that, as far as Schneider knew, was swarming with Germans—to knock out the detestable guns and rescue the survivors of Task Force A. Whether Rudder or Schneider would command Task Force C is not clear, but a startling development would set up Schneider as its commanding officer, and he would make his authority an unequivocal fact once they were on the beach.

The startling development was that, at almost the last hour, Lytle got drunk, and Rudder threw him out of the Rangers and took his place in command of Task Force A going to Pointe du Hoc. At the moment, this change threatened disaster, but in fact Lytle had changed history for the better. His misconduct and Rudder's decisive reaction put Rudder and Schneider in command of two major components of the invasion, and they performed brilliantly. The key to success was the adaptability inherent in exhaustive preparation at all levels of Rudder's command, beginning with the men he selected to become Rangers. They were prepared for the unexpected.

LYTLE'S DERELICTION

The sequence of events that led to Lytle's dereliction began a few days earlier when Rudder received unconfirmed information, originating with French civilians, that the guns on Pointe du Hoc had been removed. The French report turned out to be correct, but Rudder had no way to confirm it. After a heavy American bombing attack on April 25, the German garrison had moved the guns about a mile inland and dispersed them along a lane beside an apple orchard. However, aerial photographs indicated the guns were still in place, but the images on film were inconclusive because, as the photo interpreters suspected, the enemy had replaced the gun barrels with logs and had camouflaged their emplacements with netting.[3] From above or at a distance from the sides, the logs appeared to be the gun barrels. Even if the French report was correct, Rudder could not assume the guns were out of action. So what if they were not in their emplacements? They could be hidden nearby—as they were—and ready to fire. Furthermore, Rudder knew the Rangers had a second objective at Pointe du Hoc: to block the coastal road that paralleled the shoreline about a thousand yards inland. Blocking the road would keep the Germans from using it to reinforce their defenses at Omaha Beach and help the Americans link their two beachheads, Omaha and Utah. There was no alternative but for the Rangers to go in, make certain the guns were out of action, and cut the coastal road.

During the week before loading onto the troopships, Rudder told Lytle and others who needed to know about the French report. Lytle then tried to persuade Rudder that the assault on Pointe du Hoc was unnecessary and suicidal.[4] Even if he agreed, Rudder did not have authority to change the plan, and Lytle's protest got him nowhere.

The landing on Omaha was planned for first dawn on June 5. In order to meet the landing schedule, many ships in the invasion force set sail late on June 3. But at 4:30 AM on June 4, General Eisenhower postponed the invasion by one day until June 6 because of storms in and over the Channel. With all vessels under strict radio silence, a prearranged signal was sent to the invasion fleet, but it failed to reach every ship. Confusion reigned as some vessels continued on course for the invasion and had to be chased down by other boats. Rudder's ship *Prince Charles*—the command ship for the PRG—spent most of June 4 cruising slowly near the Isle of Wight and returned to Weymouth Bay late on the same day.[5]

After the *Prince Charles* reanchored in Weymouth Bay, Rudder learned of Lytle's drunkenness the night before on board the *Ben-my-Chree*. He had caused trouble with the ship's crew, struggled with his own officers when they tried to restrain him, and had taken a swing at the 2nd Battalion's surgeon, Dr. Block, a transgression that Len Lomell judged "tantamount to beating up your mother."[6]

Lytle's promotion from captain to major on June 3 had prompted a celebration that night around the bar. When Rudder went to the *Ben-my-Chree* to promote Lytle, he had unintentionally fueled the party by giving him a quart of gin. In the custom of British vessels, the *Ben-my-Chree* also had a bar. The drinking binge began after Rudder left. The liquor went to Lytle's head, and he began talking to his subordinates about the French report. He pulled out a sketch map showing the six gun positions. The men around him remembered his words as he tapped the map with his finger, "Whether you guys know it or not, intelligence says the guns ain't there. It's suicide, and what the chrissake for?" Lytle disparaged the mission, saying it was unnecessary and would mean death for his listeners, the men charged with carrying it out.[7]

When Rudder was told about Lytle's misconduct, he took quick action. The hour was about 7:00 PM on June 4, but he still had four hours of daylight.

(With clocks advanced two hours from Greenwich Mean Time to British Double Summer Time, twilight in early June lasted until 11:00 P.M.)[8] With the instincts of a future university president, he appointed a committee of three captains—Harvey Cook, Dick Merrill, and Frank Corder—to investigate and report back to him. Merrill wrote that they found Lytle in detention onboard the *Ben-my-Chree* by order of the ship's captain and that he "had been drunk, out of control, and had created a situation where he no longer could command the officers with whom he had the problem."[9] Upon hearing the report, if not before, Rudder decided that Lytle should be removed; he had lost faith in the mission, in the reasons for it, and in its possibilities for success. He could not be trusted to do his best. Lytle was a danger to himself and to his men. Cook tried unsuccessfully to talk Rudder out of relieving Lytle, and they never discussed it again.

Rudder instructed Cook and Merrill to take Lytle ashore and turn him over to the military police, with orders to take him to the hospital and keep him under surveillance until the invasion was underway. Keeping Lytle under surveillance was a security precaution, because he was fully briefed on plans for the invasion.[10]

In his war memoir, *A Soldier's Story,* General Bradley perpetuated a story that after Rudder relieved Lytle, he went to Maj. Gen. Clarence R. Huebner at 2:00 A.M. on June 5 to tell him that he would personally lead Task Force A in the assault on Pointe du Hoc. In Bradley's account, Huebner told Rudder: "I can't let you do that. I need you to oversee the entire Ranger operation. We may have Rangers spread out over a four- or five-mile stretch of beach. You can't risk getting knocked out in the first round." Rudder is alleged to have replied, "I'm sorry, sir, but I'm going to have to disobey you. If I don't take it, it may not go."[11]

If this conversation occurred, Rudder was certainly not serious about disobeying General Huebner. No doubt he emphasized that he had more confidence in himself than anyone else to lead the attack. Actually, neither Huebner nor Rudder may have considered the change very important, because if the Rangers' assault went off as planned, the change merely had Rudder going ashore at Pointe du Hoc about an hour earlier than he would with Schneider and Task Force C.

Exactly where Rudder would be when the landings began had been a lingering issue for Rudder and Huebner. They seem to have finally resolved the question on May 29—only three days before boarding the troopships—when Rudder went to Huebner's headquarters in Blandford Forum. A clerk typist wrote in Huebner's office diary: "Lt. Col. Rudder of Ranger group in.

He discussed his presence with the forward Bn. of the Rangers in the Assault." That's when Huebner apparently agreed that Rudder would accompany Schneider's Task Force C destined for Pointe du Hoc or Omaha Beach, depending on the speed and success of Task Force A in the escalade.[12]

Huebner's decision recognized that Rudder should be where he could see and sense the ebb and flow of the fast-moving tactical operation. His intuition and his confidence to act on hunches—his feel for situations and perceptions of men around him—were among his strengths. Some men thought his instincts were flawless. "He had," one said, "an uncanny ability to read a situation and know how to cope with it or to capitalize on it."[13] Only near the scene of action could he exercise those talents. Stale second-hand reports received on board the headquarters ship, *Ancon*, with Huebner would not do. Success could depend on minimizing the time lapse between sensing, deciding, and doing.

Although the conquest of Pointe du Hoc was planned for one day, three days would be required. The delay is more understandable if the reader knows who could overrule Rudder with orders to the PRG. Major General Huebner was in temporary command of all units that would land on Omaha Beach and Pointe du Hoc. His command included his own 1st Infantry Division plus two regiments of the 29th Infantry Division—the 115th and the 116th—and the Rangers. Brig. Gen. Norman D. Cota, assistant commander of the 29th Division, would land on Omaha Beach as Huebner's subordinate for the 115th and 116th infantry regiments until they reverted to the command of Maj. Gen. Charles H. Gerhardt, the division commander, at 5:00 PM on June 7. Cota's subordinate, Col. Charles D. W. Canham, commanded the 116th Regiment, to which Rudder's PRG was attached. Canham was Rudder's immediate superior and would exercise his authority with decisions that jeopardized the survival of the Rangers on Pointe du Hoc for the larger purpose of defending Omaha Beach.[14]

When Rudder relieved Lytle of his command, he saved the major from himself and demonstrated an ability to recognize merit in people, even when they failed. He could have filed numerous charges against Lytle in a court-martial, but holding a court-martial under the circumstances was impractical, and Rudder did not otherwise besmirch Lytle's record.[15] He judged Lytle as potentially a good combat leader who had lost his nerve under the influence of alcohol. Rather than criminalize Lytle, he hospitalized him.

His appraisal of Lytle was accurate. Released from the hospital on June 7, Lytle went to a replacement depot and became a battalion commander in the 90th Infantry Division, where he was acclaimed for his bravery. He was

awarded the Distinguished Service Cross for rowing a boat across the Moselle River under fire in the dead of winter to rescue two of his men stranded
on the other side. Called "superman" and "tiger" by other officers, he had a
high standard of performance. His subordinate Capt. John Colby observed
that Lytle "personally wrote precise operations orders for his battalion and,
then, supervised and led his men in their execution."[16] Lytle retired from
the army in 1951 to practice law in his native South Carolina, where he was
elected mayor of Fort Mill, his hometown. But after Rudder put him in the
custody of the military police in Weymouth, England, he never had anything
to do with the Rangers, nor did he see Rudder again.

Although Rudder handled Lytle's misconduct with discretion, his disgust
with the man did not mellow with the passing years. When asked during a
Ranger reunion in the 1960s, "What got into Lytle that made him do such
a thing?" Rudder snapped, "He was just trying to save his ass!"[17] This reaction typified his attitude about people who disappointed him or failed to dis-
charge their responsibilities. "I don't have time to worry about his failures,"
he would say. He did not fret about forgiving them; he simply put them out
of mind and pursued the tasks before him.

Having got rid of Lytle, Rudder had to inform his key subordinates that
he was taking Lytle's place. They were dispersed on several ships to avoid
losing the essential leadership if one went down. Since all ships were under
strict radio silence, he went to them, moving from one to the other, accompanied by his ever-present radioman, Tech. Sgt. Francis J. "Killer" Kolodziejczak. Killer—whose nickname derived from his romantic way with women
rather than murderous instincts—never understood why they puttered
around Weymouth Harbor in a small boat in the middle of the night.[18] He
did not need to know, and Rudder never told him.

On each ship Rudder shook hands with the officers and wished the men
Godspeed, knowing that he was seeing many for the last time. On the *Prince
Baudouin,* he told Maj. Richard P. Sullivan, executive officer of the PRG, that
he would now have more responsibility for the group because Rudder would
be fully occupied on Pointe du Hoc. In reality, when Rudder decided to take
Lytle's place, he effectively but unofficially handed over command of the PRG
to Sullivan. On the *Prince Leopold,* Rudder told Schneider that he would
not be with him in Task Force C as planned. U.S. Navy lieutenant (j.g.) Ben
Berger was standing near Schneider when Rudder climbed up the ladder, and
he never forgot the colonel's "short, inspirational talk from the bottom of his
heart." Rudder affirmed the dangers ahead and strengthened their resolve
with a rhetorical question that had an obvious meaning: "What better way to
die than to die for your country?"[19]

THE CROSSING

Few Rangers in the enlisted ranks were aware of the changes Rudder had made. They cared little about the command structure. They knew nothing about the French report that the guns had been removed. Their concerns were for their buddies—the men on whom they depended. They checked and rechecked their weapons and equipment to see if they had everything and it was all functioning properly. They continued talking about girls, shooting craps, cleaning rifles, sharpening knives, and playing cards.

As for Rudder, he snoozed. "Some of us actually slept," he told Cornelius Ryan twelve years later when Ryan was collecting information for his book *The Longest Day*.[20] After that uninteresting response, Ryan sought no more information from Rudder and did not quote him in the book or mention him in the movie script of the same name.

1st Lt. Elmer H. "Dutch" Vermeer, Rudder's demolition specialist, talked with the Rangers' chaplain, Father Joseph Lacy. "He told us not to take time to pray on the beach but to do our praying ahead of time." Later, when they were under fire, Father Lacy moved among them, urging, "Get up, son, and keep moving. I'll do the praying." The popular Father Lacy was respected for his secular skills as well as for his piety. "When he came into a poker game, I got out," recalled Capt. Harold K. "Duke" Slater.[21] Rudder would pin the Distinguished Service Cross on Father Lacy's chest for performing his ministerial duties under fire on Omaha Beach.

Under gunpowder gray skies on the afternoon of June 5, the *Prince Charles* sallied from Weymouth Bay at 4:45 PM with Rudder aboard. As the command ship for the PRG, the *Prince Charles* had the communications gear to assure that he would know promptly if invasion plans were changed again. With the main convoy bound for Omaha Beach, the *Prince Charles* went east along the south coast of England through mine-swept lanes to Point Z, an area of open water ten miles in diameter southeast of the Isle of Wight. Point Z—called "Piccadilly Circus"—was the convergence area for all ships before they proceeded to the Normandy coast's five invasion beaches, three British and two American. Here the largest armada ever put to sea—some five thousand ships—rendezvoused under an umbrella of fighter planes to protect them from an enemy air attack that never came. Thousands of barrage balloons floated overhead, streaming behind vessels to foul up any German fighter that tried to slip beneath the friendly umbrella and make a strafing attack.

From Piccadilly Circus troopships bound for the two American beaches steamed unmolested through more mine-swept lanes in complete blackout to their transport area about twelve and one-half miles (twenty-two thou-sand yards) off the French coast, where the men transferred to landing craft. Troopships bound for the three British beaches went closer to the shore and lowered their landing craft seven to eight miles from the coast. The differ-ence reflected the separate conclusions of U.S. Navy and Royal Navy officers about how close to the coast they would risk taking their troopships after the vessels had crossed through the enemy mine barrier that generally paralleled the coast. The British—apparently more confident that they could neutral-ize German shore batteries in their sector—permitted their troopships to go closer to the shore. The guns on Pointe du Hoc were a consideration in the American decision, but the British also had powerful enemy artillery in their sector.[22]

Rudder remained on the *Prince Charles* for the crossing to the transport area. The weather was not good but, as predicted, before darkness fell the wind moderated to about twenty miles per hour, the skies partly cleared, and the waves decreased to about five feet. Then darkness closed in, and by midnight the view from the bridge was pitch black. About three o'clock, in the colorless low light of predawn, large shadows on the port and starboard sides gradually disclosed themselves as other ships proceeding toward Nor-mandy. A little later, the throbbing of the engines ceased, and the steel-on-steel clanging of a descending anchor chain slamming against the side of the ship reverberated through the *Prince Charles*. At 3:28 AM the clanging suddenly stopped; the ship was anchored in the transport area, where troops would transfer from ships to landing craft.[23]

At 3:53 AM Rudder boarded an LCA that took him to the nearby *Ben-my-Chree,* where he assumed personal command of Task Force A, sched-uled to land beneath the cliffs of Pointe du Hoc at H-Hour, 6:30 AM. Almost unnoticed, Pfc. Theodore H. Wells, his radioman for contact with Max Schneider and the 5th Battalion, went with him. Wells would be near Rud-der on Pointe du Hoc until he was wounded in the late morning and evacu-ated. He left a fascinating and previously unpublished account of his time with Rudder.[24]

Before reaching the far shore, Rudder would face the second crisis of his Pointe du Hoc mission. The cause was an alarming but fortuitous naviga-tional error that had an ironically positive effect on the success of the land-ings on Omaha Beach and may have saved the lives of many Americans on Pointe du Hoc, including Rudder's.

The *Ben-my-Chree* hoisted Rudder and his LCA to deck level about 4:00 AM, two hours before sunrise. The Rangers were already on deck, saying goodbye to buddies going in other landing craft and grumbling about their breakfast—only two small pancakes and coffee—prescribed by Dr. Block to prevent seasickness.[25]

Above the deck, LCAs were suspended along both sides of the *Ben-my-Chree*. A few minutes after four o'clock, the davits lowered the landing craft and slung them just over the edge of the deck. The voice of a British seaman blared from the loudspeakers: "Attention on deck! United States Rangers, man your boats. Good luck, lads!"

An LCA usually carried about thirty-five men seated on three benches that ran along the sides and through the middle. For this outing they averaged twenty-two per boat to allow room for climbing equipment. Still, they were crowded. Men

James W. Eikner, an officer in the 2nd Ranger Battalion before Rudder took over, was the communications officer until promoted to Headquarters Company commander, 1943–45. (Courtesy of James W. Eikner)

in the center straddled the bench; those on the sides had their backpacks against the sides of the boat and little space for their rumps. The men in each landing craft were a climbing team that would split into several smaller assault groups to knock out the six gun emplacements. Each man boarded a preassigned LCA with the exception of 1st Lt. James W. Eikner, Rudder's communications officer in the 2nd Battalion. As he and Rudder watched the others load, Rudder decided they should not risk being in the same boat; Eikner went to LCA 222, where two of his comrades were Commando Trevor and Amos Potts, a photographer for the *Stars and Stripes*.[26]

On schedule, at 4:30 AM a British seaman shouted "Off grips" and released the brakes on the davits. Rudder's LCA 888 dropped eight feet and splashed into swirling waters that slammed it against the mother ship. Then the twelve LCAs circled slowly, lining up in two columns behind a guide launch. Two carried supplies, and the other ten carried men, their weapons, and climbing gear, including six rocket-propelled grapnel hooks with ropes attached that were mounted on the gunwales of each LCA; in addition, two men in each landing craft had smaller versions of the same devices. Each boat also carried ladders—twenty-eight sections of lightweight four-foot-long tubular steel ladders that could be assembled one on top of the other. With such redundancy, at least one method should work.[27]

The two supply LCAs carried rations (food and water), personal belongings, ammunition, explosives for destroying concrete bunkers, and
equipment for hoisting the 81 mm mortars (250 pounds each) and their ammunition (10 pounds for each round) up the cliff. An LCT (landing craft,
tank) loaded with four DUKWs trailed the LCAs. The DUKWs carried the
deck-mounted ladders, adapted from those of the London fire department,
that could be extended upward by electrical power to the top of Pointe du
Hoc's hundred-foot cliffs.[28]

The plan was to shock the Germans with speed, attacking too fast for
them to mount an effective defense. On the assumption that the fighting
would end quickly, each man carried only a minimum of weapons and food—
one canteen of water, one enriched chocolate D-Bar (six hundred calories),
two ordinary fragmentation grenades, and usually an M1 Garand rifle with
eighty-eight rounds, eight in the rifle and ten clips with eight rounds each
in his cartridge belt. A few men had a "Chicago piano," otherwise known
as a Thompson submachine gun. Men selected to go up first had the easiest
weapons to carry: a .45-caliber automatic Colt pistol or a .30-caliber carbine.
The Rangers took no machine guns because they were too heavy to carry and
fire while running in a fast-moving attack. Had they not captured German
machine guns, this deficiency could have been disastrous.[29]

Their heaviest weapons in both firepower and weight were twelve BARs
(eighteen pounds) and six 60 mm mortars (forty-two pounds).[30] Altogether
they had thirty thermite grenades, which did not explode but burned at
about four thousand degrees Fahrenheit, hot enough to melt the steel in the
German guns they intended to destroy.

BEEVER'S ERROR

With Rudder's craft at the head of the right-hand column, the landing craft
followed their guide vessel, Motor Launch 304 of the Royal Navy. ML 304
had one purpose: to lead them through the darkness, swift-running seas, and
gusting winds to a speck on the French coast twelve and one-half miles away
and due south along the first meridian west of Greenwich. Only in the last
half hour, beginning about 6:00 AM, would Pointe du Hoc become visible.

The skipper of ML 304 was Temporary Lt. Colin Beever of the Royal
Navy Volunteer Reserve. RNVR lieutenants were usually younger or older
and less experienced than other naval officers. At forty, Beever was one of the
oldest. Through no fault of his own, Lieutenant Beever's training in navigation was less than that normally required. Early in the war, the Royal Navy
decided as "matter of necessity rather than choice" to limit the navigational

training of RNVR officers in order to graduate more in less time.[31] Most of their assignments were in coastal waters within sight of land, where navigation was less challenging than at sea. Nevertheless, Beever was now leading Rudder's flotilla under conditions that demanded skills for which he had not been trained.

Visibility was so poor that Rudder and the crew of his leading landing craft could not see ML 304, only eighty feet ahead of them. The coxswain in Rudder's LCA steered by the phosphorescent glow stirred in the wake of ML 304; and each landing craft followed the wake of the one ahead. Following ML 304 in two parallel lines, the two columns of six were slightly offset to the right and left with the wake of the motor launch between them.[32]

On board ML 304, Beever had two elecronic instruments for navigation. Before nearing the shore he would depend on the "Q.H. 2 'Tree' navigation set, which relied on cross bearings from transmitters in England with an accuracy of 50 yards."[33] Closer to shore, he expected a newly designed radar set—termed Type 970—to help him identify Pointe du Hoc. When used for the first time in dress-rehearsal landings only a month earlier, Type 970 had produced reliable images of coastal features, and crews were enthusiastic about it. By coincidence, ML 304 was the second backup for the intended guide vessel; the usual substitute was sidelined with mechanical problems, and the new radar may not have been thoroughly tested on ML 304. Thus, Rudder and his Task Force A set out on a high-risk mission in rough seas with poor visibility led by a substitute guide vessel equipped with unproven radar and commanded by an officer with less than the usual navigational training.

Greatest Show on Earth

Soldiers and sailors on the water had front-row seats to this military epic. Spectacular explosions lit the night and early morning sky. Once the hammering noise began, it was unceasing. "A rending and thunderous ovation of shells whizzing overhead signaled the beginning and the breaking loose of all hell," wrote Ranger Morris Prince. "Our Navy was . . . softening up the enemy's beach defenses. The distant and distinct hum of friendly aircraft became audible and soon the planes and bombers became visible."[34]

British and American air forces began bombing the French coast about the time Rudder's LCA was put in the water. At 5:50 AM the battleship *Texas* turned broadside to Pointe du Hoc and opened up with her fourteen-inch guns, sending 226 armor-piercing and high-explosive shells, each weighing about fifteen hundred pounds, hurtling toward the German fortified area on the *pointe*. Still later, from 6:10 to 6:25 AM, seventeen American B-26 Marauder twin-engine medium bombers were scheduled to pound the target again.[35]

As the senior army officer aboard LCA 888, Rudder sat at the front, straddling the center bench. When they hit the beach, he would go out first, followed by Kolodziejczak, who sat behind him. The exit ramp was directly in front of Rudder; its four-foot width allowed only one man to pass through at a time. To his right front was an armored cabin in which the coxswain sat and steered the vessel. A British naval officer stood on Rudder's right, directly behind the cabin of the coxswain, to whom he could speak through a vent in the cabin door. The naval officer was in command of the entire LCA flotilla going to Pointe du Hoc, and the coxswain took orders only from the naval officer.[36]

Theodore Wells sat at the very back next to the stern chief in charge of the anchor and the pumps. The chief stood up all the way and gave Wells a running account of what he saw. Every few minutes Wells rose to see for himself. He saw "a huge boiling cloud along the coast several miles ahead, and in the back of the cloud, a red glow shown through. Planes roared overhead and the warships all around them were firing and [he] could see the red blast as the bombs and shells hit their targets."[37]

Men in landing craft wallowing between the *Texas* and the shore were surprised by the sequence of sights and sounds that emanated from a single round. "We could see the flash [from the muzzle], then hear the roar of the shell overhead, then hear the report as it left the muzzle, then see the flash on the shore, and finally hear the bursting shell explode [on the shore]."[38]

Cold spray blew into the LCAs, covering the men crouched inside, making it "a soggy, wet ride," in the words of Dutch Vermeer. Waves ran five to six feet in mid-Channel, diminishing to three feet closer to shore but still rough for the shallow-draft boats. Some were in trouble from the moment they were in the water, shipping more water than their internal pumps could eject, and the men bailed water with their helmets. Eight miles from shore, LCA 860 went down with company commander Capt. Harold K. "Duke" Slater and twenty men, and LCA 914, containing rations and ammunition, was lost with five men aboard.[39] The other supply landing craft jettisoned most of its cargo to stay afloat.

The British designed the LCA for stealth, primarily to put Commandos ashore on coastal raids and to recover them by lifting the landing craft to deck level on the mothership with the men in the craft. The LCA lay low in the water, its gunwales only four feet above the normal waterline. The low profile enabled it to avoid detection, and its armor afforded greater protection for troops than did that of most landing craft. On D-Day, however, many LCAs were overloaded and sat lower than usual in the water, and the weight of the water splashing over the sides made them ride even lower. A gusty fifteen-knot wind from the west increased their potential to swamp and produced a strong current that pushed them to the east all along the beachhead.[40]

Course Correction

Compounding these difficulties, Lieutenant Beever made a navigational error that delayed the landing at Pointe du Hoc. At 6:00 AM he was on course to touch down exactly on schedule at 6:30 AM, but then he changed course and made for Pointe de la Percée, three miles east of Pointe du Hoc. An officer on the nearby British destroyer *Talybont* observed his error and wrote in the ship's log that the change was difficult to understand, "as *Texas'* fall of shot on Pointe du Hoe [sic] was obvious."[41] Radio silence was in effect until 6:30 AM, and no one called Beever to tell him of his error. His radar was not functioning properly, and more than 250 men were following him with their lives in his hands.

Beever did not know that the cliffs no longer appeared as they did in the photographs he had studied because the photographs were taken before Pointe du Hoc was heavily bombed only hours before. Bombs had struck the edges and blown huge gaps along the rim of the cliff, changing its profile. More than that, Beever later told investigators that he "expected the gun battery on Pointe du Hoc [to] disclose its position, but it was not firing."[42]

Even on a clear day, Pointe du Hoc can be difficult to recognize from a mile out at sea. Compared to the blunt prominence of Pointe de la Percée, it is only a sliver of land that slices like a V into the sea, so thin and narrow that it is not easily distinguished from other headlands of similar height in the vicinity. Beever had been exactly on course for Pointe du Hoc, but in the partial light he did not recognize it, obscured as it was by clouds, mist, smoke, and dust.

After the war Rudder told Chick that he thought they were going wrong when he saw the coastline and was certain when they were about half a mile from Pointe de la Percée.[43] But the coxswain continued to follow ML 304, and the British naval officer standing beside Rudder was the only person onboard with the authority to alter course. Army officers did not give orders on naval vessels, even to naval officers of lesser rank.

At first Rudder was civil to the British officer. Getting no response, he protested, then, when the officer still took no action, Rudder suddenly raised himself to full height and shouted "Goddammit, turn right!" Kolodziejczak, sitting within the length of an arm, said the coxswain reacted so fast that he literally jerked the landing craft to the right. After LCA 888 turned west, the naval officer apparently used hand signals to instruct the other landing craft to follow. Rudder's landing craft was now in the lead. "We had to take control of the landing craft ourselves," Rudder wrote later, "and guide them to the proper landing area."[44]

Thus, at 6:30 AM, a full half hour after daylight and the exact time they were supposed to land at Pointe du Hoc, Rudder's Rangers were still three miles from their landfall. When they turned west, their course was directly into the wind and the eastward-running waves. They had lost the crucial element of surprise but had no alternative except to proceed parallel to the shore, running the gauntlet of fire from German gunners on the cliffs above. Lt. Cdr. Edmund F. Baines, commanding officer of the British destroyer *Talybont,* watched the Rangers as they slowly made their way toward Pointe du Hoc. He wrote in his log, "Their course from Raz de la Percée along the shore to Pte. du Hoc was suicidal."[45]

Shortly after changing course, 20 mm rounds fired from the cliff tops fatally punctured one of the thin-skinned DUKWs; five of the nine men aboard were killed or wounded. Several LCAs were hit with rifle fire with only minor damage. The 20 mm shots probably came from the enemy's Le Guay radar station. The rifle fire came from either Le Guay or, more likely, a small, improvised resistance nest between the radar station and Pointe du Hoc that the Germans had not designated with a number in the usual custom.[46]

The Americans knew about Le Guay radar station and the resistance nest before the invasion. Both were drawn in detail on the map that General Huebner had in his possession. Rudder knew about them, too. The radar station was bombed and destroyed, but the resistance nest—ill defined and hidden in undergrowth—was not bombed, although Rudder included it in his assault plan to be silenced soon after the escalade. But its limited size and low profile in thick brush made it difficult to pinpoint, while its location on the cliff's edge enabled its crew to fire out to sea, laterally down on the beaches, and across the east side of Pointe du Hoc. With these advantages, this resistance nest on the east side would cause difficulties for the Rangers on Pointe du Hoc from the beginning to the end.[47]

"Praise the Lord!" or "Tilt!"

Lt. Col. Max F. Schneider, with his Task Force C in a flotilla of twenty LCAs, was intentionally thirty minutes behind Rudder's Task Force A. Leaving

Capt. John C. Raaen Jr., headquarters company commander in the 5th Ranger Battalion on D-Day. (Courtesy of Maj. Gen. John C. Raaen Jr., USA, ret.)

the troopships, Schneider's group headed for an area of open water between Pointe du Hoc and Omaha Beach, where they circled slowly, waiting for a coded radio message from Rudder. If the essential men had scaled the cliffs by 7:00 AM, Rudder would transmit "Praise the Lord," and Schneider would follow him to Pointe du Hoc. Two flares fired from the *pointe* could also signal Schneider to come in.

If Schneider heard the code word "Tilt" from Rudder or got no message at all, that meant the Rangers had failed to get enough men up the cliffs to consider the escalade a success, and Schneider would take Task Force C to Omaha Beach. From there they would try to avoid fighting and get to the *pointe* as fast as possible. Schneider's Rangers much preferred to land at Pointe du Hoc rather than Omaha, from where they might have to battle the Germans all the way to the *pointe.*

Capt. John C. Raaen Jr., Headquarters Company commander in Schneider's 5th Battalion, was in a landing craft near Schneider with a radio at his feet tuned to the frequency of Rudder's anticipated message. "We laid off Pointe du Hoc . . . for better than 45 minutes. We circled and circled, praying for the message from [Rudder] that they had landed successfully. The message never came. We were supposed to wait until 0700. Schneider waited until 0710 before ordering us to divert to Omaha Beach."[48]

Beever Redeemed

In the absence of a message from Rudder at Pointe du Hoc, Schneider took Ranger Task Force C, more than 650 of the finest fighting soldiers, to Omaha

Beach. They arrived at 7:53 AM, according to the log of Royal Navy commander Stratford H. Dennis, when the landings begun at 6:30 AM were clearly in serious trouble. Dennis commanded the Rangers' troopships and their landing craft flotilla. The plan called for Task Force C to land on the west end of Omaha in the sector of the beach code-named Dog Green, but the battle-tested Schneider, making his fourth assault landing of the war, observed that Dog Green had become a killing ground. To the left he saw less German gunfire and convinced the British naval officer with him to divert half a mile to the quieter Dog White sector. Landing there, he followed Company C of the 116th Infantry and got his 5th Battalion "across the beach and up to the sea wall with a loss of only 5 or 6 men to scattered small-arms fire." This was Schneider's great contribution to the success of the assault on Omaha Beach. With his experience, he had recognized that the landing plan was flawed and did not follow it.[49]

The two companies from the 2nd Battalion in Schneider's Task Force C were not so fortunate. They were in landing craft ahead of him, and he was unable to redirect their landing. The results were tragic. Of their 132 men, only 62 got through the hail of fire to the seawall. Few men in Schneider's task force were situated to see what he had done, but Tech Sgt. Herbert Epstein was standing beside him in the lead landing craft and afterward told an interviewer: "I have always felt that Schneider was the unsung hero of Omaha Beach. He was certainly my hero and I credit him with saving my life and countless others by his savvy and decisiveness."[50]

Schneider's Rangers were exactly where they were needed to get to the top of the bluffs. Once there, they began with elements of the 116th Infantry to rout the German defenders from their flanks. Later in the day, when the west end of Omaha was vulnerable to a German counterattack, Canham ordered Schneider and Task Force C to defend it rather than continue their thrust toward Pointe du Hoc.[51] This is another way that Schneider and his Task Force C were instrumental in the success of the Omaha Beach landings.

Another benefit of Beever's error may have kept Rudder's Rangers from being bombed by American planes on Pointe du Hoc. Seventeen American B-26 Marauders were supposed to make a last strike on Pointe du Hoc between 6:10 and 6:25 AM to stun the Germans, drive them deep into their bunkers, and keep them there until Rudder's Rangers made their assault. Five minutes later, at 6:30 AM, the Rangers were to land while the Germans were still numb. However, the Marauders (only nine, because eight aborted) arrived late and dropped sixteen tons of bombs on or near Pointe du Hoc between 6:25 and 6:45 AM. If Rudder and his Rangers had arrived at 6:30 AM as planned, they could have come under aerial bombardment from the American planes. In the low light conditions, the aircrews almost certainly could not have recognized that Americans were in the target area.[52]

In his report to the Royal Navy, Beever expressed "infinite regret" that his "assistance to the Rangers was of such slight value." He attributed his navigational error to a failure of electrical power to his radar set and the navigational device.[53] He never knew that his error contributed to the success of the Omaha Beach landings and may have prevented Ranger casualties at Pointe du Hoc. Rudder believed mistakenly, as he told Chick with some exaggeration, "If we had landed on time, we would have taken Pointe du Hoc without firing a shot."

Two Errant Screaming Eagles

Huddled against the cliffs on the narrow, rocky shore, two teenaged American paratroopers watched Rudder's cavalcade of landing craft proceed along the coastline. They were Pfc. Raymond Crouch and Pfc. Leonard Goodgal of the 101st Airborne Division. When their C-47 transport plane was struck by German antiaircraft fire, they had managed to bail out. They had lost their weapons and came down in waist-deep water in front of a large cliff.

U.S. Ninth Air Force A-20 Havoc fighter-bombers over Pointe du Hoc prior to D-Day. (National Museum of the U.S. Air Force)

They had no idea where they were except that they were in France, or, more accurately, in waters off the French coast. Of one thing they were certain: Germans nearby wanted to kill them.[54]

The time was shortly after 1:00 AM on June 6. They took shelter under an overhang at the base of the cliffs. Cold, wet, shivering, they pondered how they could find their outfit—I Company of the 3rd Battalion of the 506th Parachute Infantry Regiment. During their hours of waiting, they heard the throb of heavy bomber engines and bombs exploding on the cliffs not far away. That was the bombing of Pointe du Hoc by British Lancaster bombers. They started walking west, looking for a break in the cliffs where they might climb up and head inland to find I Company. Then they heard the roar of large shells knocking off chunks of the cliffs farther west. In the early light about 6:00 AM they saw a battleship, which they later learned was the USS *Texas,* firing at Pointe du Hoc. Finally the *Texas* ceased firing, and twin-engine bombers—B-26 Marauders—came in to pound the *pointe.* Then they saw landing craft approach the shore and turn abruptly west. They shouted and waved but were not seen by the men in the landing craft. Crouch and Goodgal knew the occupants could only be Americans and followed them along the shoreline.[55]

THE BATTLE FOR POINTE DU HOC

Nearing Pointe du Hoc, Rudder had more decisions to make. He had planned for all landing craft to approach from the north and land in equal numbers on each side. Now all were approaching from the east. On his instructions, the Royal Navy officer beside him signaled for all to fan out and land on the east side. They keyed on Rudder's LCA number 888 and came in at about equal intervals from near the tip for a distance of some 550 yards along the shore. Rudder's was the first to beach. When it crunched to a stop on the jumble of stones and clay, the bow door opened, and he was the first out, followed by Kolodziejczak. Eikner noted the time at 7:08 AM; they were thirty-eight minutes late.[56]

As the Rangers dashed from their landing craft, Germans recovering from the virtually seismic aerial and naval bombardments appeared above them, shooting and dropping grenades. But when Ranger sharpshooters began picking them off, they backed away while continuing to throw grenades over the rim. Dr. Block diagnosed their predicament and drew a sketch showing two sources of enemy gunfire: the resistance nest on the far left and the huge concrete observation bunker near the apex of the *pointe* on the right.[57] From the bunker enemy observers had commanding views of the sea and could fire at the approaching Americans through a narrow slit in the thick wall as well as dart out to fire down or drop grenades on them.

The main menace was the sweeping gunfire from the resistance nest on the left. No one could get an exact fix on it because it was not in a single place but hidden along a trench in thick brush. Slugs from its automatic weapons splattered the mud and the cobblestone-size rocks on the beach like water dripping on hot grease. The German gunners were "firing on everybody as they crossed the beach. Only when we got to the cliff," Vermeer said later, "could we get out of their sight." Fifteen men were

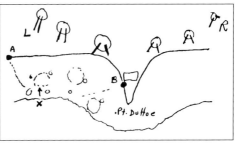

Dr. Walter E. Block's diary drawing of German gunfire on the beach below Pointe du Hoc. Beneath the drawing he wrote, "My craft lands at Pt. X. We are under machine gun fire from 2 points, A & B. We crouch in a bomb crater for a few minutes & then when the 1st riflemen reach the top, I and my medics—(Otto C.) Bayer & (Frank E.) South—go up to the top." Point A was a resistance nest obscured in brush on the rim of the cliff to the left and point B was the command bunker near the tip of the pointe. The dashed line indicates machine gun fire and the circles are bomb craters on the beach. (Ranger Collections, U.S. Military History Institute, Army War College, Carlisle Barracks, Pennsylvania.)

lost in crossing the thirty-five-yard-wide beach, "most of them from the raking fire to the left."[58] Despite the hail of lead, Rangers from each landing craft worked together as a climbing team, and the escalade went quickly. The first men were on top in less than five minutes, pulling themselves up on ropes attached to rocket-powered grapnel hooks shot over the rims or by climbing ladders assembled from the four-foot steel sections.

Unlike Omaha Beach, where the Americans found little bomb damage, Pointe du Hoc had been plastered, and the craters kept the DUKWs from reaching the base of the cliffs, rendering their extension ladders completely useless. But bombs had also struck the rim of the cliff and knocked off huge mounds of dirt and stone that stacked up against its face, some thirty-five feet high, fully one-third of the way to the top. Men near a mound had protection from the lateral fire and a higher base from which to climb. Within half an hour everyone was on top unless they were casualties or intended to remain below for a few minutes, like those in Rudder's headquarters.

Rudder did not go up immediately. His first priority was to work himself into the new situation and take stock of his force. Who had been lost? What was the condition of those who made it? What weapons, supplies, and equipment were lost? He discovered a small cave at the base of the cliff near the tip of the *pointe* and made it his command post until he went topside half an hour later.[59] His staff inched along the base of the cliff toward him.

He found that the uninjured Rangers now ashore were fit to fight. The medical section was intact. Of the twelve LCAs that had left the troopship, two had sunk. One went down with twenty-four men; twenty were picked up at sea, including the company commander, Captain Slater, who rejoined the battalion nineteen days later. One of the two supply LCAs had sunk with five men aboard; only one man survived. Those in the other supply boat (which arrived later) had thrown nearly everything overboard to avoid swamping; the loss would limit food, ammunition, and medical supplies.

Near Rudder in his temporary command post were the two radiomen, Kolodziejczak and Wells; Eikner, the communications officer; G. K. Hodenfield, a writer for the *Stars and Stripes;* and Amos Potts, a Signal Corps photographer whose film was already ruined by saltwater. Although Commando Trevor was usually close by, he was walking on the beach, ignoring enemy gunfire and the Rangers' warnings. After five years of war, he was fatalistic about his chances of survival and cowering under the cliff was contrary to his sense of duty.

All twelve men of an army-navy team called the Naval Shore Fire Control Party were safely ashore. Commanded by Capt. Jonathon H. Harwood of the U.S. Army Artillery, the fire control party was Rudder's go-between to bring the guns of British and American warships to bear on enemy targets ashore. Harwood had trained on the U.S. Navy destroyer *Satterlee,* which now lay offshore. To make certain that he could "talk navy," Harwood had naval lieutenant (j.g.) Kenneth S. Norton in his party. Everyone anticipated Harwood's contingent would be important, but not that survival would depend on them and naval guns to keep the enemy at bay.

From down on the beach, Rangers could not see what the Germans were doing above them. But they could be seen from ships that were already laying tremendous volleys of gunfire across the flat tableland of the *pointe* to keep the enemy burrowed in his holes. Cmdr. W. J. Marshall, senior officer aboard the *Satterlee,* saw Germans assembling and took "the cliff tops under fire" until the Rangers could "establish a foothold." The British destroyer *Talybont* also raked German positions with her guns. The remorseful Lieutenant Beever came close in with Motor Launch 304 and "sprayed more than a thousand 20-mm rounds across the top of the cliffs until the ascent was completed." Even so, the men on the beach, surrounded by a pandemonium of continuous violent explosions, were hardly aware of the naval gunfire. They could not distinguish one explosion from another.[60]

Amid the whirlwind of shells, Trevor continued to stroll the beach as though the excitement was nothing more than a Sunday regatta of the Royal Thames Yacht Club of Knightsbridge in London, of which he was president. He believed that "occasional acts of calculated gallantry are necessary to give men courage in battle." To the Americans, it was nonsense even when he explained, "They can't draw a bead on me. I take two short steps and three long ones, and they always miss me." Only minutes later a German marksman shot him squarely in the forehead; he survived by virtue of the steel in his American helmet. The bullet pushed the jagged edges of the hole into his head, and its impact knocked him into a bomb crater. Vermeer and Rudder ran to him. "I helped him up," Rudder told W. C. Heinz in 1954, "and the blood was starting to trickle down his forehead, but he was a great big, black-haired son of a gun—one of those staunch Britishers—and he just looked up at the top of the cliff and said 'The dirty ——.'" "We had to jerk the helmet from the back to get it off," Vermeer said. Trevor had a headache but was not incapacitated. With a white bandage wrapped around his head, he would be a calming presence in Rudder's command post over the next two perilous days.[61]

By now, the two misdropped youngsters from the 101st Airborne Division, Crouch and Goodgal, had reached Pointe du Hoc. Shouting "We're Americans!" they ran up behind an officer, who gave them a quick look and said emphatically, "Stick with me!" The officer was Rudder. Fifty years later, they still remembered "Stick with me!" It was classic Rudder verbal shorthand stating his authority and paternalistic concern.

About 7:45 AM Rudder pulled himself up the cliff on a rope, followed by the two paratroopers. As they went over the rim, a sniper fired at them. Rudder rolled to the left, and they dove into a shell hole. Crouch peeked over the edge of the crater and saw "a dead German soldier . . . a young boy with a knife in his back." Crouch was eighteen years old and had never seen a dead person. They spotted Rudder moving along the edge of the cliff toward the niche where he would reestablish his command post and crawled toward him, collecting an M1 rifle and Thompson submachine gun on the way. He gave them new instructions: "Stay put!"[62]

From his command post Rudder looked out on a wasteland literally torn to pieces by bombs and naval shells. The devastated landscape bore little resemblance to aerial photographs he had studied in England. Pockmarked with hundreds of bomb craters, the expected landmarks were gone, replaced by mounds of dirt blown out of the depressions as much as twenty-five feet deep and forty feet wide. What had been German fortifications were now large, chaotic piles of broken concrete and twisted steel, hiding places for friend and foe alike.

After the invasion, General Eisenhower's Supreme Headquarters Allied Expeditionary Force (SHAEF) analyzed the bombing of all German strongpoints on the French coast before D-Day. That analysis determined that a total of 3,264 bombs weighing 1,183 tons were dropped on the approximately 150 acres of German fortifications on Pointe du Hoc. That is almost eleven bombs and four tons per acre more than the saturation of any other target on the coast of France in preparation for the invasion.[63]

Of the total, 1,606 bombs were dropped on D-Day by British four-engine Lancaster bombers between 4:46 and 5:03 A.M. A follow-up report on the mission by the British Air Ministry found that "several sticks [series of bombs falling in a row] of 1,000 lb bombs were seen falling on the aiming point" in the center of the fortified area; no other coastal battery received so much attention. Of the 124 "Lancs" that RAF Bomber Command dispatched on the Pointe du Hoc mission, 114 completed the bombing run over the target. The flak was heavy, and three were shot down, with only one crewman surviving.[64]

After the Lancasters' heavy pounding, Pointe du Hoc was subjected to one last bombardment from the air when the B-26 medium bombers arrived twenty minutes late and dropped their bombs between 6:25 and 6:45 A.M., at the very time the Rangers would have landed if they had been on time.[65]

Within half an hour at least twenty assault groups were running toward the six gun positions.[66] Without further instruction, they knew where to go and what to do, but the heaps of smashed concrete and sod as well as the craters hampered movement across the *pointe* and forced them to deviate from their plan of attack. In coping with the clutter men got separated from their group and joined other groups or went to Rudder's command post for orders.

Two of the six gun positions were casemates—vaultlike structures with steel-reinforced concrete roofs and walls three to five feet thick—from which guns could be fired only through an embrasure (flared opening) toward the sea. The other four positions were emplacements: round concrete bases, open to the sky, on which guns could be rotated to fire in any direction. Numerous other concrete buildings, partly underground, were near the guns to house their crews and store ammunition.

As the assault groups scurried inland, Rudder remained in his command post waiting for their reports. He was in a familiar role, like a football coach sitting on the sidelines while his team executed his game plan. Having made their plan, he influenced their decisions without making them. He was not thinking about football, he later said, "but I was thankful to be with men who wouldn't run away, men who would die, if need be for the good of the team."

Rudder's command post on Pointe du Hoc, late morning, June 8, 1944, shortly after the
relief column arrived from Omaha Beach. Rudder is at top center, watching the German
prisoners. The flag is to ward off an attack by friendly aircraft. Censors whited out
the 2nd Ranger Battalion insignia on the back of several helmets. (U.S. National
Archives)

Sgt. Len Lomell also saw the similarity: "We played it just like a football game.
We ran as fast as we could, charging hard and low. We didn't stop."[67]

After knocking out the guns, the plan was to move inland and block the
coastal road. To Hodenfield, the *Stars and Stripes* writer, the way the Rangers pursued their assignments was uncoordinated and sporadic. But he was
not a Ranger, while Pfc. Alfred C. Baer clearly saw the relationship between
his training and the attack plan. In his 1945 memoir, Baer said, "Each group
would knock out the gun emplacement assigned to it. Then, one group joining with another drove down the Pointe, away from the sea, toward the road
that ran along the Normandy coast. . . . Cut the road and consolidate. The
bird's eye would have shown little groups of three or four starting out from
the cliffs. One after another, [they] formed tiny tentacles reaching out to the
gun emplacements. From there, the tentacles turned down the Pointe, toward the road, colliding with one another and merging to form one solid
body across the small peninsula."[68]

When Rudder moved topside, he made his command post in a bomb crater on the very edge of the cliff about 275 yards from the unsubdued observation bunker and 500 yards from the resistance nest to his left; from both
enemy positions the command post was within range of the standard rifle of
the German army, the Mauser Karabiner 98 Kurz. The post was in a niche
on the cliff's rim that resembled half of a broken bowl. Two square chunks of
concrete dislodged in the bombing lay in its bottom like undissolved lumps
of sugar. The inland side was the concrete base of an antiaircraft gun more
than six feet thick, ten feet high, and twenty feet long, thus shielding the
command post from enemy fire on the inland side.[69]

On its seaward side, the command post was open, with clear views of the
Channel and of the shoreline below. An advantage of the location was that
men could find it day or night simply by going toward the sound of the sea
until they reached the rim of the cliff and then following it. If they went the
wrong way, it would soon be apparent. The command post was "a very busy
place with men moving in and out at all hours."[70]

The command post was not a safe haven from German guns. It had no
roof and, except deep in the niche, was vulnerable to snipers shooting from
either side or straight ahead in the ruins. Any movement in the open was
dicey. In a dramatic demonstration of its vulnerability, the first German prisoner captured on the *pointe* "was shot right between the eyes" while standing
in front of Rudder in the command post as Vermeer questioned him. Rudder
recalled him as "a little freckled-faced kid who looked like an American. He
died instantly and fell on his face in front of me, his hands still behind his
head."[71] Another threat was a direct hit by artillery or mortar, from which
there was no protection.

Although the mounds of debris and dirt blocked more than a "worm's
eye view" of the *pointe* from the command post, Rudder was well informed
about the surrounding countryside. He had studied aerial photographs and
maps and, immediately important, he had in his possession a detailed British
sketch map of the *pointe,* stamped with Top Secret and Bigot in large dark
letters.[72]

Rudder's sketch map showed a dirt exit lane from near the tip of Pointe
du Hoc, through its middle out for a thousand yards to a T junction with
the coastal road, which was hard surfaced and sixteen feet wide with a low
hedgerow on each side. Two miles west of the junction, the road entered the
fishing village of Grandcamp, which he knew because in planning the assault he had considered landing near Grandcamp and attacking overland.
That's what the Germans expected and why they had built their defenses
primarily on the inland side of Pointe du Hoc, to the relative neglect of the

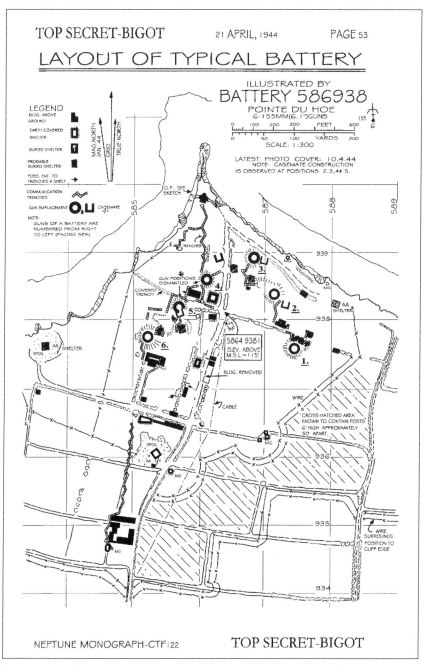

Map 7-1. *Sketch map used to plan the assault on Pointe du Hoc (misspelled Hoe). Bigot was the codeword for documents about the coming invasion of Normandy and for individuals who had been briefed on it.* (Neptune Monograph—CTF 122, April 21, 1944, 53, file reference DEFE 2/374, National Archives of the United Kingdom)

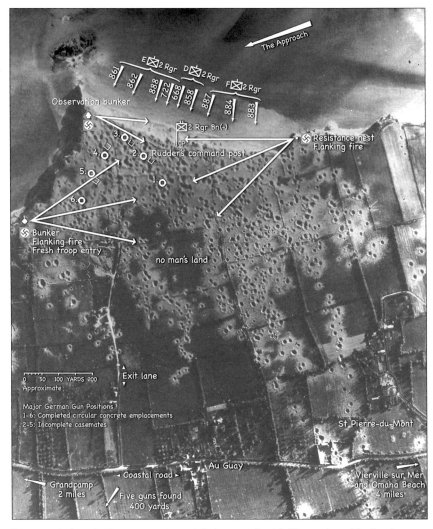

Map 7-2. Pointe du Hoc, composite aerial photograph with illustrations. The bomb craters reflect the extraordinary efforts to destroy the German gun battery before Rudder's Rangers landed. (Base photograph courtesy U.S. National Archives, graphics by David Grosvenor and David Zepeda, copyright Thomas M. Hatfield.)

seaward side, which, German survivors told their historian, Helmut Konrad von Keusgen, they believed was unassailable.[73]

West of Grandcamp around the Vire River estuary were the towns of Isigny, Carentan, and Sainte-Marie-du-Mont and Utah Beach, where another American amphibious assault was in progress. The Overlord plan called for quickly joining Omaha and Utah Beaches in one continuous front to keep the Germans from attacking them separately.

East of the coastal road's intersection with the exit lane, the road passed several sturdy stone farmhouses and barns clustered around a tall, slender chateau called Saint-Pierre-du-Mont. Four miles further east, the road passed through the village of Vierville-sur-Mer, strategically located only seven hundred yards inland from the west end of Omaha Beach, with which it was connected by a ravine through the bluffs called the Vierville Draw. The Vierville Draw was one of five ravines from the beach through the bluffs to the coastal road, but only the Vierville Draw had a paved road; the others were merely trails or tracks. Of the five draws that cut through the beach to the coastal road, the Vierville Draw was both the best and the shortest way inland from Omaha Beach. The Omaha assault plan assumed that four exit roads would be open to traffic by two hours after the first landings at 6:30, when large numbers of vehicles and mountains of supplies would begin arriving. The importance of the exit roads from the beach was as obvious to the Germans as to the Americans, and they constructed their defenses to deny them to the attackers.[74]

Rudder understood that success on Omaha required driving the Germans out of the Vierville Draw and beyond the village to gain elbow room for incoming reinforcements. But he may not have realized that doing it could jeopardize the survival of the Ranger force on Pointe du Hoc. And that is exactly what happened when the necessity of holding the Vierville Draw required Schneider's Rangers to remain there, leaving Rudder's Rangers isolated and exposed to annihilation.

Midmorning, First Day

By nine o'clock, about twenty-five men were jammed into Rudder's command post. It was too many for safety, and some could be more useful elsewhere. Some were slightly wounded or separated from their assault group. Several were from the medical and communications sections, plus Hodenfield, Potts, Vermeer, paratroopers Goodgal and Crouch, and Trevor and his aide, RNVR lieutenant Ronald F. Eades, who had wanted so much to go to Pointe du Hoc that, with Rudder's approval, he had hitched a ride on a DUKW. About ten were members of Harwood's fire control party; Rudder wanted them scouting the *pointe* and transmitting enemy locations to the ships offshore. When a nearby casemate was cleared, he moved Harwood's party there. Its intact walls and roof shielded them from snipers, had space for their maps, and sheltered their radios from rain.[75]

Trevor, with a bandage around his head and still scorning German guns, rummaged through the ruins, accusing men he found in protected places of

shirking their duties, and attempting to spot snipers by intentionally drawing their fire. He believed the odds were in his favor that an ordinary Jerry
would miss him with the first two shots, which he would hear as they passed
to either side. Then it was, he said, "time to get down, but not too fast, because the next one was coming right down the middle."[76]

While exploring the inland side of the fortification that shielded the command post, Trevor spied the entrance to the enemy gun crew's sleeping quarters under the wreckage. When the debris was cleared away, the quarters
became Dr. Block's medical aid station. In a dark subterranean room Block
set up his makeshift hospital, operating by flashlight and flickering candle-
light. Another room with fourteen beds became the hospital, and yet another
room, the morgue. At first there were few patients, but as the day wore on the
numbers increased. "Sometimes there were so many patients," Block wrote
in his diary, "that the [wounded] men had to lie outside . . . until another
patient died, or was patched up enough to go back out."[77]

As the assault groups moved inland, they made the same discovery. The
guns were gone. As the French resistance had reported, not one gun was in its
casemate or emplacement. Instead, Rangers found logs the size of telephone
poles—fake gun barrels—that had been camouflaged under nets spread over
wooden frames that had collapsed under the bombing. No one had to tell
them to press inland to find and disable the dreaded guns. Their advance
was rapid and uneven, because each group started from a different place and
moved at a different speed, depending on the terrain and enemy opposition.
The first group—twelve Rangers under Sgt. Len Lomell—reached the coastal
road about 8:15 AM and blocked it without seeing a single enemy soldier. At
that moment the only known Germans still on the *pointe* were in the observation bunker and the resistance nest, but others were hiding in unknown
numbers. During the next hour they fired on assault groups that followed,
killing seven and wounding eight Rangers.[78]

In spite of increasing German opposition, by 9:00 AM about fifty Rangers
had advanced to the coastal road. Their patrols pushed even farther inland,
searching for the guns and for the enemy thought to be present in large numbers to the south and west. The best defense was to find and destroy them
before they attacked, but the Rangers were too few in number to attack. The
alternative was to establish an observation post further inland to provide
advance notice of enemy threats. That job was given to the difficult yet proficient Sgt. William L. "L-Rod" Petty.

Petty took his squad of nine men six hundred yards beyond the coastal
road, almost a mile from Rudder's command post, and improvised his

Leonard G. "Len" Lomell in 1945.
Rudder decorated Lomell with the
Distinguished Service Cross for
his gallantry at Pointe du Hoc and
awarded him the coveted battlefield
commission in Belgium on October
10, 1944. (Courtesy of Leonard G.
Lomell)

observation post behind a rock wall on the back slope of the headland that formed Pointe du Hoc. Rudder knew the site as "Petty's Wall." Petty looked across a creek to a broad valley of farmland and the crossroads village of Cricqueville-en-Bessin, notable for its small parish church constructed in Romanesque style from fieldstones in the year 1260. The church's dark, weathered limestone tower was a useful reference for giving directions. Although separated from his fellow Rangers and most of the action, Petty was well placed to give advance warning of German movements in daylight. When German stragglers from Omaha Beach passed through the valley in front of him, Petty surprised them with the accuracy of his BAR and inflicted some thirty casualties on D-Day, including two Poles in a group of seven whose intent to surrender he recognized too late.[79]

Scouting south of the coastal road shortly after 9:00 AM, Lomell and Sgt. Jack Kuhn found five of the six missing guns, unguarded and camouflaged in a lane beside an apple orchard, by all appearances unified since the invasion began. Apparently the gun crews had been killed or wounded and were demoralized or in shock from the bombing they had sustained. The guns were aligned in the direction of Utah Beach, visible and within range on the horizon. Kuhn and Lomell had two thermite grenades. With Kuhn covering him, Lomell ignited grenades in the recoil mechanism of two guns and bashed in the sights of others with his rifle butt.[80] Thermite grenades do not explode but burn at temperatures in excess of 4,000 degrees Fahrenheit, more than enough to melt the steel of the guns. They returned to the coastal road for more thermite grenades, and Lomell sent a runner to Rudder's command post with the good news that the guns had been located.

Eikner was with Rudder when Lomell's runner arrived. To their surprise, about twenty minutes later another runner came with the news that a patrol led by Sgt. Frank A. Rupinski had rendered the same guns unquestionably inoperable by igniting a thermite grenade in the chamber of each barrel. Rudder eventually had to decide whether Lomell or Rupinski should be decorated and decided in Lomell's favor because he acted first. Lomell was awarded the Distinguished Service Cross for exceptional heroism in battle, and Rupinski got the Bronze Star for meritorious achievement. Rupinski would never get the recognition he deserved. He was captured the next day and was not around to tell his story when combat historians conducted interviews after the battle. Back home after the war, he worked for the postal service and maintained a low profile.[81]

Within two hours of landing, Rudder's Rangers had accomplished their missions. They had cut off the coastal road and disabled five of the six 155 mm guns. German soldiers who manned the Pointe du Hoc guns say the sixth gun was destroyed in a bombing attack.[82] Other accounts say a sixth gun with a damaged undercarriage was found in thick undergrowth not far from the five guns Lomell and Kuhn discovered.

At this point, Rudder may have thought he had only to hold his positions until later in the day, when Schneider's relief column would come along the coastal road from Vierville-sur-Mer. Most men with Rudder knew the D-Day plan was for Schneider's task force to penetrate inland from Omaha and sweep west to relieve them on Pointe du Hoc.[83] Events on the ground would prove the plan overly optimistic.

Unknown to Rudder, at that very moment Omaha Beach was in crisis. In General Gerow's appraisal, the Omaha forces "were disorganized, had suffered heavy casualties, were handicapped by losses of valuable equipment, and pinned down along the beach by intense enemy fire, afford[ing] good targets for the enemy." General Huebner radioed General Bradley, "These goddam Boche just won't stop fighting."[84] Delays on Omaha had already set back the invasion timetable, and Schneider would not reach Pointe du Hoc as planned. Rudder knew none of this, only that the men on the *pointe* would soon run out of the essentials: food, water, and ammunition. They had only what they had carried up the cliff on their backs. All else had been lost at sea.

Through the morning enemy resistance increased between the coastal road and Rudder's command post. German soldiers would be seen and then disappear. When Rangers came to the command post and told Rudder their frustrations, Hodenfield listened and concluded: "The Jerries knew every inch of the terrain. They had long deep tunnels through which they would dash, firing from first one spot, then another." Hodenfield probably mistook covered trenches for tunnels. On his way to the coastal road, 1st Lt. George Kerchner ran through a "zigzag trench that was the deepest I'd ever seen, eight feet deep. I went through this trench for a hundred and fifty yards." He then understood that "Pointe due Hoc was a self-contained fortress," above and below ground.[85]

German infiltrators, as individuals and in small bands, stole across the jumbled battlefield and attacked toward Rudder's command post. If they could destroy the command post, they would imperil the remaining Rangers' survival by eliminating their control center and by severing their communication with the big guns of British and American warships.

The critical terrain became the area between the coastal road and the command post. If the Germans dominated it, they would isolate the Americans in two places and use their entire force to attack them separately, destroying one then the other. Most Rangers had gone inland, leaving the command post stripped. Its weakness was not a concern to Rudder until the strength of the German revival became apparent. He had neither the manpower nor the firepower to occupy the contested area. At best, he could deny it to the enemy. As the two sides skirmished between the command post and the road, with neither in control, it became a no man's land.

As Rudder did not know about the crisis and delays on Omaha Beach, neither did he know that fresh German troops were joining the battle for Pointe du Hoc. They were slipping unseen from the direction of Grandcamp along the edge of the cliff to a bunker on the western fringe of the fortified area. The bunker's location and its underground chambers enabled them to enter no man's land unobserved through trenches and between the masses of debris. The bunker became the conduit of renewed German strength—the organizing point for attacks toward the command post and to cut off Rangers on the coastal road.[86]

With only a handhold on the Normandy coast, the men around the command post had their backs to the cliff. Rudder had no reserves, and many men were wounded. His Ranger force was divided in two parts, with neither positioned to help the other. After barely two hours ashore, their assault had been thrown on the defense, a role contrary to the Rangers' training and attack-minded attitude and also unsuited for the weapons they had brought to the battle, especially with their lack of machine guns and sufficient ammunition.

With the command post now vulnerable to a frontal attack, Rudder put Capt. Otto "Big Stoop" Masny in charge of its perimeter, which defended only a narrow strip along the cliff, 75 to 200 yards deep and about 600 to 700 yards long, altogether some thirty acres. Only 150 yards separated the command post from the nearest perimeter boundary. Snipers could hide deep in no man's land and select their targets inside the perimeter. Although Rudder dispatched numerous patrols to hunt them down, the searchers were never entirely successful. All during D-Day, Rangers told a combat historian soon after the battle, "the CP and the whole Pointe area were harassed by snipers who came out of tunnels and trenches to find plenty of cover in the cratered debris."[87]

Having established the perimeter defense as a barrier to a frontal attack from no man's land, Rudder wanted to neutralize or destroy the enemy in the three places where they were known to be: the west side bunker, the resistance nest on the east, and the observation bunker at the tip of the *pointe*, the largest fortification on the *pointe* but the least threat because, unlike the other two, its occupants were usually confined by the walls that protected them. To knock out the observation bunker, he turned to Vermeer, who undertook the task the next day with a twenty-pound bag of C-2 plastic explosive and six men to cover its exits. Vermeer put a short fuse on the charge and placed it at the base of the steel door on the inland side of the bunker. "The explosion lifted us right off the ground," he reported. "It wasn't long until we heard the Germans calling, 'Comrade,' as they were coming out."[88]

Seven Germans were captured; an eighth stepped through the doorway with a rifle in his hands and was perforated by Ranger marksmen before he could pull the trigger. Vermeer explored the interior and became the first American to peer through the narrow opening across its front with expansive views of the sea.[89] Exactly forty years later, President and Mrs. Ronald Reagan retraced Vermeer's footsteps, and her widely circulated photograph peering through the observer's slit made Pointe du Hoc and the observation bunker known to American audiences.

The resistance nest and the west side bunker demanded immediate attention. From both positions the enemy limited movement by the Rangers and consistently inflicted casualties. Getting close to the resistance nest was almost impossible, because it was two hundred yards beyond the defensive perimeter's eastern boundary across flat, exposed ground. Four unsuccessful attempts had resulted in several casualties. Two failed attempts on the west side bunker cost fifteen to twenty casualties. With the ground attacks fruitless and costly, Rudder decided to call on the navy for help.[90]

In this critical situation Rudder discovered that he had no radio contact with the outside world. When first ashore, the radios failed because they were wet. By midmorning, most had been disassembled and dried out, and they were functioning again. Then they were useless because invasion planners in charge of signal communications had neglected to give Eikner the latest instructions about call signs, frequencies, and code words to use in making radio contact with other units. Only if a Ranger on Pointe du Hoc spoke the correct code words could his listener know that he was speaking to an Allied soldier and not a German who spoke English.[91] Because of other reliability problems, Rudder did not have consistent radio contact with his men only a thousand yards inland on the coastal road. Runners were the most reliable means of communication between them but had to contend with snipers both ways, and casualty rates among the runners were high.

There was a disadvantage in transmitting radio messages, because the Germans monitored radio signals and had excellent radio direction finding (RDF) equipment. By using two RDFs and elementary geometry, they could compute the exact location of a signal's origin and aim their artillery at the transmitting site. When radio signals were transmitted from the command post, German artillery fire increased in volume and accuracy. Vermeer saw "dirt flying when the [short] rounds hit" and "water splash of those that passed over and landed in the Channel."[92]

Eikner, anticipating problems with the radios, had brought other means of communication in the form of semaphore flags, two signal lamps, and two homing pigeons. By flags and lanterns some messages got through to the destroyer *Satterlee* and were relayed to army units, but that was no substitute for direct radio communication. Through the morning of D-Day Rudder's superiors remained ignorant about the condition of the Rangers on Pointe du Hoc.[93]

By signal lantern Cpl. Lou Lisko flashed Rudder's request for a warship to take the east side snipers under fire. Whether HMS *Talybont* or USS *Satterlee* came in for the shoot is uncertain, but one or the other responded. Perched near the edge of the cliff, the core of the resistance nest was probably no more than several logs, perhaps held together with concrete. With seven thunderclap salvos, the destroyer undercut the earth beneath the logs, and the whole thing slid off the cliff into the sea as Rangers burst into cheers, prematurely; the resistance nest's crew remained and continued sniping on the Americans.[94]

To deal with the west side bunker, Rudder again called on naval gunnery, and the USS *Satterlee* fired, but the undercutting technique failed.[95]

The bunker was too far—about twenty yards—from the edge of the cliff. Firing from below the rim of the cliff, *Satterlee*'s flat-trajectory rounds either hit the rim of the cliff or passed over the bunker to strike farther inland. Thus, the two main sources of the enemy's defense—the east side snipers' nest and the west side bunker—remained viable.

Late Morning, First Day

As the threat of increasing German strength became clear in late morning, Rudder crossed the 125 yards from his command post to the casemate where he had assigned Harwood's fire control party. As he urged Harwood to disperse his observers across the *pointe,* the two men were standing at an outside corner of the casemate when Rudder heard the zing of a ricochet bullet and felt a burning sensation in the fleshy part of his thigh about six inches above the knee. The bullet made a clean wound, passing through his leg without hitting a bone or a major blood vessel, and the hot metal of the bullet seared and closed the puncture. Lisko ran to the aid station for Dr. Block, who hurried to Rudder and dressed the wound by cleaning the surface and applying topical sulfathiazole and a bandage.[96] Rudder remained at the casemate with Harwood.

Within half an hour, Rudder had another close call. He, Harwood, Harwood's naval aide, Lieutenant Norton, and Theodore Wells were standing in the casemate looking out to sea with the thick concrete wall to their right. Rudder was closest to the wall and a step deeper in the casemate than the others. A round believed to have been fired by the British cruiser *Glasgow* fell short of its intended target and struck the front of the wall, throwing fragments of concrete toward the four men. Fortunately, the projectile was not an explosive shell but a marking round with a metal casing filled with a powdered yellow dye. Harwood was struck by several fragments and died later in the day. Rudder was struck in the chest and upper left arm. Again he did not consider evacuation. For the remainder of his life a shard would occasionally work its way to the surface of his skin and fester into an ulcer. He was spared because he was standing deeper in the casemate than Harwood and next to the wall. Norton was injured, evacuated, and replaced by Lt. Ben Berger.

Theodore Wells was standing behind Harwood, whose body shielded him from most of the fragments, but he was blown backwards on the concrete floor and suffered a back injury. The yellow powder stained his skin and left a bitter taste in his mouth. Carried to the aid station, he was laid in a bunk bed and given a shot of morphine. After a while, a medic came in and said, "Take a drink of this. Just drink. Don't ask any questions." Wells complied and was surprised; it was good, smooth Scotch whisky, liberated from the Germans. Thus ended a very long day for Wells. He went to sleep, and the next day he was evacuated to the USS *Texas.*[97]

At almost the same hour Rudder was wounded, Chick was awakened in her hotel room in Austin, Texas, by the shouts of newsboys on the street below. She had stayed overnight in the Stephen F. Austin Hotel on Congress Avenue. In Texas, the clocks' hands were straight up and down, and newsboys on the street below her open window were hawking an early-morning edition of the *Austin American:* "Invasion Extra," "Invasion On," "Allies Hit in Northern France." When she read the stories, she knew intuitively that Earl was there. "I've thought so much about you since the invasion started," she wrote in her next letter. "We heard over the radio that Rangers were part of the assault forces, but newspapers here aren't carrying many details. I'm so anxious for any bit of news about you."[98]

In Amsterdam fifteen-year-old Anne Frank, in hiding with her Jewish family, listened to the BBC's broadcasts to occupied Europe. She heard the calm Midwestern voice of a man from Kansas, Gen. Dwight D. Eisenhower, proclaim that 1944 was the year of complete victory. She then wrote in her famous diary: "I have a feeling that friends are approaching. The long awaited liberation seems too wonderful, too much like a fairy tale ever [to] come true. Hope is revived within us. It gives us fresh courage and makes us strong again."[99]

When Rudder returned to Pointe du Hoc in March 1954 with his son Bud, he stood in the casemate exactly where he was when the shell hit the wall beside him. The visit was his first since the fighting ended. In an unusual moment of shared introspection, he talked about "how close it really was. . . . I've thought about this a lot. You wonder if it was as close as it seemed and how a man could live. The way I pictured it, you could just about reach up and touch the place where the shell hit, and you just about can." Absorbed in reflection about how near death had been, he ended with a vague query for himself: "You wonder so long what it would be like to come back."[100] In 1969, only a few months before his death, Rudder returned for the last time accompanied by his second son, fourteen-year-old Bob. He guided Bob around the battlefield, walking beside or behind him, his hands resting on young Bob's shoulders. Standing again where he had stood with Harwood and Norton, he told Bob the story. His account was captured on film. "I was fortunate," he said, "to be standing just far enough back that the shell fragments didn't hit me. In thirty minutes time, I was wounded twice, and it was the only time I was wounded in the entire war. If I had been standing a little closer to the front, you wouldn't be here, boy."[101]

As D-Day morning passed, Rudder was increasingly concerned about the lack of communication with his superiors, who needed to know the Rangers had accomplished their mission and were now in desperate straits. Near noon, he directed Eikner to send this message by all available means, including the homing pigeons: "Located Pointe du Hoc—mission accomplished—need ammunition and reinforcements—many casualties." Rudder's message was the only news received from him at headquarters on D-Day.[102] Three hours later, the *Satterlee* relayed a three-word reply from General Huebner: "No reinforcements available." The men on Pointe du Hoc were expendable if their sacrifice would assure a successful invasion. With the view of Omaha Beach blocked by Pointe de la Percée, Rudder had not even a visual clue of the situation there.

Nothing was heard of Eikner's pigeons until thirty years later, when an article appeared in a British magazine that reported one pigeon had returned to its roost in England late on D-Day with the "mission accomplished" message written on cigarette paper attached to its leg. Eikner always thought the Germans shot down the other pigeon; it had become attached to its Ranger keeper, had to be shooed away, and circled Pointe du Hoc until it disappeared.

Afternoon, First Day

As midday passed, Rudder remained unaware of the fragile hold on Omaha Beach and knew nothing about the progress of Schneider's relief column. All essential goods were in short supply, and casualties increased as German pressure rose. With the seriously wounded in dire need of evacuation, Trevor taught the medics how to make stretchers from the four-foot steel ladders and lower them to the beach. Eikner signaled the American destroyer *Barton*, which dispatched a small motorboat for them. However, it was driven off by gunfire from the German gunners on the east flank, confirming both the isolation of the *pointe* and the resilience of the enemy defense. Having failed to silence the Germans by land and sea, Rudder decided to try by air. He sent a request for an air strike to the *Satterlee*, which relayed it to the Army Air Corps, and in came a flight of P-47 Thunderbolts. When they dove toward his command post, Rudder asked for volunteers to spread an American flag visible from above. Crouch and Goodgal placed the flag where the planes could see it.[103] But even the air strike did not shut down the east side snipers.

In midafternoon of June 6, the Germans made two attacks toward the command post. Both attacks originated from within no-man's land and were in greater numbers than expected. The first attack came from the southeast, toward Saint-Pierre-du-Mont, and was broken up quickly. The second attack came from around the west side bunker, was stronger, and got closer. During the second attack Vermeer was in the perimeter defense: "The mortar, machine gun, and rifle fire was deafening. Fear gripped me. I wondered whether we would survive."[104]

As the shadows lengthened on D-Day, the situation became more desperate. More attacks during the night were expected. The two afternoon attacks had confirmed that the enemy could assemble enough men to make a frontal attack on the command post and possibly push the Americans off the cliff. The Rangers were low on ammunition and short of able-bodied men, and many had eaten only enriched D-bars since the light breakfast at 3:00 AM. Communication with the coastal road Rangers was erratic, and runners usually had to fight their way in both directions. Although they were connected by telephone, it was with wire laid on the ground, which the enemy cut whenever he found it.[105]

Twilight, First Day

Two hours before dark, about 9:00 PM, spirits rose on the *pointe* when twenty-three men from the 5th Ranger Battalion under 1st Lt. Charles H. "Ace" Parker walked into the Rangers' position on the coastal road. Parker was immediately connected by telephone to Rudder, whose first question was, Parker recalled, "'Where the hell is the rest of the fifth battalion?' I told him since they weren't already here, they must be right behind me, coming on the road." But they weren't. "They had been grabbed up by superior officers and were used to [defend] Vierville. That was not our mission but Schneider could hardly refuse a full colonel [Canham] and a general [Cota]." However, with Parker's mistaken reassurance, Rudder jumped to the equally mistaken conclusion that Schneider's Rangers were approaching, when, in fact, they had made little progress and were dug in near Vierville-sur-Mer, defending the draw and the west end of Omaha.[106]

In the first year after the war, the army published an authoritative booklet entitled *Omaha Beachhead, June 6–13, 1944,* by Harvard history professor Charles H. Taylor. Rudder's copy has blemishes and worn edges—indications of extensive use—but not one handwritten mark. Children growing up poor in Eden, Texas, learned not to write in books. But he left a paper clip, rusty after sixty years, on the map showing the Ranger rescue column at midnight on June 6–7 still around Vierville-sur-Mer. Rudder did not dwell on the past, but in this instance he had continued to contemplate the circumstances that delayed Schneider's relief column to Pointe du Hoc for two days.

The First Night

With darkness approaching on the night of June 6–7, Rudder was confronted with a difficult command decision. Should he consolidate his small force or leave them in two places, one defending the command post and the other on the coastal road? Of the two hundred men who had scaled the cliff, more than a third were dead or wounded, although many of the wounded were still fighting. Food and ammunition were running low, especially mortar rounds and grenades. The Germans were stronger and present in unknown numbers in no man's land. Communication with Rangers on the road was touch-and-go. The eighty-five men on the road, including Parker's twenty-three new arrivals, outnumbered those in the command post perimeter. The danger was greater than ever that the two groups might be eliminated separately. In this grim situation, Trevor remarked casually, "Never have I been so convinced of anything as that I will be either a prisoner of war or a casualty by morning."[107] He was suggesting that they should focus on defending themselves rather than on their discouraging situation.

Rudder decided to hold both positions. As he assessed the situation, two German attacks on the command post had been turned back, the Germans had not attacked the coastal road, and Schneider would arrive soon. He knew that the Germans had his command post under observation and, if he concentrated his entire force near the tip of the *pointe,* it would attract German artillery. Given these considerations, he sent a patrol to the coastal road shortly before dark with orders to hold.

Out there on the coastal road, four lieutenants coordinated the defense, but it was no substitute for a single command, and they did not have reliable communications. They formed their defense south of the road in the shape of a right angle pointed to the southwest in order to stop a German attack before it reached the road. The defense depended on each man's keeping his head and doing as he was trained. With the acute shortage of American ammunition, more men began using enemy weapons, as ammunition for them was plentiful around German positions now occupied by the Rangers.[108]

Not long after dark, the Germans launched the first of the three attacks that night against the coastal road defense.[109] The first attack began about one-half hour after dark, around 11:30 PM. It began with an outburst of whistles and shouts near the right angle of the line. Undetected, the Germans had moved in close, and immediately after the shouts and whistles, they lobbed grenades toward the American positions. The Rangers beat back the attack, but it weakened their defense at the angle. In the confusion and darkness the men were out of contact with one another, and only those at the corner angle knew about its weakened condition. The darkness and scattered state of the Ranger force compounded the problem of organizing and adjusting the defense.

The second attack began about 1:00 AM with a stronger effort, again hitting from the south and southwest. As in the first attack, the Germans got close without being seen. The attack began with whistles, followed by the shouting of names like a roll call. They followed the shouting by extravagantly firing machine guns and machine pistols and throwing grenades. Many of the rounds were tracers, high and inaccurate, blindly spraying the hedgerows to intimidate the Americans. Rudder's only information was the sound of guns firing, grenades exploding, and tracers streaking across the night sky. Although he recognized most of the gunfire was from German weapons, he was not certain that the enemy had overrun the coastal road because he knew the Rangers were also using German weapons.

The third attack developed about 3:00 AM from the southeast. This attack was even stronger than the previous ones and extended farther east toward Omaha Beach. Some of the attackers came from the no-man's land between the road and the *pointe*. Along the coastal road the Germans captured about twenty Rangers, killed several, and wounded others.[110] In the absence of effective communications, men began passing the word to fall back toward the command post, but the word missed others, leaving them scattered in hedgerows and thick vegetation. By 4:00 AM (now June 7) about forty-eight Rangers had fallen back through no-man's land and were in the defensive perimeter around the command post across the neck of the *pointe*. They mistakenly told Rudder that the force holding the coastal road had been destroyed. "Neutralized temporarily" would have been more accurate, because some were still there, unorganized and hiding.[111]

Rudder now believed that the men within the command post perimeter were all that remained of his original force. When the sun rose on his second day on Pointe du Hoc, he had about ninety men able to bear arms, including the twenty-three who had come with Parker the previous evening. With his isolated force hemmed within a few acres, he expected an increase in both German artillery and ground attacks. He had no reason to expect help in time to save his beleaguered force. Similarly, his counterparts on Omaha Beach did not know if the Rangers on Pointe du Hoc had been killed or captured, had held on, or had been pushed into the sea.[112] Hodenfield thought the end was near. "I gave up hope of getting off Pointe du Hoc alive. No reinforcements in sight, plenty of Germans in front of us, nothing behind us but sheer cliffs and [the] Channel. . . . We were up a creek not only for food and water but also for ammunition."[113]

The Second Day

Rudder, determined to learn what had happened on Omaha and to inform Cota, Canham, and Schneider about the plight of the Rangers on Pointe du Hoc, turned to Ace Parker. At 4:00 AM he told Parker to select six men and return to Omaha by way of the beach below the cliff. Parker followed Rudder's instructions exactly, with one small exception: he took seven rather than six because "one of the youngest and greenest soldiers decided to join us."[114] The youngster believed in Parker, and Parker did not refuse him.

Rudder's appraisal of his situation on the morning of June 7 was bleak. There was not much ammunition and no food. About fifty men were seriously wounded. The departure of Parker's patrol had reduced the number of men able to bear arms to about eighty-three. He expected enemy artillery to rain down on his small area. He could do nothing about the German bunker on the west side of the *pointe*. Germans could be seen around the resistance nest on the left as well as in front. He expected more enemy attacks on his command post, and there was no sign of relief from Omaha.[115]

Throughout the day the Germans harassed the command post with artillery barrages and small arms fire, apparently trying to organize an attack that did not materialize for two reasons, one unknown to Rudder and the other plainly obvious to him. The obvious reason was accurate naval bombardments on likely assembly areas for a German attack. Unknown to him was the fact that from noon into the afternoon, Germans who would have attacked Pointe du Hoc were resisting the advance of Schneider's relief column on the coastal road. Within the command post perimeter, the Rangers used the churned earth like breastworks and fired on any movement to their front. Marksmanship was second nature to many American boys, who grew up hunting rabbits and deer. Trevor's assistant, Ronald Eades, was mistaken for a German while searching for snipers and was fired upon by a Ranger. Running hard, he sprawled headlong into the command post. Knowing how lucky he was, he laughed it off with, "I say fellows, I'm glad to see that you do miss a shot sometimes."[116]

The most important event on June 7 occurred in midafternoon with the arrival of two LCVPs (landing craft, vehicle or personnel) under Maj. Jack B. Street with food, water, ammunition, and twenty-four Rangers who had been

Rudder at Pointe du Hoc, midafternoon, June 7, 1944. "Don't lose this," he wrote to his wife. "It was taken by Maj. Jack Street and holds much history for me. I have enough equipment to weight down a horse." His equipment includes a standard steel helmet with the insignia of a lieutenant colonel (silver oak leaf), normally front and center, painted over or smeared with mud. He is wearing a tanker's combat jacket. The bag in mid-chest is for a gas mask. The strap for a pistol holster is draped over his left shoulder and across his chest, but the pistol is indistinguishable from other equipment. Below the waist on his left front is a web magazine carrier for two clips of ammunition. And behind the magazine carrier his canteen is in its cover. In his right hand he is carrying a map case. The object under his right armpit above the map case may be a fighting knife. To his right is an Aldis signal lantern that was used to communicate with the ships offshore. An M-1 Garand rifle lies in the debris above his head. Nearby are climbing ropes and ammunition containers. (Courtesy of Margaret Rudder)

left behind on Omaha when the others moved inland. Although Street did not have the latest information about Schneider, he told Rudder the relief column was making progress.[117] Again, Rudder thought the crisis was over, even if the fight was not yet done. The G.I.s' spirits rose. Ammunition was again plentiful, and the Rangers ate their first American food—bread, jam, and Spam—since early D-Day morning. When the LCVPs backed away, they took with them fifty-two seriously wounded men.[118]

From the cliff's edge about a mile east of Pointe du Hoc, Ace Parker watched Street's LCVPs back away and mistakenly "decided the Pointe was being evacuated." He may have been tempted to turn back, but Rudder had given him an assignment to return with information about conditions on Omaha and in Vierville, and he intended to carry it out. En route back to Pointe du Hoc, he and his patrol skirted German strongpoints, killed snipers before the snipers got them, and crawled through minefields on their hands and knees, using bayonets to probe the soil ahead of them for mines. They had not eaten for two days. When Parker reported to Rudder, he was rewarded with punchy words that he never forgot: "You men look hungry. We have plenty of bread, jam, and Spam. Go to it."[119]

Unknown to Rudder, early on June 7 Canham agreed to let Schneider advance toward the *pointe*. The attack began before 8:00 AM. At first it was fast, thanks to close cooperation between tanks and foot soldiers. Despite enemy opposition, the column never stopped. When an enemy position was identified, the tanks drenched it with machine gun fire, and the column kept moving. German prisoners later commented on the Americans' "crazy march" past their positions.[120]

The armor and infantry one-two punch held together until early afternoon, when they came upon a huge crater in the road flanked on either side by antitank minefields. The crater was near Saint-Pierre-du-Mont and within fifteen hundred yards of Rudder's command post. While the tanks were trying to get around the crater, German resistance stiffened, and heavy artillery fire began hitting around them.[121] The ranking officers in the relief force then had the familiar dilemma of trying to make the right decision on the basis of inaccurate and incomplete information processed with imperfect reasoning ability. The unanswered questions were: Had Rudder's Rangers on Pointe du Hoc been wiped out? How strong were the Germans in front and on either side of them? Was the landing on Omaha Beach succeeding or failing?

In this ambiguous situation an officer arrived with the startling report that a German counterattack had retaken Vierville-sur-Mer and had liquidated the landing force on the west end of Omaha, and that enemy tanks were at that moment coming toward them on the coastal road. The alarming news was perfectly believable to Ranger officers in the relief column. If it were true, the column would be under attack in a few minutes. Several hours passed before they learned that the report was wrong and the "invasion was definitely a success."[122]

At five o'clock that afternoon a radioman in Rudder's command post made contact with the relief column by radio with a message from Rudder: "Try and fight thru to us." The reply was negative. On orders from Canham, there would be no further advance toward Pointe du Hoc on June 7. Schneider's relief column was held back for a second night.[123]

Men of the 2nd Ranger Battalion in the defensive perimeter of Rudder's command post on Pointe du Hoc. (U.S. National Archives)

The Second Night

As night fell on June 7–8, Schneider's relief column took up defensive positions around Saint-Pierre-du-Mont, and the tanks pulled back to Vierville; they were difficult to hide and would be especially vulnerable during a night counterattack. The 5th Battalion's headquarters company commander, John Raaen, remained in Saint-Pierre-du-Mont. Sitting on the floor of a barn with several officers and noncoms, he sketched the terrain in the dirt with twigs and adjusted his company's defensive positions for the night. He decided to send out a two-man patrol to find Rudder and selected Sgt. Willie Moody and Sgt. Howard McKissick for the mission.

The assignment, a war patrol at night across unfamiliar enemy territory studded with mines, called for extreme bravery. Their route was almost three miles round trip, and they were as likely to be shot by Americans as by Germans. Setting out, they went almost completely across the base of Pointe du Hoc to the cliff on the west side before realizing their error. They then doubled back toward the tip of the *pointe* and found Rudder's command post. Eikner remembered Moody and McKissick coming in and "how the tension in the CP evaporated" with the knowledge that help was not far away.[124] They gave Rudder his first account of the relief column's proximity to the *pointe*.

On their return to Saint-Pierre-du-Mont, Moody and McKissick led seven men to serve as guides the next day. They also carried a spool of telephone wire that unrolled on the ground behind them. Raaen's first question for them was, "Did you contact the second [battalion]?" "Yes, sir" was the reply. "Any messages? What shape are they in?" Moody handed Raaen a field telephone and said, "You can ask them, Captain."[125] For their daring venture, Moody and McKissick were decorated with the Distinguished Service Cross, and Raaen, their company commander, wrote the citations that vouched for their extraordinary deed.

The Third Day

Early on the morning of June 8, Schneider came to the barn in Saint-Pierre-du-Mont where Raaen had spent the night. Raaen could not avoid hearing as "Schneider spoke to Rudder with Moody's phone before we jumped off." At the same time, Eikner was with Rudder and heard his side of the conversation. Schneider told Rudder that relief was near, and they would approach from the southeast, south, and southwest.

Rudder lacked the means to inform men dispersed across Pointe du Hoc about the three-pronged relief plan. Instead of hearing about the plan, they heard renewed German artillery and presumed the enemy was softening them up for another attack. Taking up defensive positions to repel it, they distributed German weapons with plenty of ammunition.[126]

The relief column started about nine o'clock. The right flank left the coastal road and went straight toward Rudder's command post—diagonally across no-man's land following the guides who had come with Moody and McKissick. Meeting no resistance, they were there by ten. Only then did sniper fire finally cease on the command post.[127] With the larger force in his perimeter, Rudder could at last relax, knowing he could stop another German attack.

The second element of the relief force—five tanks and infantry—went inland from Saint-Pierre-du-Mont and then turned west. When the tanks were due south of the *pointe*, they turned north and drove toward Rudder's command post, while the third element, the foot soldiers, continued on west before turning right and sweeping back toward the *pointe* from the southwest along the road between Grandcamp and Pointe du Hoc. The intent was to trap the Germans on the west side of the *pointe* against the steep cliff.

It was a time-tested frontal attack combined with envelopment on the enemy's flank, a maneuver as old as Cannae. But it was the Americans' first attempt in combat, and it worked out badly. The infantry in the relief column advanced toward the Rangers, who were expecting a German attack from the same direction. Each mistook the other for the enemy. The relief column opened fire on the Pointe du Hoc Rangers in German positions and firing German machine guns with their unmistakable rapid cyclic rate of fire. The gallant Schneider ran out in front and shouted "Cease fire," but four Rangers were killed and three wounded in the confusion.[128]

The fratricidal conflict continued with the five tanks. Advancing toward the tip of the *pointe,* they opened fire on Rudder's command post with their 75 mm guns and quickly made two direct hits, stunning several men with the concussions. Raaen, having reached the command post with the relief column that came by the most direct route across no man's land, "was sitting on one of the concrete emplacements, looking toward the coastal road. When this happened, we all hit the dirt." Eikner, monitoring the tanks' radio network from the command post, began calling "Desist! Desist! Stop firing!" When a tank commander responded, Eikner told him that he would fire an orange flare to indicate the location of the command post. Eikner fired off the flare and that tank stopped firing, but the others continued until German mines disabled three of them. When the tanks stopped, Rangers banged on their turrets with rifle butts, demanding they cease firing.[129]

A year later, shortly after the end of the war in Europe, several men in the relief column were asked to describe their most harrowing combat experiences. They agreed that the "hottest firefight" of the war came during the relief of Pointe du Hoc, and practically all of it resulted from other Americans—the Rangers of the 2nd Battalion—firing German weapons.

On Pointe du Hoc, amid the backslapping and storytelling, the Americans momentarily forgot about the Germans in the resistance nest on the east side. The enemy gunners' zeal for sniping had collapsed when they realized they would soon be prisoners of their intended victims. Rudder sent a patrol to bring them in. The Rangers gathered around a captured German lieutenant. Capt. Harvey Cook stood in front of the prisoner with his hands around his neck as Rudder watched closely. The prisoner—short in stature, red-headed, and freckle-faced—answered each question with the same infuriating words: "We love our Fuehrer." In anger, a Ranger shouted, "Kill

that son-of-a-bitch!" The arrogant German was lucky; captured snipers were
fortunate if they were accepted as prisoners of war by either side.[130]

It was now time for the two 101st Airborne paratroopers, Raymond
Crouch and Leonard Goodgal, to leave the Rangers. Concerned that they
might be considered deserters, Goodgal asked Rudder for a letter to explain
where they had been. "Otherwise," Goodgal thought, "the guys would think
I had been goofing off." Rudder wrote a note, and they took off to find their
company. "They thought we were bragging," Goodgal told an interviewer
fifty years later. His lieutenant displayed no regard for the paper trail required
by historians to reconstruct events. "When I showed my lieutenant Colonel
Rudder's letter, he just ripped it up and told me to rejoin the company. The
company had been hit pretty hard. No one seemed interested in hearing our
crazy story."[131]

The reunion on Pointe du Hoc was memorable and short-lived. Most of
the 5th Ranger Battalion and the 116th Regiment did not stop but pushed
on toward Grandcamp with Canham in the lead. Schneider went for a brief
reunion with Rudder. The American advance and buildup of men and ma-
tériel was behind schedule. The invading forces on both Utah and Omaha
had failed to make substantial progress in joining up, and that was a matter
of concern to commanders from Eisenhower on down. They believed a rapid
expansion of the beachhead was necessary to prepare for the anticipated German counterattack. Eisenhower viewed the landing beaches from the deck of
a minesweeper and ordered an immediate drive to join the two beachheads.
Forces from Omaha, including the Rangers, were to attack through Grandcamp toward Utah Beach.[132] The hard fight to end Nazi Germany's oppression of Western Europe was just beginning.

AS THEY SAW HIM

Dutch Vermeer extolled Rudder as the steadfast leader: "Seeing Colonel Rudder control the operation saved our day on Pointe du Hoc. In spite of his
wounds, he was in command all the time." Jack Keating, a Ranger in the relief
column, "went out to the cliffs and got a look at what they had been through
for three days. They'd push inland, and then get pushed back, almost off the
cliffs and into the sea. Our colonel, James E. Rudder from Texas, was one of
the greatest men that ever lived. He was hit twice on D-Day and refused to
be evacuated." Lou Lisko was near Rudder for most of the ordeal. After the
war, he interviewed comrades and summarized their accounts, concluding,
"If Colonel Rudder had not led us in this battle, there would not have been
any survivors."[133]

For his leadership and heroism Rudder was decorated with the Distinguished Service Cross, the army's highest award after the Medal of Honor
for gallantry in the face of the enemy. Lt. Gen. Courtney H. Hodges made
the award on June 18 in the rolling Norman countryside near Colombières,
seven miles inland from Pointe du Hoc. As the battalion stood in formation,
Rudder's citation was read aloud, ending with special recognition of his perseverance while suffering from wounds.[134]

With tears on his face, Rudder called out to the battalion, "This does not
belong to me. It belongs to you." From down in the ranks, a man shouted,
"You keep it for us!" Ranger Richard P. Buehre in 1982 wrote, "The instantaneous shouts of approval left no doubt that the men felt he should have it.
He stood head and shoulders above everyone else in the eyes of every man
who served with him. He thought first of his men, then of his job, and never
of himself."[135]

"Rudder," said Ranger Len Lomell, "talked to you softly but firmly, like
a big brother. He inspired you to do your best. He was a man you would
die for."[136]

POSTSCRIPT

On the afternoon of June 8, Capt. Richard P. Merrill presented Rudder with
the army's regulation morning report to account for all the men of the 2nd
and 5th battalions. The ink of the report, handwritten with a pen, was slightly
smeared as though by the interminable mist of the Normandy coast. Of the
450 men in the 2nd Battalion who had sailed from England on June 5, 77
were dead, 152 wounded, and 38 missing. Some of the missing later returned.
Six were known to have been captured, and possibly 15 others. The casualty
rate was about 60 percent. By comparison, the 5th Ranger Battalion suffered
20 killed, 51 wounded, and 2 missing over the same period.[137]

The morning report did not tell the entire story about the casualties because it did not include the men attached to the two Ranger battalions, such
as Jonathon Harwood, who died of wounds. His example illustrates a difficulty in computing an exact casualty rate for Pointe du Hoc.

"Too Exhausted for Further Action"

Half of the 2nd Ranger Battalion landed on Omaha, where the casualties
were also high. Of the sixty-nine men of the battlion who came in on Omaha
and went sharply to the right to take out the guns on Pointe de la Percée,
twenty were killed and fourteen seriously wounded. In the attack straight in

on Omaha, Joe Rafferty, a popular company commander, was one of thirteen 2nd Battalion Rangers killed. Two officers to whom Rudder was close were seriously wounded before they reached dry land. Bob Edlin was shot through both legs as he left his landing craft, and Frank Corder was shot in the face, losing an eye and several teeth. Edlin would return to the battalion, but for Corder the war was over. No wonder a chronicler wrote without exaggeration that the 2nd Battalion was "too exhausted for further action."[138]

A strange stillness spread over Pointe du Hoc in early afternoon as men searched for their buddies. They found some intact, but others were wounded, and still others were not found at all, having become prisoners of war or having been blown to bits. Joyful reunions were restrained by the sense of loss. Casualties were taken to the newly established hospital in Vierville, but Rudder declined to go.[139] His leg wound was healing with no sign of infection, and he would not leave the battalion.

Those who remained searched the battlefield and the bodies of dead Germans for anything that could tell higher headquarters more about the enemy. Friend and foe alike, the dead lay where they fell in contorted positions, mangled, dismembered, and disemboweled. Outside Dr. Block's aid station, the dead were laid in rows, their feet pointing to the sky, as though, one man remarked, called to attention for the last time. When Rudder returned ten years later, he remembered Harwood and told his son, "We left the artillery captain right here when we took off on D plus two." In later years he would say, Pointe du Hoc is "sacred to me and to the youngsters I had the privilege of commanding there."[140]

Aside from human remains and the battered concrete and steel, Pointe du Hoc was littered with the implements and impedimenta of war: backpacks, gas masks, letters and photographs from wives and sweethearts back home, first aid kits, girlie pictures, cigarettes, broken shovels, spent cartridges, broken rifle stocks, and German weapons.

Commando Tom Trevor returned to England. His aide, Ronald F. Eades, hitched a ride to the British sector on a landing craft plying the invasion coast, only to be killed four days later. Trevor's father was notified of his head injury by a personal letter from the British War Office addressed to T. W. Trevor, Esq., c/o Guarantee Trust Co., Fifth Avenue, New York. The elder's Trevor's address implies a source for Tom Trevor's independent wealth, which became apparent when he retired from the British army in 1960 as a lieutenant colonel. Until his death in 1991, Trevor lived reclusively in the Albany, one of London's most exclusive bachelor apartments just off Piccadilly, where other residents included the novelist Graham Greene and former prime minister

Edward Heath. Trevor wrote a report for Combined Operations headquarters that praised the Rangers' assault on Pointe du Hoc: "So great was the tactical surprise and the verve and dash of the troops that . . . the first man was up in 3–4 minutes and the guns captured and destroyed in thirty minutes. An operation of this sort against a strongly defended coast is only suitable for bold and skillful troops who have had long and careful preparation. The leaders must combine a courageous spirit in the conception of the plan, with the ability to take infinite pains over minor details of the execution."[141]

In the flurry of leaving Pointe du Hoc, Rudder and Trevor failed to see each other, and their paths never crossed again. In 1965 Rudder obtained an address for Trevor in London and wrote a generous expression of gratitude for his contributions to the success of the Pointe du Hoc operation. Sadly, the address had a minor error, and the letter was returned, undelivered. They had planned a reunion in London that never materialized, to Trevor's certain regret, as he liked Rudder and obviously admired the Rangers. A month after D-Day, he sent a handwritten letter to Rudder:

Dear Rudder—

How's the leg—I was very worried that you would not go to the hospital but also realised how you felt about leaving even temporarily the Rangers. Since I got back I have been to Shaef and was able to explain some of your requirements. News of your exploits has reached the [British forces]. A brigadier . . . who works in close cooperation with the "Very Supreme" sought me out to hear about your doings. Knowing the high opinion I have of the Rangers, you can imagine that they lost nothing in the telling. You must be justly proud.

I hope you remember that you still have an engagement when you come to London. We have not had that party yet—so let me know as soon as you can—when I can book a table.

My abrasion has healed up beautifully, thanks to the doctor's excellent treatment.

Yours ever,
Tom Trevor[142]

At 4:00 PM, the men of the 2nd Ranger Battalion marched out the exit lane and turned right on the coastal road toward Grandcamp and the enemy. They went hardly a mile before veering to the right on a trail that led toward

the shoreline where they, with Rudder, bivouacked on a sloping hillside overlooking the sea and Grandcamp. Occupying trenches left by the Germans,
they quickly fell asleep despite unusually hard lumps in the bottom of the
trenches. On awakening, they discovered that the lumps were antitank mines
left by the former occupants, but "after what we had had gone through," Morris Prince said, "it was Paradise."[143]

Before them was the low-lying basin that led inland toward the village of
Cricqueville-en-Bessin. On the basin's shoreline, sluice gates normally held
back seawater, but the enemy had opened the gates to flood the basin and
create an obstacle for the invaders. Before nightfall, however, Schneider's
5th Battalion and Canham's 116th Infantry pushed into Grandcamp. One
company of the 5th Battalion "occupied a portion of the defense set up by
the Second Battalion" around its bivouac area, permitting their weary and
weakened comrades to rest. The night's sleep was interrupted by "bed-check
Charlie," a German night bomber that dropped "light bombs" nearby. The
next morning they marched through Grandcamp and eight miles farther
down the road to Osmanville, where they made camp for the nights of June 9
and 10. "Dead Americans lay on either side of the road," wrote Al Baer, "and
the gold and silver insignia of rank on the officers' collars caught the sun and
sent it back along the road in little pinpoints of dancing light."[144] The mortal-
ity rates of company-grade infantry officers were high.

In the last year of his life, Rudder affirmed his feelings about commanding Rangers when he hosted their meeting on the campus of Texas A&M
University:

23 May 1969
TO ALL RANGERS:

*The greatest privilege ever afforded me by my country was the oppor-
tunity of commanding the 2nd and 5th Ranger battalions in the invasion
of Europe, and being associated with the members of all six Ranger battalions of the Second World War. This is something that an outsider cannot comprehend; it is understood only by those of us who have had this
privileged experience.*

James E. Rudder
Former CO
2nd Ranger Battalion[145]

The Rudder Legend in Normandy

On June 9, as the battalion moved to Osmanville, Rudder looked over conditions in Grandcamp. There was a rumor about abuse of German prisoners, and he inspected a schoolhouse where some were temporarily held. Among the prisoners he saw a man who was unlike the others. He was older, and his attire was not German military but a tattered coat with a fleur-de-lis crest and badges of a French organization. The man was Robert Ravelet, the head of the Grandcamp volunteer fire department. The young G.I.s had detained him, not realizing that he was recruiting firefighters when they saw him going through the town, calling other men to follow him. They took him into custody, and as they led him away, Mrs. Ravelet ran after them, screaming, to no avail. The G.I.s locked him in the schoolhouse with the German POWs.[146]

Rudder released Ravelet, put him in a jeep, drove him through the streets of Grandcamp, and took him home to his family. In some recollections, a loudspeaker mounted on the jeep announced Mr. Ravelet's return. News of Rudder's kindhearted act quickly spread, and his name, pronounced "ker-nuhl rue-dare," was soon on the lips of everyone in Grandcamp. His treatment of Ravelet was in stark contrast to four years of harsh German rule. These gestures ensured that Rudder was immediately well known in Grandcamp and helped make him admired in the region. When Rudder revealed his generosity of spirit and genial manner, he lifted the spirits of people emerging from four years of oppression.

Rudder did not linger at the Ravelet home. Yet in the span of a few minutes he created a host of advocates, including men of the cloth, who would memorialize him and the Rangers. Ravelet became the prime mover in preserving the Pointe du Hoc battlefield and organized a committee called the Comité de la

Robert Ravelet of Grandcamp organized the Comité de la Pointe du Hoc to preserve the battlefield and erect the monument to Rudder's Rangers. On this photograph he wrote (in French), "With the fraternal regard of Robert Ravelet for his friend Earl Rudder." (Courtesy of Margaret Rudder)

Pointe du Hoc.[147] At the tip of Pointe du Hoc, on top of the German observation bunker, the committee erected a commemorative monument to the Rangers: eight feet of gray granite, roughly hewn in the shape of a dagger set upright. At the base of the blade, on each side of the hilt, a flat tablet bears an inscription, the left side in English and the other in French. In the English inscription shown below, the abbreviations in the second line refer to D, E, and F companies of the 2nd Ranger Battalion, and "1st American Division" refers to the entire assault force on Omaha Beach, including the 116th Infantry Regiment to which the Rangers were attached.

> *To the Heroic Ranger Commandos*
> *D2RN E2RN F2RN*
> *Of the 116th Inf*
> *Who Under the Command of*
> *Colonel James E. Rudder*
> *Of the 1st American Division*
> *Attacked and Took Possession of*
> *The Pointe du Hoc*

Ravelet benefited from public appearance with Rudder. Many local people thought he had been too cozy with the Germans. The whole town knew that German officers had lived in his venerable two-story stone home, with grand views of the sea and distinctive for its three gables and chimneys. It did not matter that Ravelet may have been coerced to keep the Germans from taking over his home and putting his family out on the street. Ravelet, the locals said, favored Germans in his small café. His reputation was tarnished. Who could say what the truth was? When Ravelet associated with Rudder, he identified himself with the good causes of the era: liberation, freedom, the restoration of democratic rule, and the destruction of Hitlerism. When he praised Rudder, he promoted himself, especially with Americans, whose prestige was ascendant. In these ways Rudder helped Ravelet rehabilitate his reputation. Not long after the war, Ravelet was appointed director of the local tourism bureau, which allowed him to promote his causes.[148]

Even so, many of his fellow citizens were never convinced. They believed Ravelet had collaborated unduly with the Germans. The four years of German occupation had been a difficult and confusing period. No one knew how long the Germans would rule. Five years? Ten years? Or five hundred years, as the Romans had occupied Gaul?[149] Knowing the right thing to do with conquerors at all times was difficult. Disputes over how to live under the German occupation had pitted French against French.

The inscription on the base of the Ranger monument at Pointe du Hoc, installed by the French Comité de la Pointe du Hoc, headed by Robert Ravelet. (Courtesy Robert W. Black)

In 1989, Ravelet received me with dignity in his home. He did not reveal that his family was in mourning for his son-in-law, who had drowned in the nearby sea on the previous day. We sat in his office, its wall decorated with certificates of appreciation from Americans and two honorary citizenships of the State of Texas. We talked about D-Day, the liberation, Rudder in 1944, and his first return to Normandy a decade later. With obvious emotion, Ravelet described the day Rudder freed him and brought him home to his *madame.* When I asked what Rudder meant to him, he replied, "Il représentait tout pour moi. Mon salut, c'était lui" (He was everything to me. He was my salvation).[150]

On June 9, Gen. Omar Bradley's First Army headquarters moved ashore and established his forward command post—a "tent city," he said—on the inland side of Pointe du Hoc near the area where Lomell and Kuhn found the five German guns. Bradley, having assigned Rudder the Pointe du Hoc mission, now overlooked the barren wasteland covered with bomb craters, debris, and wreckage. On June 12, General Eisenhower—Bradley's friend from West Point's class of 1915—came for lunch, and a few days later Eisenhower endorsed the esteemed Presidential Unit Citation for the 2nd Ranger Battalion. Rudder's name was now known to Eisenhower and would become more familiar. Bradley admired Rudder and included this compliment in his memoirs: "No soldier in my command has ever wished a more difficult task than that which befell the 34-year-old commander of [the] Provisional Ranger Force. Lieutenant Colonel James E. Rudder, a rancher from Brady, Texas, [who] was to take a force of 200 men, land on a shingled shelf under the face of a 100-foot cliff, scale the cliff, and there destroy an enemy battery of coastal guns."[151]

When Rudder returned to Pointe du Hoc in 1954, he stood on the edge of the cliff, gazed down at the beach and pondered aloud, "Will you tell me how we did this? Anyone would be a fool to try this. It was crazy then and it's crazy now."[152]

Cornelius Ryan and Ronald Reagan

Cornelius Ryan's compelling history, *The Longest Day: June 6, 1944,* was published in 1959 and sold more than eight hundred thousand copies in the first year, a blockbuster by any standard. Major errors and oversights in Ryan's account ignored or disparaged the Rangers' contributions to the Normandy invasion. Ryan repeatedly sacrificed facts for dramatic effect. The 1962 film of the same name, scripted by Ryan and produced by Darryl F. Zanuck, compounded the errors. Zanuck could have been speaking for Ryan when he said, "There is nothing duller on screen than being accurate but not dramatic."[153] Too few film critics appraised the movie for what it was: a pseudodocumentary that misled and misinformed its viewers.

In *The Longest Day,* Ryan wrongfully belittled the Pointe du Hoc operation as a "futile effort" that had no useful result.[154] In a scene from the movie on Pointe du Hoc, his screenplay puts despairing words in the mouth of a young actor portraying a Ranger: "We've come all this way for nothing." On the contrary, the operation was a heroic effort that achieved its intended objectives. Unfortunately, Ryan's book and Zanuck's film have probably influenced public perception of the Normandy invasion more than all other sources combined, in Europe and Britain as well as in the United States and Canada.

Ryan's flagrant errors about the conquest of Pointe du Hoc may be explained by the fact that he took all his information from one person, Sgt. William L. Petty, the erratic and dissident member of the 2nd Ranger Battalion, the same Petty whom Rudder turned down twice for the Rangers, yet whose fighting prowess was respected by his fellow Rangers.

Ryan was uninformed about historical research and revealed his flawed method without self-consciousness in the acknowledgements section of *The*

Longest Day. "I would like to thank," Ryan wrote, "Sergeant William Petty for meticulously reconstructing the Rangers' actions at Pointe du Hoc."[155] No other Ranger was cited as a source of information. With this public confession, Ryan unwittingly invalidated his depiction of the Rangers' role, because no single person possibly could have known what Petty claimed to know. And least of all, Petty, whose observation post was a mile from Rudder's command post and away from most of the action.

Every soldier has a different perspective on what happens in a desperate engagement with the enemy. At best, Ryan did not appreciate the complexity of the battle, with its many incidents and interrelated episodes. The best excuse that can be made for his shabby treatment of this momentous event is that he was a newspaperman in a hurry to meet the deadline for a book. He either did not know or did not care that the army's historical section, under the leadership of S. L. A. Marshall, had determined that interviews with individual soldiers were inadequate for unraveling what had happened in a battle. Marshall and other historians had devised after-action group interview techniques to analyze why an encounter ended in victory or defeat. The techniques were implemented for the battle of Normandy, but Ryan apparently did not use the authoritative publications that resulted from them and were readily available in many libraries.

Petty's stories to Ryan exaggerated his accomplishments while denigrating others. James W. Eikner, an officer in the 2nd Ranger Battalion's headquarters before Petty arrived, regarded him as a disciplinary problem. "Petty was demoted and then promoted," Eikner remembered, "because he was a good fighting soldier. He was such a great fighting man that I guarded and kept private a whole lot of what I knew about him."[156]

Frank South, a professor of physiology at the University of Delaware, was a medic in the 2nd Ranger Battalion from mid-1943 until the end of the war. He knew Petty during and after the war. In the late 1970s Petty visited with South and his wife on his travels up and down the East Coast while recruiting college students as counselors for a boys' camp outside New York City. South recalled, "Petty told strange tales that I tried to rationalize. He told stories that in no way he could have known about. . . . His comments were self-serving lies. . . . His stories were scurrilous, shameful, and gratuitous. He attempted to diminish the accomplishment of others in order to aggrandize himself."[157]

In South's opinion, Petty "was a very good soldier. . . . But he always wrapped himself in glory, and it was an undeserved glory." Men like Petty, effective on the battlefield and trouble otherwise, were a mystery for army psychiatrists. They did not know that his father abused him until, at the age of

Frank E. South, medic, 2nd Ranger Battalion, 1943–45, in England before D-Day. (Courtesy of Frank E. South)

fourteen, Petty fought back with a pick mattock. When his father died, Petty spat on his casket.[158]

In Ryan's movie script, the Rangers appear as an amorphous, unkempt, leaderless group of amateurs. For the movie three teen idol singers—Tommy Sands, Paul Anka, and Fabian—were cast as Rangers and depicted as buffoons. "I had to laugh when I saw those actors trying to climb those cliffs," recalled Ranger Antonio Ruggiero. "If we had taken time like that, we'd have all been killed." Even German veterans of Pointe du Hoc laughed at the movie's scenes, according to Wilhelm Kirchhoff, who was there on D-Day.[159]

While collecting information for the book, Ryan sent Rudder a questionnaire with twenty-three items. Rudder was then vice president of Texas A&M University and chief executive officer of the main campus in College Station. He had little time, seldom talked about the past, and replied to four questions from Ryan with a mere seven words:

> **Ryan:** *Where did you arrive in Normandy, and at what time?*
> **Rudder:** *Omaha Beach. H-Hour.*
> **Ryan:** *Were any of your friends killed or wounded either during the landing or during the day?*
> **Rudder:** *Yes, many.*
> **Ryan:** *Were you wounded?*
> **Rudder:** *Yes, twice.*
> **Ryan:** *Do you recall any incident, sad or heroic, or simply memorable, which struck you more than anything else?*
> **Rudder:** *No.*[160]

Rudder's lack of involvement in the film was a matter of priorities. He was two thousand miles from New York, where Ryan worked, and five thousand miles from Normandy, where portions of the movie were filmed. During the film's production, some Rangers could foresee the defects and sought Rudder's support for their protests to Zanuck. Rudder declined and said, "I have no suggestions to make except . . . I hope [the film] will be factual and portray these gallant men in their proper role."[161]

Rudder attended to his duties, and advising Zanuck was not one of them. Typically he avoided controversies that detracted from progressing with worthy projects. It would have been unlike him to complain in the slightest way on October 3, 1962, when he attended the New York premiere of *The Longest Day* and sat for dinner between Zanuck and Charles Canham, the American colonel who held back the relief column to Pointe du Hoc from June 6 to June 8.[162]

The U.S. Army's official history of the Normandy invasion, *Cross-Channel Attack,* by Gordon A. Harrison, published in 1951, does not cite Rudder as a source but refers to him and describes significant Ranger actions. Rudder was a primary source for Harvard historian Charles H. Taylor, author of the U.S. Army's 1946 sixty-three-page booklet, *2d Rangers at Pointe du Hoc: 6 June 1944.*[163] Taylor interviewed Rudder and other Rangers immediately after the battle, and Harrison used Taylor's account when he wrote *Cross-Channel Attack,* a primary source for historians. Professor Taylor's account of Pointe du Hoc on D-Day is the most authoritative one, but Cornelius Ryan gives no indication that he used it. Ryan cheated the Rangers of recognition for their contributions to the success of the Normandy invasion.

On the fortieth anniversary of D-Day, President Ronald Reagan stood beside the Ranger monument at the tip of Pointe du Hoc, with Margaret Rudder and many 2nd Ranger Battalion men in his audience, and delivered a tribute to their accomplishment:

> *Their mission was one of the most difficult and daring of the invasion: to climb these sheer and desolate cliffs and take out the enemy guns. . . . One by one, the Rangers pulled themselves over the top, and in seizing the firm land at the top of these cliffs, they began to seize back the continent of Europe.*
>
> *These are the boys of Pointe du Hoc. These are the men who took the cliffs. These are the champions who helped free a continent. These are the heroes who helped end a war.*[164]

NORMANDY RESPITE

JUNE 9–AUGUST 19, 1944

Immediately after Pointe du Hoc, Rudder's staff believed he discussed with his superiors the return of the 2nd Ranger Battalion to England. Having taken 60 percent casualties, they needed rest and time to reorganize and train replacements. Instead, they got light duty for two months escorting POWs and standing guard on the Cherbourg peninsula against the possibility of a German attack from the Channel Islands only twenty miles to the west.

By mid-June, 250 candidates for the battalion—all volunteers—had arrived from the replacement depot. Rudder was as selective as ever, and after interviews 99 were rejected and returned. Eager new men were integrated with veterans, who taught them survival skills. Such training could have been easily tested by real combat, as they were almost within view of the Germans in a forest called Bois du Molay about nine miles inland from Pointe du Hoc. The Rangers were there to help block an anticipated German counterattack. However, rather than counterattack through the hedgerows, which the Americans could use in defense, the Germans were digging in to use the hedgerows in their own defense. The invasion planners had hoped that the Americans would advance inland so fast that they would be through the hedgerow country before the Germans could reinforce them.[1]

In the Bois du Molay, many men had time to write their first letters from France, but not Rudder. When he finally wrote, he did not tell Chick about his wounds; she would learn that from the newspapers. Busy obtaining supplies and equipment from higher echelons, he wrote, "From early morning to late at night, I have been on a constant go."[2]

In reorganizing the battalion, he filled vacancies by matching individual skills with the needs of companies and platoons. This required careful study and influenced the selection of new men, one of whom was Pfc. Paul Parscenski of Springfield, Illinois. When memories of Rudder recurred a decade later, he wrote, "I'll never forget the first time I saw you. I was sitting along a hedgerow with a group of Ranger replacements when a group of officers approached us. You stopped and asked one of the GIs near me if he wanted

*Rudder in Normandy standing before men of the 2nd Ranger Battalion, who were
surprised by his vitality despite wounds and the recent ordeal of battle at Pointe du Hoc.
(U.S. Army Signal Corps photograph, courtesy U.S. National Archives)*

to go home. The GI gave the obvious answer, 'Yes,' and you answered, 'Well,
so do I.' And from then on, the familiarity that was shown between officers
and men was quite the reverse that had been pounded in my head in basic
training."[3]

Rudder did not have to go far to see fighting, as the Germans were yielding
little territory. A major American offensive was underway to take Saint-Lô,
the strategic center of the regional road network. He went to battalion and
company headquarters along the front to observe how the Germans conducted their defense, to study their strengths and weaknesses, and to learn
from his fellow commanders.

Chick did not know whether Earl was dead or alive until a front-page
story appeared in the *San Angelo Standard-Times* on June 12. The story was
the beginning of his rise to widespread public recognition in Texas as a war
hero. That same day, she wrote: "I am so excited I can't breathe normally.
There was a picture of you and a write-up this A.M. about you and the Rangers on the front page of the San Angelo paper. I wish someone had the power
to end all wars. They are such terrible things. We will try to make up for

everything you've missed when you come home. I'm praying for your continued success and safety."[4]

Stories about Earl spread through the towns and sparsely populated ranch country of West Texas. Two days later she wrote again: "So many people have asked me about you. Brady, Menard, Eden and all around here—everyone is talking about you. . . . I still haven't had a letter since the one you wrote May 14th."[5]

On June 16 the battalion made a four-mile speed march from the Bois du Molay to a more secure rest area near the seventeenth-century Château de Colombières. The training of new recruits began in earnest; otherwise, the men relaxed, except for watchfulness about air attacks. Bivouacked under trees, the foliage was their camouflage. For the first time the battalion was in a rear area where French food and drink were available to supplement army rations. Most Rangers were country boys, so they milked the handsome Norman dairy cows that grazed through the area.

War correspondents used the Château de Colombières for both their workplace and sleeping quarters. Rangers were fascinating and convenient to interview, which partially accounts for newspaper stories that appeared in the States about them and Rudder. Leaving or entering the medieval castle, they—and likely Rudder—walked across the stone bridge above its encircling moat filled with water that had not been flushed for so long that the lone white swan had trouble pushing its way through the green scum on top.[6]

Escorting and guarding prisoners of war is usually a responsibility of the military police, but the increasing number of prisoners exceeded the capability of MPs to handle them. Once again, the Rangers were assigned MP duty and moved to Valognes, twelve miles south of Cherbourg, to help guard 38,000 new POWs when the port city surrendered on June 27. Although they disliked POW duty, Rudder thought it was good experience because it taught them that Germans "were far from supermen but smart enough to ask if they could be sent to a POW camp in the United States." On July 3 the battalion moved through Cherbourg to the Cape de la Hague, the most northwestern tip of France. There they searched for German stragglers, cleared booby traps, "patrolled the beaches [and] searched out immense pillboxes with huge storerooms of ammunition, weapons and equipment."[7]

On the Cape, the Rangers were housed indoors for the first time, in French army barracks, and while they were there Bob Edlin returned to the battalion, still hobbling from leg wounds received on D-Day morning. Dr. Block examined him and sent him to Rudder, who had asked to see him immediately upon arrival. In a letter to Chick, Rudder's special regard for Edlin was clear: "This has been a very good day for me. Lt. Edlin returned from the hospital . . . sooner than expected. It is a real morale booster to have him with us again."[8]

Edlin's early return was a story in itself. Worried that he might be sent from the hospital to a replacement depot and not back to the 2nd Ranger Battalion, he persuaded a hospital administrator in England to release him, took a civilian bus to a Channel port, talked his way on board a vessel bound for Omaha Beach, and hitchhiked until he found the Rangers. Edlin talked about his reunion with Rudder. "He greeted me with a big hug and was as happy to see me as he could possibly be. He said he wanted to talk to me before deciding what we were going to do [about reorganizing Edlin's company]. He talked to me as an equal. He asked me to help him make a decision. It was inconceivable to me, but he took the advice of a young, 22-year-old lieutenant."[9]

About the same time, an incident involving Pfc. Buford L. Riddle of Evanston, Wyoming, portrays another side of Rudder's easygoing way with men in the lower ranks. Years later, something triggered Riddle's memory, and he wrote: "Do you remember the time that you, Capt. Williams & myself were in those underground billets at Cherbourg looking for whatever we could find. I found a billfold with a lot of pictures & 140 francs. You said we should split it. I said, 'Like heck we do.' Gosh, I'll never forget those days. If you ever come up to Wyo. I sure would enjoy seeing you again."[10]

At exactly twelve noon on the Fourth of July, every American artillery piece in France was fired at the enemy, catching the Germans as well as many Americans unawares with the sudden, widespread explosions. 1st Lt. John Colby was napping in his tent after pulling all-night duty, and the concussion of the eight-inch howitzers behind him blew him off his cot.[11]

In the rear area, the biggest dangers for Rudder's Rangers were German booby traps and themselves. The accidents were stupid things to be expected of young men in possession of firearms, explosives, and alcohol. Dr. Block noted in his diary that the "only casualties are men fooling around with mines and demolitions." Morris Prince wrote: "One of our boys, armed with a rifle, accidentally set it off. The bullet ripped through his lower jaw and embedded itself in his brain. He died instantly."[12]

Lt. Robert Page, a new replacement, was killed while conducting a class on the German *Panzerfaust,* an antitank weapon. When he tried to disassemble the weapon with his knife, the *Panzerfaust* exploded, blowing him apart and slightly wounding two other men. Rudder went with Dr. Block and medics Frank South and Bill Clark to collect Page's body parts in a blanket.

Afterwards Dr. Block wrote in his diary: "Last Sunday night Lt. Page was blown up. The colonel carried what was left of him on the front of a jeep covered with flowers back to camp."[13]

On the Cape de la Hague, Max Schneider's 5th Ranger Battalion and the 2nd Battalion were side by side, and Rudder saw Max often. Max's subordinates noticed that he was more easygoing and approachable than in England or during the invasion. The war, his headquarters commandant John Raaen said, "was all over for him and he knew it." He was eligible for rotation back to the States; he had fulfilled the expectations of those who denied Rudder's request for his return six months earlier.

On September 1 Max returned to a hero's welcome in his hometown of Shenandoah, Iowa, where he was descended from a pioneer family and had been a popular youngster. He was Shenandoah's most decorated war hero and honored by civic and veterans' organizations. A public reception evoked a "tremendous ovation from the crowd" at the local armory. When he walked through downtown, men rushed to shake his hand and little boys ran to touch him. Old friends got the impression that he was the same Max they had known in their school days. He stayed in touch with Rudder, plying him with questions such as, "Who has been hurt in both outfits," and "How did Sully work out as Bn. C.O.?"[14]

There was another story beneath the surface. His inner war still raged. In his private life, he was aloof and emotionally numb toward his family. After his death, his wife said that when he came home from the war, "he just crawled in a bottle." His cousin, Julia Ferguson Falk, summed up her family's observation with, "We always said the war took the best out of Max."[15] He remained in the army, was promoted to full colonel, participated in the landing at Inchon, Korea, in 1950, and held responsible commands in the United States, Japan, and Germany. And in spite of occasional short-lived tremors observed in private, like a man severely stricken with palsy, he got good efficiency ratings. He was still bothered by headaches but refused medical treatment.

The military culture was not tolerant of psychological troubles. In 1959, while en route from leave in the United States to resume his command in Korea, he disappeared for two weeks and was found wandering through the streets of San Francisco, confused and disoriented. Rather than hospitalizing him, the army charged him with absence without leave and promptly sent him on to his duty post in Korea. His family never heard from him again, and he took his own life two months later on March 25, 1959, thus ending a "brilliant military career," in the words of his hometown newspaper.[16] We can only wonder how many more of his countrymen would have died on

Omaha without Max's seasoned judgment—and how many returned home to suffer similar mental anguish for the rest of their lives.

On July 25 the long-awaited breakthrough of German defenses in Normandy finally occurred with a concentrated effort in a rectangle four miles long and one mile wide along the road west from Saint-Lô to Periers. Waves of bombers flew from England to drop more than eight million pounds of high explosives in the small area, the most intensive carpet-bombing of the European war. Rudder and most of the battalion were within five miles of the target area and witnessed the immense stream of planes passing overhead. Dr. Block estimated he saw more than eight hundred B-24 Liberator bombers in one formation.[17]

Several days later, Rudder and the battalion followed the advancing American forces through the carpet-bombed area to encamp near the Château de Canisy, six miles southwest of Saint-Lô. The grounds of the château, owned by the de Kergorlay family for almost a thousand years, were the location of a newly created school for training in coordinated infantry and tank tactics. This may not have been an entirely new experience for Rudder, but joint infantry and tank operations were a relatively neglected training exercise in the U.S. Army. In Normandy, the problem of dealing with an enemy dug into the hedgerows necessitated using infantry and tanks together. For the Rangers, the training was another indication that henceforth they would be employed mostly as ordinary infantry and not for their special skills.

The reputation of Rudder's Rangers preceded them to Canisy, where they made a vivid impression on Brigitte de Kergorlay, the twenty-four-year-old heiress to the château and surrounding estate. Their assault on Pointe du Hoc was already becoming legend in Normandy, and everyone recognized their distinctive diamond-shaped blue insignia with a gold border. In the summer of 2000, while sitting in her home near the château, she talked about the Rangers as she had observed them in 1944, rolling her eyes about their exploits at Pointe du Hoc. Then she laughed about the goose they had stolen and cooked over an open fire unwittingly in a chamber pot—a twenty-liter family-sized one that they had taken from a tenant's house.[18]

In Canisy the Rangers had a lesson in military justice under Eisenhower in the case of Pvt. Clarence Whitfield. Whitfield arrived handcuffed in the custody of military policemen and was executed by hanging in the kitchen garden of the château for raping a woman near Vierville-sur-Mer on June 14. His last duty was to dig a pit below his gallows, and his last wish, which was granted, was to smoke a cigar before he ascended the gallows.[19]

Following Operation Cobra, after breaking through the German defenses, the Americans streamed south down a narrow corridor with the Bay of Mont Saint-Michel on their right. Hitler then tried an armored offensive drive west to cut across the corridor near the hilltop town of Avranches, hoping to trap Americans who had passed through the Avranches corridor. Instead, his offensive put most of the German army in Normandy in a trap, called the Falaise Pocket, where they suffered enormous losses. Their advance was stopped with a heroic stand by elements of the U.S. 30th Infantry Division on a hilltop near the town of Mortain.

Desperate Germans trying to flee the Falaise Pocket drew Rudder and the 2nd Ranger Battalion south to help block their escape. Patton brought to Bradley's attention "the hole in our line [north of] Mayenne," and the 2nd Rangers were used to help plug the hole. In trucks, they joined the great stream of American vehicles funneling through Avranches in pursuit of the enemy. Wrecked and burned German tanks and vehicles littered the roadsides, where long lines of enemy POWs shuffled north, dirty and docile, hands folded across the tops of their heads. With the great monastery at Mont Saint-Michel visible across the bay to their right, the Ranger convoy crept up the steep slope into the war-torn town and down the other side to cross the miraculously intact bridge at Pontaubault, where they bore to the left and southeast for another fifty miles to take up positions in Mayenne, a town of about nine thousand near the inland boundary of Brittany and Normandy. From there, Rudder gave his location to Chick as "a long way into France. You should see the chateau I have my headquarters in—I am also the town mayor. We have really got the Boche on the run and we are hoping we can keep him that way. By the time you get this, I'll be in Paris, I hope."[20]

Mayenne was an important road intersection, especially for the east-west route, where the bridge was the only span still standing over the Mayenne River, a major obstacle about one hundred feet wide and five feet deep with steep banks. Rudder posted detachments he could see from the château at each end of the bridge and northeast of the town to sound the alarm if the Germans approached. None came, not even stragglers. Those who escaped the Falaise Pocket headed east across the Seine.

In Mayenne, medic Frank South, then nineteen years old, was scolded by Rudder for an incident that is an example of Rudder's exercise of authority. One evening South and his buddy, Virgil Hillis, went out carousing on the town. Returning to their quarters in the small hours of the morning, they sang lustily, doing more shouting than singing, without realizing they were passing beneath Rudder's bedroom window. Suddenly the shutters of the colonel's window flew open, and there he stood. He ordered them to come to his headquarters the next morning. They sobered up fast, had a sleepless night, and appeared before him the next morning.

Standing at attention, South trembled, expecting that his least penalty would be a reduction in rank or that "I might be court-martialed and sent to Leavenworth." To their surprise, Rudder dismissed them with, "You boys stay out of trouble. Go back to Dr. Block and 'get with it.'"[21] "Get with it" was his frequent urging, meaning "go to work."

South recounted this story after he became professor emeritus of physiology at the University of Delaware. It illustrates perfectly that Rudder was not "a chickenshit disciplinarian." He knew that the "petty harassment of the weak by the strong . . . [had nothing] to do with winning the war." Reflecting on Rudder sixty years later, South would say, "The war was bad enough and he did not make it worse."[22]

CHAPTER 9

BRITTANY
AUGUST 19–SEPTEMBER 22, 1944

In Mayenne on August 14 Rudder was surprised by new orders to take the 2nd Ranger Battalion west into Brittany. He expected to go east, where the real business was. But orders were orders, and he wrote in his black vest-pocket notebook the names of towns on the 220-mile route that would traverse the full length of the long peninsula: "Dinan, Jugon, Lamballe, St. Brieuc, Guin-camp, Morlaix, Lesneven, Plouzevede, area due west of Lesneven."[1]

For the men of the battalion the journey was seventeen hours of sitting on the unyielding wooden benches of two-and-one-half-ton cargo trucks—called "deuce-and-a-halfs"—driven by African American G.I.s from the Quartermaster Corps over heavily used roads that had seen little mainte-nance for four years. In heavy traffic, the battalion's convoy, identified by L283 on the bumper of each vehicle, averaged thirteen miles per hour, with so much stop-and-go that the trucks ran out of gasoline, causing further de-lays. Along the roads the native Bretons cheered and tossed flowers and fruit, and "every time we halted," Morris Prince told an interviewer, "the cider and wine jug would come into play. These people were conscious of the meaning of freedom, liberty, and democracy and were showing us their approval of our aid."[2]

Rudder traveled in a car with his key staff and, no doubt, discussed the needs of the battalion and the leadership of its six line companies, topics to mull over with Harvey Cook, his operations and intelligence officer. Rudder knew nothing of the vigorous debate in the American high command about this big push in Brittany, which had ended with the controversial decision to force the surrender of the German garrison in Brest. The Allies' invasion plan presumed that after the Germans were defeated in Normandy, those in Brittany would quickly surrender. When this proved wrong, the obvious question was whether the port of Brest was still needed for incoming men and supplies from the United States. An argument against subjugating Brest was that Germans across northern France were rapidly fleeing toward Germany, leaving Brest ever more distant from the front lines. Brest was heavily forti-fied and defended by between forty thousand and fifty thousand German troops, more than twice the number estimated by army intelligence officers, and tough paratroopers were the core of the German garrison.[3]

But there were other considerations. With Eisenhower's concurrence, Bradley decided to take Brest for two reasons. First, such a large enemy force could not be cordoned off and left in the Allied rear; guarding it would "require more troops than we could spare on an inactive front." The second reason was entirely subjective: "to maintain the illusion . . . that the U.S. Army cannot be beaten." In private, Bradley admitted the importance of maintaining an image of invincibility. Lt. Gen. George S. Patton agreed and wrote in his diary, "I fully concur in this view. Anytime we put our hand to a job we must finish it."[4] So it was that if the German commander in Brest, Lt. Gen. Herman B. Ramcke, obeyed Hitler's order to hold out to the last man, a brutal, punishing fight for both sides was guaranteed.

LE CONQUET

Rudder's new area of operations was the sparsely populated tip of Brittany on the north side of Brest harbor that the U.S. Army called Le Conquet, for the name of a small town. The locals called it Le Finistère—literally, the end of the earth, which it was to ancient inhabitants.[5] His exact destination was Le Folgoët, a village fifteen miles north of Brest known for its medieval church—a landmark on Christian pilgrimages—with rich stained glass and a statue of Joan of Arc. He established his headquarters near the church, and the battalion bivouacked around an open field on the edge of the village.

The American forces in the Brest offensive were unified as the U.S. Army VIII Corps under Maj. Gen. Troy H. Middleton. VIII Corps was composed of three infantry divisions (the 2nd, the 8th, and the 29th) and many attached units, including artillery, communications, transportation, and the two Ranger battalions—all told more than fifty thousand men. In addition, the French Forces of the Interior (FFI)—the French resistance organization directed from London—numbered about twenty thousand armed men and women.[6] Middleton attached the Rangers to the 29th Infantry Division under Maj. Gen. Charles H. Gerhardt, who would criticize Rudder severely, although some men thought he was averse to Rangers rather than to Rudder.

Middleton became another of Rudder's champions and would figure in his future, both during and after the war. During the First World War Middleton had been the youngest regimental commander in the American Expeditionary Force and was awarded the Distinguished Service Cross. In the 1920s he taught at the Command and General Staff School while Eisenhower was a student. "Ike used to come to my office," he recalled. "He would sit on a corner of my desk and pump me for information. He asked the most practical questions. And he wasn't after information about tests; he wanted to know what a commander would do in combat situations."[7] With Middleton as a tutor, Eisenhower graduated number one in the class of 1926.

When World War II came, Ike was Middleton's superior and wanted him as a troop commander. Although in late 1943 Middleton was in Walter Reed Hospital in Washington, D.C., suffering from painful arthritis in the knee, Eisenhower insisted on his returning to Europe: "I don't give a damn about his knees," he said. "I want his head and his heart. I will take him into battle on a litter, if we have to." Middleton, like Bradley, would become another connection to Eisenhower for Rudder. After the war, Middleton described Rudder as "one of the finest combat soldiers I ever saw."[8] The admiration between the two men was mutual. In 1950, Middleton became president of Louisiana State University, and when Rudder was inaugurated as president of Texas A&M in 1960, he invited Middleton to give the principal address.

LOCHRIST BATTERY

On Le Conquet Peninsula the Germans had installed several powerful gun batteries similar to those on Pointe du Hoc, but four of the guns were larger, and there were others of the same or lesser caliber. The most powerful were four 280 mm guns (11-inch bore diameter), each with a range of about seventeen miles. The guns were situated near the end of the peninsula, with well-prepared ground defenses to protect them. Putting the guns out of action was important to capturing Brest. It was a job for the Rangers.[9]

The Germans called the four 280 mm guns the Graf Spee Battery, because the guns were duplicates of those on their battle cruiser *Graf Spee,* which the British had sunk off Uruguay shortly after war broke out in 1939. The French called them Kéringar, the name of the farm where the guns were located. The Americans called them the Lochrist Battery, after the name of a nearby village, which is the name that will be used in this account.

Although the 2nd Ranger Battalion's primary mission was to knock out the Lochrist Battery, the battalion had two other missions in conjunction with the 5th Battalion: to screen the right flank of the 29th Division and to round up or liquidate scattered remnants of the Wehrmacht once it was beaten. Unlike the situation at Pointe du Hoc, here Rudder was not confined to a small space. He moved frequently, leading from forward positions in attacks to push the Germans into smaller areas near the tip of the peninsula and strangle their supply line to Brest.

Lt. Col. Baptiste Faucher—nom de guerre, "Colonel Louis"—commandant of the French Forces of the Interior in the Brest district in 1944, partnered with Rudder to gain the surrender of all German troops near the tip of Brittany. (U.S. National Archives)

FRENCH RESISTANCE

Brittany was fertile ground for resistance fighters. Its Breton population was proud and independent-minded. More people in Le Finistère spoke the indigenous Celtic language than in any other part of Brittany. The rolling terrain afforded good concealment for covert activities. When Rudder arrived, significant resistance against the Germans was underway, led by the FFI and aided by Jedburgh teams parachuted into France after they were trained in Britain. A Jedburgh team usually had three highly trained resistance specialists: one French, one British, and one American.[10]

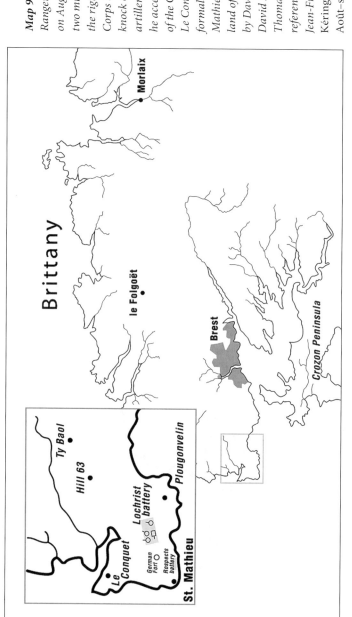

Map 9-1. Rudder took the 2nd Ranger Battalion into Brittany on August 19, 1944, where two missions were to protect the right flank of the U.S. VIII Corps besieging Brest and to knock out threatening enemy artillery. On September 9 he accepted the surrender of the German garrison on Le Conquet Peninsula in a formal ceremony at Saint-Mathieu, the most western land of France. (Graphics by David Grosvenor and David Zepeda, copyright Thomas M. Hatfield. Map reference: Jacques André and Jean-François Conq, Objectif Kéringar: Jours de libération, Août–septembre 1944, 92.)

Shortly after Rudder set up his command post, the leaders of the regional FFI and the local Jedburgh team came to see him. The FFI commander, Lt. Col. Baptiste Faucher, whose nom de guerre was Colonel Louis, had an estimated five thousand armed FFI members in Le Finistère. U.S. Army major John W. Summers, code-named "Wyoming," was the OSS officer leading the Jedburgh team, code-named "Horace," which had dropped into the area on the night of July 17. Both men knew the terrain and enemy dispositions. If the Germans caught them, the best they could hope for was to be killed quickly. Faucher, trim and ramrod straight at the age of fifty-six, came wearing a beret and the battle dress of a British officer with five parallel stripes of a French army lieutenant colonel on his shoulder straps. In neat block letters he printed his name in Rudder's vest-pocket notebook, followed by "Le Finistère." Beneath his name Rudder wrote, "Lt. Col. Louis" and "FFI oil and gas."[11]

In working with Faucher, Rudder adapted to unusual circumstances in exercising his command. Faucher was sensitive about his government's collapse and humiliation before the German onslaught in 1940. As a career army officer, he had refused to accept the French capitulation and remained in North Africa, then returned secretly to France and became head of the FFI in the Brest district. If Rudder had been intent on glorifying himself or his country, his relationship with Faucher might not have been productive. But they got along famously and often had their command posts in the same place. The payoff was the complete German surrender on Le Conquet at a low cost in human lives.[12] Faucher complimented Rudder in his 1946 report on FFI activities and in his memoir published twenty years later, which assured that he would be recognized in local histories of the liberation.

A group of about two hundred Russians, used as forced labor by the Germans and led by a mysterious man known only as Joseph 351, escaped and joined the FFI and the Americans against the common foe. It was widely believed that Major Summers engineered their escape. The Americans were fascinated with them. The Russians were fierce fighters, with bandoleers of ammunition draped from both shoulders across their chests in their customary way, and had no mercy for their former captors. They once apologized to the Americans for leaving no survivors to interrogate from a group of eight captured Germans. At one point Rangers dressed fifteen of the Russians in American uniforms to bluff the Germans, making the Rangers appear greater in numbers than they were.[13]

HILL 63

On August 25 the Rangers and the 29th Division went on the offensive to destroy or neutralize the enemy guns. War correspondents and army historians were distracted from covering the offensive by two major events that occurred on the same day: the beginning of the main attack on Brest and the liberation of Paris. Not many news accounts appeared about the fighting on Le Conquet, which Rudder considered no less difficult than that in Normandy, although Ranger casualties were fewer.[14] By August 29, a task force of two companies of the 2nd Ranger Battalion under Capt. Edgar L. Arnold had reached the Atlantic coast at the extreme tip of Brittany and identified several resistance nests along the shore.

Rudder then took command of the task force, advising Arnold, "I am attempting to have the garrison (at Pointe de Corsen) surrender," which they did, fifty-six alive and four dead. But the main German force on the Le Conquet, including the Lochrist Battery, remained intact as an enclave within the peninsula, and its supply line to Brest was still open. Rudder now concluded that the Germans, numbering more than a thousand, were concentrated in a half-dozen well-prepared defensive areas rather in a continuous line. Aggressive and costly attacks would be required to kill or capture them and cut the Brest road unless they surrendered as a whole, which seemed unlikely considering the reputed stubborn arrogance of their commander.[15]

The German defenses of the Lochrist Battery in the direction of Brest were arranged in an arc about three miles out from the battery. An important cog in the defense was the village of Goasmeur on the Brest highway, where a minor road came in from Ty Baol, a cluster of houses a mile north. The high ground in the area, Hill 63, lay beside the road junction. In possession of the hill and the stone houses of Goasmeur, the Germans were in a favorable position to block the American advance, especially with supporting fire from their artillery in the Lochrist Battery. However, repeated bombings by American B-17s and B-24s flying from England and dive-bombings by P-47s and P-38s shattered some German positions and demoralized many Germans. Still, as the Rangers advanced on Goasmeur, they skirmished with German defenders.[16]

The Le Gall family farm was a quarter of a mile up the Ty Baol road from the Goasmeur junction. On the afternoon of August 29, a Ranger patrol ran into a German patrol on the farm, and a firefight ensued around its three buildings. Several Germans were killed, but no Americans. When the Germans retreated, five or six Americans entered the Le Gall home, where the family had stayed during the shooting. Spreading their maps on a table, they gave chocolates to fifteen-year-old Rene Le Gall and cigarettes to the adults; two of the adults were Rene's uncles, veterans of World War I. Two officers climbed into the attic and used their binoculars to study Hill 63. The Americans then pulled back five hundred yards toward Ty Baol, but not before trading their canned foods for the family's fresh vegetables. Later in the afternoon a larger German patrol returned to the farm and searched fruitlessly for the Americans.

Sixty-one years later, Rene showed a visitor where the fallen Germans lay untouched until a U.S. Army graves registration team removed them several days later. Rene was absolutely certain that the American soldiers were Rangers, saying emphatically, "Ils étaient Rangers!" "They were Rangers!" Like most Bretons and Normans, he distinguished between Rangers and other U.S. soldiers by referring to Rangers as "Rangers" and to others as "Americans." He knew the difference. The Ranger shoulder patch was distinctive, and an orange diamond was painted on the backs of the helmets of men in the 2nd and 5th Ranger battalions, with the number 2 or 5 in the center of the diamond.[17]

The next morning Rangers came in force along the muddy road from Ty Baol to Goasmeur and Hill 63. Ranger officers went again to the Le Gall attic to observe the area in front of them. The ground was too muddy for tanks,[18] so the Rangers advanced on foot toward the crossroads, where they attacked the Germans.

The FFI fought in the battle around Hill 63, and their historian described the action: "Rudder commanded personally the attack. He leaped from his jeep, bullets were whizzing by and the gunfire was very dense." Although the Germans retreated, they tried to deny the hill to the Americans. Despite their artillery fire, the Rangers dug in. "Hill 63 was a bitch," wrote Al Baer. "We just sat on top of the hill and took some pretty rough shelling. With darkness came the usual nightly barrage from those 280 mm guns. We were relieved after seven days. But Hell, the night we came off the hill was the worst part of the whole deal. You've seen movies with shells exploding and men falling. Well, that's how it was the night we came off of Hill 63." Although the Rangers withdrew, they did not permit the Germans to reoccupy the hill.[19]

When the battle for Hill 63 was over, Rudder advanced his command post to the Le Gall farm or close by, as Rene recalled that Americans were in and around the family home for days. As the advance proceeded, Rudder moved closer to the Lochrist Battery, usually traveling in a jeep with a driver, his radio operator, and his interpreter, Sam Mélo, a Portuguese American linguist.[20] He went where his men were in contact with the enemy; it was the best way to know the circumstances confronting them.

Aggressive actions with the 5th Ranger Battalion pressed the Germans toward the tip of the peninsula. Gerhardt complained that he could not keep track of Rudder, and his headquarters journal is peppered with his criticisms. Ironically, the same entries confirm that Rudder was consistently working with the FFI and positioned to know the conditions on the battlefield. Gerhardt proposed using the Rangers in an amphibious attack from the Brest harbor against the German submarine pens on the shoreline of the city. Rudder disagreed, citing the lack of proper equipment and logistical support, and nothing came of the impractical scheme.[21]

Entries from Gerhardt's headquarters journal illustrate his dissatisfaction with Rudder:

September 1:

0200 From Rudder: *Artillery falling on 2nd Ranger battalion area.*

0215 From Rudder: *POW indicates location of German headquarters; Estimate 1,000 to 1,800 troops in Le Conquet; CO is Lt. Col. Furst; 4 guns of Lochrist battery still firing.*

0600 To Rudder: *Lochrist battery will be hit by air this morning.*

1145 From Rudder: *Request air [aerial bombing] on big guns.*

1301 From Rudder: *Lochrist battery still firing.*

2000 From Rudder: *Shelling on companies B, D, E & F.*

September 2:

1757 From Rudder: *FFI and POWs report three of four guns in Lochrist battery still OK.*

September 3:

0830 Gerhardt to staff officer about Rudder: *"I would just as soon can him as not."*

1030 Gerhardt: *"Get after those Rangers and get somewhere. I want to get some definite results. . . ."*

1200 Gerhardt: *"Keep after Rudder."*

1353 Staff officer: *Rudder says the big gun at Lochrist is firing on them. Can you get some air on it?*

1647 Staff officer: *The Rangers keep screaming for a [strike] time by the Air Corps. I have to put them on as they come over.*

1830 Gerhardt: *"Get after Rudder."*[22]

Two days after his "Get after Rudder" outburst, Middleton removed the 2nd Ranger Battalion from Gerhardt's command and attached it directly to his VIII Corps. Rudder brought the elements of the battalion in close proximity, and they drove toward the tip of Le Conquet. On September 6 the battalion broke the enemy's main line of resistance, cutting them off from Brest. This success led to another dispute with Gerhardt. His 29th Division newsletter, "29 Let's Go," credited the division with Rangers' achievements. The Rangers were incensed. Rudder took up for them, protesting to both Gerhardt and Middleton, and the error was corrected in the next issue of the newsletter.[23]

THE FOOL LIEUTENANT

The Rangers' attack on Lochrist Battery focused on a fortified bunker that was the command center and observation post for the German artillery. The bunker (called a "fort" by the Americans) was a man-made mound about thirty feet high in a farmer's field. Camouflaged with netting and vegetation to appear as only a natural rise on the landscape, it had five levels, two below ground level and three above. Its dimensions were astonishing: 138 feet long, 61 feet wide on the lower level, and 49 feet from the lowest level to the top, which was a small "telemeter room" for radio communications and range-finding equipment to assist their long-range artillery in firing accurately. The 280 mm guns were located about seven hundred yards east of the fort in a slight depression that was otherwise pastureland for horses and cows. Visibility from the depression was poor, and the guns were of little use without the fort's observation of their hits and directions for firing. A network of barbed wire, mines, trenches, and machine guns defended the battery as well as the fort.[24]

Overcoming the German defenses was a matter of time and breaks for the Americans. Casualties had been severe in recent days, and many more were expected in the coming attack. Dr. Block noted in his diary: "I have really worked & I know I have saved men's lives by rapid evacuation & prompt use of plasma (including Germans). Had two close calls from machine gun fire and air bursts."[25] Captured German medical units were kept intact to care for their wounded, allowing American medics to concentrate on their own.

Rudder liked to say that luck comes to those who are prepared to take advantage of it. A few minutes after a frosty sunrise on September 9, a four-man patrol led by 1st Lt. Robert T. Edlin surprised and captured a pillbox, an outpost of the fort. Shouting "Hände hoch," they crashed through the door and

German Army colonel Martin Fürst. A professional soldier since 1923, Fürst surrendered his 899th Infantry Regiment of the 266th Infantry Division to Rudder in Brittany on September 9, 1944. Fürst is shown here at the head of a column of the Wehrmacht in 1939 and in a 1944 portrait. (Courtesy of Manfred Fürst, Mannheim, Germany)

took about twenty prisoners. One was a lieutenant who had attended college in the United States and spoke perfect English. Edlin asked him, "How do we get into the fort from here and to your commander?" The German replied, "I can take you to the fort commander."

Edlin decided to attempt to enter the fort without seeking permission from Rudder, who, he believed, would consider it too risky. Taking Sgt. William J. Courtney with him, Edlin left Sgt. William Dreher Jr. to guard the prisoners. He then sent Sgt. Warren Burmaster back to their company command post with instructions to ask Rudder to stop all firing on the fort. Lewis Gannett, a well-known reporter for the *New York Herald-Tribune,* was with Rudder in the battalion command post when the message arrived. It began with, "That fool lieutenant of yours is up there already."[26] Gannett used the line in his story, and "fool lieutenant" became Edlin's handle.

The German officer led Edlin and Courtney on a path through a minefield. They carried no white flag and slung their Thompson submachine guns from their shoulders. As they entered the fort up a small concrete ramp, electric doors opened for them. They passed through a hospital and an operating room and continued past other rooms and occasional guards. The dull rumble of heavy electrical generators turning was audible throughout the fort.[27] To each group they encountered, the German lieutenant explained that he was taking the Americans to see the commander "to possibly negotiate a surrender so there would be no more casualties."

They entered the commander's office without knocking, surprising but not ruffling the commander, Col. Martin Fürst. He impressed Edlin as "calm and the smoothest character I ever saw." He spoke excellent English. Edlin asked, "Why don't you surrender this fort and get this whole thing over with?" Fürst replied, "Why should I do that? You cannot capture this fort and you cannot take the Brest peninsula." Fürst got on the telephone and learned that only Courtney was with Edlin. "You are my prisoners, now," he told Edlin. Edlin then pulled the pin on a hand grenade and put it to Fürst's stomach, or lower, while holding down the lever on the grenade to keep it from exploding and hurling its forty-eight steel fragments around the room. "Threaten[ing] with as much bravado as I could," Edlin told Fürst, "You either surrender or you're going to die right now." "Well, so are you," was Fürst's response.[28]

Cut off from Brest and isolated at the end of Le Conquet Peninsula, Fürst's situation was hopeless. American planes roaming unhindered in the skies above intensified the Germans' feelings of despair and helplessness. Edlin sensed that Fürst wanted to surrender and would under honorable conditions, especially to an officer of at least equal rank. "I did not give a rat's ass who he surrendered to," Edlin told an historian decades later. Fürst, at age forty-one, had been a professional soldier since 1923. Only a few days earlier he had been promoted to full colonel—to jack up his courage, no doubt. He needed time to think.[29]

After Edlin returned with his report, Rudder sent Harvey Cook to ascertain that Fürst was ready to surrender. Taking only an interpreter and carrying a white flag, Cook entered the fort, "worried as to who was going to surrender to who—especially after those big iron doors clanged shut with me on the inside."[30]

In Fürst's 1954 memoir, he referred to Cook as a "pathfinder." "I received him at the entrance to my command bunker and assured him and his companion that they would not be harmed." Fürst agreed to surrender the Lochrist Battery and the nearby Rospects Battery of four 155 mm guns. Using the fort's public address system, he told its garrison what he had done and that they should not take hostile action against the Americans.[31]

Rudder came to the fort at twelve noon, accompanied by Faucher, to accept Fürst's surrender of the two batteries.[32] Imagine Fürst standing in the doorway of his bunker waiting for this unknown American officer, the winner of their bloody duels across Le Conquet. Was he a fanatic or a vengeful blockhead? Rudder could have approached Fürst in a rage; men who were dear to him had been killed or maimed by followers of Martin Fürst. Fürst knew better than anyone that his future depended on the captor's state of mind.

To Fürst's relief, Rudder greeted him with a breezy "So you're the guy we've been looking for so long." It was as though Fürst was the coach of a rival football team that he was meeting in midfield for the first time. Their rapport developed from that sociable beginning. A decade later, when Fürst wrote about his surrender—the most humiliating day of his life—his first thoughts were of Rudder. He began with gratitude for his humane conduct. "I can say that in this most difficult moment of my military life—a German officer, disarmed, deprived of his freedom and declared a prisoner of war— that the friendly treatment of me and my staff by the Ranger commander was a moment of great emotional relief. I thank him very dearly for being such a chivalrous comrade. It was comforting how the commander accommodated my wishes."[33]

When Rudder arrived, the midday meal was already prepared for the garrison of Fürst's bunker. As prisoners of war, the Germans would soon be taken away with only what they could carry. They would be fed, but when was uncertain. Fürst asked Rudder if his men could have time to eat. "He gave us one hour. He left me alone for an hour in my room, a gesture of confidence in me that I appreciated. I packed up my things."[34]

At this point in his memoir, Fürst's soldierly pride interfered with his memory. He wrote that Rudder asked him to surrender all German troops in Le Conquet, not just those in the Lochrist and Rospects batteries, and that he refused. In fact, Fürst did agree to surrender all German forces on Le Conquet Peninsula. Lt. Col. Faucher wrote a detailed account that is backed up by the 2nd Ranger Battalion's after action report and individual Ranger recollections. Fürst initially declined to surrender all German forces on the grounds that, as a prisoner himself, he lacked authority to issue orders for additional forces. Then he changed his mind.[35]

While Fürst was undergoing this conversion, he and Rudder talked. Fürst hints at the familiarity that developed between the two men, one triumphant and the other despondent: "While we were sitting around, he asked me for a drink and I gave him everything I had." Rudder gained Fürst's confidence, and he may have intimidated him, which would not have been difficult. Fürst's situation was beyond hope, and he greatly preferred surrendering to the Americans rather than falling into the hands of the FFI or, least of all, the Russians; both routinely killed German prisoners. At that very moment he was wanted by French authorities in Morlaix on the north coast of Brittany for alleged atrocities committed by his men against civilians a few days earlier. French emotions were high, and vigilante justice for Fürst was a possibility. Fürst was on the edge of the great abyss of his life, with only fantasies of his fate. As he tried to decide what to do, there were other influences on his thinking.

Martin Fürst was not an ardent Nazi, and he was sympathetic to Americans. He was familiar with life in America from the experiences of his older brother, Joseph, who had immigrated to the United States in 1922 at the age of twenty-two, had become an American citizen, and lived in Connecticut, where he was an expert toolmaker in the aviation industry. Martin saw Joseph off at the railway station when he left for America and may have considered going with him. Their mother and father had died in 1917, and Germany was in dire economic conditions with limited opportunities for a young man. But Martin remained and joined the army the next year. Meanwhile, Joseph was another American success story, and his love for his adopted country was clear to Martin when Joseph visited Germany in 1938. That visit was an unconcealed display of happiness and affluence, as he brought with him his wife, whom he had met in Brooklyn, and a new American-made car.[36]

Conflicted by such notions, Martin Fürst changed his mind. He agreed to surrender all German forces on Le Conquet in a formal ceremony to be held at his central command post in the village of Saint-Mathieu at the very tip of the peninsula, only a mile away. Faucher told about going there with Rudder: "It was decided that in order to avoid shots being fired on or other incidents along the way to the central command post of the German defense on the Pointe Saint-Mathieu to execute the surrender, a German car and not a US jeep would be driven by a German officer, which car would convey the US and FFI colonels together with their assistants, Major [Summers] of the Jedburgh mission and the interpreter Mélo."[37]

The German car almost drew a Ranger attack. Sgt. William V. "Bill" Klaus was probing for Germans along the same road with a four-man patrol. The five Americans heard the car coming and jumped over a stone fence into a cemetery. As the car came closer, they saw it was a German car painted with camouflage colors and raised their weapons to fire, only to realize that the soldier sitting on the front fender was an American. Klaus told what happened. "We stopped the car and Lt. Col. Rudder [was] in the car. . . . He told me the fort had been captured [and] said, "Have your men jump on here—anywhere. So we jumped on to go with him to accept the surrender of the Germans."[38]

Holding a formal surrender ceremony was an important Rudder accommodation to Fürst's concept of honor and a conspicuous way of conveying to all under Fürst's command that they should abandon the fight. How easy, even tempting, it would have been for Rudder to humiliate Fürst or to heighten his distress, but he treated him decently. And Fürst surrendered, ending the bloodshed on Le Conquet.

"WHERE IS HIS PISTOL?"

For the surrender ceremony, troops of both sides drew up in formation and stood facing each other. Rudder and Fürst faced each other with their backs toward their own men. Rudder probably posted security guards with their weapons at the ready, should Fürst have renegades in his command. Immediately behind Rudder stood an honor guard of the "Fabulous Four," Edlin and the three Rangers of his intrepid patrol: Burmaster, Courtney, and Dreher. On Rudder's left was his battalion staff, including the battalion sergeant major, Len Lomell. Behind this group, standing at parade rest with their weapons, were as many men from the battalion as could be assembled, except for one company left at the Lochrist Battery as a holding force.[39] The Germans' weapons were stacked to the side.

Bill Klaus gave Colonel Fürst the once-over: "He was absolutely immaculate. He looked like something out of Hollywood. He had his best uniform on, all polished up. His facial features reminded me of a famous comedian of that time, Joe E. Brown. He had a huge mouth. He was of average height and good looking. I remember his appearance because he looked so sharp. The rest of us looked like bums."[40]

Fürst called the Germans to attention, and Rudder did likewise for the Americans. Fürst marched forward to present his pistol to Rudder, the symbol of his submission. Then came an awkward moment, comic in retrospect. Fürst reached for his pistol, but it was not in the holster on his belt. He had forgotten that Edlin had removed it from him during the tense confrontation in the fort. Rudder looked back over his shoulder at Edlin: "Where's his pistol?" Edlin handed the pistol to Rudder who handed it to Fürst who put it in his holster and then withdrew and presented it to Rudder.[41]

The ceremony concluded with the dismissal of both formations, thus ending the fighting on Le Conquet, except for a few die-hards. The After Action Report of the 2nd Ranger Battalion for that day, September 9, 1944, noted: "Lt Col Furst, Comdg Officer of all Germans [sic] troops in LeConquet Pinninsula [sic] surrendered to Lt Col Rudder at St. Mathieu at 1330.

Total PWs captured 814. At 1330 hrs. the entire peninsula had been officially surrendered to the Rangers. Enemy casualties were undetermined. Bn suffered no casualties." Isolated pockets of Germans resisted until noon the next day without inflicting casualties on the Rangers. Eventually, the number of German prisoners exceeded 1,400.[42]

When the ceremony ended, the Rangers dashed for German liquor. Edlin heard Rudder call, "Wait a minute. I want to talk to you." He expected Rudder to chew him out for his hazardous gamble to enter the fort. "You're the dumbest. . . . You risked the lives of you and Courtney. You risked your own life." Rudder "went on and on," Edlin said. Finally, when he seemed spent of words, Edlin asked, "'Colonel, What would you have done if you were in my position?' He looked at me with big tears running down his cheeks. 'I hope I'd have had nerve enough to do what you did.' He hit me on the back and walked away from me. That was the greatest medal I ever got in my whole life."[43]

Rudder then gave orders for the battalion to assemble at the Lochrist Battery except for one company to remain at Saint-Mathieu to ensure that the new POWs did not change their minds. Back at the battery, elements of the battalion held a ceremony in honor of Faucher. In his next letter to Chick, Rudder left no doubt that taking Fürst's surrender was an unforgettable moment. "The past 21 days I have had an experience that was more interesting than D-Day. I have been working with the French Forces of the Interior or better known as the French underground. My Bn knocked out the largest guns in the Brest area, and I had the pleasure of personally capturing the commanding officer. The experience is one I shall never forget. We are rather a long way from the main war . . . , but the fighting has been as bitter as any we have had. We are all hoping and praying . . . the war will be over before winter as it will really be tough to sleep in a foxhole in cold rainy weather."[44]

At the end of the war in Europe, Rudder returned home with Fürst's pistol, a snub-nosed double-action 7.65 mm Mauser. After his death, Margaret Rudder offered it to Edlin. Edlin declined, and she gave it to the Ranger Museum in the Norman town of Grandcamp, not far from Pointe du Hoc.

Rudder recommended Edlin for the Medal of Honor and took him to see General Middleton. Confident that Eisenhower would approve his recommendation, Middleton told Edlin, "You are not going back to your unit. You are going home today. We can't take the risk of a Medal of Honor winner being captured." Edlin immediately declined the recommendation in order to remain with the Rangers and accepted the Distinguished Service Cross, the army's second highest award for valor.[45]

Edlin's comrades remembered and told others of his incredible feat that saved the lives of countless Germans, Americans, and French civilians. A few days before his death on April 1, 2005, he received a measure of recompense from the State of Texas. A resolution was introduced in the House of Representatives to award him a Texas Legislative Medal of Honor. I testified for the resolution, which passed unanimously. Governor Rick Perry conveyed the news to Edlin by telephone on his deathbed in Corpus Christi, Texas.

With the campaign for Le Conquet completed, Faucher was awarded the Bronze Star, and Rudder sent him a personal letter—in French with numbered paragraphs in the military style—which Faucher distributed throughout the region:

> 1. During the campaign to liberate Le Conquet, the FFI took part in all the battles. They conducted themselves well under enemy fire, and their discipline was highly appreciated by the American command;
>
> 2. All information given to us by the FFI concerning enemy forces and installations was very accurate and of great value to us. This made possible the quick and definite defeat of the enemy with a minimum of losses;
>
> 3. Lt. Col. Faucher, called "Louis," and his headquarters merit the highest commendation for their organization, command, and spirit of cooperation;
>
> 4. We would like to thank the FFI for the work done which proved in every way the renewal of the martial spirit of France.[46]

In time, the town council of Le Conquet placed a commemorative plaque beside the entrance road to the German fort where Edlin boldly provoked the surrender of the two gun batteries and Rudder persuaded Martin Fürst to order all German forces in the area to lay down their arms. The inscription is a lonely reminder of one day in the history of the ancient land of Le Finistère when bravery and reason prevailed:

> On 9 September 1944
> Col Rudder
> Commander of the 2d Rangers
> and Col. Faucher
> Commander of the FFI
> received on this site
> the command post of the batteries
> of Keringar and Rospects
> the surrender of German Col. Fürst.[47]

POSTSCRIPT TO LE CONQUET CAMPAIGN

Although the Germans were finished on Le Conquet by September 10, in Brest they fought on, besieged, for nine more days. The determined defense seemed without reason to the Americans, but the German commander, General Ramcke, believed that any American troops kept fighting around Brest were that many fewer that could be brought to bear on Germany.

Until the Germans surrendered in Brest on September 19, fighting continued on the opposite side of the Brest harbor from Le Conquet on a rough, jagged cape called the Crozon Peninsula, which reached into the bay like a giant claw. Rudder and the 2nd Ranger Battalion arrived after most of the fighting was over, encountered little resistance, took about sixteen hundred prisoners, and released some four hundred American POWs, including several of their own men. Then came four days of rest. In a letter to Chick, Rudder explained why he had not written for ten days: "When you are a battalion commander in action, you simply do not have the time or opportunity for writing."[48]

The capture of Brest yielded a destroyed city and a completely demolished port that made no contribution to the Allies' supply problems. Of the approximate 50,000 Americans who participated in the siege and liberation of Brest, 9,831 became casualties, including an estimated 2,000 killed. More than 38,000 German prisoners were taken; 20,000 of them were combat troops.[49] Their daring commander had made a reputation in North Africa for raiding behind British lines, which lends credence to General Bradley's decision to force their surrender; they could have caused much trouble in the Allied rear. Virtually every building in the center of the city was damaged beyond repair. Of the 35,000 homes in Brest, 20,000 were destroyed, wholly or partially.

Standing amidst heaps of rubble on September 20, General Middleton returned Brest to Mayor Jules Lullien, and the city was free after 1,553 days of the Nazi goose-stepping.[50] The French tricolor waved over a liberated people whose children could once again begin their school day to the rousing strains of "La Marseillaise," redeemed by American blood and treasure.

CHAPTER 10

BELGIAN INTERLUDE

SEPTEMBER 22–NOVEMBER 5, 1944

While Rudder and the Rangers were absorbed in Brittany, the Allied forces had pursued the Germans in a rapid retreat across France. Paris was relieved of enemy occupation on August 25, and Brussels, 175 miles farther, on September 5. By the time the Germans surrendered in Brest on September 20, the Allies had freed northern France, Belgium, and most of tiny Luxembourg from Nazi rule. The first American patrols had slipped into Germany from Belgium south of Aachen on September 11.[1] Optimism infused the Allies' high command; they believed they could finish the German war before the end of 1944.

The result was different. As Allied supply lines lengthened, German lines shortened. When the enemy reached his homeland, he became more determined and stopped his retreat behind the West Wall, long-prepared defensive positions called the Siegfried Line by the Allies. Shortage of gasoline at the front, for lack of a port on the English Channel closer than Normandy, brought a halt to the Allies' sweep to the east. Rudder's hope in mid-September that "the war will be over before winter" would not be realized.[2] It would go on for nine more months. The biggest battles and hardest fighting of the European war were still ahead.

Rudder's new orders were to take the 2nd Ranger Battalion to Arlon, Belgium's southernmost city, situated on Luxembourg's western border. Before leaving Brittany, he came in contact with Lt. Gen. William H. Simpson, commander of the U.S. Ninth Army. In Brest, Simpson saw a late-model yellow Buick convertible that had been the personal car of the local Gestapo chief and wanted it for his official use. However, Simpson was flying to Belgium, and the question was how to get the car there. Rudder and Harvey Cook decided to drive the Buick to Simpson. On further thought, they decided that having a driver would be even better, and they selected Sgt. Edward Gurney of Cook's intelligence section for their chauffeur. The battalion's administrative journal noted simply that on September 22 at 9:00 AM, "Lt Col Rudder left on a trip."[3]

The battalion's advance party of eighty-three men traveled from Brest to Arlon by truck, followed by the rest of the battalion, more than 350 men, by train. The truck convoy required four days to cross France, 730 miles by their odometers. The trip by train was an unforgettable five days and nights of rough riding in the notorious "forty and eight" freight cars designed for forty men or eight horses—"40 hommes et 8 chevaux" was stenciled on their sides—just as their fathers were hauled across France in them during the First World War. Thirty-five men were assigned to each car with all their equipment, including weapons. The toilet was a hole in the floor or an open door. The best pillow was a helmet, and the worst was the steel baseplate of an 81 mm mortar. So crowded and uncomfortable were the twenty-foot-long, eight-foot-wide cars that some men preferred to ride, and even to sleep, on top. Morris Prince concluded in his account, "Paradoxically, our morale and spirits were never better."[4]

Meanwhile, Rudder and Cook were in no hurry to complete their tour of war-ravaged France, making stops in Chartres, Paris, and Reims. Some men who knew about their trip disapproved, but few knew they were taking the car to Simpson and still fewer that Rudder recruited new Rangers on the way. Stopping over in Paris, he went to the U.S. Army office that administered replacement depots from a hotel at number 9 rue Washington, just off the Champs-Élysées. There he came face-to-face with Nilah Pennington, a former student at Brady High School, now a lieutenant in the Women's Army Corps. Six decades later she had a clear memory of Rudder entering her office in the heart of Paris, near the Arc de Triomphe. "He came in about mid-morning. I have never in my life seen anyone who seemed so happy to see me. A smile spread all across his face. He came right over to my desk and out came all the pictures of his wife and children." She and her supervisor (who she eventually married) provided Rudder with a list of replacement depots and their locations where he could interview prospective Rangers.[5]

Rudder and Cook got to Arlon after the battalion had begun training in a new program organized by Capt. Harold K. "Duke" Slater. Slater, an experienced company commander, was a "soldier's soldier" and widely admired and popular with the Rangers. In consultation with the company commanders, he had developed a two-part program—an advanced level for veterans and a basic course for fifty-seven new men.[6]

Rudder disagreed with the two-part program, preferring to continue with a single program that integrated the new men with the veterans. It was not the first or the last time that Slater and Rudder would disagree, but their disputes were, in Slater's words, usually "one-on-one, private or semi-private." Although they disagreed in this case, Rudder relied on Slater as a leader in combat as well as in recruiting and training. In Slater's view, Rudder was "basically a good person, a good leader and politician, often back at higher headquarters politicking."[7] More than personal pleasure was involved when Rudder went to higher headquarters, usually the division or corps that the battalion was attached to, where his attendance was required at commanders' conferences. And the battalion always needed an advocate at the higher echelons of command.

To Ranger Al Baer, Arlon was "a Ranger's dream. Light filtering through the tall, interlocked fir trees created a cathedral atmosphere." There was "an abundance of beer, a theatre, and many beautiful girls eager to entertain lonely Rangers." Even Rudder relaxed. He told Chick about a Sunday in early October when he "had a good steak dinner at 12:30, Red Cross coffee and donuts at 3 P.M. and a nice ride about the countryside in my private car—a Buick Eight convertible, a snazzy job." Two days later he lost the car when General Simpson came to decorate men for the Brittany campaign and claim his automobile. On the same occasion Rudder awarded the coveted battlefield commission to Ranger Leonard Lomell for outstanding leadership.[8]

In Arlon a Belgian mother and father came to Rudder with a proposal that he could never talk about without visible emotion. He wrote Chick about it that night: "This afternoon a mother and father came to me and asked for their son to come along with us. He was a lad of 18, 6 ft tall and a really fine looking chap. They do not want to wait until the Belgian army is formed to have a go at the Boche." Rudder denied the offer and told the parents that the best thing they could do for their son was to give him a good education.[9]

Two events on October 21 foretold the future of Rudder and his battalion for the next six weeks. The first was the enemy's surrender of Aachen, Germany's historic and westernmost city, contiguous with the borders of Belgium and Holland. Aachen was important to the German psyche as the city of Charlemagne, the founder of the Holy Roman Empire and the undisputed ruler of Europe about the year 800. With Aachen in Allied hands, Cologne was only fifty miles away. As an industrial powerhouse strategically located on the Rhine, Cologne was a tempting objective for Allied commanders, who believed mistakenly that pushing on into Germany would be about the same as their pell-mell pursuit of the German army across France. Few, if anyone, on the Allied side realized the German war machine was in its strongest condition since Normandy.

The false optimism was based partly on inaccurate information about how many Germans had escaped from the Falaise Pocket. No one knew for certain, but army intelligence officers estimated the total at only 20,000 to 40,000 men. The actual number who got across the Seine River was about

240,000 plus twenty-eight thousand vehicles and several hundred tanks. (Some who crossed the Seine may not have been in the pocket.) A British study in the spring of 1945 of their crossing points on the Seine determined the larger figures, but forty years would pass before a researcher uncovered the study in British archives. Furthermore, of the estimated twenty-three German generals in the Falaise Pocket, only three were captured, leaving the enemy's command structure mostly intact and more experienced than ever to carry on the struggle.[10]

Neither did the Allied high command know that in the fall of 1944 German war production was reaching its peak. This phenomenal industrial output, combined with the astonishing escape from Normandy, meant that new tanks and weapons would replace those lost in the long retreat across France. Despite the loss of nearly four million men in the war, Germany still had more than ten million under arms. Failure to destroy the German army west of the Seine condemned the Allies to face a resurgent foe in Holland in September, in Aachen and the Huertgen Forest in October and November, and in the Ardennes in December and January.

The second event of October 21 that affected Rudder's Rangers was an order from Eisenhower for the First U.S. Army under Lt. Gen. Courtney H. Hodges to attack eastward from Aachen to the city of Duren, continue on, and possibly seize a bridgehead across the Rhine. For the Allied armies poised on Germany's frontier, Eisenhower would permit no Valley Forge; they would not move into winter quarters. He believed that interrupting the offensive effort would allow the Germans to strengthen their defenses and make their final defeat more difficult in the spring of 1945. The new attack plan included clearing the enemy from an area southeast of Aachen that the Americans called the Huertgen Forest.[11]

During its inexorable move toward Germany, the battalion was quartered for a few days in the Belgian town of Eupen. Here, Rudder saw for the first time people living in close proximity who did not have a common language. "There are people who can speak and understand only German or French," he wrote Chick. And he speculated on language barriers as a cause for their historic misunderstandings. "It is easy for these people to distrust each other when they do not understand each other."[12]

In Eupen, the aftermath of a fight between two American officers illustrates one of Rudder's qualities that inspired his men's loyalty: his willingness to take up for them. The impetuous Bob Edlin and a less-experienced fellow lieutenant, identified only as Ed, went to the officers' club one evening and became fascinated by an American nurse, who was dancing with a lieutenant colonel. Edlin and his friend had been in combat for four months without contact with American women, and Edlin encouraged Ed to cut in. "It's the normal thing to do," he explained. But the colonel declined, and Ed came back, saying, "That joker wouldn't let me dance with her."

For Edlin, the man who had held a live hand grenade against the belly of Colonel Fürst in his Brittany bunker, a stubborn lieutenant colonel on the dance floor was a trivial problem. Thinking about the incident late in his life, Edlin remembered, "By that time, we'd had a couple of poppers." He told Ed, "I'm going to talk to that guy and see if I can't convince him to be a little more courteous to combat people like us." The colonel also refused Edlin and challenged him to settle their dispute: "Why don't you and I step outside?" Edlin was pleased with the opportunity to "knock the crap out of an arrogant son-of-a-bitch" who outranked him. But while he was removing his coat with his arms bound in the sleeves, the colonel hit him with a flashlight, witnesses said. In Edlin's account, "That cutie sucker-punched me. . . . He whopped me upside the mouth and knocked me back across a jeep. I was about half out."[13]

Seven stitches were required to close his upper lip. When Edlin returned to the battalion's bivouac area, word got to Rudder about the incident. Rudder then took Edlin and several others to the officers' club, found the offending colonel, and, in Edlin's words, "the manure hit the oscillator. The colonel hit the colonel and away we went."[14] No further details were passed down about the exchange of blows, but Edlin felt fully avenged.

Called to a commanders' conference on November 1, Rudder was told about Eisenhower's orders for the attack toward the Rhine and instructed to move the battalion up to the German border on the edge of the Huertgen Forest. It was a clear indication that the battalion would soon be fighting in Germany. That night he soft-pedaled the news to Chick: "Don't worry if you don't hear from me very often," followed by, "the news is rather scarce from here."[15]

A few days after moving and setting up tents near the village of Neudorf, Rudder was astonished by a visit from the supreme allied commander. Eisenhower was visiting Allied units near the front lines to assess the situation for himself and boost the morale of men who would bear the hardships of the winter offensive. He dropped in on Rudder, accompanied by Bradley, Twelfth Army Group commander, and Gerow, V Corps commander.[16]

A visit by such luminaries to a small battalion was an extraordinary event that Rudder appreciated. He told Chick about it without revealing anyone's identity. "I have had three very distinguished visitors. One was the most distinguished we could have had. It was very kind of them to visit us—particularly in a place as muddy and cold as this is. Be sure and remind me of this date when I return and I will tell you all about it."[17]

Two days before visiting the Rangers, Eisenhower had directed American commanders to assure that "officers place the care and welfare of their men above their own comfort and convenience." As Ike mingled with roughly 150 men of Rudder's battalion—"talking, laughing and joking"—they noticed that he was wearing boot packs, insulated boots that were better footwear for the snow and mud than they had. When Ike asked, "Is there anything that you men need?" he got an unexpected response from a young man in the ranks. "How come you're wearing a boot pack to keep your feet warm and dry and you don't get out in the rain and we don't have any. Everyone back at headquarters has got them." Eisenhower quickly replied, "That will be taken care of." "God bless his soul," one man said, "a few days later the entire battalion got boot packs and wristwatches."[18]

Ike's encounter with the Rangers was still fresh in his mind when he wrote to his wife, Mamie, about his tour of the front and the unusually cold weather. "I'm comfortable enough because I can keep dry and wear enough clothes. . . . Anyone in this war, that has the slightest temptation to bemoan his lot or feel sorry for himself should visit the front line soldier!"[19]

From Rudder's command post Eisenhower went further east, entered Germany for the first time during the war at the village of Roentgen, and visited Gen. Norman Cota in his 28th Division headquarters. The next destination for Rudder and the 2nd Ranger Battalion was the Huertgen Forest, where they would fight under General Cota.

CHAPTER 11

HUERTGEN FOREST
NOVEMBER 5–DECEMBER 7, 1944

On November 1, 1944, Rudder was told to move the 2nd Ranger Battalion immediately up to the Belgian frontier with Germany and keep it in a state of readiness to enter combat on short notice. The five-mile move was a clear signal that the Rangers' six-week recess from combat would soon end. His men were ready and rested. They had new clothing. Their weapons were cleaned and oiled. They trained every day with emphasis on physical conditioning, and their mood was buoyant.

Rudder got these new instructions in a briefing at U.S. Army V Corps headquarters in Eupen, Belgium. As usual, Capt. Harvey Cook accompanied him because Rudder relied on Cook in planning and implementing orders for the six rifle companies of the battalion. The briefing concerned an American attack that would start the next day to force the enemy from Schmidt, a ridge-top farming community in Germany about twenty miles southeast of Aachen.[1] After the Americans had taken Aachen on October 21, no one, not even the German generals, was surprised they would continue to push into Germany. However, the German generals were flabbergasted that Americans would attack through the rugged terrain and dense woods of the Huertgen Forest, where they could not capitalize on their superior mobility with tanks and self-propelled artillery or bring to bear their vastly overwhelming tactical air support. It was an error that German strategists would never understand, although they would soon see that its purpose was to protect the main American offensive from Aachen eastward to the city of Duren on the Roer River. Actually, the American strategists hoped to go thirty miles further and reach the Rhine south of Cologne. The attack through the Huertgen Forest was intended to prevent a German counterattack into the right flank of their drive toward the Rhine.

The attack on Schmidt, however, was in German minds a greater threat than the Americans realized, and the Germans' fierce resistance took them aback. The Americans had not analyzed their strategy from the German perspective, and this flaw contributed to making the Battle of the Huertgen Forest one of the most difficult and futile of the European war.

Before it was over, more than 120,000 Americans, plus more thousands of replacements, would fight in the Huertgen Forest. Of these, at least 24,000 would be killed, wounded, captured, or declared missing. In the cold, wet, and depressing woodland, another 9,000 succumbed to foot infections, respiratory sickness, and psychological disorders. The casualty rate exceeded 25 percent in a war where 10 percent was considered high. German losses were at least as great but can only be estimated, because records were lost.[2] American strategists did not fully discern the factors that made the fighting in the Huertgen Forest extraordinarily difficult and futile, namely the complicated and restrictive topography, the innumerable small tactical moves dictated by higher headquarters, and the piecemeal commitment of assets to the battle.

Rudder's briefing at V Corps headquarters was a prelude to his most frustrating period of the war. In the subsequent five weeks he had the least flexibility ever in commanding his battalion, which absorbed heavy casualties and was usually kept in fixed positions that were exactly contrary to the Rangers' training and purpose. Rudder's staff believed he protested the assignment of the battalion to static defenses. Eventually his superiors tasked the Rangers with an objective more fitting to their talents: an assault to gain control of an important enemy stronghold called Hill 400 that overlooked much of the battlefield. But first the Rangers would endure other hardships in the depressing Huertgen Forest.

As Cook and Rudder looked on, the briefing officer outlined the forest on a map as an irregular area between Aachen and Schmidt that was extensively eroded by gorges and ravines with steep slopes. The Huertgen Forest was part of a much larger woodland of dense fir trees, typically 75 to 150 feet high with lateral branches to near ground level, that extended into Belgium. The forest was an evergreen wildwood, too thick to walk through without stooping, meandering, or crawling. On ridges between the gorges and ravines, villages had developed over hundreds of years with nearby clearings for agriculture. Only a few hard-surfaced roads plus a multitude of primitive trails and firebreaks crisscrossed the forest.

The deepest and widest gorge was formed by the Roer River, which defined the southern and eastern boundaries of the forest as the U.S. Army conceived it. Seven dams spanned the river, holding back substantial bodies of water. Schmidt, the objective of the attack, sprawled across a high ridge above the largest reservoir on the river. Just downstream from Schmidt, the Roer emerged from the gorge, bent to the left, and flowed northward on the Cologne plain through Duren, directly across the path of the planned American offensive from Aachen to the Rhine. By controlling the floodgates on the

Roer dams, the Germans could create impassable conditions for Americans attacking toward Cologne and isolate those who crossed the river. Inexplicably, however, the American high command did not appreciate the significance of the Roer and its dams as obstacles, at least not at the beginning of their effort to reach the Rhine by the end of 1944.

"A DARK AND BLOODY GROUND"

If the Americans underestimated the Roer as an impediment, they were completely in the dark about another reason the Germans would fight desperately to keep them from occupying Schmidt. The German high command was determined to safeguard Hitler's plan for their great counterattack in the Ardennes in mid-December that would precipitate the Battle of the Bulge. The staging ground for the German attack was only a few miles south of the Roer. If the Americans took possession of Schmidt, they might discover German preparations for the attack. With the enemy determined not to give way and the Americans resolved to take the same area, the Huertgen Forest became, as it was aptly described, "a dark and bloody ground."[3]

The main road through the Huertgen Forest ran northeast from Monschau in the south for twenty-two miles to Duren, where it crossed the Roer. Like knots in a string, as Charles MacDonald saw them, villages of sturdy stone houses were strung along the Monschau–Duren road. Most of upper half of the road was in German hands; the Americans held the lower half. The briefing officer drew Rudder's attention to the village of Germeter, about midway between Monschau and Duren, where the road was virtually the front line, with Germans on one side and Americans on the other. There the battle was, in the words of the American general James M. Gavin, "the most primitive kind of fighting, man against man at grenade distance."[4] And Germeter is exactly where the 2nd Ranger Battalion would be inserted in the battle for the first time.

The briefing officer stressed three points: First, the effort to clear the Huertgen Forest of Germans would begin the next day with an attack across the Monschau–Duren road by the U.S. 28th Infantry Division, commanded by Maj. Gen. Norman D. Cota, Rudder's acquaintance from invasion planning in England. Two prongs of the attack would start from Germeter. One would swerve to the left up the Duren road toward the next village, Huertgen. The other would smash straight across the road at Germeter through the village of Vossenack, which extended a mile along a ridge of the same name. Like a dagger, a spur from the Vossenack Ridge pointed toward Schmidt, another two miles from the nose of the ridge. At the base of the ridge a stream flowed

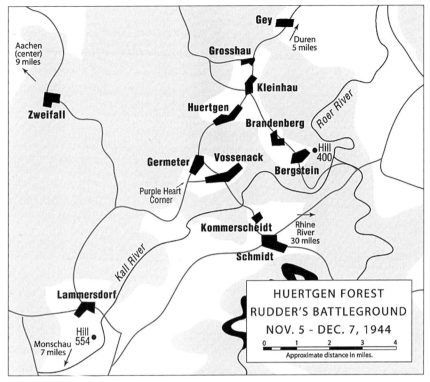

Map 11-1. *The portion of the Huertgen Forest that was Rudder's battleground for one month of unceasing peril in the fall of 1944. (Graphics by David Zepeda, copyright Thomas M. Hatfield. Map reference: Charles B. MacDonald,* The Battle of the Huertgen Forest, *72–73.)*

through a narrow, treacherous ravine called the Kall River gorge, words that would later strike terror in the memories of men who fought there, friend and foe alike. At the end of the battle, numerous dead—both German and American—were left along the gorge to be swallowed up by the forest, and sixty-five years later their remains were still occasionally unearthed.

Three battalions of 28th Division riflemen, roughly 1,750 men, were to knife their way from Germeter along the Vossenack Ridge, cross the Kall River gorge, continue through a hamlet called Kommerscheidt, and finally occupy Schmidt, whose inhabitants—reduced by war to a thousand or so women, children, and old men—had fled a few weeks earlier as sounds of heavy artillery firing rumbled across the countryside during the American conquest of Aachen.[5] The attack on Schmidt was an almost impossible order and not yet fully appreciated by American strategists.

The second point of the briefing was that the 2nd Ranger Battalion was ordered to move from permanent housing to tents about twenty miles from

Rudder and Harvey Cook traveled this or a similar road from Belgium when they entered the Huertgen Forest on Nov. 5, 1944. (U.S. National Archives)

the 28th Infantry Division's jump-off position; the third was that the battalion should be ready to move up on short notice if the 28th Division's attack on Schmidt faltered. That night Earl forewarned Chick in language that belied the danger and avoided the censor: "Don't worry if you do not hear from me very often for the next few days."[6]

Four days after the briefing, Rudder and Cook went forward into "Naziland" (Rudder's term) to reconnoiter the area where they anticipated taking the battalion. Both men would survive the war because they were careful as well as lucky, and they did not treat their "recce" into Germany as a walk in the park. Although they planned to stay in territory controlled by the Americans, there was always the danger of road hazards and jeep accidents, which were frequent, plus the possibility of mines and mistaken friendly fire. Most of the area was within range of German artillery, and enemy patrols were known to penetrate the area by coming undetected up ravines from the Kall River gorge. As a reminder of the danger, the army had erected a sign half the size of a billboard beside the road where they crossed into Germany from Belgium.

YOU ARE ENTERING

GERMANY

AN ENEMY COUNTRY

KEEP ON THE ALERT[7]

Near the sign they saw rows of dragon's teeth, the square-pyramidal blocks of concrete reinforced with steel that the Germans had built years before to obstruct and channel the movement of enemy tanks encroaching on their territory.

The purpose of their reconnaissance was to obtain information about the route and road conditions, obstacles (natural and manmade), availability of protection from enemy fire and concealment from enemy view, and the logistical situation: transportation, medical evacuation, and resupply of food, ammunition, and equipment. From recent reports of enemy activity they learned they could not go to Germeter by the direct route on the Duren–Monschau road, because they could be seen and might draw enemy artillery fire. So they traveled through the woods on firebreaks and trails, contending with mud, creeks, and gullies. Even off the main road they were vulnerable to German artillery, whose gunners searched for targets without seeing them—called interdictory fire by the military—by randomly firing rounds into the thick treetops, where the shells exploded, scattering steel fragments and wooden splinters across the forest floor. Tree bursts were an unavoidable hazard, prompting Ernest Hemingway, then a war correspondent, to describe the Huertgen Forest as a "Passchendaele with tree bursts," in reference to a British offensive during World War I that was also fought in similar misery of relentless mud and in which heavy casualties were suffered with small gains and indecisive results.

Rudder and Cook studied the battle area from a high point southeast of the village of Lammersdorf that the locals called Pausterbach Hill, labeled Hill 554 by the army. They could not see the Vossenack Ridge, where fighting was underway, but they saw enough of the area to appreciate the harshness of the terrain and the thickness of the forest. Rudder decided to make Hill 554 an observation post from which to orient his officers and NCOs to the situation they would encounter if they were called to action in Vossenack and Germeter. His decision was prescient, because that is where they found themselves only a few days later. "I have made several trips into Germany," he confided to Chick, "and the few civilians that are left won't look at you. That's the way we want it—as a matter of fact, we don't care if there are any left, after all the trouble they have caused."[8]

The attack of the three battalions of the 112th Infantry Regiment of the 28th Division made good progress at first. One battalion forced the enemy from Germeter and Vossenack, and the other two crossed the Kall River, with one holding around Kommerscheidt, the hamlet between the Kall and Schmidt, while the remaining battalion actually got into Schmidt, despite the fact that there was not a single road or trail across the jagged landscape. The rough Kall Gorge and the adjoining dense timber made the area almost impenetrable. Resupply or evacuation, one of which would be necessary, was extremely difficult. Nonetheless, for the moment it appeared the 28th Division had accomplished its mission.[9]

The next morning, however, the enemy struck back hard, driving the Americans from Schmidt and Kommerscheidt, and they did not stop there. They crossed the Kall and attacked the Americans along the Vossenack Ridge. Some defenders, newly arrived from the States, panicked and drifted away. Their company commander, also inexperienced and seeing his force diminished, ordered a withdrawal from Vossenack to Germeter on the main road between Monschau and Duren. But once the retreat began, disorder set in. The sight of men running away was contagious for other Americans, who ran and could not be stopped. The only available G.I.s to fill the void were engineers doing roadwork deep in the mud and wearing hip boots. Having first been trained as infantrymen, they dropped their picks and shovels, picked up rifles and grenades, and drove the Germans from the Vossenack Ridge almost to the Kall. They were lucky, because the enemy suffered a communications breakdown and failed to follow up on their short-lived success, and the Americans avoided a rout. But the situation was dire, and the Rangers were put on two-hour alert as a relief force in case the defense of the Vossenack Ridge collapsed.[10]

The fierce German attack should have been a tip-off about the enemy's determination to hold the Huertgen Forest, but it was not. The American strategists still failed to see that the Roer and the city of Duren downstream were essential to the defense of the Rhineland, in the valley of Europe's greatest river. After the war, the German general Rudolf von Gersdorff eloquently clarified the motive for their fierce resistance: "In view of our Ardennes offensive, which was already planned, the American intention to capture the commanding heights of Bergstein and Schmidt via Vossenack in order to cross [the Roer] and capture the dams had to be prevented at all costs."[11]

The American presence on the Vossenack Ridge was an intolerable projection toward Schmidt for the Germans, but they were unable to push it back to the Monschau–Duren road. At the same time, the Americans were stymied on the Vossenack Ridge, unable to advance across the Kall River gorge to take and hold Schmidt, the original objective of their attack. Frustrated, the opposing commanders decided, at almost the same time and unbeknown to each other, to change their strategy.

On November 8 the Americans decided temporarily to give up reaching Schmidt but to hold the Vossenack Ridge down to the Kall at the bottom of the ridge. They would settle for a right flank secure on the Kall River rather than the Roer.[12]

On November 9 the German commander decided to stop his ground attacks across the Kall on the Vossenack Ridge and to concentrate on attacking down the road from Duren through the villages of Huertgen and Germeter, with the aim of cutting off the Vossenack salient at its base on the road. Meanwhile, the Germans would continue shelling the whole area, but their ground attack would be down the main road from the north. This decision by the enemy commander determined that Rudder's war in the Huertgen Forest would be in the villages along the road and in the nearby woods.

On the morning of November 13 the American command concluded that the 28th Division's battered 112th Regiment along the Vossenack Ridge should be withdrawn. Of the regiment's some 3,000 men, it had taken 2,093 casualties since the attack began on November 2.[13] The approximately 400 men of the 2nd Ranger Battalion would take their positions, but solely as a defensive force and with a reduced area of responsibility.

GERMETER AND VOSSENACK

On the morning of November 14, in another briefing at V Corps headquarters, Rudder was told the Rangers were needed immediately in Germeter and Vossenack. From corps headquarters in Eupen, he called his battalion headquarters with instructions to prepare for the move "as quickly as possible." He dispatched an advance party to 28th Division headquarters to coordinate the transition and to get up-to-date information on the situation. Capt. James W. Eikner was in the advance party and remembered Rudder's reaction when he returned and made his report. Eikner confirmed that the battalion's mission was strictly defensive, to hold the ground against enemy attacks. "When I informed him that they were sending us up to relieve one of their battle-worn battalions, he was flabbergasted that they would put a highly trained unit such as the Rangers to be wasted away in an eroding defensive position." Eikner had little else to report: "We couldn't get anyone [at 28th Division headquarters] to give us accurate data on the enemy's positions, the minefields, theirs or ours."[14]

All the while, the Germans continued to batter Vossenack and Germeter with their artillery fire. From Schmidt and Hill 400 near Bergstein, enemy observers could see movements in the villages and along roads. Their artillery was presighted on road junctions, buildings in the villages, and likely assembly points in the forest. There was no real defense except a strong roof overhead. Men subjected to such gunnery were often overwhelmed by a sense of helplessness and fear.

Twenty-three of the ubiquitous deuce-and-half trucks hauled the men of the 2nd Ranger Battalion toward Germeter. Precluded from traveling on the main road by the threat of German artillery, the trucks went through the forest on firebreaks and primitive roads and dropped off the Rangers five miles from their destination, which was the three-way intersection where the minor road from the Vossenack Ridge came into the Monschau–Duren road at Germeter. From the drop-off point the Rangers walked the rest of the way, carrying everything through mud and snow—all the weapons and equipment as well as ammunition, food, and supplies that they would need for twenty-four hours. They were on the same latitude as Nova Scotia in mid-November, and the sun was already receding behind the trees.

The forced march though the forest was more grueling than any training exercise. "Snow had begun to fall," Morris Prince remembered, "while the frost and cold made us miserable. We were bitching and cursing, angry at the enemy for causing us all these agonies. Still we had no idea what miseries lay just ahead." On the roadsides and on trails in the woods the Rangers were amazed to see discarded U.S. Army equipment, clothing, and weapons thrown away by their predecessors in the flight from the Vossenack Ridge a few days before. The fire trails were deep in "pea soup mud," with rifles, backpacks, and bedrolls strewn about. Gruesome lumps in the snow and oozing mud appeared to be human bodies. Here and there lay a "rent field jacket or a muddy overcoat with an ugly clotted dark stain on it. One man kicked a bloody shoe, then shuddered to see that the shoe still had a foot in it." The sight of dead animals evoked Al Baer's reflection that, "If living things must die, it is only proper it should be humans who brought this war into being. But not their horses, nor these dogs, nor these cattle . . . it isn't their fault."[15]

Bob Edlin said the march through the forest was "almost more than we could overcome," loaded as they were and wearing heavy winter clothing. "We were following a fire trail. Snow was coming down and it was getting dark. Artillery fire was breaking on the ridgeline. Nothing could move." "The muddy and sloppy roads made each step one of torture. Slime and filth covered our shoes. . . . The hilly roads that twisted through the forest were a handicap that the stoutest Rangers could hardly overcome."[16]

The sun was already below the horizon at five o'clock when they slogged up to the crest of the final ridge to the T junction where the branch road from the Vossenack Ridge intersected the Monschau–Duren road. They would learn that the junction was a well-defined target to the Germans, who could place accurate fire on it, day or night. Although the battalion took no casualties this first time they passed the intersection, it soon earned the nickname Purple Heart Corner.[17] Rudder and his staff paused to confer with officers of the unit they were relieving: the 2nd Battalion, 112th Infantry Regiment, 28th Infantry Division. In the dim light Rudder must have peered down the side road into Vossenack, just two long, parallel rows of gray stone houses in ruins covered with new-fallen snow. To his immediate left was Germeter, another linear village up the main road toward Duren. Expecting German ground attacks on Vossenack from Schmidt to continue, he sent more than half of the battalion—three companies and part of a fourth—to positions along the spine of the ridge all the way to the cleared area where the road tapered into a winding trail down to the Kall Gorge, where men had first broken and run a few days before.

Passing the Vossenack church they saw a dead American soldier still gripping the steering wheel of a jeep, with his head reared back as though he had seen the shell coming that had killed him. His hands and face had turned a bluish black metallic tone, and his teeth seemed very white behind lips stretched in a wry grin. The headless corpse of a German soldier lay beside the cellar door where Al Baer's squad took cover; they removed it only when they were forewarned of an inspection by Rudder.[18]

After dispatching the remainder of the battalion more than a mile up the Duren road toward the village of Huertgen, Rudder went about five hundred yards in the same direction into Germeter and took for his forward command post the basement of the two-story family home of Josef Wolter, a forester who had fled with his wife and three daughters, as had nearly all German civilians. It was a solidly built house; although the upper portion was damaged, the ground floor was a thick slab of concrete that covered the basement. Only a few days before, an American officer, Lt. Col. Theodore S. Hatzfeld, had sat in this same location with his head in his hands as German shells fell continuously along the road, shattering the nerves of some men under his command, who refused to eat and cried like children, unashamed.[19]

The exterior entrance to the basement was at the back of the house on the north side, an important advantage because most German artillery came from the south in the direction of Schmidt. Near the entrance, a trail led into the forest. Men came and went at all hours from the limited space of the Wolter basement. Normally, it housed two or three clerks of the message center; Dr. Block's aid station; Harvey Cook and men of his two sections, operations and intelligence; and any or all of the six company commanders who came to confer with Rudder. Two rows of double bunks along the walls "were always occupied." Charcoal was burned for heat in order to avoid emitting smoke that could be seen by the Germans. Small gasoline burners were used to make coffee and warm their rations.[20]

In the crowded environment of the command post, men treated each other as equals distinguished more by function than by rank. Nearly everyone smoked, and the tobacco fumes were so thick that they would leave a yellow tinge on the walls. The basement dwellers knew each other so well they could anticipate each other's coughs.

In 1974, Barbara and Rainer Gübbels, husband and wife, acquired the Wolter homestead to establish their hotel, Zum Alten Forsthaus, "the old forest house." In the basement they found discarded U.S. Army equipment, blankets, and clothing still permeated with the stench of tobacco. The men in Rudder's command post never knew that Josef Wolter had built a false wall across the basement that constricted their space. Concealed behind lay the silverware and precious possessions of the Wolter family and their friends, protected even from the tobacco smoke that stained the interior of the command post. The Gübbelses converted the basement into a wine cellar for their hotel.

At five-thirty on the afternoon of November 14, the 2nd Ranger Battalion officially assumed the defense of both Germeter and Vossenack. The closest enemy to the command post was on a roadblock a mile up the Duren road. Rudder permitted his men to take shelter in houses but gave orders to dig trenches and fighting holes outside as refuges from artillery bombardments and to form a continuous line of firing positions to repel the anticipated ground attack, unaware that the Germans had decided to stop their ground attacks on Vossenack.

At two o'clock the next morning he distributed the plan to his company commanders, instructing them to regroup and counterattack before the enemy could consolidate his gains. At eleven o'clock, as enemy artillery and mortar rounds fell in the neighborhood, he convened a meeting with two officers from adjacent units to coordinate their defenses. In his vest-pocket notebook he wrote the major points of their discussion:"Patrol every 2 hrs to 12 Inf" referred to patrolling along the boundary with the 12th Infantry Regiment of the 4th Infantry Division in the woods to the left of the road toward Duren.

"TD's at road junction to south" meant to locate tank destroyers at Purple Heart Corner.[21]

"Every man on position at night—1/3 in position during day."

"Keep vehicle traffic down on the roads." Reducing the traffic would moderate the muddy conditions and attract less attention from Jerry's artillery.

"Dry pair of sox each night" was a preventive measure for trench foot. The constant cold rain and mist left no chance for feet to dry out; only a change of clothing would do.

"Supplies at night" meant that supplies would be brought in under cover of darkness to avoid attracting German artillery fire. Some supplies were brought by Weasels, boxlike tracked vehicles designed specifically to carry cargo in snow and mud.[22]

One-half mile down the trail into the forest from the forward command post in the Wolter basement, Eikner—now headquarters commandant—set up the rear command post, essentially a point to receive and distribute everything required by the battalion both to kill Germans and attend to personal needs. Merely watering the men in a battalion was a formidable task, not to mention feeding them and funneling forward ammunition and weapons. Certain members of the battalion, such as Capt. Frank Kennard, Rudder's assistant for personnel; company clerks; and Capt. George Williams, the supply officer, and his team for picking up and delivering goods to units, had duties in the rear command post. Still others were mechanics; communications technicians; cooks; newly arrived replacements; the armorer, who maintained weapons; and men rotated from the front for rest.

Rudder could have exercised his command from the rear command post, but Eikner never once saw him there. "He was always strictly involved at the forward CP."[23] As at Pointe du Hoc and in Brittany, he stayed in a forward position where he had superior information about the changing situation on the battlefield and could make timely decisions for the infantrymen who were in closest contact with the enemy. For them, merely the idea of the "rear" suggested a safe place, comfortable and restful, with hot meals. That is why Rudder would not be seen there and why many men would have followed him anywhere.

In disposing the battalion to defend Germeter and Vossenack, Rudder needed to know the strength of German forces on the other side of the Kall, especially in Schmidt. Were they likely to attack? What was their capability in infantry, tanks, and artillery? Who could find out for him? He sent for Edlin. Edlin did not see Rudder regularly and was surprised by his appearance: "He looked like a tired, worn-out old man. He was 34 years old and I had never seen him this way." Rudder explained that he needed to "know if there is going to be a counterattack from Schmidt. We need to know if there are enemy infantry in Schmidt."[24]

Rudder did not have to tell Edlin to take a patrol to Schmidt. Their understanding was implicit, and each would do what had to be done regardless of the personal consequences. Rudder may have seen something of himself in Edlin, with whom his bond was more fatherly than brotherly. Rudder described the situation, stated what he needed to know, and Edlin assumed the task. Men who knew Edlin only from his daring exploits may have thought he was a war lover, but he was fundamentally a comrade lover. He was combative and, no doubt, exhilarated by danger, but his main motivation was the well-being of his comrades and desire for their respect. Gerry Heaney, also a lieutenant, who knew him, spoke of Edlin sixty-four years later as a federal judge in Duluth, Minnesota: "He had a high sense of duty, and he wanted to be in the forefront with the men. He did not seek glory, but the respect of others was essential to his self-respect."[25]

To accompany him on the patrol to Schmidt, Edlin selected Courtney, Dreher, and Burmaster—the same Fabulous Four who had brazenly precipitated the surrender of the Lochrist Battery in Brittany. Now they would make the risky reconnaissance of Schmidt. Their route began along the road that ran the length of the Vossenack Ridge between long lines of war-torn houses and shops. Heaney watched them leave as fellow Rangers recognized the peril of their assignment and bantered with them as they passed by. "Don't get too close to Fritz," and "Get a Heinie for me," they called out. At the bottom of the ridge the patrol crossed the Kall River gorge and made their way cautiously up the long slope toward Schmidt. "We started out across that frozen wasteland that ran down through the valley," Edlin remembered. "We were carrying Tommy guns and fighting knives. We didn't have helmets. We were not there to get in a fight but to get information. Not only was it physically trying but mentally trying. We expected gunfire at any time."[26]

Edlin believed the entire area was mined and stayed on established paths. "I told Courtney and Dreher, instead of fanning out in a diamond patrol as we usually did, I would go out in front about 75 or 100 yards and they were to come behind me. Burmaster was another 50 yards back as the getaway man. We rotated the point man as much as possible." They went through Kommerscheidt and "up the hillside to Schmidt without seeing a German. Everything was quiet. We looked down the streets . . . and found it deserted. We could stand on the open hill at Schmidt and look down at Germeter and Vossenack and see a flea move during the daytime."

Then Edlin had a premonition that he could enter the town and return. "Hold here," he instructed the others. "If you hear any gunfire, get back to the battalion and tell them that there were no troops until we hit the first building." Leaving them, he slipped along the streets of Schmidt. "I was sneaking around buildings. Absolutely nothing. There should have been some self-propelled weapons in sight, some activity somewhere. Even though it looked like a wide open town, it smelled like a trap." The silence was spooky. Finally he decided, "I've had enough." He returned to his companions waiting at the edge of Schmidt. "Let's get back to the battalion as quick as we can."[27]

When the Fabulous Four got back, they had been gone twelve hours. Edlin's report that he had not seen any Germans drew the obvious question from Rudder: "Why?"

"I think it's a trap," Edlin replied, meaning a trick to lure the Americans into an ambush, although the actual reason was to tempt the Americans to attack Schmidt, weakening their defense along the road from Duren, where the Germans intended to attack. Since Rudder's orders were to defend rather than attack, the Rangers continued to hold their positions in Germeter and Vossenack.

For the next week the battalion was shelled regularly, at times incessantly, and took heavy casualties that reduced some companies to no more than half strength, but they were not attacked by enemy ground troops. "Moderate to intense artillery and mortar fire fell in Bn area through out day" was a regular entry in the battalion's diary.[28]

THE DEEP FOREST

At ten minutes past noon on November 19, Rudder got orders for the Ranger battalion to pull back immediately a mile southwest of Germeter and Vossenack into the deep forest, where it would be on call as a mobile reserve. Without casualties they moved into the forest that afternoon, where their only protection from enemy artillery was the earth. Most men worked in groups of three or four, digging one deep hole and roofing it with logs and shelter halves. The roads were "sluggish streams of liquid mud, churned by endless vehicle activity. Shelling from mortars and artillery was almost constant."[29]

After four days in these conditions, Rudder wrote on Thanksgiving Day with unusual vehemence about the enemy: "Every day is a day of thanksgiving to those of us that are still able to fight the enemy that has taken us from home and our loved ones. I am having a hard time writing this letter here in the middle of battle. You will have to pardon the dirt on the paper but I am not writing under the most sanitary conditions."[30]

They could not stay in dugouts all the time, and, if caught in the open, they needed new tricks to defend against the tree bursts. In their previous experience, incoming shells hit the ground and exploded upward, and the best way to avoid injury was to fall flat on the ground or jump into a hole. But in the dense forest, where the shells exploded in the treetops and sprayed their fragments below, the best protection was to stand erect against a tree trunk wearing a steel helmet and exposing the smallest possible body surface above. If a man was in a hole, he wanted it covered with logs. The Luftwaffe was more active than ever, too, once strafing a column of Rangers dashing to the trucks and another time through the battalion bivouac area.[31] An eerie distraction, German pilotless subsonic V-1s—called "buzz bombs" or "doodlebugs"—flew over day and night at about two thousand feet on flight paths to Liege and Antwerp.

Rudder had both a personal dugout and a tiny building above ground, perhaps a hunter's shelter. He described his dugout as an "underground air shelter" and reassured Chick, "We are fairly safe so long as we are inside." His above-ground shelter was furnished with a small kerosene stove, table, couple of chairs, and double bunk bed. When Edlin went to see him, he was huddled by the stove, and Edlin was impressed again that he "looked like a tired, worn-out old man." A few days later he improved his dwelling enough to call it a "cabin in the pines made of logs cut and stacked with my own hands. It is not only good protection from the weather but turns artillery shell fragments excellently."[32]

Since the battalion was a mobile reserve, Rudder placed a time limit of thirty minutes for all men to reach their trucks, fully equipped to fight, from dispersed locations usually several hundred yards away. He made this exercise a regular training routine. Because of the tree bursts, men assembled only in small numbers. Periodically Harvey Cook presented an overview of the war to small groups of a dozen or so. During one presentation, a shell burst directly overhead, killing two men and wounding nine. Cook was not wounded, and neither was Gerry Heaney, who was blown against a tree. Dr. Block confided in his diary that he got "a kick in going thru a mortar barrage" and went "out in a litter jeep to evacuate men" until Rudder told him to quit, saying, "You might get hit!"[33]

About five o'clock on the afternoon of December 5, Rudder received two sets of orders: one was urgent, requiring his immediate action, and the other permitted a day to comply. The order allowing a day to comply was for him to report in person to General Hodges' First Army headquarters, forty miles to the rear in Spa, Belgium, by noon the next day, December 6. He probably knew that this was a transfer to take command of a regiment in General Cota's 28th Division, now recuperating in the Ardennes, a quiet sector of the front lines in Luxembourg and Belgium, but apparently he did not tell anyone about the transfer except the man who would succeed him, Capt. George Williams.[34]

He got the deadline extended by one day because the order requiring immediate action instructed him to put the battalion on standby alert for deployment to Bergstein, a village at the end of a ridge that, like the Vossenack Ridge, pointed toward Schmidt, which the Germans would again defend with maximum effort. An American unit had driven the Germans from Bergstein, but its hold on the village was shaky. Furthermore, from nearby Hill 400 the enemy had an unobstructed view and was calling down "artillery fire with deadly accuracy on any observable movement."[35]

The next afternoon, December 6, at five minutes after five Rudder got a telephone call that the battalion was urgently needed in Bergstein to defend the village and take Hill 400. Lacking time to distribute the usual five-part written orders, he issued an oral field order to "establish a perimeter defense around [Bergstein]" and "attack 'Sugar Loaf' [Hill 400]. Jump off 0800." In plain English, that meant the battalion would go to Bergstein that night and attack Hill 400 at eight o'clock the next morning.[36]

So widely dispersed were the Rangers in the forest that three hours passed before the order reached all of them. When Harold Gunther and James Shalala were told, they had only fifteen minutes to decamp. In the pitch black forest, the Rangers held to each other's belts in long lines, shuffling toward trucks that would carry them toward a destination unknown to all but a few.[37]

As when they went to Germeter and Vossenack, the trucks stopped short of Bergstein, and they walked the last three miles. Edlin remembered the "cold sleet, snow, and mud as we moved up the hard top toward Bergstein. Artillery shells were beating the road around us. About five rounds hit the road in front of us. [We] hit the ditches." Memories of the ghoulish spectacle never left him: "We crawled for several yards over and around bodies, American or German. There were American tanks burning and bodies everywhere."[38]

FAREWELL TO THE RANGERS

On the road into Bergstein that night, Rudder "walked up and down the column, encouraging us," Ed Sorvisto recalled. "When you get there, dig and dig deep, boys," he advised. Silhouetted against the lapping flames of burning vehicles, while in the distance sounded the thump-thump-thump of heavy artillery, "he shook hands with every man," said Len Lomell. "His eyes glistened when I got to him. I was really touched by the whole episode. It was like losing your father. He stayed with us as long as he could. He asked us to support George."[39]

In 1967, Edgar L. "Ed" Arnold, a captain and company commander in 1944, reminded Rudder of "the night march into Bergstein when you informed me that you were leaving the battalion." Edlin encountered Rudder as his commanding officer for the last time "as we were coming to Bergstein. I saw a guy standing in the road shaking hands with everybody. I thought, 'Who is that fool standing right in the middle of the crossroads shaking hands and I'm crawling through the ditches afraid that I might get hit.' It was Colonel Rudder telling everyone goodbye and good luck. When I got to him, he put his arms around me and said, 'Bob, don't take any chances. Quit taking chances.'"[40]

Five minutes into December 7, Rudder left, and George Williams assumed command of the battalion. At seven-thirty that morning, half of the battalion attacked Hill 400, and sixty-five minutes later they had driven the Germans from its summit. Holding it would be exceedingly difficult, but they did that, too, at a frightful cost. The other half defended the village against enemy attacks. On a flat bench of land between the village and the steep slope of the cone-shaped hill, Dr. Block set up his aid station in Bergstein's rugged parish church built with hefty, uncut stones, tinted in brownish shades of tan and rust. It would be the only church in the Huertgen Forest not destroyed in the fighting, but Dr. Block never knew its fate. At ten minutes after four the next afternoon he was killed instantly by an enemy shell that burst overhead as he walked out an entrance on the south side toward Schmidt. A few steps behind him came Harvey Cook, as steeled as any Ranger to the death of friends and the horrors of war. Carrying the body of the surgeon back inside, Harvey wept for the only time in the entire war.[41]

In accomplishing their mission in Bergstein and on Hill 400, about one-third of the battalion was killed, wounded, or captured. Most casualties were in the three companies that took the hill, the same three that made the assault on Pointe du Hoc. All told, the battalion suffered twenty-three dead, 106 wounded, and four missing. Rudder learned of the losses in a gentle, euphemistic letter from Dick Merrill. "It was a bit rough just after you left. You would have been proud of the boys for they came through in great style. There are a lot of new faces here, but that has happened before and we've still made the grade. Dr. Block went to visit Joe Rafferty. . . ."[42]

Six weeks would pass before Chick heard from him again, his longest lapse between letters during the war. Then she learned he was no longer with the Rangers and had left them with a "heavy heart. No commander ever had the privilege to command a finer bunch of men. They gave their all freely as good soldiers should."[43]

Rudder molded the 2nd Ranger Battalion with his decisions in selecting and training the men who composed it and by sharing their hardships. His character was the underpinning of their devotion to duty and to each other, inculcating them with their bond to love one another as only men willing to die for each other can know and express their love. Fifteen years after the war, he concluded that the best explanation for the Rangers' success was their "dedication to country and to each other." Courage, he said, is not innate but "stems from training, beliefs, and experiences." Continuous preparation for the future was the Rudder way.[44]

Harvey Cook went on to a distinguished, thirty-year career in the army and saw front-line service in the Korean War. As chief of staff of the 24th Infantry Division, he barely escaped capture by the North Korean Communist Army in 1950. Late in life, he reflected on his military experience and passed judgment on Rudder's Rangers: "I am convinced that there will never be another outfit like the Second Ranger Battalion. We had no cowards. Scared, Yes!!! But not cowards and we never had a mission that we didn't perform."[45]

CHAPTER 12

BATTLE OF THE BULGE

DECEMBER 1944

The 28th Infantry Division that Rudder joined as a regimental commander on December 8, 1944, had in the previous five weeks suffered 6,184 casualties, amounting to about 35 percent of the entire division. A study by the army described its losses as "one of the most costly" of any division in the entire war. Percentage-wise, Rudder's 109th Infantry Regiment absorbed greater losses than the division. From its 3,142 men on November 1, the regiment had taken 1,367 casualties, or 44 percent. Although the losses were extraordinary, the proportion was higher in the regiment's nine rifle companies, each with 195 men (at full strength), who were in closest contact with the enemy. However, when heads were counted on December 1, the regiment was back up to 2,967 men, almost to its authorized strength of 3,257.[1] More than half were replacements, euphemistically called "reinforcements," many of whom had recently arrived inadequately trained from the United States.

REGIMENTAL COMMANDER

To enhance the 109th's ability to operate independently, it had been upgraded to a regimental combat team by the attachment of more artillery, engineers, tanks, signal, and other supporting units. These additions gave it a numerical strength of almost five thousand, ten times more men than Rudder had commanded in the 2nd Ranger Battalion. Competent command of a regiment in combat requires knowledge, skills and an intuitive understanding that are best learned over a period of years. The officer that Rudder replaced, Jesse L. Gibney, had graduated from West Point in 1918, when Rudder was eight years old.[2]

At age thirty-four, Rudder was six to ten years younger than most regimental commanders in the army, but few could match him in their preparation. He had planned and executed a major operation for the Normandy invasion, involving about a thousand men. He had led the Rangers during the fighting in Brittany from forward positions, solidifying his understanding of ground fighting. He had much experience in coordinating infantry fire-

and-maneuver tactics with supporting artillery fire and with tank-infantry teams. For more than three years he had dealt with the practical details of training from the basics to advanced tactics. In preparing for D-Day, he had conferred extensively with higher-ranking officers; his poise with superior officers would be important in the coming crisis. In addition to good judgment tempered by hard combat experience, Rudder brought to the dejected regiment a contagiously buoyant personality and a stoic character.

However outstanding Rudder's qualifications appeared, his fitness for command would soon be tested under battlefield conditions in the extreme when the Germans fell on the unsuspecting Americans with an enormous counterattack only eight days after he took command of the regiment.

Rudder's new headquarters were in the Luxembourg town of Ettelbruck, population forty-five hundred, in the hills of the southern Ardennes near the Belgian border. Ettelbruck would be central to his decisions in the coming battle by virtue of its location on the main road from the German border to Belgium and at the juncture of two rivers: the Sûre and the Alzette. The Sûre came from the north to Ettelbruck, where it turned abruptly ninety degrees to the east, while the smaller Alzette flowed from the south along Ettelbruck's east side to merge with the Sûre.

From Ettelbruck the road toward Germany paralleled the Sûre on its north bank, coming in three miles to Diekirch, a town of comparable size that was the administrative and cultural center of the area.[3] As Ettelbruck was at the confluence of streams, Diekirch was at the convergence of roads. In addition to the east-west road from Ettelbruck, two bridges spanned the Sûre to the south; and, to the north, a road ascended a high ridge, which the G.I.s called Skyline Drive, and continued along its crest. From Skyline Drive on a clear night the muzzle blast of an enemy artillery piece in Germany, about four miles east, stood out like a pinpoint of light on the black landscape. When Rudder drove up on Skyline Drive, he got a quick overview of the rugged Ardennes terrain, with its deep, angular valleys, numerous streams, splotches of cultivated fields curving around dense forests, and hilltop villages that would figure in the fighting.

Seven miles east of Diekirch, the Sûre flowed into the Our, the largest river in the region and the boundary between Luxembourg and Germany. On the other side of the Our, the enemy's defense was organized around long-prepared and well-camouflaged bunkers that Nazi propaganda deceptively called the West Wall, which was not a wall but a series of fortifications the Allies called the Siegfried Line. "I'm gonna hang out my washing on the Siegfried Line," was the lyric of a popular British ditty. The Americans were dug in on the west side of the Our only a few hundred yards from the

Germans. Martin Slota, a sergeant in Rudder's regiment, summarized what they were doing: "They were watching us and we were watching them watching us."[4] There were no vehicular bridges in this stretch of the Our.

"NOTHING EVER HAPPENS IN THE ARDENNES"

Most high-level Allied commanders considered the Ardennes an unlikely place for a big German attack. They thought the terrain was too rough and the narrow, winding roads inadequate for enemy tanks in large numbers. Newly arrived divisions from the States were sent to the Ardennes for indoctrination to combat, and exhausted divisions such as the 28th, spent by hard fighting, were assigned to the Ardennes for recuperation and training of replacements. The consensus on the Allied side was that the Germans used the region opposite the Ardennes for similar purposes. Otherwise, north and south of the Ardennes, across the whole front from the North Sea to Switzerland, Eisenhower intended to remain on the offensive through the winter. He would allow the Germans no reprieve from fighting to prepare for the big Allied push in the coming spring to end the war.

However, the Ardennes was an exception where the Allied command would take a chance, launch no large-scale attacks, and protect the 75-mile front with only four static divisions, which would not take the offensive. The 28th Division was responsible for 25 miles of the front line, or about three times the normal span for a division. Of those 25 miles, Rudder's regiment held 10.3 miles. The southern boundary of the regiment's sector was a mile below the Sûre, where it bounded the U.S. 9th Armored Division, newly arrived from the States, inexperienced, and at one-third of its normal strength.[5] The northern boundary was about 9 miles north of the Sûre.

Rudder's superiors recognized that he did not have the manpower to cover his front twenty-four hours a day, but there was no great worry. After all, as everyone said, "Nothing ever happens in the Ardennes," which was not really true but was a comforting illusion. Someone forgot to remind the generals that the Germans had used the Ardennes as an axis of advance in their attack on France in May 1940 as well as in August 1914 at the beginning of World War I.

Another false assumption was that the Germans were beaten. Allied commanders were still tinged with the euphoria of late summer, when they had chased the Germans across France to the borders of the Third Reich. Few Allied commanders believed that an opponent who seemed so clearly beaten could rebound with a large-scale counterattack. A flaw in their thinking was the presumption that the German generals—rational men trained like themselves—were making the decisions. They did not realize that the irrational Adolf Hitler, rather than his generals, made detailed decisions about the conduct of the war without regard to the generals' judgments. Months before, he had conceived a lightning strike through the Ardennes to reach the North Sea at Antwerp and split the British and American armies. Splitting them would cause, he thought, a strategic rift that would force them to negotiate a separate peace and abandon their ally, the Soviet Union, on which he could then concentrate all his forces. In the attack through the Ardennes, the Germans would depend on speed, which in turn depended on the validity of Hitler's long-held prejudice that the Americans—freedom-loving softies and racial mongrels—were weak and would not fight. The Americans would crumble, he told the German generals, before their powerful attack.

The four divisions in the Ardennes made up the U.S. Army VIII Corps commanded by Maj. Gen. Troy H. Middleton, who was probably responsible for Rudder's promotion from a battalion to a regimental command. Middleton had wanted to promote Rudder since observing him in the fighting around Brest. For his headquarters, Middleton selected the Belgian crossroads town of Bastogne in rolling hills twenty-five miles northwest of Ettelbruck. There was nothing distinctive about Bastogne except that it was the intersection of seven roads, and Middleton knew that transportation networks were important in fast-moving mobile warfare. Middleton, studious in manner and calm in crisis, was regarded by Bradley and Patton as one of the best tacticians in the army. However, the four divisions of his VIII Corps were not to take the offensive but "to train, rest, re-equip, and observe the enemy."[6]

Middleton dissented from the "group-think" consensus of Allied commanders that the Germans were incapable of an attack in the Ardennes—or so he apparently told the American Ninth Army commander, Lt. Gen. William H. Simpson, on December 5 and may have told Rudder three days later when the colonel passed through Bastogne en route to Ettelbruck. This could explain the extraordinary effort that Rudder made to improve his regiment's defenses in his first week on the job.

Beneath Middleton, Rudder's immediate boss was Maj. Gen. Norman D. Cota, commander of the 28th Infantry Division. They knew each other from planning and training in England and subsequent operations in Normandy, Brittany, and the Huertgen Forest, where they became more than ordinary comrades. Coming events would solidify their friendship for life.

PRELUDE TO THE CRISIS

In Ettelbruck, Rudder's headquarters were in the basement of a vocational agriculture high school called the Lycée Technique Agricole, a building with an exterior of dark stone and reddish brick. The basement was spacious and afforded good protection from artillery fire, the main danger. Rudder inherited a regimental staff that had gone through several crises since crossing the English Channel to the continent on July 22, 1944.[7] They were competent for the tasks that would soon confront them.

One of Rudder's early decisions was to have telephone wire laid from his headquarters to each company in addition to preexisting telephone connections to the battalions.[8] His experience at Pointe du Hoc had convinced him not to rely solely on radios. He also began training infantry officers in the finer points of giving precise aiming directions to artillerymen, whose targets were usually located far beyond view of their guns. Ideally, he wanted every infantryman to be an effective forward observer for artillery.

In the first week after he took command, Rudder drove across his sector, inspecting units of the regiment. He made an important visit to the 3rd Battalion, which defended the angle formed by the confluence of the Sûre with the Our. Facing the Our, the battalion was dug in along the forward edge of a steep two-hundred-foot ridge, looking across the river into Germany. At the south end of the ridge the men could also see across the Sûre. Rudder discovered that he had much in common with the 3rd Battalion commander, Maj. Jim H. McCoy. Like Rudder, McCoy was a newcomer to the regiment, had grown up in a small Texas town (Eddy), and had attended Tarleton College before transferring to Texas A&M, where he graduated in 1940.[9]

McCoy's riflemen had dug foxholes for one or two men spaced some thirty-five yards apart. The holes were deep for protection from the bitter winter wind as well as from hostile fire, and they were manned around the clock. Capt. Harry M. Kemp, commander of the third battalion's heavy weapons company, escorted Rudder along the ridgeline and briefed him on the situation. "It is easy to describe him that day," Kemp told a historian. "He was, as he always was, supremely professional and competent. The way he talked, the way he acted, and the words he spoke indicated that he was very familiar with the situation and that he knew what to do about it. When he gave instructions, they were very positive, very clear, and we understood they were to be done immediately."[10]

The men in the foxholes were surprised when Rudder came to them. Many had never seen his predecessor, who was considered "C.P. bound," meaning safe and comfortable in the command post.[11] But Rudder walked along the ridge, scrutinizing them and their weapons and asking questions about their positions. He decided, or concurred with, all arrangements for the defense. He asked the men to tell him the name of the man to their right and left. Calling a man by his name could be important in the defense, especially at night. He asked if the enemy could infiltrate between them without being seen. Leaning over a man in his foxhole and peering down the ridge, Rudder asked, "Can Jerry get behind that tree out there without you seeing him?" He wanted to know how often the men on the line were relieved or got a hot meal.

He made an impression on a soldier who was later wounded and talked about him to other G.I.s in a hospital. Rudder was wearing a heavy overcoat with, the man guessed, "about six pairs of long johns underneath." The insignia of his rank did not appear on his helmet or outer clothing; thus, if a German sniper peering through the leafless trees glimpsed him at a distance of five hundred yards, he would not know that he had a field grade officer in the crosshairs. Strapped around his waist on the outside of his olive drab overcoat was the holster with his revolver, the .45-caliber Smith and Wesson six-shooter that he preferred over the army's standard-issue automatic Colt pistol.[12]

About this time, Pfc. George Bunnell saw Rudder for the first time. Bunnell had recently been yanked out of college, told he was an infantryman, and rushed with thousands of others to the battlefields of northwestern Europe. Six decades after this first encounter an interviewer asked him what came to his mind when he thought of Rudder. Without hesitation, Bunnell replied, "He had an air about him that 'If you stick with me, you won't get hurt.' He was strict but fair and there was no bullshit about him."[13]

Both the Germans and the Americans sent patrols across the Our, probing the others' defenses and trying to capture an opposing soldier to interrogate and learn their opponent's positions, strengths, and weaknesses. The G.I.s dreaded the night patrols into Germany more than anything else. A few nights after Rudder took command, he came to the river's edge, boarded a small flat-bottomed boat with a patrol, and crossed with the men into German territory. A junior officer told how this affected the men. "After the Colonel showed up one night and took the leading boat across, the men thought he was nuts but they would go anywhere for him."[14] He was prudent, yet so purposeful in his resolve that fear seemed not a factor in his behavior.

In these ways Rudder quickly gained an understanding of the regiment's situation that he could not obtain from the reports of others. At the same time, he won the trust and confidence of the entire regiment, which bolstered the men's response to his leadership and their willingness to fight it out in the days ahead.

FIRST DAY: "KILLING FIELD"

A clue about the coming German attack occurred in the sector of the 109th Infantry. "We picked up a woman a few days before who reported a lot of activity behind the German lines," Rudder told a newspaper reporter in San Angelo, Texas, eight months later. The woman was Elise Delé from the Luxembourg village of Bivels on the Our. Abducted by German soldiers in Bivels on December 10, she was taken to Bitburg, twenty miles inside Germany. Desperate to find her thirteen-year-old son, Jean, who had gotten separated from her, she escaped and headed west toward home, unavoidably seeing the roads and villages teeming with German soldiers, tanks, and other vehicles. Near the Our she saw many small rowboats. Crossing back into Luxembourg on December 14 at the town of Vianden, she sought shelter from the damp, penetrating cold in the Heintz Hotel, which also housed the 109th Regiment's intelligence and reconnaissance platoon. The G.I.s were interested in her story and took her to the regimental headquarters in Ettelbruck, where an intelligence officer questioned her. He informed Rudder and wrote a report that went up the American chain of command: "Following is a preliminary interrogation of a Luxembourg woman. She reports that [en route from Bitburg] she observed many trucks and horse-drawn vehicles, pontoons, small boats and other river-crossing material. In addition, she observed many artillery pieces. . . . While in [Bitburg] she observed many troops in light gray uniforms with black collars (SS troops). Woman's condition is highly nervous, having stepped on a trip wire that detonated a mine."[15]

Despite the forewarning of Elise Delé and other signs, the Germans achieved complete surprise with their attack at 5:30 AM on December 16, 1944. They attacked with three great thrusts into the American lines with their objective to capture the port of Antwerp, one hundred miles northwest near the English Channel. Nearly two hundred thousand German troops came at the eighty-mile front defended by Middleton's four divisions. Two entire German divisions—the 352nd Volksgrenadier (352 VGD) and the 5th Parachute—struck the 109th Infantry Regiment. Charged with protecting the left flank of the powerful thrust toward Bastogne, both divisions were to cross the Our, and the 352 VGD was to sweep up the Sûre Valley, capture Diekirch and Ettelbruck, and push further to the west to take up defensive positions against an anticipated American counterattack. Their commanders knew about the decimation of the 28th Division in the Huertgen Forest and expected the 109th Regiment to give way in front of them.[16]

A careful study by the noted American military historian and theorist Trevor N. Dupuy calculated that the combined manpower strength of the two German divisions was 32,730, while Rudder's 109th Infantry had 4,985 with the attached units. Dupuy may have underestimated the German preponderance. Roland Gaul, Luxemburg's leading historian of the war and founder-director of the National Military Museum in Diekirch, believes the ratio of Germans to Americans in Rudder's sector was more like ten to one and as high as fifteen to one between opposing infantrymen.[17]

The attack began with an artillery and rocket barrage around Diekirch. Little damage was done aside from the destruction of a few jeeps and trucks.[18] At the same time, German infantry began crossing the Our in small boats and on footbridges used by the local inhabitants. In the soupy fog of the damp, chilly morning they were mostly unseen by the defending Americans. The German attack was not recognized immediately at any level of the Allied command as a major offensive. Rudder's first information about enemy troops coming across the Our reached him about 9:00 AM with a report from the men in the foxholes on the heights above the river that he had visited a few days before.

Only about three hundred Americans were available to defend the three-thousand-yard stretch of the ridge, but they extracted a tremendous toll on the Germans—the 916th Regiment of the 352 VGD—who struggled to climb or crawl up the steep, slippery incline while carrying heavy backpacks. By this late period in the war, most of Hitler's soldiers were men in their forties or older and teenage boys who were poorly led.[19] In no time, the Germans scrambling up the ridge had another obstacle—the bodies of comrades who had preceded them in the attack. Those who made it across the crest of the ridge found themselves on the Hoesdorf plateau in an open area surrounded by the trees and shrubbery of a natural forest, from which well-hidden machine guns cut them down. So great was the slaughter that the area became known to the Luxembourgers as the "killing field."

The 2nd Battalion of the 109th adjoined McCoy's 3rd Battalion on the north in an area where the ridge tapered off to a low-lying riverbank that was a poor defensive position. It was also where the enemy's 5th Parachute Division, in concert with the 915th Regiment of the 352 VGD, was the main attack force. In the absence of suitable terrain along the river, Rudder organized the defense as strongpoints in abandoned villages and farmhouses inland from the river. As more Germans crossed the river, they gained strength, pushed inland, and killed or captured men of the 109th in several strongpoints.

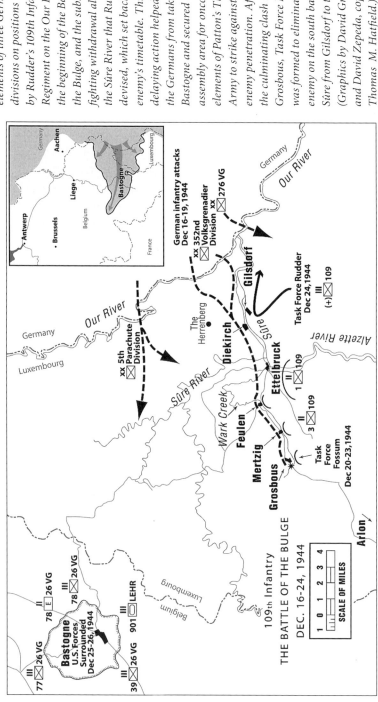

Map 12-1. The attack by elements of three German divisions on positions held by Rudder's 109th Infantry Regiment on the Our River at the beginning of the Battle of the Bulge, and the subsequent fighting withdrawal along the Sûre River that Rudder devised, which set back the enemy's timetable. This delaying action helped keep the Germans from taking Bastogne and secured an assembly area for oncoming elements of Patton's Third Army to strike against the enemy penetration. After the culminating clash near Grosbous, Task Force Rudder was formed to eliminate the enemy on the south bank of the Sûre from Gilsdorf to the east. (Graphics by David Grosvenor and David Zepeda, copyright Thomas M. Hatfield.)

Veering left, they advanced like a wedge toward the Sûre, threatening to divide the 2nd Battalion from the 3rd and cut the road along the river on which the 3rd Battalion, in the angle with the Our, depended for its supplies. In an attempt to counter the German drive, Rudder committed his only infantry reserves, the 1st Battalion, but they were unable to stop the Germans' slow but gradual drive. As concern about the attack spread in the early afternoon, Cota ordered, "No retreat. Hold at all costs. Nobody comes back." Middleton later modified the order to "Hold as long as tenable."[20]

The Germans had difficulties crossing the Our with their tanks and mechanized assault guns. On the first day they ferried across a few light artillery pieces and vehicles and improvised a roadway over a small dam.[21] The portable steel bridges for the tanks never got to the river because Allied air strikes on German railroads kept them away. As a remedy, methodical German engineers cut down trees in the nearby forest and constructed wooden bridges strong enough to support some tracked vehicles. Enemy commanders worked mightily to get more men across and to gain better control of those already west of the river.

Threatening though the German attack was, Rudder was optimistic when he crawled into his sleeping bag at the end of the first day. "We were in a good position and had a distinct advantage in terrain," he told a junior officer a few days later. "All attacks were company-size infantry but there were no tanks. Everyone was holding and I saw no cause for alarm. We did not even consider giving ground."[22] He may not have been informed about the depth and strength of the German penetrations between his village strongpoints or that their armored vehicles were assembling where a bridge was under construction across the Our from the gap in his defenses.[23] And his confidence may have been boosted in the knowledge that he had most of the regiment's tanks and two battalions of artillery with good observation and ample ammunition. Although he claimed to have slept soundly every night during the war, the first night in the Battle of the Bulge was an exception, because enemy artillery, mortars, and rockets harassed roads and road junctions as far back as Ettelbruck.

SECOND DAY: "HOLD ON THE SHOULDERS"

General Cota called Rudder at 2:40 AM on the second day, December 17, with orders to put a platoon of infantry (about thirty-five men) on a platoon of four tanks and "help out up north where things are getting hot."[24] The village of Hosheid on Skyline Drive on the boundary of the 109th with the 110th Infantry was where the Germans had broken through. Rudder complied, but the tanks never got to Hosheid. The Germans were already there and drove them back. The Germans were now between the two regiments, and the 109th was about to be cut off from its parent 28th Division.

In midmorning, German engineers completed the first wooden bridge across the Our in the defensive gap, and their infantry, accompanied by assault guns, poured across. McCoy's 3rd Battalion remained dug in on the heights above the river, but even there the enemy shot their way into the center of the line, where, a German chronicler wrote, "bloody fighting" continued. Failing to dislodge the American riflemen on the ridge by frontal assault, the Germans began outflanking them along the Sûre. Unfortunately for the enemy, forward observers for the artillery had "good wire and radio communication" with their firing batteries back around Diekirch, which stopped the flanking movement by firing 3,123 rounds during the day.[25]

As the second day ended, Rudder and the 109th Regiment were nearly isolated but not surrounded. They had lost contact with the 110th Regiment to the north. To the south, the 9th Armored Division had pulled back, and defenses along their boundary were weak. No air support had been provided or was expected because of low-hanging clouds and rain. More Germans were coming across the Our, presenting Rudder with decisions that would determine the fate of the regiment and affect the outcome of the battle, the importance of which was growing.

The 109th Regiment now stood as the main obstacle to the Germans' widening of the southern shoulder of their breakthrough. In this situation, Rudder and other American commanders knew what to do without being told: "Hold on the shoulders." It was U.S. Army doctrine—a fundamental principle—derived from the analysis of German counterattacks during World War I. The doctrine held that the way to contain and eventually recover a salient created by a major offensive was to stand fast on the sides of the breakthrough and deny the enemy room to bring in more forces. Patton asserted the doctrine at Eisenhower's conference with his commanders in Verdun on December 18, when he said: "Let the sons of bitches go all the way to Paris. Then we'll really cut 'em up."[26] But first, they had to be held on the shoulders.

THIRD DAY: "RUDDER IN THE WAY"

On the third day, December 18, the 109th's situation deteriorated further. About noon German tanks crossed the newly constructed wooden bridge across the Our in the gap and attacked toward Diekirch. The enemy also completed a second bridge across the Our below the heights held by McCoy's 3rd Battalion. The last of Rudder's six antitank guns was knocked out. His tanks were low on fuel and in need of maintenance. More than five hundred men had been lost. But the Germans had not achieved either of their objectives: they had not penetrated to Diekirch and Ettelbruck and had not widened their penetration by putting a significant force across the Our on the south side of the Sûre.

About noon, Rudder decided on his general course of action for the next three days. He could not contain the German onslaught, but he would comply with Middleton's order to "hold as long as tenable" by denying the Germans the critical terrain and roads they needed to advance. At 2:10 PM he called Cota and asked permission to withdraw his three infantry battalions to the highest ground in the area, a hill called the Herrenberg a mile northeast of Diekirch that loomed about two hundred feet above the town and the Sûre.[27] At first, Cota did not agree. He wanted Rudder to pull back northwest toward Bastogne, but Rudder convinced him that such a move would be a futile attack into the flank of the main German thrust toward Bastogne, leaving the German attack on the Diekirch–Ettelbruck road unopposed.

Reconnoitering on the Herrenberg, Rudder laid out the defense in an arc slightly behind the crest of the hill, with the right flank overlooking the road along the Sûre and the left flank across Skyline Drive, the two most likely avenues of an enemy attack. Dug in behind the crest, the Americans could not be seen by the advancing Germans until they came over the crest, silhouetting themselves as easy targets for the defenders. Rudder drove along the Sûre, watching his men blow its bridges before they made for the Herrenberg. Those who saw him told others, "If the 'old man' can be calm and unruffled in this situation, so can I."[28]

The planned withdrawal to the Herrenberg was the first of several over the next three days in which Rudder skillfully maneuvered the regiment and exercised keen judgment in using the terrain on the defense. He selected sites with good observation and fields of fire that took a heavy toll on the enemy without becoming so closely engaged that he could not easily fall back to another prepared position from which to continue to resist.

The success of the defense was more important than Rudder knew. As his regiment was moving to the Herrenberg, Eisenhower was meeting with his ground commanders. From that meeting came the decision that on December 22 elements of Patton's Third Army to the south would turn north from their eastward attack toward Germany and launch a powerful assault against the side of the bulge in the American lines created by the German offensive.

Cota may have foreseen this possibility when he told Rudder to continue fighting for time and space, both of which would be required for Patton's attack force to assemble.

Roland Gaul, the Luxembourg historian, refers to the fighting along the Sûre as "Rudder in the way." Gaul believes the 109th Infantry Regiment crippled the German advance almost completely during the first days of the offensive so that the enemy could achieve practically no noteworthy gain in territory. The American military historian John C. McManus calls the fighting "Alamo in the Ardennes," meaning that it made possible the defense of Bastogne. In the bitter fighting of the first three critical days of the German attack, the 109th used every available weapon, expending 280,000 rounds of small arms ammunition, five thousand mortar rounds, more than ten thousand artillery rounds, three thousand grenades, and three hundred bazooka rounds. Because of the fierce defense of the 109th, the 352 VGD was unable to finish crossing the Our until the fourth day of the attack and unable to attack in force until the fifth day, December 20, all of which the Germans had expected to achieve on the first day.[29]

FOURTH DAY: "USE YOUR OWN JUDGMENT"

On the morning of the fourth day, December 19, Cota directed Rudder "not to recoil any further than the Sûre River," two miles behind his defenses on the Herrenberg. (Cota was referring to the north-south segment of the Sûre before it turned east at Ettelbruck.) In the afternoon, the enemy placed heavy artillery fire on the Herrenberg. The cannonade went on for two hours and then stopped, only to resume at night when small groups of German infantry probed for weak points in the defense as their searchlights, reflected off the clouds, illuminated the terrain in front of them. Their numbers were increasing while those of the 109th declined. At 8:00 PM Rudder called Cota again, this time to tell him that the regiment could find itself surrounded by the next day. He asked Cota for permission to withdraw to the west across the Sûre and beyond Ettelbruck. Rudder told Cota that he had he had three options: He could "fight it out" where he was, but that, he said, "would be the end" of the regiment; it would be destroyed. He could withdraw to the south and "tie in closely" with the 9th Armored Division, but that would allow the Germans to continue west, unopposed. Or he could withdraw to the southwest and continue to delay the German advance; this was actually Rudder's request for Cota's approval.[30]

The commander of the 9th Armored Division favored the second option, which would have had the 109th protecting his tanks. Cota called Middleton, then almost surrounded in Bastogne. Middleton counseled that Rudder "should hold where he was, but, if forced back, he should retire to the west behind" the small Alzette River, which ran along Ettelbruck's east side.[31]

Then Middleton added the most important part of Rudder's new instructions: "Use your own judgment as you are on the ground." That was Middleton's philosophy of command if he had confidence in his subordinate. Thus, he allowed Rudder the freedom to develop his tactical plan for the next few days without further approval. And since the 109th was no longer in physical contact with the 28th Division, Middleton removed it from Cota's command and attached it to the 9th Armored Division across the Sûre, whose commander then, to Rudder's disgust, "ordered me to send my second battalion to outpost [guard] his tanks."[32] Cloth-clad foot soldiers ridicule tankers' demands for them to protect their steel jumbos.

Overwhelmed by the masses of German attackers, late on the fourth day, December 19, the 109th began carefully withdrawing from the Herrenberg toward the Sûre without alerting the enemy. It was a ticklish affair, with squads and platoons moving out on a timetable as German artillery continued to fall on their vacated positions. Those who remained increased their volume of fire to fake the firepower of the entire force. Anxiety was high. Who would be the last man off the hill? Confidence in the leadership was required for the men to remain calm and ensure that the retreat did not become a rout. Eventually the enemy caught on and harassed the withdrawal with artillery fire, inflicting thirty-four casualties. But one young lieutenant appreciated the maneuver: "The Colonel fooled the hun," he wrote home, "and they shot the hell out a hill from which he had withdrawn his troops."[33]

Another scholarly study by Trevor Dupuy concluded that, in the first four days of the Battle of the Bulge, the performance of Rudder's 109th Infantry was exceptional in comparison to that of all other U.S. Army units of similar size or larger. Dupuy collected casualty figures from German and American sources for ten engagements in the Battle of the Bulge. In each of the four days, the 109th inflicted an average of 436 casualties on the Germans while absorbing an average of 259. Only the U.S. 2nd Armored Division had a higher ratio, which occurred during a two-day period (December 25–26) against the spent 2nd Panzer Division, which had been in ten days of continuous fighting and was at the extreme depth of its penetration into the American lines about forty miles northwest of Bastogne. In those two days the 2nd Armored inflicted 408 casualties on the German force and took 108 of its own. Dupuy attributed the success of the 109th to the difficulties the Germans had in crossing the Our and to the regiment's "exceptional performance during the campaign."[34]

FIFTH DAY: "A NEW GAME PLAN"

The withdrawal from the Herrenberg and across the Sûre to the west was supervised by executive officers of the companies and battalions while Rudder kept the commanders and the regimental staff in his Ettelbruck headquarters devising a new plan. At 2:00 AM on the fifth day, December 20 he gave them a pep talk with oral orders and an overview of the plan, a fighting withdrawal that would be a precursor to victory at Bastogne, "victory" meaning to keep the Germans from taking the town, the crossroads hub of the region.

The new plan was complex, involving night marches of exhausted men in dispersed units on a timetable. Its success owes much to how it was developed and communicated. Rudder involved both staff and line officers in order to avoid the familiar problem of staff officers making a plan without input from line officers (as he had recently seen in the Huertgen Forest), who then had to implement it despite difficult or unrealistic requirements. Rudder was present during the development of the plan and during the explanations, leaving no doubt in his subordinates' minds about what he wanted them to do. The resolve of their commander gave them confidence in the outcome.

Rudder presumed the Germans would continue their attack from Ettelbruck toward Arlon in Belgium, about twenty miles southwest. Knowing he could not stop them in a head-on fight, he would try to delay and weaken them by resisting from successive positions prepared in advance and then withdrawing before a large-scale direct confrontation occurred. Having the smaller force, if the losses were equal on both sides, he would be weakened more than his foe.

As he stood before his assembled subordinates, the circumstances resembled the halftime briefings he had given his football teams on the revised game plan for the second half. He could have likened, as Cota did the 28th Division, the 109th to the guards and tackles in a defensive line that must slow down the plunging ball carrier until the secondary can come up and knock him down. When Rudder finished speaking, his staff—like assistant football coaches—went over the details with the commanders.[35]

At 3:35 AM Rudder's personal representative at the Ettelbruck bridge over the Sûre radioed that the last elements of the regiment had crossed over. Rudder then went four miles south to his new command post, the fifteenth-century castle Château de Berg, the former residence of the Grand Duchess of Luxembourg, who had fled to England with her family and all government ministers save one, left behind as caretaker.[36] Having disposed the regiment to delay the enemy along the road to Arlon, Rudder would wait with his staff, receiving reports and appraising alternative actions as circumstances changed.

Implementing the new plan, the 1st Battalion dug in to hold a ridge not far to the southwest of Ettelbruck overlooking the main road west from Ettelbruck through the villages of Feulen, Mertzig, and Grosbous. Rudder assigned responsibility for the defense of the three villages to the three rifle companies of McCoy's 3rd Battalion. He reinforced each company to the strength of a task force with antitank guns, towed artillery pieces (76 mm), mortars (60 mm and 81 mm), two Sherman tanks, engineers, and forward observers for calling aiming directions to artillerymen.[37] They were not to fight to the finish but to delay the enemy before withdrawing to hold the high ground to the south.

Capt. Embert A. Fossum commanded Task Force L, which Rudder reinforced most of all to about 180 men and sent farthest to the village of Grosbous. Half of Fossum's original company of 195 men had already been killed, wounded, captured, stricken with serious respiratory illnesses, or frostbitten from prolonged exposure to subfreezing temperatures. Fossum taught journalism at the University of Oregon after the war and wrote an unpublished monograph about his task force that was favorably critiqued at the army's infantry school. Fossum lamented the condition of his men as they retreated toward Grosbous in the predawn hours of December 20, 1944:

> After four days and nights of constant contact with the enemy, [the men] were so worn with loss of sleep and fatigue that orders did not arouse [their] interest. They were almost too tired, cold and hungry to care. Incessant attacks by the enemy and the digging of three successive positions during the withdrawal had fatigued them almost beyond endurance.
>
> There had hardly been time to eat even if food had been available. When they left their original position [nineteen miles to the east] shortly after noon on the 18th, each man had carried one-third of a K-ration [one meal] in his pocket. Another one-third of a K-ration had been issued as they left Diekirch [handed to them as they filed out town] on the night of the 19th. . . . So it was a pretty badly beaten unit that headed for Grosbous. Morale was certainly at a low ebb.[38]

Arriving in Grosbous after daylight, Fossum set up a perimeter defense in the sturdiest houses on the edges of the village. He planned against an attack from any direction, because Germans driving on Bastogne were already ten miles behind him to the northwest and could double back. Near the houses the Americans dug foxholes for themselves and emplacements for their guns and mortars in the frozen ground. Despite the drudgery of digging with picks and shovels in the hard sod, the day was restful in comparison to the previous four. It was a good time to shave and clean weapons.

Morale and manpower got a boost when fifteen Luxembourg policemen showed up and volunteered to help. Wearing white "Gendarmerie Auxiliare" arm bands and armed with captured German weapons, they were quickly integrated with the Americans. Their motivation was high because they faced almost certain death if the Germans regained control, for they had publicly executed jailed Nazi collaborators before evacuating Diekirch only two days earlier.[39]

Fossum's orders were to "communicate directly with regiment, by-passing battalion channels," but his radio contact with Rudder's command post was poor. To his relief, shortly after dark an officer sent by Rudder arrived in a jeep with two messages. The good news was that telephone wire was being strung from Rudder to Fossum. The other message was a surprise. Rudder ordered Fossum to move his entire task force post haste to a "low, wooded ridge [across the valley of Wark Creek] to the southwest that paralleled the road at a distance of 1,000 to 1,300 yards."[40] On the ridge they were to prepare additional positions for themselves and their weapons. When the new positions were completed, Fossum was to call Rudder.

It was a test of Fossum's leadership, but his men followed him across the valley. In three hours they were done, and Fossum called Rudder, only to receive another surprise. "Take your task force back to Grosbous and reoccupy your positions there!" was Rudder's new order. Amidst great grumbling about the crazy colonel, Fossum led his men back across the valley to Grosbous.[41]

Earlier in the day at his Château de Berg command post, Rudder received an officer dispatched by General Cota to brief him on the big picture. Rudder learned that Bastogne was surrounded, but that the 101st Airborne Division had gotten inside before the town was encircled. More important for Rudder's regiment, the 26th and 80th infantry divisions from Patton's Third Army would pass through the area held by the 109th to attack the left flank of the Bulge. Liaison teams from both divisions were coming to Rudder to coordinate the delicate matter of bringing together the friendly, heavily armed forces that could easily mistake each other for the enemy. The entry of the two divisions into the fray clarified the importance of containing the 352 VGD on the Ettelbruck–Grosbous road in order to guarantee the Americans a secure jump-off line when they launched their attack. Success would be measured in the hours and minutes that the 109th Regiment delayed the Germans.[42]

SIXTH DAY: "PUT RUDDER IN THE LEAD"

In a heavy fog on the morning of the sixth day, December 21, hundreds of German infantrymen with tanks and artillery began crossing the Sûre to Ettelbruck. In midmorning, a captured German officer showed a map confirming that the German plan was to go west on the road through Grosbous and on to Arlon.[43] True to the map, throughout the day the Germans pressed on along the road, where intense firefights developed with Americans defending the villages of Feulen and Mertzig.

By their numbers and persistence, the Germans fought through the villages and continued their advance after nightfall toward Grosbous. Fossum and his task force had another quiet day in Grosbous until about nine in the evening, when a large German patrol of at least fifty men noisily approached the village. Drunkenness may have caused their indiscretion, and they would pay dearly for it. The last five hundred yards of the road into Grosbous was almost straight, but entering the village it bent to the left. On the outer edge of the bend, Fossum had placed a .50-caliber machine gun aimed straight down the middle of the road on which the Germans were approaching. A long burst into the pitch-black night toward the sound of the German voices drew screams of surprise and pain. Other G.I.s sent streams of thirty-caliber rounds down the road. It was, Fossum said, like "knocking down pins in a bowling alley!" Then the German column was heard withdrawing back toward Mertzig. Early the next morning a patrol sent out by Fossum counted the bodies of thirty-one German soldiers on the road, and, from their condition, it appeared the .50-caliber had inflicted all the damage.[44]

Expecting the usual German counterattack, the men sat tight in their holes, and Fossum reported the incident to Rudder. When an hour had passed and the Germans had not struck back, Rudder told Fossum to move his task force from Grosbous to the ridge across Wark Creek, where they had prepared new positions during the previous night. Having dug them at night, they had little difficulty finding them in the darkness, although, Fossum said, the second night was darker and the mud slicker.[45] Snow fell heavily through the night on the men of Task Force L, whose only shelter from the elements was their clothing.

As an instructor of tactics, Middleton valued creative remedies to battlefield problems over the standard "school solutions" taught by the army. Speaking of Rudder after the war, he commented, "We were not fighting a textbook war in the Bulge. The average man is an imitator. Put a man like Earl Rudder in the lead, and you get an original solution. Others will do as their leaders do."[46]

SEVENTH DAY: "WE STACKED THEM IN PILES"

When daylight came on the shortest day of the year, the 352 VGD's 915th Regiment, some 3,500 strong when it attacked six days earlier, resumed its advance toward Grosbous. The German commander may have sent a reconnaissance patrol ahead of his main column that returned to tell him that no Americans were in the village. Probably inexperienced, he presumed they had withdrawn and did not dispatch patrols to find them. He had no inkling that the men of Task Force L were watching, with weapons ready to fire, the very road on which he marched his column.[47]

Until midmorning the snowfall obscured visibility from the ridge. About ten o'clock the air cleared, and a strange sight greeted the Americans. Down on the road they saw a column of men and vehicles, one and one-half miles long, with towed artillery pieces and two tanks at its tail and no patrols for security on its flanks. It was an unbelievable sight. Fossum doubted the column was German and called Rudder for instructions. He was away from his command post, and his executive officer firmly told Fossum not to fire on the column, as it might be from one of Patton's divisions, which were expected to arrive in the area that day. When Rudder returned a short while later, he called Fossum with instructions: "No American units could be on that road. Fire away."[48]

The scene could have been taken from a pulp war novel. Fossum's firing plan jelled along the ridge. He assigned targets to the most suitable weapons: artillery laid on the vehicles and tanks; mortars and machine guns aimed at personnel. The Americans waited. Discipline and restraint were necessary. One trigger-happy G.I. could spoil the ambush. The artillery would fire first on the rear of the column to destroy the vehicles and block the German retreat. When the first artillery round went out the tube, an officer shouted "On the way!" The projectile was in the air. Instantly, Fossum called out, "Commence firing!" and signaled the same with the downward wide wave of his hand. Everyone let go with all weapons, and "the German column seemed to disintegrate under the initial blast of fire." The Germans were beyond normal effective rifle fire, but it did not matter to the American sharpshooters, who poured it on. Fossum remembered: "The ridge spewed lead, flame and smoke. The enemy column, a minute before a quiet, compact dark trace against the white snow, became a melee of men, weapons and vehicles erupting in all directions. . . . Men fled in all directions, seeking cover from the destruction that threatened them. . . . The fire was kept up for twenty minutes on every enemy thing that moved, with not one shot received in return."[49]

Once again men in the 109th Infantry Regiment believed Rudder had outsmarted the Germans. One of his lieutenants wrote: "The Colonel tricked the hun on a withdrawal and killed in the region of 2000." German sergeant Wilhelm Stettler survived the slaughter, and at an advanced age shared the painful memory of the massacre with Roland Gaul, the Luxembourg historian: "Shells flew at us endlessly, plowed up the ground and destroyed everything. The crying and the screaming of the wounded and dying were terrible. We left that place of destruction like a funeral procession."[50]

Two weeks later, Rudder took the detached perspective of a commander who had set up the bushwhacking and had delegated its execution to subordinates. "On the 20th and the 21st, it was rather quiet. On the 22nd the Germans, under the impression we had withdrawn south, marched at least two battalions of infantry and one of artillery across our front. Our artillery had a field day. We stacked them in piles along that road from Ettelbruck."[51]

The stunning success of the attack sent a wave of optimism through the American high command. With unusual speed for bestowing an award, Rudder was decorated with an Oak Leaf Cluster to his Bronze Star. His citation recognized that he had kept his regiment "intact and fought a brilliant delaying action, holding [the] lines from which our forces launched a counterattack."[52] The regiment had held the high ground west and southwest of Ettelbruck, where the 26th and 80th infantry divisions could assemble for their counterattack into the flank of the German salient toward Bastogne.

The 80th Division arrived first and passed through the American lines east of Fossum's Task Force L, which remained on the ridge overlooking Grosbous until the next day, when the 26th Division came through. Although the two divisions would have difficult fighting, the 352 VGD—the first German resistance they encountered—had been reduced by Rudder's regiment to about half of the approximately twelve thousand men it had on December 16 at the beginning of the German offensive.[53]

Rudder then moved his entire regiment east of Ettelbruck on the south side of the Sûre in the sector of the 10th Armored Division (which had replaced the 9th Armored), to which the regiment was now attached.

EIGHTH DAY: "TASK FORCE RUDDER"

On the morning of December 23, Rudder and 10th Armored Division staff prepared a plan to regain territory along the south side of the Sûre. In midafternoon Rudder convened his commanders and key staff and issued an oral field order for an attack the next day. About fifteen hundred men, designated

Task Force Rudder, were to sweep the Sûre from Ettelbruck eastward for five miles to the village of Moestroff. Enemy strength in the area was believed weak, but German soldiers were not to be underestimated. The core of Task Force Rudder was the 109th Regiment's 1st and 3rd battalions plus tanks and tank destroyers from the 10th Armored who had a vengeful debt to settle with the enemy: Germans, believed to be SS, had recently murdered several of their supply men.[54]

NINTH DAY: "HAPPY TO SEE AMERICANS"

Christmas Eve dawned with a blanket of fresh snow and a temperature of twenty degrees Fahrenheit. Gilsdorf was the first village on the list for Task Force Rudder. As Rudder was about to give the order to go in, five young Luxembourger men came out and asked to take part. They wore U.S. Army jackets, were armed with German rifles, and said they were resistance fighters. After checking their identities, Rudder allowed them to mount the tanks that would lead the way into Gilsdorf. With their knowledge of the town, they guided the attack, and the Germans were quickly routed. An American lieutenant, James Christy, saw Germans taken with such surprise that they surrendered with dinner still cooking in the ovens of the homes they had taken over. Christy declared, "The operation was a great success since we had scarcely any losses to report."[55]

In due time, the people of Gilsdorf erected a monument in the center of their village to commemorate their liberation. A bronze plaque embedded in the monument bears this inscription in English:

> *GILSDORF*
> *Liberated 24 December 1944*
> *By the 28th Inf. Div. and the 10th Armd. Div.*
> *With the courageous help of*
> *Ben Bauler, Louis Dupont, Charles Breyer,*
> *Emile Pesch, Heandel Jean*
> *TASK FORCE RUDDER*
> *We Remember*

Lt. Willie Peña was in the vanguard of Task Force Rudder entering Moestroff. It was about dusk, and Peña was anxious to end the day without further casualties. "The sooner we captured the town, the sooner we could [go] back to the rear area for Christmas dinner the next day. We were extremely cold and moved about, stomping our feet to keep warm. It began to snow anew." Peña sent a twelve-man squad into Moestroff. They saw no one until a priest appeared and welcomed them at the front door of his church. Then the people began to emerge from their cellars and come out in the streets, "happy to see the Americans again."[56]

With Task Force Rudder's mission accomplished, Peña began the six-mile trek with his platoon back to the regimental area. The scene—glistening white fields against the dark conifer forest under a crystalline sky—came back to him over the years as if a dream: "The night was absolutely clear. The whole area had the illusion of daylight. I began thinking about how I could describe this lovely environment to my folks without intimating I was near the front line." Peña's platoon spent Christmas Eve night in an abandoned farmhouse not far from Rudder's château. He allowed his men to enter first. Then, searching for a place to sleep, he found a "vacant corner in an upstairs room filled with sleeping bundles."[57]

POSTSCRIPT

For his personal conduct and handling of his regiment during the Battle of the Bulge, Rudder was awarded the Silver Star, the army's third highest decoration for gallantry. His citation began with an acknowledgment that the "regiment was attacked by vastly superior numbers of enemy forces." It aptly commended him for "skillful handling of his troops [in] numerous counter-thrusts against the ... enemy ... [enabling] his Regiment to inflict high casualties on the enemy with a minimum loss to his own troops. ... At great personal risk to himself, [he] made frequent trips to subordinate units through enemy infiltrated territory and under heavy enemy artillery fire." The citation "credited [him] with stopping an enemy offensive that threatened a large area to the south and west of his defensive position."[58]

The Battle of the Bulge was a turning point in Rudder's adult life, a time when he apparently began contemplating a vocation other than coaching football after the war. His first letter to Chick after the battle was cast in a more pensive tone, his youthful exuberance chastened by close calls, other life-transforming experiences, and his world view expanded by the weight of far greater responsibilities.

"Our lives must be so complete," he wrote, "that we can make up for the time that has been stolen from us. We must plan to give the world the kind of children who can stand the tests that they are certain to face as they grow and take their places in an ever more complicated way of life."[59] He was becoming more inclusive in his concerns about society, people, and the institutions that serve them.

MISTAKEN HISTORIES OF THE BULGE

In three of the most widely read books on the Battle of the Bulge, the 109th Infantry Regiment and Rudder received slight recognition for blunting the German attack. Rudder shares the blame for this oversight with esteemed authors of the books: John Toland, Hugh M. Cole, and Charles B. MacDonald.

In 1959 John Toland produced the first substantial book, *Battle: The Story of the Bulge*. While interviewing retired veterans in San Antonio, he tried unsuccessfully to schedule an interview with Rudder, then commissioner of the Texas General Land Office, a major state agency with heavy administrative and political obligations. With five children at home under the age of eighteen and a ranch in the country, Rudder always had a good excuse to be out of town, especially when a historian who would ask tedious questions wanted to see him at ten o'clock on a Saturday morning, as Toland did. Toland did not mention Rudder or the 109th Infantry in his groundbreaking and influential book.

Neither did the U.S. Army's official historian of the Battle of the Bulge, Hugh M. Cole, get help from Rudder in researching *The Ardennes: The Battle of the Bulge*, published in 1965. His personal letter to Rudder with three questions about the 109th in the fighting withdrawal along the Sûre River got a prompt reply: "I do not remember." By contrast, Rudder's counterpart in the 110th Regiment—the regiment immediately north of the 109th that lost an estimated 2,750 men from its approximate 3,000—was verbose and got far more coverage.[60] The destruction of the 110th and the capture of its commanding officer was a more dramatic story than the fighting withdrawal of the 109th, however skillfully conducted.

Nonetheless, Cole concluded that the dogged defense of the 109th Infantry along the Sûre prevented the Germans from making a wider breach and deeper penetration on the southern shoulder: "The stubborn and successful defense of the towns and villages close to the rivers . . . blocked the road net, . . . and barred a quick sweep into the American rear areas. *The failure to open bridges over the Our and Sûre within the first twenty-four hours forced the German infantry to fight without their accustomed heavy weapons support even while American reinforcements were steadily reducing the numerical edge possessed by the attackers.*"[61] In this way Cole affirmed the importance of Rudder's leadership, albeit with meager personal recognition of him or of the 109th Infantry Regiment.

Charles B. MacDonald's *A Time for Trumpets: The Untold Story of the Battle of the Bulge* (1984) expanded on Toland's account and relied on Cole for many sources. Finding limited mention of the 109th in Cole's official history and none at all in Toland's book, he compounded Cole's oversight in failing to give the 109th Infantry credit for its role in securing the assembly areas for the oncoming 26th and 80th infantry divisions. MacDonald actually got the Grosbous massacre completely wrong, stating that the Germans "drove out a company . . . of the 109th Infantry that had been holding there," when in fact Rudder had intentionally withdrawn Fossum's Task Force L from Grosbous to the ridge, from which they slaughtered the German column marching toward Arlon. Moreover, MacDonald credited the 26th Division with the Grosbous massacre.[62]

There is a plausible explanation for MacDonald's oversight. When the newly arrived Americans passed through the 109th Regiment, they found Fossum's men on the ridge across Wark Creek from Grosbous and assumed the Germans had driven them there. They attributed the German dead and wreckage on the road to their own artillery rather than those haggard looking G.I.s they had just seen on the ridge. Subsequent written reports of their parent units reflected this misconception. Such is the "fog of war," in Clausewitz's phrase.

MacDonald used the records that were available to him. He was a responsible historian as well as my close friend and tutor on the Battle of the Bulge. We made five trips to the Ardennes and spent several weeks driving and walking over the battlefields, mostly on the northern shoulder, where he had fought. If he had begun his research with accurate sources about the 109th—perhaps Fossum's monograph—he would have investigated further and included its extraordinary achievements in his book, still an outstanding treatment of the Battle of the Bulge.

For these reasons, both the 109th Infantry Regiment and Rudder were deprived of rightful recognition for slowing down the German attack that was a major factor in the defense of Bastogne. Whatever historians and their readers may think about this oversight in recorded history, we can be certain that Earl Rudder did not spend one minute worrying about it. He would have considered it a waste of time.

CHAPTER 13

COLMAR POCKET
1945

Two days after Christmas, Rudder brought his 109th Infantry Regiment back under General Cota's command in the 28th Infantry Division. The scattered units of the division were painfully reassembling about twenty miles to the rear in Belgium to begin rebuilding for the third time in six months. They had taken the brunt of German counterattacks in Normandy, the Huertgen Forest, and the Ardennes.

Rudder's regiment, after suffering heavy casualties in November in the Huertgen Forest, had taken another 1,174 casualties (40 percent) during December in the Battle of the Bulge. New men arrived from replacement depots as truckloads of individuals rather than as the trained member of a squad or team. The depot method of replacement was fast, but few new men had combat experience, and they were, in Cota's opinion, little better than cannon fodder. "We haven't time to dig the graves," he said. "These boys don't last long enough to reach the foxholes." Some old-timers befriended newcomers only reluctantly, knowing they would likely soon be mourning their deaths.[1]

In Belgium, Cota's division protected the west flank of Gen. George Patton's forces that had come up from the south and had pierced the German ring around Bastogne on December 26. Patton was now trying to expand the breach in the German encirclement of the town. Cota set up his command post in Neufchateau, and Rudder went three miles further north to Libramont, seven miles southwest of the embattled Bastogne. The muffled roar of heavy cannon fire echoed through the cold winter air like thunder rumbling on the horizon. Germans were in the vicinity of Libramont in small numbers, but the only contact with the enemy occurred on the last day of the year, when Cota came to visit Rudder. Upon arrival, Cota followed his instincts and sent a patrol up the road to the smaller town of Saint-Hubert; the patrol flushed the foe, drawing the unmistakable ripsaw sound of the rapid-firing German MG 42. But the enemy took no initiative, and the two officers spent a quiet evening together, welcoming in the New Year with more reverence than revelry.[2]

On the second day of 1945, Rudder and the regiment moved about thirty miles into France to guard bridges along the Meuse River from Sedan to Verdun. There were credible reports that the enemy might drop saboteurs or troops into the area to disrupt communications and supply lines. G.I.s, spooked by Germans masquerading as Americans in the Battle of the Bulge, even required pregnant women to confirm that their swollen abdomens were what they claimed. For his new command post, Rudder took over a fashionable home in Sedan overlooking a sweeping bend in the Meuse River.[3]

On January 6 he wrote his first letter to Chick since December 5, the longest interval between his letters. It was also his longest letter of the war, six handwritten pages. Making no excuses, he explained the lapse with vague references to the "circumstances of war" and the "recent crisis." "So much has happened since I last wrote that it is hard to know where to start. Much will have to wait until after the war." About leaving the 2nd Ranger Battalion he wrote, "It was with a heavy heart that I went away from them." He contemplated the disconnect between people back home and men at the front: "If only our entire nation could get the viewpoint of the front line soldier we could end this war so much easier and sooner. We of the U.S. take things too easy and never become aroused until the eleventh hour." He still savored the turkey dinner on Christmas Day, but there had been no ceasefire. "It was," he wrote, "like any other day. Everyone was very busy eliminating the Germans so we can spend the next one at home. . . . New Year's Day, we gave thanks that 1944 had given us many victories and prayed that 1945 would bring about the final victory."[4]

On the home front, Americans were expecting quick victories over Germany and Japan and planning extravagant celebrations on the announcement days already designated as V-E Day for Germany's surrender and V-J Day for Japan's. Rudder deplored the planning for V-E Day: "It should not be a day for great celebration but a day of Thanksgiving and reverence for the final victory."[5]

ALL WELL AND SAFE

After posting the letter, he apparently thought about the time required for it to reach her and sent a telegram, his fastest means of getting a message to the States. The Bulge had been banner news back home, and he knew she was worried about him. Worry was an understatement. She was tormented with forebodings that she relieved by concentrating on their children and visiting her parents at the Williamson ranch. "I did not hear from him for

six weeks," she would say. With the telegram, she knew at last that he was
still alive:

MRS J E RUDDER

BRADY TEXAS

ALL WELL AND SAFE. BEST WISHES FOR THE NEW YEAR. ALL MY LOVE

DEAREST=

JAMES E RUDDER[6]

Three days later he wrote again, daydreaming about what he would do when
he returned home. "When I get home, I don't want to be disturbed for a
month. I want to be with just you and the kids. . . . I haven't had a complete
day off for rest and away from the Army since I left Texas."[7]

In Sedan on the night of January 15, 1st Lt. William M. Peña was lounging
in his quarters (also a French home) when he got a call to report to Rudder
at his nearby regimental headquarters. The unprecedented and unexplained
summons aroused Peña's anxiety. He trotted up the street along the river to
Rudder's headquarters and presented himself to a sergeant seated at a desk in
the entranceway. The sergeant led him into a large parlor with high ceilings
and a small blazing fireplace that lit up the room. Rudder was seated near
the fireplace talking with Jim McCoy. He invited Peña to sit down and join
them.

Rudder tried to make conversation; he was meeting Peña for the first
time. "I understand all three of us are Texas Aggies. When were you at
A&M?" Peña, tongue-tied at the moment, managed to say he was in the class
of 1942. Then, he recalled, "The conversation centered around the good old
days at college. I could tell this was an honest attempt to maintain close college ties, but I was having a difficult time with it. I was overawed by the famous Colonel Rudder and was ill at ease with the irascible Colonel McCoy."
Finally, at a lull in the conversation, Rudder said, "I just wanted to meet the
other Aggie," and Peña knew it was time to leave. He returned to his quarters
doubtful that he had gained any favor with his presentation.[8]

The next day orders were passed through the ranks to remove all 28th
Division insignia—the Bloody Bucket—from uniforms, equipment, and vehicles.[9] They were moving roughly 250 miles southeast into the French province of Alsace, where Germans still held the city of Colmar, thirty miles
south of Strasbourg. Few men knew their destination, because only those
who needed to know were told.

Strasbourg had been liberated on November 23, but the enemy still occupied the Colmar Pocket, an area that centered on the city and extended for

fifty miles along the west bank of the Rhine in a valley between the river and the Vosges Mountains to the west. The east bank of the Rhine was German territory. The twenty-two thousand German troops in the Colmar Pocket were a dangerous threat to the French and American forces around its perimeter that had been stretched thin when Patton moved elements of his Third Army northward to contain the German attack in the Ardennes. Tempted by this weakness, Hitler launched his last offensive of the war on the Western Front on the last day of 1944. Giving their offensive the codename Operation Nordwind, the Germans attacked toward Strasbourg, the symbolic capital of Alsace, the province lost with Lorraine to Germany between 1871 and 1918 and from 1940 to 1944.[10]

Short of troops, Eisenhower considered a strategic withdrawal from Strasbourg and the Colmar perimeter to shorten and strengthen his defensive line. However, such a withdrawal would expose hundreds of thousands of French people to German reprisals. The possibility of returning Strasbourg to the Germans, even temporarily, precipitated an international political crisis that involved Roosevelt, Churchill, and Gen. Charles de Gaulle, head of the French provisional government. Eisenhower relented, and Allied forces remained in Strasbourg. The newly liberated people would not be betrayed.

With almost no reserves to contain the German threat, Eisenhower sent Cota's exhausted 28th Division to reinforce those around the Colmar Pocket. An official appraisal found the division so depleted by casualties and fatigue that it was "capable of only limited offensive action." Nonetheless, the division did more than merely reinforce the defense of the perimeter. It led the attack on the city, with Rudder's 109th Infantry as the spear point of the final drive that forced the enemy out of Colmar. In the dead of winter, the division was transported to Alsace in the rickety, unheated, airy French "forty and eight" boxcars that jolted from side to side as they rolled over tracks that had been overused and under-maintained for years. For warmth, the men built fires in barrels set on the floor.[11]

In Alsace, American units were integrated into the First French Army commanded by Gen. Jean de Lattre de Tassigny. The 28th Division arrived as final preparations were underway to drive the Germans out of the Colmar Pocket and across the Rhine. Four American divisions—3rd Infantry, 75th Infantry, 12th Armored, and 28th Infantry—would attack from the north and the French from the south and the west. The cold, wet weather and flat terrain laced with numerous streams and canals favored the defense, as did the "Alsatian network of small towns, each of which could be turned into a small fortress."[12]

EXECUTION OF PVT. EDDIE SLOVIK

Before the attack on Colmar, Rudder was forced to participate in an event that he considered "the most difficult thing I had to do during the entire war." It was the execution of Pvt. Eddie D. Slovik for desertion.[13] Rudder's presence was required because Slovik had deserted from the 109th. It did not matter that Slovik had deserted before Rudder took command of the regiment or that Rudder had never seen Slovik. The colonel had to take part because a U.S. Army tradition, established during the Civil War, held that deserters were to be shot by a firing squad of men from the deserter's regiment. Eisenhower personally confirmed the execution order on December 23 at a moment when it was essential for Americans in the Ardennes to stand fast against the powerful German attack. The supreme commander's order specified that the execution would be carried out on January 31, 1945, "in the area of the 109th Infantry," leaving Rudder no option but to participate.

Rudder's duties were to provide the firing squad and to witness the execution. To muster the firing squad, he instructed his three battalion commanders each to select four expert marksmen, who were to aim for Slovik's heart from a distance of about twenty paces. The 28th Division's provost marshal, its "chief of police," was in charge of the execution. For the site he chose the courtyard of a private home at 86 rue de General Bourgeois on the outskirts of the town of Sainte-Marie-aux-Mines. Only authorized observers would be allowed to witness the execution, and no one outside would be able to see over the courtyard wall, which was seven and one-half feet high. Slovik, bound to a post with his head and neck covered by a hood of thick black cloth and hands tied behind him, was shot to death about ten o'clock in the morning.[14]

Unfortunately, the battalion commanders assigned to select the firing squad members had delegated the selection to the company commanders, who had declined to impose the face-to-face killing of a fellow American on their best soldiers. As a result, incompetent marksmen, perhaps nervous replacements who had arrived the day before, made up the firing squad, and not one bullet struck Slovik's heart. He did not die immediately, but he did expire before a second volley was ordered.

The pathetic scene evoked images that would never fade: the firing squad, the shouted commands in the cold mountain air—"ready, aim, fire"—the crack of rifle fire, the crumpling body, and the dark red stains on the white snow. Although Rudder told Chick about his participation, his children did not learn about it until the publication in 1954 of a well-investigated book by

William Bradford Huie entitled *The Execution of Private Slovik*. Even then, Rudder never discussed the execution with his children.[15]

Rudder and Cota knew death on the battlefield, but the organized spectacle of Americans killing one of their own disturbed them as much as did other horrors of the war. The shared trauma became one of their bonds. Cota's bodyguard said the general "cried like a kid" after the execution. Rudder hurriedly composed a memorandum to inform the men of the 109th Infantry about the execution and the reason for it. In blunt language, he stated his philosophy of military service: "The person that is not willing to fight and die, if need be, for his country has no right to life." He added that the best way to "return home at the earliest possible moment" was to "close with and eliminate the enemy."[16]

In 1968 the lasting effect of the Slovik execution on Rudder was evident to Wayne C. Hall in an office conference at Texas A&M. Hall was the university's chief academic officer and went to Rudder's office for their customary twice weekly, early-morning meeting. Rudder was nearly always there when Hall arrived, but on this day he was an hour late. "I could detect that he was not feeling well," Hall recalled. "His face was grey, he seemed in pain, and his speech was somewhat slurred and irrational. He bade me to move my chair up along the right side of his desk." Hall concluded that Rudder was distracted by "a media flagellation about his role in a . . . travesty involving the execution of a private by a firing squad." Whatever the cause of Rudder's distressing flashback—perhaps an inquiry from a newspaper reporter or writer—he could not talk coherently about it. Hall left the meeting convinced that the Slovik execution caused Rudder "more personal sorrow and pain than . . . any other unpleasant event in his life."[17]

Of the approximately forty thousand American deserters during the war, Slovik was the only one put to death. In Europe, ninety-five American soldiers were hanged for violent crimes such as rape or the murder of civilians. Only Slovik was executed by a firing squad, and his pitiful lot was Rudder's misfortune as well. In mid-1960 Rudder heard that his participation in Slovik's execution had been discussed in a history course taught by Haskell Monroe. He asked Monroe for an explanation and then remarked, "I always thought that young man had more problems than cowardice."[18]

LIBERATION OF COLMAR

While Rudder and Cota were distracted by the Slovik affair, most of the 28th Division fought their way against fierce resistance from the Vosges

Mountains across the rivers and canals of the Kaysersberg Valley to positions north of Colmar and prepared to attack straight into the city. To the east, in the ten miles between Colmar and the Rhine, the U.S. 3rd and 75th infantry divisions pressed forward in parallel with the 28th Division. The Germans were trapped. They could escape only by crossing the Rhine before they were killed or captured. Colmar was "ripe fruit ready to fall," in the opinion of Madame Lise Pommois, Alsace's leading historian of the liberation.[19] But it would not happen without effort by and casualties among both French and Americans.

Cota chose Rudder's 109th Infantry for the attack. On February 1 at 1:30 in the afternoon, Rudder issued an oral order to jump off at nine o'clock that night. The regiment was to seize the approaches on the north side of Colmar—the key road intersections, bridges, and sites with the best observation. A night attack was rare, especially against a defended city, and Colmar had forty thousand civilian inhabitants as well as more than twenty thousand German troops within the perimeter. Rudder chose the reliable Jim McCoy and his 3rd Battalion as the leading element to attack down the main north-south road into the city. There was an unusual twist to this operation: once the approach route was secured and German outer defenses penetrated, Rudder was to pull the 109th aside and permit the French 5th Armored Division to drive the hated foe out of Colmar.

The speed and the effectiveness of the attack on Colmar was influenced by the Ranger training that Rudder had prescribed for the regiment's anti-tank company. After the Battle of the Bulge, he was convinced that their 57 mm gun was no better than a peashooter against German tanks. So he reorganized the antitank company, called them the Raider Company, and gave the men Ranger training, including instruction in night fighting. Dispersed to spearhead companies, the men of the Raider Company led the regiment into Colmar, and the attack went off faster than anyone expected.[20]

Willie Peña led a platoon of about thirty-five riflemen into Colmar. The line of departure was the forward edge of a clearing in a densely wooded forest about three miles north of the city center. They entered the forest after dark in a single file with the regular platoon leader at the head and Peña at the rear. With no moonlight, it was pitch black under the tree canopy and too dark to see the next man ahead. In low tones the word was passed back: "Keep in touch with the man in front." They shuffled along a trail with each man reaching out to touch the one in front of him like a blind man following another. After progressing through the wooded abyss for a quarter of an hour, the man in front of Peña turned and whispered, "We've lost contact." Peña worked his way to the head of the remaining column and asked the soldier there, "How long ago did you lose contact?" "Ten minutes," was the reply from a private, who was likely one of 921 new men who had come to the regiment in the previous month. Peña got his group on the correct trail and caught up with the rest of the platoon just as they left the forest, crossing the line of departure. After only a few steps in the clearing, the Germans opened up on them, the platoon leader was fatally wounded, and Peña took over.[21]

He led the platoon through a vineyard out to the main road into Colmar, where they turned left. Advancing into Colmar on both sides of the street, they kept five-yard intervals between each man and held their weapons chest high, at the ready. When they approached the built-up area of the city, street fighting began in earnest. Peña's carbine jammed just as he jumped up on a barricade to fire on Germans behind it; luckily for him, others in his platoon took them under fire, and they ran away or were captured. As Peña's small band pressed into the city, snipers fired from second-story windows before they, too, fled or became casualties. Some refused to surrender and were killed.

When Peña reached the designated point inside the city's perimeter, Mc-Coy, the battalion commander, appeared seemingly from nowhere and told him to stop and disperse his platoon into houses along the street. Peña heard McCoy radio Rudder's command post that the battalion was on the objective. He had to repeat the message twice before his contact would believe they had completed their mission so quickly. After fighting through the night, Peña's men rested as the French armored column came down the street, driving toward the center of Colmar. An unexpected bonus for Peña's platoon was the capture of a German horse-drawn kitchen with hot breakfast grub ready to be served.[22]

Back at Rudder's command post, four French officers had arrived at 1:33 AM to track the progress of the attack and to plan for their units to pass through the Americans holding their positions inside the city. One of the French officers was Brig. Gen. Guy Schlesser, commander of the tanks that would pass through the Americans. Cota came at 5:45 AM to observe and to issue any last-minute instructions.

The surprise and swiftness of the three battalions of the 109th in their night attack caught the Germans off guard. By midmorning the French tanks had passed through the 109th, and before dark Colmar was freed of its oppressors for the first time in four and one-half years. The cost to Rudder's regiment was considered light: 125 men killed, wounded, or missing. By 6:00 PM Rudder had moved his command post through Colmar and had arrayed his three battalions in a horseshoe-shaped defense south of the city to prevent a German counterattack from disturbing Colmar's celebrations.

In the following week the regiment continued southeastward to the Rhine and encountered little opposition. Most of the Germans had their bags packed, but the G.I.s had to root out occasional fanatics. Rudder moved his command post to the village of Sainte-Croix-en-Plaine, six miles south of Colmar and about the same distance from the Rhine. When the enemy was finally driven across the Rhine, the Colmar Pocket was cleared out except for small groups bypassed in the rapid advance, including twenty-five who were flushed from the basement of a convent where nuns had protected them.[23]

"FAITHFUL TO A GENTLEMEN'S AGREEMENT"

French authorities selected February 8 for Colmar's victory celebration. In the grand parade, one company of the 109th Infantry Regiment represented all American forces, because men of the regiment were the first to enter the city. Rudder was at the head of the contingent with McCoy behind him.[24] On a cloudy but bright Thursday afternoon they marched down the broad avenue now restored to its historic name, Avenue de la République; it had been called Adolf-Hitler-Strasse during the German occupation. Colmar, like Paris and Strasbourg, escaped the war with little destruction, not least because the 109th's unexpected night attack kept the enemy from reinforcing the city. Photographs of Rudder in the parade with his country's flag slightly billowing behind him and thousands of cheering, ecstatic people along the street explain why this event was one of his most memorable experiences of the war.

In retrospect, Alsatian historian Lise Pommois believes the Americans made a mistake when they stood aside and permitted the French to drive the Germans from Colmar. "It left the people with the false idea that the French had liberated themselves," she says. "Even young French soldiers entering Colmar thought they, not Americans, had liberated the city. The Americans and the French should have entered together."[25]

Colmar city officials in 1945 knew how their liberation was achieved, and many were still influential ten years later when the city commemorated the tenth anniversary of its liberation. They invited an American delegation, and President Eisenhower appointed Rudder as a member. But twenty and thirty years after the liberation, most city officials had been small children in 1945 and watched the "French liberate themselves." Few knew the truth of their liberation and therefore did not fully appreciate what the Americans had done.

Rudder gave Chick a jubilant account. "My regiment really has done a fine job, and I have received much recognition because of it. All the good

Above: *Rudder
leading the American
contingent in the
Liberation Parade
of Colmar, France,
February 8, 1945.
(U.S. National
Archives)*

Right: *Rudder in
Colmar, France,
February 12, 1945,
newly decorated by
General Jean de Lattre
de Tassigny with the
French Croix de Guerre
with palm. (Courtesy
of Margaret Rudder)*

work has been done by the soldiers in the line." Rudder received more honors after the liberation parade. General Schlesser proclaimed him an honorary member of the French Foreign Legion. Rudder replied with a letter in French, written by his interpreter: "It was a rare privilege to serve such a great soldier as you are." On February 10, two days after the Colmar victory parade, the widely circulated Paris newspaper *Le Figaro* carried a story under the headline, "Brothers in Arms," praising the 109th, which, "having reached the gates of the city, halted to give the 5th Armored Division the honor of being the first to enter." Charles de Gaulle, as head of the provisional French government, signed a proclamation citing Rudder by name as well as his regiment.[26]

In a solemn ceremony on Colmar's central square, Gen. Jean de Lattre de Tassigny bestowed on Rudder the French Croix de Guerre with palm and the Legion of Honor, the superior decoration. In bestowing the Legion of Honor, he laid a sword on both sides of Rudder's shoulders. Then, in the manner of the traditional French *accolade,* the general gently took Rudder by the shoulders and grazed his cheeks on both sides. It was another profound and teary moment for Rudder. Four years later, General de Tassigny, now *maréchal* of the French army, praised Rudder in his war memoir: "Faithful to a gentleman's agreement and the traditions of chivalry, Colonel James E. Rudder stopped his 109th infantry regiment to permit Schlesser's tanks the honor of entering Colmar first."[27]

On February 18 a courier delivered a message from Eisenhower to Cota directing him to notify Rudder that he had been promoted to colonel. At age thirty-four he was not the youngest bird colonel in the army, but few were more respected for their leadership on the battlefield. He was described by a subordinate in the 109th Regiment as "one of the very select personal heroes of World War II."[28]

CHAPTER 14

END OF THE WAR

Shortly after five o'clock on the afternoon of February 9, General Cota came to Rudder's command post in a former textiles store in the center of Croix-en-Plaine. When asked about the 109th Infantry's defensive positions along the Rhine, Rudder pointed to the map locations of half a dozen squad-sized detachments (ten to twelve men) watching the other side of the river. In addition, an untold number of sharpshooters armed with sniper rifles equipped with telescopic sights were hidden along the riverbank to keep the Germans buttoned up on the other side. Cota stressed the importance of around-the-clock vigilance against a spoiling attack by the demoralized but spiteful foe.[1]

Cota informed Rudder that the division was pulling back west of Nancy to reorganize and rest before reentering the front lines further north. A Moroccan outfit with French officers would replace the regiment. Several French officers came the next morning to discuss the changeover, which began that afternoon, although Rudder remained in the area with his regiment for forty-eight hours in case the Jerries crossed the chocolate-colored stream to test the newcomers. None tried.

Before noon on February 14, the 109th began a 130-mile vehicular road march over the narrow, twisting passes of the Vosges Mountains to Vaucouleurs. The trip required most of the day, but by nine o'clock that evening Rudder had reestablished his command post in a row of houses in the center of the town. By the next morning, hot water was flowing, and the men were cleaning up and pulling on new socks, underwear, and woolen long johns. That afternoon Rudder held a meeting for all commanders to review problems in their convoy groups from Croix-en-Plaine; there had been irregularities in keeping proper distances between vehicles, and special precautions were necessary for trucks carrying high explosives. He directed them to begin preparing for another long convoy movement almost two hundred miles north and into Germany. In houses along the streets the G.I.s disassembled rifles and machine guns and laid the parts on canvas shelter halves spread on the floor, where they sat cross-legged, cleaning them with dirt-stained toothbrushes and small greasy rags. New vehicles, weapons, and men were arriving, and Rudder tried to interview all new officers. Everyone needed this relaxing week in Vaucouleurs before they departed ready to do battle again.[2]

SCHLEIDEN

Rudder's shooting war would end near the German town of Schleiden, only fifteen miles south of Bergstein, where he had left the 2nd Ranger Battalion in early December. So much had happened since then that the two and one-half months could have been half a lifetime ago. But the most important thing had not changed: the Germans had not collapsed as the Allied high command expected and still held a substantial area west of the Rhine. Eisenhower's strategy was to drive the enemy from the entire west bank of the Rhine before crossing it in strength anywhere. To that end, a major effort, codenamed Operation Lumberjack, would be made to clear all remaining German military forces from the west bank of the Rhine between the cities of Cologne and Bonn, the reason Rudder and his regiment had been moved into the area.

On the afternoon of February 23, the 109th began replacing the 9th Infantry Regiment in a hilly region of western Germany called the Eifel, an eastward extension of the Ardennes plateau that Rudder knew well from the Battle of the Bulge. His new command post was in the village of Harperscheid, about three miles west of Schleiden, which was still under German control. Schleiden, lying along the narrow valley of the Olef River, was in ruins from American artillery fired from miles to the rear. The Germans had placed thousands of booby traps and mines on roads and trails and in buildings to inflict maximum casualties on the advancing Americans. Most civilians had left on orders of the Nazi party. Scattered groups of the Wehrmacht were in the hills east of Schleiden, and a few were in the town. More pertinent to Rudder, the enemy had outposts west of the Olef, where his regiment assumed responsibility for the defense at 2:30 AM on February 24.[3]

When daylight came, Rudder appraised his new situation. The area was semiforested with conifers and had considerable open farmland above its numerous steep ravines that drained into the normally shallow and slow-flowing Olef. He kept one of his three battalions in reserve and put the other two on the high ground overlooking Schleiden and the river. Although the war was lost for the Germans, many had not lost their desire to kill Americans; the regiment would have fatalities from mines and snipers. A sniper brought down Capt. Oswald P. Ransonet, a company commander, and Lt.

Willie Peña—the plucky Aggie architect—stepped on a mine and lost his left foot. Peña would aptly label his splendid personal account of the war *As Far as Schleiden*.[4] In 1963 Rudder remembered Peña and commended him in his dedicatory remarks for Texas A&M's new architecture building.

At first, the 109th's mission was to keep pressure on the Germans while the other two regiments of the 28th Division sliced around behind Schleiden from north and south. Rudder sent strong offensive patrols across the Olef River to keep the enemy's attention while gradually pushing those west of the river to the other side. Once the western part of the Schleiden was secure, he planned for the entire regiment to cross the river and move through the town. This maneuver would be a major operation, so he moved closer to the line of departure for his rifle companies by going to a two-story farmhouse on the eastern edge of the village of Bronsfeld, at the top of a steep, curving road that led down to the valley of the Olef and into Schleiden. The attack was set for the afternoon of March 3.

About one o'clock, Rudder entered the farmhouse, whose occupant, war widow Maria Schumacher, had fled with her two children and farm animals, normally housed in the basement during the winter. The stench of the animals remained and was absorbed in the clothing of the G.I.s occupying the house, giving them an aroma that made them as unpopular with others as it did the Schumacher children when they went to school.[5] Belts of machine gun ammunition were hanging from the walls, while boxes of hand grenades and yellow-banded (high explosive) mortar shells were stacked on the floor.

By 5:30 that afternoon the Americans had reached most of the designated buildings in Schleiden, encountering no enemy troops but even more mines and booby-trapped explosives than expected. Rudder stopped them and requested additional mine clearing help from engineers before the advance resumed the next day. By early the next morning, March 7, the three battalions of the regiment were across the Olef and in Schleiden. It would be their last day of fighting. The enemy had no coordinated defense, but individual Germans continued to resist. The Americans advanced house by house, tossing fragmentation grenades into dark basements and breaking down walls between houses to avoid exposure in the streets. Everyone was determined not be the last man to die, and they knew that even the most Hitler-hating, disillusioned German who thought simply of defending his homeland could kill them as easily as could a fanatical Nazi Waffen SS man. By midafternoon they were on the high ground east of the town. Sure enough, ten men paid a price in blood on their last day of combat; two were killed and eight were wounded.[6]

When the regiment got beyond Schleiden, twelve-year-old Karl Josef Lüttgens saw his first American soldier. He and his parents had fled the town

and had taken shelter in the cellar of a farmhouse with several other evacuees, including an English-speaking Roman Catholic priest. They heard an
American tank approaching and peeped out as it crashed through a fence
and rolled to a stop on the farm's dung heap. Karl and the others were fear-
ful, because Nazi party officials had told them the Americans were cruel and
would brutalize them. In this unlikely spot, the tank commander opened
the hatch and climbed down. The priest went out to talk to him and, within
a few minutes, beckoned the others to follow. Their fears subsided when
the American smiled and handed cigarettes to the men. Karl stood so close
that he whiffed the rich odor of the tanker's glossy brown leather jacket.
When the tanker returned the package of cigarettes to his jacket, he pulled
out a small relic that immediately relaxed the worried Germans. Schleiden
was a Roman Catholic town, and "When we saw his rosary," Karl recalled
with a soft smile of fond remembrance in his seventy-third year, "we knew
everything was going to be all right."[7]

REAR AREA DUTY

For the next six weeks the regiment had rear-area security duties: patrolling
rural areas of Germany, relocating displaced persons, and accommodating
newly released Allied prisoners of war. Rudder was generous with leaves,
even taking some himself. He visited the 2nd Ranger Battalion on March 15.
By coincidence, that was the same day that the Rangers discovered thirty-
five hundred slave laborers—Russians, Poles and French—hiding in a tunnel
near Mayschoss. Rudder stayed four days in a hunting lodge, requisitioned
from a German baron, with "good table linens, dishes, silver ware, soft beds,
running water, and," he remarked, "all the things they have been depriving
us of since D-Day." He observed that Germans outside their obliterated cities
had a higher standard of living than the French or Belgians (or the British,
according to economists), and their homes were "much more modern in every respect." He concluded that "they have been living off the fat of the land
and are holding on as long as possible."[8]

He gave himself a much-deserved week off and went to London, where he
stayed in his favorite hotel, the Savoy. "My room overlooks the Thames River
near Waterloo Bridge," he wrote to Chick. "If you were only here, everything
would be perfect. I have had breakfast in bed two mornings now, then go
back to sleep until noon. I only have 72 hours here and then back to the land
of the super race."[9]

Returning to Germany, he crossed the Rhine for the first time on a
pontoon bridge at Bad Honningen, about ten miles south of the original

bridgehead at Remagen. Near Herschbach he established his command post in a school and sent patrols across the area, mostly to see and be seen by the cowed German civilians. Favoring Eisenhower's decree of no fraternization with Germans, he enforced it strictly. He ran into Jim Dan Hill, the artillery colonel from Texas he knew from preinvasion days in England. A trained historian, Hill wrote an account of their conversation: "I asked Rudder what he planned to do after the war. He opined the last two years in the army had convinced him that Mexican sheepherders had good jobs. He thought if he could get home within the next six months, he might find a good collie dog for doing the legwork, and try to chisel some good, honest Mexican out of his job."[10] If Rudder actually spoke in such a manner, he was tired or homesick— and probably both.

On April 6 Rudder participated in a high-level ceremonial flag raising at the magnificent Prussian fortress of Ehrenbreitstein high on the east bank of the Rhine above the confluence of the Moselle and Rhine Rivers at Koblenz. General Bradley came for the ceremony marking the first official raising of an American flag in Germany during the war. At Ehrenbreitstein, Rudder met Col. Harrison A. Gerhardt, who had come from Washington. Gerhardt told him about postwar plans to continue conscription and expand the army reserves. Rudder was interested and followed up with a letter to Gerhardt that is significant for his unequivocal declaration that he intended to return to civilian life, which would have surprised many of his comrades in arms. But his statement of interest in the army reserves foretold his second career for the remainder of his life: "As I told you, I am particularly desirous to participate in this program. Being a civilian myself and with the wide experience I have had in the army, I am certain I can do much to help put over a program of this type."[11]

Any temptation he had to remain in the army was overwhelmed by his sense of belonging in Texas with family, friends, the land (especially the ranch), the intimate bonds of small town life, and the heroic myths of the Lone Star State—Sam Houston, Davy Crockett, the Alamo—"all of it," he might have said. His daughters believed that being near his mother was a major reason. Even Gen. Courtney H. Hodges tried to persuade Rudder to remain in the army by promising him choice assignments, but Rudder knew his own mind and was unyielding. When Hodges told Rudder that he intended to retire near Kerrville, Texas, it was an opening for Rudder to tell him that he would not be far away in Brady.[12]

On April 23 the 109th Infantry Regiment was assigned an occupation area of about 1,475 square miles centered on the town of Kirchheimbolanden in a province of vineyards about forty-five miles southwest of Frankfurt. For his headquarters, Rudder took the manor house of a large estate, where a guest noted, "Wine at meals was plentifully evident." When an officer's war bride came to visit from England, Rudder gave up his master bedroom to the couple, prompting a man to say that he "demonstrated again his loyalty to the soldiers he commanded."[13]

COMING HOME

Following the German surrender on May 8, men began thinking more seriously about deployment to the other side of the world for the invasion of Japan. Two popular slogans made the rounds: "Two down and one to go!" and "Stay alive in forty-five!" Predictions of the number of American casualties that would result from an invasion of Japan ranged up to one million. "We knew we were going to Japan and I figured my odds were running out," said one soldier. "Japan was the last stop."[14]

The war with Japan was also on Chick's mind: "I pray that you'll get to come home for a while if you do have to go to the Pacific" and that a "miracle would happen and things would be over there in a short time." She got her "miracle of deliverance," as Churchill called it, with the bombing of Hiroshima and Nagasaki.[15]

In the immediate aftermath of the German surrender, Earl was speechless: "I have started to write you at least six times. Little [else] matters except getting home and yet there is so much to be done here that it leaves one without words. Our big problems are getting a government set up for the Germans and gathering up the displaced Russians, Italians, and Poles so they can be returned to their homes." When she asked about his health, he assured her, "I have never been sick or to a hospital since I've been over here."[16]

Men of the 2nd Ranger Battalion also expected to be sent to the Pacific, and Rudder got a touching letter from Lt. Bob Edlin in Pilsen, Czechoslovakia. Edlin's intrepid Fabulous Four, renowned for their daring patrols into hostile territory, wanted to rejoin Rudder if they were going back into combat. Edlin could only write from the heart:

Dear Colonel:

   Sorry to bother you, but several of the boys have asked me to write you. We received the dope several days ago, that the 2nd Ranger Bn. is all finished. It is possible for us to transfer to other units, so Sgts. Courtney and Dreher, I'm sure you remember them and myself, have volunteered

Rudder lifts a toast on V-E Day, May 8, 1945. Major James H. McCoy, commanding officer of the 3rd Battalion of Rudder's 109th Regimental Combat Team, is second from the left. Others in the photograph cannot be identified. (Courtesy of Margaret Rudder)

for further duty. The chances are that we'll be separated unless we all stick together in transferring and we know of no-one we would rather serve with than "Big Jim."

If you're going into some more fighting we would like to go with you. The old out-fit is still the best in the world and all the fellows still miss you. Wish the Bn. could fight again together but guess this is for the best. Please excuse the informality Colonel, but you are our last hope of sticking together. Thanks very much, and we'll be waiting for an answer.

Respectfully yours,
Bob[17]

Fast-moving events overtook Edlin's request and brought an end to the war. Rudder vacationed for a week on the French Riviera where hotels had been taken over by the army for men of all ranks to rest and relax. On the first anniversary of D-Day, he talked far into the night with Lt. Gen. Leonard T. Gerow about the invasion. He drove into the mountains on Route Napoléon to a perfume factory in Grasse, sailed on the Mediterranean, and walked

Rudder in Germany, summer of 1945, while his 109th Infantry Regiment had occupation duties with responsibility for 1,450 square miles of territory southwest of Frankfurt. (U.S. Army photograph, courtesy of Margaret Rudder)

through Monte Carlo casinos without dropping a chip on the tables, so he said. His time on the Riviera was "the first real sunshine I've had in two years."[18]

Back in Germany, he moved with the regiment on July 8 to an assembly area near Reims, France, called Camp Pittsburgh, considered merely a way station to Japan via the States. Only a fool would go AWOL now, and most hours of the day were unscheduled, allowing men to talk and to reflect on what they had done in the liberation of Europe. Such relaxed conditions continued during their trans-Atlantic voyage, permitting almost a month for soldiers to unwind, loosen up, and let go with anything they had on their minds. During the crossing the seas were calm, and church services were held almost every day. Music was piped through the intercom.

Swapping stories as they came home together was, in a sense, one long session of unstructured group counseling. It was talk therapy. A man had opportunities to open up and clear his mind of anxiety or guilt for anything he had done or not done during the horrors they had been through. It was a sharp contrast to the Americans who served in Vietnam two decades later. Then, when a man left Saigon, he was usually on a jetliner with a couple of hundred other G.I.s, most of them strangers, and was back in the United States within a single day with little conversation or group talk.

From Camp Pittsburgh the 109th moved to a transit camp near the port of Le Havre, certain evidence that they were returning stateside, at least for a brief leave at home. In expectation of their future, the army sent lecturers to orient the regiment on Japan—its history, its army, uniforms, and tactical methods. By July 30, when the regiment sailed for New York on the transport ship *Mormacport*, Rudder knew the army planned for the regiment to re-assemble at San Luis Obispo in California for intensive amphibious training to prepare for the seaborne attack on Japan. But on August 6, the day before the *Mormacport* entered New York harbor, the atomic bomb was dropped on Hiroshima, followed three days later by another on Nagasaki, in effect ending the war.

Chick and Earl, unable to communicate between France and the United States except by letter, tried to anticipate when and where he would arrive on American soil. When he learned that *Mormacport* would go to New York, he wrote, "I am sorry you will not be able to meet me. I will call you when I arrive. I will still have troops to look after until we reach San Antonio. . . . The smart thing for you to do is to meet me in San Antonio."[19]

Unknown to Earl, Chick was in New York waiting for him even before he boarded the ship in Le Havre. How she had learned the details of his arrival is a tribute to her resourcefulness. At the movie theater in Menard, she overheard the owner, Henry Reeves, say that a cousin in the 28th Division's advance party was already in Philadelphia. She called the cousin, and he referred her to the officer coordinating the arrival of the *Mormacport* in New York. She contacted him and was told, "I know you want to see him get off the boat, but you can't do that."

"Would I be crazy to go up there without him knowing I was there?" she asked herself. A few days later a Brady friend, whose husband was in New York, came to her with a proposal: "You've got to go to New York with me." Chick seized on the idea, and they found a sailor and a woman whose naval husband was stationed there to travel with them. Ten dollars from each of the three passengers paid for the gasoline, and they drove straight through to New York. In midtown Manhattan she stayed with Alice Wilkins, the wife of Earl's former adjutant who was seriously wounded on Omaha Beach, the same Alice Wilkins that Earl had instinctively called a *damnyankee,* the proper term for Northerners in his childhood home.[20]

In New York, the army officer in charge of disembarking the regiment sent Earl a radio message while his ship was still at sea: "Your wife is in New York. Please telephone her, Whitehall 3–6110." Knowing his arrival day, Chick made a reservation at the upscale Pierre Hotel at Fifth Avenue and 61st Street across from Central Park. The *Mormacport* docked about nine o'clock on the morning of August 7, and at four that afternoon he knocked on her door. "That was pretty exciting," she sighed longingly in 2002. "I had not seen him for two years."[21]

When the Japanese surrendered, plans to deploy the 28th Division to the Pacific were cancelled, and it was sent to Camp Shelby, Mississippi, for de-activation. Chick wanted Earl home as soon as possible, but he wanted to keep drawing his colonel's pay and allowances until he had a cash flow in civilian life. His attitude about money had not changed since he counted pennies as a poor boy in Eden. Chick and Earl, like tens of thousands of other couples at the end of the war, were in a transitional period that required unprecedented adjustments. "It will be some time before we can adjust ourselves to a normal life again," he cautioned. At age thirty-five, Earl was between a past filled with the unceasing urgencies of war, exhilarations, and thunderous noise and the prospect of a tranquil civilian life of routine consistencies: sitting in a familiar church pew, driving country lanes, and working in the quietude of the ranch, disturbed only by the wind in the trees and bleating of sheep. If the predictability of civilian life was a trap, it was also a refuge. Even in ordinary times he was entering a critical period in the lives of many men; the last four months of 1945 proved to be the most vacillating period of his adult life.

QUANDARY

Earl was trying to decide between two incompatible future occupations while his wife wanted him home—now! On the one hand he had agreed to partner with Frank Corder in a new business on the Brady square to sell appliances (General Electric) and tires (Goodyear). At the same time, Dean Davis was expecting him to return as Tarleton College's football coach, and he had not told Davis otherwise. "I will ask [Tarleton] to delay my return for four months," he informed Chick in November. "That will give me a better chance to decide if I want to go back or not." At that moment Frank Corder was in Brady organizing their new business, and Chick was uneasily writing checks on their personal bank account to purchase goods to stock the business that she did not fully understand.[22]

Ranching was also a business. Her father wanted to retire and give sheep and cattle to Chick and Earl, but Earl asked for time to study the gift tax implications. As for their own ranch, he had been away for more than four years, and maintenance was long overdue on corrals, loading chutes, roads, fences, water wells, and windmills. "There is so much to be done," he said, "that if we rely on someone else it will be unsatisfactory."[23]

Their lives were in flux, Earl was away, and Chick was at home with the two small children managing frustrating responsibilities. His absences were always a grievance, and this period was the most difficult for her to tolerate. He needed time to sort things out and decide on the future direction of his life. So when the army asked him to remain temporarily on active duty in charge of a Victory Loan Train filled with captured booty that was crisscrossing the country to promote the sale of war bonds, he accepted. Chick objected, especially when she learned that Bess Meyerson, the unmarried former Miss America, would also be on the train. Meyerson seems to have spent little, if any, time on the train and did not mention the Victory Loan Train in her autobiography.

The assignment gave Earl time to think through alternatives while continuing to generate an income. He finally reached their Brady home two days before Christmas, and, with his accumulated leave time, he collected his salary until mid-April 1946. His warm welcome, both public and private, quickly resolved any lingering uncertainty he had about where they would live and what he would do. His nephew, ten-year-old Johnny Rudder, remembered his homecoming as "the first time I realized the meaning of family love."[24] Earl had a gift for each child, and Johnny's was a German army helmet.

PART THREE

PUBLIC SERVANT

The credit belongs to the man who is actually in the arena,
whose face is marred by dust and sweat and blood, who strives valiantly,
who errs and comes up short again and again, because there is no effort
without error or shortcoming, but who knows the great enthusiasms,
the great devotions, who spends himself for a worthy cause; who, at the best,
knows, in the end, the triumph of high achievement, and who, at the worst,
if he fails, at least he fails while daring greatly, so that his place shall never be
with those cold and timid souls who knew neither victory nor defeat.
—*Theodore Roosevelt*, Citizenship in a Republic, *1910*

CHAPTER 15

RISE TO PROMINENCE
1946–1954

Rudder had gone to war as a man of faith, believing in the basic goodness of people in the small towns of his early life, in the cohesion and bonds of his family, and in the religious teachings of his childhood. They were the psychological pillars that inspired him with confidence, shielded him from doubt, and buttressed his spirits in times of peril. He returned from the war with his faith strengthened, eager to reconnect with ordinary folk, to be a contributing citizen, and to use his life to make a positive difference in the lives of others on a wider and wider scale.

He looked much like the same person, but he was different within, and he would often say to his family, "I was saved for a purpose." The main thing he wanted to do was to enjoy the peace for which such an exorbitant price had been paid. That's why he and millions of others did not talk about the war. If introduced as "Colonel Earl Rudder," he would quickly say, "Not Colonel anymore. I'm just plain Earl Rudder."[1] And unlike returning veterans who vowed never again to wear khaki (or navy blue), he wore the same khaki pants he brought home from active duty until his girth exceeded their capacity.

Shortly after New Year's Day 1946, he told his friend, Smitty Smith, of the *Brady Standard,* "I am back in the best little town with the best people in West Texas." He was planning for the future. The first decision confirmed that Brady was home; Chick and Earl would rear their children in their adopted hometown. Three other decisions were public news: He would not resume coaching football at Tarleton College; in partnership with Frank Corder he would start a new business enterprise, the Corder-Rudder Tire and Supply Store, to sell General Electric appliances and Goodyear tires; and he would be on the April ballot for mayor of Brady.[2]

Two private decisions were to buy a new home and to ranch. The two-bedroom frame house where Chick had lived with Sis and Bud since mid-1943 was too small for the family they intended. The second was hardly a decision; he would ranch their twelve square miles of pastureland that her parents had helped them obtain. West Texas was ranching country, and anyone with enough land used it to graze cattle and usually sheep in his area.[3]

Earl and Frank located their business at the busiest intersection in town, where Bridge Street emptied onto the McCulloch County courthouse square. Frank managed the business, and Earl did not keep regular hours, or so it seemed to the gaunt old men who watched from under the pecan trees around the courthouse. The business served two purposes: it kept him in contact with his friend, Frank Corder, and it was a niche from which he could reenter civic life with the possibility of financial gain. The challenge of operating a retail business had appealed to Rudder since his boyhood, when the successful tycoon was an American icon. In this case, however, the experience undercut his enthusiasm for it. The partnership ended a year later when he bought Corder's interest. They continued to operate under the same name until Corder withdrew the next year. Two years later, in 1950, Rudder sold out, ending his retail ventures in Brady or elsewhere.[4]

Unlike Chick, he did not come from a ranching family. She told his biographer, "Earl was a town boy, not a ranch boy. So he hired somebody to do it for him." Fortunately, a spread of more than seventy-six hundred acres normally generated sufficient revenue to hire a foreman, who knew what to do, and ranch hands for the endless repetitive chores. "He jumped into ranching with both feet," said his son Bud, while his daughter Anne, or "Sis," thought of her father as "part and parcel of the land."[5] Rudder tended the business side: buying and selling livestock as well as marketing wool. He studied range management and animal husbandry and initiated projects to conserve water and improve the land for grazing. Ranching was, and would remain, one of his main interests.

Those first nine years after the war in Brady were the most tranquil era of his adult life, as relaxed as he permitted it to be. His wife recognized no symptoms of posttraumatic stress disorder. He organized his days by the sun rather than the clock, and except for city council and army reserve meetings, his obligations were not imposed by others. He purchased two small farms that brought his total holdings to more than eight thousand acres and began developing a herd of black angus cattle, while most ranchers still preferred white-faced herefords. In buying and selling livestock he partnered at times with Frank Corder and Chick's younger brother, Alton "Rusty" Williamson. Alone with Rusty, he occasionally asked, "Am I treating your sister all right? . . . Does she say anything that I've done wrong?" "No," Rusty would reply, "She's perfectly happy."[6]

His mother lived nearby, and he saw her often. On Sundays he made two trips to the Methodist church. The first was to take the children and his

Rudder shipping cattle to better grazing land in Illinois during a prolonged drought. Left to right: *Frank Corder, Frank "Buddy" Corder Jr., Rudder, and Ed Campbell in the stockyards of Brady, Texas. (*Brady Standard, *April 15, 1952)*

mother; then he would return for Chick, who had stayed behind to get the noon meal in the oven. After church his mother came home with them for dinner and sat beside him. He ignored the moments of tension between his wife and his mother, who might admonish him with, "Earl, you're too hard on these chil'ren."

MAYOR OF BRADY

Rudder became mayor of Brady in the usual way that he rose to leadership positions in organizations: he was asked. He did not seek the job; he merely agreed to put his name on the ballot, and he did not campaign. He did not maneuver for control of groups, and he seldom promoted his personal views except on important public issues.

His supporters remembered him as a popular high school teacher and coach of winning football teams. Now he was the best-known local hero of the war. In postwar America veterans had a distinct advantage, especially those who had served in dangerous situations. When votes were counted on

April 2, his nonveteran opponent, who had been in office for three years, polled 244 votes, and Rudder had 624. The term was for two years. He ran unopposed for reelection in 1948 and again in 1950. When his third term ended in 1952, he declined to run again, saying, "My decision not to seek office again is based on my firm belief that no individual should monopolize any public office."[7]

He went to the mayor's office almost every day, a three-minute walk from the Corder-Rudder store. As mayor, he was the equivalent of a corporate CEO and chairman of the board. Brady's mayor-council form of government relied on a strong mayor who, the townsfolk said, "ran the city." By law he "inspected all city offices, called meetings of the council and recommended improvements of the finances, the police, health, security, cleanliness, comfort, and good government." All department heads reported to him: sanitation, fire and police, streets, water, electricity, parks, and health. The monetary compensation remained six dollars a month for his entire tenure in office.[8]

Two weeks after taking office, Rudder presided over his first council meeting with a typical agenda: to approve paying a long list of routine bills, including the fire marshal's travel to an out-of-town meeting, plus moving a fireplug.[9] Preparing the city council's agenda was in sharp contrast to the topics he had written in his vest-pocket notebook only twelve months earlier: "draw sniper rifles," "get back wounded and bodies from night patrols," and the hospital addresses of wounded men. Nonetheless, he transitioned easily to the mayor's office, and his satisfaction confirmed that he was a civilian first and a soldier second.

The issues that most concerned him as mayor were flood control on Brady Creek and the conversion of Curtis Field, a wartime aviation training center three miles north of Brady, to civilian use as an airport and industrial park. Personal attention to concerns of individual citizens rekindled his appreciation for shut-ins and low-profile citizens. A self-declared heiress in Mississippi, unknown to Rudder, asked him "to find out about [her] uncle and let me know. He has not replied to my letters, but he told me that if there was anything remaining in his estate when he died, it would go to me. Please inquire at the banks and see if he had an account and, if he is dead, what was done with it. I am very concerned." Rudder found the uncle, who invited him into his home to sit near a wood-burning stove and talk. Rudder then replied to the niece without mentioning an inheritance. "Dear Madam: I have located your uncle and had rather a long talk with him. He appears to be in perfect health for a man of his age, says he needs nothing, and is evidently very happy."[10] On a brisk winter day an elderly woman called to ask a favor.

She had left her gloves on top of the garbage can when she pulled it to the curb in front of her home. Would he bring them to her? He did.

He declined to write a positive reference for Julius "Rocky" Belcher, one of his Rangers, who was decorated with the Distinguished Service Cross, wounded four times in combat, and called a "one-man army" by other men. Belcher was charged in Ohio with manslaughter in the death of a woman for allegedly striking her in the face and causing a cerebral hemorrhage. Belcher's attorney and his company commander, Ralph Goranson, asked Rudder to "vouch for [Belcher's] traits of character." Rudder replied to Goranson with a friendly personal letter that mentioned the accused only to say, "I am sorry to hear that Belcher has been involved in a serious incident."[11]

In another case, Rudder pleaded for leniency in the court-martial of a young soldier from Brady charged with a minor offense at Fort Sill, Oklahoma. Rudder informed an officer of the court that the young man's parents "were honorable people" who had "worked very hard" and "did not have time to spend with him as a boy," but "if he is given a second opportunity and sufficient guidance, I believe he will make a worthwhile citizen of our country. I trust your court will be lenient with him."[12]

Seventeen men from McCulloch County had been killed during the war. Their coffins arrived in Brady by train, one by one, for four years after the war. Each arrival was followed by memorial and funeral services. "I thought I would never stop going to funerals," said long-time Brady resident Vivian Smith, "and I got to know every cemetery in the county." On the day of memorial services, Rudder issued a proclamation asking business houses to close during the service. He noticed how the bodies were transported and insisted on proper dignity. After one arrived "on a mixed train of cattle cars and freight cars," he protested to the army "on behalf of the Gold Star Mothers of Brady." Writing as both the mayor and "James E. Rudder, Colonel—Infantry," he recommended a routing that placed the coffins on trains with only passenger cars, which remedied the army's carelessness.[13]

As mayor he played a leading role in the conversion of Curtis Field to peacetime purposes. Completed in early 1941 as an aviation training center, it could house more than twenty-five hundred servicemen and servicewomen on a 354-acre site. The deactivation of the field in August 1945 dealt a blow to the local economy. In Mayor Rudder's first meeting of the city council, he signed an agreement with the federal government allowing Brady to use temporarily a portion of Curtis Field as a municipal airport. The relevant federal agencies could not make clear-cut decisions about the rest of the site, which was potentially useful as both an airport and an industrial park. The issue was finally settled when Rudder went to Washington and, with the help of his friend, U.S. Senator Lyndon B. Johnson, negotiated Brady's purchase of the entire complex for a mere twenty-three thousand dollars.[14]

Brady benefited significantly in other ways from Rudder's friendship with Johnson. In 1951 Congress adopted legislation to permit federal support for housing related to national defense, and the Brady city council applied to have Brady designated a "critical defense housing area." Brady's eligibility for the award was questionable, but Rudder pursued the application with Johnson's support until Brady was approved for the construction of fifty housing units in January 1952. Rudder also got Johnson's help to extend Social Security coverage to all Brady city employees, an exception to rules in effect at the time.[15]

Rudder put much effort into flood control of Brady Creek, which could overflow the central business district around the courthouse square, the lowest-lying area of the city. The creek was normally a small stream, but it drained about five hundred square miles before reaching the town, which had no levees to protect it. In July 1938 Rudder had witnessed record-breaking floodwaters that rose twelve feet inside the Rudder Drug Store he owned with his brother John. In his second month in office, he led a group of Brady civic leaders to Vicksburg, Mississippi, for a meeting with the U.S. Army Corps of Engineers. To study the problem, the Corps of Engineers had constructed a model that replicated the 1938 flood, when twenty-five inches of rain fell on the watershed in seven days. The corps proposed enlarging the creek's channel and constructing levees and floodwalls to protect the town and quickly move the water downstream.[16]

Rudder favored an alternate plan set forth by the U.S. Soil Conservation Service. The SCS emphasized dams to hold back the water and an overflow channel to bypass the business district if the dams were not sufficient. The SCS plan permitted the water, in Rudder's words, "to walk off the land" rather than "run off" under the Corps of Engineers' plan. He preferred to hold back floodwaters as long as possible, permitting the water to percolate through the soil into aquifers, where it seeped gradually into springs and streams and could be drawn from wells in dry periods.

The big challenge was to obtain the money necessary to build the dams and a bypass channel along the edge of town. Brady could not afford the costs alone. More than twenty years were required to complete the system, and Rudder was involved until it was done—long after he had moved from Brady. Files in the Lyndon B. Johnson Presidential Library contain an extensive correspondence between Rudder and Johnson, as well as between Rudder and Congressman O. C. Fisher, about Brady Creek. The correspondence ended in 1966 when federal money for soil and water conservation funded the completion of the system of dams and embankments that finally tamed the stream's floods. Rudder was then president of Texas A&M University, and Johnson was president of the United States.

Rudder's ascendance in Texas state government began in the spring of 1946, not long after he was elected mayor of Brady, with a visit from J. J. "Jake" Pickle, Chick's friend from student days at the University of Texas.[17] Pickle was an Austin public relations man specializing in political campaigns; his clients included two ambitious politicians, Congressman Lyndon B. Johnson and State Senator Allan Shivers.

Shivers was campaigning for lieutenant governor, and Pickle was traveling the state setting up county organizations for him. At the same time, Johnson was considering a run for the U.S. Senate in 1948. When Pickle came to see Rudder, Rudder did not know Johnson or Shivers, but they were interested in West Texas voters, including McCulloch County, population thirteen thousand, and Brady, its county seat, population about six thousand.[18] And both politicians wanted Rudder, a well-known war hero with demonstrated voter appeal, in their camps.

Shivers's race for lieutenant governor would be close, and he needed help in conservative West Texas, where voters favored his opponent, Boyce House, a folksy radio personality who told old-fashioned entertaining stories about Texas. Shivers's endorsement by his hometown newspaper, the *Port Arthur News,* as a "liberal without being radical" was a handicap in Rudder's West Texas, which Shivers subsequently lost by a wide margin. However, he carried the state, and when he was sworn in as lieutenant governor in January 1947, Rudder had a conduit through Pickle to the most influential office in Texas government relative to the state budget, which had its advantages.

Rudder did not actively campaign for Shivers in 1946, but neither did he turn a deaf ear to Pickle. So soon after returning home after an absence of almost five years, he was preoccupied with home and family life, the new business, ranching, and governing Brady. He deferred but did not reject Pickle's proposal indefinitely. More political campaigns were on the horizon.

LYNDON B. JOHNSON

When Jake Pickle solicited Rudder's support of Shivers in 1946, he also cultivated him for Lyndon Johnson and his 1948 race for the U.S. Senate. Johnson, a protégé of President Franklin Roosevelt, had supported FDR's program of social and economic reforms. Elected to Congress in 1937, Johnson ran for

the Senate four years later only to lose by 1,311 votes of 350,000 cast. He believed the election had been stolen by fraudulent votes in several East Texas
counties, and he did not intend to lose again.[19]

In early 1948 Johnson came to see Rudder. "I remember him coming to
the house to get Earl to help him," Chick recalled. The three of them sat in
the kitchen and drank coffee while LBJ played with Linda, not yet a year
old. Later, Lyndon pushed Bud and Sis in their swings suspended from the
branches of the tall pecan trees in the backyard.[20]

Johnson's opponent in the coming campaign was former governor Coke
Stevenson from nearby Kimble County, whose achievements made him a
respected figure throughout the region. He was a self-educated lawyer and
perhaps the most popular governor in Texas history (1941–47), esteemed for
his homespun philosophy about government, for having the sharp mind of
a good trial lawyer, and for his ethics. Stevenson's legislative colleague A. M.
Aiken observed that "Coke cared not only about what was done but how it
was done."[21] Chick's father knew and supported Stevenson, a fellow rancher,
as did most people in the area at the beginning of the campaign.

To Chick's surprise, Earl agreed to manage Johnson's campaign in Mc-
Culloch County. Many people were surprised and some were disappointed,
including Chick's father. "My parents could hardly stand the idea of Earl taking over Johnson's campaign." Her father asked, "Why do you support Lyndon Johnson? He's not a real rancher. Coke is the rancher. Johnson is nothing
but a drug store cowboy." After the election Earl told Pickle, "I had to walk on
eggshells through all that campaign, trying to be helpful [but] not too political in the sense that I was out to get Coke." Yet, Rudder was unequivocal in
assuring LBJ of his support: "We are here at Coke's front door. . . . Your supporters in McCulloch County stand ready to do whatever is necessary until
we have elected you our United States Senator."[22]

Earl's support of Johnson did not cause a family rift. His explanation may
have been as simple as keeping a promise to Pickle, or that he liked Johnson
and considered him a friend. More likely, he saw Johnson as a man for the
future, while Stevenson, born in 1888, represented the past.

A fundamental issue was Stevenson's and Johnson's differing attitudes
about government and how to use government to best benefit people. The two
main causes of suffering and deprivation in Rudder's life had been the Great
Depression and the war. Only the federal government had been capable of
coping with them, and most Americans believed President Roosevelt's leadership in both calamities had been important to success. Stevenson opposed
many policies of the Roosevelt administration. He criticized the increase in

federal regulatory authority and size under Roosevelt's New Deal programs and during the war. By contrast, Johnson usually voted for Roosevelt's policies in both domestic and foreign affairs. Stevenson seemed not to realize that nuclear weapons, rocketry, and long range aircraft had undermined historic American security based on distance from potential enemies. An active engagement in international affairs was now essential.

Unlike Stevenson, Johnson and Rudder had seen other parts of the world. Rudder had enjoyed comradeship with men from all across America and from other nations—British, French, Belgians, and Luxembourgers. He had walked the streets of New York, London, and Paris. He had seen rows of tenement houses where people lived in crowded circumstances unthinkable to those in West Texas. He had observed industrialized areas where people worked under conditions equally unbelievable. Texas had industrialized rapidly during the war, drawing people in large numbers to cities—people who did not return to the country. Texas was changing from a rural and agricultural state to an urban, industrial society.

Johnson and Rudder could understand the emerging social and economic circumstances of Texas, as Stevenson never could. They thought of the future and could dream beyond what had been imaginable on December 7, 1941. Lyndon had ideas about how to cope with the changes. Complex issues could not be solved by assertions of sterling character and old-time values but might be with new ideas and pragmatic compromises.

Race was an underlying issue in the Stevenson-Johnson campaign. Like most Southern politicians, both were willing to appeal to the racial prejudices of white voters when necessary to win votes, but Stevenson went further by defending a wartime lynching. "Certain members of the Negro race," he said, "from time to time furnish the setting for mob violence by the outrageous crimes which they commit." Johnson had, as historian Lewis Gould pointed out, "the capacity to grow" on matters of race.[23]

To this point in his life, Rudder had little direct exposure to racial issues, but his wartime experiences muted his notions about racial stereotypes. At a critical time, six months before the German surrender, African American troops volunteered to serve as infantrymen in the front lines, often taking reductions in grade, and they had performed creditably. He had seen the consequences of racial hatred in Nazi Germany. His sense of humanity was heightened by firsthand knowledge of Hitler's inhumanity toward those who did not conform to the fallacious idea of Aryan superiority. Men who served under Rudder during the war contended that his fundamentally humane spirit could be seen in the way he treated people. They saw it in his conduct toward enlisted men, toward newly liberated peoples in France, Luxembourg, and Belgium, and toward prisoners of war as described in the memoir of the German colonel Martin Fürst.[24]

Johnson left Rudder that day in early 1948 with Earl's promise of support in a region where most people, including LBJ, believed Stevenson was unbeatable. Chick heard him say to Earl, "I know you can't carry your own county, but do the best you can."[25] Everyone would be surprised when the votes were counted.

During the campaign, for the first time in the history of politics, a candidate traveled by helicopter, then in an early developmental stage and unseen by most civilians. Johnson was the helicoptering candidate, while Stevenson traveled by car—a clear example of their future-versus-past orientation. Rudder was waiting for LBJ in Brady on Saturday, July 3, when his blue and white Sikorsky "Flying Windmill" set down at 11:30 AM in the Dutton cotton yard, two blocks west of the courthouse square. As the whop-whop-whop of the helicopter's blades slowed, Rudder greeted him, and then he carried the candidate to the square in a Ford convertible borrowed from a local dealer after the Cadillac dealer, a Stevenson man, refused Rudder's request. He introduced LBJ to a crowd of more than two thousand people, a third of the town's population, and a greater number than had attended a political rally that same evening at the local fairgrounds for Stevenson and other gubernatorial candidates. Most people were probably there to see the chopper, as the *Brady Standard* noted in its headline, "Helicopter Outdraws Candidates."[26]

Johnson spoke directly to national defense and tax policy: "If you want one who is aggressive and progressive, who has seen the world and the horrors of war, and who knows you cannot win peace with appeasement and isolation, then you're for me. If you want tax cuts for big men, then vote for someone else."[27]

Two other elections in 1948 concerned Rudder. One was his unopposed second term as mayor. The other was Shivers's campaign for reelection as lieutenant governor, which he won handily. Since Shivers favored Johnson rather than Stevenson, when Rudder organized a precinct or county for Johnson, he also organized it for Shivers. In the election, Shivers carried McCulloch County by a three-to-one margin, and Rudder's relationship with him soared.[28]

In the historic statewide race between Stevenson and Johnson, LBJ won by a mere 87 votes from a total vote of 988,295. The vote in McCulloch Country was 1,461 for LBJ and 1,245 for Coke, a margin of 216 in favor of LBJ. Even Johnson's inner circle of advisors were surprised that he carried McCulloch County by more votes than his statewide victory margin.[29] In the campaign there was much to criticize about Johnson. Allegations about voter fraud in South Texas plagued him for the remainder of his life. But Rudder was far removed. He had delivered on his promise, and Johnson never forgot it.

Rudder's support of Johnson did not waver, remaining steadfast through the White House years that ended in January 1969. After Johnson's election to the Senate, Rudder on his own initiative took charge of LBJ's political organization in the twenty-seven counties of the 21st Congressional District of Texas, more than thirty-one thousand square miles inhabited by about 265,000 people. He built LBJ's organization for future elections by appointing county chairmen and meeting with them and other Johnson supporters. At his expense, he traveled the district, sometimes accompanied by Jake Pickle. In 1951, J. Edward Johnson, no kin and a Dallas lawyer, accompanied them around the district and described the trip to LBJ: "Earl has many acquaintances throughout the District and is favorably known, and Jake Pickle is one of the best public relations men I have ever known." LBJ followed with a letter to Earl: "I want to tell you how grateful I am for your generous offer to help me. . . . It is mighty comforting to know that I can call on you. I want to work with you on all matters to the interest of West Texas, so please call them to my attention as they arise. I will call on you for advice."[30]

Jake Pickle referred to Rudder as "LBJ's West Texas representative. . . . Earl was committed to helping Johnson. He did not go up and down the streets. He was not a backslapper, but we used his name, and he helped us find the right people and get committees organized. Just the fact that Earl Rudder was on LBJ's team helped out one hell of a lot. He stayed with us. He was loyal."[31]

Legacies of the 1948 campaign reverberated for the remainder of Rudder's life. As Chick said, "From then on, Earl was in solid with LBJ." He befriended Johnson's campaign manager, an Austin lawyer named John B. Connally, yet another acquaintance of Chick's from student days at the University of Texas. Pickle and Connally were close, and Jake cemented the Rudder-Connally friendship. Decades later, Jake reminisced about both men: "John Connally and I just kind of elected Earl to be a politician. He was a natural and we developed him. John and I got Earl involved with LBJ. We set it up to begin with."[32]

Rudder's rapport with Connally bode well for the future. Connally was elected governor in 1962 and reelected by wide margins in 1964 and 1966. His six years in office was within the ten years that Rudder was president of Texas A&M.[33] He appointed influential and visionary men to A&M's governing board who supported Rudder in putting Texas A&M on a path toward national and potentially international stature. The Pickle-Rudder friendship also stood the test of time. In 1963 Pickle was elected to Congress and served fifteen consecutive terms, thirty-one years in all, wielding constructive influence from the House Ways and Means Committee. Yet Rudder's most important political benefit from the 1948 senatorial campaign was his close friendship with LBJ, senate majority leader in 1955, vice president in 1961, and president of the United States from 1963 to 1969.

THE SHIVERCRATS

Less than a year after the 1948 political campaign, Allan Shivers became governor when the incumbent, Beauford Jester, died in office on July 11, 1949. Rudder now had two powerful champions, Johnson and Shivers, who could not have been better placed to advance him and his interests. In the one-party state of Texas, Shivers was the leader of the prevailing conservative wing of the Democratic Party. Johnson led the moderate Democrats and displaced Shivers as the party's leader in 1956. Through them Rudder was, by the early 1950s, on a first-name basis with most statewide officeholders and acquainted with many U.S. senators and congressmen.

Insights about Rudder can be gained by comparing his demeanor in the company of Shivers and Johnson. Around Shivers he was uncharacteristically stiff, seemingly ill at ease. With Johnson, he was the opposite, slapping his knee, laughing easily and often. Their impoverished boyhoods in the resource-poor Texas Hill Country were nothing like that of Shivers, whose lawyer father was relatively prosperous in Port Arthur, a center of the state's oil and chemical industry.

Rudder admired much about Shivers that had little to do with political philosophy. Shivers exercised his authority and insisted on party discipline and unity. He rarely hesitated or backed away from a political confrontation—qualities that Rudder equated with decisiveness and courage. Shivers was strong in his convictions, persuasive with many people, and magnetic to his followers.[34] To Rudder's thinking, that added up to good leadership. But he was too different in style and manner to become his easy-going friend like Johnson.

In 1950, Rudder became a political insider during the bitter confrontations between rival factions of the Texas Democratic Party. Jake Pickle brought Rudder into the Shivers crowd and used him, perhaps unwittingly, to help Shivers gain control of the Democratic Party in Texas. Fifty years later, Pickle summarized what he did: "Earl came in unknowingly, but John Connally and I initiated him and got him involved. He was a natural, but we taught him a lot."[35]

Allan Shivers, governor of Texas, 1949–57, brought Rudder into state-level politics by appointing him to the Public Welfare Board in 1953 and commissioner of the General Land Office in 1955. (Courtesy of Margaret Rudder)

Shivers was elected governor in 1950 with 76 percent of the 1,086,564 votes cast in the first Democratic Party primary, which determined the outcome of the general election.[36] His election set up Rudder's entry into high-level decision making in the Democratic Party of Texas. It opened with Shivers taking control of the party's decision-making body, the State Democratic Executive Committee (SDEC), whose members were selected informally by county delegates in the state's thirty-one senatorial districts. Meeting in their senatorial districts, the county delegates selected one man and one woman, whose actual appointment as members of the SDEC was normally a formality, just routine business at the state convention—a procedure that Shivers would change with Pickle's help.

The year 1952 was a presidential election year, and Shivers wanted to control the votes of the Texas delegation to the Democratic National Convention. If he could control the Texas votes, he could be a power broker at the national convention and influence the selection of the presidential nominee. An obstacle to Shivers's ambition was that delegates to the national convention were selected by the SDEC. To control the Texas delegates at the national convention, he had to stack the SDEC with his supporters. This could be done by not approving in the state convention the SDEC's presumptive members selected in the senatorial districts and by replacing them with others who would vote as he directed.

To orchestrate this takeover of the SDEC, he turned to Jake Pickle, whose assignment was twofold: to replace SDEC members selected at the level of the senatorial districts with others acceptable to Shivers and to ratify their selection at the state convention. In the weeks leading up to the state convention, Shivers talked about party unity to calm the concerns of Democrats who feared that he might not support the national party's nominee for president. At the same time, Jake kept Shivers's supporters on the SDEC in line and collected the proxies of delegates who could not attend the state convention.[37]

Pickle brought Rudder into the scheme to manipulate the convention with a request from Shivers: "The Governor would like for you to serve as the assistant to the temporary chairman of the convention whose duties are to direct the work of the convention." It was one of the few times in Rudder's life that he was an assistant to anyone, but he was a cub in a den of old lions. Pickle later told University of Texas historian Joe B. Frantz that when the senatorial districts presented their nominations for the SDEC, "the governor would look over the people nominated in the district caucuses and, if he saw someone on there who was personally obnoxious, he would say 'Knock them off.'"[38] In this way the SDEC was packed with Shivers supporters, and one of them was Earl Rudder.

Shivers led the Texas delegation—derisively called "Shivercrats"—including Rudder, accompanied by Chick, to the 1952 Democratic National Convention in Chicago. The Shivercrats had sharp differences with leaders of the national Democratic Party. There is no clear indication of Rudder's attitude about the major issues that divided the Texas delegation from the national party: racial integration of schools, the Korean War, the Communist threat both foreign and domestic, labor unrest, and disputes over state and federal rights, particularly Texas's jurisdiction over the oil-rich seabed in the Gulf of Mexico called the Tidelands.

Texas was a swing state at both the Democratic and Republican national conventions and in the presidential election. Although the Democratic convention nominated Adlai Stevenson for president, the Texas delegation, led by Shivers, voted against him at the convention, as did the state's electorate in the general election in November. After the Republicans nominated Dwight D. Eisenhower, Shivers organized "Democrats for Eisenhower." Shivercrats, allied with Republicans, carried Texas, and Eisenhower was elected president.

Rudder would probably have supported Eisenhower regardless of his party affiliation. Ike's victory was in large part more personal than political. All across America, veterans, and their families and friends, usually voted for veterans. Eisenhower exemplified qualities that Rudder admired most in a man.

Soon after the elections in November 1952, Shivers brought Rudder into Texas state government by appointing him to the three-member State Board of Public Welfare (SBPW). The board dispensed almost one-fourth of the state's budget to help counties assist "aged, blind and dependent and neglected children."[39] Most public welfare monies came from federal sources. An appointment to the board was a significant public responsibility with impositions and token compensation of ten dollars for each meeting.

Rudder's acceptance of the appointment indicates how his ideas about what to do with his life had changed between his twenties and his early forties. In his twenties his career interest was coaching football. His thirties were consumed by the war and reentering civilian life. From the time he went on the SBPW at the age of forty-two, he devoted the greater part of his time and energy to working for the benefit of others through public institutions. In the art and science of governing he discovered that his gifts of perception, analysis, and decisiveness helped people resolve complex problems whether concerned with public sanitation in Brady, organizing a political campaign, or, eventually, building a great university. He often expressed his commitment to public service in the following way: "If you don't want war again, you had better get busy on the home front to keep it from happening." This was clear example of how the war had changed his values.

While serving on the SBPW and becoming its chairman, Rudder drove three hundred miles round-trip from Brady to Austin to attend eighteen of its twenty meetings in twenty-four months, the best attendance record of any member of the board. Since SBPW monies were an important revenue source for local governments, county officials made it a point to know members of the board, yet another way that Rudder got acquainted with elected officials across the state.

Meetings of the SBPW were a recurring seminar about the social and economic conditions of his fellow citizens. Rudder could not avoid exposure to the grim statistics that large numbers of people lived in deprivation, that more women than men lived in poverty, that malnutrition was commonplace among certain populations, that more than a third of family dwellings in Texas were without flush toilets, and that Texas ranked last among the then forty-eight states in providing aid to dependent children. Such background information was useful when he became a member of numerous education commissions and president of a university with grass-roots service to the public as a primary mission and extension programs in every county of the state.

AN AMERICAN HERO RETURNS TO NORMANDY

On June 11, 1954, Rudder was propelled to national prominence by an article in *Collier's* magazine, one of America's most widely circulated publications, selling more than four million copies every two weeks. The cover was a color illustration of him standing with fourteen-year-old Bud on the cliffs of Pointe du Hoc. Photographs of them appeared in a highly readable text based on their conversations as they walked around the battlefield.

Three months before the publication date, Earl and Bud went to France at the magazine's expense with a photographer and the well-known sports writer W. C. Heinz, who proposed the story to *Collier's*. The trip was Rudder's first return to Europe since the war. Heinz titled his article "I Took My Son to Omaha Beach: An American Hero Returns to Normandy" and wove Earl's comments into a captivating text.[40]

The Brady post office was flooded with letters from wartime comrades, friends, and just plain admirers—even some from France. They were reminded of or learned for the first time about the Rangers' extraordinary feats at Pointe du Hoc. If Rudder had done nothing noteworthy after the war, the *Collier's* article would have assured him public acclaim for years to come.

When "An American Hero Returns to Normandy" hit the newsstands, Rudder's political value rose spectacularly, and Shivers quickly capitalized on it. Ten days after the article appeared, Rudder introduced Shivers on a Texas-wide radio network, the primary broadcast medium at the time, of more than sixty stations. The occasion was Shivers's announcement that he was running for an unprecedented third term as governor. His opponent was Ralph Yarborough, formerly a state district judge and a leader of the liberal

Rudder on his first return to Pointe du Hoc, March 1954. (Courtesy of James Earl Rudder Jr.)

wing of the Democratic Party. As predicted, the bitter campaign involved harsh accusations about the dominant issues of the era: racial integration, organized labor, and communism.

Citing the *Collier's* article and emphasizing Rudder's heroism in the Normandy invasion, Shivers's campaign headquarters played up—and almost certainly wrote—his introduction of their candidate. He lauded Shivers in his introduction as "a man of integrity, of a warm heart and raw courage, who won't run away, a man [to] follow with complete confidence." He included a unique and unlikely public reference to his role in the Normandy landings: "When I landed with the Second Ranger Battalion and looked up at the sheer 100-foot cliffs of Pointe du Hoc. . . ." The introduction ended with "I've been around long enough to know a *man* when I see one."[41]

Shivers followed Rudder to the podium with one of the most problematic speeches of his political career. Tinged with demagogic and racist

Rudder in his Normandy Invasion command post on Pointe du Hoc, March 1954. He is on the left with W. C. Heinz (wearing a hat). Robert Ravelet, chairman of the local committee to preserve the battlefield, is in the center, and James Earl "Bud" Rudder, age fourteen, is to the right. (Courtesy of James Earl Rudder Jr.)

implications, it linked three negatives—school integration, communism, and "ruthless, dictatorial Northern labor overlords"—with his opponent's candidacy. The idea of linking labor unrest, racial integration, and an alleged domestic communist threat to discredit Yarborough was cooked up in Jake Pickle's advertising firm of Syers, Pickle and Winn. Pickle later denied any personal responsibility for this smear on Yarborough.[42]

Rudder cited Shivers's speech in letters to army reserve subordinates in official correspondence concerned with army business. His recipients read that Shivers "really 'laid it on the line,'" and Rudder urged them to "join me in doing all we can to see that he gets elected." This partisan political activity in the conduct of official army business was contrary to the written ethics for officers in the U.S. military and to army regulations, which could not have been more explicit: "No person in military service will use his official authority or influence for the purpose of interfering with an election or affecting the result thereof."[43] In this error of judgment Rudder was unfortunately caught up in the temper of the times.

Shivers's 1954 gubernatorial campaign occurred at a time of great uncertainty in the American body politic. Government employees and performing artists were accused of being communists with and without evidence, and many people did not know who or what to believe when they heard members of Congress, the Supreme Court, and other institutions of government described as disloyal, even treasonous. Of particular concern in the South was the U.S. Supreme Court's decision, in the case *Brown v. Topeka Board of Education,* that racial segregation in public schools was unconstitutional. The Supreme Court's decision occurred only one month before Shivers announced his candidacy. It was a tense and confused time.

Shivers prevailed in the 1954 election, with 53 percent of the 1.5 million votes cast,[44] but his popularity had begun to wane. The decline was related to bankruptcies in the state-regulated insurance industry, overseen by Shivers appointees, who were decried by Yarborough's supporters as unqualified cronies. Hundreds of thousands of policyholders lost their savings, and many of them blamed Shivers.

Although the hatred between Shivers and Yarborough never healed, Rudder and Yarborough were congenial. Yarborough was a member of the U.S. Senate while Rudder was president of Texas A&M, and they had mutual interests in education-related legislation. Rudder also knew that Yarborough, once a West Point plebe, had a good war record and was active in the army reserves.

BRIGADIER GENERAL

During the last month of 1954, Rudder got his long-awaited promotion to brigadier general in the army reserves, effective on December 8. He had been a colonel since February 1945. The army's press release for the promotion ceremony described him as holding "every decoration awarded except the Congressional Medal of Honor, which makes him one of the most decorated soldiers in American history."[45]

Since 1946, eight long years, he had been on the list of colonels eligible for promotion. Spokesmen for army review boards attributed the delay of his promotion to fluctuation of national defense policies while demobilizing, the contemplation of atomic weapons, and the threat posed by the Soviet Union. Those were the stated reasons. The real reason was the army's reluctance to promote any reserve colonels while coping with excessive pressure by members of Congress for some of them. In addition, review boards considered him too young to be a general; he turned forty-four on May 6, 1954. He learned that his age was an issue from a boyhood friend at Eden High School, John Frank Day, a staff officer in the headquarters where the records of eligible colonels were reviewed. Day wrote Rudder an off-the-record letter with "the true facts" of his situation: "You and your reputation," he said, "are very firmly established here . . . but your age is an embarrassment in that to give you a senior appointment now might discourage many outstanding officers of merit who are much older than you."[46]

Rudder refused to "pull one string" for the appointment, "purposefully because I feel certain that, should I warrant [the promotion], I would get it without any pressure." He could easily have called on Senator Lyndon Johnson to nudge the promotion along, but he informed the top levels of the Pentagon that his promotion was to be considered only on his merits, a condition acknowledged by a secretary to the Joint Chiefs of Staff, who wrote: "Concerning the status of your promotion, General Ryder was informed that you had specifically asked that no intervention be made in your behalf."[47]

The army's refusal to promote Rudder to brigadier general over older colonels led to his command of the 90th Infantry Division while he was still a colonel, a highly unusual appointment. An unknown action officer high up the army's chain of command resolved Rudder's promotion impasse by making him the acting division commander and then promoting him on the basis of his performance. Thus, in March 1954 Rudder got oral instructions to assume command of the division. Not until July, after he commanded the division in its annual summer training and was commended for his performance, was he issued written orders to assume command.[48]

When Rudder took command of the 90th Infantry Division, Joe W. Neal was a major in the intelligence section of his headquarters. Eventually he promoted Neal to full colonel and made him head of the section. In civilian life, Neal was a professor of communications and a seasoned administrator at the University of Texas. With a Ph.D. in government, he was both trained and experienced in evaluating organizations and leadership. Joe Neal described Rudder's effect on men in the division:

> We knew him by reputation and simply having him there made everyone do their best. There was a lot of talk among the ranks about him. Earl always had a little smile on his lips and he was pleasant, but it was no sign of weakness. He seemed soft and easy-going, but you had a feeling there was steel underneath. Everyone around him worked at maximum capacity just because of the force of his personality. Everyone I knew was doing their best not to cross him but to gain favor with him. He was not a man to cross. He was a strong man, no doubt about that.[49]

While Rudder was stalemated as a colonel, Senator Johnson gave him a boost by calling him to Washington, D.C., as an adviser to the Senate Subcommittee on Military Preparedness. The assignment began with a routine letter from Johnson to Rudder inquiring what he could do to better serve McCulloch County. When Rudder replied, he first mentioned the importance of schools for veterans and federal price supports for wool, mohair, and cotton. Then he offered his opinion about defense preparedness, ending with, "There are many problems in our Reserve program which I would like to discuss with you personally in the near future."[50]

Rudder's letter hit Johnson's desk as he was preparing to hold hearings on the training of draftees and reservists called to active duty for the Korean War. Rudder was an expert on training and the army reserves. At Johnson's request, the army called Rudder to thirty days' active duty in February 1951 as a congressional liaison to the subcommittee on military preparedness. Rudder began and ended his tour of duty in Washington. In between, he conducted on-site inspections at five training posts across the nation before returning to Washington to make his report.[51]

Rudder became known in the Pentagon and on Capitol Hill, especially with Johnson's colleagues in the U.S. Senate. He helped the army in its relationship with Johnson, and his stature with Johnson rose. From this period until Johnson left the White House, he would often say to those around him, when grappling with issues pertaining to the Texas or the armed forces and later about higher education, "I want you to ask Earl Rudder about this."[52]

Rudder ended 1954 with a well-established and growing reputation. In the nine years since the war he had moved easily from local to state politics, learning much that would be indispensable in the days to come. He was a man with a future in Texas. He had risen to prominence, and his influence would expand. The summit of his career was still ahead.

CHAPTER 16

TEXAS LAND OFFICE COMMISSIONER
1955–1958

Texas governor Allan Shivers had growing political problems that defied solution. He had been reelected in early 1954 with 54 percent of the vote in the Democratic primary runoff that determined the winner of the general election in November. Yet almost from the day of the Democratic primary, his administration had been plagued by allegations of unethical conduct in state agencies. A major scandal concerned the state-regulated insurance industry overseen by Shivers's appointees to the state insurance board. In the last half of 1954, seventeen Texas-incorporated insurance companies went belly-up, taking with them the savings of hundreds of thousands of policyholders, who bitterly blamed Shivers for their losses. Shivers's opponents condemned him and attacked his appointees as unqualified cronies. To no one's surprise, his popularity began to wane.[1]

A second sensational scandal involved the state-sponsored Veterans Land Program, which helped veterans buy land with small down payments and low-interest loans. The program was administered through the General Land Office and governed by the three-member Veterans Land Board, composed of Shivers, Attorney General John Ben Shepperd, and Bascom Giles, commissioner of the General Land Office and administrator of the Veterans Land Program as well as chairman of its board. All three—governor, attorney general and land commissioner—were statewide elected positions with two-year terms. (The terms of office became four years in 1974). Unknown to Shivers and Sheppard, Giles created and took advantage of loopholes in the way the program was administered. He and several accomplices were eventually convicted of unlawfully exploiting the program through fraud and bribery.[2] Several investigations cleared Shivers and Shepperd of misconduct, but the scandal discredited them with the public, and neither ran for elective office again.

After allegations implicating Giles in the scandal became public in late 1954, he declined to take the oath of office for the two-year term to which he had just been elected for the ninth consecutive time. As governor, Shivers was obligated to fill the vacancy, and he appointed Earl Rudder to succeed

Giles. Rudder was well known, had an impeccable reputation, and had not been sufficiently associated with Shivers to be considered his crony. Rudder, vetted by Shivers's cabinet—the heads of executive departments—was considered by Texas secretary of state Thomas M. Reavley, later a federal judge, as a "paragon of integrity and heroism." The Shivers people hoped Rudder would clean the governor's tarnished image.[3]

The duties of the commissioner of the General Land Office were important and sensitive, because the Land Office administered the vast landholdings of the State of Texas and the assets they generated. The complexity of these historic functions had been compounded by the discovery of oil on state lands in the early twentieth century. The state did not drill or mine its lands, but contracted with private firms that drilled for or excavated minerals— oil, gas, and "hard rocks"—and paid the state a commission, or royalty, on their value. The Land Office was the agent for the state in these transactions, a complex series of negotiations and agreements. When such transactions were not managed properly, whether through incompetence or fraud, the loss of revenue was borne by the public, especially the public schools. Rudder would characterize this process as a "sacred trust" and made the improvement of leasing and collecting royalties a high priority, resulting in significantly improved revenue streams during the three years that he held office.[4]

Ironically, Rudder learned Shivers's intention when he met with him to recommend Bill Allcorn of Brownwood for the job. The date was Monday, January 3, 1955. Allcorn was a lawyer and, like Rudder, a combat veteran with wounds to show for it. After Shivers listened to Rudder praise Allcorn, he said, "We're way ahead of you. We've already decided who it will be." "Who is it?" Rudder asked. "It's you, Earl."[5]

Rudder did not accept immediately. "I drove back to Brady, got home at midnight, and wore out two sheets before morning." One consideration in his decision was the discouraging multiyear drought that had devastated farming and ranching, on which his livelihood largely depended. He had shipped cattle to Illinois for better grassland. Profits were way down, the situation was getting worse, and when the drought would end was anyone's guess. He decided to accept the appointment and was sworn in the next morning, Wednesday, January 5, 1955, in the governor's office as Shivers and more than one hundred state and federal officials looked on.[6]

Rudder made no public statement, but Shivers made a brief speech, calling Rudder "sincere, honest and courageous." The governor declared, "With his help I will take full responsibility for the administration of the Land Office and the Veterans Land Program . . . and put the affairs of the General Land Office and the Veterans Land Board in order" The governor's office

Rudder and his family in the Texas capitol on January 5, 1955, when he was sworn in as commissioner of the General Land Office. Left to right: *James Earl "Bud" Rudder Jr., Anne Rudder, Margaret, and Earl. (Courtesy of Margaret Rudder)*

issued a press release describing Rudder as an "outstanding hero of the Normandy invasion in World War II," and newspapers across the state cited his war record. One observer who interviewed him that day said he was "blunt, jovial, unequivocal, the opposite of egotistical, whose innermost desire is to serve his fellow man without ostentation."[7]

Rudder would later say that he assumed his duties "with the avowed purpose of restoring the General Land Office to its proper place in the government of Texas and a place of respect in the eyes of the citizens of Texas." There was no time to lose. He went immediately from the swearing-in ceremony to begin his review of both the Land Office and the Veterans Land Program. Accompanied by Shivers and Shepperd, he walked through the capitol grounds and entered the Land Office Building that thirty-three years later would be renamed in his honor.[8]

Fraught with anxiety for their jobs, about seventy-five quickly assembled Land Office employees breathed a sigh of relief when Rudder told them, "I'll need the help of each and every one of you in getting the job done." Then he went to another level in the same building to the offices of the Veterans Land

Program—a separate administrative entity from the Land Office—where he ordered all files examined in a joint investigation with the state auditor, the attorney general, and the Texas Department of Public Safety. There would be no stonewalling. Cooperation with authorized investigations was a pathway to cleansing the record.[9]

Rudder could not spare time to search for a family home in Austin. January was in the middle of the school year, and four young Rudders were attending Brady public schools: Jane was in the first grade, Linda in the second, Anne ("Sis") in the sixth, and Bud in the eighth.[10] Leaving Chick and the children in Brady, he took a room in the Commodore Perry Hotel, only five minutes' walk from the Land Office.

When Jake Pickle, a widower, heard that Rudder was living out of a suitcase in a hotel, he called to say, "This will not do," and insisted that Earl move to his home. Earl lived in Pickle's home until Chick and the children moved to Austin in August. Jake remembered, "I can still hear Earl snoring like a fire engine in the front bedroom."[11]

Back in Brady, people were proud of Earl—even his political opponents. Bill Cobb, the man Rudder had beaten in his first election for mayor, praised him, saying, "He's honest and he's a doer. The town's proud of him and we'll miss him."[12]

RUDDER TAKES CHARGE

Rudder took office in the midst of legislative and grand jury investigations, lawsuits, and newspaper exposes—all hot political issues. The alleged scandals were the basis of the controversy, and the investigations were also controversial because members of the legislature vied to participate and gain attention for themselves. His immediate tasks were to restore order, calm anxieties, remove Giles's accomplices, and correct administrative procedures. While stabilizing the management, he had to make certain that both the Land Office and the Veterans Land Program carried out their functions as well as placate the legislature, which began its session only six days after he took office. His most urgent task was with the Veterans Land Program, which he vowed to transform from "chaos and confusion to an honest, orderly, and well-regulated business-like program."[13]

A few days after he began his review of the Veterans Land Program, he confided to Chick, "I don't know who in that office was in cahoots with the previous commissioner. I've got to get someone around me that I can trust." Convinced that obtaining valid land appraisals as the basis for making loans was a critical part of the Veterans Land Program, he recruited his reliable

friend Frank Corder to become its chief appraiser. They set up new procedures concentrating responsibility at the local level, which Rudder called
"one of the strongest safeguards we have for integrity in the program." Seeking an accountant with an unimpeachable reputation, Rudder lured Clark
Diebel from the state auditor's office and asked him to reform the accounting
system and collect unpaid balances. As Diebel's assistant, Rudder brought
Arthur Scharlach from Brady, a 1932 classmate at Texas A&M, to become
executive secretary to the board while Rudder retained authority over the
program as chairman.[14]

Shortly after Rudder took office, Attorney General Shepperd appointed
Bill Allcorn as a special assistant to investigate the veterans land scandals.
Allcorn, the friend Rudder had asked Shivers to appoint as commissioner,
and Sam Kimberlin, an assistant attorney general, called on Rudder in his
office. Going into the meeting, Kimberlin knew nothing about Rudder, but
he came away with the unforgettable impression that Rudder "was very per-
ceptive about the situation and what needed to be done. I liked his whole
approach and left his office convinced that he would straighten it out."[15]

Rudder's initial reviews confirmed misdoing in the Veterans Land Program while finding out that the Land Office functions were "in proper order,
but chaotic." Part of his dilemma was that while he was engaged in making
internal reforms of both agencies, the legislature insisted on calling him
before committees for guidance about proposed new statutes affecting the
operations that he was trying to comprehend. Fortunately, he was a quick
study. He also had to protect the integrity of the Veterans Land Program
from individual members of the legislature; one was State Senator Jimmy
Phillips, ambitious to run for governor. Phillips personally removed Veterans Land Program files and took them to the Capitol. Rudder insisted that
the law required the records remain in his custody. When Phillips refused,
Rudder asked to appear before the Senate Investigating Committee to resolve the dispute. It was a bold maneuver for a newcomer, but he prevailed,
and the records were returned. The piqued Phillips criticized disorganization in the Land Office and the Veterans Land Program. Rudder could have
blamed Giles; instead, he apologized to the intemperate senator and told the
committee that the failure of his staff to find a particular file for Phillips was
"a matter of internal management on my part."[16]

TARGET CONSTITUENCIES

From the beginning Rudder based his actions on the assumption that he had
to gain the confidence of three constituencies: employees of the Land Office

and Veterans Land Board, members of the legislature, and the general public. He attempted to rally support for the Land Office and the Veterans Land Program by testifying before legislative committees, meeting with newspaper reporters, and speaking to civic clubs and professional associations across Texas. He used his office as a bully pulpit to proclaim two deeply held personal convictions: that individuals should accept responsibility for their actions and that they should build for the future. The Land Office, he told his audiences, was also about the future because it managed the main endowment for the public schools—the public domain, their land, and its subterranean treasures of oil and gas. He spoke to parent and teacher organizations about parental responsibilities and the healthy development of children—an odd topic for a land commissioner, but not for Rudder personally. The same was true when he spoke to leaders of the Boy Scouts, Girl Scouts, and even Cub Scouts about the importance of their work for coming generations. He visited high schools and reviewed military formations of students enrolled in ROTC. When he met with conservation-minded farmers and ranchers to discuss watershed improvements and the proper use of the land, he was in his element, speaking from his knowledge about projects similar to those on his own land.[17]

Rudder found two passionate callings as land commissioner. One was helping war veterans and their families; the other was stewardship of about eight hundred thousand acres of Texas, its waters, minerals, and, implicitly, its wildlife and vegetation. He identified with men and women who worked on the land, and he did not confine his speaking engagements to population centers in the Houston–San Antonio–DFW triangle of the state. He went to cities on the perimeter: Beaumont, Lubbock, Amarillo, El Paso, Corpus Christi, and Laredo. He lectured oilmen about their responsibility to develop mineral resources on their leases of state lands wisely in order to ensure the future education of Texas schoolchildren. Before leaders of the petroleum industry, he enunciated an operating principle of the Land Office: "Whether your organization is large or small, you will get the same treatment from us. There will be no favors. Once you start doing favors, there is no way to stop." At a statewide meeting of sheep and goat raisers, he asked for advice to help him solve state land problems.[18]

Crisscrossing the state, he surprised editors of small-town newspapers by dropping in to visit. En route to Clarendon in the eastern Panhandle to make a speech, he dropped in on the *Childress Index,* circulation eight hundred. He went to Muleshoe near the New Mexico border and to sparsely populated counties like Fisher and Hockley in the lower Panhandle to tell veterans about the benefits of the Veterans Land Program. He spoke off-the-cuff, and reporters flavored their stories with his phrases, such as: "I have no doubt that there have been some irregularities by a bunch of two-bit chiselers, and that those same two-bit chiselers were at home getting fat off of deals during the time that the veterans we are trying to help were risking their lives on behalf of Texas and the nation."[19]

He talked about requirements for good government: "Some folks feel that their vote is insignificant in that if they lift their voices to learn about the government, they would be drowned out by lobbyists and the VIPs. That is the quickest road to a dictatorial government. Every individual has a stake in democratic government."[20]

Across the state Rudder spoke directly to the people, hoping the public would influence the legislature to pass the bills that he supported. He extolled the value of the Veterans Land Program. Promising a new era of responsible management, he placed the veterans land scandal in a larger historical context. "We find in the records of the Land Office, even in the early days of our Republic, that fraudulent land schemes were widespread. . . . I hope to keep the Land Office operations free of fraud, so that the Veterans Land Program will be administered for the benefit of the veteran." He invited scrutiny of his every move. "Keep a close surveillance on my conduct as land commissioner," he advised, "and I strongly urge you to do the same toward the conduct of all other public officials. I do not wish to operate in an official vacuum separated from the desires and the will of the people who it is my duty to serve."[21]

Rudder petitioned the legislature to place before the voters a constitutional amendment that would continue the Veterans Land Program and double its size with an additional $100 million in bonds backed by the state. Monies generated by the sale of bonds would be loaned to veterans, who would repay the loans with interest. That is how the program was financed. The "Veterans Land Program was," he said, "not all bad despite reports of fraud and excess profits from some fast-dealing land promoters." Critics in the legislature maintained that the program was scandal-ridden and had helped only fifteen thousand out of eight hundred thousand eligible veterans. Even the Veterans Land Board was divided two to one on whether to support Rudder's proposal; Shivers favored it, and Attorney General Shepperd opposed it.[22]

To counter the critics, Rudder cited letters from veterans who had participated in the program. "It has been good for some," he said. "It can be made good for all by proper supervision and management." Eventually, the legislature agreed to put the sale of $100 million in bonds for the Veterans Land Program to a referendum on the November 1956 ballot.[23]

The legislature went along with Rudder's request to increase the number of field inspectors, whose job was to confirm that oil and gas producers on public lands obeyed the state's drilling laws and paid their royalties in full. Similarly, he increased the staff for seismic exploration and toughened the professional qualifications for its staff. As a consequence, more oil wells were drilled on state land, and the royalties from them increased considerably. He fired five Land Office seismologic inspectors who had profit-making business relationships with the same private companies whose operations they were supposed to inspect. By August 1955, seven months after taking office, Rudder was able to tell investigators from the attorney general's office that "the veterans' land program is now functioning as it should and, so far as humanly possible, protecting veterans' interests."[24]

GENERAL LAND OFFICE: INTERNAL REFORMS

The basic functions of the Land Office were threatened by disorganization and confusion. While the demoralized staff was pressured by official investigations and news media inquiries, they had to carry out the essential functions of collecting and keeping records of land transactions, providing maps and surveys, and issuing titles. Accuracy in these functions was required for public schools and universities to obtain optimal benefits from oil and gas on public lands. But Rudder found that documents were missing, the filing system was disorganized, and equipment was outmoded.

Since the Land Office also managed the funds derived from the land, which required investment expertise, he asked the state auditor to determine if the staff was sufficient in number and qualifications to meet their responsibilities. The state auditor confirmed Rudder's judgment that the state had been losing money from oil and gas royalties because the staff was not up to the task. With this endorsement the legislature approved Rudder's request for funds to hire more and better qualified people.[25]

Within the General Land Office, Rudder embarked on three major reforms. His first reform was the restoration and preservation of records. This involved two innovative processes that later became routine: microfilming and laminating original documents. He personally confirmed that many fragile documents in the archives, especially from the Spanish period in the late 1700s, had been neglected and were deteriorating from handling and decay. It was a serious problem because their texts were necessary to validate land titles. "There is nothing so exasperating and frustrating," he said, "as to open a book of old letters where you expect to find a vital piece of correspondence . . . and to discover that the letters and the writing have been reduced to nothing more than a mass of crumbled confetti and dust."[26]

The second reform in the Land Office was the establishment of tidal boundaries in a way that would reconcile industrial and recreational development of the Texas coastline, permitting each to occur while respecting public rights. Rudder described the seventeen-hundred-mile coastline as "the last frontier left for recreational development in the United States." Development was erasing natural boundaries. In order to protect the state's ownership of minerals in such areas, he undertook to permanently demark the natural boundaries by persuading the legislature to authorize him, as commissioner of the General Land Office, to negotiate agreements with the federal government to settle boundary issues.[27]

Rudder's third Land Office reform was the improvement of working conditions for its staff, which he asserted were underpaid, overcrowded, and insufficient in number. He condemned their "deplorable working conditions" to the press, to the legislature, and to the governor. "They [are] badly handicapped," he wrote, "in the performance of their duties by the heat and the crowded working conditions. Besides the poor working conditions, . . . salaries of employees [are] wholly inadequate." The legislature did not fund his full request for pay raises, but it funded two projects that improved working conditions: air-conditioning of the Land Office Building and renovation of another floor of the building, thus enlarging the available work space.[28]

STATEWIDE ELECTORAL CAMPAIGN

In the closing weeks of 1955, some eleven months after Rudder had taken office, the recovery of confidence within the General Land Office and the Veterans Land Program was clearly evident. Everyone knew that in the coming statewide elections of 1956, the land commissioner's job would be on the ballot, but no one knew whether Rudder would be a candidate. No group of voters was more interested in the commissioner's election than the employees of the General Land Office and the Veterans Land Board. In December 1955 they presented Rudder with a petition signed by the entire staffs of both organizations urging him to be a candidate. If he would enter the race, every last one of them promised the "fullest cooperation in his campaign and throughout his tenure of office."[29]

Months passed with no commitment from Rudder. Widespread rumors held that Shivers was grooming him for governor. Early in 1956 Ned Price declared his candidacy for land commissioner. Price was a former member of the legislature and had been a widely respected county judge from Smith

County, where Tyler was the principal city. By April, Rudder had decided to run, but he kept it to himself even as he spoke at Aggie Muster Day—April 21—on the Texas A&M campus in College Station. The five thousand people who turned out for the 6:30 AM ceremonies in front of the Memorial Student Center heard serious reflections about public service and politics. The speech marked his transition from a problem-solver to a serious thinker about the democratic process, people, and their government. "In government," he said, "there is no middle ground; either we govern ourselves, or someone else will move in to govern us. In a democracy, people can have government as good as they demand, but they usually get government as bad as they will tolerate." From the porch of the MSC, standing beside the plaque bearing the name of 953 Aggies killed in World War II, he ended his oration with, "We need men who will defend freedom as vigorously in the county courthouse as they will on a battlefield. It is as important to fight with ballots in peacetime as with bullets in time of war."[30]

Two days later, Rudder paid the $875.00 filing fee and announced his candidacy for a full term as commissioner of the General Land Office, trumpeting what he had done to clean up the Veterans Land Program and close loopholes that "enabled promoters and sharp dealers to use this fine program for their own selfish motives." Despite these accomplishments, he claimed that "much remains to be done and it is my desire to help complete the job. To refuse to offer my services for two more years, in my opinion, would be to shirk an important public duty."[31]

Rudder had the assets of a successful candidate. Handsome and accomplished, he had strong name recognition, an unexcelled war record, and a cohesive family. A visitor to his home described the Rudders as "five energetic youngsters, a charming mother and a famous father."[32] Chick stopped using her childhood nickname and reverted to her given name, Margaret. "Chick," she thought, might be misunderstood by people who did not know her, and it lacked proper dignity for the wife of an important state official.

Earl was his own campaign manager and had no paid consultants, employees, or pollsters. The Rudder home at 2000 Elton Lane in central Austin was campaign headquarters. The campaign workers, all volunteers and many from the Land Office, gathered in the Rudder home at the end of the workday and worked in the backyard at tables under electric lights suspended from trees. For the Land Office employees there were no ethical or legal conflicts as long as they did not use state equipment or work on the campaign during business hours.

Ned Price was a strong contender, and Rudder's biggest disadvantage was apparently his close association with Allan Shivers, whose public approval rating had fallen to 22 percent in late 1955. Rudder and Price had difficulty attracting public attention to their campaigns, because the ballot was unusually long. In addition to the land commissioner's race, voters had to choose among six candidates for governor, four for lieutenant governor, four for attorney general, and three for agricultural commissioner, plus those running in local and regional elections. The land commissioner's race was near the bottom on the list of names on the ballot.

Most newspaper coverage focused on the six candidates for governor. Even the *Austin American,* the state's most politically oriented daily, devoted little space to the land commissioner's race. Rudder worried that people would be more likely to vote for a "Price" than for a "Rudder," which he thought was too guttural to catch on. John Lindsey, his campaign chairman in Houston, suggested a campaign slogan—"None udder but Rudder." Rudder did not like it, but it caught on.[33]

Ned Price and Earl Rudder had similar backgrounds, except that Price was not a war veteran and Rudder had not been elected to the legislature. Both were experienced in local government. Rudder's primary constituencies were veterans, former students of Texas A&M, and army reservists. Ned Price had graduated from the Southern Methodist University law school and was known to officeholders in every county through the statewide association of county judges and commissioners, of which he was a former president. He had well-placed friends from his service in the Texas House of Representatives from 1940 to 1945.[34] Price was definitely not a "Shivercrat," but a Democrat who had been loyal to national party candidates. His wife had served on the State Democratic Executive Committee until 1954, when Shivers and Pickle had supplanted her along with others preferred by Shivers, one of whom was Rudder.

Both Price and Rudder were active Methodist laymen. Neither was wealthy, but both were generous with people in need and charities that they believed in. Their children attended the same high school, and they would remember the campaign as "clean and without backbiting or mudslinging," which was true except for a last-minute flurry of allegations by Price advocates in paid newspaper advertisements.[35]

The 1956 political campaigns were the last before television became the dominant electioneering medium. Most campaigning was grassroots, walking the streets and making speeches. Back and forth across the state Rudder campaigned in a style that would seem almost apolitical in comparison to later norms. Unable to attract attention from major newspapers, he went to smaller cities and towns, speaking to service clubs and veterans organizations, telling them what the Land Office was and what it did. He urged voters to support the constitutional amendment on the November ballot that would strengthen and extend the Veterans Land Program by authorizing the sale of $100 million in bonds for loans to veterans to buy land, which he had recommended to the legislature. During the last month of the campaign he placed small ads in farm and ranch journals calling attention to his commitment to soil and water conservation.

Ned Price campaigned against Shivers rather than Rudder. He presented the real issue of the campaign as Shivers's corruption, with Rudder as an appointed hack and a Shivers clone. Only in the final days did the Price campaign attack Rudder directly by contemptuously dismissing his military service: "Yes, we, too, like a hero. We have heard so much about the 'big hero'—it has been rehearsed and rehashed, morning, noon, and night, for years, until we are sick and tired of it—fed up on it. We have heard this story so often we can close our eyes and recite it from memory. We want our land commissioner to be one that was 'appointed' and 'chosen' by us—not by Allan Shivers—never."[36]

Rudder prepared a response that may not have been released to the public but made fascinating counterpoints, accusing Price of using "dark whisperings and insinuations" as his major campaign weapons. In a quid pro quo for Price's ridicule of his war record, Rudder's rejoinder was, "I have no patience with men who prate about freedom, but are unwilling to fight for it. During the war, some of us didn't have time to think of the fellows who chose to remain at home in their comfortable legislative swivel-chairs. When we got back, we found that some our wartime indispensable lawmakers had created state jobs for themselves. Some men are invincible in peace, but invisible in war."[37]

Television was little used in the 1956 political campaigns except by the leading gubernatorial candidates, so on Thursday, July 26, two days before the Democratic primary election, the Price campaign was caught off guard by a fourteen-minute prime-time statewide telecast featuring Rudder and his family. The telecast was mostly the story of Earl's life, with emphasis on his efforts to clean up the veterans land scandal and his war service. Ned Price always believed the Shivers crowd had raised the money for the production, and his supporters thought the telecast tipped the vote in Rudder's favor. Jake Pickle implicitly supported Price's contention with the observation that Rudder "didn't have any organization or people, except the Shivers people."[38]

In the final days of the campaign, newspapers in the largest cities—Dallas and Houston—and notably those in medium-sized cities such as San Angelo and Corpus Christi that were owned by Harte-Hanks, the largest newspaper

Keep **EARL RUDDER** on the job

as

COMMISSIONER of the GENERAL LAND OFFICE

EARL RUDDER deserves your support in the July Democratic primary BECAUSE . . .

- He is cleaning up and restoring confidence in the Veterans Land Program.

- No more "block deals" . . . Earl Rudder runs this office for the benefit of the veterans and the people, not the slick promoters.

- Earl Rudder is the veteran's veteran. He was a battlefield soldier himself in World War II. And Earl Rudder knows the problems and will protect the rights of his fellow veterans.

- General Omar N. Bradley, Commander of U.S. ground forces in Europe, has written that the D-Day mission he assigned to Earl Rudder was the toughest he ever gave any soldier in his entire military career. (The capture by Rudder's Rangers of a German coastal battery on 100-foot high cliffs overlooking both Omaha and Utah beaches.)

- The cleaning up of the scandal-ridden affairs of the Veterans' Land Board has been one of the toughest jobs ever assigned a public official in Texas.

- Earl Rudder's friends KNOW that he will continue his untiring efforts on behalf of his fellow veterans and all of the people of Texas.

VOTE FOR
EARL RUDDER
(MEMBER V.F.W. POST 856)
— and —

KEEP A VETERAN IN A VETERAN'S JOB!

(Political Advertisement Paid for by Friends of Earl Rudder)

A sample of Rudder's literature in the campaign for commissioner of the General Land Office in 1956. (Courtesy of Margaret Rudder)

chain in the state, endorsed Rudder. Nonetheless, the vote was so close that Rudder did not declare victory until two days later. In the final tally, he had 647,443 votes (51.2 percent) and Price had 616,459, a margin of 30,984 out of 1.7 million cast. Of the 254 counties in Texas, Travis County gave Rudder his greatest numerical edge, 25,687 to 11,864 for Price. The 13,823 margin in Rudder's favor was a surprise, because Travis County—strongly anti-Shivers—was projected to go against Rudder. Word-of-mouth praise of Rudder by Land Office staff and other state employees apparently gave him the advantage.

Three counties where Rudder was best known voted overwhelming for him: McCulloch, where he had been mayor of Brady, with 72.3 percent; Concho, his birthplace, with 78.9 percent; and Menard, where he ranched, with 75.6 percent.[39] These three counties, plus Travis, provided Rudder with more than half of his margin over Ned Price. Winning the Democratic primary guaranteed that he would prevail in the general election in November.

Nonetheless, Rudder was stung by the closeness of the vote. He had campaigned believing that he had rightfully earned the public's trust and confidence. In his disappointment he may have overlooked the fact that he was the biggest vote getter of all candidates in all races. He outpolled a popular U.S. senator in the race for governor, Price Daniel, who pulled in twenty thousand fewer votes than Rudder.[40] Supporters advised Rudder that the narrow margin was not personal disapproval but an anti-Shivers backlash.

Rudder sought the viewpoints of supporters across the state. "I had the scare of my life," one wrote, "when the returns started coming in from Lufkin and South East Texas. Judge Price must certainly have spread the discord about Shivers and you being an appointee of his." Another echoed the idea that "people who are anti-Shivers thought you were an associate of his because he appointed you. Your opponent had a very common name and this got him a number of votes. In this county a number of people voted for Mr. Price because he was from East Texas and you were from West Texas."[41]

Although he was personally disappointed with his 51.2 percent of the vote, 69 percent of the electorate approved the $100 million bond issue to expand the Veterans Land Program. This overwhelming but indirect endorsement of his accomplishments suggests that Rudder's identification with Shiver was indeed his primary liability in the campaign.

Three months into his new term of office he was promoted to major general in the U.S. Army Reserves on May 7, 1957. Meanwhile, he got an enticing but confidential proposition that finally became public on November 27, 1957, when headlines across the state announced, "Rudder to Resign, Take A&M Duties." Many Aggies were happy about the rumors, while other supporters pleaded with him to remain as land commissioner. "Your service can hardly be replaced," wrote an attorney in Linden. "The people of Texas, particularly the veterans, have great confidence in you. In a short time you have brought the Veterans Land Board from chaos and great distrust to orderliness and trust." Another wrote, "You are needed to help us keep one or two oil companies from cramming selfish and self-serving legislation through the Legislature. Stay in there and pitch. Forget your personal desires and think of the greater benefit you can be to the public."[42]

SUMMING UP

Rudder was proud of his accomplishments as commissioner of the General Land Office. When the first $12.5 million of the $100 million in bonds for the Veterans Land Program were sold at a favorable (low) interest rate to the state on December 16, 1956, he was unrestrained in saying that it represented "the completion of the mission which I had undertaken as land commissioner and chairman of the Veterans Land Board on January 5, 1955."[43]

Otherwise, his proudest accomplishments were the increases in the permanent endowments for schools and universities derived from lands managed by the General Land Office during his tenure. Wanting the public record to show what he had done, he prepared a report on the growth of these endowments from the day he took office in January 1955 until his last day in office, January 31, 1958. The report stated that the increases "had been accomplished in spite of a recession in oil and gas leasing activity during 1957." Never published, the report indicated that the Permanent School Fund had increased by 26.18 percent and the Permanent University Fund by 29.67 percent.[44]

As expected, Texas A&M offered Rudder an appointment, and he submitted his resignation to Governor Price Daniel on December 21, 1957. "Having been appointed by the Board of Directors of Texas A&M College to an executive position at Texas A&M, beginning February 1, 1958, I hereby respectfully submit my resignation as Commissioner of the General Land Office of the State of Texas effective that date. I can report to you in all sincerity that with the help of many dedicated Texas citizens and faithful state employees this mission [to clean up the Veterans Land Program] has been accomplished."[45]

Rudder disliked form letters, but so many people sent congratulatory messages that he prepared a standard reply, ending with his commitment to Texas A&M: "I leave the General Land Office to become vice president of Texas A&M College where I believe I can be of greatest service to my state and nation."[46]

CHAPTER 17

TEXAS A&M PRESIDENTIAL YEARS
1958–1970

When Rudder was offered an executive position at Texas A&M, he was as eager to go as he had been in 1943 when offered command of the 2nd Ranger Battalion. As when he took charge of the Land Office and the Veterans Land Program, he was going to an organization in crisis, but this time he could not leave immediately.[1] He was nine months into a two-year elected term as commissioner of the General Land Office of Texas, and his conversations with the A&M Board of Directors were confidential. Careful to show proper respect for Governor Price Daniel, whose authority over A&M included appointing its directors and reviewing its budget requests, he waited to announce he was leaving office.

The directors and Rudder agreed in a closed-door meeting on September 27, 1957, that he would resign as land commissioner at an unspecified early date and become vice president of Texas A&M College, the principal institution in a system of several colleges.[2] Vice president was temporarily the top administrative position in the institution.

Willing to bide their time for Rudder, the nine-member Board of Directors instructed the chancellor of the Texas A&M College System, Marion Thomas Harrington, to assume the college presidency while continuing as chief administrator of the system. Harrington had been president of Texas A&M College from 1950 to 1953, one of five in the previous decade. The directors gave Rudder a mandate "to take charge," which meant that his authority devolved from them, and he would not have to clear his decisions with Harrington. Individual directors further strengthened his role by saying he would become president at an unspecified later date.[3]

Ten days after the board's confidential agreement with Rudder, Harrington met with him in Austin. Initially, they would divide the presidential duties, with Harrington as the outside man and Rudder the inside decision maker. As president of the Texas A&M System and of A&M College, Harrington would represent the college with professional organizations and A&M's alumni, the Association of Former Students. Legislative relations were a top priority for both men.[4]

A month later, Harrington was again in Austin. Unable to see Rudder, he sent him a handwritten note that the Board of Directors would meet in late November and wanted to "make the announcement of your appointment at that time." But Rudder put it off. "Please keep this confidential until I get further word from the governor." Despite the secrecy, newspaper columnists were soon speculating that Rudder might quit the Land Office to "become a professional Aggie."[5]

When the A&M Board of Directors convened on November 27, Rudder still had not met with Governor Daniel, who stayed much of the time on his ranch near Liberty, Texas. So the board officially appointed him in executive session and delayed until three days before Christmas to announce that on February 1, 1958, he would become "Vice President of the A. and M. College of Texas" at a salary of sixteen thousand dollars per year with a house and utilities.[6]

With Rudder taking over, the arch defenders of Aggie traditions—the Old Army Aggies—breathed deep sighs of relief. He seemed the preeminent Aggie: a heroic soldier, a former A&M football star, and a public servant who had won a statewide election. He had a fine family—a wife of twenty-two years and five children—to whom he was obviously devoted. The Old Army Aggies were so proud of him that they did not question whether he was one of them. In his 1956 Muster Day speech he had implied that he was in accord with A&M's great traditions. Twice he drew on words of the time-honored school song, "True to each other as Aggies can be," and emphasized his "firm resolve to keep the heritage handed down by those we honor today."[7]

But Rudder was not a traditionalist by disposition or by indoctrination. Neither was he a typical Aggie, and he knew it. He told his staff not to play up the fact that he had been an A&M student for only two years.[8] He was a Tarleton College man as much an Aggie. During his two years as an A&M student, he was not a mainstream cadet. He was never an underclassman, and his part-time jobs and his participation in intercollegiate athletics kept him from many experiences that were the everyday life of most cadets.

Rudder was a reformer, a pragmatist for whom dwelling on the past was a waste of time. He was a problem-solver, an activist, and a hardnosed do-gooder, intent upon making the world better for others. He was in the Aggie culture but not its prisoner, and he was already a legend, endowed with the talents of the change agent that A&M desperately needed. One of his talents was an inborn ability to blend in with almost any group, which was important because his only real concern about going to Texas A&M was whether he would fit in "with those Ph.D. types," as his wife would say. It was not a matter of holding his own with them intellectually and verbally, but whether they would accept him as their leader, a man with only a bachelor's degree in industrial education and no experience in collegiate administration except coaching a junior college football team. That he need not have worried is illustrated by an incident later related by the presidents of the University of Houston and Rice University, who attended with Rudder a weeklong seminar for twenty new presidents at Harvard University. On the third day, at the end of a session discussing the challenges of their jobs, one of the presidents remarked that it was obvious to him that "none of us are old broken down generals or retired politicians. We have all come up through the ranks." Rudder, having schmoozed so well that the man thought he came from an academic background, laughed as he exclaimed, "It looks like you've got me on all counts!"[9]

Rudder had a strong ego, but helping others was an overriding value. He was, his children thought, always on the lookout for someone in need. Twenty-two-year-old Marsha Jensen was driving between Texas A&M and Austin on a Sunday afternoon in 1963 when her car had a flat tire. She pulled to the side of the road to replace it with the spare in the trunk. A light rain was falling, and changing the tire would be a major physical challenge. Then another car stopped behind her. A portly man dressed in coat and tie got out and changed the tire for her. She wanted to know who he was and what he did. He admitted to having a job at A&M, but when she asked what he did, he replied, "I work all around the campus," leaving her with the impression that he had something to do with buildings and grounds. Only when she told a friend that a nice man named Earl Rudder had changed her tire did she learn who he was.[10]

Rudder's demeanor was nearly always natural and relaxed, which had its downside when he popped off and revealed his biases and preferences, but even then it was usually beyond the earshot of anyone who would take offense. In common with infantry officers who have risen to high rank, he could give orders, be demanding, and blister anyone who assumed prerogatives or disappointed him. Yet in such moments he kept his composure, which inspired respect and confidence even from those he reprimanded.

VICE PRESIDENT, FEBRUARY 1, 1958–JULY 1, 1959

On January 26, 1958, the Rudder family moved into the two-story Victorian frame house near Sbisa Hall built for Lawrence Sullivan Ross after he became president in 1891.[11] Earl made his office on the second floor of the Richard Coke Building. When he sat down at his desk that first day, he had a sobering professional appraisal that outlined the major challenges he would confront in the coming decade. At the request of Harrington and the directors, the evaluation had been prepared by Durwood B. "Woody" Varner, a prominent 1940 Aggie alumnus, then vice president of Michigan State University and destined to become chancellor of the University of Nebraska. It was a five-page, single-spaced letter composed," Varner said, "in the spirit of constructive criticism about the problems of Texas A&M as one who might be president."[12]

Varner had visited the A&M campus and had conferred with colleagues in land-grant colleges across the nation before reaching his main point: "A and M College is not highly regarded," and "no one would say it is a first-class institution." He attributed A&M's deplorable condition to six causes:

> **Required military training.** Varner noted that "the glamour associated with being part of a military college" had declined since World War II. "Texas A&M has not been willing to adjust to this new situation and is rapidly falling behind other land grant colleges."
>
> **Hazing.** The deeply engrained Aggie tradition of harassing underclassmen, especially freshmen, was retarding A&M's enrollment while other institutions were growing rapidly. "Prospective students are discouraged from attending A&M," and "the price," Varner declared, "in the loss of competent students is more than we can afford."
>
> **All-male student body.** "A and M's full potential will never be realized as long as it continues as an all-male school. The very fact that every other land-grant college has become co-educational is cause to review this longstanding policy."
>
> **Faculty deficiencies.** "The morale of the faculty is quite low. The extremely low salary scale is one of the serious problems . . . but not the entire problem. There is no positive dedication to moving ahead vigorously with a program of real scholarship and scholarly activities."
>
> **Overemphasis on the Corps of Cadets and the athletic department.** "Too much emphasis has been placed on their problems and too little support has been given to developing and retaining a faculty of the highest caliber."
>
> **Old Army Aggies.** "Many former students seem more dedicated to preserving traditions and memories than in contributing to the changes that must be made to take Texas A&M where it should be and keep it there."[13]

Although each item on Varner's list cried out for action, Rudder's first imperative was to stem the awesome number of freshman dropouts threatening the viability of the college and to make A&M more appealing to potential

Rudder visiting with Texas A&M students in their dormitory, October 29, 1969.
Margaret Rudder described these occasions as "what Earl liked to do best." (Battalion,
Texas A&M University)

students. His first concern was to give students more time to study, especially
freshmen, who needed relief from abuse by upperclassmen. In the opinion of
many professors, this would involve changing customs of the Corps. Rudder
aligned himself with the faculty by consistently supporting their primary role
in the educational process. He was a fundamentalist for academic achievement. Everything else about a student's college experience was subordinate
to classroom performance. His unceasing question to students was, "What is
your grade point average?" and they joked that they were soldiers in Rudder's
"Grade Point Army."

Rudder made an early visit to the counseling center, where he told the
staff to concentrate on boosting academic achievement. They replied, as if he
did not know, that hazing presented a major obstacle by infringing on a student's time. Having struggled with grades while juggling hours for study and
work as a student, he took action, and the counseling center began receiving

additional funds to augment its services. Lannes Hope, a specialist in testing
and measurement, was convinced that Rudder "believed in counseling. The
presidents before him had no use for testing and psychology but, with him,
we made a lot of progress."[14]

Only a few days after he assumed office, he met with the two senior students who held the highest ranks in the Corps of Cadets, Jon Hagler and Ray
Bowen, making it "clear he was in charge." Then he announced new policies
to take the pressure off freshmen. Upperclassmen would be punished "who
detain students en route to class," and good study habits would be stressed.
Bowen advised fellow cadets, "Anything that doesn't complement good study
habits and conditions is being removed." Rudder condemned hazing; he had
no patience with the argument that hazing enhanced military discipline.[15]

Unlike most new appointees to his position, he did not need to travel
widely to meet people with deep pockets and speak to alumni groups, because many already knew him. The same was true for A&M's most important external constituents: the governor and leaders in the state legislature.
Indeed, his appointment rested on his standing outside the college. He devoted himself to learning Texas A&M from the inside, from which, he anticipated, internal respect would follow.[16]

He met the faculty initially by presiding over the academic council,
which was composed of about fifty deans and department chairmen—an
exasperating initiation to stodgy academic processes for a man accustomed
to taking counsel only of himself before acting. He could have delegated this
task, but he deliberately plunged into A&M's innards to learn the issues and
hear individual concerns. He could have abolished some faculty committees
as impediments to change, but he kept most of them. When he could not
work with them, he worked around them, devising his own processes. More
quickly than he expected, the A&M faculty accepted him, relieved by his appointment, which transformed uncertainty and ambiguity into definiteness
and clarity. Some already knew him because they, too, were A&M graduates
and active in the Association of Former Students, which he had served as a
member of its executive board.[17]

Those who met with him spread the news that he was reasonable, firm,
and fair, with his full attention focused on the development of Texas A&M.
He had no other agenda, and he did not play games. As Rudder's knowledge
of the campus grew, the faculty realized they could take a proposal to him
and get an immediate yes or no on a proposed project. Such decisiveness was
new to them, but it was possible with Rudder because he had the confidence
of the Board of Directors.[18] He walked the campus at night, both to relax

and to inspect the lighting and the landscaping, especially the trees, often accompanied by a daughter.

Rudder understood authority and how to exercise it in a complex organization better than most college executives did. He did not pretend knowledge that he did not have. He learned on the job from subordinates by practicing two ingrained personal habits that he had adopted long before they became principles of modern management. One was to ask people at all levels for their ideas about how to achieve greater productivity; the second was to evaluate himself critically to improve his own performance.[19]

Coeducation: The Main Issue

As Rudder was taking office, lawsuits and court judgments confirmed that the admission of women was the most controversial issue affecting the long-term development of Texas A&M. Three other issues—racial integration, military training, and the institutional name—were important, but none packed the emotion and complexity of coeducation. Only three days before Rudder took office, litigation over coeducation became headline news that continued unabated for the next fourteen months as it progressed through the courts. The case began on January 29, 1958, when a Bryan attorney filed a suit against the A&M registrar, President Harrington, and the Board of Directors seeking a court order directing them to admit two Bryan women. The district judge ordered A&M to admit the women, but the decision was reversed in the circuit court and refused by the state supreme court, which had the effect of supporting the directors' male-only policy.[20] Many people thought the issue had run its course, but the women and their attorney intended to keep challenging the policy.

When Rudder was asked about the Texas Supreme Court's decision, he evaded the question: "The decision is in keeping with the Board of Directors' desire. It is my job to run A&M as the Board wants it run." Asked how the court's ruling would affect the future of the college, he laughed and said, "I don't have a crystal ball."[21] He would try to stay out of the public controversy. He was intent on improving campus life before taking on big policy issues.

However, he could not ignore the issue. Aggie factions were passionate, and their gabbiness appealed to reporters and newspaper editors, with the result that A&M's troubles were magnified and publicized. In a speech to the Dallas A&M Club, Rudder tried to cool the agitation: "The best thing A&M alumni can do is settle down, quit making so much publicity, and let students resume their studies. I can't blame them for being upset."[22]

Privately, though, he confided to his wife, "If A&M does not change, it will become less important than the smallest junior college." He spoke similarly to Lester Harrell, deputy director of the Commission on Higher Education. As the head of a major state agency, Rudder had acquired respect for counterparts in other agencies. "Earl had not been at A&M very long," Harrell recalled, "before he began talking about what he had found. His comments were different from all other college presidents. They'd come in and say, 'What we need is more money.' He said, 'We need to change.'"[23]

In his first thirty days in office he was exposed to organizations that would try his patience during his entire twelve-year administration. One was the American Association of University Professors, and the other was the journalism department—and journalists generally. Harrington had approved the creation of a chapter of the AAUP, a national organization to help create conditions under which teachers could do their best work in the classroom. Like most other chapters, the A&M faculty interpreted the purpose broadly and created a committee on faculty-administrative relations. Rudder largely rendered the committee redundant by the effectiveness of his direct communications with the faculty. For the AAUP's first outside speaker he invited a former neighbor in Austin, James P. Hart, liberal Democrat, former associate justice on the state supreme court, and former chancellor of the University of Texas. Rudder introduced Hart to his audience, and Hart stated perfectly Rudder's personal philosophy that "too much emphasis was placed on leisure and acquiring material gains and not enough on serving our fellow man."[24]

Rudder expressed his skepticism about the journalism department by denying, with no explanation, a routine request to establish an honorary society for high-achieving students. It was a minor decision and obviously inconsistent with his emphasis on recognizing academic achievement, but he did not envision Texas A&M as a training ground for journalists.

Two months after he took office, he was implicated in the dismissal of the director of student publications. The director, Ross Strader, had incurred Harrington's displeasure when he failed to prevent the student newspaper, the *Battalion,* from publicizing a dispute between the faculty and the Board of Directors about mandatory military training. Harrington fired Strader by leaving him out of the budget for the coming year. When Strader sought to avail himself of a policy that permitted an appeal to the directors, Rudder let him go immediately, explaining afterwards that "since he has chosen to make the decision a matter of public debate, the best interests of the college require the immediate termination of his connection."[25]

Soon after the Strader firing, Rudder ordered the destruction of all copies of *The Commentator,* a student magazine that published racy articles.

He believed his responsibilities for students resembled those of a parent. In law, the concept is known as *in loco parentis,* "in place of a parent." Once widely practiced, the doctrine was already fading when Rudder articulated his "duty to see that A&M does not endorse anything that could tend to destroy the moral fiber of the young men attending this school. A&M is not going to support any activity that can degrade the morals of its students, to any degree, at any time."[26]

Rudder's resolve not to permit anything that tended to "destroy the moral fiber of the young men" at Texas A&M extended to art exhibits in the Memorial Student Center, whose director was art connoisseur J. Wayne Stark. Rudder had preconceived ideas about art that were based on little information and experience. He had never been in an art museum, and he believed almost to the end of his life that paintings were concerned only with nude feminine forms. His first and only visit to an art museum occurred three months before his death, when he was in Chicago on a business trip with two A&M benefactors, director Ford Albritton and future director John Lindsey. Only Lindsey's insistence persuaded Rudder to accompany them to a Rembrandt exhibit at the Art Institute of Chicago. Rudder was enchanted by landscape scenes, and he stayed until the janitors escorted him to the door to lock up for the evening.[27]

That mind-expanding experience was far in the future, however, and Stark had to contend with a supervisor whose ideas about acceptable art were far more limited than his own. The two men had the similar goal of "educating the whole person," but Stark's concept was broader than Rudder's. In addition to art exhibits, Rudder and Stark sparred over outside lecturers, foreign travel for students, and Stark's promotion of Ivy League graduate schools to A&M's best students when they completed their bachelor's degrees. Rudder believed that if bright young men such as Jon Hagler and Henry Cisneros did not return to Texas after graduate study at Harvard or Columbia, Texas would lose potentially valuable assets that it had invested in heavily. The Rudder-Stark differences produced guffaws across the campus, especially about works of art that Rudder criticized in student center exhibits. More than once Stark returned to his office after meeting with Rudder to say, presumably in jest, "Well, I just got fired again."

In 1955 Stark had organized a Student Conference on National Affairs (SCONA), which became an annual event and a widely admired model for other university unions. Rudder was initially skeptical of SCONA, but he could not ignore it. SCONA brought to the campus politicians such as Lyndon B. Johnson, Hubert H. Humphrey, and Robert F. Kennedy, and the news media followed them. As for politicians, he was circumspect about those with

Rudder with Robert F. Kennedy at Texas A&M in 1959 while Kennedy was chief counsel for the U.S. Senate Labor Rackets Committee. (Courtesy of Margaret Rudder)

whom he was seen or photographed. One was Ralph W. Yarborough, the junior U.S. senator from Texas, who Rudder had campaigned against on behalf of Allan Shivers in the bitter gubernatorial campaigns of 1952 and 1954.

As Rudder went about familiarizing himself with A&M, he visited support units across the campus and came to know many of the staff by name. Such familiarity was unusual for some college presidents, but not for a combat-experienced army officer who knew to respect the people on whom he depended, regardless of their rank or duties. In a relatively short time most A&M employees saw him up close and were left with the remarkable first impression that was his gift. He projected purposefulness and was meticulous in his attire, invariably wearing a dark suit and tie. When he went home for lunch, Margaret ironed his trousers to restore the crisp crease down the length of the front.

Rudder's friendliness with staff may have been mistaken for micromanagement. Workmen were overheard asking his opinion about the shade of the new paint on the water tower and his preference for the time of day that they should mow the grass near his office. His preferred mowing time was an appropriate question, because campus buildings were not yet air-conditioned, and the windows to his office were open to lawnmower noise. He was approachable, so they asked him, and they avoided going through his office staff for an answer. Rudder respected people who worked with their hands, who performed the tasks that made life easier for others, whether it was sweeping out buildings at night or unlocking them at dawn.

While he was making changes in the first months on the job, he had to learn the college—the key people, the facilities, and the services and installations required for it to function. A&M was a community of more than ten thousand people: students, faculty, and staff interwoven in numerous departments and informal groups. He could make a few changes by edict, but the really complex changes required study, analysis, making choices, involving others in formulating plans, and cajoling still others to implement them. Obtaining cooperation depended on his ability to persuade key people, and that required time and patience. If they were to follow him, they had to believe in his proposals and ultimately in him.

Rudder got so much done in the first eight months that he was asked in the first faculty meeting of the next academic year, 1958–59, how he dealt with his responsibilities. He explained, "Solutions came after discussion and research. Many officials met in my office and together we came up with the best solution for the situation, considering the tools available. We don't always agree but we do try to find the best solution."[28] Deliberation often frustrates resolution, but they were combined as hallmarks of the Rudder administration.

PRESIDENT RUDDER, JULY 1, 1959

To no one's surprise, the Board of Directors elevated Rudder from vice president to president of A&M College on July 1, 1959. His promotion attracted slight attention in the news media, overshadowed as it was by A&M's disputes over coeducation and military training. With Rudder's move up, Harrington dropped his title as president of A&M College and became chancellor of the

The Rudder family in 1960 when Earl was inaugurated president of the Agricultural and Mechanical College of Texas. From left: *Jane, Bob, Linda, Margaret, Earl, James Earl Jr., and Anne. (Courtesy of Margaret Rudder)*

Texas A&M System. Little was changed in the relationship of the two men or in their duties, but formalizing Rudder's title as president made him the unquestioned leader and spokesman for A&M College in all venues with all constituencies.[29]

The scant public recognition accorded Rudder's promotion may have been a consideration in making his presidential inauguration a grand event attended by some five thousand people. Delegates from 244 colleges and universities, attired in their academic regalia and mixed with the heraldry of military decorations worn by scores of army and air force officers, formed a colorful procession in the G. Rollie White coliseum. President Eisenhower sent a telegram of congratulations, and Rudder's wartime commander in Brittany and the Ardennes, Troy H. Middleton, now president of Louisiana State University, gave the principal address. He depicted Rudder as "the kind of person who will direct his efforts to the problems of the future and not dwell on those of the past."[30]

Rudder in his square academic cap, often called a mortar board, and gown on March 26, 1960, when he was inaugurated president of Texas A&M. (Courtesy of Margaret Rudder)

Rudder took the title of his inaugural address from Charles Wesley's hymn "A Charge to Keep," which he had sung as a boy in Eden. He predicted that college enrollments would double in ten years but despaired that "Americans spent more money on cigarettes, liquor, recreation, and legalized gambling than on higher education." In conclusion, he spoke directly to the Board of Directors: "You charge me with the care, supervision, the education, and the training for responsibilities of citizenship of the most precious resource of the State of Texas. . . . It is a charge I will do my utmost to keep. May the Almighty guide and grant me wisdom in this undertaking."[31]

After the inauguration he hosted a luncheon for twelve hundred guests in Sbisa Hall, where he had waited tables while earning his way through Texas

Rudder with Troy H. Middleton, president emeritus of Louisiana State University, 1969.
Middleton, Rudder's superior as commander of VIII Corps in Brittany and the Ardennes,
described him as "the bravest man I have ever seen in action." (Courtesy of Margaret Rudder)

A&M as a student. Afterwards, he told the assembly, "I deserve only small credit for this or any of the good things that have come my way. I owe more than I can repay to many people who have helped me." Making no mention of his father, he praised his mother and his wife as the two most important people in his life: "I owe much to my good Mother for my upbringing," and "for the strongest influence on my mature years, I owe much to the one here beside me today."[32]

The pageantry and oration of Earl Rudder's presidential inauguration on March 26, 1960, had the intended effect. Texas A&M was praised for producing leaders in public life as well as soldiers, and Rudder was more widely recognized as a leader in higher education. "In Earl Rudder," the *Houston Post* editorialized, "Texas A and M College has a president of whom it can be proud—a true A&M man and an exemplar of the college's highest traditions."[33] When Aggies saw their professors in processions with counterparts from leading universities in Massachusetts, Illinois, and California, it raised their aspirations for Texas A&M.

In the slightly more than two years that Rudder had been in charge, the threatening decline in enrollment had been stopped, mainly by improvement in the freshman retention rate. Now he could focus attention on advancing A&M academically. For this undertaking he required a small group of collaborators to study issues, solve complex problems, and consider ways of going forward. In the weeks following the inauguration, he made two appointments for this team. He selected Dorsey E. McCrory, a retired army colonel, as his executive assistant and Wayne C. Hall as the dean of the graduate school. He had not met McCrory until he interviewed him, and he had only recently met Hall.

McCrory was recommended by fellow officers in the Pentagon, and, although campus detractors called him "the general's aide," he was no intellectual slouch. McCrory had taken his bachelor's degree at A&M as a Distinguished Military Graduate in 1939, standing sixth scholastically in his class. After serving as an infantry officer in the European war, he remained in the army and earned a master's degree in political science from Yale. Like Rudder, he came from a Methodist family in a small town: Waelder, Texas, population about one thousand.[34]

McCrory's résumé was easy for Rudder to understand in comparison to Wayne Hall's curriculum vitae, which listed seventy-five published scientific botanical articles, with titles replete with Latin words, in addition to several honorary societies with Greek names. An eminent plant scientist, Hall had been on the A&M faculty since 1949 and was head of the plant physiology and pathology department. He had grown up dirt-poor on the family cattle and wheat farm in Montana and later worked his way through the University of Iowa, where he returned after the war for his doctoral degree.[35]

Hall first met Rudder while planning a new building for plant sciences. In contrast to previous presidents, Rudder involved himself in the project and insisted on two changes contrary to A&M customs. One was that the occupants of the new building should participate in its design, and the other was that each professor should have a private office.[36] When Hall was summoned to Rudder's office, he presumed the new building was the subject, only to learn upon arrival that it was a job interview. Rudder seated Hall in a straight-backed chair in front of his large desk. Hall was psychologically disarmed as Rudder grilled him, asking questions, listening, and observing his body language.

Rudder began with, "Dr. Hall, you seem to know what research and graduate work is all about and that is what I want to discuss with you. *My purpose is to develop Texas A&M into a graduate and research institution.* Do you have what it takes to head up this mission for me?" From that opening

Professor Wayne C. Hall, an eminent plant scientist, was Rudder's chief academic officer at Texas A&M from 1959 to 1968. Committed to eliminating A&M's "virtual albatrosses" and creating an "immutable marriage" between teaching and research, he influenced Rudder's vision for A&M and helped shape the recommendations that transformed the institution. (Courtesy of Janice Hall Zapata)

Rudder launched into an inquiry of Hall's entire life that in another decade would border on invasion of privacy. "Tell me about yourself, what is your background, and where would you like to go in your career?" When Hall described "A&M as a sleeping giant with unlimited potential" that "lacked only leadership and vision," Rudder's interest in him soared. More of an interrogation than an interview, the meeting left Hall "mentally, physically and emotionally exhausted." Later, Rudder got an opinion about him from his parish priest.[37]

When Rudder learned that Hall had served as a naval officer during the war, he asked, "Where were you during the Normandy invasion?" Hall replied that he had been in the waters off Omaha Beach on board a destroyer, the USS *Frankford,* and recounted the coincidence that he had directed fire support for Rudder's Rangers under Max Schneider. From the bridge, Hall had watched the fighting on the shore with binoculars and had called aiming directions to naval guns that had silenced enemy artillery and induced the surrender of German troops to the Rangers. "Our eyes locked as brothers in a war," reminisced Hall, "where by chance we had shared the bonds of a common horrible experience."[38]

When Hall agreed to join Rudder's team, he found he had the equivalent of three full time jobs. Officially, he was dean of the graduate school, but Rudder did not appoint a dean of the undergraduate college and gave the work to Hall. Neither did Rudder appoint a replacement for Hall as head of his plant sciences department, where he also taught part-time and tried to continue his research.[39] Rudder took satisfaction in running A&M with a minimal number of administrators, and he thought nothing of assigning his subordinates additional duties.

In Wayne Hall, Rudder chose both A&M's chief academic officer and his personal tutor about academic life, customs, and attitudes, especially of the faculty. Rudder respected scholars in applied sciences, but he required persuasion to accept the faculty's concerns with academic freedom, their desire to participate in professional appointments and curricular changes, and their rank consciousness. Hall believed in the mutual benefits of interactive relationships among teaching, research, and extension. He referred to this potential as the "Holy Grail of the land grant institution," and his professional passion was to create an "immutable marriage" between teaching and research.[40]

Hall's convictions would echo through Rudder's speeches with confident assertions that there was no contradiction between A&M's commitment to good teaching and greater emphasis on research. As Rudder's confidence in Hall grew, he persuaded the Board of Directors to transfer A&M's principal extension and experiment components from the A&M System to A&M College. Approval of the transfer occurred in the same meeting where Hall's appointment as dean was confirmed, which placed him in charge of them. Like Rudder, Hall was the right man at the right time, as he would say, to lead A&M "to its rightful place in the sun."[41]

Rudder's firm declaration that "my purpose is to develop Texas A&M into a graduate and research institution" was the fundamental goal of his presidency. At first, he did not talk about the conspicuous issues confronting

Texas A&M, namely gender and racial integration and whether military training should be required or voluntary, the issues that Wayne Hall called "A&M's virtual albatrosses." He had yet to learn that remedying them would be necessary to accomplish his fundamental goal. Many changes that he instigated followed his growing comprehension of issues and the expansion of his vision for A&M.

Where did Rudder get the idea of transforming Texas A&M into a powerhouse of graduate education and research? It was a far-reaching concept, which he knew little about when he set out to foster it in an institution that was considered suboptimal by some of its most faithful supporters. When asked the origins of Rudder's vision for A&M, his son Bud suggested, "Never overlook the influence of 'Tiger' Teague and Lyndon Johnson." Olin E. "Tiger" Teague was a member of Congress whose district included Texas A&M; he was a highly decorated war veteran, Rudder's A&M classmate, and one of his most intimate friends. Lyndon Johnson was then the senior U.S. senator from Texas and the Senate majority leader. Teague was a member of the House Committee on Science and Astronautics, later Science and Technology; Johnson, soon to be vice president of the United States, chaired the Preparedness Subcommittee of the Senate Armed Services Committee. The Cold War was in full swing, countering the threat of the Soviet Union was a matter of national survival, and the race for superiority in outer space was an important part of it.

Teague or Johnson could easily have convinced Rudder that pushing back the frontiers of science and technology was essential. No one needed to tell him that A&M had potential in both areas. Teague and Johnson were influential in the congressional appropriations process, and their influence was growing. Keenly aware of the huge sums of federal money that went to the nation's universities, especially on the east and west coasts, for research and training, they wanted Texas to have a larger share of the bounty, and Rudder wanted Texas A&M to be a major recipient. The Rudder-Teague-Johnson alliance was a convergence of mutual interests that would materially help Rudder put Texas A&M on a path to realize his expansive ideas.

The Coke Building Trio

With Hall and McCrory installed near Rudder's office by the summer of 1960, the second floor of the Richard Coke Building became the operational center of Texas A&M. Their daily routine was to gather in Rudder's office about 5:30 in the afternoon. "Alone and at length" they discussed any-and-everything about A&M. Rudder permitted freewheeling discussions while leaving no doubt that he was in charge. To McCrory and Hall, he was usually "General," sometimes "Mister" or "President" and never "Earl." Hall was usually "Doctor" to Rudder, occasionally "Wayne" and simply "Hall" when the president was miffed.

Rudder ignored the clock, and the meetings typically ended about eight o'clock or frequently after nine. In the beginning they identified institutional weaknesses and discussed what to do about them. One of Rudder's first questions was, "How sound are fiscal affairs?" Reassured, he waited a while before hiring Thomas D. Cherry from Trans-World Airways to direct business affairs. Cherry was an A&M graduate who had taught economics there.[42] After appointing Cherry, Rudder persuaded Clark Diebel to leave the state auditor's office to become A&M's controller of accounts. Diebel had helped clean up the Veterans Land Board after Rudder installed him as its executive secretary in 1955. Hall recognized that Diebel was Rudder's trusted "financial confidant," a mole in Cherry's camp, not from distrust but as a precaution. The mutual respect between Diebel and Rudder was deep; long after Rudder was gone, his photograph remained on view in the Diebel home.[43]

Texas A&M provided important services to students, beginning with processing their admissions applications, followed by registering them, scheduling classes, awarding scholarships, checking on degree requirements, and enforcing disciplinary rules. Management of these services was decentralized, and Rudder had complaints about inconsistencies. He brought in James P. Hannigan as dean of students to oversee them. As with McCrory and Hall, Hannigan was not a crony; he was recommended by mutual acquaintances. He was a graduate of the U.S. Military Academy, a retired brigadier general, and a linguist with a diploma in French civilization from the Sorbonne. He had taught at West Point and held diplomatic posts. Hannigan would not be intimidated by professors, and he was further evidence that Rudder respected both academic and military credentials.[44]

Rudder consolidated public information services under Jim Lindsey, who resigned as managing editor of the *Midland Reporter-Telegram* to accept the position. Unlike other key appointments, Lindsey was a sidekick; he was the public information officer for Rudder's 90th Infantry Division. Lindsey virtually campaigned for the job by lavishing publicity on Texas A&M and Rudder, to the relative neglect of Texas Tech University, where he was vice chairman of the governing board. In an assignment that would have debatable repercussions, Rudder also made Lindsey responsible for student publications, including the student newspaper, the *Battalion,* and various magazines and newsletters.[45] With responsibility for supervising students, Lindsey had duties that were beyond his experience and knowledge. How-

ever, Rudder liked him; he complied with instructions and kept a lid on
student criticisms as well as their ideas about exercising first-amendment
freedoms on campus.

The Coke Building trio—Rudder, Hall, and McCrory—deliberated the
big issues of A&M's future. McCrory, a skeptic about changes, was Rudder's
follow-up man with the Association of Former Students, the Corps of Cadets, student leaders, and the commandant of the Corps of Cadets, a regular
army officer. In Hall's view, McCrory was "brilliant, tireless and innovative,"
had a "creative mind," and was the "perfect match for Rudder."[46]

Hall was Rudder's representative to the faculty and his resident expert
on teaching, research, and any other academic question that arose. When
Hall recommended that A&M needed someone to administer the growing
research enterprise, Rudder readily agreed and gave him the job in the same
breath: "O.K., you are it. Add the title of Coordinator of Research to your
title as Dean." Later, Rudder created A&M's first position for a full-time vice
president for research. He delegated Hall to interview all prospective faculty
members while he interviewed all prospective department heads and deans.
As time permitted, Rudder met important guests and prospective faculty.[47]

One all-encompassing question was inescapable for the Coke Building
trio: What would it take to make Texas A&M renowned academically for its
degree programs and for research? The crux of the challenge was to develop
several projects that were widely respected for their excellence. Only if other
institutions acknowledged the importance and quality of A&M's educational
endeavors could it achieve the prestige that they sought. Since every program
could not be equally strong, the question was what programs to emphasize.
Nor could they escape the "virtual albatrosses"—racial and gender discrimination and mandatory military training—that would have to be remedied or
eliminated before their academic aspirations would be feasible.

Since changing the institutional name was nonsubstantive, Rudder took a
shot at it in late November 1960, just six months after the trio began strategiz-
ing. He appointed an internal College Name-change Committee of eight faculty, staff, and students to consider including the word "university" in a new
name. The charge to the committee was "whether or not the official name of
the College should be changed to incorporate the word 'university,' and, if so,
what new names would be acceptable."[48] His initiative presumed that everyone could see that Texas A&M had developed beyond its origins as an "agricultural and mechanical college" and was a "university" in all but name.

When newspapers published a bland story about the committee, a
firestorm erupted that was minor only in relation to those about coeducation that came later. The only groups in favor were A&M's international

students, led by the Indians and Pakistanis. Having "university" on their diplomas would enhance their status back home. The student senate voted "no change." The 368 dues-paying members of the Corpus Christi A&M Club "were emphatically and unanimously opposed," as was the Tyler club. For some Old Army Aggies, merely posing the question confirmed the existence, they said, of a "general policy to destroy the College," and two of them informed Rudder that it was part of a continuing "Communist plot to destroy our heritage."[49] So Rudder pulled back, took no action, his initiative a conspicuous failure.

The Coke Building trio returned to discussing how to achieve a broad-based consensus to move A&M toward academic eminence. Racial integration was an issue, but it was already the "law of the land," and they were only waiting for the Board of Directors to authorize it. The lack of positive movement was more a concern about political repercussions than opposition to it.

The issues of admitting women on the same basis as men and making military training voluntary were so sensitive that they "could hardly agree on how to discuss them." At one point Hall despaired of further progress, but they kept talking.[50] Talking was their only way to come to grips with difficult issues. Hall thought he was the strongest advocate for admitting women and making the Corps optional, and McCrory became convinced before Rudder came around.

Rudder may have held back because he knew better than McCrory and Hall what opinion makers were saying across the state through the gossip grapevine that fed into the president's office. He had to think widely about the ramifications of whatever was done, for he would bear most of the opposition and criticism. Perhaps he pretended disagreement to test their convictions and draw out varying perspectives on how to proceed. Also, Rudder had to consider the attitudes in the legislature (A&M's main source of operating funds) and the Board of Directors, which, with three new appointees by Gov. Price Daniel, seemed slightly more flexible on some issues. However, Daniel had qualified his appointees on their opposition to the admission of women.

One new member of the board, Sterling C. Evans, had been outspoken in favoring the admission of women but had gained the governor's appointment only after assuring him that "any effort to push coeducation at this time would be counterproductive, and I will not do so." However, when Daniel left the governor's office in January 1963, Evans was freed from his promise and became instrumental in the reforms.[51] For any significant change, Rudder had to have a convincing rationale for thousands of people in A&M's

widespread constituencies. The key to success might rest on how he framed his proposals and explanations. Analyzing the strength of the opposition was a constant mental exercise.

The spectrum of Rudder's choices about what to do varied from simply transacting daily business (routine communications, budget, and personnel decisions) to making a frontal attack on the virtual albatrosses. Essentially, he had to decide what kind of president he would be. By disposition he could only be an activist, determined to leave any situation better than he found it. He recognized that he had two interlocking challenges: One was to heal the bitter disagreements in the Aggie community over the divisive issues of coeducation and compulsory military training, and the other was to obtain a broad-based endorsement for Texas A&M to progress academically with higher standards and expanding in research and graduate studies. Rudder concluded that both the healing and the consensus building could be accomplished in the same process. It was a gamble that would require careful planning and deft management. A single misstep that alienated an influential person could set back the entire reform effort.

TRANSFORMING A&M

Informed and chastened by the name change debacle, by early 1961 Rudder had a change of strategy to transform Texas A&M. It would begin with the creation of two study groups, one internal and the other external, that would involve most A&M constituencies.[52] Each group would examine Texas A&M for a year before recommending goals on how A&M should change to achieve preeminence by 1976, the hundredth anniversary of its founding. Rudder would appoint the internal group of twenty-four faculty, staff, and students, called the Committee on Aspirations, to be chaired by Wayne Hall. The other group would be a high-profile Century Council, made up of one hundred leading citizens of Texas appointed by the Board of Directors. The theme of the entire effort was "Planning Advancement toward Pre-eminence." Each group was to submit a written report to the board with recommendations of ways A&M should change to become more widely esteemed.[53]

To start the process, Rudder conferred with members of the Association of Former Students, although its policy making body had consistently opposed the admission of women and a noncompulsory Corps of Cadets. He assembled a joint committee from the association and the Board of Directors to generate a proposal that he submitted to the board on April 22, 1961. The board's resolution created the Century Council, charged with making recommendations to guide development of A&M for the next fifteen years to

1976. The recommendations of both the Century Council and Hall's Committee on Aspirations were to cover four areas: the kind of graduate A&M should produce by 1976, the mission of the college for the next fifteen years, realistic aspirations for A&M's academic and scholastic attainment, and the size and scope of A&M in the year 1976.[54]

Of the one hundred members of the Century Council, no fewer than fifty-six were A&M graduates, five were newspaper executives, four were school superintendents, and three were women, including two heirs of fortunes: Oveta Culp Hobby of Houston and Mary Moody Northen of Galveston. Others were Maj. Gen. Alvin R. Luedecke, Rudder's A&M classmate and general manager of the Atomic Energy Commission; former governor Allan Shivers; Rudder's Brady friend L. B. "Smitty" Smith, publisher-editor of the *Brady Standard;* and rancher Walter Pfluger, a friend and prominent citizen in Eden, in addition to Dolph Briscoe, a future governor, and Lloyd Bentsen, a future U.S. senator.[55]

The initial meetings of the Century Council and the Committee on Aspirations were prominent events in which Rudder's goal of transforming Texas A&M was clearly stated. He hired outside consultants to advise both groups and presided over their opening sessions. He asked the internal Committee on Aspirations to "look at A. and M. College with the future in mind, visualizing how all of us as a team can improve this institution and better serve the people of Texas, especially the youth of this state." He compared A&M to the "American republic," saying the "rise and fall of a nation depends on its response to challenge." Texas A&M was at a crossroads and should be reappraised to assure its future.[56] Leaders of land grant colleges and universities from Pennsylvania and California spoke to the committee about long-range planning and trends in their institutions.

The Century Council convened for a two-day Forecast Conference in September 1961, preceding a football game to attract a larger turnout. Rudder told its members that the "future of Texas in large measure depends on how successfully its institutions of higher education plan now to meet the challenges anticipated in the next fifteen years."[57] As the keynote speaker he enticed Jenkin Lloyd Jones, editor of the moderately conservative *Tulsa Tribune.* Jones had covered the Nuremberg war crimes trials, and his weekly column on values in public life was syndicated in more than a hundred newspapers. So carefully did Rudder try to manage the event that he sent Jones a suggested outline of his speech, which Jones revealed to the conference, promising to ignore it. But he was positive about Rudder's request to "emphasize the requirements of American citizenship that will confront A&M's future graduates."

"This would be," Jones orated, "a happier and sounder nation if more presidents of distinguished technical and scientific schools were more concerned over the citizenship of their products." He asked, "How do you intensify a scientific or technical education and at the same time broaden it with the humanities?" which he deemed indispensable for citizenship education.[58] Jones's speech was hardly the first time Rudder had considered the issue of "educating the whole man," as he often phrased it. But afterwards he spoke more emphatically about this complex duality of academic goals, and he contemplated major expansion of humanities programs at A&M. In this he was influenced by the ideas of C. P. Snow, a British scientist and novelist, who proposed in a 1959 essay that the communications gap between the sciences and the humanities—the inability of scientists and humanists to appreciate the work of the other—was a "hindrance to solving world problems." From Rudder's handwritten notes it is apparent that he thought Texas A&M should have a "humanities research institute."[59]

The Century Council met several times in the next twelve months. One subcommittee arrived at the unpleasant conclusion that A&M was rapidly losing its claim as the second school in the state, after the University of Texas, to faster-growing institutions such as Texas Tech University and A&M's own branch campus, Arlington State College. The University of Houston, a private institution soon to attain public status, was also growing rapidly. The subcommittee attributed A&M's decline to six causes: the lost monopoly on vocational, agricultural, and engineering programs; the limited scope of A&M's curriculum; its designation as a college rather than as a university; its male-only student body; compulsory military training and Corps of Cadets membership; and the poor quality of many academic programs.

The indictment was serious, but the Century Council as a whole was unable to translate the subcommittee's findings into recommendations, preferring instead to endorse the status quo in its final report. On the paramount issue of coeducation, the council merely recommended "careful and objective studies of some degree of coeducation." It recommended continuing compulsory military training and dismissed concerns over its adverse effect on enrollment, thus concurring with the Old Army Aggies' contention that A&M should concentrate on the quality of its students rather than the quantity. The council even hedged on a name change, stating that there was "not unanimity but *Texas A and M University* was strongly favored."[60]

Nonetheless, the Century Council adopted the main recommendation that Rudder needed, namely that "the attainment of excellence should be the long range aim of all activities of the College."[61]

In comparison to the Century Council's diluted recommendations and failure to suggest remedies for the major problems, Wayne Hall's Committee on Aspirations produced bold, detailed, and far-reaching proposals. Rudder had less control over Wayne Hall than over the staff assistant he assigned to help the Century Council, who was not a professor with market value but a factotum who responded to inquiries and gathered information. The staff assistant helped compose the Century Council's report, which included the usual Rudder phrases about A&M producing "leaders in wartime and peace-time," "good citizenship," and "belief in a Supreme Being."

Hall was under no such constraints, and he was almost indispensable to Rudder's team. He could always return to teaching and research if Rudder became dissatisfied with him. He and members of his committee were wise to the ways of A&M's academic jungle. They knew the issues inside and out, were informed about developments in other land grant institutions, and were indifferent to Old Army Aggies. As a result, Hall's committee proposed

> *Construction of a new library with more books and periodicals*
> *A faculty tenure policy in accord with national norms*
> *Increases in salary levels, merit pay, and endowed chairs*
> *Recognition for outstanding teaching and research*
> *Funding and released time for research*
> *Changing the institutional name "to foster and maintain a university image"*
> *Ending compulsory military training*
> *A building program and fringe benefits to make A&M more attractive to faculty*

The Committee on Aspirations also reported that the faculty and staff pre-ferred "an end to compulsory military training and all-male admissions policy by a margin of more than six-to-one." Further, the report boldly de-clared, "In housing, feeding, and recreation of students, the military empha-sis has limited the true pursuit of scholarship and the development of an environment which will contribute to scholarship." Professors on the com-mittee were concerned about the quality of extension teaching across the state beyond faculty review and recommended, "All educational activities . . . not properly a function of resident teaching and research should be brought together under a Division of Continuing Education."[62]

When the Committee on Aspirations completed its work, Hall gave Rud-der a preliminary draft to review. Rudder wrote notes in the margin and

returned the draft to Hall, who passed it to Haskell Monroe, an energetic
young history professor who was secretary of the committee. Hall asked
Monroe to revise the recommendations in accordance with Rudder's notes.
Monroe found that Rudder's notations had disclaimers such as "No," "Cannot do," and "Where'd you get this?"

Knowing how strongly committee members felt about the recommendations, Monroe went back to Hall and explained, "I cannot make changes
that go against the committee's recommendations. Our assignment was to
recommend to the president what we thought the college should aspire to
be by 1976 and that's what we have done. The vote was unanimous on all
major points." When Hall was assured that Rudder's criticisms were actually
contrary to the recommendations, he promised Monroe, "I will stake my job
on your right to express what the committee recommended."[63] Hall's ability
to stand up to presidential authority was an affirmation of his character, of
his importance to Rudder, and of the value of a professor's job security in a
showdown when sticking with principles was important.

Whatever initial doubts Rudder had about the recommendations of
Hall's Committee on Aspirations, the ideas percolated through his mind,
gradually impressing him with their significance. In time, the recommendations became a virtual to-do list for A&M's progressive thinkers, prompting
A&M historian Henry C. Dethloff to conclude, "It is startling to see how very
many of these recommendations were implemented by President Rudder, or
by his successors." Rudder was growing with the challenges and eventually
commented to Monroe with obvious satisfaction, "You guys got everything
you asked for except the name change." The committee had recommended
"Texas State University."[64]

In the summer of 1962, Rudder's staff molded the two studies, internal
and external, into a single document for Rudder to lobby through the Board
of Directors. He wanted the directors to adopt a single set of recommendations as a Blueprint for Progress to be presented at a grand public event called
the Century Convocation on November 16, 1962.

More than four thousand people attended the Century Convocation, anticipating recommendations that would transform A&M. Local A&M clubs
came in chartered buses from across the state, former governor Shivers and
Governor-elect John B. Connally were conspicuous attendees, and the *Dallas Morning News* informed its readers that "the spirit of Aggieland never
seemed stronger."[65]

However, advocates of prompt changes on the big issues were disappointed
that the Blueprint for Progress endorsed keeping the virtual albatrosses by
making no reference to racial integration, no commitment to the admission

of women or to a new name, and no change in the policy of mandatory military training. It endorsed the status quo on all issues except advancing A&M academically. In adopting the Blueprint for Progress, a majority of the Board of Directors, perhaps on Rudder's initiative, had decided to avoid divisive recommendations and focus on "excellence": upgrading the academic quality of A&M in every respect—facilities, faculty, students, and programs. Who could oppose excellence except possibly a few Old Army Aggies who were opposed to any change? Everyone could define *excellence* as they wished, and it was invariably positive. The report ended with a charge from the directors to "all members of the faculty and staff that their watchword and goal shall be EXCELLENCE."[66] The Blueprint for Progress was a compromise that sacrificed perfection for progress under the encompassing call for excellence.

Despite the compromises, Rudder had the backing he needed to advance A&M academically. With "excellence . . . as the long range aim of all activities," he would determine what excellence required and do whatever was necessary to achieve it. Excellence was an elusive quality, a moving target, and he would have to cultivate broad-based support continuously to keep the goal alive. Pursuing the new challenge, he took on the issues incrementally and opportunistically, sometimes initiating, at other times reacting or temporizing.

The adoption of the Blueprint for Progress was the end of the beginning for Rudder's presidency. Tough problems lay ahead, but an energetic, determined executive intent on progress will always precipitate issues and controversies. That was the nature of the president's job, and Rudder knew it. Overcoming A&M's virtual albatrosses would be left to him, his administrative team, and amenable directors.

Texas A&M's self-evaluations in 1962, consolidated as the Blueprint for Progress, spawned four initiatives that by 1966 had laid the foundation for the institution that A&M would become over the next half-century. The intense controversy over the admission of women virtually swamped the other three: adopting a new name, Texas A&M University, in 1963; admitting African Americans in 1963; and making military training optional in 1965.

The name change satisfied almost all constituents. The first African Americans were enrolled without public notice, even on the campus. The controversy over voluntary membership in the Corps of Cadets was muted when the army and air force announced their intention to limit the number of students in ROTC. A study by the Rudder's staff rationalized that "an effective ROTC program and a Corps of Cadets can best be attained from the optional participation by [qualified male] students," and the Board of Directors adopted that policy effective September 1, 1965.[67]

Few Aggies were neutral about the admission of women. They were divided by two polarizing beliefs. The opponents clung to A&M's masculine and military traditions with the slogan All-Male, All-Military. The proponents were generally aligned in two groups: advocates of equal opportunities for men and women, and pragmatists who believed that the admission of women was essential for the institution's future. Some may have preferred an all-male A&M but concluded that gender integration was necessary if, as Rudder told them in April 1963, A&M "was to achieve its rightful place among institutions of higher education."[68] Some Old Army Aggies advocated mandatory military training as a tactic to keep out women, citing the male-only West Point to support their argument. West Point began accepting women as cadets in 1976.

When women were finally permitted to enroll at Texas A&M on the same basis as men, the reasons were both legal and pragmatic. The legal basis was the equal protection of the law under the U.S. Constitution, and the pragmatic motive was A&M's continuation as a significant institution. Under state law A&M might have remained all male, but it could not limit the admission of women based on restricting qualifications such as kinship with a male student or an A&M employee. A&M had to admit women on the same basis as men or not at all.

Rudder and Sterling C. Evans, class of 1921, led the movement for change. Evans, a member of A&M's Board of Directors (1959–71), had believed in coeducation at Texas A&M from the time he enrolled as a student in 1917. His role as a catalyst and consensus builder was indispensable. Rudder tried to stay above the public fray, insisting that he only administered the directors' policies. In reality, he dealt constantly with conflicting personalities, responded to critics, and devised proposals and countermeasures to resolve the issues to promote A&M's long-term interests.

The main obstacle to changing Texas A&M was the Old Army Aggies and the attitudes they stood for. To change the A&M they remembered was to diminish it, and anything that diminished A&M diminished them. Many men in the Aggie brotherhood had been formed by their shared experiences at A&M. Separated from home and family, a boy who went to A&M in his late teens grew to become a man surrounded by thousands of boys who did everything together. They performed collective rituals, marched in close-order drill, studied, and chased girls together, even mouthed a unique lexicon of earthy terms such as *serge butt* and *pisshead* that generations of Aggies had created and passed down. For most who remained at A&M four years, fraternal bonds were forged for life. In the whole world, they were quick to tell you, there was nothing like Texas A&M. Aggieland was hallowed ground, revered by its graduates and a religion for some.

While engaged in altering A&M's Old Army culture, Rudder maintained the stability of the institution as opponents of coeducation attempted to undermine it. In making his plans and conferring with allies and adversaries, he balanced the inevitable tension between daily operational challenges and long-term goals that would truly transform the only Texas A&M anyone had ever known. Throughout these changes, Rudder was, to use Theodore Roosevelt's metaphor, "the man in the arena," day in and day out, contending with the issues and contentious personalities for the cause of advancing Texas A&M.

Governor John B. Connally

The possibilities for positive change in Texas and at Texas A&M rose dramatically on January 15, 1963, when the forty-four-year-old John B. Connally was inaugurated as governor. He and Rudder were friends from the 1948 campaign to elect Lyndon B. Johnson to the U.S. Senate. As President John F. Kennedy's secretary of the navy in 1961 and 1962, Connally became keenly aware of scientific advances, of the challenges of space, and of the overall potential, as he proclaimed, "for the economic, industrial, political, and cultural expansion" of Texas. But progress was possible for Texas only, he made plain, with a competitive educational system on a par with that of other leading states. During his gubernatorial campaign, Connally shocked his listeners, telling them that contrary to myths about the superiority of Texas, it was actually "a depressed educational area. . . . We have not given enough attention to the educational task and the investment we must make in the important human resource for our region."[69]

Connally and Rudder were in complete agreement about what needed to be done. As Rudder wanted to transform Texas A&M into a high-quality research university, Connally was determined to transform Texas government into an instrument of efficient and progressive change, and he became, in the words of Paul Burka, "nothing less than the architect of modern Texas."[70] Connally advisor Julian Read observed, "In Washington, he got his eyes opened as to what was happening in terms of what other states were doing to prepare for the future." As secretary of the navy, he saw that "federal research grants for science and technology were going to California, New York, and Connecticut—not Texas. He saw where the world was moving, and Texas was not in the forefront. He saw that investment followed education."[71] It was no coincidence that much of Texas A&M's progress during Rudder's presidency (1959–70) occurred during Connally's six years as governor (1963–69).

Three weeks after taking office, Connally appointed three new members to the nine-member Texas A&M Board of Directors and effectively shifted the sentiment of the board toward reform. In Margaret Rudder's view, "Earl could not have asked for a better Board than the one appointed by John Connally."[72] They were industrial executives, informed about the national economy, and in frequent contact with counterparts beyond Texas. Two were not A&M graduates, which limited former A&M students to a simple majority of five to four.

The two non-Aggies, A. P. Beutel and Gardiner Symonds, were CEOs of large firms that applied science and technology to productivity on a scale that provided thousands of jobs. Beutel was the executive of Gulf Coast operations for Dow Chemical, and Symonds headed up Tennessee Gas Transmissions and was a director of several Fortune 500 corporations. Symonds was also a trustee of Stanford University, where he earned his undergraduate degree, which he followed with an M.B.A. from Harvard. The third Connally appointee was Leland F. "Pete" Peterson, a petroleum executive from Fort Worth and president of A&M's Association of Former Students.[73]

Unfortunately, the Rudder family suffered a stunning loss of household goods and personal possessions as the new directors were taking office. On January 26, 1963, fire destroyed the two-story frame president's home that had stood near the center of the campus since 1895. The winds of a "Texas norther" whipped cinders from the fireplace chimney onto dry wooden planks, and the flames were quickly out of control. The fire occurred at midday while Margaret Rudder and four of their children were downstairs. They fled the house without difficulty as Rudder dashed from his office two blocks away, but his military decorations, wartime mementos, and other belongings were burned.[74] The positive side of the loss was that planning began within a few days for a much needed new home for A&M's presidents, built to the Rudder family's specifications.

Four days after the fire, Rudder introduced Connally to a conference of college and university presidents in Austin and spoke on the importance of research to the Texas economy. He mentioned the importance of MIT and Cal Tech to their regional and state economies. "It is not," Rudder said, "water, or real estate, or labor or power, or cheap taxes alone that attracts industry, it's brainpower." Throughout his presidency he would cite MIT as an example for Texas A&M to emulate. In the same week, Connally addressed the legislature and hit hard on the same issues: "Unless our nation produces more and better brainpower, our system of democratic government, our

Seven members of the Board of Directors of the Texas A&M University System in 1965–66 plus W. T. "Doc" Doherty, a member from 1953 to 1959, and Rudder. Presided over by Sterling Evans and H. C. Heldenfels from 1963 to 1967, these directors adopted policies to implement the major reforms and stood by them despite vigorous protests. Left to right: H. C. Heldenfels, Gardiner Symonds, Clyde Thompson, Clyde Wells, Dr. A. P. Beutel, Sterling Evans, L. F. "Pete" Peterson, Doherty, and Rudder. Doherty was an executive of the Robert A. Welch Foundation, whose gifts were significant and timely for A&M's development in the Rudder era. Directors not pictured were Wofford Cain and Samuel B. Whittenberg. (Courtesy of Margaret Rudder)

personal liberties, will soon perish." He went on to compare universities in Texas unfavorably to those in California and Massachusetts.[75]

Sterling C. Evans

With Connally's appointees voting for the first time on February 23, 1963, the new Board of Directors elected Sterling C. Evans as its chairman. With Evans as chairman, advocates of coeducation had a policy maker with authority, and Rudder had a capable partner for progress. In the same meeting, the Board of Directors voted to ask the legislature to rename the institution Texas A&M University. Rudder was at pains for the public to know that the letters A and M were not short for agricultural and mechanical, but were "retained only as a traditional symbol."[76] The legislature passed a bill with the name change that Connally signed into law, and on August 22, 1963, A&M became officially Texas A&M University.[77]

After the directors' quick action to change A&M's name, rumors spread that they would vote on coeducation at their next regular meeting on April 27. Newspapers assigned reporters to investigate the rumors. To the man, the directors denied that a vote was planned, although several admitted that they had discussed coeducation, and it could be voted on anytime.[78]

Opponents of coeducation did not wait to see an agenda for the meeting before organizing. Travis L. Smith, class of 1898 and an oilman in Houston, emerged as an early leader of the opposition. He tried to rally Aggie alumni to his cause with hundreds of letters, declaring that "A&M should continue to be a FIRST CLASS MAN'S ALL MILITARY SCHOOL," or the result would be "numerous panty raids and other foolishness."[79]

The A. & M. Club in Beaumont was one of the most active. Hectored by cantankerous Aggie alum Charlie Babcock, the club passed a resolution "unanimously in opposition to coeducation" and sent a copy to each A&M director. Babcock sent a copy directly to Rudder with a gratuitous note: "Earl. *Blind copy* for your information. Charlie."[80] His courtesies toward Rudder would soon end, and time would show that not every member of the Beaumont Club opposed the admission of women.

Sterling Evans pampered the press, saying he was "disappointed that this matter hit the headlines before we gave formal consideration to it." Rudder declined to make a public statement, but in a candid, off-the-cuff comment he asserted that his overriding purpose was "building a great university with high academic standards rather than getting involved in any controversy. The board's job is to establish policy, and my job is to build this university within the framework established for us."[81]

The A&M campus was abnormally quiet when the Board of Directors assembled for their meeting on Saturday, April 27. Few cadets were seen, which was unusual because mandatory drill practice was held every Saturday except for one Saturday in each semester—and April 27 was the exception. A&M cadets, generally vociferous opponents of coeducation, considered any Saturday without drill practice a free weekend and left town.

On Friday night, April 26, the directors discussed coeducation behind closed doors. Although the recorded vote on coeducation the next day was officially unanimous, a reliable source said the Friday night meeting lasted into the morning hours, "with members bitterly divided over the issue." No record was kept of the closed meeting, but the next morning, on the motion of new member Gardiner Symonds, the directors voted unanimously, with three members abstaining, "to accept on a day-student basis the wives and daughters of faculty and staff, and wives of students in residence, and women staff members to the undergraduate programs," effective June 1, 1963.[82]

Then all directors voted to "admit qualified women on a day-student basis to all graduate programs and to veterinary medicine."[83] The phrase "on a day-student basis" meant that housing for women was not available, but those qualifying under the new policy could attend A&M year-round and earn degrees. In addition to coeducation, in its closed meeting on April 26 the A&M Board of Directors probably discussed the admission of African Americans, because five weeks later, in an orchestrated event behind closed doors, the Rudder administration admitted and registered three black men for degree courses.

The new policy allowing the limited admission of women was front-page news in newspapers across the state. "Tradition Shattered" read a bold headline in the *Dallas Times-Herald*. Other headlines were "Famed All-Male School Will Be Coeducational" and "A&M Admits Girls, Girls, Girls." Travis Smith, the elder statesman of the anticoed movement, promptly conceded defeat with a clarity that Rudder commended. "As good Aggies, we must follow the decisions of constituted authority."[84]

Opposition to Coeducation

Not everyone followed Smith's lead. Robert W. Rowland, class of 1957 and advertising director for radio station KFMK in Houston, continued organizing the opposition. Well placed to publicize his efforts, he harshly criticized the directors, calling the decision "asinine" and a "tragedy" and blaming it on Sterling Evans, who he claimed presided over a board of directors that was destroying the college. He publicized his rancor by threatening to return his class ring, with the hope that other Aggies would follow suit.[85] Many opponents leveled their criticisms at Rudder. Thirteen A&M graduates in Brownwood, Texas, telegrammed: "We hold you and you only responsible for taking the only asset left to A&M." Another disgruntled Aggie tore his 1954 A&M diploma in two pieces and mailed it to Rudder with a handwritten note accusing him of selling the college out "for a *mess* of cheap Texas coed pottage" and turning it into a "countrified" version of the University of Texas.[86]

Letters from women were as intemperate as those from men. The president of the A&M Mothers Club in Abilene asked the statewide federation of clubs to stop all financial support of the college until the coeducation admission policy was rescinded.[87] Much of the criticism was childish, and some was actually written by children:

> Did you ever see a good horse race where a mare was entered? It will tear a good race up every time.[88]
>
> We know what a fix Eve got us in the Garden of Eden. Let's not let that happen at Texas A&M.[89]
>
> I am very sorry that the board of directors let coeds go to A. and M. I'm only 11 years old but my father, grandfather and uncle went to A. and M. I predict something will happen because of coeds.[90]

Rudder was not deterred by the criticism. On the Monday following the directors' decision to admit women as regular students although limited to day students in certain categories, he invited the student body to the coliseum, ostensibly for an explanation of the directors' decision and its authority.[91] He had another motive. They needed to see and hear him say unequivocally that there was no turning back. In essence, he told them that Texas A&M would embrace the future, order would be maintained, and it would not be run by student opinion.

When an estimated four thousand students heard Rudder say there was no possibility of rescinding the policy to admit women, they began hissing and chanting "We don't want to integrate," referring to gender rather than racial integration. Rudder emphasized, "The Board of Directors has absolute authority on this and other matters. The United States Supreme Court has twice upheld the Board's authority." Some cadets knew that Rudder had no room for compromise. "There is nothing you can do," he said. "A&M has not gone to hell nor will it unless we abandon our responsibilities. [All changes] are aimed at helping A&M achieve its rightful place among institutions of higher education. You have a basic decision to make: you can pick up your marbles and leave and throw in with some other school. Or you can suck up your guts and work to make A&M great. Those that choose to defect should know they leave A&M in the hour of her greatest need."[92]

Rudder cited an important reason to admit women that was beyond the comprehension of his listeners. He stated publicly for the first time A&M's growing concern about the rise of Texas Tech University as a rival in direct competition for students, degree programs, political support in the agricultural economy, and, ultimately, money. While A&M was stalemated in the 1950s, Texas Tech had developed rapidly, adding degree programs in agriculture and engineering similar to those offered by A&M. Texas Tech's overall profile resembled that of the typical land grant college in other states even more than did Texas A&M, namely because it was coeducational with degree programs in liberal and fine arts, and ROTC was voluntary. Texas Tech's growing popularity was intense across West Texas, formerly an Aggie stronghold.

The competition between A&M and Tech was a simmering, long-term issue that was obscure to outsiders. Even as Rudder spoke, a bill was pending in the Texas legislature to create a second state-supported school of veterinary medicine at Texas Tech, despite the fact that A&M graduated more veterinarians each year than could be absorbed by market demand in Texas, more than 10 percent of all new veterinarians in the United States. Although every college or university in the state was an actual or potential competitor for A&M, the main threats were Texas Tech and the University of Houston, two rising institutions with influential supporters.[93] If A&M refused to admit women, the state would likely permit them and other institutions to duplicate A&M's programs for the benefit of women.

Cadets, and their elders who egged them on, feared that admitting women would result in abolishing or weakening the Corps of Cadets, while Rudder's concern was the wellbeing of the institution. Aggie alums across the state, individually and through their clubs, encouraged the cadets to protest Rudder's leadership and the changes occurring during this period of his administration. The hissing drowned out his closing statement: "If the Corps of Cadets does what it stands for, its future is bright." In truth, many cadets wanted girls on the campus, but few admitted it because of pressure from upperclassmen and alums.[94]

For many Aggies, young and old, regardless of their attitude about coeducation, the students' treatment of Rudder tarnished Texas A&M's traditions of discipline and respect for constituted authority. The mere thought of cadets mocking and jeering their president was unconscionable. "The spectacle," wrote Heidi Ann Knippa, an A&M graduate and authority on the history of the admission of women, "was incomprehensible to anyone who knew of Rudder and A&M. He personified all that A&M stood for: military heritage, courage, success, and loyalty."[95]

Rudder did not talk afterwards about the student jeers on April 29, 1963. That was past, and he knew that former students shared in the blame. Leaving no doubt that A&M was in firm and capable hands, he told faculty advisors that "Mickey Mouse behavior in the Corps indicates unrest and uncertainty." But the jeering incident was always a sore topic for Margaret Rudder. Thirty years later she addressed a reunion of the class of 1963 and asked her listeners to raise their hands in response to three questions. "Were you there?" "Did you boo Earl?" and "How many of you have daughters who have graduated from A&M?" When more raised their hands for the third question than for the first two, she took it as further vindication of her husband's wisdom and leadership.[96]

In the week following the Board of Directors' decision to admit women on a limited basis, opponents approached the state legislature to overturn the decision. However, since the legislative session would soon adjourn, it was too late to enact a bill even if the members were sympathetic. The legislature would not meet in regular session again until the spring of 1965, an interim of almost two years that the anticoed faction used to organize a campaign to persuade the legislature to overrule the directors' policy of admitting women. A poll of A&M's Association of Former Students in 1963 found that most members opposed the general admission of women, which implied that many opposed admitting them even on a limited basis.[97] The poll forewarned Rudder and Sterling Evans to prepare for another battle in the legislature in the spring of 1965.

By noon on the day after the cadets jeered Rudder, a dozen women had applied for admission. The Rudder administration was now saddled with deciding who could qualify for admission. Simple though the task appeared to the novice, it was difficult to determine the eligibility of some applicants. An admissions officer identified almost fifty ambiguous situations. Could the wife of a local man who lived at home and enrolled for a one-hour course enroll as a full-time student? Was a woman who had initially qualified for admission on the basis of her husband's enrollment eligible to continue if they later divorced? So uncertain was Rudder about the future of coeducation that all female students were required to sign a form agreeing "to voluntarily withdraw at the end of any semester in which a change of status occurs that would make me ineligible to enroll."[98]

Racial Integration

While the Rudder administration was coping with the complicated challenge of admitting women in ill-defined categories, it broke the color barrier that had existed since A&M held its first classes in 1876. By careful planning, that was accomplished without public notice or controversy. On June 3, 1963, three African Americans enrolled as regular degree-seeking students. Each was a mature student with a good record and almost certain to succeed academically. George D. Sutton and Vernell Jackson were high school science teachers attending an institute at A&M funded by the National Science Foundation. Neither had applied for admission, but they welcomed it as an opportunity to earn another degree. The third was Leroy Sterling, a resident of Bryan and a third-year undergraduate at Texas Southern University, a predominantly black institution in Houston. Trying to stretch his savings to complete his degree at TSU the next year, Sterling wanted to attend A&M because it was "close to home and would save me money."[99]

In the spring of 1963 Sterling applied for admission to A&M in the coming summer term. As expected, he was denied. "We are not admitting Negroes at this time," read the letter refusing his admission. "They could tell," Sterling told an interviewer, "that you were black by looking at your transcript and seeing the schools you had attended." Shortly after Sterling returned to Bryan for the summer, he was surprised to receive a telegram accepting him into A&M with instructions to come to the A&M registrar's office at three o'clock on Monday, June 3, 1963. When he got there, he encountered Jackson, who had been his high school science teacher. In the private office of the registrar, H. L. Heaton, they selected their courses, completed the required enrollment forms, and paid their tuition. "We did not want this special treatment but it didn't bother us," Sterling recalled.[100]

Rudder was not present. He was in summer training with the army reserve at Fort Hood, Texas, but he told Margaret Rudder how the three students were registered. "Instead of having the black students out in the line to register, we had them come inside and register privately. They were never out in the line. Then they just appeared in their classes."[101]

So inconspicuous was their registration that even *Battalion* reporters failed to notice them. Three days later a student editorial observed that "the registration of the trio was unannounced and conducted quietly. With scarcely any effort A&M took a big step forward."[102] Several more days passed before the major dailies got wind of it. By then it was old news, and the stories were buried on the inside pages with almost no public reaction. The front-page news concerned racial integration troubles all right, but they were at Ole Miss and the University of Alabama, not at Texas A&M. Registrar Heaton told Sterling and Jackson that Secret Service agents would attend classes with them, but they would not know the agents' identities. He also asked them not to give any interviews, and they did not.

"We just wanted to go to school, not to be in the middle of trouble," said Sterling. On June 5 he attended class for the first time, and that night he wrote to his fiancée: "There were no incidents. The students are very nice." When his mother worried for his safety, he reassured her: "There are lots of students on campus who are darker than I am."[103] They were from Ethiopia, and their presence created an ironic contradiction that would have been amusing except for its injustice. It had been acceptable to have African students at A&M, but not African American students until the enrollment of Leroy Sterling, George D. Sutton, and Vernell Jackson.

Committee for an All-Male Military Texas A&M

In the summer of 1963, Robert W. Rowland formed the Committee for an All-Male Military Texas A&M to bring about "a reversal of the recent decision to abolish our state's only all-male facility at Texas A&M." By late June he claimed to have mailed fifteen thousand letters to former A&M students, elected officials, and businessmen to organize the opposition. Aligned with the Beaumont businessman Charlie Babcock, Rowland aimed to destroy confidence in the Rudder administration and the Board of Directors.[104]

Rudder responded with a public information campaign aimed at selected groups, one of which was students on the campus. During the summer he and his staff met with student leaders, especially those who worked on the *Battalion,* to inform them about Babcock and Rowland and their committee. As a result, when the student body returned in September, articles in the *Battalion* played down passions as Babcock and Rowland tried to undercut the directors and Rudder's administration. About the same time, Rowland wrote an ingratiating, overly familiar letter to Rudder that went unanswered, a rarity for Rudder:

Dear Earl:

I hope this finds you enjoying good health and the peace of mind which only the Lord can provide. I traveled throughout the state this summer . . . and have found that the disgust [over the Board's decision to admit women] is widespread and probably deeper than most people realize. . . . We won't give up on this fight and feel that the next Legislature will pass legislation overturning the Board's action.[105]

In planning for the next legislative session, Rowland relinquished his Committee for an All-Male Military Texas A&M to Charlie Babcock. Almost forty years older than Rowland, Babcock had been editor of the *Battalion* before graduating in 1920. Later, he was president of the Association of Former Students and of the Beaumont A&M Club. As an independent businessman, Babcock could devote almost full time to rolling back the Board of Directors' policy. In the subsequent acrimony, Babcock snubbed Rudder. In a receiving line he stepped away as he neared Rudder to avoid shaking his hand or making eye contact. When Earl and Margaret Rudder encountered him in an airport, "he just turned his head," she recalled. "He didn't speak."[106]

In the fall of 1963, 183 women availed themselves of the new admissions policy by enrolling at Texas A&M, as Babcock flooded the campus with pamphlets and letters to stir resentment against coeducation and the Rudder administration. His disruption—agitating one group of students against another and seeking to undermine the governing authority—could have had serious consequences. As an illustration of Babcock's distracting influence, one male student wrote to him: "A lot of things have been building up inside of me after reading your Committee's pamphlets. . . . I would like to do more if you will tell me what to do. President Rudder and Dean Hannigan are against us."[107]

As time and events moved toward the anticipated showdown in the legislative session in the spring of 1965, Aggies were sharply divided among themselves. From Rudder's vantage point, however, there were encouraging developments. More people were beginning to speak in favor of coeducation or in support of his administration. State Senator George Moffett copied Rudder on a letter scolding Babcock's committee and commending Rudder and the Board of Directors.

John Lindsey

The split over coeducation was a serious problem for A&M's Association of Former Students. Its members were at odds with each other, the Board of Directors, Sterling Evans, and Rudder. Until January 1964 the Association's policy making body was unable to reach a consensus on the coed issue. Then, John Lindsey of Houston was elected president of the association to serve until February of 1965.[108] Lindsey was a friend of Rudder's from the 1956 Land Commissioner's campaign, when he had chaired the Harris County committee that garnered a majority of the votes for Rudder.

When Lindsey took office, the A&M directors were about evenly divided on the coeducation issue. Although they had voted unanimously for the limited admission of women, they were actually split five to four against further opening up A&M to women. Their attitudes varied from full admission to continuing the limited admission of women. As the board's presiding officer, Sterling Evans needed the assurance of one more favorable vote among the nine members. One of the wavering directors promised Evans that he would vote for full coeducation if the Association of Former Students took a position in favor. The issue was on a razor's edge, and it would fall to John Lindsey to swing the balance by putting the association on record in favor of coeducation.

When the governing body of the association met on Saturday, February 6, 1965, it was the last meeting over which Lindsey would preside. The meeting began routinely by acting on recurring business items, electing officers for the coming year, and hearing an annual report from Rudder. By then they had been sitting for a couple of hours, and Lindsey called for a brief recess. After the recess, he expected to conclude the meeting by recognizing the newly elected president of the association, who would speak briefly and preside over an appreciative resolution to Lindsey for his service, including, Lindsey reminisced, "presenting me with my President's Chair. . . . I was standing there during the recess with a cup of coffee when

Earl said, 'John, I've got one more resolution I want you to pass.' 'Okay, what is it?' I asked. He handed me the resolution, and it was for the admission of women to A&M. I just threw it back at him and said, 'Oh, come on, Earl, this is not the time for jokes.' He said, 'I am not joking.' Quickly scanning the resolution, Lindsey saw that it addressed the two most controversial issues: the admission of women and a voluntary Corps of Cadets. The text of the resolution was:

> The Council recommends that the Board of Directors study ways to con-
> tinue to improve A&M student life with a view of making it more effec-
> tive and attractive for all students. This includes possible change to a
> non-compulsory military program, and improvements in the limited co-
> education program.[109]

"I was absolutely horrified at the thought of it, but deep down I knew it was best for Texas A&M. The majority of A&M people didn't want coeducation or any talk about it."[110] He returned to the podium and called the meeting back to order. Estimating about three hundred members were present, he noticed that the first three or four rows were filled with Old Army Aggies, men over eighty years old, "the ones who always remembered, 'All male, all military, compulsory military,' and forget everything else." He reckoned the resolution would not pass on an up-or-down vote, and its only chance was to ram it through. He prevailed on Bob Latimer, his classmate of 1944, to read the resolution: "Bob, I need you to read this resolution and then I'll talk about it."

"I called the meeting to order, he read it. I talked about it for a few min-utes and said General Rudder wants this. He has worked on it for years and he has looked at it from every angle. I'm in favor of this and I want a 'yes' vote from this group because I think it will be best for A&M." Then Lindsey called for a voice vote. "I said, 'All in favor, say aye.' There were some ayes and a hell of a lot of no's but I said, 'The ayes have it,' and banged the gavel down. They were booing and shouting 'No! Ballot vote! Ballot vote!' I said, 'No, it's over. The ayes have it' and went out the back door. I went to my room and locked the door and did not answer the telephone."[111]

Two days later Lindsey had a lunch meeting in Houston with Sterling Evans, who said the resolution would help him work with the Board of Di-rectors toward the full admission of women.

Only two weeks before John Lindsey rammed the resolution through the Association of Former Students, the legislature had convened. As expected, bills were introduced in both houses to eliminate or restrict coeducation at

Texas A&M: "No persons other than males shall be admitted" during the fall and spring semesters was the exact language in both bills. The *Bryan Eagle* called the bills "a declaration of war on women at Texas A&M." When contacted by reporters, Lindsey said, "Our university must change to fit the times," and Sterling Evans told them that the resolution rammed through the association by Lindsey would be discussed at the next meeting of the Board of Directors on February 26–27.[112]

The Rudder and Evans scheme of one event deliberately precipitating another was now apparent. Rudder, accompanied by students and former students who were enthusiastic about coeducation, took the association's resolution to the Board of Directors meeting. Surrounded by such positive supporters, the board directed Rudder to "study the impact of full coeducation and noncompulsory military training" and present his study to them by the next meeting in June.[113]

With a majority of the Board of Directors now on their side, Rudder and Evans focused on the legislature and concluded that the opponents of coeducation were unlikely to succeed. Even if their bill passed the Texas senate, the house of representatives had just elected a new speaker, Ben Barnes, who believed that an all-male Texas A&M was inherently unfair. Closely identified with Connally, Barnes was the rising star in state politics. Furthermore, they were confident that Governor Connally would veto any adverse bill that reached his desk.

Frank Denius

Confident that they had little to fear from the legislature, Rudder and Evans quietly moved the issue from political considerations to addressing serious legal questions. On March 16 they conferred with thirty-nine-year-old Austin attorney Frank Denius. Denius was a partner in an influential law firm whose senior partner, Edward Clark, was well connected across the state capitol complex and was an advisor to Governor Connally and President Johnson. Two months before, Denius had cochaired the inauguration committee for Connally, who had just appointed Denius's uncle, Wofford Cain, to the A&M Board of Directors. Cain had graduated from A&M in 1913 with a degree in civil engineering, and his position on coeducation was moderate to conservative. Denius's extraordinary four Silver Stars for gallantry in the European war impressed Rudder. Furthermore, Denius was the president of the alumni association of the University of Texas and familiar with laws that governed higher education. Besides these assets, Denius had an insightful and retentive mind and was highly respected in the legal profession.

Although the directors were not of one mind about coeducation, all were concerned about the effects of the recently enacted federal Civil Rights Act of 1964. They wanted to know if Texas A&M's policy of discriminating against women would disqualify the institution from receiving federal funds. Rudder had tried to stay out of the controversy by insisting that coeducation was a policy matter for the Board of Directors, but within the privacy of the lawyer's office he clarified his attitude. "General Rudder was outspoken," Denius recalled. "He wanted a policy change that would impact the future of A&M for all time to come. He carried the discussion."[114]

Denius told Evans and Rudder that he would "do some briefing [on A&M's policy of limited admitted admission for women] and advise them accordingly." Three weeks later they met again, and Denius advised that limiting the admission of women students to certain categories or conditions, such as county of residence or kinship to employees or students, was probably unconstitutional. Such limitations "seemed illogical to me," he would later say.[115]

Rudder, Evans, and Denius then discussed how best to obtain a legal judgment about the legality of the admissions policy. The choice was between filing a friendly lawsuit or requesting an opinion from the attorney general of Texas, Waggoner Carr. An attorney general's opinion would have the force of law unless superseded by a court order or statute. They decided against filing a friendly lawsuit, as it would be too controversial and expensive. Instead, they would challenge the policy by requesting an opinion from the attorney general. Denius was well acquainted with Carr and had assisted him in raising money for political campaigns. Twice Rudder returned alone to confer with Denius, and Denius met several times with Carr or his assistants, notably T. B. "Tibbie" Wright, who supervised the opinion committees.

On the morning of August 19, Rudder arrived in Austin by A&M's small twin-engine maroon and white plane. Denius picked him up at the airport, and they discussed their meeting with Carr as Denius drove to the attorney general's office. During the meeting Carr agreed to an unusual procedure for dealing with A&M's opinion request. Normally, in dealing with an opinion request, a committee of assistant attorneys general was formed, and one member would agree to draft an opinion subject to review by the whole committee, which would eventually reach a consensus. The A&M request would be handled differently but within the rules of the office.[116] Without a public announcement, the opinion committee would conduct an informal hearing similar to a court hearing, with two adversarial lawyers presenting the viewpoints of the opposing factions of the Board of Directors. Frank Denius would represent the directors led by Sterling Evans, who believed the law required the full admission of women.

Before the hearing occurred, H. C. "Tony" Heldenfels, a contractor from Corpus Christi, succeeded Sterling Evans as chairman of A&M's Board of Directors. Evans had been chairman for two years, and the change was not a power struggle but was in keeping with the directors' policy on terms of office. However, in contrast to Evans, Heldenfels sided with directors who were opposed to the admission of women on the same basis as men. He would later say the decision that fundamentally changed the character of A&M was not admitting women but building residence halls for them. The Heldenfels faction on the board selected Dee Kelly, a Fort Worth lawyer, to represent them before the opinion committee. He would argue that the directors had the authority to limit the admission of women to certain categories, as in the existing policy.[117]

The situation was rife for destructive infighting between directors that could have delayed or diverted A&M's progressive momentum. That it did not confirms the quality of Governor Connally's appointees. Heldenfels was as committed as Evans to assuring that all directors would be heard; the minority and majority points of view would be aired in the same circumstances. He differed with Evans in his "opposition to full coeducation," but he was equally "determined to do all in [his] power to effect greater growth at A&M." "We must aim," he said, "at the future if we expect to come on target for the present."[118]

Heldenfels was also under the Rudder spell. In 1974, four years after Rudder's death, David Chapman, A&M's archivist, asked him, "What kind of man was Rudder—privately, out of the board room?" Heldenfels replied, "He was great company. You just loved to be around him. He was a good conversationalist and just the type of person I could spend the day with."[119]

On September 9, 1965, the parties gathered for the hearing before the opinion committee in the offices of the attorney general. Heldenfels and fellow director Peterson came with Dee Kelly, who argued that the Board of Directors was within its discretionary power to accept "certain women relatives of students, faculty members and employees, unless it violated federal law," which he contended it did not. Denius argued that the admissions policy was "discriminatory in that the daughter of a grounds keeper at A&M could attend . . . but the daughter of a highway engineer in Dallas could not."[120] He emphasized that he believed the discrimination—admitting women only in selected arbitrary classes—violated the U.S. Constitution.

A month later, Waggoner Carr issued his opinion, a seventeen-page public document with three conclusions. First, the federal Civil Rights Act of 1964 did not apply to discrimination on the basis of sex; hence, the policy need not be changed to comply with the act. Second, the Board of Directors had the authority to make A&M "either all male or all coeducational." In the third conclusion, which shaped the policy that enabled women to be admitted on the same basis as men, the attorney general agreed with Denius's contention that the exclusion of applicants for the sole reason that they were not "wives or daughters of staff members or students, or widows or daughters of deceased staff members was discriminatory and an unreasonable class distinction."[121]

The divided A&M Board of Directors then faced the challenge of agreeing on an admissions policy that did not discriminate against women but, for the Heldenfels faction, did not admit women on the same basis as men. In another act of fair play, Heldenfels appointed a four-member committee with closely balanced sentiments, but neither the committee nor the board could find new language on which they could agree.

"For Any Reason"

In trying to reach an agreement, the nine directors were hung up on three words: "for any reason." The five members led by Sterling Evans wanted to say that a woman could be admitted "for any reason" if she met the other qualifications. Tony Heldenfels and the other three members wanted less inclusive wording.[122] The phrase "for any reason" had actually originated with Rudder the previous June when the directors asked him—in the aftermath of the resolution adopted by the Association of Former Students—"to study the impact of full coeducation and noncompulsory military training and present it to the Board."

When the directors studied the attorney general's opinion, they found themselves again debating Rudder's all-inclusive phrase, "for any reason." With the majority pro-coeducation bloc unwilling to force the issue, the directors remained stalemated until the following March, one year after Rudder and Evans had asked Denius to help them resolve the legal quagmire. It was only a matter of time before someone would file a suit against Texas A&M for the admission of a woman as a regular student and cite the attorney general's opinion to support their case.

When the directors met on March 5, 1966, they were still unable to agree on the wording of a policy change, but they found an administrateve remedy on which all would agree: they would delegate decisions about the admission of women entirely to Rudder. They adopted a policy that began with the usual restrictions on the admission of women but ended with "in addition, the President of the University is authorized to make such further amendments to the admissions policy . . . to keep our program in compliance with the Attorney General's opinion."[123]

Rudder promptly instructed the admissions office to admit women on the same basis as men and issued an admissions statement for public distribution that began with the usual limitations but ended with the provision that a woman could enroll if she was "seeking an academic goal which *for any reason* can best be achieved at Texas A&M University." Thus, a woman could be admitted as a regular student as a matter of personal convenience or preference, perhaps because her father or grandfather had attended A&M.[124]

Edwin Cooper, the admissions officer, recalled, "We were completely open about the admission of any qualified woman; it was no big deal." By 1969, when Rudder presided over his last commencement, A&M had "graduated hundreds of female students and more entered each year." Until 1970 the official admissions policy was printed with the same list of limitations, followed by the "for any reason" proviso. Gradually, as Heidi Knippa observed, the opposition to women "faded into passive acceptance." Finally, on February 21, 1969, in a closed-door meeting the directors agreed to an explicit coeducational policy. Then it was typed for Rudder to read in the public meeting where it was officially adopted by the Board: "Texas A&M University is a co-education University admitting men and women to all academic studies on the same basis. It should be noted, however, that no housing is currently available to women." In the typed copy prepared for Rudder to read, the word *currently* did not appear; he inserted it above the line with the small inverted V that proofreaders call a caret. At that moment, Texas A&M had fewer than a thousand women among its total enrollment of 12,340. He usually saw a bigger and better world than did those around him. In the fall of 2010, Texas A&M University enrolled 49,129 students, of whom 22,791 were women, with 3,953 housed on the campus.[125]

The new policy took effect on September 1, 1970, eight months after Rudder's death.[126] Would he have been disappointed not to witness this acknowledgement of a major accomplishment of his life? Perhaps, but he was more interested in the substance of things than in their appearances. From his point of view, Texas A&M was coeducational from the day the Board of Directors turned the decision over to him in 1966, and he directed the admissions office to admit women for any reason if they met other requirements.

SCIENTIFIC ADVANCEMENT

When President John F. Kennedy was killed and Texas Governor John Connally wounded, Rudder was barely two miles away awaiting their arrival at
the Dallas Trade Mart. A luncheon was planned with local citizens and leaders of the Democratic Party in Texas. With his friend Lyndon B. Johnson as
vice president, Rudder was an enthusiastic supporter of the Kennedy administration. He had kept a low profile during their 1960 campaign, but he was
active behind the scenes throughout Texas, which the JFK-LBJ ticket carried
by about 46,000 votes of 2.5 million cast. He explained his low profile by
saying he was "president of a university which has students and faculty members who feel strongly about another party," the Republicans led by Richard
Nixon.[127]

When Johnson moved into the White House, he concentrated on legislation related to civil rights and education. "There is no time for delay," he told
a joint session of Congress five days after becoming president. "It is time for
action—strong, forward-looking action on the pending bills to help bring
the light of learning to every home and hamlet in America." Later, he sent a
message to the House and Senate that education "is our primary weapon in
the war on poverty and the principal tool for building a Great Society." Before leaving office in January 1969, Johnson signed into law about sixty bills
that almost tripled the federal appropriation for education.[128]

Among leaders in American higher education, Rudder was the closest
to the president. By an extraordinary coincidence, the folksy congressman
Rudder helped win his U.S. senatorial seat in 1948 was determined to be the
"education president" at the same time Rudder was striving to elevate Texas
A&M. Rudder's calls to the White House were returned, and his desk calendar began having notations to "Call White House," or "Call Cliff Carter,"
LBJ's liaison to the Democratic National Committee, or "Call Douglass
Cater," a White House specialist on higher education. More than once Johnson's assistants apologized for missing his telephone calls, as Marvin Watson
did when he wrote: "I am sorry to have missed your calls today. I look forward to seeing you at the first opportunity."[129]

If Rudder was in Washington, Johnson might be informed with notes
such as, "Earl Rudder is staying at the Shoreham Hotel in room B 327
through tomorrow," or by typewritten memos such as, "MR. PRESIDENT: A
reminder—Earl Rudder will be in Washington tomorrow. Do you want to
see him briefly?"[130]

Rudder was an occasional overnight guest in the White House, sometimes
accompanied by Margaret. She told of a surprise summons one morning to

Rudder with Vice President Lyndon B. Johnson at Texas A&M, 1962. (Courtesy of Anne Rudder Erdman)

the president's bedroom. When she and Earl entered, Lyndon was in his paja-mas in bed talking on the telephone to Florida senator George Smathers. She heard Johnson say, "I can get almost anyone to do almost anything for me but I cannot get Earl Rudder to do a damn thing." Johnson was exaggerating; Rudder accepted numerous assignments, but none of the full-time ones, such as ambassador to Pakistan, that LBJ wanted. Rudder withstood LBJ's famous persuasion by always insisting that his calling was at A&M working for the future with young people. He also resisted occasional pleas from conserva-tive Democrats that he should run for governor. In the mid-1960s he emerged as their informal choice to succeed Connally as governor, but he turned them down emphatically: "My main interest is the building of a university for the youth of Texas. I am not interested in any political job."[131]

Johnson brought Rudder into the government's domestic war on pov-erty by appointing him to the National Advisory Commission on Rural Pov-erty in 1966.[132] Similarly deprived childhoods in rural areas was one of their bonds. Disappointed that the overall War on Poverty was neglecting rural America, LBJ hoped the commission would bring balance to the effort. But

Lady Bird Johnson, left, and Margaret Rudder at Texas A&M, December 13, 1962, during a speech by Lyndon B. Johnson, then vice president of the United States. (Courtesy of Margaret Rudder)

whatever good the commission might have done, its recommendations were overwhelmed by the escalating war in Vietnam.

Johnson named Rudder to a fifteen-member task force that went to South Vietnam to study the people's health and education in hopes of assisting its government in developing an infrastructure that would improve the lives of its people. On the ground in Southeast Asia, Rudder observed that although most people were engaged in agriculture, there was little in the way of technical or agricultural education, and while the people spoke the Vietnamese language, most books were in French. His pertinent recommendations influenced the U.S. government to issue contracts for the publication of materials in the native languages and for the construction of several engineering, agricultural, and teacher training schools.[133] While in Vietnam, he made an unrelated visit to the U.S. 1st Infantry Division, where chatting with A&M graduates at a base camp of the Big Red One was a special pleasure.

Upon his return to the United States, Rudder was interviewed on NBC's "Today" program. He appeared ill at ease while giving an upbeat assessment of the situation: "We have many programs in Vietnam that should make

Rudder visiting Cal Farley's Boys Ranch near Amarillo, Texas, August 1965. (Courtesy of Margaret Rudder)

Americans proud. We are building schools and producing teachers. It will take time to establish the national cohesion to create a just and democratic government. And the war will not be won quickly."[134] There is no evidence that Johnson conferred with Rudder about conduct of the Vietnam War.

As long as improving higher education with new money and programs was a high priority in LBJ's Great Society agenda, the Johnson presidency was an extraordinary period for Rudder's influence and the enhancement of Texas A&M. His easygoing friendship with Johnson got Texas A&M

In 1966 Rudder was the Texas statewide chairman of the March of Dimes Foundation's annual fund drive. He is shown here with four-year-old Donna Dill of Hillsboro. (Courtesy of Margaret Rudder)

The 1966 Ranger reunion in Pittsburgh, Pennsylvania. Seated, l. to r.: Andrew Mlay, James Kerr, Rudder, Lou Lisko, William Matty, Francis "Killer" Kolodziejczak. Standing, l. to r.: Gerard Rothoff, [unavail.] Rogers, Guy Shoaf. (Courtesy of Margaret Rudder)

professors appointments to advisory panels and help from the president's staff in obtaining funding for their projects from federal agencies. Several wrote freely to White House assistants such as Bill Moyers, Marvin Watson, Jake Jacobson, and Jack Valenti as well as to cabinet officers. Rudder proposed A&M professors for advisory committees on federal programs and legislation on matters ranging from financial assistance for students to a federal tax on alcoholic beverages "to establish hospitals and treatment centers across the nation where alcoholics can go for treatment on a 'no charge' basis." He told Johnson that he supported his Great Society goals: "The fact that we have a President who continues to have a concern for the unfortunate of this nation is a source of great satisfaction and pride to all thinking people."[135]

The elections in November 1966 were humbling, though not disastrous, for Johnson's policies. The Democrats retained majorities in both houses even though they lost forty-seven seats in Congress and three in the Senate. Rudder tried to boost Johnson's spirits with a letter asking an assistant to tell "the President not to let the elections worry him. The great majority of the people know what he is doing and support him." After Johnson announced on March 31, 1968, that he would not seek reelection, Rudder telegrammed: "Many more people believe in you and the service you are rendering to your country than it is possible for you to know. I hope you [will] reconsider your decision."[136]

The Cyclotron

The upswing in federal grants and contracts for Texas A&M began a few weeks after Johnson became president, when the institution's application to the Atomic Energy Commission for funds to construct a cyclotron was approved after languishing for two years far down in the ranked evaluations of similar requests from other universities. The approval was the beginning of a stunning surge in federal grants and contracts that transformed Texas A&M from an agriculture and engineering school into a more comprehensive modern scientific research university. The cyclotron was a highly desirable addition to A&M's scientific capability because it could be used for both theoretical research about the nature of matter and practical applications that lay people could understand and put to immediate use. It was the almost perfect instrument to enhance respect for Texas A&M in both the scientific community and in the general public, especially with members of the state legislature, who appropriated the money for A&M's operating budget.[137]

About mid-January 1964 Rudder got a message to send someone to Washington to pick up a check from the Atomic Energy Commission for three million dollars. When Rudder's courier arrived, he found the AEC staff indignant at disbursing the grant for political reasons on a project that was judged inferior to unfunded applications from other institutions. Fortunately, Rudder's courier was a competent nuclear scientist who assured the disgusted staff that A&M would use the money as intended with satisfactory results, which proved to be correct. A&M became recognized for research, for educating students, and for applying the cyclotron to a wide variety of challenges in space science, materials science, and nuclear medicine. Long after LBJ had left office, federal agencies continued to support A&M's cyclotron.[138]

While Johnson leaned decisively on the AEC to fund A&M's cyclotron, Rudder had strong support from the inside. His A&M classmate and friend, Maj. Gen. Alvin R. Luedecke, had retired from the Air Force in 1958 to become general manager of the AEC. He was one of five members on the commission that approved the $3 million disbursed to Texas A&M. "I considered it one the projects the AEC should support," he said later. In 1968 Rudder appointed Luedecke associate dean of engineering and engineering research coordinator. When a building was constructed for the cyclotron, it was appropriately named in honor of Alvin Luedecke.[139]

The cyclotron complemented A&M's Nuclear Science Center, established in 1962 under the leadership of Richard E. Wainerdi, as a teaching facility and as a launch pad for the expansion of nuclear engineering education. The Nuclear Science Center, with the first nuclear reactor in the Southwest owned by a university, was a unique development.[140]

With the cyclotron the Rudder administration could concentrate resources for distinction in a narrow, though expensive, area of research rather than attempting several areas at the same time. And since the AEC promised to provide up to 80 percent of the cyclotron's annual operating expenses, A&M could undertake this research with money largely from federal sources. Rudder called the cyclotron "a real breakthrough into excellence," and it clearly staked out A&M as a national center for nuclear studies that would attract top scientists, graduate students, and more grants. He delayed a public announcement of the grant until he and Director Sterling Evans could brief Governor Connally, still recuperating from wounds suffered in the Kennedy assassination. When Connally emerged from their meeting in the state capitol, he told the press, "The cyclotron will lead to steps in scientific development beyond anything which has occurred."[141]

The cyclotron was exactly the kind of acquisition that Connally wanted to boost Texas higher education. Almost two years earlier, when Connally was campaigning for governor, he had conferred with Rudder about improving the teaching of science in colleges and universities. Both men believed the improvements would require attracting first-class scientists to Texas, and Connally maintained they would only come if they had the "proper tools like the cyclotron to do exacting research." He told audiences that the physical sciences, as represented by the cyclotron, were the basis for industrial expansion that would translate into jobs and a stronger economy. "If I could get an Einstein down here," he told a Waco audience, "do you think I would have trouble getting research funds from outfits like the Ford and Rockefeller Foundations. The answer is obviously, 'No.'"[142]

When the legislature met again, Connally recommended an additional $2 million for the cyclotron. Then the Robert A. Welch Foundation added another million dollars, and Rudder had the $6 million required to build the cyclotron. It made big news across the state. Newspapers carried the story under such headlines as: "Texas A&M to Get Huge Atom Smasher," and "Texas A&M to Become South's Strongest Nuclear Center." As proof that it would attract highly talented scientists, Dr. George J. Igo was hired away from Berkeley to direct the new Cyclotron Institute. Igo told the state's newspapers that the cyclotron would "increase the state's economy many times over its $6 million cost by creating new industries."[143]

More than three years were required to complete the cyclotron. Once done, it got the attention of scientists throughout the nation. Cancer patients traveled great distances for treatment with A&M's "atom smasher." The renowned University of Texas M. D. Anderson Hospital and Cancer Center in Houston sent patients to College Station for treatment. In 1966 A&M began offering the first nuclear engineering degree in the Southwest, which made the institution even more appealing to highly qualified students and eminent faculty. When the cyclotron was dedicated, the principal speaker was the chairman of the Atomic Energy Commission and 1951 Nobel Laureate in Chemistry, Glenn T. Seaborg, who alluded to the misgivings of the AEC staff in making the initial grant: "Through your daring, imagination and determination, you have accomplished what many have thought, with reason, was impossible."[144]

Space Science

In 1946, Rudder's friend and 1932 Aggie classmate, Olin E. "Tiger" Teague, was elected to Congress from the district that included Texas A&M. Tiger Teague and Earl Rudder were more than ordinary friends. The pleasure of their companionship was, in the words of Rudder's son, "total, nothing less than the most that old friends can be." A psychologist observing the two of them alone would have noticed that they relaxed completely, regressing occasionally to their undergraduate days as A&M cadets for the pure and harmless fun of it.

By coincidence, at almost the same time Rudder became president of A&M in 1959, Teague went on the House Committee on Science and Astronautics—later, Committee on Science and Technology. The United States and the Soviet Union were spending extraordinary and increasing sums of money trying to outdo each other in the race for space. The spending drove scientific research and development along at a phenomenal pace, and much of the R&D occurred in universities with monies provided by contracts with agencies of the federal government, especially the National Aeronautics and Space Administration. Rudder would get a bountiful share for A&M.

In May 1961 President Kennedy announced a national goal of putting a man on the moon by the end of the decade and signed legislation making the vice president, Lyndon Johnson, the presiding officer of the National Aeronautics and Space Council. Johnson believed "we must be first in space and in aeronautics to maintain first place on earth." A few months later, Tiger Teague became chairman of the House subcommittee on manned space travel, which handled all spending authorizations of NASA's manned space flight programs. When this happened, as his booster Murray Watson said, "Tiger Teague held the purse strings on appropriations" for space and aeronautics. Once again, Rudder had well-placed friends to help advance A&M in scientific and technological development. He formed a new entity called the Space Technology Division to shore up A&M's credibility as a recipient of space and aerodynamic research contracts. In this decision Rudder was probably advised by his friend, General Luedecke, who left the Atomic Energy Commission to become deputy director of the Jet Propulsion Laboratory at California Institute of Technology, where he played a major role in space research.[145]

The first NASA heavyweight to visit A&M was its administrator, James Webb, a former president of MIT. Teague brought him and introduced him at the Convocation Conference at which Rudder and the A&M Board of Directors presented the Blueprint for Progress in November 1962. Webb gave the keynote at the conference. Before long, Teague brought his entire eleven-member subcommittee to the campus. Then he brought a delegation of NASA officials, including Wernher von Braun, director of the Marshall Space Flight Center.[146] Von Braun was impressed by a campus "Space Fiesta," which attracted thousands, and he was clearly excited about the possibilities of a moon probe device designed by Professor Wainerdi with grants from the Atomic Energy Commission and NASA.

Congressman Jake Pickle represented the district centered on Austin, the location of the University of Texas. He and Tiger were friends of long standing in Congress and in Democratic Party politics of Texas. In retirement Pickle described how Tiger Teague wrangled federal money for A&M: "As chairman of the space technology committee, Tiger was in the middle of all the planning for the flight to the moon. He needed a front man to get all those grants and programs. He'd have Earl come up to Washington, stay a week, and maybe they'd travel together to NASA sites. For a few years, A&M got so many grants and new buildings that I think the Gulf Coast tilted two feet into the ocean with all that weight."[147]

Pickle thought Rudder was essential to Teague's success in channeling grants to A&M. "Earl was so polite and friendly. He had a great smile about him. He would listen and be very agreeable. Based on what his A&M scientists told him, he'd ask 'What are the plusses for A&M?' and finally make up his mind. He got a lot of programs started at A&M because he was in the right place and made the right decisions fast and implemented them with authority. When he made up his mind, believe you me, he'd go into action."[148]

When Rudder established a Bioengineering Division, he strengthened Texas A&M's credibility as a grant recipient for other monies that Tiger

Rudder in 1969 with J. J. "Jake" Pickle, member of the U.S. House of Representatives from the tenth district of Texas, 1963–95. In 1946 Pickle recruited Rudder into the political organizations of Texas lieutenant governor Allan Shivers and Congressman Lyndon B. Johnson. Pickle's connection to Rudder began with Margaret Rudder, his friend from their student years at the University of Texas. (Courtesy of Margaret Rudder)

Teague influenced. As Rudder had formed the Space Technology Division that capitalized on Tiger's importance as chairman of the manned space flight subcommittee, the Bioengineering Division took advantage of Tiger's long-standing chairmanship of the Veterans Affairs Committee. The R&D purpose of the new division was to "apply engineering principles and techniques to medical and other biological problems sponsored primarily by NASA and the Veterans Administration," both under the oversight of Teague's committees. The benefits of these grants were not merely in gaining revenue and attracting outstanding faculty, but also in providing opportunities for students. With the faculty and knowledge base attained by the grant money, A&M began offering in 1971 a bachelor of science degree in bioengineering, the first such program in Texas and among the first in the United States.[149]

By late 1965, Texas A&M was playing a major role in America's bid to conquer space and land a man on the moon. From a small NASA grant three years earlier to investigate remote activation analysis of the moon, its space research projects now involved more than 140 faculty members and hundreds of graduate students, many of them participating in the investigations. "Aggie engineers, chemists, physicists, mathematicians, statisticians, psychologists, biologists—professors in virtually every discipline—[were] at work to unlock the secrets of this new dimension." Their projects were as diverse as placing a device on the surface of the moon to analyze and telemeter data back to A&M computers, the effect of gamma radiation on human ability to perform in space, methods of powering space capsules, controlling the attitude (angle) of satellites, testing materials to withstand the temperatures of outer space, and predicting solar flares.[150]

However, A&M's space research facilities were dispersed, and housing them together would have the obvious advantages of bringing scientists and equipment in close proximity. In this situation, no one should have been surprised that Tiger Teague, running for reelection, announced an appropriation to construct a "space center" at A&M. Rudder garnered additional monies from NASA and the National Science Foundation for the building, which was named the Olin E. Teague Research Center in honor of the congressman who helped unlock the federal treasury for A&M.[151]

Soon after the Teague Center opened, Rudder announced a grant from NASA for A&M to participate in designing a "futuristic space shuttle" as part of a larger study that led to a manned orbiting satellite. He declared publicly that Tiger Teague "was the strong right arm of A&M in Congress." Noting A&M's progress, the *Dallas Times Herald* took a balanced perspective, agreeing that Tiger was indispensable, but Rudder was an essential partner. "Rudder," the *Times Herald* editorialized, "knows his way around in Washington and Austin, where the money comes from."[152]

Sea Grant College

"The most important effort of Texas A&M University in recent decades," declared A&M's historian, Henry C. Dethloff, on the eve of its centennial in 1976, "has been in the areas of marine science and marine resources."[153] The effort contributed to the designation of A&M as a sea grant college, which complemented its status as a land grant college. Both functions were supported with monies from the federal government.

The National Sea Grant College Act, signed into law by President Johnson in 1966, paralleled the land grant act of a hundred years earlier, usually considered one of the best investments the United States has ever made. When the sea grant act's sponsor in the U.S. Senate, Claiborne Pell of Rhode Island, referred to his bill as establishing centers of excellence in marine and coastal studies, he got Rudder's attention. Designation as a sea grant college would virtually assure Texas A&M of greater capability in marine science, an area of increasing scientific and economic importance. The sea grant colleges would be a network of top universities conducting research, education, and training to foster science-based decisions about the use and conservation of aquatic resources.

Texas A&M was a strong candidate for sea grant status by virtue of its programs in oceanography and meteorology, historic achievements as a land grant institution, and, uniquely, a campus on an island—Pelican Island in Galveston Bay—called the Texas Maritime Academy. The development of Texas Maritime Academy and its evolution into Texas A&M University at Galveston can be traced directly to Earl Rudder.[154]

In 1931 the Texas Legislature authorized the creation of a nautical school to provide instruction related to ships, shipping, navigation, and seamanship. However, the country was mired in the Great Depression, and the legislature provided no money for the school. Moreover, the enabling statute prohibited state funding, and nothing came of the plan. The law was mostly forgotten until 1958, when the Galveston Chamber of Commerce appointed a committee to investigate the possibility of establishing a maritime academy in that city. Nowhere on the Gulf of Mexico could a person get the necessary training for a career in the merchant marine. The committee reviewed the 1931 statute and discovered that it required any nautical school to be managed by Texas A&M. Galveston advocates went to College Station and were encouraged by A&M president Tom Harrington. They returned home anticipating that A&M would support their request to the legislature to appropriate money for the school during its coming 1961 session.[155]

Then they got distressing information. In early 1960 they were informed that A&M had agreed with other state colleges and universities not to ask the legislature to fund any new programs in 1961. State revenues were tight, and higher education officials decided to limit their requests for funding to existing programs. The meaning was clear: since funding for Galveston's maritime school would be new money, it would not be included in A&M's budget request to the legislature. For a while, Texas A&M was not popular with Galveston civic leaders, who felt they had been snubbed.

The Galveston Chamber of Commerce was discouraged until Rudder, recently inaugurated as A&M's president, came to meet with them. As a former commissioner of the General Land Office, he was experienced in dealing with the legislature. He suggested that Galveston should make its request directly to the legislature and leave A&M out of it. He assured them that, if the legislature approved their request, he "would do everything possible to administer a first rate maritime academy." After the meeting, one man commented that Rudder "smiled at the Galvestonians; they smiled at him and at each other. Given his military background, his suggestion seemed more of a marching order than a hint."[156]

Galveston boosters took Rudder's advice and lobbied the legislature. When they testified before legislative committees, he was with them, lending credibility and support for their request. As hoped, the legislature came through and appropriated money to operate the academy for two years but made actual receipt of the money contingent upon the academy obtaining a ship and money to operate it, neither of which was available. It fell to Rudder to inform the Galvestonians that A&M could not activate the school until the ship issue was settled. He then negotiated a contract with the Federal Maritime Commission, which provided a ship that was renamed the *Texas Clipper* and converted to a seagoing classroom.[157]

There were unforeseen benefits. When Rudder helped start the Texas Maritime Academy, the federal sea grant program was several years in the future. After President Johnson signed it into law in 1966, A&M filed an application that was strengthened by already having the academy. After A&M received a major grant for the maritime institute in mid-1968, the university was designated one of the first four sea-grant colleges in the United States.[158]

IMAGE CHALLENGES

Early in Rudder's presidency, if not before, he became convinced that "the boisterous fellow with an overdose of blind school loyalty had been the wrong Aggie image for too long." All college and university presidents must concern themselves with public relations, and given A&M's declining trajectory when Rudder took office, he was more intent than most. Many, though not all, of A&M's staunchest supporters agreed with him, and they gave him plenty of advice about it. An ardent Aggie of years past sent him a "to do" list on the eve of taking office that included this: "Public relations—big problem. We Aggies must quit talking to ourselves—inform the general public about A&M.[159]

To a large extent, A&M's image problem resulted from the positive accomplishments of its graduates during the first half of the twentieth century in fields that had become outmoded. As one described the image problem, "Too many Texans think of A&M primarily as a good old boys' military school that specializes in teaching courses about farming. We're proud of our agricultural courses but we want to correct false impressions."[160]

The image problem was inherent in Woody Varner's letter to Chancellor Tom Harrington in mid-1957, in which he declined to be considered for the

A&M presidency. Varner, the student Corps commander in 1940 and then a vice president of Michigan State, concluded that Texas A&M "is not as highly regarded as it should be."[161]

Soon after Rudder took over, he asked coworkers for reports about other colleges and universities they visited. He was interested in their administrative organizations, but his special interest was their public relations programs. He instructed his director of information services to survey counterparts about "how to conduct research for our basic information program." Recipients of the inquiry read that A&M's main concern was its "image among prospective students and their parents."[162]

Rudder brought up the image issue in many circumstances. When some five hundred noncadet students marched on his campus home one night to protest a policy that made boarding fees mandatory for residential students, he admonished them. "You're bringing discredit to A&M," he said as members of the Corps of Cadets stalked conspicuously in uniform around the outskirts of the crowd.[163]

Like most college presidents, Rudder thought the public would view his institution more favorably if they saw and heard directly from its faculty. He encouraged A&M's faculty and staff to seek speaking engagements about their areas of expertise, whether it was controlling soil erosion, eradicating the screwworm fly, or winning the space race. Early in his presidency he asked A&M's English Department to conduct public speaking courses on Saturday mornings, and he took a course himself. Although public speaking was not one of his strengths, Rudder had more speech invitations than he could accept. His assistant, John Mobley, who later worked for Governor Connally, overheard a conversation between Lyndon Johnson and Connally in which LBJ said, "We should run Earl Rudder for something." Connally, who had studied dramatics and performed on the stage, exclaimed, "He cannot make a speech worth a damn!" But it was a different story in small groups. "President Rudder," wrote a student, "I can tell the world that you are much more pleasant in meetings with small numbers where your humor and true nature can show through the thorny vestiges of your office."[164]

The Battalion

Rudder believed that student publications significantly influenced public perception of A&M and that he should control them, especially the newspaper, the *Battalion*. "A student newspaper is bound to be regarded as the voice and the mirror of the university," he told a reporter. He further believed he "had the right and the responsibility to regulate its contents and conduct."[165]

Rudder with Texas governor John B. Connally at the airport in Waco, Texas, October 23, 1968, waiting to greet Vice President Hubert H. Humphrey, the Democratic Party nominee for president of the United States. (Courtesy of Nelda Rowell Green)

His approach was legally defensible, but he did not understand the press and provoked reactions that were detrimental to the very image of Texas A&M he wanted to enhance. When he imposed or sanctioned censorship, newspaper reporters rallied against him, which led to more unfavorable publicity than if he had overseen the *Battalion* with an organization that he created, as many universities did.

He appears to have opposed the preparation of professional journalists at A&M, whether in the classroom or by experience producing the *Battalion*. From the outset of his presidency, he declined to support the journalism department, even symbolically. He turned down a request to establish a chapter of an honorary journalism fraternity with the purpose of instilling the ideals of "a truthful, honorable press" in students. He declined to attend banquets that recognized student achievement in journalism, and his general lack of support was a factor in the departure of the journalism faculty.[166]

John Mobley was with Rudder in a receiving line when the parents of an
A&M student told him how happy their daughter was majoring in journalism. When they were gone, Rudder muttered, "And she's getting a damned
sorry education, I'm sorry to say."[167] He may have considered journalism a
trade to be learned on the job by covering the courthouse and pecking out
stories on a typewriter, rather than a profession with a code of ethics deserv-
ing formal preparation. Perhaps correspondents he observed during the war
were his ideal of good journalists—men like Ernie Pyle, Andy Rooney, and
Walter Cronkite, seasoned professionals. They were on the team to win, followed orders, and did not divulge damaging information. Rudder's crusade
was to elevate A&M in the academic world, and he expected the college reporters who worked on the *Battalion* to promote A&M, which meant doing
as he said.

His approach might have been successful at a military college in the 1940s,
but not in the rebellious 1960s with the caliber of students who were drawn
in increasing numbers to the new Texas A&M he was building. Few students
interested in newspaper work could countenance the *Battalion* as a public
relations organ for Texas A&M. The more vigorous and curious the student
editors were, the more likely they were to conflict with Rudder. When an editor of the *Battalion* criticized his administration, Rudder rebuked him: "I'm
not about to let one smart-aleck kid tear down what I've built up."[168]

Before the 1960s, the *Battalion* was cited for excellence as a college newspaper historically free of censorship. But in the fall of 1966 Rudder summar-
ily removed its editor, Thomas M. DeFrank, who would graduate at the end
of the year at the top of his class and be nominated for a Rhodes scholarship.
He replaced DeFrank with Jim Lindsey from his own staff, who was also his
public information officer in the 90th Infantry Division. On September 28,
1966, the masthead of the *Battalion* showed DeFrank as the editor, and the
next day Lindsey was listed as editor-in-chief. Lindsey explained that the
change was "to pave the way for a better atmosphere in which the newspaper
could operate," while Rudder defended his stand on the grounds that "the
newspaper should be operated in a professional manner."[169]

In a three-hour meeting with the Texas A&M Student Senate, Rudder
told them that "editors all over the state have recommended this type of
newspaper setup and I believe in it." A few publishers and editors may have
supported Rudder's organization of the *Battalion,* but he would learn that
virtually no writer who actually wrote for their newspapers favored heavy-
handed editorial control. When a female student senator asked the purpose
of a student newspaper, he replied that it was "to train good journalists." In
an afterthought, he tagged on, "If you want a University of Texas type of

newspaper, then go there." Although Rudder barred out-of-town reporters from his meeting with the Student Senate, tape recorders were running, and the big city dailies quickly had the story. "A&M President Bars Reporters at Meeting," next day's headline read.

When another young woman asked, "Can the *Battalion* criticize the administration?" he dodged, saying, "It would be in poor taste and you'll have to ask Mr. Lindsey." Her question raised a fundamental difference between Rudder and student editors. In his view, the A&M administration was the publisher, and newspapers do not criticize their publishers. However, student editors considered the administration as the government and fair game for investigative reporting and criticism; they pointed out that newspapers permitted letters to the editor that criticized the publisher and editor.[170]

Unfavorable letters to the editor printed in the *Battalion* were a sore spot with Rudder, and Jim Lindsey often stopped their publication. Rudder told student senators that there is no need for letters to the editor, as they would expose A&M's internal problems to the detriment of the university. "If I make a mistake, you come in and tell me about it," he reminded them of his open door policy.[171] His administrative style was direct and personal rather than detached and formal, even with students.

Cashiering Johnny Cash

Rudder's controversies with the *Battalion* were brewing long before he removed DeFrank as editor. They began moving toward a new high one year before, in mid-November of 1965, when he terminated a contract with Johnny Cash, the country and western singer, to perform on the campus only a week later. Stories about Rudder's decision were carried in Dallas and Houston newspapers. A campuswide committee of faculty, students, and staff had proposed the Cash performance to the administration, which negotiated the contract with his agent. Six weeks before Rudder canceled the contract, Cash had been arrested on a federal drug charge in El Paso. Rudder's rationale was stated by Dean of Students James Hannigan: "Cash put us in an untenable situation of having to promote and sell tickets for a person under indictment for smuggling and concealing illicit drugs."[172]

Cash's manager described Rudder's termination of the contract a "unilateral action without complete and accurate knowledge of the facts." Joe Buser, Rudder's former aide and now on the staff of the Association of Former Students, used Rudderlike expressions when he said that "to permit Cash to fulfill his engagement would reflect unfavorably and generate a poor image" for A&M. Petitions circulating among students to reinstate the contract quickly garnered almost three thousand signatures, but Rudder did not budge. In an unusual act of belligerence for A&M students, they formed a Committee for Johnny Cash, with no connection to the university, and made a deal for him to perform at a nearby dance hall at the same time he had been scheduled on the campus.[173]

The dance hall had no seats or benches and was jammed with young people sprawled across the floor on blankets and cushions. *Battalion* editor Glenn Dromgoole, near the front, thought the Man in Black was "high as a kite." The crowd roared when Cash dedicated the song "Dirty Old Egg Sucking Dog" to Rudder[174]

> *Well he's not very handsome to look at*
> *Oh he's shaggy and he eats like a hog*
> *And he's always killin' my chickens*
> *That dirty old egg-suckin' dog.*

In his deep, bass-baritone voice, Cash sang the verse again and again as his audience joined him in singing the last line: "That dirty old egg-suckin' dog." Rudder could enjoy ribbing by his soldierly comrades, but not likely the mockery of students led by a degenerate songster. His favorite vocalist was Anita Bryant, and for instrumentals he preferred the "jus' wunnerful" melodies of Lawrence Welk. A few days later he explained his decision to the campus committee that had originally proposed the Cash performance. "The Cash decision was mine alone," he said without equivocation. "I did not try to prejudge Johnny Cash because only a court of law can do that, but no one can dispute that he had been caught with pep pills."[175]

Within a month Cash entered a plea of guilty before a federal judge on charges of possessing 668 Dexadrine and 475 Equanil tablets when arrested in the El Paso airport. In making his decision, Rudder may have considered that six months earlier Cash had spent a night in jail in Starkville, Mississippi, after his arrest for public intoxication and relieving himself in public.[176] Cash had not yet taken the road to redemption, and Rudder would not risk his repeating such acts on the A&M campus.

Since Rudder was sitting with the committee that recommended campus events in the visual and performing arts, he clarified their purely advisory role by telling them that in the future he "would not hesitate to step in and stop anything that would bring discredit on the university." In a more telling revelation, he confirmed that he had removed the painting of a nude feminine figure from an exhibit in the Memorial Student Center. But, he added, he had done that "only once in my tenure of office."[177] Arbitrary and uninformed though his judgments were, they were probably in accord with those of A&M's principal patrons, beginning with members of the state legislature.

Following the cancellation of the Johnny Cash performance, a *Battalion* editorial criticizing the Rudder administration was eliminated by Jim Lindsey, who followed by removing letters to the editor that also criticized the administration for the same reason. A student reporter's account of a labor strike at the cyclotron construction site was cut by Lindsey, who then deleted stories about the Vietnam War picked up from the Associated Press wire service. So it went in the first months of 1966, with Lindsey or his assistants censoring the *Battalion*.[178]

Lindsey tried to hand off the *Battalion* to the journalism department, headed by the steady Delbert McGuire. McGuire had been in the position for six years after eleven years on the journalism faculty at the University of North Texas, where he also advised the student newspaper. He was an experienced newspaper reporter with two degrees in journalism and had worked as the chief editor of two trade publications. But Lindsey imposed restrictions that made it impossible for McGuire to use the *Battalion* as a laboratory to teach students to be professional journalists, a primary purpose of college newspapers. Discouraged and disillusioned with the "direction journalism was going at A&M," McGuire simply resigned.[179]

With the controversies continuing, Rudder invited the *Battalion*'s current editor (1965–66), Glenn Dromgoole, and other student staffers on the newspaper to his home one evening to discuss their differences. Trying to find a way out of the ongoing disputes, Rudder asked them to send him an analysis of the situation with recommendations. They sent him a professional-quality document called "State of the *Battalion*," seventeen pages of detail ending with twelve recommendations and not even an executive summary. This was too much for a university president already overburdened with raising money, schmoozing the legislature, recruiting faculty, and placating noisy alums whose main interest was football while reconciling an increasingly diverse and restive student body—all in addition to managing the operations of the university. He continued to delegate the *Battalion* to Lindsey and told a reporter that he was "not interested in the technicalities" of an oversight organization for student publications.[180]

Thus, nothing came of the student editors' recommendations. Rudder was the publisher of the *Battalion* and would not tolerate anything in print that reflected adversely on A&M, which, the students contended, included himself. They talked about Rudder's objection to a clever, satirical essay by Dromgoole about the lack of pencil sharpeners in classrooms while "millions were spent on research." After reading Dromgoole's piece, he grumbled, "If they had come to me first, we could have taken care of it without airing any dirty linen."[181] References to "dirty linen" became a Rudder tagline for his displeasure with the *Battalion*.

About the same time that Rudder canned Johnny Cash, an incident of campus vandalism occurred that would have ramifications decades later with a powerful politician. In the early hours of October 22, 1965, thirteen A&M buildings were painted with BU '69 or Baylor '69 in Baylor University's green and gold colors. At 3:00 in the morning, A&M security officers apprehended a Baylor freshman, Richard J. Ream, on the campus. He would not admit any wrongdoing but he gave A&M security officers the names of a dozen other Baylor freshmen who had planned the escapade.[182] One of them was Thomas Dale "Tom" DeLay, a premedical student and later a congressman from Texas called "the Hammer" and known for his self-righteous assertions of moral superiority. In his 2007 autobiography, DeLay remembered Ream as the "Bible-thumping, goody two-shoes, hymns-in-the-morning type."

"I was put on probation," DeLay said, "and marked by the administration as a certain source of trouble." Eventually "I was notified that my presence on the Baylor campus was no longer required." As DeLay did not have favorable memories of Richard Ream, his turncoat classmate, neither did he have high regard for Baylor and Texas A&M. In 1992 he told a Baptist church congregation near Houston, "Don't send your kids to Baylor and don't send your kids to A&M. Send them where they can get a good, solid, godly education."[183]

Defrocking DeFrank

Thomas M. DeFrank became the *Battalion* editor at the beginning of the 1966–67 school year. He was smart, capable, energetic, full of ideas and initiative, and well informed about how other universities governed student newspapers. People with important sounding titles did not intimidate him, and that included Maj. Gen. and President Earl Rudder. Shortly after classes began in September 1966, DeFrank scheduled two half-hour conferences with Rudder to clarify editorial guidelines for the *Battalion*. Ed Davis, the student Corps commander and DeFrank's friend, was frequently in Rudder's office at the time and understood that the meetings could be summarized in one sentence, with Rudder telling DeFrank, "Tommy, we do not wash our dirty linens in public." When Rudder declined to assure DeFrank the latitude he sought as editor of the *Battalion*, DeFrank requested a meeting with the Board of Directors. He expected them to side with Rudder but hoped "I might at least receive some straightforward black and white policy concerning the *Battalion*. The censoring of student publications was becoming increasingly worse."[184]

DeFrank met with the directors on September 27, and by the time DeFrank left the boardroom the board had eliminated any confusion about who was in charge by passing a resolution "that policies pertaining to student publications are matters to be handled within the structure of the University administration." And the next day Lindsey notified DeFrank of his removal as editor.[185] DeFrank had lasted less than a month. He was ahead of his times, too aggressive, and too professional to edit the *Battalion*.

DeFrank maintained that he was not surprised, and he was not repentant. "We had been warned we would be fired if we continued to talk," and "they were reasonably sure I would continue to oppose their policy of censorship." The twenty-year-old put his finger on the basic issue: "The university is so concerned with its public image that it went overboard and damaged that image. That's the big thing right now, A&M's image. As long as A&M has policies like these, people will laugh at us when we try to call ourselves a first class institution.[186]

DeFrank kept writing and talking. At Sam Houston State University his speech criticizing Rudder was printed in the student newspaper. "General Rudder seems to think the whole world is one big infantry division and he's the commander. I didn't get fired because I violated any ethics of journalism. I got fired because I crossed Earl Rudder. My firing was not to punish me but to get me out of his hair." Later he would say, "It's not the smartest thing I ever said," but he followed it with a resolution that censured Texas A&M for censoring student publications and was passed overwhelmingly by student delegates from twenty-four universities. Afterward, DeFrank commented, "Someday I want to go back to the *Battalion* and see it as a respected newspaper, instead of the joke it is now." He would return to A&M many times. While this book was in progress, he was the Washington bureau chief for the *New York Daily News*. Earlier he was *Newsweek*'s deputy Washington bureau chief and senior White House correspondent.[187]

Thomas E. Turner covered A&M and a broad swath of Central Texas for the *Dallas Morning News*, perhaps the most widely read newspaper in the state. Turner wrote flattering articles about Rudder and the 90th Infantry Division in summer training at Fort Hood, and Rudder considered him a friend, but their friendship was severely strained by a story of forty column inches that Turner wrote for a Sunday issue under the title, "Feud Over A&M Campus Newspaper Continues Unabated." Turner opened with a comparison that displeased Rudder: "It is not stretching a point much to say that the two bravest men on the campus of Texas A&M University at the moment are James Earl Rudder and Thomas Michael DeFrank." Rudder fired off an out-of-character letter to Turner. "Dear Tommy: I don't need any adversaries with friends like you!" He softened his second and closing line by inviting Turner to "stop by" the next time he was on campus.[188]

Turner's story appeared in April 1967, and DeFrank graduated from A&M the next month as one of eight students with high honors in a graduating class of 655. At the commencement ceremony, Rudder shook hands with the other seven but not with DeFrank. When DeFrank approached him across the stage, Rudder stepped behind a table stacked with diplomas. The ostensible reason was to permit the donor of a scholarship held by DeFrank to congratulate him, but DeFrank always thought it was personal. Upon graduation, DeFrank was commissioned as a reserve officer. Two years later, while he was on active duty in the Pentagon, he met Rudder by chance in Washington's Dulles airport. Attired in his army greens, Tommy spoke to Rudder, who snapped, "If your grades hadn't been so good, I'd have thrown your ass out of school." Tommy's instinctive reply was disarming: "That's what my mother told me."[189]

To many people, Rudder was a "noble person," in the phrase of Oliver Sadberry, one of A&M's few black students in the 1960s. "You had to admire him," Sadberry remarked with a smile decades later as director of the Brazos Valley African American Museum. Yet Rudder's conduct toward the *Battalion* and its student writers seems ignoble and spiteful. Second-guessing him is difficult, because it is impossible to re-create the circumstances in which he made the decisions.

Despite the conflict between Rudder and DeFrank, longtime observers of Texas A&M recognized that any student criticism of institutional policy "would have been unthinkable ten years earlier when the school was under strict military discipline." Rudder's attitude was evolving, and within a month after removing DeFrank as the *Battalion* editor, he approved the formation of a "political forum" for outside speakers "to speak about various facets in the broad spectrum of politics." However, he did not agree to politically partisan student organizations.[190]

As the years passed, DeFrank mellowed as Rudder might have. When DeFrank delivered the spring commencement address at A&M in 2007, he reminisced about their differences and reached a different conclusion than he had in his student days: "As I walked around this magnificent campus, General Rudder's presence was everywhere. His vision of what Texas A&M could be is the underpinning of today's world-class university, and all of us should honor his memory. I certainly do."[191]

After an extraordinary career as a Washington journalist covering the White House under three presidents, DeFrank was asked what he learned in his storied conflict with Rudder forty years earlier. "Most of all," he replied, "I learned that you can stand up to authority and live to tell the story to your children. It was fabulous training for the White House beat. More than one President of the United States has threatened, cajoled, poked me in the chest, and otherwise attempted to intimidate me. I've discovered that it doesn't faze me much and I can thank Rudder for that."[192]

Censured by the AAUP

Professor Leon W. Gibbs baffled his colleagues in A&M's College of Veterinary Medicine. They thought they knew him well. When he completed his doctoral degree under their supervision in 1949, they offered him a position teaching anatomy. The anatomy department had fewer than ten faculty members, and they were close-knit professionally and socially. In a small, somewhat isolated college town, their families were well acquainted, too, an extended family that included Gibbs and his wife. The faculty friendships were based on common interests, ethnicity, education, and gender. All were male, as were their students; the only women in the department were clerks and secretaries.[193]

At some point Gibbs began making unwelcome advances toward women in the department. He placed his hands on one woman and possibly others in "such a manner," his department chairman determined, "as to frighten and humiliate" them. He spent excessive time in the break room, where he made women feel uncomfortable by sitting too close and initiating conversations about sex and religion. Long after these incidents occurred, a faculty committee declared that his behavior had interfered with the "mission, procedures and purpose" of the department. The finding was not disputed, only the failure to create a record of it and take timely action.[194] Failure to take action implied that the faculty was too friendly to enforce standards of good conduct and efficiency.

By the mid-1970s Gibbs's conduct probably would have been unlawful and called sexual harassment, but such laws did not exist in the 1960s, and the concept had not become prominent in public consciousness. Since there was no formal grievance procedure for the offended women, Gibbs's offenses did not become matters of record, and he was not disciplined for his infractions against the unwritten code of proper conduct. The tendency was to hope such affronts would not happen again and fade away as a forgotten secret. As the years went by, Gibbs was commended as a teacher and promoted to full professor. When a committee finally got around to investigating his conduct, even his sympathizers agreed that his "improprieties were condoned, largely out of compassion for his family."[195] It was an example of misguided compassion.

The reluctance to discipline Gibbs began to unravel in April 1965 when his wife made an appointment with the dean of the college and informed him that her husband was involved with another woman, that he had moved from their home, and that she was filing for a divorce. Few academic deans are trained marriage counselors, but they usually have opportunities to learn on the job. Within a month the dean and department chairman decided Gibbs's employment should be terminated, and they did so by simply leaving him out of the budget for the coming year. When Gibbs was told his position was being eliminated, no mention was made of his job performance, only his marital problems. Rudder approved the budget without Gibbs in it; a line item salary for his unnamed replacement was included in the same budget. Most people subjected to such treatment left without causing trouble, but not Gibbs.

Rather than go into obscurity, Gibbs went to the American Association of University Professors (AAUP), the national organization founded in 1915 to protect the rights of professionals in higher education. On the advice of the AAUP, he appealed in writing for Rudder to review his case, because he was being fired, he claimed, "on the basis of gossip and rumor."[196] Rudder, always an activist ready to solve a problem, immediately asked to meet with Gibbs. Fully briefed beforehand by the dean and department chairman, Rudder listened but backed up their decision that Gibbs had to go. Still, Gibbs did not leave. Instead, he asked the AAUP to investigate his case. Wanting to avoid conflict with the AAUP, Rudder included Gibbs in the budget for the coming year as a researcher rather than a teacher.

Then Gibbs was moved out of his office and assigned to a laboratory that was improvised space in a breezeway without furniture, electricity, water, or gas connections. Eventually he got a filing cabinet, a microscope, and a typewriter. When the lock was changed on the door, he had difficulty finding anyone to give him the correct key. When he asked technicians for help, they were always busy with other projects. As for his coveted close-in parking space, he was reassigned to one a quarter of a mile from his office and told that if he complained, it would be moved further away. Still he did not leave.[197]

He then asked for a meeting with the Board of Directors, a permissible appeal under A&M's regulations. In Gibbs's account of the meeting, Rudder introduced him by saying, "Professor Gibbs has something to discuss with you." Gibbs told the directors that he could not reply to the charges against him because they had not been formalized in writing, which was true. The directors talked about faculty responsibilities for some ten minutes, ending in silence until Rudder announced gruffly, "That will be all, Gibbs." Gibbs was insulted by being called only by his last name. If the directors took any action on his appeal, he was not informed.

For more than a year Rudder and representatives of the AAUP sparred, corresponding and conferring, trying to find common ground to resolve the dispute over Gibbs's future. Rudder was intent on avoiding censure, but he was in unfamiliar territory and did not realize that he was getting into a no-win situation. For the AAUP, the issue was legal. "The Gibbs case was probably A&M's first exposure to due process," said James B. "Jimmy" Bond, a lawyer and later general counsel for the Texas A&M System.[198]

From Rudder's perspective, the issue was not legal but ethical. Rudder did not have legal counsel in dealing with the Gibbs case, perhaps by choice. "He was not inclined to accept that he needed legal help," says Bond. By contrast, the AAUP was fully aware of the implications of the new standards regarding individual rights as shown in the 950-page transcript of a four-day hearing at A&M about the Gibbs situation.[199] Two lawyers retained by the AAUP represented Gibbs at the hearing; no lawyer represented Texas A&M. Within a few years, however, the state's attorney general would routinely participate in such cases.

Eighteen months after Gibbs was told that he was losing his job, he still did not have written charges of his offense. Having made no progress toward resolving his situation, the AAUP's national executive sent an investigating committee of three respected professors to confer with knowledgeable people at Texas A&M and write a report that would form the basis for action, if any, against the university. When the AAUP informed Rudder about the coming visit of the committee, he replied that the proposed dates "are not convenient for me." He did not reply to the suggestion of alternative dates or to the request for a "suitable room on the campus" for use by the committee.[200]

In Rudder's view, the AAUP was attempting to interfere in the operation of Texas A&M and his authority. At the same time, Rudder genuinely wanted to avoid censure, which could be tantamount to a boycott of A&M by some professors and stigmatize the image he was desperately trying to enhance. H. C. Heldenfels, a director during this period, would later say that Rudder regarded AAUP censuring "as a real threat. General Rudder felt it would leave a black mark on the university, and he couldn't hire the caliber of professors needed."[201]

By coincidence, one of the three professors sent by the AAUP to investigate Texas A&M (actually, the Rudder administration) was Frank E. South Jr., a physiologist then at the University of Missouri—the same Frank South who was a medic in the 2nd Ranger Battalion, who scaled the cliffs at Pointe du Hoc, and whose robust singing aroused Rudder in the wee hours of a morning in Mayenne just before the big push into Brittany in August 1944. South had never heard of Earl Rudder; he was not on a first-name basis with his battalion commander, whom he knew as Col. James E. "Big Jim" Rudder. Only after South arrived in College Station did he realize that he was there to investigate his old commander. Since Rudder refused to deal with the committee, South made a private appointment to see him in his office.[202]

The date was April 21, 1967—the traditional Muster Day for all Aggies—and Rudder had a full schedule from morning into the night. But his secretary, Nelda Rowell, recognized South's connection to Rudder and squeezed him in at 10:45 AM as a "personal friend" between a visiting general and a budget conference. After Rudder warmly greeted South with a bear hug, they did not talk about old times but about the Gibbs case for thirty minutes straight before Rudder broke it off for his next appointment. In that half hour Rudder convinced South that Gibbs had repeatedly exhibited character flaws that made him unfit to serve on the A&M faculty. When South informed the AAUP committee about meeting with Rudder, the chairman, a law professor at the University of Arizona, told him that he had compromised their work, that he could not be objective, and that he should resign and go home, which he did.[203]

Within a week after the AAUP committee left the campus, the A&M Board of Directors discussed the Gibbs case in a closed session, leaving no record except the notes of the board's secretary, Robert G. Cherry. After Rudder briefed the members "on recent developments," the board "confirmed that it would not compromise its authority" over employees and that "censureship is to be avoided."[204] The clear statement about avoiding censureship probably explains why Gibbs was kept on the payroll for another eight months. Rudder was still trying to avoid the reprimand, but the dispute was irreconcilable.

In April 1968 the members of the AAUP voted to censure Texas A&M. In the run-up to the AAUP vote, Rudder was not spared the negative publicity that he detested. Headlines in major Texas dailies read: "Censure of University Possible: Academic Freedom at A&M Questioned" and "Texas A&M Censure Predicted over Dismissal of Dr. Gibbs." Even the *Battalion*, exercising newly granted freedoms, carried an article headlined, "A&M Faces AAUP Censure for Handling of Gibbs' Case: Krise Says List Not 'Place To

Rudder upon retirement from the U.S. Army Reserve on July 12, 1967, after thirty-five years of service, newly decorated with the Legion of Merit. President Johnson also awarded Rudder the Army Distinguished Service Medal for his command of the 90th Infantry Division, USAR, December 1954 to June 1967. (Courtesy of Nelda Green)

Be.'" (George Krise was chairman of A&M's AAUP chapter.) The A&M directors finally terminated Gibbs's employment in January 1969, more than three years after his salary line had been removed from the budget.[205]

Texas A&M was one of fifty-one institutions on the AAUP's censured list. Six were in Texas, the most of any state, including the University of Texas of the Permian Basin. Not until 1982 was A&M removed from the censured list. Two questions remain about AAUP's censuring of Texas A&M: What damage was done, and could Rudder have avoided it? It was embarrassing, but it probably did not significantly affect Rudder's A&M goals. He was trying to build an institution emphasizing science and engineering rather than arts and humanities. He hired scientists whose inquiries are normally objective—discovering and applying knowledge about the physical world—rather than describing and debating human behavior and thought. The AAUP censure could have been devastating if he had been molding a liberal arts college and recruiting a faculty to teach political science, philosophy, and literature. But his priority was hustling federal R&D contracts and hiring faculty to implement them and teach, which depended on the quality of A&M's laboratories and the ability of investigators in charge of the projects.

In hypothetical terms Rudder could have avoided the Gibbs scandal and AAUP censureship, but in practical terms it seems unlikely. He was transforming Texas A&M where its needs for modernization were paramount: new degree programs, research projects, and facilities as well as the elimination of the "virtual albatrosses" of a segregated, all-male, military college. He focused on correcting those deficiencies because they blocked A&M's progression to the upper ranks of American universities. Refining internal personnel procedures was left to others, but it is improbable that he, or those around him, recognized that A&M was deficient, because most colleges and universities were similarly at fault.

Another factor against an appropriate internal resolution of the Gibbs case was A&M's heritage of decision making heavily concentrated in the president rather than delegated to others with authority to act and technocrats to help them comply with increasing governmental regulations. Added to that was Rudder's insistence on having a bare minimum of administrators to help him. Except for secretaries and an aide, the president's office had virtually no staff.

By comparison, the army division that he commanded had an elaborate and highly differentiated line and staff organization. He declined to create a similar organization for an increasingly large and complex university. If he recognized that A&M needed more staff, his frugality precluded him from adding positions to the budget, which was self-defeating in the long term. His frugality was not a factor in the 90th Infantry Division, because the army both prescribed and provided the administrative organization.

He and most of his contemporaries in academic administration conducted official business on a personal basis, guided by thin policy manuals, if any, in comparison to those that came a few years later, largely as a result of state and federal requirements. Thomas D. Cherry, his director of business affairs, once retained a consultant to prepare an organization chart for A&M to be included in a budding policies and procedures manual. When the consultant showed Rudder the organization chart, he reached across the table, tore it up, and threw it in a trashcan. Unlike his attitude while on active duty with the army, he objected to the implication that he could only deal with individuals and issues at Texas A&M through a hierarchy of subordinates.[206]

Such was the management style that men of Rudder's generation and earlier knew—how they functioned as executives over large organizations without review of their decisions, before and after, by MBAs, CPAs, lawyers, and human resource specialists. That's how he did it in the General Land Office and at Texas A&M. He was an extraordinary leader who made many tough decisions, and most of them were right.

THE SIXTIES

The assassination of President Kennedy had a latent and immeasurable impact on the period of unrest in the decade of the sixties. JFK's death did not precipitate the sixties but it seemed like it did. Challenges to the old order— to authority figures, traditions, laws, and lifestyle restrictions—increased in frequency, size, and intensity. Much of the initiative for these challenges occurred on university campuses, where students organized protest demonstrations to express their opposition on two overriding issues: the Vietnam War and racial discrimination. The demonstrations were exacerbated by President Johnson's conduct of the Vietnam War. As more and more young men were drafted and sent to Vietnam, the protests increased, and their leaders challenged the policies of universities, whose presidents symbolized and embodied institutional authority. By speaking out and condemning the disorders of the sixties, Rudder distinguished himself among university presidents across the nation.

On some campuses, demonstrations were violent, property was damaged, and in a few instances demonstrators were injured, even killed. People became polarized over the war and civil rights. They were further antagonized and divided by the unruly demonstrations and police reactions. Regardless of what Rudder thought about the substance of the issues, he was profoundly repelled by the protesters' disrespect for authority, law, and order. And the fact that the protesters were mostly university students assured that he would take action. Had he not reacted so vigorously, he would have lacked the very qualities for which he was so widely admired.

There were hints even in the late 1950s of coming confrontations over racial segregation. Two signal events were the Montgomery bus boycott (1955–56) to oppose racial segregation on the city's public transit system and President Eisenhower's use of regular army troops to protect African

American children during the integration of Little Rock's Central High School (1957). We cannot be sure of what Rudder thought about these episodes, but we do know that he was not inclined to criticize Eisenhower. Years after Eisenhower left office, Rudder cited him to students as a model of leadership.

The triggering event for college students to become involved in the civil rights movement occurred on February 1, 1960, when four black male students staged a "sit-in" in the Woolworth's store in Greensboro, North Carolina. They sat at a lunch counter that by state law was only for whites and asked a white waitress for a cup of coffee. She refused to serve them, but they did not leave as blacks ordinarily did. Instead, they remained seated, and the police declined to intervene as long as they were peaceful, which they were, as well as quiet and respectful. This act of nonviolent defiance of the law and social custom defined the sit-in as a form of civil disobedience that students would use to protest segregation and to oppose the Vietnam War and the policies of many universities, but not Texas A&M.

Rudder condemned civil disobedience of all forms and prohibited any manifestation at Texas A&M. In his usual forthright style, he declared that "civil disobedience, however righteously disguised, must be stopped. When we are free to choose which laws will be obeyed and which will be violated, we have no system of laws." One must wonder if an Aggie history professor dared suggest that the Boston Tea Party was an act of civil disobedience and that the women's suffrage movement had depended on it. Whatever the cause or nature of a campus demonstration, Rudder considered it a "rebellion against the authority of the college administration." That was his statement in 1966 in speaking to a faculty meeting from prepared notes. However, the revolutionary sixties sensitized him (as they did many thoughtful adults) to imperfections in American society. Three years later he could say to an audience of high school students and their parents, "Those who suffer from injustice have the right to protest." He did not say how, only that they should not "foment disorder, disrespect for the law, and violence."[207]

The second day of the Greensboro sit-ins established the pattern for the movement when more students joined in and went to lunch counters in other retail stores. Sit-ins quickly spread to fifteen cities in nine states. In each place a group of students would go to a segregated cafe or lunch counter and ask to be served. If they were, they'd move on to the next. If they were not, they would not move until they had been. If they were arrested, they did not resist, and a new group would take their place. And if that group was arrested, another would take their place. Then students above the Mason-Dixon Line began picketing local branches of national chain stores such as Woolworth's,

Kress, and Sears that were integrated in the North but segregated in the South. That summer (1960), northern students, white and black, went to the Deep South to work in the burgeoning civil rights movement.

When students at the University of Michigan returned north in the fall of 1960, they organized the Students for Democratic Society (SDS), composed mostly of white college students. The founders of the SDS envisioned it as an ideological crusade to "battle against racism, war, and policies of oppressive institutions," however construed by the protesters. When President Johnson expanded the war in Vietnam, the SDS organized protest demonstrations and became the primary vehicle of student opposition. Eventually, more than 250 universities had an SDS chapter, but not Texas A&M.[208]

Most student demonstrations against universities were motivated by objections to three institutional policies: conducting research for the Department of Defense, permitting the Central Intelligence Agency to recruit on campus, and providing information that the U.S. Selective Service System used to decide which men to call up for military service. As more and more students were drafted and sent to Vietnam, conscription became the most powerful motivator of antiwar sentiments on university campuses. This was reprehensible to Rudder. In speeches he cited three reasons for supporting President Johnson's war policy: he was the elected commander in chief, he had the "nation's welfare in mind in establishing policy," and he had the "best information available in making his decisions."[209]

The potential for SDS-inspired disruptions to create turmoil on a campus was made evident in a series of escalating demonstrations at the University of Wisconsin–Madison in 1967 and 1968. A group of students protesting the university's cooperation with the U.S. Selective Service took over a building and held it for several days. Then students staged a sit-in that blocked access to a building where the Dow Chemical Company, which manufactured napalm used in the Vietnam War, was interviewing prospective new employees. When police tried to remove them, a riot broke out in which seventy-four students were reportedly injured. Thousands of students boycotted classes.

Later, when African American students asked the Wisconsin administration for more black studies courses, the administration responded positively by forming a committee on race relations, adding the courses, and expanding efforts to recruit minority students. The motivation may have been altruistic, but it was perceived as a weakness. White students took cues from black students and confronted the faculty, demanding an equal voice in grading, curriculum, and decisions about granting tenure to faculty. Black students began boycotting classes, and white students joined in, which led to a mass protest involving up to eight thousand demonstrators. The protests turned violent with considerable property damage. A major goal of the demonstrators was to shut down the University of Wisconsin, and they failed only when the National Guard was called out to maintain order. But the lesson that many presidents took from the incident was that giving in to any request or demand, however reasonable it seemed, could be perceived as weakness and lead to more difficulties.

Rudder's Stance

As a rational person, Rudder understood the injustice of racial discrimination. Reflective, educated men who saw him often during the war believed his values were humanely affected by the unspeakable cruelty of racism in Nazi Germany. He went to a slave labor camp where thirty-five hundred men, women, and children, mostly of Slavic origin, had taken refuge in a tunnel. For several weeks he was responsible for thousands of displaced persons. "Our big problem," he told Chick, "is to gather up the displaced Russians, Italians, Poles and others so they can be returned to their homes. It is unbelievable that so many were brought in for slave labor." He had also seen that American troops in combat could rely on one another regardless of race. To his staff at A&M, he confided that he had seen the blood of black men and white men and it was all the same. In 1958, when he assumed command of the mostly volunteer army reserve 90th Infantry Division, he had encouraged the recruitment of African Americans in contrast to his predecessor's indifference.[210]

Having planned the admission of A&M's first black students, perhaps Rudder thought he had done what should be expected of him. In any case, he did not fully comprehend the complaints of African American students about their experiences on the A&M campus. It may be more accurate to say that he did not act on their complaints because he was uncertain about what to do. He was, as Oliver Sadberry said, "a product of his times," and there was nothing in his background that enabled him to see the campus environment as they saw it. They felt prejudices and slights that he could not. In his whole life, he had never experienced, even momentarily, the discomfort and sense of vulnerability that comes with being in a very small minority of any kind.

The black students weighed the overwhelming numerical and political imbalance between themselves and white students, while Rudder believed they should put such matters out of their minds and concentrate on preparing for the future by studying and making good grades. For him, the college experience was not to foment social change but to pursue a profession. That had been his attitude as a student. Wasn't the same approach right for them?

His inability to resolve the difficulties of African American students was his greatest frustration and probably the biggest disappointment of his presidency. Clearly, it evoked the most tension and worry.

Taken literally, his insistence that African American students should concentrate on their courses without regard to the social revolution sweeping the nation was contrary to their view of themselves as part of the historic crusade for Americans to live up to the ideals of the Constitution. They wanted a campus rally to show support for freedom marches and greater rallies elsewhere. Rudder opposed demonstrations of any kind. Until the murder of Martin Luther King by a white man on April 4, 1968, Rudder's concern was likely for no more than the possibility of Greensboro-style sit-ins.

King's death undermined the confidence of civil rights leaders in non-violence as their primary method, and black students became more militant. On many campuses they petitioned for recognition of an organization of their own and for courses on their history, culture, and literature. Rudder's reaction was similar to many university presidents, white or black; he was reluctant to agree to any request, especially if was posed as a nonnegotiable demand, however reasonable, for fear that it would lead to more extreme demands. A few months after King's murder, black students brandishing weapons at Cornell University occupied the student union building to protest the administration's delay in approving a black studies program. The Cornell incident confirmed a radical escalation of campus confrontations, which Rudder would soon have reason to fear at A&M.

On one occasion, he met in his office for three hours with fifteen African American students who were not happy with their experience in Aggieland. Their spokesman, Allen Giles, described their frustration with him. "Our hang-up was that the president refused to acknowledge that we had problems. Instead he was interested in the 'educational process,' which he implied did not include social transgressions." Few white people understood the "social inequity" that students told Rudder was one of their difficulties. In the soft-spoken words of Oliver Sadberry four decades later, "It meant the separateness we felt on the campus. We were basically ostracized without a sense of belonging. To talk about being ostracized is no big deal but to live it is a big deal. In class, there was always an empty seat by me. That changed over time, and the first time someone said 'Howdy' [a traditional Aggie greeting] to me, I didn't know what to do."[211]

When Rudder was asked about the students' dissatisfaction with their discussion, he replied, "If there is anything in the way of their education, I'll remove it."[212] What was in the way was the lack of a special sense of belonging that the black students could see was the essence of being an Aggie.

White students might brush off racist remarks, but black students took them seriously. Regardless of efforts on the campus to make them feel welcome, elsewhere they faced discrimination and heard racial slurs in cafes, taverns, and business houses that were external to the university.

Rudder's worries became more concrete on May 2, 1969, when a group of students referring to themselves as members of the Afro-American Society presented eight demands (later rephrased as requests) that ranged from recognition of their organization to more African American literature in the library, more about "black men" in history courses, and the hiring of a black counselor "as an intercessor between black students and the administration." That same night three students, one allegedly an SDS member, were found in the Administration Building (later named the Williams Building) about midnight. Although they were initially accused of burglary, their statement that they had entered through an unlocked door was later accepted.[213]

Three days later the Board of Directors held a special meeting in Dallas to reject the demands of the black students and to issue a manifesto stating that it would not tolerate or consider changes "thrust upon this institution under the ugly veil of threat or demand."[214] The directors' emphatic rejection was typical of governing boards and ironic because by the midseventies most universities had implemented the requests that black students made in the threatening atmosphere of the sixties.

Tensions were rising at a time Rudder was beginning to have serious health problems. Only a few days later, he had even more to worry about when a student, presumably African American, submitted an essay in an English composition course asserting, apparently based on facts, that "a riot can occur if there are the necessary attitudes, certain conditions, and agitators. Agitators could easily come to A&M from the SDS and the Black Panthers." More threatening was this statement: "At A&M, there is an Afro-American group. The leader has several weapons on campus as do many other students. Some claim they have weapons off campus and can get weapons, including machine guns, from Houston. Negroes organized at Cornell University and captured a building with the use of numerous rifles."[215]

The Wisconsin and Cornell experiences were cause for concern. "Rudder was greatly disturbed about what SDS was doing on other campuses," said his former aide, Ed Cooper. "He could not bear the thought of riots and blocking entrances to buildings. He had a dreadful fear of anything like that happening here, and he took it on himself to find out who were the leaders of SDS in Texas."[216] One of his methods was to capitalize on information collected covertly by the army and the FBI, usually called counterintelligence.

The local office of the FBI, headed by agent Bob Wiatt, was actually on the A&M campus. Wiatt and Rudder had both arrived at A&M in 1958 and quickly gained each other's confidence. In the 1960s they collaborated to keep SDS organizers away. Wiatt described his cooperation with Rudder: "I shared with the General information that I was privy to so he could be forewarned about any matter of concern that might happen on the campus, and he did the same with me. I dealt directly with him and his close associates. He was not out to stifle free speech. His only concern was the wellbeing of the students and preventing disruption or destruction. Some of the agitators we had coming here were not kids."[217]

In one case Rudder learned that an "SDS ring leader" had enrolled at A&M and had him watched. After a few months there was no disruption, but Rudder had reports that the student was trying to stir up unrest and called him to his office. Cooper remembered that when the young man came in, Rudder said to him, essentially: "I know who you are, where you're from, and what you stand for. If you cause the kind of problems that are occurring on other campuses, you will have to fight me personally." "That boy," Cooper recalled, "came out of the office pale as paper and we never had a problem."[218]

Shortly after he left the Board of Directors in 1973, H. C. Heldenfels told David Chapman how Rudder and Wiatt capitalized on their counterintelligence information. "Rudder would let us know," Heldenfels recalled, "that a certain agitator had caught a bus and was headed our way. They'd pick him up at the bus station in Bryan and search him to see if he had a weapon. This was one way that General Rudder saw to it that we had security at all times." An SDS organizer confronted in the bus station by a Rudder aide was told to go home for his own safety. "If you burn an American flag in College Station, someone will kill you."[219] Thus intimidated, potential agitators might take the next coach to Houston, Dallas, or Austin, the site of a vibrant SDS chapter and the home of an underground newspaper, *The Rag.*

On many university campuses students produced and distributed underground newspapers to raise awareness of issues. At least three such mimeographed tabloids—*Paranoia, The Screw,* and *Evolution*—circulated at Texas A&M in the year following the King assassination. Their columns objected to the draft and the Vietnam War, disparaged the administration's ban on political clubs, alleged that the Corps of Cadets was racist (citing the prevalence of Confederate flags in dorms) and sexist (lack of women members) and satirized Rudder's belittling of professors with beards. He had always objected to hairy faces but opened himself to ridicule by telling a group, when asked about professors with beards, "I think we hired the wrong professor. A prof who wears a beard in the classroom is just trying to substitute a beard for knowledge."[220] His quip was widely publicized in newspapers.

On this issue Rudder's sentiments were in tune with A&M students, civilian or military, who petitioned for enforcement of institutional rules forbidding beards and requiring socks with shoes and a "proper haircut." Joe Buser, Rudder's special assistant, used his boss's words in letters to parents concerned about underground newspapers, saying that their influence was "overwhelmingly rejected" by the students and "young men have come to Texas A&M down through the years to learn about this world before they set about to change it."[221]

Rudder permitted no political clubs and partisan political activity on the A&M campus—unlike the situation at almost every other university in America. He probably had two reasons, although he did not summarize them in this way: one was his belief that they detracted from scholarly pursuits, and the other was his determination to avoid disruptions of any kind that might be inspired by impassioned partisan speeches.

In the spring of 1968, students in favor of Eugene McCarthy's presidential bid were denied a table in the Memorial Student Center to collect signatures. The *Battalion* editorialized that Rudder violated his own rule by holding a dinner on campus in honor of Congressman Teague. And a student's letter to the editor criticized Rudder's legal rationale that partisan political activities on the campus of a public university were contrary to state law, pointing out that other institutions had permitted them. So while other universities experienced the burning of draft cards and bras and had teach-ins or sit-ins, there were not even political clubs at Texas A&M.

In affirming his "control over the university," Rudder told the faculty that "real freedom can exist only when there is order and reason." He believed justice could be achieved only with order, which he connected to his oft-stated belief in a Superior Being. In that vein he told a meeting of Future Farmers of America at A&M that "spiritual problems are the basic reasons for student distrust and revolt. . . . If you don't believe in a being greater than yourselves that brings order into our world, then you are missing out on a great experience."[222]

With few exceptions, students at Texas A&M supported Rudder in maintaining a calm campus, and, unlike many of his counterparts, he was not seriously challenged to yield on his authority. Day-to-day life at Texas A&M continued mostly as in the past—relatively quiet and stable in comparison to that at other universities. With A&M's strong military traditions and location away from an urban area, Rudder had a far less contentious environment than did his counterparts in Morningside Heights or the Bay Area or even Austin. Although he was greatly concerned about the disturbances on other campuses, Rudder remained focused on his goal of advancing Texas A&M as a high-quality research university.

The year 1967 seemed the worst possible with riots, looting, and arson in several cities, notably Detroit, Buffalo, Milwaukee, Oakland, and Washington. Criticism of the Johnson administration grew more widespread and strident because of the increasing number of Americans killed in Vietnam, which rose from a monthly average of 172 during 1965 to an average of 770 a month in 1967. But 1968 was the turning point for the decade. Martin Luther King and Bobby Kennedy were assassinated, North Vietnam launched the Tet Offensive, American involvement in Vietnam began to decline, LBJ decided not to seek reelection, and many Americans were radicalized by police conduct during the massive demonstrations that accompanied the Democratic Party's convention in Chicago.

After SDS students at Columbia University occupied several buildings for days, J. Edgar Hoover, director of the FBI, warned that the SDS used college dissidents to incite campus disorders "under the guise of academic freedom and freedom of speech when their real motive was confrontation with established authority to provoke disorder." In a speech two weeks later, Rudder warned potential agitators that "Texas A&M University will not submit to tyranny, regardless of its guise. There will be no Columbia, no Berkeley here. We will maintain a healthy environment for education, a climate that fosters the free exchange of ideas in the orderly democratic way that has its roots in the constitution of the United States."[223]

His vivid language made news across the nation, and he made another speech on the same topic. "We must meet their power with power if they threaten our society," he said. "I would use whatever force I could command to keep the educational processes at A&M continuing on an orderly basis. The dissidents will have a hell of a fight, and this pot-bellied president will be up in the front ranks leading it." The speech was widely quoted, and within a week Rudder had letters urging him to run for governor. "Dear General," one read. "Anytime you want to run for governor, I'll campaign for you full time, no charge."[224]

One of many who took note of Rudder's defiance was Leon Jaworski, soon to be president of the American Bar Association and later the famed Watergate prosecutor. As a war crimes prosecutor in Germany immediately after the war, he had studied the violent disorders involving the Hitler Youth that helped Hitler come to power in 1933. He saw parallels between the Hitler Youth and SDS demands on university administrations. Speaking before lawyers in Memphis, Tennessee, Jaworski singled out Rudder for special praise that was cited in newspapers throughout the nation. "Today in America," he said, "the reasonable and peaceful majority are reluctant to take a stand against the lawless minority." Quoting from Rudder's speeches, Jaworski told his audience, "Earl Rudder is a courageous man who loves his country." Then he asked: "Is Earl Rudder to be alone or are others to join him in one hell of a fight to preserve our democratic institutions?"[225]

SILVER TAPS

The decline of Rudder's health occurred so gradually that even his wife did not recognize it until she saw him in the film *Ten Men Went to War*, shot for British television in Normandy in April 1969. "I could tell," she said, "that something was wrong." He was significantly overweight, and she noticed that he became short of breath just rambling around Pointe du Hoc.[226]

The trip to France, with a nostalgic stopover in London to stay at the Savoy Hotel, was only one in a relentless travel schedule during the last full year of his life that took him away from home for seventy-seven nights. With Lyndon Johnson no longer in the White House, Rudder made only three trips to Washington, but then he overcompensated with the time he spent in Austin. The first five months of the odd-numbered years are always taxing for presidents of Texas public universities, because the state legislature convenes and decides how much money their institutions can spend for the next two years. He made thirteen trips to Austin in the spring of 1969 for presentations before legislative committees, which were more trying because he no longer had an ally in the governor—quite the opposite, in fact.

John Connally had declined to run for reelection and was succeeded in January 1969 by Preston Smith, whose personal agenda was elevating not Texas A&M but its archrival, Texas Tech University, even at the expense of A&M. Rumors were rife that Smith might attempt to transfer A&M's college of veterinary medicine to Texas Tech, or duplicate it, which would inevitably detract resources from A&M's school. When Wofford Cain, one of Connally's appointees to A&M's Board of Directors, came out for Smith in the election, Connally asked, "Wofford, what are you going to do if Preston tries to move the vet school to Lubbock?" Cain blushed and did not answer.[227]

However, in the final hours of his gubernatorial tenure, Connally thwarted Smith and did one last favor for A&M and Rudder by reappointing three progressive and devoted members to the Board of Directors: Albert Beutel, Ford Albritton, and Pete Peterson. In appointing them, Connally usurped the traditional prerogative of an incoming governor and colluded with Rudder in doing it. Rudder dropped a hint in his office that Governor Connally had asked if making the reappointments was a good idea. He had agreed that it was, and at the next closed-door meeting with the directors, Rudder "expressed his gratification" for Connally's final favor.[228]

To many men of Rudder's background, disclosing a health problem was a sign of weakness. Such men were reluctant to talk about their frailties, even to a physician. That Rudder's health was a forbidden topic was made clear to Wayne Hall not long after he became a member of Rudder's administrative team. Noticing that Rudder appeared pale, he casually asked, "Are you feeling well?" Rudder glared back and paused before saying, "There's nothing wrong with me, and I don't know why you ask." Rudder retained the self-image of an athlete and the appetite that went with it, although he had long been sedentary. If he sensed trouble with his health, he did not complain. "He was a master stoic," Wayne Hall thought.[229]

His time away from home in 1969 included one-week stays in two cities with well-known hospitals—Scott & White Clinic in Temple, Texas, in April and the Ochsner Clinic in New Orleans in July, where he told physicians about pains in his shoulder, neck, and occasional generalized headaches. The New Orleans doctors diagnosed "hypertension, gout, obesity, and muscle spasms." His attending physician noted that the "gout and elevated blood pressure were of several years duration."[230] Follow-up efforts, if any, to alleviate these symptoms cannot be determined.

In May he checked into a hospital in Bryan for several days, only to leave for a stressful meeting with African American students about race relations and to fly to Dallas for a special meeting of the Board of Directors on the same subject. Shortly after he left the hospital, he flew to the Dominican Republic to inspect A&M extension projects. Returning home at midnight, he left at seven the next morning for Calgary on business related to funding for A&M by the Superior Oil Company.

His last trip outside of Texas was to Chicago with Director Ford Albritton and John Lindsey, A&M's generous former student. They flew in Albritton's plane to discuss a partnership with executives of the J. Walter Thompson public relations firm to improve A&M's image. Lindsey used the time to persuade Rudder to hire an executive vice president to relieve him of the ceaseless burdens he had carried for a dozen years.

"Earl," said Albritton over cocktails at thirty thousand feet, "Heaven forbid, but if something should happen to you, you have no second in command and we know of no one to come in and take your place. That's something you should think about." Rudder replied that he had been thinking about Jack Williams, formerly Texas commissioner of higher education and currently vice president of the University of Tennessee. Williams—a history Ph.D.

with a Phi Beta Kappa key—would be another kind of leader for A&M. But he was also in the Rudder mold as a decorated Marine Corps officer with the scars of two Japanese bullets from Saipan as evidence.[231]

Rudder's health declined before periodic health examinations were a prevalent practice. Most people only went to a doctor when they were sick or injured. And not until 1968 did Kenneth H. Cooper publish his famous book *Aerobics,* which revolutionized thinking about physical fitness. There is no comparative baseline data for Rudder's blood chemistry and pressure; recommended upper limits then were much higher than they would be twenty years later. Since the risks of his illness were not recognized in the months preceding his death, when the end came, it seemed sudden.

On January 29, 1970, he developed a severe headache at his home on the A&M campus and was taken to Saint Joseph Hospital in Bryan, where he was diagnosed as suffering from a heart ailment. The next day he was taken to Saint Luke's Episcopal Hospital in Houston's Texas Medical Center, where the diagnosis was changed to cerebral hemorrhage. He was then transferred to Methodist Hospital in the same medical complex for surgery to remove a clot in the brain; his condition was listed as serious but not critical.

Dr. Denton Cooley, the famed cardiovascular surgeon, was a friend of the Rudder family and visited him in Methodist Hospital's intensive care unit. Margaret Rudder told Cooley, "If Earl's problem is anything in your area, I want you to take care of it." On the day after Rudder's brain surgery, Cooley asked her permission to operate to stop stomach bleeding brought on by a stress ulcer. When she asked if he could withstand another surgery, Cooley explained, "You don't have any choice. You either operate or he bleeds to death." So she consented. Since Cooley practiced in Saint Luke's rather than Methodist, Rudder was transferred between the two hospitals through a tunnel on a rolling stretcher. On the way, Cooley's humor momentarily lifted the family from their distress. "Dr. Cooley was in the lead," Margaret Rudder remembered, "with five doctors around the bed. Two young men were guiding the bed and several nurses were minding all of those tubes. The family troops were right behind them and it was a tense situation. Then, Dr. Cooley looked over his shoulder said, 'All we need now is the Aggie Band.'"[232]

Earl underwent two more surgeries to control the stomach bleeding. He remained in the hospital, and his condition was upgraded to "satisfactory." On February 24 his doctors told Tony Heldenfels that he had suffered no brain damage. Barring unfavorable changes, Heldenfels understood he could be home by the middle of March. But Rudder did not improve, and on March 22 he was diagnosed with a kidney infection. As his condition deteriorated, his blood pressure became irregular. The next day his condition was considered critical, and he died that afternoon, Monday, March 23, at 5:10 P.M. The immediate cause was attributed to a "circulatory collapse brought on by a kidney infection."[233]

Texas A&M then set about venerating its fallen leader in the manner of a university abundantly endowed with military and academic traditions. The east entrance to the campus was lined with more than a hundred American flags at half mast. On the morning after his death, an estimated ten thousand people attended the flag-lowering ceremony in the center of the campus. They returned that evening for the traditional Silver Taps salute for fallen Aggies. On Wednesday morning the homage continued as his body lay in the rotunda of the Administration Building flanked by an honor guard from the Ross Volunteers, an elite Aggie military society, in dress whites as some three thousand people shuffled past his flag-draped coffin. Col. Jim H. McCoy, commandant of the Corps, was in charge of the military protocol—the same Jim McCoy who Rudder had first met on the heights above the Our River in Luxembourg looking into Germany that December morning a quarter-century before.

Shortly before two o'clock, students escorted Rudder for the last time to G. Rollie White Coliseum for a memorial service attended by five thousand mourners, including former president and Mrs. Johnson; it was LBJ's first public appearance since suffering a heart ailment only a month earlier. He told the reporters that Rudder's wartime heroism was "only a prelude to his contribution in peace as an educator, public official, and concerned citizen." Members of the A&M Board of Directors were there along with University of Texas regents, whose chairman, Frank C. Erwin Jr., extolled Rudder with a widely quoted compliment that "We shall not see his likes again soon."[234]

Conducted by civilian pastors, the memorial service was rich in U.S. Army symbolism: a floral replica of the 90th Division's famous TO—Texas' Own—patch and large displays of red, white, and blue flowers. Rudder's former pastor, the Rev. James B. Argue, came from Little Rock to eulogize him "as a man of love. He loved this great university, his country, and was the perfect example of the citizen-soldier." Nelda Rowell, Rudder's secretary, made notes of a prayer that captured her sense of him: "He came from the heart of America, geographically and spiritually—strong, courageous, honest, compassionate—one of the greatest men we've seen in our day."[235]

Rudder's wartime comrades presented two flags, the banner of the French province of Normandy and the ensign of the Rangers, to commemorate his legendary leadership of the 2nd Ranger Battalion. "We know of no man who has worn the mantles of leadership and of humility so well at the same time," Ranger William Henderson told the crowded coliseum. Robert L. Boone,

The funeral bier of James Earl Rudder at Texas A&M University, March 25, 1970. The honor guard was formed from the Ross Volunteers, a select group of students in the Corps of Cadets. (Courtesy of Margaret Rudder)

director of A&M's Singing Cadets, sang Earl's favorite hymn, "A Charge to Keep." The service concluded with the singing of "The Spirit of Aggieland" by the Singing Cadets.[236]

He could have been buried in Arlington National Cemetery with other heroes of America's wars or with renowned public servants in the Texas State Cemetery. But Margaret Rudder—escorted by Ed Cooper, Dick Bernard, and Maj. Edmond S. Solymosy, McCoy's assistant and A&M graduate of 1960—chose his, and her, last resting place in the city cemetery of College Station, not far from the campus. Eight students, four uniformed cadets and four in dark suits, carried his coffin to the grave. A squad from the Ross Volunteers, the cadet honor guard, fired a twenty-one-gun salute at the conclusion of the ceremonies as four buglers from the Aggie Band played "Silver Taps."[237]

As the mourners went their separate ways, Nelda Rowell noticed thirteen middle-aged men standing together. They were U.S. Army Rangers from the war, eight of the 2nd Ranger Battalion, three decorated with the Distinguished Service Cross on Rudder's recommendation: Len Lomell from New Jersey, Ralph Goranson from Ohio, and Bob Edlin, his fair-headed boy from Corpus Christi, Texas. Reluctant to part with each other and from their old commander, they were curious about his comings and goings as a university president and the final days of his life.

Nelda led them on their last patrol, a search for the man he became after the perils they had shared. They went to his office and sat at a table, not morbid but serious, remembering that they were better together under him than any one of them had been before. Nelda gave them photographs of Rudder in academic regalia and copies of recent newspaper articles about him. Lomell had the crisp words of an epitaph: "He understood how to be a good citizen and its importance. He was reared properly, educated, and he worked hard. He was fair-minded and honorable. He could be trusted and all men believed in him."[238]

On the credenza behind his desk, flanked by the state and national flags, they recognized a small bust of Lyndon Johnson and photographs of two generals: Omar Bradley and Norman Cota. In a letter ten months before, Rudder had reminded the Rangers of their unique bond forged in war, that "an outsider cannot comprehend" and are "understood only by those of us who have had this privileged experience." The bond had been the difference between defeat and victory. Soldiers once, they could say goodbye to comrades who died before their time and keep their memories evermore.

NOTES

PROLOGUE

1. Thomas M. DeFrank, commencement address, Texas A&M University, May 11, 2007, copy in the possession of the author; Thomas M. DeFrank, telephone interview with the author, January 12, 2009.

CHAPTER 1. EDEN, TEXAS

1. *Eden Echo,* Friday, July 29, 1921. The public timetable for the Santa Fe Railroad dated March 1, 1921, shows the scheduled arrival time in Eden as 5:20 PM on train number 53. A copy is in the Railroad and Heritage Museum, Temple, Texas.

2. *Texas Almanac and State Industrial Guide, 1926* (Dallas: A. H. Belo, 1926), 241. According to this source, the population of Eden in 1920 was 593.

3. "John Lapp's Body Returns," *Eden Echo,* Friday, July 29, 1921.

4. *San Angelo Standard-Times,* July 29, 1921; "The Ministry of Pastor Ludwig Karcher: History of Lutheran Church, Eden, Texas, 1916–1966," collection of Margaret Loveless, Eden, Texas, and copy in the possession of the author. Karcher wrote in his diary that more than two thousand people attended the funeral of John Lapp.

5. Margaret Rose Loveless, interview with the author, September 17, 2004.

6. For an extensive discussion of the boundaries and influences of the Great American Desert, see W. Eugene Hollon, *The Great American Desert: Then and Now.*

7. The quotation about the fields of bluebonnets was made often by Mallie Jones, born in 1898, to her daughter, Clara Dobson, of San Angelo, Texas. Clara Dobson, telephone interview with the author, October 5, 2007.

8. *Eden Echo,* September 9, 1937; Ron Tyler et al., eds., *New Handbook of Texas* (Austin: Texas State Historical Association, 1996), 2:217, s.v. "Concho County," and Handbook of Texas Online, http://www.tshaonline.org/handbook/online/articles/CC/hcc21 .html (accessed July 2, 2010). McCall quote from Hazie Davis LeFevre, *Concho County History, 1858–1958.*

9. *Dallas Morning News,* January 9, 1955; quoted in the *Texas Aggie,* March 1955.

10. *San Angelo Standard-Times,* May 24, 1970.

11. *Eden Echo,* 1923 (month and day illegible).

12. LeFevre. *Concho County History,* 37.

13. Edward Earl Rudder, Sr., "Rudder Family Genealogy," copy in the possession of the author. The masculine form, "Francis," was the actual, if misspelled, spelling of the name given to the girl, Francis Jane Tyler Rudder.

14. Francis Tyler Rudder, "Widow's Application for Confederate Pension," January 14, 1925, Texas State Library and Archives.

15. *New Handbook of Texas,* 6:565–67, s.v "Trinity County," and Handbook of Texas Online, http://www.tshaonline.org/handbook/online/articles/TT/hct9.html (accessed July 2, 2010); Rudder, "Rudder Family Genealogy." Annie Clark (Powell) Rudder was born in 1871 and died in 1952.

16. Rudder, "Rudder Family Genealogy." In chronological order of birth, the children who lived to adulthood were Francis Simmie (1893), J.D. (1899), A.P. (1902), John (1905), James Earl (1910), and Marshall (1913). During April 8–10, 1905, Annie Francis Rudder gave birth to four children (quadruplets), of whom only John survived. Edward Earl Rudder Sr., son of Marshall Rudder and a student of his family's lineage, found no documents stating names for J.D. and A.P. other than their initials.

17. Petition filed by Annie C. Rudder, March 21, 1939, Records of Concho County Probate Court, 6:151, Estate of D. F. Rudder, deceased. D. F. Rudder died intestate.

18. "City upon a hill" is a phrase associated with John Winthrop's sermon "A Model of Christian Charity," given in 1630. The phrase is derived from the metaphor of Salt and Light in the Sermon on the Mount of Jesus given in the Gospel of Matthew. Winthrop warned the Puritan colonists of New England who were to found the Massachusetts Bay Colony that their new community would be a "city upon a hill" watched by the world.

19. Rudder, "Rudder Family Genealogy."

20. Thomas M. Cable, interview with the author, March 5, 2006. Cable is coauthor of *A History of the English Language,* the standard and most frequently quoted textbook in the field.

21. Evelyn Whitfield Hendricks, interviews with the author, August 14 and September 17, 2004. Evelyn Whitfield was born in Concho County in 1912 and has lived in or near Eden for her entire life. Two years younger than Earl Rudder, Hendricks was his fellow student at Eden High School, where she graduated in 1930. At the time of the interviews, Mrs. Hendricks possessed a remarkably lucid and detailed memory of the Rudder family and Eden during the 1920s. Stephens quoted in *San Angelo Standard-Times,* May 24, 1970.

22. *Texas Almanac, 1925* (Dallas: A. H. Belo, 1925), 202; Eden Village Council minutes, July 18, 1925, Book A, 137. Certain business houses had electric lights at an earlier date with electricity produced by small gasoline-powered generators.

23. Blu Bell Maddox, telephone interview with the author, September 11, 2004.

24. In 1984 the National Rural Electric Cooperative Association published a book whose title, *The Next Greatest Thing,* was adapted from this anecdote, which may have originated in east Tennessee in the 1940s.

25. William Green, M.D., interview with the author, August 14, 2004; this informa-

tion is also the author's personal knowledge from boyhood in the Texas Hill Country in the 1940s.

26. Hendricks, interview with the author, August 14, 2004.

27. Maddox, telephone interview, September 11, 2004.

28. Ibid.

29. Earl Rudder to his wife, June 1, 1944, copy in the possession of the author, courtesy of Margaret Rudder.

30. There have been three army posts in Texas called Camp Bowie in honor of James Bowie, a hero of the Alamo. The first was established in Jackson County for the Army of the Republic of Texas in 1837; the second, to which the text refers, near Fort Worth in 1917; and the third, near Brownwood in 1940.

31. *New Handbook of Texas,* 2:1111, s.v. "Fort McKavett," also available online at Handbook of Texas Online, http://www.tshaonline.org/handbook/online/articles/FF/qbf36 .html; and 2:1095, s.v. "Fort Concho," available online at http://www.tshaonline.org/hand book/online/articles/FF/qbf11.html (both accessed June 23, 2010).

32. Ben Cox, one year ahead of Earl Rudder at Eden High School, saved the materials from the civics class taught by Mr. LeFevre. Rudder was also taught by LeFevre, who created his own curriculum materials. Ben Cox passed the papers from the class to his daughter, Margaret Cox, and she made them available to the author.

33. Earl Rudder holographic speech notes for a conference of Texas A&M students on leadership, September 10, 1959, Personal and General Correspondence Papers (unprocessed) of James Earl Rudder, Cushing Memorial Library and Archives, Texas A&M University.

34. James Parton, *Air Force Spoken Here: General Ira Eaker and Command of the Air,* 21–22, 493. During World War II Eaker commanded the U.S. Eighth Air Force based in Britain, the largest assemblage of aircraft in history, and later took charge of the U.S. Fifteenth Air Force in the Mediterranean. "Eden High School Scores Again," *Eden Echo,* November 10, 1927.

35. *San Angelo Standard-Times,* August 30, 1945.

36. M. J. Green is the complete name given to the boy at birth. For information about class officers and favorites, see the Eden High School yearbook, the *Bulldog,* for 1926 and 1927.

37. *Bulldog,* 1927:47. In Earl Rudder's 1927 yearbook, John Miller wrote in red ink under a sketch of a bulldog, "Long live the Bulldog of E.H.S." Under his own full-page photograph as Most Popular Boy, he wrote "To the guy with the massive physique. The big, true, loyal and foolish—still cool and capable friend when necessity demands—Your best friend. Miller." See also R. W. Fogel et al., "Secular Changes in American and British Stature and Nutrition," *Journal of Interdisciplinary History* 14, no. 2 (Autumn, 1983): 462–63.

38. *San Angelo Standard-Times,* May 24, 1970.

39. *Bulldog,* 1926; Maddox, telephone interview, September 11, 2004.

40. *Bulldog,* 1926. The author of the note was identified as M. J. Green.

41. *100 Years of Texas High School Football,* 85. Helmets were not required until 1939, and shoulder pads became mandatory only in 1974.

42. Elmer H. Vermeer, "Pointe du Hoc, France: D-Day: June 6, 1944," typescript, no date, 11. A copy sent by Vermeer to Margaret Rudder is in the possession of the author.

43. *Bulldog,* 1926.

44. Ibid., 1927:11.

45. Ibid., 1926; the authors of these three notes were identified as Culver Johnson, Carl Pfluger, and Grady Smith.

46. Ibid.

47. Margaret Rudder, interview with the author, May 9, 2002; Rudder, "Rudder Family Genealogy," 150. Dee Forrest Rudder was born in Goliad County, Texas, on December 21, 1872, and died September 7, 1935, in Eden, Texas.

48. Hendricks, interview, September 17, 2004.

49. *San Angelo Standard-Times,* December 5, 1948; *Eden Echo,* September 6, 1959.

50. Parton, *Air Force Spoken Here,* 442.

51. Hendricks, interview, September 17, 2004.

CHAPTER 2. TARLETON COLLEGE

1. The John Tarleton Agricultural College, henceforth Tarleton College, was a lower-division branch of the Agricultural and Mechanical College of Texas. Unlike A&M, Tarleton enrolled women, but, like A&M, it required military training (ROTC) for men. Its athletic teams competed in football, basketball, and baseball against other junior colleges and the freshmen teams of four-year institutions, most often Abilene Christian College, Howard Payne College, Texas Christian University, and Southern Methodist University.

2. W. J. Wisdom, personal letter to Earl Rudder, July 15, 1959.

3. Athletic scholarships did not come into existence officially until 1945, when colleges and universities began subsidizing athletes, usually paying for all or part of their room, board, tuition, and incidental expenses.

4. The statement "We set the best training table in the state" was a familiar selling point by W. J. Wisdom to scholarship prospects, according to Jerry Flemmons, *Plowboys, Cowboys and Slanted Pigs,* 6.

5. C. Richard King, *The John Tarleton College Story: The Golden Days of Purple and White,* 208. Wisdom coached football for nine years, 1924–28 and 1932–35.

6. Christopher E. Guthrie, *John Tarleton and His Legacy: The History of Tarleton State University, 1899–1999,* 294–95. An undated copy of Ripley's "Believe It or Not" illustration is in the possession of the author.

7. Flemmons, *Plowboys, Cowboys and Slanted Pigs,* 3. The phenomenal winning streak in basketball occurred between 1934 and 1938.

8. Charles A. Lindbergh, *The Spirit of St. Louis,* 510.

9. *Bulletin of the John Tarleton Agricultural College* 10, no. 7 (March 15, 1927): 48, John Tarleton Agricultural College Collections, Dick Smith Library, Tarleton State University,

Stephenville, Texas. The 1927 catalog for the college gave the estimated expenses for the spring semester as $160.75. Tuition and fees were included in the estimate: $13.25 for the spring. Margaret Rudder, telephone interview with the author, June 9, 2002; Margaret Rudder, holographic speech notes for the dedication of the James Earl Rudder State Building, November 24, 1988; *Houston Post,* May 9, 1955, report of an interview with Earl Rudder in which he said that he "started out with $100 in his pocket. . . ."

10. Earl Rudder, letter to W. Doyle Graves, February 28, 1969.

11. *Texas Almanac, 1927* (Dallas: A. H. Belo, 1927)., map insert with legend for road condition.

12. *Grassburr* (yearbook), John Tarleton College, 1928:66, 76; 1929:78, John Tarleton Agricultural College Collections, Dick Smith Library, Tarleton State University.

13. Ibid., 1928, 44.

14. The characterization of Rudder as "just an ordinary boy" is attributed to Will Loveless by his daughter, Carolyn Moody. Rudder had worked on the Loveless ranch while in high school.

15. Quotes from Willie Tate, interview with the author, December 10, 2004. Of the 184 students in Tarleton's "senior" class of 1929, seventy-six, or 41 percent, were women, based on my count in the college yearbook, the *Grassburr.* In the college year 1929–30, thirty of the seventy-three instructors at Tarleton were women. "College of etiquette" from the *Fort Worth Press,* February 18, 1933, quoted in J. Rice Finley, "The History of John Tarleton College" (master's thesis, University of Texas, 1933), 63.

16. For the requirement to attend chapel, see the *Bulletin of the John Tarleton College,* 1928:34.

17. *Bulletin of the John Tarleton College,* 1928:31–32. Chambray is a fine lightweight fabric woven with white threads that run lengthwise across a fabric of another color. The sewing instructions for making the dress were: "The school uniform shall be a blue chambray dress made of Parkhill's Imperial Chambray No. 7588 [using] McCall's pattern No. 4017. . . . Make a straight belt of chambray . . . the collar of No. 60 white cambric. Sleeves . . . either long or elbow lengths . . . Four-inch hem . . . cloth shrunk before making."

18. *Bulletin of the John Tarleton College,* 1928:30.

19. John Tarleton Agricultural College, *The Purple Book,* 5th ed., 1925: 20, 21, 48, John Tarleton Agricultural College Collections, Dick Smith Library, Tarleton State University.

20. Samuel Hopkins Adams [Warner Fabian, pseud.], "Flaming Youth," *Metropolitan Magazine* with *The Girl of Today,* February–March 1923, 51.

21. Tate, interview, December 10, 2004.

22. The lines from Grantland Rice are from his poem, "Alumnus Football," published in 1923, which became better known as a result of his 1941 book, *Only the Brave and Other Poems.* Tate, interview, December 10, 2004. Willie L. Tate is not to be confused with Willis MacDonald Tate, who played football for Southern Methodist University (and against Earl Rudder) in the early 1930s and later was president of the institution.

23. Flemmons, *Plowboys, Cowboys and Slanted Pigs,* 8.

24. *Grassburr,* personal copy of Earl Rudder, 1928:203.

25. James Earl "Bud" Rudder Jr., telephone interview with the author, April 30, 2008. Bud Rudder concluded that his father approached most complex tasks as a challenge to learn and master the correct procedure. If done properly, success would usually result.

26. W. J. Wisdom to Earl Rudder, July 15, 1959; Earl Rudder to W. J. Wisdom, July 29, 1959.

27. *Eden Echo,* November 24, 1927; *Grassburr,* 1928:122.

28. *Grassburr,* 1930:34; Student's official record card for Earl Rudder, at Tarleton College, 1927–30, copy in the possession of the author, courtesy of the registrar, Tarleton State University. My conclusion that Rudder was considering a coaching career is based on a matter-of-fact note to him by classmate Hayden Duke of Wheeler, Texas: "May you someday be a great football coach and a civil engineer."

29. *Grassburr,* 1929:131, 138.

30. *Grassburr,* 1930:116.

31. *J-Tac,* October 26, November 16, December 6, 1929, John Tarleton Agricultural College Collections, Dick Smith Library, Tarleton State University.

32. The game was played in Stephenville on November 11, 1929. *Grassburr,* 1930:77; *Texas Almanac and State Industrial Guide, 1931* (Dallas: A. H. Belo, 1931), 331. According to the 1930 census, Stephenville's population was 3,944.

33. *Grassburr,* 1930:64.

34. Ibid., 1928:78; 1929:54–55, 96, 176–77; Nathan Miller, *New World Coming: The 1920s and the Making of Modern America,* 253.

35. *Grassburr,* 1928:121; 1930:35, 64, 66, 46, 47, end pages.

36. Margaret Rudder, telephone interview with the author, July 18, 2003.

37. *Grassburr,* 1930:166.

CHAPTER 3. TEXAS A&M COLLEGE

1. Henry C. Dethloff, *A Centennial History of Texas A&M University, 1876–1976,* 561.

2. An untitled document found in the Texas A&M registrar's office indicates that Rudder would be in the class of 1933.

3. *Longhorn* (yearbook), Agricultural and Mechanical College of Texas, 1932:114–27. Personal copies of Earl Rudder, 1931 and 1932, are in the possession of the author. For ROTC training, see William O. Odom, *After the Trenches: The Transformation of U.S. Army Doctrine, 1918–1935,* 108. The 1932 *Longhorn* has material about the summer camps that A&M cadets attended in 1931.

4. James Earl "Bud" Rudder Jr., telephone interview with the author, January 29, 2005; Edwin Cooper, interview with the author, February 11, 2005.

5. Margaret Rudder, interview with the author, May 5, 2002. Alfred I. Davies was born in Fort Worth on September 22, 1912, and lived with his parents in Bowie until he entered Texas A&M in 1930. He earned a bachelor of science degree in economics and a master's degree in marketing finance. He had an outstanding career with Sears, Roebuck

and Co., and he served on the Texas A&M University System Board of Regents from 1975 to 1981.

The proper name of the governing board of the Agricultural and Mechanical College of Texas was the Board of Directors from its establishment until 1975, when it was changed to Board of Regents. For simplicity, it is cited hereafter as Texas A&M Board of Directors.

6. E. J. Howell to Earl Rudder, September 1, 1927, registrar's office, Texas A&M University.

7. Earl Rudder to E. J. Howell, August 29, 1930, registrar's office, Texas A&M University.

8. Donald D. Carter, registrar, Texas A&M University, provided the enrollment figure in a telephone interview with the author, January 26, 2005.

9. John O. Pasco, *Fish Sergeant,* 62; A. I. Davies to Earl Rudder, June 14, 1954; Margaret Rudder, interview, May 5, 2002. In his letter Davies wrote, "Through you I got into the Aggieland Inn and, as you remember, received probably more education working there than I got from classroom routines. . . . I sometimes wonder if some of the selling principles that we used in selling book cases, etc., to freshmen and sophomores might not have been the thing that eventually guided me toward Sears."

10. Mike Dillingham, interview with the author, February 12, 2005; Bud Rudder, telephone interview, January 29, 2005. Dillingham graduated from Texas A&M in 1935. He became acquainted with Rudder during the 1931–32 academic year and was actively involved with the Texas A&M Association of Former Students during Rudder's presidency.

11. Fred Hervey, former executive director, Texas A&M University Association of Former Students, telephone interview with the author, February 23, 2005.

12. *Bulletin of the Agricultural and Mechanical College of Texas, Record of the Session 1930–31,* 41; and Board of Directors, Agricultural and Mechanical College of Texas. "Record of the Session 1930–31, Minutes of the Board of Directors," May 30, 1930, Cushing Memorial Library and Archives, Texas A&M University.

13. James Earl Rudder, *Application for Admission,* Agricultural and Mechanical College of Texas, September 15, 1930; Transcript of James Earl Rudder, Office of the Registrar, Agricultural and Mechanical College of Texas, 1932. The transcript lists every course for which he enrolled at both the John Tarleton Agricultural College and Texas A&M, indicating that he took ten courses in physical education and coaching, the equivalent of the course work for one academic year.

14. Dethloff, *Centennial History,* 409, 426. Dethloff quotes the minutes of the Texas A&M Board of Directors, May 30, 1930, IV, 153 (in the office of the Texas A&M University System Board of Regents). See also *Bulletin of the Agricultural and Mechanical College of Texas, Record of the Session 1930–31,* 39.

15. Nelda Green, telephone interview, July 25, 2010. Green was executive secretary to President Jack K. Williams when Guion Hall was razed in 1970 for structural deficiencies and to make room for construction of Rudder Tower, which was completed in 1974.

She got her information from Tony Heger, long-time employee of the TAMU System Facilities Planning and Construction Office.

16. Thomas C. Morris, interview with the author, Waxahachie, Texas, November 10, 1985; Pasco, *Fish Sergeant,* 17–18.

17. *Longhorn,* 1931:173, 178, 179.

18. *The Olio,* 1895, 32, as quoted in Dethloff, *Centennial History,* 167.

19. Dethloff, *Centennial History,* 437.

20. Dillingham, interview, February 12, 2005.

21. William Manchester, *American Caesar,* 161.

22. Lou Maysel, interview with the author, March 1, 2005; *Longhorn,* 1931:280. Quotation from *Longhorn,* 1932:237. Maysel, born in 1922, is a retired sportswriter for the *Austin American-Statesman* and a noted authority on the history of football and the Southwest Conference.

23. *Longhorn,* 1932:237; *New Handbook of Texas,* 1:471, s.v. "Bell, William Madison," and Handbook of Texas Online, http://www.tshaonline.org/handbook/online/articles/view/BB/fbebf.html (accessed June 24, 2010).

24. *Bryan Daily Eagle,* September 19, 1931.

25. Ibid., September 26 and 28, 1931.

26. Ibid., October 5, 1931.

27. Ibid.

28. Dillingham, interview, February 12, 2005; *Bryan Daily Eagle,* October 15, 19, 1931.

29. *New Handbook of Texas,* 6:210, s.v. "Tate, Willis McDonald," and Handbook of Texas Online, http://www.tshaonline.org/handbook/online/articles/view/TT/fta58.html (accessed June 24, 2010). Willis McDonald Tate is not to be confused with Willie L. Tate, who played basketball at Tarleton and was later an all–Southwest Conference basketball player at the University of Texas.

30. *Longhorn,* 1932:236; Wayne C. Hall, *The Glory Years: Making of a University,* 135–36.

31. *Bryan Daily Eagle,* November 25, 1931.

32. *Longhorn,* 1932:182; *Houston Post-Dispatch,* November 27, 1931.

33. Dillingham, interview, February 12, 2005.

34. *Newsweek,* June 8, 1964, 18.

35. A&M men from Rudder's period assert that the printing of individual photographs in the yearbook other than the class photo, such as those for club members or class officers, required a fee payment by the student.

36. *Longhorn,* 1932:39.

37. After Rudder's death, Margaret gave the ring to the Association of Former Students.

38. Dethloff, *Centennial History,* 433. See also Harry J. Carman and Harold C. Syrett, *A History of the American People,* 2:505. Rudder's graduation date was July 8, 1932.

39. *Houston Post,* May 9, 1955.

CHAPTER 4. COACHING YEARS

1. Minutes, Trustees of Brady Independent School District, April 24, September 11, 1933; *Houston Post,* May 9, 1955.

2. *Brady Standard,* September 5, 1933.

3. *Bulletin of the Agricultural and Mechanical College of Texas, Record of the Session 1930–31,* 199; and Board of Directors, Agricultural and Mechanical College of Texas. "Record of the Session 1930–31, Minutes of the Board of Directors," May 30, 1930, Cushing Memorial Library and Archives, Texas A&M University. The full quotation by Henry Ford, as published in the *Chicago Tribune* on May 25, 1916, is, "History is more or less bunk. We want to live in the present and the only history that is worth a tinker's dam is the history we made today."

4. Margaret Rudder, interview with the author, May 9, 2002.

5. Bill Roberts, interview with the author, April 25, 2005.

6. Haskell Monroe, ed., *James Earl Rudder in the Words of His Wife, Margaret Rudder,* 7.

7. Ibid., 8. The dormitory was Littlefield Dormitory for freshman women.

8. Vivian Smith, interview with the author, April 25, 2005.

9. Larry Smith, telephone interview with the author, May 5, 2005; *Brady Standard,* September 8, 1933.

10. Larry Smith, interview with the author, April 7, 2005. Smith succeeded his father as editor and publisher of the *Brady Standard.* In the early 1930s the elder Smith was the *Brady Standard* sports editor and later told the story about Powell and the San Saba coach to his son.

11. Karl Steffens, Charlie Dye, and Bill Roberts, interviews with the author, Brady, Texas, July 23, 2003; John Rudder, interview with the author, Brady, Texas, April 26, 2005. John Rudder described the strength of his two uncles, Earl and Marshall Rudder, saying they wrestled each other for the simple joy of the experience.

12. Steffens, Dye, and Roberts interviews, July 23, 2003.

13. Ibid.

14. Ibid.

15. *Brady Standard,* November 23, 1934.

16. Ibid., November 27, 1934.

17. Ibid.

18. Leonard Jacoby, telephone interview with the author, May 14, 2005.

19. Minutes, Trustees of Brady Independent School District, August 3, 1936; Monroe, *Rudder in the Words of His Wife,* 10.

20. Monroe, *Rudder in the Words of His Wife,* 12–13.

21. *Brady Standard,* June 15, 1937.

22. Monroe, *Rudder in the Words of His Wife,* 12.

23. Alton "Rusty" Williamson, interview with the author, August 13, 2004. Originally, there were five Williamson children, but Weyman died in 1928 at the age of sixteen.

24. Omar N. Bradley, *A Soldier's Story,* 269.

25. Monroe, *Rudder in the Words of His Wife,* 15.

26. *Brady Standard,* December 10, 1937.

27. *Brady Standard,* December 14, 1937.

28. J. Thomas Davis to Earl Rudder, April 6, 1938. Rudder's wife and children quote him as saying he "went for the Tarleton job as never for another position in his entire life."

29. G. Rollie White was a member of the Texas A&M Board of Directors from 1929 to 1955. He founded the Commercial National Bank in Brady, Texas, in 1906 and remained its president until his death in 1965.

30. Earl Rudder to J. Thomas Davis, April 12, 1938.

31. Earl Rudder to J. Thomas Davis, April 12, 1938; Joseph Utey to Earl Rudder, April 16, 1938. Utey was a member of the Texas A&M Board of Directors.

32. J. Thomas Davis to Thomas O. Walton, August 11, 1938.

33. *Brady Standard,* August 12, 1938.

34. J. Thomas Davis to B. E. Masters, March 15, 1938.

35. "The Estate of W. W. Williamson for the Calendar Year 1952: An Analysis of Gifts Made by W. W. Williamson and Lucy Williamson of Community Property," Supplement Schedule G, Lawrence Williamson, executor, Golda Mauldin, Eden, Texas, preparer, March 10, 1953. The calculation of equivalent purchasing power was based on Lawrence H. Officer and Samuel H. Williamson, "Purchasing Power of Money in the United States from 1774 to 2007," Measuring Worth, 2008, http://www.measuringworth .com/ppowerus/result.php; Haskell Monroe, *Rudder in the Words of His Wife,* 16.

36. The win-loss record for Rudder's teams was compiled from the Tarleton College *Grassburr,* 1939, 1940, and 1941, John Tarleton Agricultural College Collections, Dick Smith Library, Tarleton State University.

37. Office of the Erath County, Texas, Clerk, Book 267, Page 89, File No. 934, Fount Taylor to J. Earl Rudder, filed July 9, 1940.

38. Ralph Steen, "Texas in World War II," *Handbook of Texas,* ed. Walter Prescott Webb (Austin: Texas State Historical Association, 1952), 2:952; Department of the Army, *American Military History, 1607–1953,* 373. The latter book is also referred to as ROTC Manual No. 145–20.

39. Margaret Rudder, interview with the author, May 9, 2002.

CHAPTER 5. STATESIDE

1. Department of the Army, *American Military History, 1607–1953,* ROTC Manual No. 145–20; Margaret Rudder, interview with the author, May 9, 2002.

2. Headquarters, First Military Area, San Antonio, Texas, Special Orders No. 129, June 4, 1941, copy in the possession of the author, courtesy of Margaret Rudder; Earl Rudder to his wife, undated (envelope postmarked San Antonio, Texas, June 25, 1941).

3. Earl Rudder to his wife, undated (June 25, 1941); Margaret Rudder to her husband, January 2, 1943.

4. In classrooms and in the field, the subject matter also included .45-caliber pistols, .30- and .50-caliber machine guns, the 61 mm and 85 mm mortars, and musketry: the use of the rifle in a squad, platoon, or company. There was also instruction on patrols, formations, communications, and differences in rifle ammunition—ball, tracer, and armor piercing—as well as teaching soldiers how to use the weapons.

5. Earl Rudder to his wife, undated (envelope postmarked Columbus, Georgia; stamped date is indistinct but appears to be either August 16 or 18, 1941); Margaret Rudder to her husband, undated; Earl Rudder to his wife, undated (envelope postmarked Columbus, Georgia, August 1941).

6. Ronald H. Bailey, *The Home Front: U.S.A.*, 115.

7. James Earl Rudder Jr., e-mail to author, June 23, 2006; Earl Rudder to his wife, September 30, 1943; Earl Rudder to his wife, undated (envelope postmarked Freeport, Texas, February 19, 1942).

8. The address was 500 East Main Cross, Edinburgh, Indiana. Between February 25, 1942, when Rudder returned to Fort Sam Houston, and November 1942, when he left Camp Atterbury for Fort Leavenworth, there are no extant letters from Margaret to Earl.

9. Roy Conyers Nesbit, *Eyes of the RAF: A History of Photo-Reconnaissance* (Gloucester, U.K.: Alan Sutton Publishing, 1996), 325 (appendix); Allied Central Interpretation Unit, #04665, sortie 613, August 18, 1942, Aerial Reconnaissance Archives, Keele University, Staffordshire, United Kingdom; Allan Williams, director, Aerial Reconnaissance Archives, e-mail to author, September 20, 2007.

10. Headquarters, VIII Army Corps, Brownwood, Texas, Special Orders No. 145, June 25, 1942, and Headquarters, 83rd Infantry Division, Camp Atterbury, Indiana, Letter Order No. 11–25, November 17, 1942, copies of both in the possession of the author, courtesy of Margaret Rudder; Margaret Rudder, to her husband, undated (postmark is illegible except for January 1943); Haskell Monroe, ed., *James Earl Rudder in the Words of His Wife, Margaret Rudder*, 17.

11. War Department, Washington, D.C., Special Orders No. 323, November 27, 1942, copy in the possession of the author, courtesy of Margaret Rudder; Margaret Rudder to her husband, undated (postmarked December 6, 1942, Edinburgh, Indiana).

12. "Subject: Activation of 2nd Ranger Battalion to Commanding Officers, 11th Detachment of Special Troops, to issue the necessary letter orders activating the 2nd Ranger Battalion on April 1, 1943," by command of Lieutenant General Lear, March 11, 1943, complete typescript in Ronald Lane, *Rudder's Rangers: The True Story of the 2nd Ranger Battalion D-Day Combat Action*, 15, 22. Ben Lear retired as a general in the U.S. Army. He fought in World War I and then trained soldiers for World War II. In 1940 he took command of the Second Army, essentially a training command wholly within the United States, headquartered in Memphis, Tennessee.

13. Typescripts dated June 18 and June 19, 1943, copies in the possession of the author, courtesy of Margaret Rudder. Each bears the statement "This is a true copy" and is signed "R. G. Harrell, Major, AGD, Asst. Adj. Gen." Colonel Van Brunt was presumptuous when he said Rudder was a Ranger. It would be more correct to say that he

was a *de facto* Ranger for having conducted Ranger-type training. Col. R. T. Beurket, GSC, was the executive officer of the Training Division, Army Service Forces. A more complete biography of Colonel Van Brunt could not be found. During World War II six Ranger battalions were formed. The 1st Battalion, formed in Britain, saw action in North Africa, Sicily, and Italy and provided the nucleus for the 3rd and 4th battalions in the Mediterranean Theater and the training cadre for the 2nd and 5th battalions in the United States. The 5th Battalion, organized in September 1943, joined the 2nd Battalion in Britain for the Normandy invasion. In September 1944 the 6th Battalion was formed in New Guinea.

14. *Houston Post,* May 9, 1955; Headquarters, 83rd Infantry Division, Camp Atterbury, Indiana, Special Orders No. 152, June 21, 1943, as amended July 1, 1943, copy in the possession of the author, courtesy of Margaret Rudder.

15. Earl Rudder to his wife, July 4, 1943.

16. Ronald Lane, *Rudder's Rangers,* 18.

17. Ibid., 22.

18. Robert W. Black, *The Battalion: The Dramatic Story of the 2nd Ranger Battalion in World War II,* 19–20.

19. Lane, *Rudder's Rangers,* 22.

20. James W. Eikner, ed., *2nd Ranger Battalion: The Narrative History of Headquarters Company, April 1943–May 1945,* 16, 25, 26; Stanley E. White memoir, quoted in Black, *The Battalion,* 25.

21. Ibid.; Eikner, *2nd Ranger Battalion,* 16; Alfred E. Baer, *"D-for-Dog": The Story of a Ranger Company,* 4.

22. Lane, *Rudder's Rangers,* 20, 21.

23. Earl Rudder to his wife, September 1, 1943.

24. Earl Rudder to his wife, July 18, 1943. The envelope was postmarked July 19. He wrote the letter the previous day, which was a Sunday. He noted, "We are supposed to go the coast some place for *amphibous* [his emphasis] training (hope that is spelled right)."

25. Earl Rudder to his wife, September 11, 1943; Eikner, *2nd Ranger Battalion,* 30; Lane, *Rudder's Rangers,* 29.

26. Baer, *"D-for-Dog,"* 12.

27. Robert A. Taylor, *World War II in Fort Pierce,* 18–19; Lane, *Rudder's Rangers,* 29; Baer, *"D-for-Dog,"* 11. Baer identifies the man with twelve charges only as Kettering: "Kettering . . . was charged for court-martial on the following morning under an even dozen Articles of War." The name of Charles E. Kettering appears on a list of 2nd Ranger Battalion men compiled by Robert W. Black, *Rangers in World War II,* 369. Other memoirs refer to the battalion's last night in Fort Pierce and the subsequent punishment; see, for example, Eikner, *2nd Ranger Battalion,* 30.

28. Lane, *Rudder's Rangers,* 30; Baer, *"D-for-Dog,"* 13.

29. Edwin M. Sorvisto, *2nd Ranger Bn: Roughing It with Charlie,* 9; Eikner, *2nd Ranger Battalion,* 33.

30. Earl Rudder to his wife, October 16, 1943.

31. Monroe, *Rudder in the Words of His Wife,* 18. "Bounced" meant that someone

with priority duties related to the war effort was given her seat on the plane; it was a common occurrence in public transportation during the war.

32. Ibid., 22; Earl Rudder to his wife, October 16, 1943, November 2, 1943. The effective date of Rudder's promotion to lieutenant colonel was November 3, 1943.

33. Earl Rudder to his wife, no date, but written after he boarded ship on November 21, 1943, and before the ship sailed on the evening of November 23.

34. Lane, *Rudder's Rangers*, 35.

35. Earl Rudder to his wife, no date, but written on board ship, November 21–23, 1943.

CHAPTER 6. BRITAIN

1. Andrew A. Watson, Historian, U.S. Army Military Police Corps Regimental Museum, Fort Leonard Wood, Missouri, e-mail to author, July 2, 2008; James W. Eikner, ed., *2nd Ranger Battalion: The Narrative History of Headquarters Company, April 1943–May 1945,* 36, 37, 40.

2. Vincent Gillen, Curator, McLean Museum, Greenock, Scotland, e-mail to author, April 10, 2007. Mr. Gillen cited records in the McLean Museum: "According to my sources the first troop ship arrived on the 11th May 1942. A total of 339 troop ships arrived from then till 31st December 1944, carrying a total of 1,319,089 American service personnel."

3. Headquarters, First United States Army, Special Orders No. 28, November 11, 1943, copy in the possession of the author, courtesy of James F. Schneider. The same orders directed Schneider to Bude in County Cornwall on November 16. Richard Tregaskis, a war correspondent for International News Service, identified Schneider as the first American ashore at Salerno in the *Shenandoah (Iowa) Evening Sentinel,* September 1, 1944. Schneider participated in the assault landings in North Africa (Arzew, Algeria), Sicily (Gela), and Italy (Maori near Salerno). His son, James F. Schneider, compiled a chronology of his father's life, including significant events such as transfers, promotions, and awards, and gave me a copy.

4. The National Institute of Mental Health includes the following statements about posttraumatic stress disorder on its website: "Post-Traumatic Stress Disorder, PTSD, is an anxiety disorder that can develop after exposure to a terrifying event or ordeal in which grave physical harm occurred or was threatened. Traumatic events that may trigger PTSD include violent personal assaults, natural or human-caused disasters, accidents, or military combat. People with PTSD have persistent frightening thoughts and memories of their ordeal and feel emotionally numb, especially with people they were once close to. They may experience sleep problems, feel detached or numb, or be easily startled."

5. The Fifth Ranger Battalion crossed on HMS *Mauritania,* which docked in Liverpool on January 18, 1944.

6. Maj. Gen. John C. Raaen Jr., e-mail to the author, April 7, 2007. The uniforms were made of wool, dyed a particular shade of olive green officially designated OG 33. "Route

step" is a march with reduced discipline, a mode of marching in military formation in which there is no requirement to keep in step and talking and singing are allowed.

7. Gerald Heaney, telephone interview with the author, July 17, 2005. At the time of his interview, Heaney was the senior U.S. Eighth Circuit Court judge in Duluth, Minnesota. He retired from the federal judiciary in 2006.

8. Earl Rudder to his wife, December 3, 1943. Some men may have been bussed elsewhere and entrained for Bude from other stations. Whether they were all consolidated in one train en route to Bude cannot be determined. Luggage and weapons were off-loaded with equipment in Glasgow, which may account for the lack of mention in any Ranger memoir of weapons in their possession while boarding the *Queen Elizabeth* or on the way to Bude.

9. Morris Prince, *The Road to Victory: The Story of the Elite WWII 2nd Battalion Rangers,* 20.

10. Heaney, telephone interview, July 17, 2005; Prince, *Road to Victory,* 20–21. While aboard the *Queen Elizabeth,* most enlisted men had only cold saltwater for bathing. Thus the conclusion that many had not bathed.

11. Earl Rudder to his wife, June 1, 1944.

12. Jim Dan Hill, "Brady Mayor's Feats As Combat Leader Unique," *Brady Standard,* April 15, 1947; Trevor Bate, interview with the author, June 17, 2005; Frank South to the Clark family in Bude, May 25, 1992, quoted in Robert W. Black, *The Battalion: The Dramatic Story of the 2nd Ranger Battalion in World War II,* 53. Trevor Bate was six years old in 1943 when the 2nd Ranger Battalion arrived in Bude. His family home was next door to Rudder's battalion headquarters in the Links Hotel. His mother did laundry for the headquarters staff.

13. Earl Rudder to his wife, December 3, 22, 25, 1943; January 27, April 18, May 7, 1944; David Dobson, Bude, e-mail to author, August 10, 2004.

14. Black, *The Battalion,* 51.

15. Earl Rudder to his wife, December 12, 1943. Jim Dan Hill was a historian by training. He returned to the presidency of Superior State Teachers College after the war and oversaw the college's development as the University of Wisconsin–Superior. In retirement, Hill returned to Texas, where he served as president of the West Texas Historical Association. He died in 1983 in Abilene, Texas. Among his books was a history of the navy of the Republic of Texas (1836–46), which was published by the University of Chicago Press. See the Jim Dan Hill Papers, Southwest Collection/Special Collections Library, Texas Tech University, Lubbock.

16. Jim Dan Hill, "Brady Mayor's Feats," *Brady Standard,* April 15, 1947.

17. Martin Gilbert, *Road to Victory: Winston Churchill, 1941–1945,* 593; Stephen E. Ambrose, *Eisenhower,* Vol. 1, *Soldier, General of the Army, President-Elect, 1890–1952,* 271.

18. In their organization and equipment, U.S. Army Ranger battalions were modeled on British Commando units—lean, expected to strike hard, and able to move fast without the encumbrance of heavy weapons. At full strength in 1944, a Ranger battalion had 516 officers and men, including the medical attachment of one medical doctor and

eleven medics; or, about 60 percent of an infantry battalion's 855. The big difference was that an infantry battalion had three rifle companies of 192 men, a weapons company, and a headquarters company, whereas a Ranger battalion had six companies of only 68 men each and a headquarters company to support the commander and his staff. Each Ranger company had two platoons with 34 men each. Another big difference was that the infantry battalion had a weapons company armed with four heavy water-cooled machine guns and four large 81 mm mortars. The Ranger battalion had no heavy weapons but had four times as many light machine guns (twenty-four) and twice as many light 60 mm mortars (eighteen).

19. Earl Rudder to his wife, December 9, 1943; Jim Dan Hill, "Brady Mayor's Feats," *Brady Standard,* April 15, 1947; Maj. Gen. John C. Raaen Jr., e-mail to author, April 7, 2007.

20. Ronald Lane, *Rudder's Rangers: The True Story of the 2nd Ranger Battalion D-Day Combat Action,* 40; Prince, *Road to Victory,* 23.

21. Brian Woolcott, interview with the author, Bude, Cornwall, June 5, 2005.

22. Lane, *Rudder's Rangers,* 38, 54.

23. Gerald Heaney, interview with the author, New Orleans, La., August 21, 2002.

24. Brian Woolcott, interview with the author, Bude, Cornwall, June 19, 2005.

25. Brian Woolcott, e-mail to author, July 28, 2005.

26. Woolcott, interview, June 19, 2005. The medication was confirmed by University of Delaware physiology professor emeritus Frank South, then a medic in the medical section of the 2nd Ranger Battalion.

27. Bill Young and Bryan Dudley Stamp, *Bude: Past and Present,* 43; Hill, "Brady Mayor's Feats."

28. Earl Rudder to his wife, December 18, 1943; Brian Woolcott, interview with the author, June 18, 2005. Woolcott received the information from Ranger Sidney Salomon. See also Sidney A. Salomon, *2nd U.S. Ranger Infantry Battalion: Germeter-Vossenack-Hurtgen-Bergstein-Hill 400 Germany: 14 Nov.–10 Dec. 1944.*

29. Edwin M. Sorvisto, *2nd Ranger Bn: Roughing It with Charlie,* 13; Eikner, *2nd Ranger Battalion,* 42; Earl Rudder to his wife, December 25, 1943.

30. Lucian K. Truscott Jr., *Command Missions: A Personal Story,* 37–38; Eikner, *2nd Ranger Battalion,* 46; Bernard Fergusson, *The Watery Maze: The Story of Combined Operations,* 415.

31. *Houston Chronicle,* May 9, 1955.

32. Richard P. Merrill to John Raaen, December 2, 1993. Merrill was an officer on Rudder's staff in the 2nd Ranger Battalion; Raaen was a company commander in the 5th Ranger Battalion.

33. James Altieri, *The Spearheaders.* (New York: The Bobbs-Merrill Company, Inc., 1960), 56.

34. Omar N. Bradley, *A Soldier's Story,* 222–23.

35. Gordon A. Harrison, *Cross-Channel Attack: The European Theater of Operations: United States Army in World War II,* 182, 196; Helmut Konrad von Keusgen, *Pointe du Hoc: Rätsel um einen deutschen Stützpunkt* (Riddles of a German strongpoint), 82.

36. W. J. Heinz, "I Took My Son to Omaha Beach: The Story of An American Hero's Return to Normandy," *Collier's,* June 11, 1954, 24. Heinz quoted Rudder as saying he was "coaching football a year and a half before," but it was actually two and a half years.

37. Harrison, *Cross-Channel Attack,* 182. The decision to add Utah Beach to the landing plan was made at the end of January 1944.

38. Samuel Eliot Morison, *History of United States Naval Operations in World War II,* vol. 11, *The Invasion of France and Germany, 1944–1945,* 125–26; U.S. War Department, Historical Division, *Omaha Beachhead: 6 June–13 June 1944,* 25; Forrest Pogue, *Pogue's War: Diaries of a WWII Combat Historian,* 30; Lane, *Rudder's Rangers,* 68.

39. Bradley, *A Soldier's Story,* 269. Bradley should have written Provisional Ranger Group, not Provisional Ranger Force.

40. James Altieri, *The Spearheaders,* 52; catalog reference WO 373/71, National Archives of the United Kingdom, http://www.nationalarchives.gov.uk/documentsonline/. Eisenhower's letter to Trevor is found on the website "Combined Operations," http://www.combinedops.com/No%201%20Commando.htm. Thomas Hoult Trevor was born near Liverpool on October 13, 1911, and graduated from staff college at Camberley in 1932. He was commissioned in the Territorial Army in 1932 and in the Welch Regiment in 1933. During World War II he commanded No. 1 and No. 6 Commandos. He was awarded the Order of the British Empire on September 23, 1943. In early 1944, he was assigned to Combined Operations Headquarters as a staff officer in military planning and began working as an advisor to the Rangers. Among other projects, he wrote "A Manual on Cliff-climbing in Amphibious Assaults" for the British Ministry of Defense, Combined Operations, in 1944 (copy in the possession of the author, courtesy of James W. Eikner). He retired from the army in 1960 and died July 29, 1997, at Albany, Piccadilly, London.

41. Harrison, *Cross-Channel Attack,* 174.

42. Headquarters, 2nd Ranger Battalion, to Commanding General, First United States Army, "Rotation and Return of Military Personnel as Individuals on Duty Outside Continental United States," January 7, 1944.

43. Medical Detachment, 2nd Ranger Battalion, to Commanding Officer, 2nd Ranger Battalion, "Transfer of Major Max F. Schneider, 0384849," January 17, 1944; Headquarters, European Theater of Operations, U.S. Army, August 26, 1944, to Adjutant General, Washington 25, D.C., "AG 201-Schneider, Max F," Para. 1: "Request an exception be made to the present rotation policy and authority be granted to return officer without replacement." The document summarized the request from the original memorandum from Rudder on January 7, 1944, through several endorsements and its retraction.

44. Harold K. "Duke" Slater, interview with the author, New Orleans, La., August 30, 2002. Slater was a company commander in the 2nd Ranger Battalion, 1943–45, and accompanied Rudder to recruit Rangers from other U.S. Army units in Britain. Dermot L. Richardson is identified in the register of British army officers as "Temporary Lieutenant-Colonel D. L. (Dermot Lindesay) Richardson of The King's Regiment. From 24 Sept 1943 onwards (Apr 1944 still showing as such) he was General Staff Officer, 1st grade (GS01)

for Plans & Combined Operations Advice of the Military Section of the Combined Operations Headquarters." The information about Richardson was found at http://www.unithistories.com/officers/persons_british.html.

45. Prince, *Road to Victory,* 43.

46. Conrad E. Epperson, interview with the author, New Orleans, La., August 30, 2002.

47. Marcia Moen and Margo Heinen, *The Fool Lieutenant: A Personal Account of D-Day and World War II,* 64–65.

48. Ibid., 63–64.

49. William Petty memoir quoted in Black, *The Battalion,* 4. See also ibid., 25, and James Eikner, interview with the author, August 5, 2005.

50. Earl Rudder to his wife, February 20, 1944.

51. Thomas M. Morris, interview with the author, Waxahachie, Texas, November 10, 1985.

52. The 5th Ranger Battalion disembarked in Liverpool on January 18, 1944. It went to Scotland on March 1. Schneider became its commanding officer on March 26, and Rudder was officially appointed commanding officer of the Provisional Ranger Group on May 19, although he was apparently its presumed commander when the planning of the Pointe Du Hoc operation began.

53. Lane, *Rudder's Rangers,* 74.

54. Ibid., 69–74; Thomas H. Trevor, "After Action Report: Assault on Pointe du Hoe [*sic*], for Combined Operations Headquarters," July 12, 1944, 1, copy in the possession of the author, courtesy of James W. Eikner. Trevor wrote that when he "started to work on the project, the plan was to land Rangers on Omaha Beach in the second wave, pass them through the forward troops and for them to advance along the coast for 4–5 miles and attack the Battery from the landward (Southeast) side."

55. Capt. F. W. H. (Francis William Hugh) Jeans, Royal Navy, was director of the Department of Miscellaneous Weapons Development. Rudder cited three others in the DMWD who helped him: Temp. Lt. Cdr. R. C. (Robert Cecil) Byng, RNVR; Temp. Lt. D. F. (Donald Felix) Currie, RNVR; and Temp. Lt. (Special Branch) R. F. (Ronald Frank) Eades, RNVR. Their names were provided by J. N. Houterman, a research-specialist of the British military in World War II, who lives in Middelburg, Netherlands. See Department of Miscellaneous Weapons Development, File ADM 277/20, National Archives of the United Kingdom; see also http://www.unithistories.com/officers/persons_british.html for information about their naval careers.

56. Trevor, "After Action Report," July 12, 1944, 1, 2. In the report, Trevor wrote that the Germans had created "an artificial inundation which restricted the line of advance and forced the attack over open country up a hill on ground dominated by prepared positions on commanding ground."

57. Combined Operations, "Mechanical Aids for Scaling Cliffs," quoted in Jonathan Gawne, *Spearheading D-Day: American Special Units of the Normandy Invasion,* 198–202.

58. Maj. Gen. Clarence R. Huebner, "Diary: 3 March 1944 to 26 September 1944," Stanhope Collection, McCormick Research Center, Cantigny, First Division Foundation, Wheaton, Illinois, copy in the possession of the author.

59. Eikner, *2nd Ranger Battalion,* 50.

60. Moen and Heinen, *The Fool Lieutenant,* 75; Prince, *Road to Victory,* 42.

61. Judyth Gwynne, interview with the author, Bude, Cornwall, June 18, 2005.

62. Eikner, *2nd Ranger Battalion,* 42. The British Home Guard was a defense organization active in the United Kingdom during World War II. Some 1.5 million local volunteers, otherwise ineligible for military service, usually because of their age, acted as a secondary defense force in case of invasion by the forces of Nazi Germany. The Home Guard watched coastal areas and other important places such as factories and explosives stores.

63. Prince, *Road to Victory,* 44.

64. Eikner, *2nd Ranger Battalion,* 51.

65. Prince, *Road to Victory,* 51.

66. Hill, "Brady Mayor's Feats," *Brady Standard,* April 15, 1947.

67. Sayre Van Young, *London's War: A Traveler's Guide to World War II,* 55.

68. Bradley, *A Soldier's Story,* 239.

69. Alex Danchev and Daniel Todman, eds., *Field Marshal Lord Alanbrooke, War Diaries, 1939–1945,* 538; Gilbert, *Road to Victory,* 730–31; Dwight D. Eisenhower, *Crusade in Europe,* 243.

70. Earl Rudder to his wife, April 9, 1944.

71. Richard P. Merrill to John C. Raaen Jr., December 12, 1993; James Schneider e-mail to author, June 24, 2008. James Schneider is the son of Max F. Schneider.

72. Huebner Diary, April 23, 1944.

73. Harrison, *Cross-Channel Attack,* 270.

74. Headquarters, Regimental Combat Team 116, by authority of the commanding general, 1st U.S. Infantry Division, Field Order No. 1, May 11, 1944, Copy no. 19, pp. 3, 5, copy in the possession of the author, courtesy of James W. Eikner.

75. Harrison, *Cross-Channel Attack,* 270; Prince, *Road to Victory,* 51, 67.

76. Earl Rudder to his wife, May 28, 1944; Huebner Diary, May 29, 1944.

77. Earl Rudder to his mother, May 31, 1944.

78. Marcia Moen and Margo Heinen, *The Fool Lieutenant,* 87.

79. Alfred E. Baer Jr., *"D-for-Dog": The Story of a Ranger Company,* 40; Earl Rudder to his wife, June 1, 1944.

CHAPTER 7. POINTE DU HOC

1. To modify the channel steamers, life rafts were replaced with the much heavier landing craft. This required strengthening the davits, the small cranes that lowered and raised life rafts and, as modified, landing craft.

2. Quoted in Joseph Balkoski, *Omaha Beach: D-Day, June 6, 1944,* 114. The full name of Pointe de la Percée is Pointe el Raz de la Percée.

3. Helmut Konrad von Keusgen, *Pointe du Hoc: Rätsel um einen deutschen Stütz-punkt* [Riddles of a German strongpoint], 70–71; SHAEF, Theatre Intelligence Section, Dossier No. 4, April 28, 1944, WO 219/1897, National Archives of the United Kingdom.

4. James W. Eikner, interview with the author, August 5, 2005.

5. F. Harry Hinsley, *British Intelligence Operations in the Second World War,* vol. 3, part 2, *Its Influence on Strategy and Operations,* 125; George Kerchner, oral history transcript, no date, World War II Oral History Archive, Eisenhower Center, University of New Orleans.

6. Leonard Lomell, telephone interview with the author, July 20, 2005.

7. Edward K. "Duke" Slater, telephone interview with the author, February 21, 2007; Ronald Lane, *Rudder's Rangers: The True Story of the 2nd Ranger Battalion D-Day Combat Action,* 96–97.

8. L. F. Ellis, *Victory in the War,* vol. 1, *Normandy,* 143.

9. Richard P. Merrill to John C. Raaen, December 12, 1993.

10. Harvey Cook to his son, Donald G. Cook, December 9, 1979, copy in the possession of the author, courtesy of Donald G. Cook. In addition, the 2nd Ranger Battalion's morning report for June 3 (copy in the possession of the author, courtesy of James W. Eikner) states that Lytle was promoted to major on that day and transferred to the hospital on June 4.

11. Omar N. Bradley, *A Soldier's Story,* 269; Lane, *Rudder's Rangers,* 97.

12. Maj. Gen. Clarence R. Huebner, "Diary: 3 March 1944 to 26 September 1944," McCormick Research Center, Cantigny, First Division Foundation, Wheaton, Illinois. Copy in the possession of the author. The 2nd Ranger Battalion's staging area immediately before embarking for Normandy was near the Dorset village of Warmwell in Camp D-5. See James W. Eikner, *2nd Ranger Battalion: The Narrative History of Headquarters Company, April 1943–May 1945,* 17.

13. James Earl Rudder Jr., e-mail to the author, August 12, 2008.

14. Gordon A. Harrison, *Cross-Channel Attack: The European Theater of Operations: United States Army in World War II,* 337; U.S. War Department, Historical Division, *Omaha Beachhead (6 June–13 June 1944),* Armed Forces in Action Series, 8–10.

15. Artices of War prescribed in the 1928 *Manual for Courts-Martial* (rev. April 1943) that might have applied are 95 (conduct unbecoming to an officer), 96 (conduct prejudicial to good military order and discipline), 85 (drunkenness), 137 (striking another officer), and 66 (mutiny).

16. John Colby, *War from the Ground Up: The 90th Division in World War II,* 493.

17. James W. Eikner to William Jordan, November 16, 1999. Jordan, an Englishman living in Caen, France, sent an inquiry to Margaret Rudder, and Eikner answered it for her, sending her a copy of his letter. Under his signature, Eikner wrote a postscript: "Sorry, Margaret, but that is what he [Rudder] said."

18. Lane, *Rudder's Rangers,* 97.

19. Ben Berger, telephone interview with the author, March 8, 2007.

20. Cornelius Ryan sent Rudder a questionnaire. Rudder kept a copy of his responses (in the possession of the author), which is the source of the quote.

21. Elmer H. Vermeer, "Pointe du Hoc, France: D-Day: June 6, 1944," 4, typescript, no date, p. 11, in the possession of the author; Eikner, interview, August 9, 2005; Harold K. Slater, interview with the author, New Orleans, La., August 28, 2002. On the first page of Vermeer's typescript is a holographic inscription, which reads, "To the family of General James Earl Rudder who we value. Dutch and Joy."

22. Harrison, *Cross-Channel Attack,* 196; Ellis, *Victory in the War,* vol. 1, *Normandy,* 187; L. J. Pitcairn-Jones, *Operation Neptune: The Landings in Normandy 6th June 1944,* British Naval Staff History, Battle Summary No. 39, 87.

23. HMS *Prince Charles,* "Report of Proceedings, Assault Group O-4, Operation Neptune, on the 6th of June 1944," 7, Ranger Collections, U.S. Military History Institute, Army War College, Carlisle Barracks, Pennsylvania. The captain's log states that the *Prince Charles* anchored in the transport area at 3:28 AM.

24. Ibid.; John C. Raaen Jr., "Intact: A Story of D-Day and the 5th Rangers," copy in the possession of the author. Major General Raaen, U.S. Army (ret.), is a 1943 graduate of the U.S. Military Academy. He was a captain and Headquarters Company commander of the 5th Ranger Battalion. He led his company ashore on the Dog White sector of Omaha Beach at about 8:00 AM on D-Day. Pfc. Theodore Wells was Rudder's radioman for communicating with the 5th Ranger Battalion and made notes about how things appeared from his seat in Rudder's landing craft. Afterward he gave his account to Raaen, his company commander, who included Wells's account in "Intact."

25. Walter E. Block, M.D., medical officer, 2nd Ranger Battalion, unpublished combat diary, 1, Ranger Collections, U.S. Military History Institute, Army War College, Carlisle Barracks, Pennsylvania, copy in the possession of the author. Sunrise on Omaha Beach on June 6, 1944, occurred at 5:58 AM British Double Summer Time. First light was at 5:16 AM.

26. Charles H. Taylor to Earl Rudder, November 11, 1944; U.S. War Department, Historical Division, *Small Unit Actions: France; Second Ranger Battalion at Pointe du Hoe* [sic], 14. In civilian life, Taylor was a professor in the history department at Harvard University. During the war he was an officer in the army's historical section in the European Theater of Operations. He wrote the account of the 2nd Ranger Battalion's assault on Pointe du Hoc. His letter to Rudder enclosed a draft copy.

27. There is disagreement about whether the launch time was 4:30 AM or 4:45 AM. The 2nd Ranger Battalion's After Action Report, June 6, 1944 states it was 4:45, whereas the *Ben-my-Chree* log states 4:30. I accept the ship's version because it was prepared soon after the event in circumstances that were more conducive to accuracy than the battalion's report, which was dated July 22, 1944, more than six weeks later. The after action reports for the 2nd and 5th Ranger battalions, June 6 through December 8, 1944, are in Ranger Collections, Military History Institute, Army War College, Carlisle Barracks, Pennsylvania. Concerning the equipment, see War Department, *Small Unit Actions,* 4–5. The three pairs of rockets were mounted on the LCA's gunwales at the bow, at the stern, and amidships. Rope ladders were attached to the bow rockets, smooth rope to the stern rockets, and toggles (wooden handles) on the rockets amidships.

28. War Department, *Small Unit Actions,* 4–5; Vermeer, "Pointe du Hoc," 4. Light

machine guns—Lewis guns designed in the United States before World War I and widely used in armies of the British Empire—were mounted on the ladders. They fired .30-caliber rounds, either .303 British or .30–06 American.

29. War Department, *Small Unit Actions,* 5. More detail about what was taken to Pointe du Hoc may be found in Rudder's reply, dated December 26, 1944, to Charles H. Taylor's letter of November 11, 1944, drafted by 1st. Lt. Frank L. Kennard, his former adjutant in the 2nd Ranger Battalion. Rudder wrote to Taylor on December 9, 1945, that "I was so busy that I had no time to make the corrections you asked for" in the transcript, explaining that he was hit with "von Rundstedt's counter-offensive on 16 December." There is no indication that Rudder did not concur with Kennard's reply, a copy of which is in the possession of the author. The Rangers took 81 mm mortars to Pointe du Hoc but did not raise them to the cliff tops because they weighed 250 pounds each, and the hoisting equipment was lost at sea.

30. Four BARs were allotted to each of the three companies, and two 60 mm mortars per company.

31. Kenneth Edwards, *Operation Neptune,* 83–84. Temp. Lt. Colin Beever, RNVR, assumed his post on December 6, 1943, and belonged to the 11th Motor Launch Flotilla, which formed part of the Western Task Force's Force O bound for Omaha Beach. Beever was born in 1904 near Yorkshire, England, and joined RNVR in 1942.

32. The distance between the leading landing craft and the guide vessel was about twice the length of the LCA, which was forty-one feet. Landing craft followed other landing craft in the column by the same distance. The assertion that the LCAs followed the wake of their leading motor launch is based on the experience of RNVR Lt. George Edward "Jimmy" Green, who was near Rudder's LCA in command of the flotilla of LCAs that took the 2nd Ranger Battalion's Company C (Task Force B) to Omaha Beach. I interviewed Green by telephone on August 31, 2005. He lives nears Axminster, Devon, U.K.

33. Steven J. Zaloga, *Rangers Lead the Way: Pointe du Hoc, D-Day 1944,* 30.

34. Morris Prince, *The Road to Victory: The Story of the Elite WWII 2nd Battalion Rangers,* 78.

35. HMS *Prince Charles,* "Operation Neptune: Chronological Report, June 6, 1944," Ranger Collections, U.S. Military History Institute, Army War College, Carlisle Barracks, Pennsylvania; and Joseph Balkoski, *Omaha Beach: D-Day, June 6, 1944,* 84; Allied Expeditionary Air Force, Daily Intelligence/Operations Summary Number 133 for 6 June 1944, Record of Air Effort in Support of Operation Overlord, AIR 37/60, National Archives of the United Kingdom. Between 5:50 AM and 6:30 AM the *Texas* fired 126 armor-piercing and 100 high-explosive shells at Pointe du Hoc.

36. George Edward "Jimmy" Green, telephone interview with the author, December 24, 2007.

37. Theodore Wells account in Raaen, "Intact."

38. Balkoski, *Omaha Beach,* 85.

39. Vermeer, "Pointe du Hoc," 5; James W. Eikner, "D-Day Ranger Landings," sketch map of the flotilla route drawn by Eikner, not included in book but a copy in the

possession of the author. It is consistent with but in more detail than the authoritative War Department, *Small Unit Actions,* 5.

40. Harrison, *Cross-Channel Attack,* 300.

41. War Department, *Small Unit Actions,* 8.

42. Lt. Colin Beever, RNVR, commanding officer, HMML 304 [ML 304], official letter to Cmdr. Stratford Dennis, RN, commanding officer, HMS *Prince Charles,* who also commanded, Assault Group O-4, June 12, 1944, in Rowe Collection, U.S. Military History Institute, Army War College, Carlisle Barracks, Pennsylvania. The letter has no title but is described in its text as "Report of Proceedings on the Far Shore on the Morning of 6th of June 1944," 1–4.

43. Estimates of the distance the landing craft were from Pointe de la Percée when they turned toward Pointe du Hoc vary from 300 to 1,000 yards. Lieutenant Beever stated 1,000 yards in his report, but Rangers say the distance was less. I have used half a mile (880 yards), the same distance stated in the lucid report of RNVR Sub. Lt. W. L. Eccles, commanding officer of an LCT carrying a DUKW. His craft sank after making the turn into the wind and current toward Pointe du Hoc.

44. Eikner, interview, August 9, 2005; Earl Rudder to G. K. Hodenfield, May 6, 1959; Cmdr. Stratford Dennis, RN, Commanding Officer, Assault Group O-4, "Report of Proceedings on 6th June 1944," June 17, 1944, 4, Ranger Collections, U.S. Military History Institute, Army War College, Carlisle Barracks, Pennsylvania. As Rudder's communications officer, Eikner was Kolodziejczak's supervisor and got this account from him. I could find no evidence to support a widely told story that Rudder pulled his pistol and threatened the British officer to effect the change of course.

45. Quoted in Robert W. Black, *The Battalion: The Dramatic Story of the 2nd Ranger Battalion in World War II,* 95.

46. Von Keusgen, *Pointe du Hoc,* 12–13. Also, von Keusgen e-mail to author, December 31, 2007. Von Keusgen is a German investigator and archaeologist who has made extensive studies of Pointe du Hoc and other fortifications along the Atlantic Wall.

47. The map of enemy gun positions along Omaha Beach prepared for General Huebner shows only light machine guns in the small resistance nest; see also War Department, *Small Unit Actions,* 35. In his attack plan, Rudder assigned the suppression of the resistance nest to the 2nd Ranger Battalion's Company F.

48. Raaen, "Intact." The U.S. Army's account of the first day on Pointe du Hoc states that Schneider received and acknowledged by radio the code word "Tilt" from Rudder, indicating he should take Task Force C to Omaha Beach. See War Department, *Small Unit Actions,* 8. There are several accounts of radio messages sent from Pointe du Hoc. An important one involves the Royal Navy, which was responsible for delivering the three Ranger task forces to the proper beach. The vessels that carried the Rangers, called Assault Group O-4, were commanded by Cdr. Stratford Dennis, RN. The LCAs carrying the Rangers were under his command and had prearranged code words to send messages to Dennis. Their code word for success by Task Force A in getting the essential men up the cliffs at Pointe du Hoc was "Bingo." Dennis never heard "Bingo," but at 7:09 AM he heard "Crowbar," which meant Rudder's Rangers had landed at Pointe du Hoc. Dennis

prepared his report on the operation on June 17, 1944, stating that he then "decided [he] had no option but to send the remaining Rangers to Dog Green where they touched down at 0753." The "remaining Rangers" were Schneider's Task Force C, and Dog Green was the code name for one of the landing areas on Omaha Beach. I use Raaen's account in the text because (1) it correlates with Schneider's action and (2) his personal account has a compelling immediacy.

49. Balkoski, *Omaha Beach,* 167; War Department, *Omaha Beachhead,* 53. In the latter publication, map number VI indicates clearly the planned landing sector and the actual one.

50. Ibid.; Epstein quoted in Balkoski, *Omaha Beach,* 174.

51. Harrison, *Cross-Channel Attack,* map XII appended.

52. U.S. Army Air Forces, Evaluation Board, "The Effectiveness of Third Phase Tactical Air Operations in the European Theater, 5 May 1944–8 May 1945," August 1945, 46. It should be noted that inaccurate bombing could have saved Rudder's Rangers from the last aerial bombardment.

53. Beever, official letter to Dennis, June 12, 1944.

54. Christopher J. Anderson, "Two Screaming Eagles: Unlikely Rangers on D-Day," *America's War Heroes: Unsung and Legendary,* 2002, 61–63.

55. Ibid. Goodgal and Crouch remembered that this bombing of Pointe du Hoc occurred after *Texas* ceased firing at 6:25 AM. Their recollection supports the contention that Rudder's Rangers could have come under the aerial bombardment if they had landed on time.

56. Lane, *Rudder's Rangers,* 80–81; Raaen, "Intact," 10.

57. War Department, *Small Unit Actions,* 11; Block, handwritten combat diary with the sketch, 1.

58. War Department, *Small Unit Actions,* 10, 11; Vermeer, "Pointe du Hoc," 6–7.

59. War Department, *Small Unit Actions,* 14.

60. W. J. Marshall to Rudder, January 13, 1947, with enclosure titled "Excerpts from Action Reports and War Diaries of Comdr. William J. Marshall"; Beever, official letter to Dennis, June 12, 1944, 3; Vermeer, "Pointe du Hoc," 15. The *Satterlee* was 348 feet long and armed with four 5-inch guns and four 40 mm guns.

61. Thomas H. Trevor, interview with the author, London, March 17, 1989; W. J. Heinz, "I Took My Son to Omaha Beach: The Story of an American Hero's Return to Normandy," *Collier's,* June 11, 1954, 25; Vermeer, "Pointe du Hoc," 13. The standard German rifle was the Mauser Karabiner 98 Kurz (often abbreviated Kar98k or K98k) in caliber 7.92 mm. If the sniper who shot Trevor fired from two hundred yards, the bullet's energy on impact was about two thousand foot-pounds.

62. Anderson, "Two Screaming Eagles," 62. The Thompson submachine gun— model M1, also known as "Chicago Piano" or "Tommy gun," used .45-caliber automatic Colt pistol ammunition. It could be fired either semiautomatic or fully automatic with a cyclic rate of fire of about 600 rounds per minute. See Jim Thompson, *Machine Guns: A Pictorial, Tactical, and Practical History* (Boulder, Colo.: Paladin Press, 1989), 200–201.

63. Supreme Headquarters, Allied Expeditionary Force, "Attacks on Batteries on the

French Coast Prior to H-Hour on D-Day, Bombing Analysis Unit Report No. 10," November 29, 1944, 2, table VII, National Archives of the United Kingdom.

64. Air Ministry, Air Historical Branch, Royal Air Force Narrative, "The Liberation of North West Europe, vol. 3, The Landings in Normandy," 1946, 120–27, National Archives of the United Kingdom; Stephen Darlow, *D-Day Bombers: The Veterans' Story,* 155–56.

65. U.S. Army Air Forces, Evaluation Board, "Effectiveness of Third Phase Tactical Air Operations in the European Theater," 46.

66. War Department, *Small Unit Actions,* 28.

67. Earl Rudder speech, quoted in the *Brady Standard,* June 21, 1954; Jack Keating, transcript of interview with Peter S. Kalikow, World War II Oral History Archive, Eisenhower Center, University of New Orleans, quoted in Alissa Quistorff, "The U.S. Army's 2nd Ranger Battalion: Beyond D-Day," M.A. thesis, Florida State University, 2005, 23.

68. Baer, *"D-for-Dog,"* 35–36.

69. Von Keusgen, *Pointe du Hoc,* 70–71.

70. James Eikner, e-mail to author, January 7, 2008.

71. Vermeer, "Pointe du Hoc," 9; Earl Rudder, transcript of comments in the documentary film *Ten Men Went to War.* Filmed in black-and-white, the original footage, in two canisters, is in the Rudder Collection of the Cushing Memorial Library and Archives, Texas A&M University. See also *Collier's,* June 11, 1954, 26.

72. Baer, *"D-for-Dog,"* 36. In a map case slung over his shoulder, Rudder presumably had a copy of the map carried ashore by his intelligence officer, Capt. Harvey Cook, who saved his map and gave it to his son, Gen. Donald G. Cook, USAF, ret., who gave me an exact copy. The sketch map in Rudder's possession was a planning document map from p. 53 of *Neptune Monograph—CTF 122,* April 21, 1944, file reference DEFE 2/374, National Archives of the United Kingdom.

73. Von Keusgen, *Pointe du Hoc,* 82. Von Keusgen quotes a German soldier, Wilhelm Kirchhoff, who was in the Pointe du Hoc garrison.

74. Harrison, *Cross-Channel Attack,* 309.

75. James Eikner, e-mail to author, December 24, 2007. Rudder moved the fire control party to casemate number 2.

76. Trevor, interview, March 17, 1989.

77. Dr. Walter E. Block, handwritten combat diary, 2–3.

78. War Department, *Small Unit Actions,* 22, 26–27, 28; Joanna M. McDonald, *The Liberation of Pointe du Hoc: The 2d Rangers at Normandy, June 6–8, 1944,* 109.

79. War Department, *Small Unit Actions,* 46.

80. Ibid., 30–31.

81. Ibid., 34; Headquarters, 2nd Ranger Battalion, General Orders No. 16, May 31, 1945, 6, in Ranger Collections, Military History Institute, Army War College, Carlisle Barracks, Pennsylvania, also cited in Lane, *Rudder's Rangers,* Appendix D.

82. Von Keusgen, *Pointe du Hoc,* 70. Based on interviews with German soldiers who were there, von Keusgen printed a photograph provided by one of them with the caption: "The cannon in emplacement number 5 was totally destroyed and left on its back."

83. War Department, *Omaha Beachhead,* map IV. Maps I through XVI are inside the back cover and thus lack page numbers.

84. The excerpt from the After Action Report of General Gerow's V Corps, including all forces involved in the assault on Omaha Beach, is quoted in Don Congdon, ed., *Combat WWII Europe: Unforgettable Eyewitness Accounts of the Momentous Military Struggles of World War II,* 501; Bradley, *A Soldier's Story,* 280.

85. G. K. Hodenfield, "I Climbed the Cliffs with the Rangers," *Saturday Evening Post,* August 19, 1944, 98; Kerchner, oral history transcript, World War II Oral History Archive, Eisenhower Center, University of New Orleans.

86. War Department, *Small Unit Actions,* 38. The bunker on the western fringe of the fortified area was a duplicate of the fortification that shielded Rudder's command post on the other side of the *pointe.* Both were emplacements for 37 mm antiaircraft guns.

87. Ibid., 35, 38, and map on 32–33. The map shows the defensive perimeter on the morning of June 7 extending from near the observation bunker for 400 yards to the east, where it curved to intersect the cliff. Page 61 describes assigning men to hold the perimeter from gun positions no. 3 to no. 5, which formed the western side of the perimeter. The acreage within the perimeter defense increased slightly when the German observation post surrendered on June 7. I measured the distances and arrived at about thirty acres' ground area. Vermeer estimated thirty-five acres, and his judgment was excellent in measuring distances and areas.

88. Vermeer, "Pointe du Hoc," 17.

89. Ibid. The observation bunker was neutralized on June 7.

90. War Department, *Small Unit Actions,* 39.

91. Ibid., 39–41; James Eikner, interview with the author, September 27, 2005.

92. Eikner, interview, September 27, 2005; Vermeer, "Pointe du Hoc," 15; War Department, *Small Unit Actions,* 37.

93. Balkoski, *Omaha Beach,* 238.

94. War Department, *Small Unit Actions,* 36. HMS *Talybont* was an escort destroyer of the Hunt (Type III) class commissioned May 19, 1943. Its armaments normally included four four-inch guns.

95. Ibid., 46.

96. Frank South, e-mail to author, November 15, 2005.

97. Theodore Wells manuscript, quoted in Raaen, "Intact," 12–13.

98. *Austin American,* June 6, 1944; Margaret Rudder to her husband, June 11, 1944.

99. Anne Frank, *Anne Frank: The Diary of a Young Girl,* 217.

100. W. J. Heinz. "I Took My Son to Omaha Beach: The Story of an American Hero's Return to Normandy," *Collier's* magazine, June 11, 1954, 26.

101. Earl Rudder, transcript of comments in *Ten Men Went to War.* Robert Rudder was born April 16, 1954, in Brady, Texas.

102. War Department, *Small Unit Actions,* 40.

103. Ibid., 43; Anderson, "Two Screaming Eagles," 63.

104. Vermeer, "Pointe du Hoc," 15.

105. War Department, *Small Unit Actions,* 48. D-bars were a type of chocolate bar

issued for special purposes, including use during severe emergencies. They were some-times erroneously called rations, but they were not rations in the true sense because they did not contain adequate nutrients for a soldier for one day.

106. Charles H. "Ace" Parker, as told to Marcia Moen and Margo Heinen, *Reflections of Courage on D-Day and the Days That Followed,* 98–101; War Department, *Omaha Beachhead,* map IX.

107. War Department, *Small Unit Actions,* 51.

108. Ibid., 53, noted, "Ammunition for German weapons was in good supply."

109. The summary of the three German attacks on the night of June 6–7 is derived from ibid., 54–58.

110. Ibid., 59–61.

111. Ibid., 61.

112. Ibid., 59–61. To determine the exact number of men and their condition on the Pointe du Hoc at any given time is probably impossible. Following are numbers that may be useful for making an estimate. A related issue is how many in the total force were Rangers and how many were not; it is generally accepted that 225 Rangers were in the force of about 252 that set out to make the amphibious landing on Pointe du Hoc on D-Day. Twenty-three of the approximate 252 men who left the troopship *Ben my-Chree* were lost when their landing craft sank, which means 229 actually landed on D-Day. Another twenty-three Rangers arrived with Ace Parker from Omaha on D-Day night, returning the total to 252. At dawn on June 7, about 90 men were able to bear arms, including many wounded like Rudder. That means that 162 had been killed, captured, or were too seriously wounded to bear arms. Depending on which figures are used, the casualty rate was between 60 percent and 70 percent by dawn on June 7.

113. McDonald, *Liberation of Pointe du Hoc,* 147.

114. Parker, *Reflections of Courage,* 111.

115. Charles H. Taylor, "The Ranger Force in the Omaha Beach Assault, Part II, Pointe du Hoe [*sic*]," 63, sent to Rudder for review with cover letter dated November 24, 1944, copy in the possession of the author, courtesy of Margaret Rudder.

116. Quoted in Black, *The Battalion,* 139.

117. 2nd Ranger Battalion, After Action Report, June 8, 1944 (typescript dated July 22, 1944), 3.

118. Taylor, "Ranger Force in the Omaha Beach Assault," 61; Raaen, "Intact," 53. The reinforcements were from F Company of the 5th Ranger Battalion.

119. Parker, *Reflections of Courage,* 115.

120. Raaen, "Intact," 16.

121. Ibid., 16; Taylor, "Ranger Force in the Omaha Beach Assault," 109.

122. Taylor, "Ranger Force in the Omaha Beach Assault," 111.

123. 2nd Ranger Battalion, After Action Report, June 8, 1944.

124. James Eikner, telephone interview with the author, October 19, 2005.

125. Raaen, "Intact," 36; Taylor, "Ranger Force in the Omaha Beach Assault," 111.

126. McDonald, *Liberation of Pointe du Hoc,* 151.

127. 2nd Ranger Battalion, After Action Report, June 8, 1944.

128. Eikner, *2d Ranger Battalion,* 62. Casualty figures are in the narrative by James W. Eikner, commanding officer of the 2nd Ranger Battalion's Headquarters Company at the end of the war; Eikner's figures agree with those from the battalion's After Action Report of June 8, 1944. Henry S. Glassman's history of the 5th Ranger Battalion, *Lead The Way, Rangers,* 20, cites two Rangers killed and four wounded by the non-Ranger elements in the relief column. The account of Schneider going in front of his men to stop their "blue-on-blue" firing is from a statement by Lou Lisko to Sylvie Chapelie and quoted in McDonald, *Liberation of Pointe du Hoc,* 156. The German machine guns were the MG 42, called "Hitler's saw," which fired at least twice as fast as the American machine guns or the Browning automatic rifle.

129. John Raaen, e-mail to author, October 27, 2005; Raaen, "Intact," 37.

130. Eikner, telephone interview, October 19, 2005.

131. Anderson, "Two Screaming Eagles," 63.

132. Harrison, *Cross-Channel Attack,* 351–52.

133. Vermeer, "Pointe du Hoc," 11; Kalikow, World War II Oral History Archive, University of New Orleans, quoted in Quistorff, "U.S. Army's 2nd Ranger Battalion," 125; Lou Lisko to Rudder, May 26, 1962.

134. Headquarters, First United States Army, General Orders No. 28, June 20, 1944, copy in the possession of the author, courtesy of Margaret Rudder:

> *Lieutenant Colonel James E. Rudder, 0294916, Infantry, United States Army. For extraordinary heroism in action on 6 June 1944 at Pointe du Hoc, France. Lieutenant Colonel Rudder commanding Force A of the Rangers landed on the beach with his unit which was immediately subjected to heavy rifle, machine gun, mortar and artillery fire. Devastating fire was also directed from the cliffs overlooking the beach. Completely disregarding his own safety, he repeatedly exposed himself in directing the reorganization of his unit to assault the cliffs. As soon as the first elements had scaled the cliffs, Lieutenant Colonel Rudder immediately scaled the cliffs in order to better direct the attack. Though wounded, he refused to be evacuated and continued to direct the attack. By his determined leadership and dauntlessness he inspired his men so that they successfully withstood three enemy counterattacks. Though wounded again, he still refused to be evacuated. Lieutenant Colonel Rudder's heroic leadership, courage and complete devotion to duty are in keeping with the highest traditions of the service.*

In addition to Rudder, nine other men from the 2nd Ranger Battalion were awarded the Distinguished Service Cross for gallantry on D-Day: Capt. Edgar L. Arnold, Sgt. William J. Courtney, Pfc. William E. Dreher, Capt. Ralph E. Goranson, 1st Lt. George F. Kerchner, 1st Sgt. Leonard G. Lomell, Capt. Otto Masny, Sgt. John W. White, and 1st Lt. William D. Moody. The source for this list is Harrison, *Cross-Channel Attack,* Appendix I, 473–76.

135. Richard P. Buehre to Margaret Rudder, postmarked Saint Paul, Minnesota, April 29, 1982.

136. This quotation from Len Lomell combines two sources. The first part is from

the *Dallas Morning News,* June 5, 1994. The last sentence is from Lomell's interview with me in New Orleans, La., on August 25, 2005.

137. Capt. Richard P. Merrill, administration and personnel officer, 2nd Ranger Battalion, Morning Report, 2nd and 5th Ranger Battalions, June 8, 1944, unpaged holographic manuscript, Ranger Collections, Military History Institute, Army War College, Carlisle Barracks, Pennsylvania.

138. Eikner, *2nd Ranger Battalion,* 62.

139. Contrary to other historical writings, the evidence is conclusive that Rudder did not go a hospital for his leg wound. The Ranger medic, Frank South, affirmed it (e-mail to author, November 15, 2005), as did Jim Eikner, the communications officer, in several interviews with me, and Trevor stated it in a letter to Rudder dated July 5, 1944. Moreover, on June 15, 1945, a month after the German surrender, Rudder informed his wife, "I have never been sick or to a hospital since I've been over here."

140. Headquarters, 2nd Ranger Battalion, After Action Report, June 8, 1944; Heinz, "I Took My Son to Omaha Beach," *Collier's,* June 11, 1954, 26; Earl Rudder to Mrs. Margaret Allen, Attorney General's Office, Austin, Texas, August 15, 1969.

141. British War Office to T. W. Trevor, July 12, 1944, copy in the possession of the author, courtesy of James W. Eikner; Trevor, interview with the author, London, March 17, 1989; Thomas H. Trevor, "After Action Report: Assault on Pointe du Hoe [*sic*], for Combined Operations Headquarters," July 12, 1944, copy in the possession of the author, courtesy of James W. Eikner.

142. Thomas H. Trevor to Earl Rudder, postmarked London, July 5, 1944.

143. James W. Eikner, interview with the author, October 27, 2005. Apparently, A and B companies of the 2nd Ranger Battalion entered Grandcamp with the 5th Ranger Battalion on June 8. Map XII of War Department, *Omaha Beachhead* depicts both Ranger battalions in or immediately south of Grandcamp on the night of June 8, 1944. The same publication does not describe the bivouac of the 2nd Ranger Battalion, but the battalion's own After Action Report does, and Eikner confirms its location. Map VIII of *Omaha Beachhead,* p. 129, shows a trail leading to the bivouac location described by Eikner.

144. 5th Ranger Battalion, After Action Report for June 8, 1944, copy in the possession of the author, courtesy of John C. Raaen Jr.; Heinz, "I Took My Son to Omaha Beach," 26; Baer, *"D-for-Dog,"* 47.

145. Copy of letter in the possession of the author, courtesy of Margaret Rudder.

146. Robert Ravelet, interview with the author, Grandcamp-Maisy, France, August 28, 1989.

147. James W. Eikner, speech at Pointe du Hoc on the thirty-fifth anniversary of D-Day, June 6, 1979, typescript copy in the possession of the author. "Monsieur Ravelet conceived the plan to preserve the battlefield in memory of the brave lads who fought here. He founded the Comité de la Pointe du Hoc."

148. Tourism brochure for Grandcamp les Bains brought back by Earl Rudder in 1954, in the possession of the author.

149. The period of Roman Gaul is usually dated from about 58–51 BC to AD 486.

150. Ravelet, interview, August 28, 1989.

151. Alfred B. Chandler Jr., ed., *The Papers of Dwight David Eisenhower,* vol. 5, *The War Years,* 156; Bradley, *A Soldier's Story,* 269.

152. Heinz, "I Took My Son to Omaha Beach," 25.

153. Lawrence H. Sud, *Guts and Glory: The Making of the American Military Image in Film.* (rev. ed., Lexington, Ky.: University Press of Kentucky, 2002), 174.

154. Cornelius Ryan, *The Longest Day: June 6, 1944,* 239.

155. Ryan, *The Longest Day,* 333.

156. James W. Eikner, e-mail to author, August 31, 2005. Eikner was an officer in Headquarters Company of the 2nd Ranger Battalion. Initially he was the battalion's communications officer and later the headquarters commandant.

157. Frank South, interview with the author, September 19, 2005; Frank South, e-mail to author, January 9, 2006.

158. Frank South, e-mail to author, January 9, 2006; Lee Kennett, *The American Soldier in World War II,* 137; Petty's memoir in Black, *The Battalion,* 3–4.

159. Antonio Ruggiero, telephone interview with the author, January 12, 2006; Von Keusgen, *Pointe du Hoc,* 82. Von Keusgen quotes a German soldier, Wilhelm Kirchhoff, who was in the Pointe du Hoc garrison.

160. A copy of the questionnaire completed by Rudder is in the possession of the author.

161. Earl Rudder to W. J. Syring, November 10, 1961. Syring was president of the World War II Rangers Battalions Association at the time.

162. "Tribute-Reunion Dinner" preceding the preview showing of *The Longest Day,* Imperial Ballroom, Americana Hotel, New York, October 3, 1962, seating document in the possession of the author. Other attendees included Gen. James M. Gavin, Gen. Omar N. Bradley, Gen. Matthew B. Ridgeway, and Francis Cardinal Spellman.

163. War Department, *Small Unit Actions.*

164. President Ronald Reagan, speech commemorating the fortieth anniversary of D-Day, Pointe du Hoc, Normandy, France, June 6, 1984.

CHAPTER 8. NORMANDY RESPITE

1. Headquarters, 2nd Ranger Battalion, After Action Report, June 15 and June 18, 1944, in Ranger Collections, Military History Institute, Army War College, Carlisle Barracks, Pennsylvania; Frederick E. Morgan, *Overture to Overlord,* 163–64.

2. Earl Rudder to his wife, July 4, 1944.

3. Paul Parscenski to Earl Rudder, June 17, 1954, copy in the possession of author.

4. Margaret Rudder to her husband, June 12, 1944.

5. Margaret Rudder, to her husband, June 14, 1944.

6. W. W. Chaplin, *The Fifty-Two Days: An NBC Reporter's Story of the Battle That Freed France,* 52.

7. U.S. Army, European Theater of Operations, "Activities of Military Police," no date or page number, U.S. Army Military Police Museum, Fort Leonard Wood, Mo.;

Morris Prince, *The Road to Victory: The Story of the Elite WWII 2nd Battalion Rangers,* 103–104.

8. Earl Rudder to his wife, July 22, 1944.

9. Marcia Moen and Margo Heinen, *The Fool Lieutenant: A Personal Account of D-Day and World War II,* 122.

10. Buford L. Riddle to Earl Rudder, June 23, 1954.

11. John Colby, *War from the Ground Up: The 90th Division in World War II,* 103.

12. Dr. Walter Block, unpublished combat diary, July 25, 1944, Ranger Collections, U.S. Military History Institute, Army War College, Carlisle Barracks, Pennsylvania, and copy in the possession of the author; Prince, *Road to Victory,* 107.

13. Block, unpublished combat diary, July 25, 1944.

14. "More Honors Are Paid To Lt. Col. Max Schneider," *Shenandoah (Iowa) Evening Sentinel,* September 5, 1944; Max F. Schneider to James Earl Rudder, November 8, 1944.

15. James Schneider (son of Max F. Schneider), e-mail to author, July 6, 2008; Julia Ferguson Falk, telephone conversation, December 20, 2005.

16. James Schneider, e-mail to author, July 6, 2008; *Shenandoah (Iowa) Evening Sentinel,* March 28, 1959.

17. Richard P. Hallion, *D-Day 1944: Air Power Over the Normandy Beaches and Beyond,* 20; Dr. Walter Block, unpublished combat diary, July 25, 1944.

18. Brigitte de Kergorlay, interview with the author, June 25, 2000.

19. Carlton Joyce, *Stand Where They Fought: 150 Battlefields of the 77-Day Normandy Campaign,* vol. 1, *The American Sector,* 258–59.

20. Martin Blumenson, *The Patton Papers,* vol. 2, *1940–1945,* 506; M. Mathien, Office of the Mayor, City of Mayenne, e-mail to author, January 5, 2006 (the population figure is the mayor's estimate for 1944); Earl Rudder to his wife, August 13, 1944. Rudder referred to himself the mayor of Mayenne because most of the civilian population had fled, and he was the temporary authority figure there.

21. Frank South, telephone interview with the author, February 2, 2008.

22. Paul Fussell, *Wartime: Understanding and Behavior in the Second World War,* 80; South, telephone interview, February 2, 2008. Fussell was an English professor at the University of Pennsylvania and combat infantryman in the European war.

CHAPTER 9. BRITTANY

1. James Earl Rudder, personal vest-pocket notebook, in the possession of the author.

2. Ibid., 1944; Morris Prince, *The Road to Victory: The Story of the Elite WWII 2nd Battalion Rangers,* 112–13.

3. Joseph Balkoski, *From Beachhead to Brittany: The 29th Infantry Division at Brest, August–September 1944,* 30–31.

4. Martin Blumenson, *The Patton Papers,* vol. 2, *1940–1945,* 532.

5. The local people do not refer to the area either as Le Conquet or as a peninsula. Le Finistère is a department in the province of Brittany. It includes the land both north

and south of the Brest harbor. The south part called *le Finistère sud,* and the north part, *le Finistère nord,* corresponds to the area that the U.S. Army called "Le Conquet peninsula."

6. Blumenson, *Breakout and Pursuit,* 634. Forces Françaises de l'Intérieur was the formal name for French resistance fighters formed under Charles de Gaulle in 1944 and directed from London.

7. Frank James Price, *Troy H. Middleton: A Biography,* 91.

8. Ibid., 171, 191.

9. Blumenson, *Breakout and Pursuit,* 638.

10. M. R. D. Foot, *SOE in France: An Account of the Work of the British Special Operations Executive in France, 1940-1944,* 267. Jedburgh was an operation during World War II in which men from British Special Operations Executive, U.S. Office of Strategic Services, Free French Bureau Central de Renseignements et d'Action ("Intelligence and Operations Central Bureau") and Dutch or Belgian Army parachuted into Nazi-occupied France, Holland, or Belgium to conduct sabotage and guerrilla warfare and lead the local resistance forces against the Germans.

11. Jonathan Gawne, *Americans in Brittany, 1944: The Battle for Brest,* 67; Rudder vest-pocket notebook, 1944.

12. Holbrook Bradley, "Bradley Visits HQ Unit of FFI in Brittany," *Baltimore Sun,* September 1944; Jacques André and Jean-François Conq, *Objectif Kéringar: Jours de libération, Août–septembre 1944,* 79.

13. Headquarters, 29th Infantry Division, "Operations of Task Force Sugar," 3, Box 24035, RG 407.270.56.6.2, National Archives; Gawne, *Americans in Brittany,* 60–62, 67.

14. Earl Rudder to his wife, September 9, 1944.

15. Balkoski, *From Beachhead to Brittany,* 198–99.

16. Henri Floch and Alain Le Berre, *L'Enfer de Brest: Brest—Presqu'île de Crozon, 25 août–19 septembre 1944,* 293 (map 7, "La Poche de Conquet"); André and Conq, *Objectif Kéringar,* 92; Alfred E. Baer Jr., *"D-for-Dog": The Story of a Ranger Company,* 53–54.

17. Rene Le Gall, interview with the author, June 21, 2005; Gawne, *Americans in Brittany,* 61.

18. Alfred Baer, *"D-for-Dog,"* 53.

19. Floch and Le Berre, *L'Enfer de Brest,* 138; Baer, *"D-for-Dog,"* 55; Headquarters, 2nd Ranger Battalion, After Action Report, September 4, 1944, in Ranger Collections, Military History Institute, Army War College, Carlisle Barracks, Pennsylvania.

20. Headquarters, 29th Infantry Division, "Operations of Task Force Sugar," 7.

21. James W. Eikner, e-mail to author, July 9, 2010; Harold K. Slater, telephone interview with author, August 5, 2005. See also Balkoski, *From Beachhead to Brittany,* 189.

22. Headquarters, 29th Infantry Division, Journal of Latitude Advance, September 1–11, 1944, Box 8628, RG 407.270.56.5.7, NA.

23. James W. Eikner, ed., *2d Ranger Battalion: The Narrative History of Headquarters Company, April 1943–May 1945,* 18; "Peninsula Falls," *29 Let's Go!* September 10, 1944, 1.

24. Gawne, *Americans in Brittany,* 64. I obtained schematic drawings of the fort from the Archives de Memorial de Montbarey. Bernard Paich, an authoritative French archaeological historian of the Atlantic Wall, prepared the drawings of the German fort, which show two levels below ground and three above. In 1984 the Brest harbor fortification known as Fort Montbarey was placed under the control of the Memorial Association to be a museum and repository of archives about the events in Le Finistère during World War II. A related article by Hubert Chanson with information about the German fort appeared in the journal of the American Shore and Beach Preservation Association, *Shore and Beach* 72, no. 4 (Fall 2004): 10–12.

25. Dr. Walter E. Block, unpublished combat diary for September 2–8, 1944, 14, Ranger Collections, U.S. Military History Institute, Army War College, Carlisle Barracks, Pennsylvania, and copy in the possession of the author.

26. Marcia Moen and Margo Heinen, *The Fool Lieutenant: A Personal Account of D-Day and World War II,* 172.

27. Ibid.

28. Ibid., 164.

29. "Martin Fürst," File no. 13392, Bundesarchiv-Militärarchiv, Freiburg im Breisgau, Germany. The file consists of twenty-four sheets, most of which concern the personality of Fürst. For obtaining and translating these documents I am indebted to my friend Karl Josef Lüttgens of Schleiden, Germany.

30. Personal note from Harvey Cook to his son, Donald G. Cook, July 26, 1998. The note was written on the back of a photograph of the fortress.

31. Martin Fürst, "Supplement to 266th Infantry Division, June–August 1944," MS no. P-176, 46, RG 319, NA, German copy, trans. Robert D. King, University of Texas at Austin (hereinafter cited as Fürst Report); Moen and Heinen, *The Fool Lieutenant,* 165.

32. Headquarters, 2nd Ranger Battalion, After Action Report, September 9, 1944.

33. Fürst Report, 46.

34. Ibid., 46–47.

35. Ibid., 47. Not every participant remembers the surrender at Saint-Mathieu in the same way. Some of the Rangers participated in several surrender ceremonies in Brittany and may confuse one with another. Confusion is easy, because on September 9, 1944, there were three surrenders by Fürst: to Edlin in the fort in mid-morning; then the battery to Rudder at 12 noon, and third, of all German forces on Le Conquet to Rudder at 1:30 PM. I have relied on four documents that are in general agreement: (1) Edlin's account in his biography, *The Fool Lieutenant,* published in 2000; (2) the After Action Report of the 2nd Ranger Battalion for September 9, 1944, which was typed on October 22, 1944; (3) the account of FFI Lt. Col. Faucher, which was prepared within one year after the event; and (4) the book *Objectif Kéringar,* by Jacques André and Jean-François Conq, published in Brest in 2002.

36. Joseph Fürst Jr., telephone interview with the author, Rocky Hill, Conn., February 12, 2008.

37. Baptiste Faucher, "Participation des FFI et des FTPF prés des formations de la 29e

DI/USA du VIII CA/USA aux opérations de la Libération des régions côtires: Reddition de las Defense Allemande," Brest, 1946, copy in the possession of the author.

38. Moen and Heinen, *The Fool Lieutenant,* 167.

39. 2nd Ranger Battalion, After Action Report, September 9, 1944.

40. Moen and Heinen, *The Fool Lieutenant,* 167–68.

41. Ibid., 169–70. Fürst's pistol was a double-action Mauser HSc, circa 1937, in 7.65 mm (.32 ACP) caliber.

42. 2nd Ranger Battalion, After Action Report, September 9, 1944 (date of preparation was October 22, 1944); Headquarters, 29th Infantry Division, "Operations of Task Force Sugar," 10; Gawne, *Americans in Brittany,* 66.

43. Moen and Heinen, *The Fool Lieutenant,* 170–71.

44. Jacques André with Alain Le Berre. *Le Bataillon F.F.I. de Ploudalmézeau: Brest-Été 44 Les combats autour du Conquet,* 236; Eikner, *2d Ranger Battalion,* 69; Earl Rudder to his wife, September 13, 1944.

45. Moen and Heinen, *The Fool Lieutenant,* 177–78.

46. André and Conq, *Objectif Kéringar,* 175.

47. Copy of inscription and photograph in the possession of the author. Inscription reads as follows in French:

Le 9 Septembre 1944
Le col. Rudder
Commandant du 2d Rangers
et le col Faucher
commandant des FFI
ont reçu en ce lieu
poste de commandement des batteries
de Keringar et des Rospects
la reddition du col. Allemand Fürst

48. Blumenson, *Breakout and Pursuit,* 652; 2nd Ranger Battalion, After Action Report, September 18, 1944; Earl Rudder to his wife, September 23, 1944.

49. Blumenson, *Breakout and Pursuit,* 653.

50. Floch and Le Berre, *L'Enfer de Brest,* 249.

CHAPTER 10. BELGIAN INTERLUDE

1. Charles B. MacDonald, *The Battle of the Huertgen Forest,* 9.

2. Earl Rudder to his wife, September 13, 1944.

3. Martin Blumenson, *Breakout and Pursuit,* 637; James W. Eikner, e-mail to author, February 3, 2005; Headquarters, 2nd Ranger Battalion, S-1 Journal, September 1–30, 1944, Ranger Collections, Military History Institute, Army War College, Carlisle Barracks, Pennsylvania. Rudder confirmed the prior owner of the car to his wife in a letter

dated October 8, 1944. Harvey Cook added details to the story in conversation with his son, Donald Cook, who told the author, February 11, 2005.

4. Headquarters, 2nd Ranger Battalion, S-1 Journal 44; Morris Prince, *The Road to Victory,* 136–37

5. Nilah Pennington Andrews, telephone interview with the author, January 18, 2005. The office administered European Theater (ETOUSA) replacement depots

6. Headquarters, 2nd Ranger Battalion, After Action Report, October 3, 1944, in Ranger Collections, Military History Institute, Army War College, Carlisle Barracks, Pennsylvania. Thirty-one new men arrived on October 3; another twenty-six came in on October 17.

7. Harold K. Slater, interview with the author, New Orleans, August 28, 2002.

8. Alfred E. Baer Jr., *"D-for-Dog": The Story of a Ranger Company,* 60–61; Earl Rudder to his wife, October 8, 1944; James W. Eikner, ed., *The Narrative History of Headquarters Company, 2nd Ranger Battalion, April 1943–May 1945,* 18, 61.

9. Earl Rudder to his wife, October 8, 1944.

10. The estimate that 20,000 to 40,000 Germans escaped from the Falaise Pocket was stated in the U.S. Army's 1961 official history of the Normandy campaign, *Breakout and Pursuit* (555), by Martin Blumenson. However, in 1993 Blumenson came out with *The Battle of the Generals: The Untold Story of the Falaise Pocket: The Campaign That Should Have Won World War II* and corrected the error by citing a British study conducted in the spring of 1945, but only recently found, which concluded that about 240,000 enemy troops escaped from Normandy; see p. 259. For an elaboration of this issue with extensive German documentation, see Jean Paul Pallud, *Rückmarsch! The German Retreat from Normandy, Then and Now,* 176–230.

11. David Eisenhower, *Eisenhower at War, 1943–1945,* 490–91.

12. Earl Rudder to his wife, October 22, 1944.

13. Marcia Moen and Margo Heinen, *The Fool Lieutenant: A Personal Account of D-Day and World War II,* 186–87.

14. Ibid.

15. Earl Rudder to his wife, November 1, 1944.

16. Alfred D. Chandler Jr., ed., *The Papers of Dwight David Eisenhower,* vol. 5, *The War Years,* 171. This volume is Eisenhower's appointment schedule from June 23, 1942 through May 5, 1945. On November 8, 1944, he was on an inspection trip along the Belgian-German border, accompanied by Generals Bradley and Middleton. The text does not mention the 2nd Ranger Battalion but refers to the 5th Armored Division, to which the battalion was then attached. Rudder's letter to his wife confirms the date, and Edlin's account (Moen and Heinen, *The Fool Lieutenant,* 194) confirms that Eisenhower was the visitor.

17. Earl Rudder to his wife, November 8, 1944.

18. Eisenhower quoted in Stephen E. Ambrose, *Eisenhower: Soldier, General of the Army, President-Elect, 1890–1952,* 358; Marcia Moen and Margo Heinen, *The Fool Lieutenant,* 194.

19. Eisenhower, *Eisenhower At War,* 493.

CHAPTER 11. HUERTGEN FOREST

1. 2nd Ranger Battalion, After Action Report, November 1, 1944, in Ranger Collections, Military History Institute, Army War College, Carlisle Barracks, Pennsylvania.

2. Douglas E. Nash, *Victory Was Beyond Their Grasp: With the 272nd Volks-Grenadier Division from the Huertgen Forest to the Heart of the Reich,* 250–51; Charles B. MacDonald, *The Battle of the Huertgen Forest,* 195–96.

3. U.S. Army, Center of Military History, *American Military History,* Army Historical Series, 494; Edward G. Miller, *A Dark and Bloody Ground: The Hürtgen Forest and the Roer River Dams, 1944–1945.*

4. James M. Gavin, *On to Berlin: Battles of an Airborne Commander, 1943–1946,* 260–61.

5. Ludwig Fischer, mayor of Schmidt, e-mail message, April 7, 2008. Fischer stated, "In 1944 Schmidt had about 1,000 inhabitants, most of them small farmers, old men, women and children. The army issued the order to evacuate and the Nazi Party executed it. The order came in the first days of September 1944, but the majority of the population left in the first two weeks of October, when they could hear the strong noise of the battle in the Hürtgen Forest not far away."

6. 2nd Ranger Battalion, After Action Report, November 1–3, 1944; Vic Hillery and Emerson Hurley, *Paths of Armor: The Fifth Armored Division in World War II,* 154; Earl Rudder to his wife, November 1, 1944.

7. Rainer Monnartz, *Hürtgenwald 1944/1945: Militärgeschichtlicher Tourenplaner* (Aachen: Heilos Verlags und Buchvertriebsgesellschaft, 2006), 8.

8. 2nd Ranger Battalion, After Action Report, November 5, 1944; Earl Rudder to his wife, November 12, 1944. The after action report states that Rudder selected an observation post near the village of Lammersdorf. Traveling by jeep with a driver and Cook, he probably crossed the German border east of Raeren, Belgium and continued about three miles to Rott, Germany (location of 28th Division headquarters), for orientation to suitable sites from which to look over the landscape and, ideally, to observe the ensuing battle. However, there was no place from which he could safely view the fighting then underway along the Vossenack ridge. The best viewpoint was from Hill 554 southeast of Lammersdorf, some six miles southeast of Rott.

9. *Historical and Pictorial Review of the 28th Infantry Division in World War II.* This publication is a well-documented account of selected actions and units of the division.

10. 2nd Ranger Battalion, After Action Report, November 8, 1944.

11. Generalmajor Rudolf von Gersdorff, quoted in Miller, *Dark and Bloody Ground,* 52.

12. Charles B. MacDonald, *The Siegfried Line Campaign,* 369.

13. Ibid., 373–74.

14. 2nd Ranger Battalion, After Action Report, November 14, 1944; James W. Eikner, e-mail to author, March 20, 2008.

15. Morris Prince, *The Road to Victory: The Story of the Elite WWII 2nd Battalion Rangers,* 147; Charles B. MacDonald, *The Mighty Endeavor: The American War in Europe,*

385; Alfred E. Baer Jr., *"D-for-Dog": The Story of a Ranger Company*, 78; James W. Eikner, ed., *2d Ranger Battalion: The Narrative History of Headquarters Company, April 1943–May 1945*, 72.

16. Marcia Moen and Margo Heinen, *The Fool Lieutenant: A Personal Account of D-Day and World War II*, 207; Prince, *Road to Victory*, 151–52.

17. Sidney A. Salomon, *2nd U.S. Ranger Infantry Battalion: Germeter-Vossenack-Hurtgen-Bergstein-Hill 400 Germany: 14 Nov.–10 Dec. 1944*, 15.

18. Alfred Baer, *"D-for-Dog,"* 81.

19. MacDonald, *The Battle of the Huertgen Forest*, 112–13. Hatzfeld was the commanding officer of the 2nd Battalion, 112th Infantry Regiment, 28th Division.

20. Eikner, *2d Ranger Battalion*, 72.

21. A tank destroyer was a vehicle that mounted a high-velocity antitank gun but that had an open turret or no turret at all. By late 1944, U.S. tank destroyers ran on tracks rather than wheels or half-tracks.

22. The M29 Weasel was a World War II tracked vehicle designed specifically for operation in snow. The first weasels had 15-inch-wide tracks; later versions, 20-inch tracks. The M29C Water Weasel was amphibious, with buoyancy cells in the bow and stern as well as twin rudders. Other specifications were weight, 3,800 pounds; length, 10 feet, 6 inches; width, 5 feet (later 5 feet, 6 inches); height, 4 feet, 3 inches; crew, 4.

23. James W. Eikner, e-mail to author, September 6, 2009.

24. Moen and Heinen, *The Fool Lieutenant*, 210.

25. Gerald W. Heaney, telephone interview with the author, March 20, 2008.

26. Moen and Heinen, *The Fool Lieutenant*, 210–15. See also Salomon, *2nd U.S. Ranger Infantry Battalion*, 15.

27. Moen and Heinen, *The Fool Lieutenant*, 210–15.

28. Frank U. Roquemore, "The Operations of the 2nd Ranger Battalion in the Hurtgen Forest, 6–8 December 1944 (Rhineland Campaign) (Personal Experiences of a Platoon Leader), 9, prepared for the Infantry School, Advanced Infantry Officers Course, 1948–49, Fort Benning, Ga., World War II Collection, Donovan Research Library, Fort Benning; 2nd Ranger Battalion, After Action Report, November 19, 1944.

29. 2nd Ranger Battalion, After Action Report, November 19, 1944; Eikner, *2d Ranger Battalion*, 73. Four companies were pulled back on November 19, leaving companies A and B in place for twenty-four hours. The new location was specified in a paper at the U.S. Army Infantry School in 1948 as "some two thousand yards southwest of Vossenack" and that the "Ranger companies were under-strength, some as much as fifty per cent, due to casualties suffered while occupying defensive positions." See Roquemore, "Operations of the 2nd Ranger Battalion," 9.

30. Earl Rudder to his wife, November 23, 1944.

31. MacDonald, *Siegfried Line Campaign*, 336; Eikner, *2d Ranger Battalion*, December 3, 1944.

32. Earl Rudder to his wife, November 23, December 2, 1944; Moen and Heinen, *The Fool Lieutenant*, 217.

33. Roquemore, "Operations of the 2nd Ranger Battalion," 9, 11; Dr. Walter E. Block, unpublished combat diary, Ranger Collections, U.S. Military History Institute, Army War College, Carlisle Barracks, Pennsylvania, and copy in the possession of the author.

34. 2nd Ranger Battalion, S-2 and S-3 Journal, December 5, 1944, Ranger Collections, Military History Institute, Army War College, Carlisle Barracks, Pennsylvania. The entry reads: "Army G-1 called C.O. to rpt to Army G-1 by noon tomorrow." Williams was promoted to major at 10:27 PM on December 6, 1944, according to the S-2 and S-3 Journal, December 6, 1944.

35. Generalmajor Rudolf von Gersdorff quoted in Miller, *Dark and Bloody Ground;* Nash, *Victory Was Beyond Their Grasp,* 84.

36. MacDonald, *Siegfried Line Campaign,* 460–61; 2nd Ranger Battalion, S-2 and S-3 Journal, December 6, 1944.

37. Harold W. Gunther and James R, Shalala, *2nd Ranger Bn: Company E, 1943–1945,* 34.

38. Moen and Heinen, *The Fool Lieutenant,* 228–29.

39. Edwin M. Sorvisto, *2nd Ranger Bn: Roughing It With Charlie,* 52; Leonard Lomell, telephone interview with the author, May 18, 2005. Apparently, Sorvisto's undated booklet was first printed in Pilsen, Czechoslovakia. It was reprinted by the Antietam National Museum, Williamstown, N.J., with no date of publication.

40. Edgar L. Arnold to Earl Rudder, April 17, 1967; Marsha Moen and Margo Heinen, *The Fool Lieutenant,* 228–29.

41. 2nd Ranger Battalion, S-2 and S-3 Journal, December 7, 1944; Eikner, *2d Ranger Battalion,* 76; Salomon, *2nd U.S. Ranger Infantry Battalion,* 68. The Bergstein church also functioned as the battalion's forward command post.

42. Robert W. Black, *The Battalion: The Dramatic Story of the 2nd Ranger Battalion in World War II,* 232; Richard P. Merrill to Earl Rudder, January 25, 1945.

43. Earl Rudder to his wife, January 5. 1945.

44. Earl Rudder to David Carlson, June 19, 1965; Newsletter (undated) for a Ranger reunion in 1963. The writer, Lou Lisko, quoted Rudder that the Rangers' "dedication to country and to each other is their outstanding quality and reason for their success."

45. Harvey Cook to his son, Donald G. Cook, December 1, 1979.

CHAPTER 12. BATTLE OF THE BULGE

1. 109th Infantry Regiment, Unit Journal, Dec. 8, 1944–Feb. 15, 1945, Personal and General Correspondence Papers of James Earl Rudder, Cushing Memorial Library and Archives, Texas A&M University (hereinafter cited as CMLA); Charles B. MacDonald, *The Siegfried Line Campaign,* United States Army in World War II: European Theater of Operations, 373; Harry M. Kemp, *The Regiment: Let the Citizen Bear Arms! A Narrative History of an American Infantry Regiment in World War II,* 202. The figure of 6,184 casualties includes an unknown number in attached units. An internal count by the 28th Division arrived at 5,700—5,454 enlisted men and 248 officers. According to

Headquarters, 109th Infantry Regiment, General Orders No. 32, Rudder arrived at the command post of the 109th Regimental Combat Team in Ettelbruck, Luxembourg, on December 8, 1944, at 2:00 PM (1400 hours) and took command.

2. J. D. Morelock, *Generals of the Ardennes: American Leadership in the Battle of the Bulge*, 17; Robert A. Miller, *Division Commander: A Biography of Major General Norman D. Cota*, 131; Kemp, *The Regiment*, 189. The authorized strength of an infantry regiment in late 1944 was 3,257, and 836 for an ordinary infantry battalion. By comparison, the authorized strength of a Ranger battalion was 516 officers and enlisted men, although the 2nd Ranger Battalion usually had only 450 to 460. The units attached to the 109th Infantry Regiment were a company of the 103rd Engineers (175), a medical company (112), a signal platoon (54), the 707th Tank Battalion minus one light tank company (391), the 107th Field Artillery Battalion (497), the 108th Field Artillery Battalion (497), the 447th Antiaircraft Artillery Battalion, towed (628), for a total of 2,354 at full strength as shown on the tables of organization and equipment. An estimate that the attached units were at about 70 percent of full strength yields about 2,000 actual. The estimate was made with the assistance of Maj. Gen. John C. Raaen Jr., USA (ret.).

3. Joseph Flies, *Ettelbruck: Die Geschichte einer Landschaft*. The population of Diekirch in 1944 was about thirty-eight hundred.

4. Roland Gaul, *The Battle of the Bulge in Luxembourg: The Southern Flank, December 1944–January 1945*, Vol. 2, *The Americans*, 85.

5. Trevor N. Dupuy, *Hitler's Last Gamble: The Battle of the Bulge, December 1944–January 1945*, 104; Hugh M. Cole, *The Ardennes: Battle of the Bulge*, United States Army in World War II: European Theater of Operations, 55. The 9th Armored Division comprised three combat commands, designated A, B, and R. Only combat command A was along the Sûre River.

6. Frank James Price, *Troy H. Middleton: A Biography*, 191; Cole, *The Ardennes*, 55.

7. Dupuy, *Hitler's Last Gamble*, 101.

8. Harry M. Kemp, interview with the author, San Antonio, Texas, August 8, 2002. Richard P. Sullivan, personal communication with John C. Raaen Jr. Sullivan became commander of the Fifth Ranger Battalion in August 1944. He and Rudder were friends. After Rudder became commander of the 109th infantry, Sullivan went to see him. Rudder told Sullivan about laying the wire from the regimental command post to company command posts and Sullivan told Raaen, who told the author. The exact date of Sullivan's visit is not known.

9. Kemp, interview, August 8, 2002. Jim H. McCoy was assigned as Texas A&M University's commandant of cadets from his job as deputy chief of staff for logistics at the Pentagon in May 1967 while Rudder was president of A&M (1959–70), a certain indication that Rudder thought highly of him. His assignment as commandant lasted until June 1971. See John A. Adams Jr., *Keepers of the Spirit: The Corps of Cadets at Texas A&M University*, 220.

10. Kemp, interview, August 8, 2002.

11. Kemp, *The Regiment*, 213.

12. Frederick G. Wilkins to Margaret Rudder, May 30, 1945.

13. George Bunnell, interview with the author, Lavenham, Maryland, September 18, 2002.

14. Frederick G. Wilkins to Margaret Rudder, May 30, 1945.

15. *San Angelo Standard-Times,* August 30, 1945; Charles B. MacDonald, *A Time for Trumpets: The Untold Story of the Battle of the Bulge,* 12–14; Jean Delé, interview with the author, Bivels, Luxembourg, June 27, 2005. When Jean Delé became separated from his mother, he returned to their home in Bivels and hid in the basement until his mother came back. At the time of the interview he lived in the same house.

16. For an elaboration on this point, see John C. McManus, *Alamo In The Ardennes: The Untold Story of the American Soldiers Who Made the Defense of Bastogne Possible,* 30–31.

17. Dupuy, *Hitler's Last Gamble,* 105–106, 113–15, 501; Roland Gaul, interview with the author, February 20, 2005. Exact numbers in warfare, especially those of large magnitude, are almost never correct and should be taken as estimates or approximations. The 352nd Volksgrenadier Division had three regiments (the 914th, 915th, and 916th) with about three thousand men in each. The 915th and 916th made the initial assault across the Our to the heights and near its confluence with the Sûre. The 5th Parachute Division had three regiments (the 13th, 14th, and 15th) with about twenty-five hundred men in each. The 13th and 15th regiments attacked across the Our between Roth and Vianden and in a low-lying stretch of the river bank on the 109th's left flank.

18. Kemp, *The Regiment,* 291. During the battle the 109th Infantry lost twenty-six jeeps, fourteen jeep trailers, and eight 1 1/2-ton trucks.

19. I counted the 414 gravestones of a German military cemetery from the 1939–45 war on the grounds of an abbey, Ehrenfriedhof Abtei Mariawald, not far from the fighting that occurred in the Huertgen Forest and the Battle of the Bulge. All gravestones indicated that 1944 was the death year. Many gravestones were for men born in the first years of the twentieth century: 1901, 1902, or 1903. The oldest was born in 1892. Numerous gravestones were inscribed with a birth year of 1925 or 1926. Three were born in 1927.

20. John Toland, *Battle: The Story of the Bulge,* 76.

21. Cole, *The Ardennes,* 219. The "small dam" was a "weir," built to moderately raise the water level.

22. Lt. Col. Earl Rudder, interview, Buzancy, France, January 6, 1945, transcript in Personal and General Correspondence Papers, CMLA. The interviewer was 1st Lt. Henry G. Jackson of the 2nd Information and Historical Service. See also Dupuy, *Hitler's Last Gamble,* 523.

23. Cole, *The Ardennes,* 218.

24. Ibid.

25. Roland Gaul, e-mail to author, February 20, 2005; Cole, *The Ardennes,* 221.

26. Carlo D'Este, *Patton: A Genius For War,* 679.

27. Cole, *The Ardennes,* 223. *Herrenberg* translates literally as the "hill of gentlemen."

28. Ibid., 224; Kemp, interview, August 8, 2002. "Old man" was army slang for the commanding officer, who was usually the oldest man in the unit.

29. Gaul, *The Battle of the Bulge,* 2:46; McManus, *Alamo In The Ardennes;* Cole, *The Ardennes,* 224.

30. Cole, *The Ardennes,* 225.

31. Ibid.

32. Ibid.; Maj. Gen. Troy H. Middleton, Headquarters, VIII Corps, U.S. Army, "Report of the VIII Corps After Action against Enemy Forces in France, Belgium, Luxembourg and Germany for the Period 1–31 December 1944," April 6, 1945, 19, copy in the possession of the author; Earl Rudder, interview with Henry G. Jackson, Buzancy, France, January 6, 1945, Personal and General Correspondence Papers, Rudder Collection, CMLA.

33. Frederick G. Wilkins to Margaret Rudder, May 30, 1945.

34. Trevor Dupuy, *Hitler's Last Gamble,* 501.

35. Kemp, *The Regiment,* 262.

36. Ibid.; Maj. Harry M. Kemp, "The Operations of the 3rd Battalion, 109th Infantry (28th Infantry Division) in the Vicinity of Diekirch, Luxemburg, 16 December–25 December 1944, (Ardennes-Alsace Campaign) (Personal Experience of a Battalion Executive Officer)," unpaged, hand-drawn map attached, prepared for the Infantry School, Advanced Infantry Officers Course, 1949–50, Fort Benning, Ga., World War II Collection, Donovan Research Library, Fort Benning. The Grand Duchess of Luxembourg with her family and all but one minister fled to France when the Germans invaded on May 10, 1940. Later they went to Canada via Portugal and England.

37. Kemp, *The Regiment,* 268–69.

38. Maj. Embert A. Fossum, "Operations of 'Task Force L,' 109th Infantry (28th Infantry Division) near Grosbous, Luxembourg, 20–23 December 1944 (Ardennes-Alsace Campaign) (Personal Experience of a Task Force Commander)," 14–15, prepared for the Infantry School, Advanced Infantry Officers Course, Fort Benning, Ga., 1948–49, World War II Collection, Donovan Research Library, Fort Benning.

39. Kemp, *The Regiment,* 271; Fossum, "Operations of Task Force L," 23.

40. Fossum, "Operations of Task Force L," 24.

41. Ibid., 24–25.

42. Kemp, *The Regiment,* 272, 274.

43. Ibid., 273. The German officer was captured on December 21, 1944. Rudder had the captured map in his possession when he was interviewed by combat historian Henry Jackson in Buzancy, France, on January 6, 1945.

44. Fossum, "Operations of Task Force L," 26–27.

45. Ibid., 27. After discussing the Grosbous massacre with other officers, Fossum wrote in 1949 that he had erred when he did not leave adequate listening posts near the road or village when the task force moved to the ridge. He had reason to believe that a sizeable German force slipped by later that night or early the next morning and ran into lead elements of the U.S. 26th Division further east. See ibid., 38.

46. Price, *Troy H. Middleton,* 91, 270.

47. Fossum, "Operations of Task Force L," 35–36.

48. Ibid., 32.

49. Ibid., 33–34.

50. Frederick G. Wilkins to Margaret Rudder, May 30, 1945; Gaul, *Battle of the Bulge*, 1:75. Estimates of the number of Germans killed in the Grosbous massacre range upward from 400 to 2,000.

51. Earl Rudder, interview with Henry G. Jackson, Buzancy, France, January 6, 1945, Personal and General Correspondence Papers, CMLA.

52. Headquarters, 10th Armored Division, General Orders Number 45, "Award of Oak Leaf Cluster" (to Bronze Star medal previously awarded), December 23, 1944, CMLA.

53. Kemp, *The Regiment*, 381.

54. Cole, *The Ardennes*, 500–501; Dupuy, *Hitler's Last Gamble*, 208; Kemp, *The Regiment*, 280–84. Maj. Gen. John C. Raaen Jr., USA (ret.) estimated the approximate strength of Task Force Rudder from a composite list of the units involved and a description of their condition. The men in Task Force L from the armored division may have been from the 9th Armored Division, which was attached to the 10th Armored Division.

55. Gaul, *The Battle of the Bulge*, 2:75.

56. William M. Peña, *As Far As Schleiden: A Memoir of World War II*, 124.

57. Ibid., 125–27.

58. The citation reads in full as follows:

The Silver Star *is awarded to Lieutenant Colonel James E. Rudder, 0294916, Infantry, Headquarters 109th Infantry, for gallantry in action against the enemy from 16 to 27 December 1944. Lieutenant Colonel Rudder's regiment was attacked by vastly superior numbers of enemy forces on an extended position held in the vicinity of Bastendorf, Vianden and Brandenburg [Luxembourg]. Lieutenant Colonel Rudder, as Regimental Commander, quickly estimated the difficult situation at the beginning of the attack. Through skillful handling of his troops he was able to direct numerous counter-thrusts against the forceful attacking enemy. At great personal risk to himself, Lieutenant Colonel Rudder made frequent trips to subordinate units through enemy infiltrated territory and under heavy enemy artillery fire. After assigning new and more advantageous defensive positions to his Combat Team, Lieutenant Colonel Rudder directed, during heavy enemy shelling, the destruction of bridges in the path of the enemy after his troops had passed over them. His outstanding tactical ability permitted his Regiment to inflict high casualties on the enemy with a minimum loss to his own troops. During this action, he is also credited with stopping an enemy offensive that threatened a large area to the south and west of his defensive position. By his gallant and skillful leadership, Lieutenant Colonel Rudder reflects great credit upon himself and the Armed Forces of the United States.*

Headquarters, 28th Infantry Division, General Orders Number 10, "Award of Silver Star," February 2, 1945.

59. Earl Rudder to his wife, January 6, 1945. Hugh Cole asked about the river that Middleton instructed Rudder to get behind in the retreat along the Sûre. It was the Alzette, but Rudder said he did not remember its name.

60. Dupuy, *Hitler's Last Gamble,* 192.

61. Cole, *The Ardennes,* 225. Emphasis added.

62. MacDonald, *A Time for Trumpets,* 518.

CHAPTER 13. COLMAR POCKET

1. Ivan H. Peterman, "They Took the Nazis' Sunday Punch," *Saturday Evening Post,* September 28, 1946, 20.

2. Harry M. Kemp, *The Regiment: Let the Citizen Bear Arms! A Narrative History of an American Infantry Regiment in World War II,* 292–93.

3. Maj. Gen. Troy H. Middleton, Headquarters, VIII Corps, U.S. Army, "Report of the VIII Corps After Action against Enemy Forces in France, Belgium, Luxembourg and Germany for the Period 1–31 December 1944," April 6, 1945, 25, copy in the possession of the author; William M. Peña, *As Far As Schleiden: A Memoir of World War II,* 133.

4. Earl Rudder to his wife, January 6, 1945.

5. Ibid.

6. Earl Rudder, Western Union telegram to his wife, received in Brady, Texas, on January 13, 1945.

7. Earl Rudder to his wife, January 10, 1945.

8. Peña, *As Far As Schleiden,* 136. McCoy was a major at the time, not a lieutenant colonel.

9. Ibid., 137.

10. Jeffrey J. Clark and Robert Ross Smith, *Riviera to the Rhine,* 505–507, 538.

11. Ibid., 534; Peña, *As Far As Schleiden,* 141; Robert Miller, *Division Commander: A Biography of Major General Norman D. Cota,* 157.

12. Clark and Smith, *Riviera to the Rhine,* 535, 538. One French division was on the north side of Colmar with the Americans and, similarly, an American division was on the south with the French.

13. Haskell Monroe, interview with the author, June 19, 2007.

14. William Bradford Huie, *The Execution of Private Slovik,* 198; Kemp, *The Regiment,* 305–306. The judge advocate general in the ETO was Brig. Gen. Edward D. Betts. The review for Eisenhower was conducted by Betts's subordinate, the chief of military justice, who was Col. Hardy Hollers of the law firm of Hollers and O'Quinn in Austin, Texas. Nine reviewing officers worked under Hollers. The house where Slovik was executed was torn down after the war, and a new house was constructed on the site.

15. Huie, *The Execution of Private Slovik,* 208, 232–33. A made-for-television movie, *The Execution of Private Slovik,* starring Martin Sheen as Slovik, appeared in 1974 four years after Rudder's death. Neither Rudder nor Cota were portrayed in the movie.

16. Kemp, *The Regiment,* 308; A copy of Rudder's message to the 109th Infantry Regiment about Slovik's execution, January 31, 1945, is in the Cushing Memorial Library

and Archives, Texas A&M University, College Station (hereinafter cited as CMLA), and another is in the possession of the author.

17. Wayne C. Hall, *The Glory Years: Making of a University,* 150. I was unable to learn if publicity about the Slovik execution in the late 1960s would have upset Rudder. The provocation could have been a writer who called him for an interview on the subject. The first edition of the Huie's book, *The Execution of Private Slovik,* was published in 1954.

18. Earl F. Ziemke, *Stalingrad to Berlin: The German Defeat in the East,* 433; Headquarters, European Theater of Operations, U.S. Army, *The United States vs. Pvt. Eddie D. Slovik,* 36896415, Review by Staff Judge Advocate, quoted in Huie, *Execution of Private Slovik,* 187; Monroe, interview, June 19, 2007.

19. Lise Pommois, interview with the author, February 9, 2006.

20. Kemp, *The Regiment,* 312.

21. William M. Peña, *As Far As Schleiden,* 159.

22. Ibid., 160–62.

23. Kemp, *The Regiment,* 318–19.

24. Ibid., 319.

25. Pommois, interview, February 9, 2006.

26. Earl Rudder to his wife, February 12, 1945; Earl Rudder to Guy Schlesser, April 12, 1945, copy in Rudder Collection, CMLA; Jacques Le Conquet, *Le Figaro,* February 10, 1945; Charles de Gaulle, "Sur la Proposition du Ministre de la Guerre, le President du Gouvernement Provisoire de la Republique Francaise, Chef, Decision No. 565: Cite a l'Ordre de l'Armee le 109 Regiment d'Infanterie Americaine [Proposed by the president of the provisional government of the French Republic, decision no. 565: citation by order of the army]," Paris, March 27, 1945, copies in French and English translation in Personal and General Correspondence Papers, CMLA.

27. Maréchal Jean de Lattre de Tassigny, *Histoire de la Premiere Armée Française: Rhin et Danûbe,* 429.

28. Original copy of the February 18, 1945, message from Eisenhower to Cota regarding Rudder's promotion to colonel is in the possession of the author; Kemp, *The Regiment,* 212. The effective date of the promotion was February 16, 1945, per Special Order No. 47 from Headquarters, European Theater of Operations, issued on the same date, copy in the possession of the author.

CHAPTER 14. END OF THE WAR

1. 109th Infantry Regiment, Unit Journal, February 1–9, 1945, Personal and General Correspondence Papers of James Earl Rudder, Cushing Memorial Library and Archives, Texas A&M University.

2. Ibid., February 10–19, 1945.

3. Harry M. Kemp, *The Regiment: Let the Citizens Bear Arms! A Narrative History of an American Infantry Regiment in World War II,* 324.

4. William M. Peña. *As Far As Schleiden: A Memoir of World War II,* 193–94.

5. The details of this account of Rudder and the 109th around Schleiden owe much to the local historian, Karl Josef Lüttgens.

6. Kemp, *The Regiment,* 333.

7. Karl Josef Lüttgens, interview with the author, Schleiden, Germany, June 23, 2005.

8. James W. Eikner, editor and publisher, *2d Ranger Battalion: The Narrative History of Headquarters Company, April 1943–May 1945,* 87; Earl Rudder to his wife, March 16 and April 15, 1945.

9. Earl Rudder to his wife, March 29, 1945.

10. Jim Dan Hill, "Brady Mayor's Feats As Combat Leader Unique," *Brady Standard,* April 15, 1947.

11. Earl Rudder to Col. Harrison A. Gerhardt, May 3, 1945.

12. Earl Rudder to his wife, October 21, 1945.

13. Kemp, *The Regiment,* 343, 344.

14. Ibid., 348.

15. Margaret Rudder to her husband, June 15, 1945; Ronald H. Spector, *Eagle Against the Sun: The American War with Japan* (New York: Random House, 1985), 559.

16. Earl Rudder to his wife, May 20 and June 15, 1945.

17. Robert T. Edlin to Earl Rudder, June 18, 1945.

18. Earl Rudder to his wife, June 6, 8, and 12, 1945. For the Normandy invasion, General Gerow commanded the U.S. Army V Corps, which comprised all the forces landing on Omaha Beach.

19. Earl Rudder to his wife, July 14 and 20, 1945.

20. Margaret Rudder, transcript of interview, Bryan, Texas, May 9, 2002, 10, in the possession of the author.

21. 1st Lt. R. E. Carey to Col. James E. Rudder, interoffice memorandum (radio message) from New York Port of Embarkation to the troop transport *Mormacport,* August 4, 1945, original in the possession of the author; Haskell Monroe, ed., *James Earl Rudder in the Words of His Wife, Margaret Rudder,* 29. Some accounts have the *Mormacport* arriving on August 4, but that was the *Excelsior* to Boston with other components of the 28th Division, including the 3rd Battalion of the 109th.

22. Earl Rudder to his wife, November 11, 1945. One check was for $4,000, the estimated equivalent of $43,400 in 2005 purchasing power. This estimate was calculated from the website of Lawrence H. Officer and Samuel H. Williamson, "Purchasing Power of Money in the United States from 1774 to 2009," http://www.MeasuringWorth.com/ppowerus/.

23. Earl Rudder to his wife, November 11, 1945.

24. John Rudder, interview with the author, Brady, Texas, April 7, 2006.

CHAPTER 15. RISE TO PROMINENCE

1. Alton "Rusty" Williamson, interview with the author, August 13, 2004.

2. *Brady Standard,* January 18, 1946; *San Angelo Standard-Times,* January 18, 1946.

3. Haskell Monroe, ed., *James Earl Rudder in the Words of His Wife, Margaret Rudder,*

33. The new home was located at 605 West 13th Street. The construction was of cream-colored Austin cut stone. The purchase price was $10,000, according to a deed record filed in McCulloch County on March 6, 1946.

4. Frank Corder, contract of sale to Earl Rudder, January 1, 1947, copy in the possession of the author. The sale price was $100.00 cash and a $9,000.00 promissory note. Rudder assumed "all accounts and notes payable" by the firm of Corder-Rudder. In a contract of sale dated January 28, 1950, three brothers whose family name was Hicks purchased the business from Rudder (copy in the possession of the author).

5. Margaret Rudder, interview with the author, May 9, 2002; Earl Rudder to Robert B. Woodin, October 16, 1952. James Earl "Bud" Rudder Jr., telephone interview with the author, August 24, 2006; Anne Rudder Erdman, e-mail to author, October 30, 2007. Rudder cited survey and abstracts numbers for twenty-two tracts of his land in Menard County, amounting to 7,700 acres. See also Monroe, *Rudder in the Words of His Wife*, 75–76. For his ranch manager Rudder hired Frank Wootan, an experienced rancher from Junction, Texas (Earl Rudder to Frank Wootan, prescribing several tasks to be carried out by a ranch manager, February 5, 1947, copy in the possession of the author).

6. Earl Rudder to J. H. Howell, April 8, 1950; Williamson, interview, August 13, 2004.

7. *Brady Standard*, April 5, 1952. The document quoted is an undated four-page typescript described in its text as "a report to the citizens and taxpayers of Brady on your City government for the past six years," copy in the possession of the author.

8. *Vernon's Civil Statutes* (1948), Cities, Towns and Villages, 296; Minutes, Brady (Texas) City Council, 1946–52.

9. Minutes, Brady (Texas) City Council, April 16, 1946.

10. Letter dated February 19, 1949 (name and address of sender withheld), copy in the possession of author; Earl Rudder to inquiring heiress (name withheld), March 4, 1949, copy in the possession of author.

11. Ralph Goranson to Earl Rudder, December 11, 1953; Harold Lutz to Earl Rudder, January 7, 1954; Earl Rudder to Ralph Goranson, February 20, 1954. If Rudder wrote a character reference for Belcher, it was misfiled or lost, which was unlike him.

12. Earl Rudder to 1st Lt. Myron H. Atkinson, legal assistance officer, Fort Sill, Oklahoma, February 22, 1954.

13. Vivian Smith, interview with the author, Brady, Texas, May 25, 2005; Earl Rudder to Maj. Thomas O. McCall, U.S. Army Quartermaster Corps, September 5, 1949.

14. *Brady Standard*, April 19, 1946; "Curtis Field Formally Deeded to the City of Brady," ibid., December 24, 1946.

15. Lyndon B. Johnson, Western Union telegram to Earl Rudder, January 25, 1955, copy in the possession of the author; Lyndon B. Johnson to Earl Rudder, March 25, 1952.

16. *Brady Standard*, June 21, 1946; "Engineering Plans About Completed," ibid., August 15, 1947.

17. James Jarrell "J. J." or "Jake" Pickle, 1913–2005, member of the U.S. House of Representatives, 1963–95.

18. *Texas Almanac, 1945–1946* (Dallas: A. H. Belo, 1945), 113. The U.S. census of 1940 listed Brady's population at 5,002. The estimate for middecade was based on government wartime rationing figures, school attendance, and utility connections.

19. Robert A. Caro, *The Years of Lyndon Johnson: The Path to Power,* 740.

20. Linda Rudder was born March 17, 1947.

21. State Senator A. M. Aiken, personal conversation with the author, ca. 1975.

22. Lyndon B. Johnson to Earl Rudder, June 5, 1948; Claud C. Wild to Earl Rudder, June 5, 1948; Monroe, *Rudder in the Words of His Wife,* 34; Margaret Rudder, interview, May 9, 2002; J. J. "Jake" Pickle, interview with the author, June 18, 2002; Earl Rudder to Lyndon B. Johnson, September 27, 1948.

23. Lewis L. Gould, "Likable? Maybe. Knowable? No," supplement to *Austin American-Statesman,* October 28, 2005.

24. Charles B. MacDonald, *The Last Offensive,* 54, 334–35; Martin Fürst, "Supplement to 266th Infantry Division, June–August 1944," 46, German copy, MS no. P-176, RG 319, NA. See chapter 10, "Brittany."

25. Margaret Rudder, interview, May 9, 2002.

26. *Brady Standard,* July 6, 1948.

27. Ibid.

28. *Texas Almanac, 1949–1950* (Dallas: A. H. Belo, 1949), 473.

29. Personal files of James Earl Rudder, 1953. The document may have been attached to a letter from J. J. "Jake" Pickle to Rudder dated October 19. 1953. It has a list of the twenty-seven counties of the 21st Congressional District, exhibiting their votes in the 1948 race for the U.S. Senate between LBJ and Coke Stevenson and the 1952 presidential race between Eisenhower and Adlai Stevenson.

30. Earl Rudder to Lyndon B. Johnson, April 4, 1949; *Texas Almanac, 1952–1953* (Dallas: A. H. Belo, 1951), 335; J. Edward Johnson to Lyndon B. Johnson, July 23, 1951; Lyndon B. Johnson to Earl Rudder, April 6, 1949. Johnson, a Dallas lawyer, accompanied Pickle and Rudder while they traveled to each county in the 21st Congressional District to shore up the Johnson organization in each county. He wrote their report, "Analysis of Twenty-first Congressional District from an Organizational Standpoint and Otherwise."

31. Pickle, interview, June 18, 2002.

32. Monroe, *Rudder in the Words of His Wife,* 35; Pickle, interview, June 18, 2002.

33. Handbook of Texas Online, s.v. "Connally, John Bowden, Jr.," http://www.tsha online.org/handbook/online/articles/CC/fcosf.html (accessed June 29, 2010). Rudder was appointed president of Texas A&M on July 1, 1959, and died on March 23, 1970, while still president.

34. Sam Kinch and Stuart Long, *Allan Shivers: The Pied Piper of Texas Politics,* foreword by Weldon Hart, 5–6.

35. Pickle, interview, June 18, 2002.

36. *Texas Almanac, 1952–1953* (Dallas: A. H. Belo, 1951), 495.

37. Ricky F. Dobbs, *Yellow Dogs and Republicans: Allan Shivers and Texas Two-Party Politics,* 63–64.

38. J. J. "Jake" Pickle to Earl Rudder, September 7, 1950; Dobbs, *Yellow Dogs and Republicans,* 63.

39. Allan Shivers, Western Union telegram to Earl Rudder, January 8, 1953; *Dallas Morning News,* January 9, 1953; *Texas Almanac, 1956–1957* (Dallas: A. H. Belo, 1955), 461.

40. W. C. Heinz, letter to Earl Rudder, January 13, 1954; W. C. Heinz, "I Took My Son to Omaha Beach: An American Hero Returns to Normandy," *Collier's,* June 11, 1954, 25.

41. Allan Shivers Papers, Texas State Library and Archives, Box 1977/081–305.

42. The document quoted is the unpublished draft by Dave Cheavens, a reporter for the *Lufkin News,* which published an edited version of the article on June 22, 1954; Patrick Cox, *Ralph W. Yarborough: The People's Senator,* 16.

43. Earl Rudder to Robert H. Travis, June 23, 1954; *The Officers' Guide: A Ready Reference on Customs and Correct Procedures Which Pertain to Commissioned Officer of the Army of the United States,* 9th ed., 396.

44. *Texas Almanac, 1956–1957* (Dallas: A. H. Belo, 1955), 553.

45. Copies of the promotion order from the army and the Western Union telegram to Rudder are in the possession of the author. The effective date of his promotion to brigadier general was December 8, 1954, but official notification came in February 1955. U.S. Army, Fourth Army, Texas Military District, Public Information Section, "Colonel Rudder Presented General's Stars," news release, Austin, Texas, February 15, 1955, copy in the possession of the author.

46. John Frank Day to Earl Rudder, February 24, 1948, copy in the possession of the author. Day was a lieutenant colonel and an aide to the chief of staff at Fourth Army headquarters, Fort Sam Houston, Texas.

47. Earl Rudder to John Frank Day, February 27, 1948; Anne Floryan, secretary to Maj. Gen. G. W. Ryder, special assistant for civilian component affairs, to the U.S. Army chief of staff, Office of the Joint Chiefs of Staff, November 14, 1949, copy in the possession of the author.

48. Headquarters, Fourth Army, General Orders Number 82, Announcement of Acting Division Commander, July 6, 1954, copy of promotion order to brigadier general from the army and the Western Union telegram to Rudder, Personal and General Correspondence Papers of James Earl Rudder, Cushing Memorial Library and Archives, Texas A&M University.

49. Joe W. Neal, interview with the author, Austin, Texas, January 12, 2005. Neal served in World War II and afterwards earned a doctor of philosophy degree in government from the University of Texas. He became a professor of government and speech communications while serving for many years as the imaginative and innovative director of the University's International Office.

50. Lyndon B. Johnson to Earl Rudder, October 20, 1950; Earl Rudder to Lyndon B. Johnson, November 14, 1950; Lyndon B. Johnson to Earl Rudder, March 19, 1951.

51. Earl Rudder to his brother, Marshall, April 11, 1951. He listed the military posts that he had inspected: Fort Chaffee, Arkansas; Camp Breckenridge and Fort Knox, Kentucky; and Fort Jackson and Parris Island, South Carolina.

52. Liz Carpenter, numerous personal interviews with the author on various dates. Carpenter was executive assistant to Vice President Johnson, 1961–63, and staff director and press secretary to Mrs. Johnson during the Johnson's White House years, 1963–69.

CHAPTER 16. TEXAS LAND OFFICE COMMISSIONER

1. *Texas Observer,* September 21, 1955.

2. Robert A. Calvert, Arnoldo de León, and Gregg Cantrell, *The History of Texas,* 3rd ed., 397–99. In 1950 the Texas electorate created the Veterans Land Program to help veterans buy land cheaply. The Veterans Land Board governed the program. The usual procedure was for a veteran to select a tract of land and notify the board, which would send an appraiser to determine its value. If the board authorized the transaction, it bought the land and then resold it to the veteran at a low rate of interest (as low as 3 percent), giving him up to forty years to pay off the note. Giles exploited the program by selecting corrupt appraisers and having purchases of large tracts (for subdividing and selling to veterans) sent directly to his office, thus avoiding scrutiny by the board; as secretary, he would later add notice of large-tract purchases to the board's minutes, making it seem as if the board had discussed them. In collusion with real estate dealers, he also authorized land to be sold at inflated prices to nonexistent or defrauded veterans. Giles was indicted, convicted, and sentenced to six years in the state penitentiary in Huntsville. He served his sentence from January 1956 to December 1958 before being released for good behavior. He also paid eighty thousand dollars to settle civil suits arising from the fraud.

3. *Fort Worth Star-Telegram,* January 9, 1955; *Handbook of Texas* 3:1066, and Handbook of Texas Online, http://www.tshaonline.org/handbook/articles/VV/mqv1.html (accessed June 30, 2010); Thomas M. Reavley, senior judge, U.S. Court of Appeals for the Fifth Circuit, telephone interview with the author, October 3, 2006.

4. Andrea Gurasich Morgan, *Land: A History of the Texas General Land Office,* viii. Other sources include Calvert, de León, and Cantrell, *History of Texas.*

5. Margaret Rudder, interview with the author, May 9, 2002. A slightly different version of this story appears in Haskell Monroe, ed., *James Earl Rudder in the Words of His Wife, Margaret Rudder,* 40. See also Gov. Allan Shivers Western Union telegram to Earl Rudder, January 4, 1955, copy in the possession of author.

6. *Fort Worth Star-Telegram,* January 9, 1955.

7. *Bryan Eagle,* January 5, 1955; *Austin American-Statesman,* January 5, 1955; Office of the Governor, Austin, Texas, press memorandum, January 4, 1955, Personal and General Correspondence Papers of James Earl Rudder, Cushing Memorial Library and Archives, Texas A&M University, and copy in the possession of the author; *Dallas Morning News,* January 9, 1955.

8. Earl Rudder, *Report of the Commissioner of the General Land Office, 1954–1956,* 1. The former Land Office Building at 1019 Brazos in Austin was officially dedicated as the James Earl Rudder State Office Building on November 24, 1988. Copies of the press release, the invitation, and newspaper stories are in the possession of the author.

9. *Austin-American,* January 6, 1955.

10. Jane Rudder was born June 16, 1948; she died September 2, 1984, of liver cancer.

11. J. J. "Jake" Pickle, interview with the author, June 18, 2002.

12. *Fort Worth Star-Telegram,* January 9, 1955.

13. Rudder, *Report of the Commissioner.*

14. Margaret Rudder, interview, May 9, 2002; Earl Rudder, "Report to the Governor and Members of the Legislature of the State of Texas," January 31, 1958, Personal and General Correspondence Papers, CMLA; "Probe Panel Subpoenas 7," *Austin American-Statesman,* January 26, 1955; Haskell Monroe, *Rudder in the Words of His Wife,* 42, 44. Rudder and Corder's new procedures established three-man committees appointed by the commissioners' court (the county judge and the four precinct commissioners) in each county to review each veteran's application before sending it to the Land Office. An applicant was required to meet with a Land Office appraiser on the tract to be acquired, and the appraiser was required to inform the applicant of the loan terms and the features of the property. Two commitments by insurance agents who previously had been approved by the Land Office were required on all improvements on the property.

15. Sam Kimberlin, interview with the author, Austin, Texas, August 10, 2006.

16. Rudder, *Report of the Commissioner,* 1; Rudder, "Report to the Governor and Members of the Legislature"; *Austin American-Statesman,* February 15, 1955; *Texas Observer,* April 18, 1955; Texas Senate, General Investigating Committee, "Hearing Concerning the Administration of the Veterans' Land Program," 3:290, Texas State Library and Archives. Rudder signed the "Report to the Governor and Members of the Legislature" on his last day in office. He described the document as "a report of my administration . . . for the three year period covered by my tenure in office."

17. *Austin American-Statesman,* November 29, 1955; *Houston Press,* May 11, 1955; *Lampasas Dispatch,* October 6, 1955. In the last case, Rudder met with members of the Hill Country Soil Conservation District on a ranch near Lampasas.

18. *Fort Worth Star-Telegram,* December 9, 1955.

19. *Childress Index,* September 25, 1955; *Sweetwater Reporter,* October 16, 1955; *Beaumont Enterprise,* March 3, 1955.

20. *Abilene Reporter-News,* September 24, 1955.

21. Earl Rudder, "Land and the Lions," speech delivered before the Austin Lion's Club, Austin, Texas, August 11, 1955, 5, Personal and General Correspondence Papers, CMLA, and copy in the possession of the author.

22. *Texas Observer,* April 18, 1955.

23. *Cuero Record,* March 15, 1955; Garry Mauro, "The Land Commissioners of Texas: 150 Years of the General Land Office," 83.

24. Rudder, *Report of the Commissioner,* 9; Mauro, "Land Commissioners of Texas," 83–84; *Texas Observer,* August 10, 1955.

25. *Austin American-Statesman,* April 24, 1956.

26. Rudder, *Report of the Commissioner,* 11.

27. Rudder, "Report to the Governor and Members of the Legislature."

28. Rudder, *Report of the Commissioner,* 10. "Within 30 minutes after I assumed the duties of Land Commissioner, a meeting of the Veterans Land Board was held in my

office. I was amazed to find such inadequate facilities for holding a meeting. A large contingent from the press was present and the available space was so crowded and confused that it was extremely difficult to conduct the meeting properly."

29. Christmas card signed by all General Land Office employees with the enclosed resolution of support, 1955, copy in the possession of the author.

30. Earl Rudder, Muster Day address, Agricultural and Mechanical College of Texas, April 21, 1956, Personal and General Correspondence Papers, Rudder Collection, CMLA, and copy in the possession of the author.

31. *Austin American-Statesman,* April 24, 1956; AP wire service report, April 24, 1956, copy in the possession of the author; Dawson Duncan, "Land Office Chief Asking Full Term," *Dallas Morning News,* April 26, 1956.

32. *Austin American-Statesman,* October 2, 1955.

33. Margaret Rudder, interview, May 9, 2002; Nelda Rowell Green, interview with the author, Bryan, Texas, May 9, 2002; John Lindsey, interview with the author, Houston, Texas, October 25, 2005.

34. Biographical sketch of Ned Price on file in the Texas Legislative Reference Library, Austin, Texas.

35. Ned Price Jr., telephone interview with the author, October 12, 2005. Rudder's checkbooks show numerous gifts of twenty-five dollars or less to charitable organizations. As for Ned Price, the author once walked with him along Guadalupe Street in Austin. As he put money in the hand of a homeless person, he explained, "I am afraid not to give."

36. "Voters . . . Let's Go To The Polls," *Brady Standard,* July 27, 1956.

37. This quotation was taken from a three-page finished typescript on yellow paper that was apparently intended as a press release. However, no published record of it could be found. Rudder may also have used it as a source of talking points. The document is in the Rudder Papers, CMLA; a copy is in the possession of the author.

38. Earl Rudder television film for telecasting July 26, 1956, Personal and General Correspondence Papers, Rudder Collection, CMLA, copy of transcript and film in the possession of the author; Pickle interview, June 18, 2002; Price, telephone interview, October 21, 2005.

39. George W. Sandlin, "Tabulated Statement Showing Votes Cast for Commissioner of the General Land Office, First Democratic Primary Election, July 28, 1956, By Counties," 3, in Texas State Library and Archives, and copy in the possession of the author. In the five counties along the Rio Grande from Brownsville to Laredo, where votes were usually influenced by the *patrón* system, Rudder and Price divided 38,922 votes almost evenly. In Zapata County, Rudder took 91.6 percent of a mere 834 votes, and in adjoining Starr County, Price got 3,214, or 82.3 percent of 3,903 cast.

40. *Texas Almanac, 1958–1959* (Dallas: A. H. Belo, 1958), 453.

41. Harvey Bayne of Crockett, Texas, to Earl Rudder, August 1, 1956; Joe L. Buford of Mount Pleasant, Texas, to Earl Rudder, August 12, 1956. Copies of both are in the possession of the author.

42. "Rudder to Resign, Take A&M Duties," *Fort Worth Star-Telegram,* November 27, 1957; "Rudder May Quit Politics to Be Professional Aggie," *Austin American-Statesman,* December 2, 1957; Burr S. Cameron of Linden, Texas, to Earl Rudder, December 10, 1957, copy in the possession of the author; J. Stuart Boyles to Earl Rudder, December 1, 1957, copy in the possession of the author.

43. Rudder, "Report to the Governor and Members of the Legislature."

44. Ibid.

45. Earl Rudder to the Honorable Price Daniel, Governor of Texas, December 21, 1957, copy in the possession of the author.

46. Earl Rudder to Edmund Bader, January 24, 1958, copy in the possession of the author.

CHAPTER 17. TEXAS A&M PRESIDENTIAL YEARS

1. James Earl Rudder Jr., Margaret Anne Rudder Erdman, and Linda Rudder Williams, personal interviews with the author.

2. The Texas Agricultural and Mechanical College System was composed of the Agricultural and Mechanical College of Texas, called A&M College or Texas A&M; a historically black institution called Prairie View Agricultural and Mechanical College; Arlington State College; Tarleton State College, and several statewide extension services. ASC and TSC were two-year institutions. See *Bulletin of the Agricultural and Mechanical College of Texas,* Sixth Series, 5 (April 1, 1958): 4.

3. *The Texas A. & M. System News: Published for all Members of the Statewide Staff of The Texas A. and M. College System* 11, no. 2 (February 1958): 1. See also H. B. "Pat" Zachry, speech at the dedication of the Rudder Tower and Conference Center in 1973: "I was a member of the committee from A&M's Board of Directors instructed to find and recommend a new president. We found Earl; we brought him to A&M. It was my privilege to work with him for four years, to share many of his dreams, his plans."

4. Marion Thomas Harrington, letter to Earl Rudder, October 10, 1957. The title of the chief administrator of the Texas A&M System has switched several times between president and chancellor. When Rudder came as vice president of the college, Harrington was president of both the college and the system. When Rudder became president of the college on July 1, 1959, Harrington's title was changed to chancellor. The changes can be traced in the pre-pages of Texas A&M College's undergraduate catalogs for 1958–59 and 1959–60.

5. Marion Thomas Harrington to Earl Rudder, November 5, 1957; Earl Rudder to Marion Thomas Harrington, November 21, 1957; "Rudder May Quit Politics To Be 'Professional Aggie,'" *Austin American,* December 2, 1957.

6. Texas A&M Board of Directors, Minute Order 285–57 of November 27, 1957, as amended by Minute Order 89–58 on April 25–26, 1958. All minutes and minute orders cited hereinafter are found in the office of the Texas A&M University System Board of Regents. When Rudder completed the standard application for employment at Texas

A&M, he wrote that his salary as land commissioner was $17,500 per year and his estimated annual income from ranching was $10,000. He did not indicate whether the ranch income was gross or net.

7. Earl Rudder, Muster Day speech, April 21, 1956, Personal and General Correspondence Papers of James Earl Rudder, Cushing Memorial Library and Archives, Texas A&M University, and copy in the possession of the author. The origin of the term "Old Army Aggie" is uncertain. By one account it was adopted by younger students when older students and graduates departed the campus for service in World War II. The younger men promised to keep A&M as it was and called it "Old Army."

8. Haskell Monroe, interview with the author, May 21, 2007.

9. Margaret Rudder, handwritten notes for a speech, undated, copy in the possession of author. The speaker was the president of Principia College, a church-related institution in Saint Louis, Missouri. Rudder's Texas counterparts in attendance were Kenneth S. Pitkin, president of Rice University from 1961 to 1968, and Philip G. Hoffman, president of the University of Houston from 1961 to 1977.

10. Marsha Jenson, interview with the author, Austin, Texas, February 9, 2005.

11. Margaret Rudder, undated holographic notes for a speech, copy in the possession of author. The notes indicate that the move-in date was January 26, 1958, and the location of the home was "where Lechner and McFaddin dorms now stand."

12. Durwood B. Varner, letter to Marion Thomas Harrington, June 11, 1957.

13. Ibid.

14. Lannes Hope, interview with the author, College Station, Texas, February 11, 2005. Hope is retired from Texas A&M's Department of Educational Psychology. Hope was not a member of the counseling center staff when Rudder first came to the campus, but was a testing and measurement specialist whose job interested Rudder as a way of measuring student progress and screening those who were admitted.

15. John A. Adams Jr., *Keepers of the Spirit: The Corps of Cadets at Texas A&M University, 1876–2001*, 201; *Battalion*, February 21, 1958.

16. *Texas Aggie*, January 1958, 1.

17. "Land Commissioner Earl Rudder Becomes College's Vice-President," *Texas Aggie*, January 1958:1.

18. Harry Kunkel, interview with the author, February 11, 2005. Kunkel is Emeritus Dean and professor of agriculture at Texas A&M University.

19. There are many accounts of how Rudder involved others in his decision making, in both military and civilian life. Subordinates occasionally speculated that he had made up his mind before asking their opinion. It was probably a mixture.

20. *Dallas Morning News*, January 19, 1959, quoted in Dethloff, *A Centennial History of Texas A&M University, 1876–1976*, 559. The Texas Supreme Court refused to review the circuit court's decision on April 6, 1959.

21. *Battalion*, April 7, 1959.

22. *Midland Reporter-Telegram*, "Rudder Urges Aggies 'Settle Down,'" March 30, 1958.

23. Margaret Rudder, interview with the author, May 5, 2002; Lester Harrell, telephone interview with the author, June 11, 2005.

24. *Battalion,* February 4 and 27, 1958.

25. Ibid., April 9, 1958.

26. Ibid., May 28, 1958.

27. John Lindsey, interview with the author, Houston, Texas, October 5, 2005.

28. *Battalion,* October 10, 1958.

29. Dethloff, *Centennial History,* 560–61.

30. *Battalion,* March 29, 1960; "Proceedings of the Inauguration of James Earl Rudder as President of the Agricultural and Mechanical College of Texas," March 26, 1960, 11, President's Office Papers, CMLA.

31. "Proceedings of the Inauguration," 27.

32. *Texas Aggie,* April 1960, 3; "Proceedings of the Inauguration," 64.

33. *Houston Post,* March 31, 1960.

34. *Texas Aggie,* May 1960.

35. Ibid., July 1960. This issue of the *Texas Aggie* stated that Hall earned his Ph.D. at Iowa State, but he wrote in his memoir, *The Glory Years,* that it was the University of Iowa.

36. Wayne C. Hall, *The Glory Years: Making of a University,* 65.

37. Ibid., 71–72, 73, 74.

38. Ibid., 74

39. Ibid.; *Texas Aggie,* July 1960.

40. Hall, *Glory Years,* 80; *Texas Aggie,* June 25, 1960.

41. Hall, *Glory Years,* 66. The five components were the Texas Agricultural Experiment Station, Texas Agricultural Extension Service, Texas Engineering Experiment Station, Texas Engineering Extension Service, and Texas Transportation Institute.

42. Tom D. Cherry was appointed director of business affairs for Texas A&M College in the summer of 1962. See *Texas Aggie,* August 1962.

43. Phil Diebel, son of Clark Diebel, interview with the author, September 15, 2007. Clark Diebel joined Rudder's staff at Texas A&M College in the summer of 1964. He came from the state auditor's office, where he was in charge of audits conducted of public colleges and universities. Regardless of his title, he was considered Rudder's chief financial officer by some observers. See Hall, *Glory Years,* 82.

44. *Texas Aggie,* August 1959.

45. Ibid., October 1962.

46. Hall, *Glory Years,* 76.

47. Ibid., 76, 77; *Texas Aggie,* August 1962. The first appointed vice president for research was Andrew D. Suttle Jr.

48. *Houston Chronicle,* December 3, 1960; Lee Duewall, chairman, Name-change Committee, memorandum to Earl Rudder, January 19, 1960, in Box 49–44, Name Change, President's Office Papers, CMLA.

49. M. A. Aziz, secretary of the Pakistani Students Association, to Earl Rudder, January 14, 1961; C. K. Parekh, president of the U.N. Club and Indian Student Association, to

Earl Rudder, January 17, 1961; W. C. Longquist to Earl Rudder, January 19, 1961; George R. Harper to Earl Rudder, December 6, 1960; R. E. Layton Jr. to Earl Rudder, January 13, 1961, all in Box 49–44, Name Change, President's Office Papers, CMLA.

50. Hall, *Glory Years,* 84.

51. Sterling C. Evans was appointed to the Texas A&M Board of Directors in early 1959, and he served twelve years. See *Battalion,* March 6, 1959, and William N. Stokes Jr., *Sterling C. Evans: Texas Aggie, Banker, Cattleman,* 60–67.

52. There was actually a third concurrent study, the decennial self-study required by the regional accrediting agency, the Southern Association of Colleges and Schools. However, its format followed a template with specific requirements that do not appear to have figured directly into the change strategy.

53. Texas A&M Board of Directors, Minute Order 103–61, April 22, 1961.

54. Dethloff, *Centennial History,* 551; *Texas Aggie,* April and May 1958; Texas A&M Board of Directors, Minute Order 103–61, April 22, 1961; Texas A&M Board of Directors, "Declaration of Policies Creating the Establishment of a Century Council and the Implementation of Said Council's Organization and Administration," adopted April 21, 1961, Personal and General Correspondence Papers, CMLA.

55. The analysis of Century Council membership was made from a list published in the *Texas Aggie,* September 1961.

56. Earl Rudder, speech in Speeches, 1961, Personal and General Correspondence Papers, CMLA; Dethloff, *Centennial History,* 562. The Committee on Aspirations met for first time on July 25, 1961.

57. The Forecast Conference was held on September 21 and 22, 1961. About seventy-five of the one hundred Century Council members attended. Rudder quote in the *Battalion,* February 2, 1962.

58. *Battalion,* September 21, 1961.

59. After Rudder's death, his executive secretary, Nelda Green, collected undated, handwritten notes from his desk. The notes included references to Snow's essay and to a "humanities research institute" for Texas A&M.

60. "Report of the Century Council to the Board of Directors," 1962, 11, 57, 59, Personal and General Correspondence Papers, CMLA.

61. Ibid., 10.

62. "Faculty-Staff-Students Study on Aspirations," resolution passed by the Texas A&M Board of Directors, September 27, 1966, 21–27, in the office of the Texas A&M University System Board of Regents, quoted in Dethloff, *Centennial History,* 563–64.

63. Haskell Monroe, telephone interview with the author, September 24, 2007, confirmed by e-mail, September 25, 2007.

64. Dethloff, *Centennial History,* 564; Haskell Monroe, interview with the author, June 19, 2007.

65. *Dallas Morning News,* November 17, 1962.

66. Texas A&M Board of Directors, Minute Order 259–62, Blueprint for Progress, unpaged, CMLA, copy in the possession of the author; *Texas Aggie,* November 1962. The

Blueprint for Progress has seventeen pages without numbers, and this reference is on the last page.

67. Texas A&M Board of Directors, Minute Order 106–65, April 24, 1965.

68. Earl Rudder, prepared remarks for April 29, 1963, meeting with the student body, Speeches, 1963, Personal and General Correspondence Papers, CMLA.

69. Connally's remarks were made on June 4, 1963, to the newly appointed Governor's Committee on Education Beyond the High School. See State of Texas, Governor's Committee on Education Beyond the High School, *Education: Texas' Resource for Tomorrow*, 5.

70. Quoted in Brian McCall, *The Power of the Texas Governor: Connally to Bush*, 11.

71. Ben Barnes with Lisa Dickey, *Barn Burning, Barn Building*, 58.

72. Margaret Rudder, interview, May 5, 2002.

73. *Battalion*, February 8, 1963.

74. *Texas Aggie*, February 1963.

75. James Earl Rudder, January 30, 1963, Speeches, Personal and General Correspondence Papers, CMLA; Connally quoted in McCall, *Power of the Texas Governor*, 13–14.

76. *Houston Post*, February 24, 1963; Texas A&M Board of Directors, Minutes of regular meeting, February 23, 1963. Minute Order 40–63 by Heldenfels, seconded by Peterson, directed Chancellor Harrington to seek legislation changing the name of the college to Texas A&M University and the system to the Texas A&M University System. In the same meeting, Minute Order 2–63 documents the election of Sterling C. Evans as president of the Board of Directors without stating the nominator or recording the vote.

77. *Battalion*, May 8, 1963.

78. Ibid., March 21, 1963.

79. Ibid., April 23, 1963.

80. Resolution of the Beaumont A. & M. Club, 1963, in Personal and General Correspondence Papers, CMLA.

81. Evans quoted in Heidi Knippa, "Salvation of a University: The Admission of Women to Texas A&M," M.A. thesis, University of Texas at Austin, 1995, 98; see also open letter from Sterling C. Evans to the Texas A&M Board of Directors, April 10, 1963, President's Office Papers, CMLA. Rudder quoted in *Houston Post*, April 25, 1963.

82. Minutes of the regular meeting of the Texas A&M Board of Directors, April 27, 1963, Minute Order 66–63. Eight of the nine members of the Board of Directors were present. The absent member was S. B. Whittenberg. See Stokes, *Sterling C. Evans*, 66.

83. Minutes of the regular meeting of the Texas A&M Board of Directors, April 27, 1963, Minute Order 65–63.

84. *Austin American-Statesman*, April 28, 1963; *Bryan Eagle*, April 28, 1963; *Houston Post*, April 28, 1963.

85. *Houston Post*, April 28, 1963. If Rowland actually returned his ring to Texas A&M, it was not found in the possession of President's Office Papers, CMLA.

86. Brownwood, Texas, Aggies to Earl Rudder, Western Union telegram, dated May 1, 1963, at 8:44 AM; handwritten note to Earl Rudder, undated, President's Office papers,

CMLA. I invited the writer of the note to comment on his attitude in 1963 and now, but received no reply. In 2007 he was a member of the Association of Former Students' Century Club, indicating that he contributes financially to the alumni organization.

87. Knippa, "Salvation of a University," 66.

88. Ralph Ashlock to Earl Rudder, November 22, 1965.

89. Gordon Wisenbaker to Earl Rudder, May 8, 1963, quoted in Knippa, "Salvation of a University," 110.

90. Rick Walker to Earl Rudder, April 28, 1963.

91. Rudder handwritten prepared remarks, dated April 29, 1963, in Speeches, 1963, Personal and General Correspondence Papers, CMLA. Another handwritten copy of his remarks is dated September 26, 1963. He may have used the same notes to make a speech on that date, but the text indicates that the notes were prepared for his meeting with students protesting the Board of Directors' policy on the limited admission of women adopted on April 27, 1963.

92. Ibid.; Rudder's prepared comments are also quoted in the *Houston Post,* April 30, 1963.

93. John Lindsey, interview with the author, October 5, 2007.

94. Frank Muller, interview with the author, February 11, 2005; *Houston Post,* April 30, 1963; *Dallas Morning News,* April 30, 1963.

95. Knippa, "Salvation of a University," 104.

96. Earl Rudder, typescript notes for a meeting with faculty advisors, November 6, 1963, copy in the possession of the author; Margaret Rudder, interview, May 9, 2002.

97. J. B. "Dick" Hervey to Sterling C. Evans, June 20, 1963, in Box 61–32, A&M and Coeds, April 1963 to August 1963, President's Office Papers, CMLA.

98. Form in President's Office Papers, CMLA; facsimile in Knippa, "Salvation of a University," 106.

99. *Dallas Morning News,* June 5, 1963.

100. Leroy Sterling, interview with the author, June 25, 2007.

101. Margaret Rudder, interview, May 5, 2002.

102. *Battalion,* June 6, 1963.

103. Sterling, interview, June 25, 2007; Leroy Sterling to Rose Marie Solomon, June 5, 1963.

104. File "A&M vs. Coeds," Box 61–32, A&M and Coeds, President's Office Papers, CMLA; *Beaumont Enterprise,* June 25, 1963; Newsletters of the Committee for an All-Male Military Texas A&M, November 30, 1964, and March 3, 1965, Personal and General Correspondence Papers, CMLA, copies in the possession of the author.

105. Robert W. Rowland to Earl Rudder, August 21, 1963, Box 61–32, A&M vs. Coeds, April 1963 to August 1963, President's Office Papers, CMLA.

106. Margaret Rudder, interview, May 5, 2002.

107. Office of the Director of Admissions and Registrar, Texas A&M University, "Women Enrollees at Texas A&M University, Long Session Only," September 3, 1965, Coeducation Correspondence, Box 75–9, November 1963 to August 1965, President's

Office Papers, CMLA; James Hannigan, memorandum to Earl Rudder, quoted in Knippa, "Salvation of a University," 115. Babcock enclosed the purported letter from a student with a memorandum to A&M alums, which he ended with, "We are withholding the student's name for obvious reasons."

108. *Texas Aggie,* February 1964, 1.

109. Lindsey, interview, October 25, 2005; *Texas Aggie,* May 1965.

110. Lindsey, interview, October 25, 2005.

111. Ibid.

112. *Houston Post,* February 11, 1965; *Bryan Eagle,* February 11, 1965; *Houston Chronicle,* February 10, 1963.

113. *Bryan Eagle,* February 28, 1965.

114. Frank Denius, interview with the author, March 6, 2006.

115. Ibid.

116. T. B. Wright, interview with the author, March 8, 2006, and telephone conversation, November 8, 2007. Mr. Wright was the "first assistant" to Attorney General Waggoner Carr when the informal hearing was held before the opinion committee.

117. Texas A&M Board of Directors, Minute Order 120–65, June 26, 1965; H. C. Heldenfels, interview with David Chapman, Corpus Christi, Texas, July 5, 1974, CMLA; *Fort Worth Star-Telegram,* September 10, 1965.

118. H. C. Heldenfels to State Senator Andy Rogers, April 2, 1965, Box 75–9, Coed Correspondence, November 1963–August 1965, President's Office Papers, CMLA. Quote by H. C. Heldenfels in *Corpus Christi Caller-Times,* June 29, 1965.

119. Heldenfels interview with Chapman, July 5, 1974.

120. *Fort Worth Star-Telegram,* September 10, 1965.

121. Opinion No. C-525, October 14, 1965, Office of the Attorney General of Texas.

122. H. C. Heldenfels, memorandum to members of the Texas A&M Board of Directors, September 2, 1965; *Bryan Eagle,* February 28, 1965.

123. Texas A&M Board of Directors, Minute Order 37–66, March 6, 1966.

124. Fritz Lanham, "Changing: 20 Years Ago, Texas A&M Opened Its Doors to Women," *Bryan Eagle,* April 23, 1963, quoted in Knippa, "Salvation of a University," 126; Texas A&M University, *General Catalogue: Announcements for the Session 1967–68,* 8, CMLA.

125. Lanham, "Changing," quoted in Knippa, "Salvation of a University," 126–27; Robert Cherry, secretary to the Board of Directors, kept holographic notes of meetings in executive session. On February 21, 1969, he recorded that the board "discussed the present policy on admission of women [and decided] it was not desirable to publicly reopen the question." Cherry kept the notes in a loose-leaf notebook entitled "Informal Sessions of the Board of Directors." The notebook is kept in the records of the executive secretary, Texas A&M University System Board of Regents. Enrollment numbers are from Donald D. Carter, Registrar, Texas A&M University, to the author, October 21, 2010.

126. Texas A&M University, *General Catalogue: Announcements for the Session 1970–71,* 8, CMLA.

127. *Texas Almanac, 1961–1962* (Dallas: A. H. Belo, 1961), 460. The quotation is from a letter that Rudder wrote on October 8, 1964, to Millard Ruud, a professor at the University of Texas School of Law, explaining his low profile in the presidential campaign of 1964. It is evident from his papers that he maintained a similar low profile in the campaign of 1960. Interestingly, he was active in the 1968 campaign for Democrat Hubert H. Humphrey. A copy of the letter is in the possession of the author.

128. *Congressional Record,* November 27, 1963, 22, 839; *Public Papers of the Presidents of the United State: Lyndon B. Johnson,* Book 1 (January 1 to March 31, 1965), Philip Reed Rulon, *The Compassionate Samaritan: The Life of Lyndon Baines Johnson,* 178, 226.

129. W. Marvin Watson to Earl Rudder, March 23, 1966.

130. W. Marvin Watson, memorandum to LBJ, November 14, 1966; Jack Valenti, memorandum to LBJ, March 21, 1966.

131. "Rudder Named Future Choice for Governor," *Dallas Morning News,* June 7, 1964; "Rudder Denies Interest in Governorship," *Battalion,* June 18, 1964. The Rudders stayed overnight in the White House on May 16, 1966, after attending a dinner in honor of Henry Cabot Lodge, U.S. ambassador to South Vietnam.

132. Lyndon B. Johnson to Earl Rudder, September 22, 1966.

133. Rulon, *Compassionate Samaritan,* 259.

134. Joe Buser, Texas A&M News, University Information (copy in the possession of the author). No date or title appears on the document. Obviously, the date was shortly after Rudder returned from Vietnam in 1966.

135. Earl Rudder to W. Marvin Watson, special assistant to the president, July 15, 1966. Geyer was appointed to the Committee on Marine Science, Engineering, and Resources created under the "Magnuson Bill for Oceanography"; Earl Rudder to Lyndon B. Johnson, January 26, 1966.

136. Randall B. Woods, *LBJ: Architect of American Ambition,* 743; Earl Rudder to W. Marvin Watson, November 14, 1966; Earl Rudder, Western Union telegram to Lyndon B. Johnson, April 1, 1968.

137. Three academic leaders in the acquisition of the cyclotron were Vice Chancellor John C. Calhoun Jr., engineering dean Fred J. Benson, and Richard E. Wainerdi, research scientist and associate dean of engineering.

138. On January 25, 1964, Rudder updated a committee of the Association of Former Students on institutional developments and included a reference in his notes to the approval of the cyclotron. If he actually revealed that news, his talk was not the official announcement, which would wait until he had briefed Governor Connally.

The account of how the three million dollars for the cyclotron came to Texas A&M was told to me by Richard E. Wainerdi, president, CEO, and COO of the Texas Medical Center. Wainerdi spent twenty years at Texas A&M University in both scientific and academic affairs. In his biography he states that he founded the university's Nuclear Science Center, was a professor of chemical engineering, and served as associate vice president for academic affairs.

139. "General Luedecke Tells of U.S. Space Plans," *Texas Aggie,* June 1966:7; "Alumni Notes," *Texas Aggie,* July 1968:4; Henry C. Dethloff with John A. Adams Jr., *Texas Aggies*

Go to War: In Service of Their Country, 102, 235. A related biography is found online at http://www.astronautix.com/astros/luedecke.htm (accessed July 1, 2010). General Luedecke was general manager of the Atomic Energy Commission from 1958 to 1964.

140. *Texas Aggie,* September 1962, 1; "A&M Nuclear Study Facilities Dedicated," *Houston Post,* May 26, 1962.

141. "A&M Gets Cyclotron," *Houston Post,* February 17, 1964; *Texas Aggie,* special edition published for Former Students of Texas A&M, 3.

142. "Connally Will Woo 'Big' Science Names," *Waco Tribune-Herald,* August 5, 1962.

143. "A&M's Cyclotron To Be Dedicated," *Houston Chronicle,* November 5, 1967; *Texas Aggie,* special edition, 3. Other details about funding the cyclotron may be found in "Dr. Seaborg Hails A&M Cyclotron," *Houston Chronicle,* December 5, 1967. When the Robert A. Welch Foundation made its $1 million contribution, its vice chairman was Wilfred T. Doherty, a graduate of Texas A&M and former chairman of its Board of Directors.

144. "Cyclotron Provides Fast Neutron Therapy," *Texas Times,* March 1977; "Nuclear Engineering Degree Announced," *Battalion,* September 29, 1966; "Dr. Seaborg Hails A&M Cyclotron," *Houston Chronicle,* December 5, 1967.

145. "Rep. Teague Named Space Panel Head," *Houston Post,* February 25. 1962; "Dallas Changes Mind About Rep. Teague," *Houston Chronicle,* May 14, 1967; Dethloff, *Centennial History,* 594; "Gen. Luedecke Named Acting President," *TAMU Today* 9, no. 2 (Spring 1970): 1.

146. "Space Experts Visit A&M," *Texas Aggie,* April 1964.

147. J. J. "Jake" Pickle, interview with the author, June 18, 2002. By "front man," Pickle presumably meant someone to vouch for his position and provide professional advice via the faculty at Texas A&M.

148. Ibid.

149. Dethloff, *Centennial History,* 594.

150. "Texas A&M Plays Major Role in America's Race to the Moon," *Texas Aggie,* November 1965:4.

151. "NASA Signs Agreement to Build $1 Million Space Center at A&M," *Battalion,* April 29, 1964; "Teague Concerned About Space Plan," *Dallas Morning News,* September 17, 1967. The *Houston Post* reported on August 1, 1965, that NASA and the National Science Foundation granted $1,170,000 of the $2,200,000 needed for the building; see also Handbook of Texas Online, s.v. "Teague, Olin E.," http://www.tshaonline.org/handbook/online/articles/TT/fte32.html (accessed July 1, 2010).

152. *Houston Post,* July 10, 1969; "Texas A&M Banquet Honors Rep. Teague," *Dallas Morning News,* November 7, 1965; "Others Collect Aggie Jokes While A&M Collects Goodies," *Dallas Times Herald,* December 10, 1967.

153. Henry C. Dethloff, *A Centennial History of Texas A&M University, 1876–1976,* 595.

154. Stephen Curley, *Aggies By The Sea: Texas A&M University at Galveston,* 47.

155. Ibid., 13.

156. "Texas Maritime Academy," *Texas Aggie,* January 1970:6.

157. Ibid.

158. Curley, *Aggies By The Sea,* 65.

159. "Aggie Image Blurred For Many Years," *Amarillo Globe-News,* November 28, 1960. The Aggie's memo is an unsigned typescript that seems to have been written by an acquaintance but not a close friend. Although the note is not dated, it was surely written in December 1957 or January 1958, when Rudder was still commissioner of the General Land Office but after the announcement that he would take the job at Texas A&M on February 1, 1958. A copy is in my possession.

160. "Aggies Seek New Image for School," *Dallas Morning News,* February 15, 1966.

161. Woodrow Varner, letter to Thomas M. Harrington, June 11, 1957.

162. Lee Duewall to Lyle Nelson, April 6, 1961, in Box 53–14, Image Study, April 1961–August 1961, President's Office Papers, CMLA. Nelson was vice president for university relations at the University of Michigan.

163. "Aggies Protest Board Fee Rule," *Daily Texan* (by the Associated Press), April 28, 1967.

164. "The Graduate," *Battalion,* April 30, 1969. The author was Mitty C. Plummer, who earned a Ph.D. in engineering in 1969.

165. "Feud over A&M Campus Newspaper Continues Unabated," *Dallas Morning News,* April 2, 1967.

166. Earl Rudder to D. D. Brouchard, head of the journalism department, April 21, 1958, President's Office Papers, CMLA; "A&M Journalism Head Resigns; Blames Conflict over Program," *Houston Chronicle,* February 16, 1967.

167. John Mobley, interview with the author, Austin, Texas, December 8, 2007.

168. Thomas M. DeFrank, "The Control Dilemma of the College Press: A Case History," M.A. thesis, University of Minnesota, 1968, 71.

169. George Sessions Perry, *The Story of Texas A and M.,* 107; "President's Stand Remains Unchanged," *Battalion,* October 7, 1969.

170. "A&M University President Bars Reporters at Meeting," *Daily Texan,* October 7, 1967.

171. "Freedom of the Press at Texas A&M," *Texas Observer,* October 14, 1966, 3.

172. "Johnny Cash Concert Cancelled; 'Unfavorable Publicity' Bars Performance," *Battalion,* November 16, 1965.

173. Ibid.; "CJC Announces Local Cash Show," *Battalion,* November 19, 1965.

174. Glenn Dromgoole, telephone interview with the author, December 19, 2008.

175. "Rudder Explains Cash Decision to MSC Council," *Battalion,* November 23, 1965.

176. "Facts Mix With the Johnny Cash Legend on the Road to Redemption," *New York Times,* October 20, 2008; see also "The Man in Black(mail)," El Paso Times online, http://elpasotimes.typepad.com/morgue/2008/04/the-man-in-blac.html (accessed July 1, 2010).

177. "Rudder Explains Cash Decision to MSC Council," *Battalion,* November 23,

1965. Rudder probably did not physically remove the painting but instructed J. Wayne Stark, the MSC director, to remove it.

178. Nelda Green, e-mail to author, October 14, 2005.

179. "A&M Journalism Head Resigns; Blames Conflict over Program," *Houston Chronicle,* February 16, 1967.

180. Glenn Dromgoole, "State of the Battalion: April 1966," unpublished manuscript, copy in the possession of the author, courtesy of Thomas M. DeFrank; "Feud over A&M Campus Newspaper Continues Unabated," *Dallas Morning News,* April 2, 1967.

181. DeFrank, "Control Dilemma of the College Press," 71.

182. "Baylor Freshman Held after Painting Incident," *Battalion,* October 22 and 26, 1965.

183. Tom DeLay and Stephen Mansfield, *No Retreat, No Surrender: One American's Fight,* 42; "DeLay's Advice: Don't Send Your Kids to Baylor or A&M," *Houston Chronicle,* April 19, 2002.

184. Rudder's desk calendars for September 12 and 22, 1966, in Personal and General Correspondence, CMLA, and in the possession of the author; Ed Davis, interview with the author, May 16, 2007; "A&M Now 'Publisher' of Student Newspaper," *Houston Post,* October 5, 1966.

185. Certified copy of resolution passed by the Texas A&M Board of Directors, September 27, 1966, signed by Robert G. Cherry, secretary to the board; "Editors Fired in A&M Shuffle," *Daily Texan,* October 9, 1966. In addition to DeFrank, Dani Presswood, the managing editor, and Gerald Garcia, the sports editor, were also fired. Each student had a successful career in journalism, and Garcia became editor of the *Houston Post.*

186. "Editors Fired in A&M Shuffle," *Daily Texan,* October 9, 1966; "Fired Editor Says A&M Will Be Hurt," *Houston Chronicle,* October 9, 1966.

187. "Ex-Editor Says A&M Could Be 'A Berkeley,'" *Houstonian,* February 24, 1967; Thomas M. DeFrank, telephone interview with the author, January 12, 2009; "Journalists Condemn A&M at Southwestern Meet," *Battalion,* March 14, 1967.

188. "Feud over A&M Campus Newspaper Continues Unabated," *Dallas Morning News,* April 2, 1967; Earl Rudder to Thomas E. Turner, April 12, 1967, President's Office Papers, CMLA.

189. Thomas M. DeFrank, commencement address, Texas A&M University, May 11, 2007, copy in the possession of the author. In a telephone interview with the author on January 12, 2009, DeFrank insisted that Rudder had used the word *ass* in their Dulles airport encounter rather than *butt,* as in his printed commencement address. The number of undergraduates awarded degrees on May 27, 1967, was provided by Donald D. Carter, registrar of Texas A&M University, by e-mail on February 2, 2009.

190. "Rudder Guides A&M with a Firm Hand," *Houston Post,* February 9, 1967; "Political Forum a Wise Decision," *Battalion,* October 6, 1966.

191. DeFrank, commencement address, Texas A&M University, May 11, 2007; DeFrank, telephone interview, January 12, 2009.

192. Thomas M. DeFrank, e-mail to author, January 12, 2009.

193. "Academic Freedom and Tenure: Texas A&M University," *AAUP Bulletin: A Publication of the American Association of University Professors* 53, no. 4 (December 1967): 378.

194. Texas A&M University Committee on Academic Freedom and Tenure to President Earl Rudder, January 13, 1969, 5

195. Ibid., 16. For a definition of sexual harassment, see http://en.wikipedia.org/wiki/Sexual_harassment (accessed July 1, 2010).

196. Alvin A. Price, Dean, College of Veterinary Medicine, "A Brief of the Case of Dr. Leon W. Gibbs, Professor of Veterinary Anatomy," 1967, CMLA. The brief is an undated chronology of major developments in the case from April 6, 1965, to October 25, 1965.

197. "Academic Freedom and Tenure" *AAUP Bulletin* 53, no. 4:379.

198. James B. Bond, telephone interview with the author, January 15, 2009. Bond held several titles in the Texas A&M System while continuing as its chief legal officer.

199. Bond, telephone interview, January 15, 2009. The hearing was conducted at Texas A&M during September 23–27, 1968. According to Nelda Green, Rudder's secretary at the time, no legal counsel was immediately available in the president's office.

200. "Academic Freedom and Tenure," *AAUP Bulletin* 53, no. 4:378, 381.

201. Heldenfels, interview with Chapman, July 5, 1974.

202. "Academic Freedom and Tenure," *AAUP Bulletin* 53, no. 4:378.

203. Ibid., 378; Frank South, telephone interview with the author, August 15, 2005; see also Rudder's desk calendar for April 21, 1968. The account printed in the *AAUP Bulletin* implies that Frank South voluntarily resigned from the committee, which contradicts his statement to the author.

204. "Informal Notes of Proceedings of the Board of Directors," Texas A&M University System, April 24–25, 1967, 2, in office of the Texas A&M University System Board of Regents.

205. *Houston Post,* April 7, 1968; *Houston Chronicle,* April 4, 1968; "Action Regarding Dr. Leon W. Gibbs," Texas A&M Board of Directors, Minute No. 40–69, January 22, 1969, 1, in the office of the Texas A&M University System Board of Regents.

206. Ed Davis, interim president of Texas A&M University, interview with the author, June 19, 2007.

207. "Indifference Main Enemy, Ex-POW's Told By Rudder," *Longview Morning Journal,* July 28, 1968, newspaper clippings, 1968, Personal and General Correspondence Papers, CMLA; Earl Rudder, speech to the Athens, Texas, Chamber of Commerce, January 20, 1966, copy in the possession of the author; Earl Rudder, "The Impact of Change," commencement address, Westbury High School, Houston, Texas, May 30, 1969, Personal and General Correspondence Papers, CMLA.

208. Harvey Pekar, *Students for a Democratic Society: A Graphic History,* vii.

209. Earl Rudder, speech in the American Legion Hall, Cuero, Texas, February 2, 1968.

210. Gerald W. Heaney, interview with the author, New Orleans, La., August 8, 2002; Earl Rudder, letter to his wife, May 20, 1945. Richard E. Wainerdi quoted Rudder's statement that the blood of black and white men was the same. Heaney was the 2nd Ranger

Battalion's training officer in Rudder's headquarters from mid-summer 1943 until Rudder left the battalion on December 7, 1944.

211. Allen C. Giles, letter to the *Battalion* editor, May 15, 1969; Oliver Sadberry, interview with the author, July 7, 2007.

212. "Rudder Advises Orderly Change," *Battalion,* May 16, 1969.

213. James P. Hannigan, Texas A&M Dean of Students, official letter and completed questionnaire to Maryl C. Levine, Urban Research Corp., Chicago, Illinois, August 4, 1969, Box 110–25, President's Office Papers, CMLA.

214. "Afro-American Society: A Difficult Beginning, 1967–69," *In Fulfillment of a Dream: African-Americans at Texas A&M University,* exhibit catalog, CMLA, Spring 2001, unpaged. A copy of the Board of Directors' manifesto may also be found in Box 110–25, President's Office Papers, CMLA.

215. Holographic document in ink, with the following written in the upper right corner: "Jim Bates, Section 130, 5-8-69," Box 110–20, President's Office Papers, CMLA.

216. Edwin Cooper, interview with the author, February 11, 2005.

217. Bob Wiatt, telephone interview with the author, February 11, 2005.

218. Edwin Cooper, interview with the author, February 11, 2005.

219. Heldenfels, interview with Chapman, July 5, 1974; Richard E. Wainerdi, interview with the author, Houston, Texas, September 20, 2005.

220. "Rudder: Hell of a Fight for Any Troublemakers," *Houston Chronicle,* April 1, 1969.

221. "Good Taste Ordered: Beards Banned for Aggies," *Houston Post,* February 8, 1967; Joe Buser to Mrs. L. D. Bounds, October 4, 1968, "Students, Underground Newspapers, April 1968–May 1969," Box 110–28, President's Office Papers, CMLA.

222. Earl Rudder, speech at the Texas A&M Annual Faculty Meeting, October 16, 1968, copy in the possession of the author; "Rudder Says He Will Meet Would-Be Agitators Head-On," *Bryan Daily Eagle,* March 28, 1969.

223. "Campus Turmoil: Hoover Warns of New Left Plans," *Houston Post,* September 1, 1968, I-2; "No Battleground at A&M, Rudder Declares," *Houston Post,* September 15, 1968.

224. "Rudder: Hell of a Fight for Any Troublemakers," *Houston Chronicle,* April 1, 1969; H. L. Somerville to Earl Rudder, April 7, 1969, Box 110–25, Students, Afro-American Demands, June 1969–August 1969, President's Office Papers, CMLA.

225. Leon Jaworski, "An Address at Law Day Banquet of Memphis and Shelby County Bar Association," copy in the possession of the author. Jaworski sent this copy to Rudder on May 6, 1969.

226. Haskell Monroe, *James Earl Rudder in the Words of His Wife,* 76–77.

227. John Mobley, interview with the author, April 17, 2007. Mobley was an assistant to Connally at the time.

228. Nelda Green, interview with the author, November 15, 2007; Robert G. Cherry, "Notes on the Proceedings of the Informal Session of the Board of Directors," February 21, 1969, in office of the Texas A&M University System Board of Regents.

229. Wayne C. Hall, *The Glory Years: The Making of a University*, 110–11.

230. Attending Physicians Statement, Ochsner Clinic, New Orleans, La., October 7–11, 1969, Personal and General Correspondence Papers, CMLA.

231. Ford Albritton Jr., interview with the author, Dallas, Texas, July 24, 2004; Rudder's desk calendar for November 20–21, 1969, Personal and General Correspondence Papers, CMLA, and copy in the possession of the author.

232. This account was synthesized from several sources. The anecdotes and quotations are from a draft transcript of an interview by Mark Sicilio, M.D., with Margaret Rudder on June 19, 1998. Similar information may be found in Haskell Monroe's interviews with Mrs. Rudder. Specific sequential data can be found in an excellent but anonymous article, "Rudder Dead at 59," *Battalion,* March 24, 1970.

233. Margaret Rudder, interview with Mark Sicilio, M.D., June 19, 1998, draft transcript, Personal and General Correspondence Papers, CMLA, and copy in the possession of the author.

234. "LBJ Attends Rites for A&M President: Gen. Rudder Funeral Crisp, Military," *Waco News-Tribune,* March 26, 1970; "Gen. Rudder's Memorial Rites Held at A&M," *Houston Post,* March 26, 1970; "Rudder Rites at 2 P.M. Today," *Austin American-Statesman,* March 24, 1970; "Rudder Gets Military Salute in Funeral at College Station," *Dallas Times Herald,* March 26, 1970.

235. Nelda Green, personal notes, copy in the possession of the author.

236. "LBJ Attends Rites for A&M President: Gen. Rudder Funeral Crisp, Military," *Waco News-Tribune,* March 26, 1970.

237. Brig. Gen. Edmond S. Solymosy, telephone interview with the author, February 4, 2009; "Gen. Rudder's Memorial Rites Held at A&M," *Houston Post,* March 26, 1970.

238. Leonard G. Lomell, telephone interview with the author, May 18, 2005.

BIBLIOGRAPHY

ARCHIVES AND MANUSCRIPT COLLECTIONS

Rudder, James Earl, Papers, Cushing Memorial Library and Archives, Texas A&M University; and the Dolph Briscoe Center for American History, University of Texas at Austin

My main sources were Earl Rudder's papers and memorabilia as substantiated by a number of memoirs and reliable historical records. However, I found fewer than a half-dozen documents that he composed before he was called to active duty for World War II in June 1941 at the age of thirty-one. Therefore, for the early period of his life I relied primarily on the recollections of friends and family members, newspaper accounts, occasional court records, and seven yearbooks published by the three schools that he attended between 1925 and 1932, all of which he kept in excellent condition. The extensive notations in the yearbooks by his classmates and teachers afforded useful insights into his personal development from the age of fifteen to twenty-two.

Eventually Rudder became a prolific letter writer. From June 1941 until his death in March 1970, he (or his wife and various assistants) kept much of his correspondence in good order. As he did not clearly distinguish between professional endeavors and personal activities, neither did he separate related documents in his otherwise well-organized files that include letters sent and received with newspaper clippings and photographs valued for their connection to events or experiences worthy of remembrance. Rudder never kept a diary, but two semblances were found. One was a vest-pocket notebook he carried during the last nine months of the war (August 1944 until May 1945) with haphazard undated entries that I was able to sort out and make sensible. The other was his desk calendar of appointments for most of the 1960s while he was president of Texas A&M.

His widow, Margaret Williamson Rudder, gave me unrestricted access to all materials accumulated during his entire life and subsequently by her, including their extensive wartime correspondence. She kept all of his letters, and he apparently got home with all of hers at the end of 1945. For this and other reasons, the unpublished documents used in this biography were so numerous that I did not include them in the bibliography but cited them in the endnotes for curious readers and future researchers.

Most of the Rudder papers are in the Cushing Memorial Library and Archives at Texas A&M University. They are in two parts: the Presidents' Office Papers, which came from his office files concerned with routine university operations; and his Personal and General Correspondence, which were most interesting to me because they contain substantive and sensitive materials regarding state and national political activity, public relations, army reserve assignments, letters from friends and detractors, as well as certain personnel matters. Other papers and memorabilia are in the Sam Houston Sanders Corps of Cadets Center, also at Texas A&M. The Office of the Board of Regents, Texas A&M University System, holds records of the governing board while he was president and, in some instances, notes made by secretaries during closed-door discussions that preceded voting on major policy issues in public meetings.

Voluminous copies of original documents from the aforementioned sources are in my collections at the Dolph Briscoe Center for American History at the University of Texas at Austin.

Bundesarchiv-Militärarchiv, Freiburg im Breisgau, Germany

John Tarleton Agricultural College Collections, Dick Smith Library, Tarleton State University

Lake Superior Maritime Collections, Jim Dan Hill Library, University of Wisconsin–Superior

National Archives of the United Kingdom

Stanhope B. Mason Collection, McCormick Research Center, Cantigny, First Division Foundation, Wheaton, Illinois

Texas Legislative Reference Library, State Capitol, Austin

Texas State Library and Archives, Austin

U.S. Army Military Police Museum, Fort Leonard Wood, Missouri

U.S. Military History Institute, Army War College, Carlisle Barracks, Pennsylvania Rowe Collection, Ranger Collections

U.S. National Archives and Records Center

World War II Collection, Donovan Research Library, Fort Benning, Georgia

World War II Oral History Archive, Eisenhower Center, University of New Orleans

OFFICIAL DOCUMENTS

Brady, Texas, City Council. Minutes, April 16, 1946–April 14, 1952. Office of the City Clerk, Brady, Texas.

Brady, Texas, Independent School District. Minutes, April 24, September 11, 1933; August 3, 1936. Heart of Texas Museum, Brady, Texas.

Carr, Wagoner. Attorney General of Texas Opinion No. C-525, Austin, Texas, October 14, 1965. http://www.oag.state.tx.us/opinions/opinions/43carr/op/1965/pdf/wc0525.pdf.

Concho County, Texas. Probate Court Records, vol. 6, 1939. Office of the Concho County Clerk, Paint Rock, Texas.

"The Estate of W. W. Williamson for the Calendar Year 1952: An Analysis of Gifts Made by W. W. Williamson and Lucy Williamson of Community Property." Supplement Schedule G, Lawrence Williamson, executor, March 10, 1953. Office of the Menard County Clerk, Menard, Texas.

Johnson, Lyndon B. "President Lyndon B. Johnson's Address before a Joint Session of the Congress," *Congressional Record,* 88th Cong., 1st sess., November 27, 1963.

Supreme Headquarters, Allied Expeditionary Force, Bombing Analysis Report Number 10, *Attacks on Batteries on the French Coast Prior to H-Hour on D-Day.* November 29, 1944, Vol. 2, table VIII, National Archives of the United Kingdom.

Texas, Governor's Committee on Education Beyond the High School. *Education: Texas' Resource for Tomorrow.* Austin: The Committee, 1964.

United Kingdom, Air Ministry, Air Historical Branch, Royal Air Force Narrative. *The Liberation of North West Europe.* Vol. 3, *The Landings in Normandy,* 1946. n.p.: Royal Air Force Centre for Air Power Studies. http://www.airpowerstudies.co.uk/historical sources.htm.

United Kingdom, British Naval Staff History, Battle Summary Number 39. *Operation "Neptune": The Landings in Normandy 6th June 1944.* First printed 1952; reprinted London, HMSO, 1994.

U.S. Army, Center of Military History. *American Military History.* Army Historical Series. Washington, D.C.: The Center, 1989.

U.S. Department of the Army. *American Military History, 1607–1953.* Washington, D.C.: U.S. Government Printing Office, 1956.

U.S. War Department. A Manual for Courts-Martial, 1928 (corrected to April 1943). Washington, D.C.: U.S. Government Printing Office, 1943.

U.S. War Department, Historical Division. *Omaha Beachhead (6 June–13 June 1944).* Armed Forces in Action Series. Washington, D.C.: Government Printing Office, 1945.

———. *Small Unit Actions: France: Second Ranger Battalion at Pointe du Hoe [sic].* Washington, D.C.: Government Printing Office, 1946.

BOOKS AND ARTICLES

"Academic Freedom and Tenure: Texas A&M University," *AAUP Bulletin* 53, no. 4 (December 1967): 379–80.

Adams, John A., Jr. *Keepers of the Spirit: The Corps of Cadets at Texas A&M University, 1876–2001.* College Station: Texas A&M University Press, 2001.

Adams, Samuel Hopkins [Warner Fabian, pseud]. "Flaming Youth," *Metropolitan Magazine* with *The Girl of Today,* February–March 1923.

Agricultural and Mechanical College of Texas. *Bulletin,* Sixth Series, 5 (April 1, 1958).

———. *The Texas A. & M. System News: Published for all Members of the Statewide Staff of The Texas A. and M. College System* 11, no. 2 (February, 1958).

Alanbrooke, Field Marshal Lord. *War Diaries, 1939–1945.* Ed. Alex Danchev and Daniel Todman, eds. Berkeley: University of California Press, 2001.

Altieri, James. *The Spearheaders.* New York: Bobbs-Merrill, 1960.

Ambrose, Stephen E. *Eisenhower.* Vol. 1, *Soldier, General of the Army, President-Elect, 1890–1952.* New York: Simon & Schuster, 1983.

Anderson, Christopher J. "Two Screaming Eagles: Unlikely Rangers on D-Day," *America's War Heroes: Unsung and Legendary* (a single-issue magazine), 2002.

André, Jacques, and Jean-François Conq, *Objectif Kéringar: Jours de libération, Août–septembre 1944.* Brest: Editions le Telegramme, 2002.

Atwood, T. Bagby. *The Regional Vocabulary of Texas.* Austin: University of Texas Press, 1962.

Badsey, Stephen, and Tim Bean. *Battle Zone Normandy: Omaha Beach.* Series ed. Simon Trew. Stroud, Gloucestershire: Sutton Publishing, 2004.

Baer, Alfred E., Jr. *D-for-Dog: The Story of a Ranger Company.* Memphis, Tenn.: n.p., 1946.

Bailey, Ronald H. *The Home Front: U.S.A.* New York: Time-Life Books, 1978.

Balkoski, *From Beachhead to Brittany: The 29th Infantry Division at Brest, August–September 1944.* Mechanicsburg, Pa.: Stackpole Books, 2008.

———. *Omaha Beach: D-Day, June 6, 1944.* Mechanicsburg, Pa.: Stackpole Books, 2004.

Barnes, Ben, with Lisa Dickey. *Barn Burning, Barn Building: Tales of a Political Life from LBJ through George W. Bush and Beyond.* Albany, Tex.: Bright Sky Press, 2006.

Black, Robert W. *The Battalion: The Dramatic Story of the 2nd Ranger Battalion in World War II.* Mechanicsburg, Pa.: Stackpole Books, 2006.

———. *Rangers in World War II.* New York: Ballantine, 1992.

Blumenson, Martin. *The Battle of the Generals: The Untold Story of the Falaise Pocket, the Campaign That Should Have Won World War II.* New York: William Morrow, 1993.

———. *Breakout and Pursuit.* United States Army in World War II: The European Theater of Operations. Washington D.C.: U.S. Army Center for Military History, 1961.

———. *The Patton Papers.* Vol. 2, *1940–1945.* Boston: Houghton Mifflin Company, 1974.

Bradley, Omar N. *A Soldier's Story.* New York: Henry Holt, 1951.

Calvert, Robert A., Arnoldo de León, and Gregg Cantrell. *The History of Texas,* 3rd ed. Wheeling, Ill.: Harlan Davidson, 2002.

Carlton, Joyce. *Stand Where They Fought: 150 Battlefields of the 77-Day Normandy Campaign.* Vol. 1, *The American Sector.* Newman, Ga.: Battlefield Publishing House, 1999.

Carman, Harry J., and Harold C. Syrett. *A History of the American People.* 2 vols. New York: Knopf, 1952.

Caro, Robert A. *The Years of Lyndon Johnson: Means of Ascent.* New York: Alfred A. Knopf, 1990.

———. *The Years of Lyndon Johnson: The Path to Power.* New York: Alfred A. Knopf, 1982.

Chandler, Alfred B., Jr., ed. *The Papers of Dwight David Eisenhower.* Vol. 5, *The War Years.* Baltimore: Johns Hopkins University Press, 1970.

Chanson, Hubert. "The Atlantic Wall in North Brittany (Bretagne Nord) France," *Shore & Beach: Journal of the American Shore and Beach Preservation Association* 72, no. 4 (Fall 2004).

Chaplin, W. W. *The Fifty-Two Days: An NBC Reporter's Story of the Battle That Freed France.* New York: Bobbs-Merrill, 1944.

Clark, Jeffrey J., and Robert Ross Smith. *Riviera to the Rhine.* United States Army in

World War II: European Theater of Operations. Washington, D.C.: U.S. Army Center of Military History, 1993.

Colby, John. *War from the Ground Up: The 90th Division in World War II.* Austin: Nortex Press, 1991.

Cole, Hugh M. *The Ardennes: Battle of the Bulge.* United States Army in World War II: The European Theater of Operations. Washington, D.C.: U.S. Army Center of Military History, 1965.

Congdon, Don, ed. *Combat WWII Europe: Unforgettable Eyewitness Accounts of the Momentous Military Struggles of World War II.* New York: Galahad Books, 1996.

Cox, Patrick. *Ralph W. Yarborough: The People's Senator.* Austin: University of Texas Press, 2001.

Curley, Stephen. *Aggies by the Sea: Texas A&M University at Galveston.* College Station: Texas A&M University Press, 2005.

Darlow, Stephen. *D-Day Bombers: The Veterans' Story.* London: Grub Street, 2004.

DeGroot, Gerard J. *The Sixties Unplugged: A Kaleidoscopic History of a Disorderly Decade.* Cambridge: Harvard University Press, 2008.

DeLay, Tom, and Stephen Mansfield. *No Retreat, No Surrender: One American's Fight.* New York: Sentinel Press, 2007.

D'Este, Carlo. *Patton: A Genius for War.* New York: HarperCollins Publishers, 1995.

De Tassigny, Maréchal Jean de Lattre. *Histoire de la Première Armée Française: Rhin et Danube.* Paris: Presses de la Cité, 1949.

Dethloff, Henry C. *A Centennial History of Texas A&M University, 1876–1976.* College Station: Texas A&M University Press, 1976.

———, with John A. Adams, Jr. *Texas Aggies Go to War: In Service of Their Country.* College Station: Texas A&M University Press, 2006.

Dobbs, Ricky F. *Yellow Dogs and Republicans: Allan Shivers and Texas Two-Party Politics.* College Station: Texas A&M University Press, 2005.

Dupuy, Trevor N. *Hitler's Last Gamble: The Battle of the Bulge, December 1944–January 1945.* New York: HarperCollins, 1994.

Eden High School (Texas). *Bulldog* (yearbook), 1926, 1927. Personal copies of James Earl Rudder, in possession of the author.

Edwards, Kenneth. *Operation Neptune.* London: Collins Clear-Type Press, 1946.

Eikner, James W., ed. *2nd Ranger Battalion: The Narrative History of Headquarters Company, April 1943–May 1945.* Comp. George M. Clark, William M. Weber, and Ronald Paradis. Houston: privately published, 1946.

Eisenhower, David. *Eisenhower at War, 1943–1945.* New York: Random House, 1986.

Eisenhower, Dwight D. *Crusade in Europe.* Garden City, N.Y.: Doubleday, 1948.

Ellis, L. F. *Victory in the War.* Vol. 1, *Normandy.* London: Her Majesty's Stationery Office, 1962.

Fergusson, Bernard. *The Watery Maze: The Story of Combined Operations.* London: Collins, 1961.

Finley, J. Rice. "The History of John Tarleton College." Master's thesis, University of Texas, 1933.

Flemmons, Jerry. *Plowboys, Cowboys, and Slanted Pigs.* Fort Worth: Texas Christian University Press, 1984.

Flies, Joseph. *Ettelbrück: Die Geschichte einer Landschaft.* Luxembourg: Imprimie Sainte-Paul, 1970.

Floch, Henri, and Alain Le Berre. *L'Enfer de Brest: Brest--Presqu'ile de Crozon, 25 août–19 septembre 1944.* Bayeux: Editions Heimsal, 2001.

Foot, M. R. D. *SOE in France: An Account of the Work of the British Special Operations Executive in France, 1940–1944.* London, HMSO, 1966.

Fossum, Embert A. "Operations of 'Task Force L,' 109th Infantry, 28th Infantry Division near Grosbus, Luxembourg, 20–23 December 1944: Personal Experiences of a Task Force Commander." Prepared for the Infantry School, Fort Benning, 1948–49. World War II Collection, Donavan Research Library, Fort Benning, Ga.

Frank, Anne. *Anne Frank: The Diary of a Young Girl.* Trans. B. M. Mooyaart-Doubleday. New York: Doubleday, 1952.

Fussell, Paul. *Wartime: Understanding and Behavior in the Second World War.* New York: Oxford University Press, 1990.

Gaul, Roland. *The Battle of the Bulge in Luxembourg: The Southern Flank, December 1944–January 1945.* Vol. 1, *The Germans;* Vol. 2, *The Americans.* Atglen Pa.: Schiffer Publishing Ltd., 1995.

Gavin, James M. *On to Berlin: Battles of an Airborne Commander, 1943–1946.* New York: Viking Press, 1978.

Gawne, Jonathan. *Americans in Brittany, 1944: The Battle for Brest.* Paris: Histoire & Collections, 2002.

———. *Spearheading D-Day: American Special Units of the Normandy Invasion.* Paris: Histoire & Collections, 2001.

Gilbert, Martin. *Road to Victory: Winston Churchill, 1941–1945.* London: William Heinemann Ltd., 1986.

Glassman, Henry S. *"Lead the Way, Rangers": A History of the Fifth Ranger Battalion.* Markt Grafing, Bavaria: Buchdruckerei Hausser, 1945. Reprint, Washington, D.C.: Ron Lane, 1980.

Gunther, Harold W., and Shalala, James R. *2nd Ranger Bn: Company E, 1943–1945.* Pilzen, Czechoslovakia: Novy Vsetisk, 1945.

Guthrie, Christopher E. *John Tarleton and His Legacy: The History of Tarleton State University, 1899–1999.* Acton, Mass.: Tapestry Press Ltd., 1999.

Hall, Wayne C. *The Glory Years: Making of a University.* College Station, Texas: privately published, 1989.

Hallion, Richard P. *D-Day 1944: Air Power over the Normandy Beaches and Beyond.* Washington D.C.: U.S. Government Printing Office, 1994.

Harrison, Gordon A. *Cross-Channel Attack.* United States Army in World War II: The European Theater of Operations. Washington, D.C.: U.S. Army Center of Military History, 1951.

Heinz, W. J. "I Took My Son to Omaha Beach: The Story of an American Hero's Return to Normandy." *Collier's,* June 11, 1954.

Hillery, Vic, and Emerson Hurley. *Paths of Armor: The Fifth Armored Division in World War II*. Nashville: The Battery Press, 1986.

Hinsley, F. Harry; E. E. Thomas; and C. A. G. Simkins. *British Intelligence in the Second World War*. Vol. 3, pt. 2, *Its Influence on Strategy and Operations*. London: HMSO, 1988.

Historical and Pictorial Review of the 28th Infantry Division in World War II. Atlanta, Ga.: Albert Love Enterprises, 1945.

Hodenfield, G. K. "I Climbed the Cliffs with the Rangers," *Saturday Evening Post*, August 19, 1944.

Hogan, David W., Jr. *U.S. Army Special Operations in World War II*. Washington, D.C.: U.S. Army Center of Military History, 1990.

Hollon, W. Eugene. *The Great American Desert: Then and Now*. New York: Oxford University Press, 1966.

Huie, William Bradford. *The Execution of Private Slovik*. Yardley, Pa.: Westholme Publishing, 1954.

John Tarleton Agricutural College. *Grassburr*, 1928, 1929, 1930.

Kemp, Harry M. *The Regiment: Let the Citizen Bear Arms! A Narrative History of an American Infantry Regiment in World War II*. Austin, Texas: Nortex Press, 1990.

Kennett, Lee. *The American Soldier in World War II*. New York: Charles Scribner's Sons, 1987.

Kinch, Sam, and Stuart Long. *Allan Shivers: The Pied Piper of Texas Politics*. Austin: Shoal Creek Press, 1973.

King, C. Richard. *The John Tarleton College Story: The Golden Days of Purple and White*. Austin: Eakin Press, 1998

Knippa, Heidi Ann. "Salvation of a University: The Admission of Women to Texas A&M." Master's thesis, The University of Texas at Austin, 1995.

Lane, Ronald. *Rudder's Rangers: The True Story of the 2nd Ranger Battalion D-Day Combat Action*. Manassas, Va.: Ranger Associates, 1979.

LeFevre, Hazie Davis. *Concho County History, 1858–1958*. Eden, Texas: self-published, 1959.

Lindbergh, Charles A. *The Spirit of St. Louis*. New York: Charles Scribner's Sons, 1953.

MacDonald, Charles B. *The Battle of the Huertgen Forest*. Philadelphia: University of Pennsylvania Press, 2003.

———. *The Last Offensive*. United States Army in World War II: European Theater of Operations. Washington, D.C.: U.S. Army Center for Military History, 1984.

———. *The Mighty Endeavor: The American War in Europe*. New York: William Morrow, 1969.

———. *The Siegfried Line Campaign*. United States Army in World War II: The European Theater of Operations. Washington D.C.: U.S. Army Center for Military History, 1963.

———. *A Time for Trumpets: The Untold Story of the Battle of the Bulge*. New York: William Morrow, 1984.

Manchester, William. *American Caesar: Douglas MacArthur, 1880–1964*. Boston: Little, Brown and Co., 1978.

Mauro, Gary. *The Land Commissioners of Texas: 150 Years of the General Land Office.* Austin: Texas General Land Office, 1986.

McDonald, Joanna M. *The Liberation of Pointe du Hoc: The 2d Rangers at Normandy, June 6–8, 1944.* Redondo Beach, Calif.: Rank and File, 2000.

McManus, John C. *Alamo in the Ardennes: The Untold Story of the American Soldiers Who Made the Defense of Bastogne Possible.* New York: NAL Caliber Books, 2007.

Miller, Edward G. *A Dark and Bloody Ground: The Hürtgen Forest and the Roer River Dams, 1944–1945.* College Station: Texas A&M University Press, 1995.

Miller, Nathan. *New World Coming: The 1920s and the Making of Modern America.* Cambridge, Mass.: De Capo Press, 2004.

Miller, Robert A. *Division Commander: A Biography of Major General Norman D. Cota.* Spartanburg, S.C.: Reprint Co., 1989.

Moen, Marcia, and Margo Heinen. *The Fool Lieutenant: A Personal Account of D-Day and World War II.* Elk River, Minn.: Meadowlark Publishing, 2000.

———. *Reflections of Courage on D-Day and the Days That Followed: A Personal Account of Ranger "Ace" Parker.* Elk River, Minn.: DeForest Press, 1999.

Monnartz, Rainer. *Hüertgenwald 1944/1945: Militärgeschichtlicher Tourenplaner.* Aachen, Germany: Heilos Verlags und Buchvertriebsgesellschaft, 2006.

Monroe, Haskell, ed. *James Earl Rudder in the Words of His Wife, Margaret Rudder.* College Station: Texas A&M University, Sterling C. Evans Library, Heritage Preservation Program, 2002.

Morelock, J. D. *Generals of the Ardennes: American Leadership in the Battle of the Bulge.* Washington, D.C.: National Defense University Press, 1994.

Morgan, Andrea Gurasich. *Land: A History of the Texas General Land Office.* Austin: Texas General Land Office, 1992.

Morgan, Frederick E. *Overture to Overlord.* London: Hodder & Stoughton Limited, 1950.

Morison, Samuel Eliot. *History of United States Naval Operations in World War II.* Vol. 11, *The Invasion of France and Germany, 1944–1945.* Boston: Little, Brown, 1957.

Nash, Douglas E. *Victory Was Beyond Their Grasp: With the 272nd Volks-Grenadier Division from the Huertgen Forest to the Heart of the Reich.* Bedford Pa.: The Aberjona Press, 2008.

Odom, William O. *After the Trenches: The Transformation of U.S. Army Doctrine, 1918–1935.* College Station: Texas A&M University Press, 1999.

Officer, Lawrence H., and Samuel H. Williamson. "Purchasing Power of Money in the United States from 1774 to 2009." MeasuringWorth, 2010. http://www.measuringworth.com/ppowerus/.

The Officers' Guide: A Ready Reference on Customs and Correct Procedures Which Pertain to Commissioned Officer of the Army of the United States. 9th ed. Harrisburg, Pa.: The Military Services Publishing Company, 1942.

100 Years of Texas High School Football. Dallas: Dallas Morning News, 1999.

Pallud, Jean Paul. *Rückmarsch! The German Retreat from Normandy, Then and Now.* Hobbs Cross, Essex, U.K.: Battle of Britain International, 2006.

Parton, James. *Air Force Spoken Here: General Ira Eaker and the Command of the Air.* Maxwell Air Force Base, Ala.: Air University Press, 2000.

Pasco, John O. *Fish Sergeant.* Sonora, Texas: n.p., 1940.

Pekar, Harvey. *Students for a Democratic Society: A Graphic History.* New York: Hill and Wang, 2008.

Peña, William M. *As Far As Schleiden: A Memoir of World War II.* Houston: n.p., 1991.

Perry, George Sessions. *The Story of Texas A and M.* New York: McGraw-Hill, 1951.

Peterman, Ivan H. "They Took the Nazis' Sunday Punch." *Saturday Evening Post,* September 28, 1946.

Pogue, Forrest. *Pogue's War: Diaries of a WWII Combat Historian.* Lexington: University Press of Kentucky, 2001.

Price, Frank James. *Troy H. Middleton: A Biography.* Baton Rouge: Louisiana State University Press, 1974.

Prince, Morris. *The Road to Victory: The Story of the Elite WWII 2nd Battalion Rangers.* Elk River, Minn.: Meadowlark Publishing, 2001.

Public Papers of the Presidents of the United States: Lyndon B. Johnson. Book 1 (January 1–March 31, 1965). Washington, D.C., Government Printing Office, 1965.

Quistorff, Alissa. "The U.S. Army's 2nd Ranger Battalion: Beyond D-Day." Master's thesis, Florida State University, 2005.

Roquemore, Frank U. "The Operations of the 2nd Ranger Battalion in the Huertgen Forest, 6–8 December 1944: Personal Experiences of a Platoon Leader." Prepared for the Infantry School, 1948–49, Fort Benning, World War II Collection, Donavan Research Library, Fort Benning, Ga.

Rudder, Earl. *Report of the Commissioner of the General Land Office, 1954–1956.* Austin: Texas General Land Office, 1956.

Rulon, Philip Reed. *The Compassionate Samaritan: The Life of Lyndon Baines Johnson.* Chicago: Nelson-Hall, 1981.

Ryan, Cornelius. *The Longest Day: June 6, 1944.* New York: Simon and Schuster, 1959.

Salomon, Sidney A. *2nd U.S. Ranger Infantry Battalion: Germeter-Vossnack-Hurtgen-Bergstein-Hill 400 Germany, 14 Nov.–10 Dec. 1944.* Doylestown, Pa.: Birchwood Books, 1991.

Shabazz, Amilcar. *Advancing Democracy: African Americans and the Struggle for Access and Equity in Higher Education in Texas.* Chapel Hill: University of North Carolina Press, 2004.

Sorvisto, Edwin M. *2nd Ranger Bn: Roughing It with Charlie.* Pilsen, Czechoslovakia: Novy Vsetisk, n.d.; reprint, Williamstown, N.J.: Antietam National Museum, 1978.

Stokes, William N., Jr. *Sterling C. Evans: Texas Aggie, Banker, Cattleman.* College Station: Texas A&M Libraries, 2003.

Sud, Lawrence H. *Guts and Glory: The Making of the American Military Image in Film.* Lexington: University Press of Kentucky, 2002.

Taylor, Robert A. *World War II in Fort Pierce.* Charleston, S.C.: Arcadia Publishing, 1999.

Ten Men Went to War. Southampton, U.K.: Southampton Productions, 1969. Film. Copy and transcript in Rudder Collection, Cushing Memorial Library and Archives, Texas A&M University. 1969.

Texas A&M College. *Longhorn,* 1931, 1932.

Toland, John. *Battle: The Story of the Bulge.* New York: Random House, 1959.

Truscott, Lucian K., Jr. *Command Missions: A Personal Story.* New York: E. P. Dutton and Co., 1954.

29 Let's Go! The Story of the 29th Infantry Division. Paris: *Stars and Stripes,* 1945.

Van Young, Sayre. *London's War: A Traveler's Guide to World War II.* Berkeley, Calif.: Ulysses Press, 2004.

Von Keusgen, Helmut Konrad. *Pointe du Hoc: Rätsel um einen deutschen Stüzpunkt* (Riddles of a German strongpoint). Garsben, Germany: HEK Creative Publishing, 2006.

Woods, Randall B. *LBJ: Architect of American Ambition.* New York: Free Press, 2006.

Young, Bill, and Bryan Dudley Stamp. *Bude: Past and Present.* Redruth, Cornwall, U.K.: Cornwall Litho, 1995.

Zaloga, Steven J. *Rangers Lead the Way: Pointe du Hoc, D-Day 1944.* Oxford: Osprey Publishing, 2009.

Ziemke, Earl F. *Stalingrad to Berlin: The German Defeat in the East.* Washington, D.C.: U.S. Army Center of Military History, 1968.

Newspapers and Magazines

Abilene Reporter-News

Amarillo Globe-News

Austin American-Statesman

Battalion (Texas A&M University)

Beaumont Enterprise

Brady Standard

Bryan Daily Eagle

Chicago Tribune

Childress Index

Cuero Record

Daily Texan (University of Texas at Austin)

Dallas Morning News

Dallas Times Herald

Eden Echo

Fort Worth Press

Fort Worth Star-Telegram

Houston Chronicle

Houston Press

Houston Post

Houston Post-Dispatch

Houstonian (Sam Houston State University)

J-Tac (Tarleton State University)

Lampasas Dispatch

Longview Morning Journal

Lufkin News

Midland Reporter-Telegram

New York Herald Tribune

New York Times

Newsweek

San Angelo Standard-Times

Shenandoah (Iowa) Evening Sentinel

Sweetwater Reporter

Texas Aggie

Texas Observer

Waco News-Tribune

Waco Tribune-Herald

INDEX

Page numbers in *italics* refer to photographs, maps, and captions under the photos. JER in index refers to James Earl Rudder.

communism, 280, 283–84

Concho County, Tex.: Civil War veterans in, 9, 14, 15; economy of and weather in, 7–9; and JER's election as Land Office commissioner, 300; Native Americans in, 13–15; real estate business of Dee Forrest Rudder in, *10, 23*; Rudder family's move to, 9–10; stock farms in, 9; terrain of, 45. *See also* Eden, Tex.

Connally, John B.: and cyclotron at Texas A&M, 355, 450*n*138; education of, 55, 277; as governor, 331–33, 343; gubernatorial successor for, 349; and JER, 277, 278, 331, 362, *363*, 386–87; photograph of, *363*; and Pickle, 277, 278; on public speaking skills of JER, 362; and scientific advancement, 331, 355; shooting of, in Dallas, 348, 355; support for education by, 331; and Texas A&M, 328, 331–33, 343, 386–87

conscription. *See* draft

Cook, Donald G., xviii, 416*n*72, 426*n*3

Cook, Harvey: and automobile for Simpson in Belgium, 194, 195, 426*n*3; and Block's death, 216; on courage of 2nd Ranger Battalion, 217; and D-Day mission, 91, 101; and Huertgen Forest Battle, 200, 201, 204–5, *204,* 210, 214, 216; in Korean War, 217; and Lytle's misconduct before Pointe du Hoc mission, 114; as operations and intelligence officer of 2nd Ranger Battalion, 78, 83, 176; photographs of, *102, 204;* and Pointe du Hoc mission, 101, 155, 416*n*72; and surrender of Germans on Le Conquet Peninsula, 187; travel from France to Belgium by, 194, 195

Cooley, Denton, 388

Cooper, Edwin, 347, 382, 383, 390–91

Cooper, Kenneth H., 388

Corder, Frank: and Corder-Rudder Tire and Supply Store, 262, 263, 267, 268, 436*n*22, 437*n*4; injuries of, on D-Day, 158; and Lytle's misconduct before Pointe du Hoc mission, 114; photograph of, *269;* recruitment of, for Rangers in World War II, 100; and Veterans Land Program, 291–92, 441*n*14

Corder, Frank "Buddy," Jr., *269*

Corder-Rudder Tire and Supply Store, 262, 263, 267, 268, 436*n*22, 437*n*4

Cornell University, 381, 382

Cornwall. *See* Bude, Cornwall

Cota, Norman: in Ardennes for recuperation and training of 28th Infantry Division, 214; and Battle of the Bulge (1944), 227, 229–34; and Colmar Pocket, 245, 249; as commander of 28th Infantry Division, 199, 214, 221, 242; Eisenhower's visit to headquarters of, 199; and Huertgen Forest Battle, 202; meetings between JER and, 242, 253; and military execution of Slovik, 247; Neufchateau command post of, 242; Omaha Beach landing by, 115; photograph of, in JER's office at Texas A&M, 391; and Pointe du Hoc mission, 147, 150; on replacements for 28th Infantry Division, 242

court-martials, 77, 88–89, 115, 174–75, 404*n*27

Courtney, William J., 186, 190, 212, 258–59, 419*n*134

Cox, Ben, 395*n*32

Cox, Margaret, 395*n*32

Crockett, Davy, 257

Cronkite, Walter, 364

Cross-Channel Attack (Harrison), 167

Crouch, Raymond, 127–28, 131, 137, 146, 156, 415*n*55

Crozon Peninsula, Brittany, 193

World War II (*continued*)
colonel (1943), 79, 405*n*32; promotion of, to major (1942), 72; public recognition of, as war hero, 169–70; return of, to U.S. at end of war, 261–63; return to civilian life after, 257, 262–63, 267–68; stateside assignments for (1941–1943), 69–80, 73, 404*n*24
—*See also* American prisoners of war (POWs); Brittany; casualties of World War II; D-Day; German army; German prisoners of war (POWs); Normandy; Pointe du Hoc (June 6–8, 1944); Infantry Division *headings;* Ranger Battalion *headings; and specific generals*
World War II Rangers Battalions Association, 160, 421*n*161
wrestling, 39, 47, 58, 401*n*11
Wright, T. B. "Tibbie," 344, 449*n*116

Yarborough, Ralph, 282–84, 312

Zachry, H. B. "Pat," 443*n*3
Zanuck, Darryl F., 164, 167